AT DUXBURY,
we think you know best

Introducing a different kind of learning system . . .
Whether it's interactive software or a self-study lab manual, now <u>you</u> can
decide what will help you learn statistics more effectively. All of the
books and software below work in tandem with other Duxbury texts to
provide you with learning options that offer innovation, flexibility, and choice.

MINITAB HANDBOOK, 3/E
Ryan and Joiner
Ideal for hands-on sessions
in the computer lab. Updated
to reflect new features of
Releases 8 and 9.

**JMP IN,
STUDENT'S EDITION**
SAS Institute, Inc
Combines classical statistics
with today's most interactive
graphics. Completely menu-
driven and easy to learn.

STATAQUEST, Release 2
DeLeon and Anagnoson
Powerful, easy-to-use,
graphically superior, and
inexpensive software with a
250 page user's guide. DOS
and Macintosh versions.

**STATAQUEST
TEXT COMPANION**
Anagnoson and DeLeon
Inexpensive software and an 80
page software manual with
essential information to get up
and running in StataQuest.

**STUDENT EDITION OF
EXECUSTAT 3.0**
Strategy Plus, Inc
Exceptional analytical power
in an easy-to-use, intuitive
format. Menu-driven, with
highly interactive graphics.
For IBM PC and compatibles.

**STUDENT EXECUSTAT 3.0
MINIGUIDE**
S. Christian Albright
Offers clear, step-by-step
instructions and tutorials for
mastering Student Execustat
3.0 software.

**LEARNING SAS IN THE
COMPUTER LAB**
Rebecca Elliott
An easy introduction to basic
data analysis techniques using
SAS—with worked
examples, exercises, and
computer output.

**STATISTICS LABORATORY
MANUAL**
Gerald Keller
Includes 65 experiments
requiring Minitab use that
illustrate how basic statistical
techniques work.

To order your copy of any of these products, please visit your nearest bookseller.

STATISTICS
FOR MANAGERS

STATISTICS
FOR MANAGERS

ULRICH MENZEFRICKE
University of Toronto
Faculty of Management

Duxbury Press
An Imprint of Wadsworth Publishing Company
I(T)P™ An International Thomson Publishing Company

Belmont Albany Bonn Boston Cincinnati Detroit London Madrid Melbourne
Mexico City New York Paris San Francisco Singapore Tokyo Toronto Washington

Editor: Curt Hinrichs
Assistant Editor: Jennifer Burger
Editorial Assistant: Janis Brown
Marketing Manager: Joanne Terhaar
Signing Representative: Peter Jackson
Print Buyer: Randy Hurst
Permissions Editor: Peggy Meehan

Production: Greg Hubit Bookworks
Text Design: John Edeen
Cover Design: Image House Inc.
Copy Editor: Caroline E. Jumper
Illustrations: Interactive Composition Corporation
Compositor: Interactive Composition Corporation
Printer: R. R. Donnelley / Crawfordsville

This book is printed on acid-free recycled paper.

For more information, contact Duxbury Press at Wadsworth Publishing Company:

Wadsworth Publishing Company
10 Davis Drive
Belmont, California 94002, USA

International Thomson Editores
Campos Eliseos 385, Piso 7
Col. Polanco
11560 México D.F. México

International Thomson Publishing
Berkshire House 168-173
High Holborn
London, WC1V7AA, England

International Thomson Publishing GmbH
Königswinterer Strasse 418
53227 Bonn, Germany

Thomas Nelson Australia
102 Dodds Street
South Melbourne 3205
Victoria, Australia

International Thomson Publishing Asia
221 Henderson Road
#05-10 Henderson Building
Singapore 0315

Nelson Canada
1120 Birchmount Road
Scarborough, Ontario
Canada M1K 5G4

International Thomson Publishing Japan
Hirakawacho Kyowa Building, 3F
2-2-1 Hirakawacho
Chiyoda-ku, Tokyo 102, Japan

1 2 3 4 5 6 7 8 9 10—01 00 99 98 97 96 95

Library of Congress Cataloging-in-Publication Data

Menzefricke, U.
    Statistics for managers / Ulrich Menzefricke.
        p. cm.
    Includes bibliographical references and index.
    ISBN 0-534-23538-7 (acid-free paper)
    1. Management—Statistical methods. 2. Statistics. I. Title.
HD30.215.M46 1995
001.4'22—dc20   94-40386

For Bob and Thomas,
and in memory of Daniel

CONTENTS IN BRIEF

CONTENTS

3

DATA SUMMARY   44

4

5

6

Time Series Analysis: Random Walks   228

7

Making Inferences in Cross-Sectional Studies   263

8

MAKING INFERENCES IN TIME SERIES STUDIES   331

9

SIMPLE REGRESSION ANALYSIS   381

10

MULTIPLE REGRESSION ANALYSIS   442

11

TIMES SERIES ANALYSIS WITH AUTOREGRESSION   539

12

FURTHER TOOLS FOR TIME SERIES ANALYSIS   580

PREFACE

Purpose and Intended Audience

Statistics for Managers is just that. It is intended to show managers and future managers how to use statistics to solve everyday business problems. This book helps them make informed decisions based on available data.

This book is an introduction to statistics for students and faculty requiring a practical business orientation. It was written with their needs in mind—their needs both in other academic courses and in the businesses in which they are likely to work. *Statistics for Managers* would be highly suitable for advanced undergraduates as well as for MBA candidates.

Emphasis

Statistics for Managers emphasizes all the steps and procedures required to successfully solve business problems in which data are useful—from definition of the managerial problem to statistical formulation of the problem, to data collection, to data analysis, and finally to conclusions about the statistical problem and an understanding of how it relates to the managerial problem.

Because it is important that students understand the managerial issues underlying any statistical analysis, the book emphasizes that managerial questions must determine the statistical questions and that the managerial concerns must be addressed by the statistical study. The book also stresses the distinction between cross-sectional studies and time-series studies. Readers will learn appropriate statistical models, the underlying assumptions, and how to check those assumptions for both types of studies.

Many traditional statistical tools were developed for cross-sectional studies, and many business problems can be solved with these tools. It has been my experience, however, that many other business applications involve data from time series studies. Users of statistics must therefore learn both the conditions under which tools for cross-sectional studies can be used in the context of time series and the conclusions that can be drawn from such analyses.

Organization

The organization of this book will help students with all the steps needed to carry out a statistical study in business. In particular, the organization emphasizes the distinction between cross-sectional studies and time series studies; features common to both types of studies are stressed as well.

Chapter 1	Briefly introduces the book.
Chapter 2	Discusses data collection, focusing on experimental and observational studies on the one hand, and cross-sectional studies and time series studies on the other.
Chapter 3	Introduces graphical and numerical data summaries.
Chapter 4	Focuses on simple cross-sectional studies.
Chapter 5	Explores simple time series studies in the context of statistical process control.
Chapter 6	Discusses the random walk, a simple time series model that has many uses in finance, to describe movement in the stock market.
Chapter 7	Returns to cross-sectional studies and how to make inferences from random samples to populations.
Chapter 8	Covers inferences in simple time series and develops several control charts.
Chapters 9 & 10	Explore the subject of regression analysis.
Chapters 11 & 12	Apply regression analysis to time series modeling through autoregression.

Design of statistical studies is first discussed in Chapter 2. Further ideas related to design are discussed throughout the book, for example in Section 5.12, where blocking is introduced.

Most of the material in this book can be covered in a 15-week course that meets twice a week for 90 minutes. A course that meets only once a week for 90 minutes can cover most of the material in Chapters 1 through 5 and 7 through 9.

Features

Statistics for Managers offers the following features:

- Emphasis on understanding and formulating managerial questions first, with statistical questions following from them.

- Reinforcement of the idea that data analysis is greatly facilitated by proper data collection.

- Many real business examples illustrate statistical ideas to show how managers implement them in practice.

- Discussion of the differences between cross-sectional studies and time series studies, as well as coverage of their common features.

- Stress on the interpretation of statistical graphs and summaries and how they help solve managerial problems, rather than focusing on how to obtain the numbers.

- De-emphasis of hypothesis testing in favor of interval estimation in accordance with current recommendations of many business practitioners.

- Incorporation of Minitab into the design of the book. Analysis of most business problems is impossible without computer software. A variety of graphical displays and data summaries are needed for the analysis of real data sets. Because computer output from different software packages is similar, readers can easily use programs other than Minitab with this text. In fact, the data disk that accompanies each new copy of the book is formatted for many such packages.

Exercises and Projects

The concepts and procedures in *Statistics for Managers* are best learned by doing. To this end, there are three kinds of exercises at the end of all chapters except Chapter 1.

- *Problems for class discussion.* These are somewhat unstructured and allow students to share their learning experiences in class and to bring together the material they have learned.

- *Exercises with short answers given in Appendix C.* Some of these are short drill problems, others are longer. All are intended to help students check their understanding. Although the answers in the appendix will provide immediate feedback, students are cautioned not to turn to them immediately when they are unsure how to proceed. Instead, it is preferable to set aside such exercises and return to them in a day or so, since new material often takes a while to "sink in."

- *Supplementary exercises.* Some of these are short, others relate to complex business problems. Answers are not given in the book.

All data sets used in this book are stored on the accompanying diskette. Many are listed in the text where they are first referenced. Since the data sets are stored in ASCII mode, all of them can easily be listed to get an impression of the data values.

An additional tool to help students learn by doing is a project taken from a business setting in which they are interested. Such a project allows students to synthesize many of the ideas discussed in the book, from problem definition, via data collection and analysis, to problem resolution. I highly recommend the use of such a project, and I have included an outline in Appendix B.

An Instructor's Resource Manual accompanies this book for adopters. It contains answers to all problems and exercises, and it discusses my approach to using this book as a teaching device.

Acknowledgments

This book was written over a period of several years, and I owe thanks to many people. My students at the University of Toronto have been very encouraging and have helped me improve it by making detailed comments and by contributing statistical problems from their places of work. I thank them and hope that readers of this book will be as diligent as they in suggesting ways to improve it.

My colleagues, Dmitry Krass, James E. Dooley, and Roger Wolff, have used drafts in their own classes, and they have provided useful comments to make the text a better teaching and learning tool. Richard A. Drapeau of Lamar University in Beaumont, Texas, and his students have been very encouraging and have made many comments to improve the book.

I have received generous assistance from Duxbury Press. My editor, Curt Hinrichs, has been very enthusiastic about the ideas underlying my text; Alan Venable and Susan Schwartz have been most supportive to make the text more readable. I would like to thank the following manuscript reviewers, who made many helpful suggestions: S. Christian Albright, Indiana University; John S. Y. Chiu, University of Washington; Richard A. Drapeau, Lamar University–Beaumont; Richard A. Meese, University of California at Berkeley; Ruth K. Meyer, St. Cloud State University; William I. Notz, Ohio State University; Joseph Nowakowski, University of North Carolina at Greensboro; Carl J. Schwarz, University of Manitoba; Patrick A. Thompson, University of Florida; and Mary Sue Younger, University of Tennessee.

I would also like to acknowledge the cooperation of those at Minitab Inc. who made available to me a preproduction version of their most recent release for Minitab Statistical Software (Minitab for Windows).

In the preparation of any work, writers use many different sources that are not explicitly referenced. I have done the same in this work, but two sources that deserve special mention are H. Roberts's *Data Analysis for Managers* (1991) and W. E. Deming's *Out of the Crisis* (1986).

Ulrich Menzefricke
Toronto, Ontario, Canada
October 1994

INTRODUCTION

PURPOSE OF *STATISTICS FOR MANAGERS*

The purpose of this book is to provide the student with statistical and data-analytical tools useful for managers. These tools will be developed by explaining the concepts, giving examples, and discussing detailed computer output.

The book's objective is to assist managers in planning, executing, and evaluating their businesses.

Upon course completion, the student will be able to:

- Identify and formulate problems where statistics can have an impact

- See the relevance of statistics and apply what has been learned to other business courses and to career practice

- Distinguish between routine and special problems requiring statistical analysis

- Understand statistical methods for quality improvement

- Assess data with healthy skepticism and seek expert help when needed

- Recognize when better data and information are needed for decision making

To put the use of statistics in perspective, here is the mission statement for Ford Motor Company, Detroit (1984).

> Ford Motor Company is a worldwide leader in automotive and automotive-related products and services as well as in newer industries such as aerospace, communications and financial services. Our mission is to *improve continually our products and services to meet our customer's needs,* allowing us to prosper as a business and to provide a reasonable return for our stockholders, the owners of our business. [Emphasis added.]

The emphasis in this course is on how statistics can help managers to continually improve products and services that meet the needs of a company's customers (see Figure 1.1). Useful statistical tools will be discussed that can be applied in any area where work is done, the output exhibits variation, and there is a desire for improvement. Examples will show how the tools are used to meet goals such as manufacturing products whose dimensions are consistently close to the targets, reducing bookkeeping error rates, or establishing the performance characteristics of a computer information system.

quality

Improving products and services typically means improving their **quality**. But how should quality be defined and measured? Who is to judge quality? The definition of quality depends on the product or service at hand. The challenge is to translate future needs of customers into *measurable characteristics* so that a product or service can be designed and then produced satisfactorily at a price the customer will pay. The quality of output—a product or a service—depends on the

system

overall *system* (or *process*) through which the output is designed, produced, made

process

available to customers, and serviced. Remember that quality considerations must start at the design phase; that is, quality must be "built into" the output.

It is a manager's job to *continually improve the process.* In this view, a process encompasses machinery and data processing, but also includes recruitment, training, supervision, and aids to service and production workers.

variable

A measurable characteristic of any unit or subject of interest, such as a product, service, or customer, is generally called a *variable*. For example, customers

FIGURE 1.1

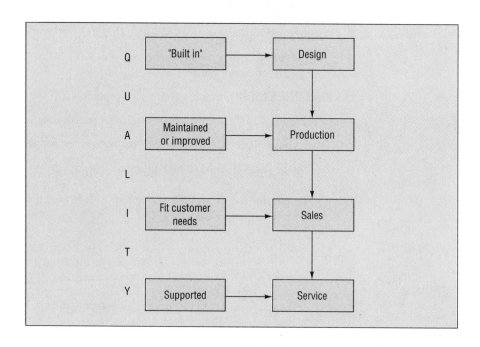

may be the subjects of interest, and the number of monthly purchases may be the variable whose value will differ from one customer (subject) to another.

As another example, consider a study done to better estimate the time required in a wholesale book company to pick and pack book orders. In this case, the unit of interest was the order. One variable was the time it took to pack each order; a second was the number of items on the order. These two variables were used to see if the number of items was a good indicator of how long it took to pick and pack the order.

1.2

TYPES OF STATISTICAL STUDIES

variation   A feature common to all problems where statistics is useful is *variation.*

> The central problem of management in all its aspects, including planning, procurement, manufacturing, research, sales, personnel, accounting, and law, is to understand better the meaning of variation, and to extract the information contained in variation.
>
> —L. S. Nelson of Nashua Corporation, as quoted in W. E. Deming (1986, p. 20).

Variation is an intrinsic element of every physical and social system. In particular, no two products or characteristics are exactly the same because any system that gives rise to them contains many sources of variability. For example, the time required to process an invoice could vary according to the

- People performing various steps

- Reliability of any equipment used

- Accuracy and legibility of the invoice itself

- Procedures followed, and

- Volume of other work in the office

In a sense, statistics is the systematic study of variation. Understanding the nature and causes of variation in a system is essential to its management. Once they are understood, it may be possible to remove important causes of variation. Thus the output will become more and more uniform, and the system will be improved; it is, of course, preferable to improve the system rather than just to make it work according to specifications.

To improve a system for which a manager is responsible, the manager needs a personal database for the system. The information that should be in the database will depend on

- What kinds of data are most worth collecting and analyzing

- How the data should be analyzed

- How the results of the analysis can be clearly and succinctly presented, both to the people to whom the manager is responsible, and to the people who are responsible to the manager

- What specific information is needed at various times

design and analysis Statistics embraces two activities: **design** and **analysis**. This book mainly deals with analyzing a given set of data, but in doing so it frequently touches upon questions of proper design of the statistical study. In the design phase, the manager must decide what data to collect and how to collect it. A first step is to distinguish what type of study is appropriate.

experimental study One useful way to distinguish types of statistical studies is by whether they are *experimental* or *observational*. In an *experimental* study, data are obtained by carefully carrying out planned experiments in which the manager can control the values of *factors* (often called *treatments*) thought to influence the outcome of the experiment. For example, in deciding on the sweetness of a new beverage, potential customers can be asked which of several sweetness levels they prefer. Here "sweetness" is the factor of interest, and there are several factor levels (that is, sweetness levels) chosen by the manager.

observational study That kind of intervention or control is not available in an *observational* study. For example, when studying the number of passengers bumped per flight, an airline manager can only observe what that number is. A further example is the picking and packing study discussed in the last section. In that case, several customer orders were selected for inclusion in the study. Since the orders came from actual customers, the manager could not intervene—say, to control the number of items on each order—so this was also an observational study.

time series study A second way to classify types of statistical studies is by whether they are time series studies or cross-sectional studies. In a *time series* study (often called an *analytic study*), values for a variable of interest are recorded over time. For example, a hotel manager may be interested in the proportion of "no-shows" (people who do not show up after making a reservation) on a daily basis. Time order is also important in studying weekly sales for a department store, since any analysis is likely to focus on trends or seasonal effects. In analyzing a time sequence of data, questions related to the time order in which the values were gathered are important: Is there an upward or downward trend? Is there an effect due to the day of the week? Is there a seasonal effect? To answer these questions, it is essential to know the time order of the data.

cross-sectional study In a *cross-sectional* study (also called an *enumerative study*), this time series aspect is not present. For example, the manager of a chain of hotels may be interested in the proportion of no-shows during a particular week for the various hotels in the chain. For proper comparisons to be made among the hotels, it is important that all data refer to the same week, but the order in which information is received is immaterial.

The picking and packing study is another example of a cross-sectional study. Here several orders were selected from those recently received, but the time order in which the orders were received was considered immaterial and was ignored.

1.3

SOME POTENTIAL CONTRIBUTIONS OF STATISTICS TO MANAGEMENT

FIGURE 1.2

MANAGERIAL
USES OF
STATISTICS

Understand past
performance

Understand cause
and effect

Forecast

Find unexpected
ways to improve

Statistics can help managers in several areas.

Description and Evaluation of Past Performance.   Many measures are useful to describe the past performance of a system—for example, profitability, sales, product quality, or personnel turnover. A wide variety of graphical displays and numerical summaries is available to display the information appropriately; some of them are useful for comparative purposes, either to show change over time or to facilitate comparisons across units. Typical questions are: What happened last month? What happened in another store?

Chapter 3 discusses many graphical and numerical tools that are useful to describe and evaluate past performance.

Study of Cause and Effect.   When cause and effect are to be studied with observational data (that is, through passive observations), the attribution of cause is often difficult. When two factors tend to vary together, it does not imply that one causes the other. Another possible explanation is that a third, unobserved factor causes both of them. For example, church attendance and suicide rate tend to be highly correlated over time, but this does not imply that high church attendance leads to a high suicide rate or vice versa. The underlying—and varying—economic conditions may explain both.

Demonstrating cause and effect is often easier using experimental studies or active observation where management intentionally varies the value of a factor of interest. For example, consider a new chemical product that is made in a reactor. To learn the potential effect of temperature on the quality of the product, several batches can be made by systematically varying the temperature settings for the batches. If all other important factors are unchanged for the batches, then the resulting output can be used to find the temperature setting that leads to the highest quality.

Chapter 2 discusses the attribution of cause and effect in experimental and observational studies.

Forecasting.   Forecasts can be unconditional or conditional. When what is likely to happen will not be influenced by what management does, we speak of an unconditional forecast. For example, the next quarter's GNP and next week's rate on treasury bills are unconditional forecasts. On the other hand, when we are interested in the effect of management actions, we talk of conditional forecasts.

Many chapters discuss forecasting, starting with Chapters 5 and 6. Chapters 11 and 12 discuss unconditional forecasting in detail.

Serendipity.   Serendipity is the unexpected finding of valuable or agreeable things. If a surprise is found in an analysis of data, examination of its cause often can lead to ways of improving the system. Such surprises should never be rationalized away or assumed to be mistakes.

1.4

BRIEF OUTLINE OF THIS BOOK

This book uses many studies from business practice to illustrate and motivate the use of statistics. In this section, some of these studies are outlined briefly to give an idea of the range of applications. The studies are then used to briefly summarize the contents of subsequent chapters.

Brief Summary of Several Studies

STUDY 1

Airborne Particulates in "Clean Rooms"

The cleanliness of the working environment is crucial to the final quality of many high-tech products made by a large multinational company. At one of the company's plants there are several clean rooms in the manufacturing area, and the achievement and maintenance of good standards of cleanliness in them are vital to product quality. The variable used to measure cleanliness level is particles per cubic foot of air. A study was conducted to evaluate the current sampling procedure and to decide whether airborne particle counts indicate satisfactory cleanliness levels.

STUDY 2

Document Translation for the Workers' Compensation Board of Ontario

Between October 1986 and October 1987, the French Translation Bureau of the Workers' Compensation Board of Ontario translated 12,411 documents (more than 4 million words) from French into English and from English into French. Accurate and timely translation of these documents was essential to providing a satisfactory service. The documents were categorized (or *stratified*) by type—correspondence, form, brochure, decision, special item, and other. A study was carried out to answer various questions related to document turnaround time.

STUDY 3

Student Survey at Durham College

Durham College's part-time enrollment in the fall semester of 1989 was approximately 9,000 students. Analyzing its economic and demographic environment, the College determined that there will be considerable opportunities for increased enrollment in part-time programs. To ensure that Durham College's system is responsive to the needs and perceptions of its part-time customers, a survey was undertaken asking part-time registrants to answer five questions about issues related to registration.

STUDY 4

Customer Service in a Dispatch Operation at IBM

The dispatch operation at an IBM subsidiary receives service calls from customers. To maintain a high level of service quality, it is essential that customers' service calls be taken promptly and efficiently, so the length of time customers are on hold is of interest. The target maximum value for time on hold is 16 seconds. A study was undertaken to determine whether the dispatch operation was meeting the target value.

STUDY 5

Analysis of Weight and Volume Data at Abitibi-Price

A division of Abitibi-Price was using two different methods of measuring wood delivered to three pulp and paper mills. Wood was delivered by trucks. The volume of each truckload was physically measured by a government-licensed individual. At the same time, each load was also weighed by a company employee. The purpose of taking both measurements was to obtain information on weight-to-volume ratios for the wood. A study was done to learn whether government-set weight/volume ratios (used as a basis for collecting charges for the wood harvested by the company) accurately reflected the company's ratios, and whether it was practical to stop the costly practice of measuring each truckload of wood and instead to rely upon a sampling process.

The five studies briefly described above—and several others—will be analyzed in many problems throughout this book to illustrate the use of statistics by managers.

Brief Summary of Subsequent Chapters

The following discussion briefly outlines the contents of the remaining chapters.

Chapter 2 discusses several issues related to data collection. One important idea relates to how sampling should be carried out. For example, in performing Study 2 (document translation), it was not possible to examine all 12,411 documents. The problem was then which documents to select for the study. The way in which documents are selected depends partially on the questions to be answered. For example, if translation performance in the past year is of interest, a representative sample from the past year's 12,411 documents may give the required information. But if turnaround time for *future* documents is of interest, data collection may have to be different, since performance may have been improving in recent months. If such an improvement is expected to persist, then the more recently translated documents may be more informative about future performance than documents translated earlier.

As a second example, how should particle counts be obtained in Study 1 (clean rooms)? It may not be possible to count *all* particles in a room, and so a small part of the room will have to be examined. If the particle count is to be monitored over time, should the count always be taken in the same part of the room or in different parts?

Chapter 3 deals with presenting graphical and numerical summaries of the data. For example, how can the frequency of different document turnaround times in Study 2 be graphically represented? What is a one-number summary for a typical value of turnaround time? What is a one-number summary for variation in turnaround times? For Study 1, is there a graph that facilitates monitoring the clean-room particle counts over time? For Study 5, how is the relationship between weight and volume of truckloads of wood best described, both graphically and in a numerical summary?

Chapter 4 presents some results for cross-sectional studies. It introduces the basics of statistical modeling, where the term *model* denotes a simplified description of reality that is useful for explanation and prediction. Frequency distributions are discussed, and the normal distribution is introduced.

Chapter 5 discusses a very important application of statistics, statistical process control, which is a group of methods by which statistics can be used to monitor and regulate a process. Chapter 5 describes simple time series and introduces the widely used model of a stable process—that is, a process that is in statistical control. The discussion of statistical process control introduces many ideas important in the study of statistics. For example, in Study 4, IBM customers' total time on hold was recorded for a number of weeks. Is there a pattern to the variation in daily waiting times? If so, the reasons for such a pattern should be uncovered: Staffing on a particular day of the week may be unusually low (leading to long waiting times), or equipment problems may be increasing (leading to more calls and thus longer waiting times). The causes for the pattern in the variation in waiting times should be identified so that the causes can be removed. How can statistics help detect such causes?

The analysis of time series is further pursued in Chapter 6, where random walks are studied. The model of the random walk is used in finance to describe stock market behavior, and it has important implications for prediction of the stock market. It turns out that there is a close relationship between the statistical model of a random walk and that of a stable process.

Chapter 7 introduces further ideas for the analysis of cross-sectional data. It discusses samples, how representative they are, and how to generalize from a sample to the whole. One crucial problem is how to describe the error likely when generalizing from a sample to the whole. For example, consider Study 3 (part-time students at Durham College). Without having to question each part-time student, what can we say about the proportion of the 9,000 part-time students who would recommend Durham College courses to others? If we used the sample proportion for 100 representatively chosen part-time students as an estimate of the overall proportion, by how much could our estimate be off?

Chapter 8 applies the ideas introduced in Chapter 7 to the study of time series data. It introduces several types of control charts useful for monitoring a process. For example, Study 1 examines whether airborne particle counts in clean rooms are satisfactory. It was expected that there would be no discernible time series pattern to particle counts. If this expectation is correct, what can be said about the average number of particle counts in the clean rooms in the near future?

Chapters 2 through 8 deal with statistical ideas relating to information about one variable, or about several variables examined independently. Chapters 9 and 10 show how to explore relationships among several variables using what is called regression analysis. For example, Study 4 (customer service at IBM) examines the relationship between time on hold and the number of calls and the staffing level. For a given number of calls, can staffing level be used to predict waiting time? If such a prediction is possible, how accurate is it?

A similar question arises in Study 5 regarding the relationship between weight and volume of truckloads at Abitibi-Price. Can we use the weight of a truckload to predict its volume? If such a prediction is accurate, then only weight may have to be measured.

As a third example, consider again the new chemical product that is made in a reactor. Several factors were identified to have a potential effect on the quality of the product, including temperature, pressure, and reaction time. Good settings for these factors were to be found to achieve high product quality.

Finally, Chapters 11 and 12 describe time series analyses in further detail, and combine the ideas discussed in Chapters 5 and 6 with regression analysis to arrive at good forecasting models. For example, Marshall Field & Company needed to forecast their sales for the next 2 quarters. Quarterly sales figures were available for the last 15 years of stable growth. The sales patterns for the last 15 years displayed strong seasonality, were expected to persist for at least the next year, and were to be used to make the forecasts.

This book will familiarize you with many important statistical tools and the ideas underlying them. The tools will be useful for the solution of many day-to-day problems as well as special problems that occasionally arise.

1.5

USE OF COMPUTERS AND MINITAB

A manager must be both a consumer and a practitioner of statistics. A computer can give the manager invaluable assistance, since it frees the user from having to carry out tedious numerical calculations. In this course, we will use the software package Minitab, which is a registered trademark of Minitab Inc. and is available for IBM and Macintosh personal computers, minicomputers, and mainframe computers.[1] Many other software packages are available, but Minitab is very user-friendly and easy to use.

Minitab Release 9 for Windows was used to generate many of the figures and tables in this book; this release has excellent high-resolution graphics capabilities. Some of these capabilities are not available in earlier releases, so your version of Minitab may generate output that looks a little different. Note that Minitab has very good Help facilities.

Try out Minitab as soon as possible. The easiest way for you to start may be to try to replicate some of the graphs in this book. The commands for many graphs are given at the end of the respective chapter in the section Using Minitab for Windows. In all graphs, the Minitab output is in black. Any added lines or annotations are in a different color. Likewise, the keystrokes to be used to produce the graphs, both in the text and in the figures, are in color. The first use of Minitab in this book is in Section 3.2. The data sets used there and all other data sets used in this book

---

[1]Minitab is available from Minitab Inc., 3081 Enterprise Drive, State College, PA 16801-3008. The telephone number is (814) 238-3280, and the fax number is (814) 238-4383.

are stored as non-Minitab files on the data diskette that accompanies this book. The data files are in ASCII format, and they are easy to read into Minitab.

It is important for you to get a firm grasp of the concepts underlying statistics. The computer is a useful tool for this, but is not always necessary. Also, the computer is not essential to do all statistical work; one important example is the control chart discussed in Chapter 5.

References

Deming, W. E. (1986), *Out of the Crisis,* Massachusetts Institute of Technology Press, Center for Advanced Engineering Study, Cambridge, MA.

> This text is an important contribution to quality control and the statistical ideas underlying it.

Roberts, H. (1991), *Data Analysis for Managers with Minitab,* Scientific Press, Redwood City, CA.

> This is a good introductory statistics book that concentrates on time series analysis.

2

DATA COLLECTION

This chapter will help you solve the following kinds of problems:

- A manager is concerned about the influence of two raw materials on the quality of a product. How should she design a study to compare the effect of the two raw materials?

- A manager wants to monitor the extent to which employees follow security procedures for information stored in personal computers. What kinds of data should be collected, and how should data collection be done?

2.1

INTRODUCTION

In this chapter, you will learn some basic concepts related to different types of data collection. Major topics include:

- Further differences between experimental and observational studies

- Design of experiments

- Further differences between cross-sectional and time series studies

- Statistical populations, processes, and samples

- A brief introduction to surveys

2.2

EXPERIMENTAL VS. OBSERVATIONAL STUDIES

This section points to the iterative nature of most statistical investigations and then explains further differences between experimental and observational studies.

Typically, when a problem is to be investigated, data must be collected. Some preliminary information is usually available, but often these preliminary data only help formulate the problem, stimulating questions more than providing answers. From preliminary knowledge, some guesses can be made or hypotheses set up. Then data usually must be collected and analyzed to shed light on the validity of the guess or hypothesis. Often, this sequence of hypothesis formulation and data collection does not solve the initial problem. Rather, it leads to revised hypotheses that require further data collection and analysis. A satisfactory solution to the problem often is found after a few iterations of the sequence, and can then be tentatively implemented. But the implementation must be monitored to check whether it works. The monitoring process may raise new questions. If so, the cycle of hypothesis formulation and data collection is started again.

This cycle is sometimes called the *PDCA cycle* (for Plan, Do, Check, Act). Extensive planning precedes actions, followed by checking on and refining the change. If everything goes well, the change is standardized across the work area, followed by new plans for further improvement—and the cycle starts again. Learning is iterative and cumulative. This process is the embodiment of continual changes leading to continual improvements.

Depending on the way in which data are collected, we can distinguish two types of studies: **experimental** and **observational** studies. (These classifications were briefly introduced in Chapter 1.) In an experimental study, the manager can control the values of factors thought to influence the outcome of the experiment; we will see in this section how such control enables the manager to draw cause-and-effect conclusions. In an observational study, the manager cannot exert such control; cause-and-effect conclusions are then very difficult to make.

In planning either type of study, we must always keep two questions in mind:

1. What will the data be used for?

2. How will they be analyzed?

If we do not keep these questions in mind, we may collect unneeded data, which is a waste of our time and resources, or we may not collect data that are appropriate for the intended purpose.

FIGURE 2.1

Experimental Studies

In business, the purpose of many experimental studies is to provide a basis for action on a service, product, or process to improve its performance in the future. Experiments help managers with continual improvement of quality. Typically they are done to design a new service, product, or process, or to redesign an existing service, product, or process. Managers should keep in mind that the design stage offers more potential for the improvement of quality than stages downstream in the provision of a service or the manufacture of a product.

Suppose a new or improved service is to be delivered, or a new or improved product is to be produced. How should the manager design an experiment to examine the product's or the service's effectiveness? In the following example of an experimental study, we consider the introduction of a TV commercial.

EXAMPLE 2.1

A company testing the effectiveness of a new commercial for an established dog food brand recruited a large number of dog owners entering a shopping mall. They were asked to come into a room, from which they were randomly assigned to one of two small TV-viewing rooms. Both groups were shown identical videos about dog care, but one group also saw a new commercial for a particular brand of dog food. After watching the video, the participants were given coupons to be redeemed in the shopping mall that day with the purchase of *any* brand of dog food. The managerial question for this study was:

Should the new commercial be aired commercially?

We will use this example to introduce some statistical terminology. The experiment is done on a number of **subjects,** the dog owners. The investigator is interested in the values of several **variables** for these subjects. The variable of primary interest, called the *response variable,* is consumer purchase behavior. It measures whether a subject buys the particular brand of dog food in the shopping mall on that day, so it can take on only two values, "yes" and "no." The investigator is interested in the relationship of the response to other variables, one of which is "Watched TV commercial?" Others might include the subject's sex, age, and length of dog ownership. Some of these variables can be influenced by the investigator. For example, whether a subject has watched the commercial can be determined by the investigator, but the dog owner's sex is beyond the influence of the investigator. The variable whose influence on the response variable is of main interest is called a *factor;* different values or *levels* of the factor are compared with respect to the response variable. Other variables that should be accounted for are called *background variables.* In the dog food study, the factor of interest is "Watched TV commercial?"; it has two levels, "yes" and "no." Two background variables are age and sex. Note that in this experiment the investigator can determine the value of "Watched TV commercial?" whereas this is not possible for the variables age and sex. Of course, there are typically many background variables in an experiment. Unfortunately, some of them may not even be known, though they may affect the response variable. Such unknown background variables are called *nuisance variables.*

FIGURE 2.2

> **Units** are the basic entities for which measurements are available or are to be made. When these units are people, they are called **subjects.**
> **The response variable** is the variable of interest.
> **Factors** are variables whose effect on the response variable the investigator is interested in. The factors are studied at different **levels.**
> **Background variables** are variables that may have an effect on the response variable and should be accounted for.
> **Nuisance variables** are unknown background variables.

Let us discuss a few more examples. Consider a study of the effect of display size on sales of a frequently purchased product in a retail store: Since displays were changed on a weekly basis, the unit chosen was a week. The response variable was weekly sales of the frequently purchased product. The factor, display size, had two levels, "normal size" and "twice normal size." There were many background variables—for example, price of the product, price of competing products, and display activity for competing products. The study was carried out over several weeks during each of which one level of display size was chosen. The two groups of weeks with normal and twice normal display size were then compared with respect to sales.

In this study the unit was a week, so sales were aggregated for the week. The unit could also have been chosen to be a day, leading to a much larger data set. Since display size was changed weekly, however, it was not considered necessary to analyze data on a daily basis; the additional information would have shed little additional light on the question regarding the effect of display size.

As another example, consider a study of the uniformity of two competing brands of a product, say, brands A and B: The product characteristic of interest was weight, whose target value was 1 kg. The unit was a product item. The response variable was deviation from the target weight. The factor was brand, with two levels, A and B. No important background variables were identified. The two brands were compared with respect to closeness to target weight.

It should be clear from the above examples that the question to be addressed by a study determines what the unit is and what data should be collected on each unit. Sometimes the unit is an individual product, sometimes it is a period of time.

As a further example, consider the following:

EXAMPLE 2.2

A large university library is planning to introduce a new interactive computer system so that its customers can examine the library's holdings and related information. Two competing computer systems, systems A and B, are being considered. One important managerial question is which system the customers find more user-friendly. In an experiment, each system is rated by several customers carrying out a predefined task. In this case, the *subjects* are the customers, and the *response variable* is a rating of user-friendliness. The *factor* of interest is which system the customer used; it has two levels, system A and system B. There may be several *background variables,* such as the customer's age or familiarity with interactive computer software used in libraries.

treatment vs. control group

Let us now introduce the "treatment versus control group" terminology. In Example 2.1 (p. 13), the factor of interest, "Watched TV commercial?", was studied at two levels, "yes" and "no"; the responses at these two levels are to be compared. Corresponding to these two levels, there are two groups of dog owners—the *treatment* group, which watched the TV commercial, and the *control* group, which did not. The responses of these two groups will be compared. All subjects in the treatment group have the same value ("yes") for the controllable factor "Watched TV commercial?"; all subjects in the control group have the same value ("no"). We can also interpret subjects who were shown the TV commercial as having been given the *treatment* "watched TV commercial." Thus treatment group is characterized by *presence* of the "treatment" and the control group by *absence* of the "treatment." Figure 1.13 illustrates these remarks.

The idea underlying the treatment versus control group terminology is important for the method of *comparison* that is basic to experimentation. The treatment group is given a treatment, and the control group is not. If, except for the treatment, the two groups are quite similar, then any difference in the response variable between the two groups may be due to the treatment.

In Example 2.2, library customers can be asked to evaluate one of the two computer systems. In this case, the factor of interest (system) has two levels (system A and system B). Alternatively, we can say that there are two treatments, systems A and B, and no control.[1] What is important is to compare the responses in the two groups.

FIGURE 2.3

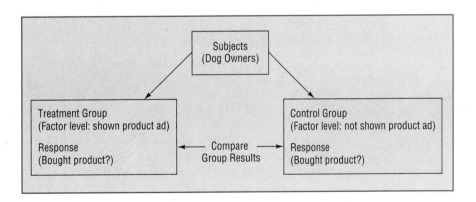

<hr>

[1]Some people would arbitrarily call one of the systems the "treatment" and the other the "control," which is also acceptable terminology.

**controlled
experiment**

An experiment is said to be *controlled* when the investigator can assign units to the levels of the factor of interest, that is, to the groups to be compared. In Example 2.2, the library manager can assign the library customers participating in the experiment to one of the two systems. In Example 2.1, the investigator can assign dog owners to one of the two groups; the treatment group will watch the TV commercial and the control group will not.

Some way must be found of assigning dog owners so that the two groups are as similar as possible with respect to *all* background variables, whether known or not. If this is achieved, then any differences in the response variable between the two groups can be attributed to the factor of interest.

The managerial question for the TV commercial study was:

Should the TV commercial be recommended for commercial airing?

This managerial question can now be translated into a statistical question:

Is the percentage of dog owners in the treatment group who buy the dog food shown in the commercial larger by at least a given number of percentage points than the corresponding percentage in the control group?

randomization

Randomization is the best way to make the groups representing the levels of the factor of interest as similar as possible with respect to all background variables, including the nuisance variables. Randomization is an impartial method that assigns units to the levels by a chance device, such as the toss of a coin, rather than by the investigator's judgment, which may include unknown biases. In Example 2.1, the treatment and control groups are to be of equal size, so randomization will give every dog owner an equal chance to be in either group. In general, it is not necessary for the groups to be of equal size.

Note that the investigator typically cannot identify all background variables. Some of them, the nuisance variables, are not even known. Randomization nevertheless helps in making the groups to be compared similar with respect to all background variables, whether those variables are identified or not.

In the following example, randomization would not be possible: A company planning to use a TV commercial in a large, ethnically varied city wants to know whether native and nonnative English speakers react differently. The response variable is "reaction to the TV commercial." The factor of interest is "native versus nonnative English speaker"; it has two levels, "native English speaker" and "nonnative English speaker." Two possible background variables are age and income. Here again, two groups are to be compared, native and nonnative English speakers. In this case the investigator cannot assign people to a group: People were already part of one of these two groups *before* the experiment was even thought up.

confounding

Randomization helps rule out problems of **confounding,** that is, mixing up the effects of the factor of interest and of background variables on the response. For example, if users of the brand of dog food under study were all in one group, any difference in the response variable (purchase behavior) between the two groups might be due to the TV commercial *or* the fact that the brand was regularly purchased by dog owners in one group but not the other. In such a case, we say that the effects of the two variables ("watched TV commercial" and "previous user") on the response variable (purchase behavior) are confounded. If randomization is used to assign units to the treatment and control groups, then the two groups are likely to be roughly similar with respect to all background variables. For example, it is then unlikely that there will be a much larger number of previous users in the control group than in the treatment group.

Another example of confounding can arise in medical experimentation. It involves the *placebo effect,* which occurs when subjects respond positively to *any* treatment, even a sugar pill. This is supposedly a psychological effect, and can be due to the belief that one is getting treatment. Suppose a group of several subjects is given a new drug, and they feel better. If there is a control group, whose subjects receive a placebo, it might be possible to tell whether the subjects in the treatment group felt better because of the treatment or because of the placebo effect. But if there is no control group, it would be impossible to say if the subjects felt better because of having been given the treatment or because of the placebo effect. Without a control group, the effects of the new drug and the placebo effect are confounded.

order effect

The following example shows how to deal with *order effect,* another problem that is sometimes encountered in experimentation.

EXAMPLE 2.3

The comparison between the two library systems discussed in Example 2.2 could be done differently. Rather than assigning some customers to system A and some to system B, each customer participating in the study could be asked to evaluate both systems. In that case, the response variable might be which system is considered more user-friendly. It would be dangerous, however, to have each customer first try system A and then system B. If there were some kind of learning effect, then preference for system B might be due to this learning effect. In this case, the effect of the system used and the learning effect would be confounded: if the second system tried were preferred, this preference could be due to (1) the second system being more user-friendly, (2) a learning effect being present, or (3) both. If an order effect might be present, it is wise to have two groups for which the two systems are tried in different order. If customers are randomly assigned to each group, it will be possible to distinguish between the effect of the system and the order effect.

Summarizing, in an experimental study we randomly assign subjects to the levels of the factor of interest so that we can study the factor's effect on the response variable. Randomization is necessary to make the resulting groups as similar as possible with respect to all background variables so that the effect of the factor of interest will not be confounded with the effect of background variables. Many randomized controlled experiments can be graphically represented as shown in Figure 2.4.

Example 2.1 can also be graphically represented this way. Dog owners were randomly assigned to the treatment group that watched the TV commercial or to the control group that did not. Recall that the participating dog owners were given a coupon for any brand of dog food, to be redeemed in the shopping mall that day. By

FIGURE 2.4

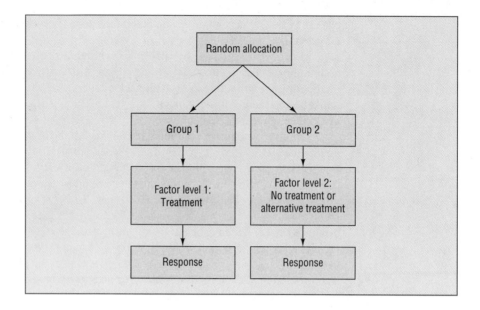

the end of the day, the merchants who redeemed the coupons returned them to the investigator, indicating the brand of dog food that was chosen. Each dog owner's response—the brand for which the coupon was redeemed—was thus available. The results from the experiment were then analyzed by comparing treatment and control groups with respect to the proportions of dog owners who redeemed the dog food coupon to purchase the product advertised in the TV commercial.

Observational Studies

It is always advisable to conduct an experimental study so that randomization can be used to avoid problems of confounding. When this is not possible, we resort to an observational study. Experimental studies use *controlled* experiments where subjects *can* be assigned a level of the factor of interest for the purpose of the experiment. Such an assignment is not possible in observational studies. Randomization is then not possible, and confounding variables may be present. For example, to study the effect of smoking on health, people cannot be assigned to smoke or not to smoke for a number of years. Since people who smoke tend to have lower incomes and education than nonsmokers, and therefore poorer overall health care, a study of health may confound the effect of smoking with the effects of income and education. This problem has to be dealt with in any smoking study.

Randomization is used in controlled experiments to avoid problems of confounding, that is, to make the groups as similar as possible with respect to all background variables, *identified or not.* Lack of randomization in observational studies implies that there is danger of confounding the effect of the treatment with the effect of other variables distinguishing the groups. This is particularly serious for nuisance variables.

As you will see shortly, the treatment/control terminology often is used in observational studies as well, even though there is no treatment in the experimental sense.

EXAMPLE 2.4

To understand the problem of confounding in observational studies, consider the possibility of gender bias in the hiring policy of a company with four departments, A, B, C, and D. Here, you could arbitrarily call the group of all men "treatment," and the group of all women "control," or vice versa. In 1 year, 31.4% of the 1,632 male applicants and 23.0% of the 834 female applicants were hired. Assuming that the applicants were on the whole equally well qualified for the jobs they applied for, the difference in hiring rates looks like strong evidence that men and women are treated differently in the hiring procedure. The company seems to prefer men to women by a ratio of 31 to 23.

For this example, the subject is an applicant, the response variable is "hired or not," and the factor of interest is gender.

Hiring in this company is done by department, and Figure 2.5 shows the breakdown of applications and hiring by department. In each department the percentage of women hired is slightly higher than the percentage of men hired, even though overall the percentage of men hired is higher than that of women hired. This sounds paradoxical, but there is a fairly easy explanation. The first two departments had a high hiring rate, and their applicants were mostly men. The last two departments had a low hiring rate and more female than male applicants.

So men tended to apply to the departments where it was easy to get hired, whereas women tended to apply to the difficult departments. When the analysis is broken down by department applied to, there is little difference in hiring rates between men and women. Before doing the analysis by department, the effects of the variable under study (gender) and another variable (department) were confounded. Since hiring is done by department, it is wrong to compare overall hiring rates in the company. The data at hand thus do not show that there is a gender bias in hiring practice. On the other hand, the data do not prove that there is no gender bias. Other variables that were not measured in this study may uncover such a gender bias.

FIGURE 2.5 Number of Applicants (Num) and Percentage Hired (%H) by Gender

Department	A		B		C		D		Total	
	Num	%H	Num	%H	Num	%H	Num	%H	Num	%H
Male	710	39.4	520	35.4	198	12.6	204	11.8	1,632	31.4
Female	97	41.2	215	38.6	312	13.2	210	13.3	834	23.0

stratification

Analyzing the hiring data by department is an example of *stratification*. Stratifying data means splitting them into groups based on one or more *background* variables, such as males vs. females, newly hired vs. other employees, first vs. second shift, etc. This is a valuable approach for finding patterns that can point toward the underlying causes of a problem.

Stratification is useful in experimental as well as observational studies. Consider Example 2.2 (p. 14) again, in which familiarity with interactive computer software may influence a customer's rating of the user-friendliness of systems A and B. Computer novices may prefer one system and experts prefer the other. In such a case, the data should be stratified by the background variable "familiarity with interactive computer software"; the user-friendliness of the two systems could then be compared at each value of familiarity—for example, for "computer novices" and "computer experts."

controlling for a
variable

In the hiring example, we can say that "the analysis was stratified by department." We can also say that "we controlled for department in the analysis." In general, we should "stratify by" or "control for" all important confounding background variables. The problem in observational studies is that we may not have been able to identify important confounding variables, and therefore we cannot control for them.

2.3

OPERATIONAL DEFINITIONS

When taking measurements or making observations, we must have clear definitions of what is to be measured or observed. It is not enough to have a conceptual definition that will evoke the correct idea. For example, in a study of dog owners, we must **operationally define** who a dog owner is. Do we consider the 4-year-old child who was given a pet dog to be the dog owner? Or is it one of the parents? Is it the parent who cleans up after the dog or who purchases the dog food? In a study of the purchasing behavior of tennis players, we may need a definition of a "tennis player." Is it someone who plays once every 3 years? What about somebody who plays once a year?

An operational definition is such that it can be used by somebody who is not knowledgeable about the problem at hand to determine unambiguously if a person or unit meets the conditions of the definition.

2.4

MEASUREMENT SCALES

All statistical studies measure one or more variables for each unit. The values of a variable typically differ across units or subjects, and we distinguish three kinds of variables according to the relationship among these values. As we will see in later chapters, the statistical analysis of data depends in part on what kind of measurement scale was used for each variable.

1. A **categorical** variable, also called a *nominal scale* variable, has values among which there is no numerical order. The variable "color" may take on the values "red," "blue," "green," and "yellow." It does not make sense to say that "red" is more than "blue" or that "yellow" is less than "green." We could arbitrarily associate the four digits 1, 2, 3, and 4 with the four distinct values, but the magnitudes of the digits have no meaning in this context. Another categorical variable is "sex."

2. An **ordinal** variable has values that have a numerical order, but the differences between successive values cannot be compared. For example, when subjects' incomes are classified as "low," "medium," and "high," these three values are ordered, but they do not allow us to assume that medium would be equidistant between low and high on a numerical scale. We can assign the numbers 1, 2, and 3 to low, medium, and high, respectively, without implying that the classes would be equidistant. In fact, we could equally well assign the numbers 10, 20, and 100 to the values without implying any numerical scale relationship. It would not make sense, however, to associate the number 1 with low, number 3 with medium, and number 2 with high, because both the numbers (1, 2, 3) and the words (low, medium, high) do have a natural order. Another ordinal variable is "agreement," measured as "strongly disagree," "disagree," "neutral," "agree," and "strongly agree."

3. A **quantitative** variable has values that fall into a numerical order and are scaled to allow differences between pairs of values to be compared. For example, the Celsius and Fahrenheit temperature scales are quantitative scales. Consider the following four temperatures, measured on the Celsius scale:

(a)	(b)	(c)	(d)
$-18°$	$0°$	$50°$	$100°$

The numerical difference between temperatures (b) and (c) is the same as that between (c) and (d), so we can say that the temperature differential between (b) and (c) and that between (c) and (d) are equal. However, the temperature differential between (a) and (b) is less than that between (b) and (c). For other examples of quantitative scaling, consider weight as measured in kilograms or pounds, and height as measured in centimeters or inches.

Three **measurement scales** can be distinguished:

1. A **categorical** variable has qualitatively different values among which there is no numerical order.

2. An **ordinal** variable has qualitatively different values that have a

FIGURE 2.6

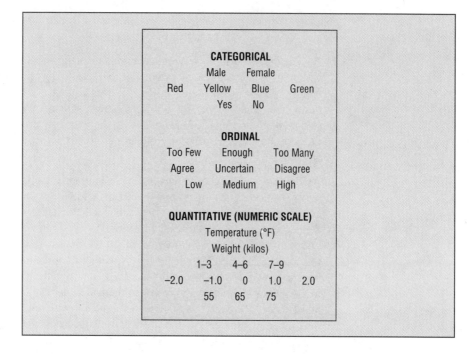

numerical order, but the differences between successive values cannot be compared numerically.

3. A **quantitative** variable has values that have a numerical order according to some quantitative scale; differences between pairs of values can be compared numerically.

2.5

DESIGNING A SIMPLE EXPERIMENT

In Section 2.2, you learned about the differences between experimental and observational studies. In this section, you will learn how to design a simple experiment regarding quality improvement.

One of the first steps is to identify *measurable* quality characteristics. Consider a company that produces a fusion-bond coating of pipelines used for the transmission of natural gas. A study was to be done to compare two alternative suppliers of raw material. Raw material from both sources had been used for some time, but recently some concern had arisen regarding quality. A key measure of quality is the strength of the bond. Strength was measured by an elaborate laboratory procedure established by the national standards association. This procedure was destructive, that is, the coating was damaged, and the extent of damage was measured. The resulting measurement, called disbondment, was measured in millimeters (mm), with values close to 0 most desirable and values exceeding 13 mm unacceptable.

The *unit* in this experiment was a pipe, the *response variable* was disbondment (a quantitative variable), and the *factor* of interest was raw material (a categorical variable). There were two possible values (levels) for the factor, that is, the two types of raw material (say, A and B). An important *background variable* was the diameter of the pipe, and it was controlled for by choosing only 120-cm pipes for the experiment.

Production of pipelines was done in batches, and two batches were produced each day. One 120-cm pipe was to be selected at random from each of 30 successively produced batches, so the experiment was expected to be completed in 2 weeks. *Randomization* was used as follows: Each material, A and B, was to be used in an equal number of batches. So 15 A's and 15 B's were intermingled in random order; raw material A was to be used in a batch if the corresponding value was an A, and material B was to be used otherwise. (This is best done with a computer software package, letting 0 stand for A and 1 for B. In Minitab, you can store 15 zeroes and 15 ones in a data column and then randomly reorder the zeroes and ones in the column. The substitution of 0 for A and 1 for B is necessary in Minitab since Minitab can randomly reorder numerical data only.) The resulting sequence of raw material used for the 30 batches was as follows:

Batch Number:	1	2	3	4	5	6	7	8	9	10
Raw Material:	B	B	A	B	A	A	A	A	B	A

Batch Number:	11	12	13	14	15	16	17	18	19	20
Raw Material:	A	A	B	B	A	A	A	B	B	A

Batch Number:	21	22	23	24	25	26	27	28	29	30
Raw Material:	B	B	B	B	B	B	A	A	B	A

design matrix

In this example, the correspondence between batch and type of raw material is called the *design matrix*. In general, the design matrix is a table associating each unit with a level of the factor of interest.

It is important to have a proper *data collection form* for an experiment. The form should provide space for the values of the response variable and preferably for a simple graph of these values arranged in order of collection. In addition, the form should have space for comments regarding unusual events that might influence the results of the experiment.

After data collection, the pipeline data were first to be analyzed graphically and then to be summarized more succinctly in numerical form. The cost of the experiment was not considered to be high since the study could be done during 2 weeks of regular production. The details of the experiment are summarized in Figure 2.7.

Randomization was used in this experiment to help prevent the effects of nuisance variables from being confounded with the effects of the factor of interest.

FIGURE 2.7 Documentation Form for Comparison of Two Raw Materials

1. **Objective:** Compare two raw materials used in the coating of pipelines.

2. **Background information:** The two suppliers providing raw material have been used for some time, and recently some concerns have arisen regarding their quality. The current raw material provided by each supplier has not been formally compared, and it is thought that the raw material of one of the suppliers will lead to a higher quality bond.

3. **Experimental variables:**

A. Response variable	Measurement technique	Target level
1. Disbondment	Laboratory test prescribed by standards association	≤13 mm

B. Factors	Level
1. Raw material	Type A, type B

C. Background variables	Method of control
1. Pipe diameter	Only pipes with 120-cm diameter were to be used

4. **Replication:** One 120-cm pipe will be selected by a random device from each of 30 successively produced batches. The experiment is expected to be completed in 2 weeks.

5. **Methods of randomization:** Each material is to be used in an equal number of batches. So 15 A's and 15 B's were arranged in random order. Raw material A is to be used in a batch if the corresponding value is an A.

6. **Design matrix:** (attach copy) See p. 23.

7. **Data collection forms:** (attach copy) Data will be recorded and graphed in order.

8. **Planned methods of statistical analysis:** Graph of disbondment values; graphs of disbondment values grouped by raw material

9. **Estimated cost, schedule, and other resource considerations:** The study can be done during the next 2 weeks of production.

SOURCE: This documentation form is adapted from Moen, Nolan, and Provost (1991).

There was only one identified background variable, pipe diameter, which was set to 120 cm. Pipe diameter was not thought to influence the quality of the bonding process. If it did, a more complex experiment would have to be run. Two batches were produced each day, but shift and day of the week were not considered to be important background variables in this application.

We will have more to say about design of experiments in subsequent chapters. The text by Moen, Nolan, and Provost (1991) is a good introduction to the topic.

2.6

POPULATIONS, PROCESSES, AND SAMPLES

The idea of a population is useful in cross-sectional studies, and that of a process in time series studies. In both cases, we shall speak of *samples,* which are limited sets of units or data drawn from a larger pool.

What ultimately determines whether we have a cross-sectional or a time series study is not what questions the study was *intended* to answer, but how the study was actually *carried out.*

Whether a time series or a cross-sectional study is appropriate depends on the questions to be answered and the availability of data. When interest focuses on the behavior of a system or process, a time series study is warranted since the process evolves *over time;* what is typically of interest is whether the process measurements are stable over time, increasing or decreasing, or changing according to some other time series pattern. Data for a cross-sectional study, on the other hand, are recorded to show the state of a population *at a particular point of time*—interest focuses on getting a "snapshot" picture.

What ultimately determines whether we have a cross-sectional or a time series study is not what questions the study was *intended* to answer, but how the study was actually *carried out.*

Populations and Cross-Sectional Studies

Cross-sectional studies, also called *enumerative,* examine characteristics of a set of units or subjects at a particular point in time. The **population** consists of all units or subjects that are of interest to the study.

For example, the medical records department of a hospital has 10 interdependent sections, each overseen by a front-line supervisor. In 1988 its total staffing complement was 120 employees. Because increasing absenteeism was affecting departmental efficiency, productivity, and staff morale, a study was done to examine the overall incidence of absenteeism in the department and in each section for one year. Here the *population* consisted of the 120 employees, and each employee is a *subject.* The *variables* measured for each subject are (1) number of absences in one year and (2) section. The response variable is "number of absences." The factor is "section."

As another example, consider an auditor who wants to know whether the book value for balance sheet items is fairly stated at year-end. One important component of the balance sheet is inventory, which can be viewed as a *population* of individual inventory *units.* Each unit is characterized by several *variables,* such as inventory number, date of purchase, location of unit, book value, and actual value. In order to check exactly whether the total book value for all inventory units is fairly stated, the auditor must investigate every unit in inventory and verify that its book value equals its actual or audit value. That is, the auditor will carry out a **census:** In a census, every unit in the population (every item in the inventory account) must be examined with respect to the variables of interest.

census

The following definition is important:

The **frame** is a list of all units or subjects in the population.

In the medical records department example, the population consists of the 120 employees, and the **frame** is a *list* of these 120 employees. In the inventory example, the population consists of all inventory units at year-end, and the frame is a list of all these inventory units. Two additional examples are: (1) If a company is interested in its present customers' satisfaction with a particular service, the frame will be a list of all present customers. (2) If a manufacturer wants to know the proportion of defective products in a batch of output produced with a new manufacturing process, the frame will be a list of all products in the batch.

sample

When a census is impractical, the investigator can examine only a *sample* of units drawn from the population. A census may not be feasible when its cost is prohibitive or when taking the entire population is destructive. For example, when you go to the doctor to have your blood tested, you will clearly prefer that the doctor take a few million blood cells rather than your entire blood supply. In the auditor's case, it may be too costly to investigate all inventory units, so only a few hundred units will be drawn from the population of units.

population parameter

sample statistic

Often we want to know a numerical aspect of a population, such as the average audit value of all inventory units. Such a numerical summary is called a population **parameter.** When summarizing the values in a sample drawn from a population, the numerical summary is called a sample **statistic.** For example, the average audit value of inventory units in the sample is a statistic. (Note that statisticians never use the word "parameter" in relation to a sample or "statistic" in relation to a population.) Typically, one would like to know population parameters, but when they are not available, they often can be estimated by sample statistics. Subsequent chapters discuss the problem of imprecision (the *error margin*) that can result when a statistic is used to estimate a parameter.

Samples can be drawn in various ways. The main intent is that we can *generalize* from the sample to the population. A *judgment* sample consists of a set of units drawn according to the investigator's judgment. If the judgment is not good, we cannot generalize from the sample. Since hidden factors (such as preferences, likes, and dislikes) can enter into the investigator's selection process, a judgment sample may not allow generalization, and should be avoided.

A *systematic* sample is obtained by including, for example, every third, fifth, or tenth unit in the sample. Such systematic samples may not allow generalization to the population because of some periodicity in the data. For example, if the population consists of all working days in a particular year and if every fifth unit (that is, day) is selected to be part of the sample, then the sample might consist only of data for Mondays. If the variable of interest were related to the day of the week, this sample would be seriously biased.

To prevent nuisance variables from biasing the sample, impartial selection is needed. This can be achieved by drawing a **random sample** which is defined as follows:

> A **random sample** is drawn by (1) selecting units sequentially from the frame of the population, and (2) giving each unit in the frame the same chance of being selected at each point in the sequence.

The operational steps required to obtain a random sample will be described more fully in Section 4.3.

In addition to avoiding biases from unidentified factors, a random sample has other advantages: The main one is that statistical tools allow generalizations from the random sample to the population. In particular, the margin of error can be determined when estimating a parameter from a statistic.

To continue with the inventory example, the managerial question was:

Is the reported total book value at year-end close enough to the actual total value at year-end?

The statistical question could be:

What is the actual total value for the population at year-end?

Suppose that there are 10,000 items in inventory, so the population consists of 10,000 units. Rather than using the population total, we can also use the population mean, which is simply

$$\text{Population Mean} = \frac{\text{Population Total}}{10,000}$$

Either the population total or the population mean might be the parameter of interest here. (We will say much more about means and related measures in Chapter 3.)

In this kind of auditing situation, a census is prohibitively expensive, so the population mean cannot be obtained exactly. Suppose that the auditor decided to randomly sample 100 units from the population frame, record their actual value, and compute the sample mean of these 100 values, which turned out to be $70. The sample mean is the statistic, and its value ($70) can be used to *estimate* the population mean, the parameter of interest.

Later chapters will show how we can supplement this estimate with a statement about how much it is likely to differ from the population mean. In Chapter 7 we will gain the tools to construct statements such as: "The estimate of the population mean is $70, and we are highly confident that the margin of error for this estimate is no more than $5."

When statistics obtained from a random sample are used to estimate population parameters, we can compute information regarding the margin of error, that is, the amount by which the statistic is likely to differ from the value of the unknown **sampling error**   parameter. This error, which is due to chance alone, is called the *sampling error.*

Often a random sample cannot be obtained. A list of all units or subjects in the population may not be available, or it may be too costly to include particular units or subjects in the sample. For example, in studying preferences of U.S. customers, it may not be possible to include customers who live in Alaska or Hawaii because of travel costs.

nonsampling error

Errors or biases that enter the study because the sampling procedure was not random are called *nonsampling errors,* because they are *not* due to the random sampling procedure. There are many possible sources of nonsampling error, and the investigator must plan carefully to avoid them.

For example, suppose that a software company is interested in its customers' attitudes toward a change in a·popular software product. The population of interest might be all customers who presently have licensing agreements. A random sample could be taken from this population to gauge customer attitudes. If, however, last year's list of customers with licensing agreements is used as the frame from which the random sample is chosen, errors may be introduced into the analysis because today's customer population differs from last year's.

nonresponse

One important, but frequently ignored, source of nonsampling error is *nonresponse.* Even if a sample is randomly drawn from the correct frame, the resulting sample *available for analysis* may not be random because of nonresponse. For example, some people may refuse to participate in a study, or working people may be missed by a daytime telephone survey. The nonrespondents may be characterized by certain factors that will influence the outcome of the study, which may make the sample nonrepresentative of the population of interest. Ignoring nonresponse is often a serious source of bias.

neutrality of nonresponse

The important question to ask is whether nonresponse is *neutral* with respect to the variables of interest. For example, suppose you want to conduct a survey, and one of the questions is the respondent's age. Some people may not return the survey because they do not want to give their age. Unless age is entirely unrelated—that is, neutral—to the response to all questions, this nonresponse will bias the results. This bias can be seen easily by dividing the population into subpopulation A (those subjects who will not return the survey because of the age question) and subpopulation B (all others). (We have ignored the fact that there may be reasons for nonresponse other than presence of the age question.) If these two subpopulations differ with respect to the variables of interest, then nonresponse implies that the resulting analyses can be generalized only to subpopulation B instead of to the entire population of interest.

Processes and Time Series Studies

Cross-sectional studies can be viewed as providing a "snapshot" of a phenomenon at a particular point in time, whereas time series studies (also called *analytic* studies) examine properties of a *process* that is evolving over time. A frame cannot be obtained for such a study. For example, we may be interested in the error rate of a check-processing system for a bank. Here our interest extends not only to the checks already processed, but also to checks to be processed in the future—although future checks clearly cannot be included in the frame.

system, process
In this and similar situations, managers are interested in the characteristics of a **system** or **process** (this book uses the terms interchangeably), which is "a set of causes and conditions that repeatedly come together to transform inputs into outcomes" (Moen, Nolan, and Provost, 1991). In the study of a process, the idea of a "population" is elusive since a frame does not exist, and so it is not useful. When a frame does not exist, we cannot draw a random sample, and we must take considerable care in generalizing from the sample to the process.

When studying a process, the *unit* is often, but not necessarily, a unit of time. For example, Study 4 described in Chapter 1 (customer service in an IBM dispatch operation) was a study of a process. The unit was the work day in the dispatch operation, and several variables were collected daily. The unit was not an individual customer call since no data were collected (that is, observed) for individual calls. Instead, data were aggregated for all calls received throughout the workday. One of the important *variables* was the number of calls received per day.

As a second example, consider Study 1 from Chapter 1, airborne particulates in clean rooms. The unit was a particular clean room on a given day at a particular time. Its condition was monitored daily.

When studying a process, managerial questions are typically related to the *future* behavior of the process. The sample from the process, to be used to help answer the managerial questions, usually consists of observations from a recent time segment of the process. For example, Study 4 in Chapter 1 was undertaken to determine whether the dispatch process at an IBM operation was meeting the stated objective of responding to customer calls within 16 seconds. The sample consisted of the most recent 70 days in the life of the process. But what managers really wanted to know was whether the process would continue to meet the stated objective in the near future.

Cross-Sectional vs. Time Series Studies

This subsection directly contrasts cross-sectional and time series studies, and gives examples of when each is appropriate. In a cross-sectional study, we want to characterize an *existing* population; once the frame is available, either a census or a random sample can be taken and described. Based on the results, some action can then be taken on the population. In a time series study, we want to characterize a process over time and, in particular, predict its *future* behavior. A frame does not exist in a time series study. A time series study "is one in which action will be taken on a cause-and-effect system to improve performance of a product or a process in the future" (Deming, 1975).

One important business application of a cross-sectional study is the survey. In general, business applications are more often time series studies than cross-sectional studies. Distinct statistical tools are often needed for these two types of studies. However, we will see that time series studies can sometimes be analyzed with the same tools that are appropriate for cross-sectional studies: This will be so whenever there is no information in the *sequence* of values as they are recorded over time, so that the sequential order can be ignored.

When managers need to project into the future or show the development over time, a time series study is in order, and data should be recorded consecutively.

When a population is to be described, a cross-sectional study is in order and a random sample must be taken from it to allow for proper inferences (unless a census of the population can be taken).

Let us now look at some examples to illustrate how to distinguish whether a study is cross-sectional or time series.

EXAMPLE 2.5

The aggregate behavior of the stocks traded at many stock exchanges is often described by an index, such as the Dow Jones index or the Toronto Stock Exchange composite index (TSE 300). Investors want to know how the index has developed over time, to discern any patterns, and to make predictions.

The stock index is used as a proxy for the health of the economic system whose stocks are traded on the exchange. A value of the index is computed for every trading day, so a time series of index values is available for successive trading days. With appropriate time series tools, the past patterns in this time series can be described. These patterns may then be useful to forecast the behavior of the stock index in the future.

EXAMPLE 2.6

The surgical suites of most hospitals are available 24 hours a day, mostly to accommodate urgent or nonelective operations. When staff surgeons wish to perform nonelective surgery, they book the operating room with the charge nurse. Management at a large hospital is concerned about long waiting times for nonelective surgery, where waiting time is defined as the time from booking nonelective surgery to the patient's arrival in the operating room. A study is to be done to obtain average waiting time for nonelective surgery.

At first glance this may appear to be a cross-sectional study, since there is no obvious time series aspect to the study. The unit is a "booking" and the variable of interest is "waiting time." But what is the population? The concept of population is elusive here, since bookings are done consecutively, and so all conceivable bookings of interest do not exist at a given point in time—bookings *evolve over time*. Though the managerial question does not have a time series component, it is tacitly assumed that recent bookings will be informative about bookings in the near future. For these reasons, a time series study of the process is in order, with the process defined as bookings of nonelective surgery at the hospital. If there is no time series pattern to recent waiting times (we call such a process *stable*), then it may be reasonable to assume that the process will be stable in the near future as well. Average waiting time for recent bookings will then be a good guide for waiting times in the near future. But if there is a time series pattern to recent waiting times, then we should describe this pattern and possibly project it into the future. For example, if waiting times tend to be increasing, then further increases should be expected in the near future, and average waiting time for recent bookings will be a poor guide for waiting times in the near future.

EXAMPLE 2.7

In June 1991, Statistics Canada carried out a census of the Canadian population. Such a census is an extremely complex data-gathering effort. Some of the questions related to demographic variables such as age, marital status, and sex. Other questions related to housing and employment. A main purpose for the census was to gather information useful for business and for social and economic policy decisions.

The information gathered in the census provides a snapshot of the Canadian population at a particular point in time—the day or year when the census was taken, depending on the question. The census is thus a very large-scale cross-sectional study of a population whose subjects are the residents of Canada when the census is taken.

EXAMPLE 2.8

A company was interested in the picking and packing activities of its shipping department. Once an order had been received and entered into the order-entry system, a pick slip was sent to the distribution department so that the order could be prepared and shipped. A study was undertaken to answer two questions:

- Is there a relationship between the time taken to pick and pack an order and certain other characteristics of the order?

- Is it possible to estimate accurately the time required to pick and pack an order for shipment to a customer?

The data were collected as follows. Using the order-entry system, 98 orders were randomly picked from all orders shipped in October 1988. Six variables relevant to the study were measured for each order.

As carried out, the study is *cross-sectional.* The population of interest consists of all orders shipped in October, and the order-entry system contains the frame of all these orders. The unit is an order, and the number of units in the population was not given. The results from the study can be used to answer the two questions for the population of interest only, that is, the orders shipped in October 1988.

If the intent of the study had been to describe the picking and packing *process* and to predict its behavior in the near future, then the study should have been conducted as a time series study, and the data-gathering effort should have been different: One order could have been picked at random each day from July through October 1988, yielding about 100 orders. Keeping the observations in their original time order, information would have been available to examine whether the process was changing over time. This knowledge might have been useful for predicting process performance for a time period after the conclusion of the study.

As actually carried out, the study did not collect information regarding the time order for the 98 orders, and so the study did not yield information about the picking and packing *process,* but only about the *population* of orders shipped in October 1988. The data, as collected, do not justify generalizations to later time periods, say, November 1988.

2.7

BRIEF INTRODUCTION TO SURVEYS

FIGURE 2.8

SURVEY STEPS

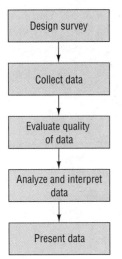

One important type of cross-sectional study is the **survey,** which consists of a standardized set of questions posed to numerous organizations or individual respondents. For example, an opinion poll of eligible voters regarding an upcoming election is a survey. Another example is the Current Population Survey of the U.S. Bureau of Labor Statistics, which gathers basic information on the labor force, employment, and unemployment. Yet another example is auditing, where auditors estimate account balances.

A proper survey is carried out by carefully planning and executing a sequence of steps. The important steps in a survey are designing of the survey, collecting survey data, evaluating the quality of the data, analyzing and interpreting the data, and presenting the data.

Carrying out a survey can be expensive and time-consuming. To complete a survey involving a few thousand individuals may take anywhere from a few months to more than a year. It is therefore important that the quality of the survey be built into the process from the initial planning stage.

Typically, the data are collected from a sample of the population. Samples are chosen scientifically, that is, by some form of random selection. Random selection is essential since it makes it possible to project the results reliably to the larger population from which the sample was chosen.

The data from many surveys are collected with questionnaires. The results are presented in the form of graphical, tabular, and numerical summaries.

An important point in the design of a survey is the choice of sample size. No general advice on specific sample size is possible since the size needed depends on the reliability needed, which in turn depends on how the results will be used. (Note that, in many opinion polls, the sample size is about 1,000–1,500, which is sufficient for a large population such as that of Canada or the United States.)

Surveys are done by many organizations, private (such as the Gallup Poll) and public (such as Statistics Canada and the U.S. Bureau of the Census). Many individual companies, for example, use surveys to find out their customers' satisfaction with their services and products. Local transportation authorities use surveys to establish people's commuting and travel habits.

There are many types of surveys, and they can be distinguished by characteristics such as

- Population group studied

- Method of data collection

- Content

- Type of question

The population can be the entire population of a country, or it can be a special group such as business leaders or the unemployed. Methods of data collection range from interviews (by mail, by telephone, or in person) to the use of special devices attached to television sets to record which channels were watched during a particular time period. The survey content can probe opinions or attitudes, or it can establish factual characteristics. The type of question used can be open-ended, where the respondents can write in a response as they see fit, or closed, where respondents choose one of several listed options. Of course, many surveys combine different types of questions in various ways.

When collecting information through a survey, all reputable survey organizations are concerned with maintaining the privacy of the information supplied by survey respondents and the identities of the respondents.

We will discuss surveys in a little more detail in Chapter 4. For additional information, see the booklet by Ferber, Sheatsley, Turner, and Waksberg (n.d.) and the text by Scheaffer, Mendenhall, and Ott (1990).

2.8

FURTHER NOTES ON THE TERM *RANDOM*

So far in this chapter, we have encountered the term *random* in two ways: in random sampling and randomization. Random sampling refers to sampling methods that ensure the absence of bias in the selection of the sample from the population so that no part of the population is favored. It also permits us to determine a margin of error when generalizing from the sample to the population. Using a larger random sample increases our confidence in generalizations from the sample to the population. Later chapters will say more about the methods of random sampling.

Randomization refers to methods that ensure the absence of bias in the allocation of units to treatment and control groups, that is, to the different levels of the factor of interest. Units with special properties are not favored in choosing any group. The allocation of units may differ in repeated trials. Using larger randomly chosen treatment and control groups increases our confidence that the groups are similar before the treatment is applied.

Random sampling and randomization both try to achieve the same goal—to ensure the absence of biases by impartial selection of units. Of course, there are no guarantees that the sampling error is small: Just due to chance, the sample can be quite different from the population.

2.9

DATA SOURCES

It is not always necessary to gather the data for a study. Often existing data sources can be used. In addition to government statistics, such as figures from the U.S. Bureau of the Census or Statistics Canada or data from the federal, provincial, state, or municipal governments, there are many other sources, such as employers' organizations, trade associations, research institutes, and existing data within a firm.

2.10

SUMMARY AND OUTLOOK

In this chapter, we have discussed aspects of the data collection phase and its planning. We distinguished between experimental and observational studies and between cross-sectional (enumerative) and time series (analytic) studies. The ideas of randomization and random sampling were also introduced.

In the next chapter, we assume that data have been collected for a study. We discuss how the information in the data can be summarized graphically and numerically.

Key Terms and Concepts

unit, subject, variable	cross-sectional study
experimental study, observational study	*population, frame, census, random*
randomization, confounding	*sample, survey*
operational definition	time series study
measurement scale	*process*
categorical, ordinal, quantitative	parameter, statistic

References

Deming, W. E. (1975), "On Probability as a Basis for Action," *The American Statistician,* Vol. 29(4), pp. 146–152.

Ferber, R., Sheatsley, P., Turner, A., and Waksberg, J. (n.d.), "What Is a Survey?", American Statistical Association, Washington, D.C.

This little booklet gives a good nontechnical introduction to surveys.

Moen, R. D., Nolan, T. W., and Provost, L. P. (1991), *Improving Quality Through Planned Experimentation,* McGraw-Hill, New York.

This book gives an excellent introduction to the design of experiments at an elementary level.

Scheaffer, R. L., Mendenhall, W., and Ott, L. (1990), *Elementary Survey Sampling,* 4th Edition, Duxbury Press, Belmont, CA.

This book gives a thorough introduction to survey sampling.

2.11

PROBLEMS FOR CLASS DISCUSSION

2.1 Industrial Product Inc.

Industrial Product Inc.[2] (IPI) designs and builds an industrial product. The drawings are produced in the drafting department by a staff of 12. A full set of drawings consists of one general arrangement (GA) drawing and between 6 and 30 detail drawings, depending on the number of accessories that have been ordered as part of the industrial product. GA drawings are always on size D paper; detail drawings may be on A, B, C, or D size paper. D paper is twice the size of C paper, which in turn is twice the size of B paper, which in turn is twice the size of A paper; that is, D paper is 8 times the size of A paper. After the drawings are done, revisions are often required.

A study was done to answer several questions. The main concern was as follows:

The sales department wanted to know how much time was spent on the drawings for the industrial product so that they could more accurately estimate the delivery date of an order and the labor costs of doing the drawings.

Predicting the time spent on an order was also important for scheduling different jobs. The following questions were to be answered:

1. Can the time spent to do the GA drawings be predicted from the number of detail drawings, taking into consideration that the latter can be of different sizes?

2. Is there a relationship between the time to do the detail drawings and the time spent on revisions? Are some jobs done too quickly?

How should the study be conducted? Should this be a cross-sectional or a time series study? What is the population or process? What is the unit? What variables should be measured? Which is the response variable? Are there important background variables?

2.2 Bell Canada

Extended Area Service (EAS) is Bell Canada's official name for a local calling area (the area within which calls can be made without additional charges). For example, in 1989 Toronto exchange customers could make local calls to over 1.3 million telephone numbers in their base Toronto exchange plus over .6 million in 26 adjacent exchanges. These 27 exchanges composed Toronto's local calling area. In general, as the size of a local calling area increases, so does the fixed monthly rate, which was about $13 for Toronto residents in 1989.

If the local calling area is to be extended, public support is needed. Bell Canada carries out surveys to gauge public support for any proposed EAS. The Canadian Radio-

---

[2] The name of the company is withheld to protect confidentiality.

television and Telecommunications Commission (CRTC) requires that certain criteria be met before a local calling area is extended (and the monthly rate is increased). These criteria are that (1) the switching centers of the two exchanges in question be no more than 40 miles apart, (2) at least 60% of the customers in one exchange call the other exchange at least once monthly, and (3) a simple majority of those customers whose monthly flat-rate charge for telephone lines would increase must support the proposal in a mail survey.

In May 1989, the 15,772 Bell Canada customers in the Whitby telephone exchange were surveyed regarding their exchange's inclusion in the Toronto local calling area. The Whitby exchange is 27 miles east of downtown Toronto. It is known that 75% of Whitby customers call Toronto at least once a month and that the average Whitby caller makes 12 calls to Toronto per month. Bell Canada proposed to eliminate long distance toll charges on calls from Whitby to Toronto and to increase the monthly flat rate by $10.25, from $8.75 to $19. Only 44.5% of respondents, however, voted for this proposal. This was somewhat surprising since (1) Bell estimates that if 35% of the customers break even on the toll/local call equation, then more than 50% of customers will vote in favor of EAS, and (2) it was known from toll records that the average call from Whitby to Toronto cost $0.94.

To learn more about differences between the pro-EAS and the anti-EAS voters in Whitby, a study was to be done to answer the question:

Do "for" voters differ from "against" voters in any of the following respects?

- The number of calls to Toronto

- The monthly dollars spent on calls to Toronto

- The total monthly telephone bill

- The extent to which they subscribe to Custom Calling Features (such as call-forwarding)

How should the study be conducted? Should this be a cross-sectional or a time series study? What is the population or process? What is the unit? What variables should be measured? Which one is the response variable? The factor of interest? Are there important background variables?

2.3 Northern Telecom

To ensure that proprietary information is properly protected at its headquarters building, Northern Telecom has developed security procedures to be followed by its employees. A study in 1988 examined the extent of compliance with these procedures, in particular, regarding security after regular working hours. There were 284 employees at the headquarters building whose adherence to the procedures was relevant to the study. The following questions were to be addressed:

What is the extent of compliance with the policy regarding "clean and locked" desks outside working hours?

What is the extent of compliance with the policy regarding security of personal computers and related media?

How should the study be conducted? Should this be a cross-sectional or a time series study? What is the population or process? What is the unit? Which variables should be measured? Which one is the response variable? Are there important background variables?

2.12

EXERCISES

Although answers are given in Appendix D, do not turn to them right away if you cannot find an answer on your own. Return to the exercise the next day and try again before turning to Appendix D.

Exercises for Section 2.2

2.4 This exercise relates to Example 2.4 (p. 19).
   a From the information given in Figure 2.5 (p. 19), derive the overall proportions of men and women hired, 31.4% and 23.0%.
   b Figure 2.5 does not suggest a gender bias. List factors not measured in the example that could be used for stratification and that might uncover a gender bias.

2.5 Magazine publishers carefully monitor rates of renewal of expiring subscriptions. For example, at *American History Illustrated* in early 1979, the publishers were pleased to note an increase in the overall renewal rate from 51.2% in January to 64.1% in February. These data are taken from the following table where renewals are given for selected subscription categories. "Total" refers to the total number of subscriptions up for renewal, and "Renewals" refers to the number of renewals. Did the publishers have reason to be pleased? Present your results in a suitable table.

Source of Current Subscriptions

Month	Gift	Previous Renewal	Direct Mail	Subscriptions Service	Catalog Agent	Overall
January						
Total	3,594	18,364	2,986	20,862	149	45,955
Renewals	2,918	14,488	1,783	4,343	13	23,545
February						
Total	884	5,140	2,224	864	45	9,157
Renewals	704	3,907	1,134	122	2	5,869

SOURCE: C. H. Wagner, *The American Statistician*, 1982, p. 46.

2.6 In 1976, Pepsi-Cola ran an advertising campaign on TV featuring an experiment. Regular drinkers of Coca-Cola were given a glass of Coke marked only as "Q," and then a glass of Pepsi marked only as "M." More than half of the subjects said brand "M" tasted better.
   a What is the population of interest? The unit? What is the response variable?
   b Which variables with a potential effect on the response variable are explicitly mentioned above? Can you think of other influential variables?
   c Is this an experimental study or an observational study? Discuss.

> **d** Coca-Cola said that this experiment was invalid because the effects of the brand of cola and an extraneous variable were confounded. Can you see where the confounding lies? Discuss.
>
> **e** In a repetition of the experiment, what would you do to avoid the confounding described in (d)? With this modification, answer (c).

Exercises for Section 2.4

2.7 One of the questions in a survey relates to age and reads:

Please give information about your age by making a check mark on the appropriate line:

25 years or younger	_____
over 25 years up to 35 years	_____
over 35 years up to 50 years	_____
over 50 years up to 60 years	_____
over 60 years	_____

What kind of measurement scale is being used here?

2.8 Consider the 7 days of the week, Monday to Sunday, and let Monday = 1, Tuesday = 2, etc. If possible, describe a situation where the coding for weekdays represents (a) a categorical measurement scale, and (b) a quantitative scale.

Exercises for Section 2.6

2.9 Advice columnist Ann Landers was once asked whether having children was worth the problems involved. A few weeks after asking her readers, "If you had to do it over again, would you have children?" her column was headlined "70% of parents say kids are not worth it," for 70% of the parents who responded wrote that they would not have children if they could make the choice again.

a Describe the population and the unit. What is the response variable? Is the sample of respondents a random sample from the population?

b Is this sample biased? Why, and in what direction?

2.10 If you want to sample public opinion quickly and inexpensively, Bell Canada will set up "900" telephone numbers for you and will inform you of how many calls were made to each number. All you need to do is announce your question on TV, give one number for "Yes" and one for "No," and wait. The respondents simply dial the number appropriate for their response; no word from them is needed. Bell Canada will either charge you for the calls or add a small fee to a respondent's telephone bill (50¢ in 1987).

a Describe the population and the unit. Is the sample of respondents a random sample from the population?

b Are such call-in polls likely to be biased? If so, can you suggest the direction of the bias?

2.11 Some market research is obtained by phone from samples chosen from telephone directories. The sampling frame therefore omits households having no phones or having unlisted phone numbers.

    a What is the population of interest? What is the unit?

    b What groups of people will be underrepresented by such a sampling procedure?

    c Can you suggest a way of including households with (i) unlisted numbers, and (ii) with no phones?

2.12 A study of the effect of living in public housing on family stability in poverty-level households has been proposed. The sample selection procedure is to be as follows: A list of applicants who were accepted for public housing and a list of applicants who were rejected are to be obtained. A random sample from each list is to be drawn, and the two groups are to be observed for several years.

    a What is the population? What is the unit? What is the response variable?

    b Which variables with potential effects on the response variable are explicitly mentioned above? Can you think of other influential variables?

    c Is this an experimental study? Why or why not?

    d What is the treatment? What is the control?

    e List one or more confounding variables that may introduce bias into the sample results.

2.13 Treat Study 2 (document translation), described in Chapter 1 (p. 6), as a cross-sectional study and answer the following questions.

    a What is the unit? What is the population of interest? What is the frame?

    b What are the important variables? Is there a response variable? If so, what is it? What purpose do the other variables serve?

2.14 Treat Study 2 (document translation), described in Chapter 1 (p. 6), as a time series study and answer the following questions.

    a What is the unit? What is the process?

    b What are the important variables? Is there a response variable? If so, what is it? What purpose do the other variables serve?

2.15 Given the very limited information about Study 1 (clean rooms) in Chapter 1 (p. 6), would you do Study 1 as a cross-sectional or as a time series study? What about Study 3 (student survey) (p. 6)? Depending on your conclusion, answer the questions in Exercise 2.13 or 2.14.

2.16 In each of the following two situations, briefly identify the population, the unit, the variables measured, and the sample. If enough detail is not provided, complete the information in a reasonable way. Be sure that from your description it is possible to tell exactly when a unit is in the population and when it is not.

    Each situation described contains a serious source of probable bias so that the sample conclusions will probably differ from the truth about the population. Discuss the reason for the bias and its likely direction.

    a A legislator is interested in whether her constituents favor a proposed abortion bill. Her staff reports that letters on the bill have been received from 400 constituents and that 250 favor the bill.

    b The police department of a large city wants to know how Chinese residents feel about police service. A questionnaire with questions about police service is prepared. A sample of 500 mailing addresses in predominantly Chinese neighborhoods is chosen, and a police officer is sent to each address to administer the questionnaire to an adult living there.

2.17   Ralston Purina Canada Inc. distributes its agricultural products to its customers through a network of independent franchised dealers. Each dealer operates in a defined trading area or *market* that is made up of a number of townships. Each market has one or more dealers. Ralston Purina's objective is to achieve maximum market share with its line of feed products through this franchise network. To this end, markets must be selected in such a way that they are large enough to allow dealers to reach a profitable sales volume, yet small enough to ensure that dealers quickly reach a targeted share of the market. A study was undertaken to answer the following questions.

What is the relationship between market share and market potential for Ralston Purina markets in Ontario?

How is market share in 1987 related to that in 1988?

Data were collected for all 96 markets in Ontario. Three variables were measured for each market: (1) 1987 feed purchases made by producers in the market (in metric tons), (2) Ralston Purina's market share in 1987 (in percent), and (3) Ralston Purina's market share in 1988 (in percent).
Is this a study of a population or a process? What is the unit?

2.18   Company X specializes in printing various types of labels. Since new printing orders require allocation of considerably more resources (such as for equipment set-up) than repeat orders, the management was interested in determining the proportion of new orders among all printing orders processed by the company. A recent study collected data for the last 50 orders processed. Identify the study as cross-sectional or time series. Describe either the population or process, the unit, and the response variable. Is the response variable categorical, ordinal, or quantitative?

2.13

SUPPLEMENTARY EXERCISES

2.19   Consider the following questions regarding the TV commercial experiment, Example 2.1 (p. 13):
a   Define the group of people toward whom the company would like to address its advertising effort; that is, define the population of interest. What is the unit?
b   What is the relationship between the volunteer group in the study and the viewing audience for the commercial, if it is aired?
c   What is the relationship between the volunteer group and the population of interest? Between the viewing audience and the population of interest?
d   Is the volunteer group a random sample from the population of interest? If not, what biases might this introduce?
e   How useful is it to use coupons to check purchasing behavior? What biases might this introduce, given that the company wants to know what the effect on purchasing behavior will be of a future airing of the TV commercial?
f   Can you think of other factors that would make you be careful about judging the effectiveness of the TV commercial based on the results of this experiment?
g   Give an operational definition of "dog owner" useful for this kind of a study.
h   What are the implications of telling subjects which dog food company is conducting the study? Should this be done or not? Justify your answer.

2.20 Give an operational definition for "mother with small children" to be used by somebody who is to hand out questionnaires to such mothers at the entrance to a supermarket.

2.21 Response to a proposal often varies with its source. Try the following: Tell several of your friends that you are collecting opinions for a course. Ask some,

> Thomas Jefferson said, "I hold that a little rebellion, now and then, is a good thing, and as necessary in the political world as storms are in the physical." Do you generally agree or generally disagree with this statement?

Ask others the same question, but replace "Thomas Jefferson said" with "Lenin said." Be sure to ask each privately. To avoid bias, randomize the question you ask each person by tossing a coin. Record the opinions you obtain and briefly discuss your results.

2.22 In 1975, the Dutch government introduced random selection for admitting students to university programs in medicine and a few related areas because there were many more applicants than openings. The random selection is stratified so that students with higher grades have a greater chance of being chosen.
a What is the population? What is the unit?
b Do you favor such a system? Why?

2.23 In many questionnaires, ethical problems arise because two conflicting goals must be balanced, (1) not deceiving respondents as to what the questionnaire will tell about them, and (2) not biasing the sample by scaring off certain types of people. To check the hypothesis that orthodox religious beliefs tend to be associated with an authoritarian personality, a questionnaire is prepared to measure authoritarian tendencies and to ask religious questions. Write a description of the purpose of this research to be read to potential respondents.

2.24 **a** Given the very limited information about Study 5 in Chapter 1 (p. 7), would you do Study 5 as a cross-sectional or as a time series study? Depending on your conclusion, answer the questions in Exercise 2.13 or 2.14.
b Consider Study 4 in Chapter 1 and the very limited information given about it. Aggregate daily data were automatically collected by the dispatch operation. In particular, three variables were measured each day: the total waiting time for all customers, the number of incoming calls, and the number of operators on duty. Since these daily data were readily available, it had been proposed to use them for this study. Given the use of these available data, would you do Study 4 as a cross-sectional or as a time series study? Depending on your conclusion, answer the questions in Exercise 2.13 or 2.14. How useful are the available data to determine whether the dispatch process was meeting the stated objective for responding to customer calls?
c Answer the questions in (a) with respect to the following study:

> In 1988, a Campbell Soup Company mushroom farm produced 160,000 pounds of mushrooms per week. Each day, between 100 and 200 employees were needed to manually harvest the mushrooms from the bed. It was easy to misjudge the number of people required, so the job could not always be finished on time. When this happened frequently, the employees became demoralized and angry since they were often asked to work through supper. Furthermore, the product lost value if left unpicked overnight, since a viral disease could result, causing yield reductions of 50% and revenue losses of $15,000 per day. To improve the situation, a model was developed that was used each morning to estimate harvest completion time that day. This estimate could be used to take appropri-

ate action if estimated completion time was longer than 10 hours. The estimate was based on the estimated size of the harvest, the number of harvesters who had been scheduled for that day one week earlier, the harvesting group's average speed, and any factors that might affect that speed. A study was done to examine the stability and precision of these estimates.

2.25 Consider Examples 2.2 and 2.3 (pp. 14 and 17), which are concerned with two library software systems. Two possible experimental set-ups were described in the text. Briefly list the advantages and disadvantages of both, and indicate which one you would recommend.

2.26 Control Data is a manufacturer of several computer series. Whenever changes to the series are made, documents regarding it must be revised. Such revisions are initiated by "change orders."

A study was undertaken to answer the following questions.

How long does it take for change orders to be approved?

How do change order processing times vary

1. over time?

2. due to the workload of the personnel responsible for processing the change order?

3. due to the number of documents revised by the change order?

Can change order processing time be estimated?

a   Do you think this is a study of a population or a process? Briefly discuss the advantages and disadvantages for both views.
b   What should be the unit?

2.27 One of the major and more expensive programs that the Workers' Compensation Board of Ontario (WCB) delivers to injured workers is the vocational rehabilitation program. This program is delivered throughout Ontario by two different operating divisions, the Head office and the Regional offices, which have different organizational structures but deliver identical services. The WCB wants to use one organizational structure throughout Ontario. A study was undertaken to compare the efficiency of the two divisions. Two questions were to be addressed:

1. Which division delivers the services more efficiently?

2. What level of productivity can be expected from each division in the near future?

Efficiency was to be measured by the proportion of successful closures and the average duration of service extended to those injured workers whose files were closed.

A "successful (unsuccessful) closure" refers to the closing of an injured worker's file after suitable employment is (not) found for the worker. Duration of service refers to the time in months from the time a file is referred to vocational rehabilitation to the time that it is closed.

a   Treat this study as a cross-sectional study. Carefully define the unit and the populations (there are, in fact, two populations). How would you obtain the frames so that random samples can be taken? Which variables would you measure? Give their operational definitions. Is there a response variable?

b Treat this study as a time series study. Carefully define the unit and the two processes. Which variables would you measure? Give their operational definitions. Is there a response variable?

2.28 A sample of 20 teenagers will be asked the following questions:

a What is your favorite cereal? (The interviewee is given a list with 15 choices, labeled 1 to 15.)

b How old are you (in years)?

c How tall are you (in centimeters)?

d What color was your father's hair this morning? (1 = brown, 2 = black, 3 = red, 4 = blond, etc.)

For each question, state whether the answers will be categorical, ordinal, or quantitative measurements.

3

DATA SUMMARY

This chapter will help you answer the following kinds of questions:

- A manager at TV Guide magazine wanted to know whether a 10–week promotion had been successful in increasing newsstand sales. What graphical tool would help her?

- A portfolio manager wants to compare the riskiness of investing in two stocks. What numerical summary measure would help him?

3.1

INTRODUCTION

In the last chapter, we discussed data collection strategies. We examined the difference between experimental and observational studies, in particular, with respect to the extent to which confounding can prevent us from drawing causal conclusions from the collected data. We briefly contrasted cross-sectional and time series studies, and we noted that time series studies are more frequently used in business applications than cross-sectional studies.

In this chapter, we assume that a study was designed to answer some managerial questions, that relevant data were collected, and that a *sample* data set is available. In order to answer the questions convincingly, the data must be properly prepared for presentation. This chapter deals with several topics related to the presentation of data:

- How to summarize data graphically and numerically, and why a proper graph is the most effective way to convey information quickly

- How numerical summary measures are useful when a lot is known about the structure of the data, but the details of the data are not known, and how different measures can each describe a particular salient aspect of the data

- How numerical summary measures can be used to compare several different data sets

- How numerical summary measures can describe the relationship between two variables

- Why understanding variability is important for managers.

Let us first review a few definitions.

> A **variable** is a characteristic of a unit or subject. The name *variable* derives from the fact that its values vary across the units or subjects whom it characterizes.
>
> A **sample** is the collection of units or subjects for whom measurements are available on one or more variables of interest.
>
> The **sample size,** usually denoted n, is the number of units or subjects in the sample.
>
> The arithmetic **average** of a list of numbers equals their sum divided by the total count of numbers in the list.

Graphical summary measures will be discussed first, followed by numerical summary measures.

3.2

GRAPHICAL DISPLAYS OF DATA

At the beginning of *any* data analysis, you should graph your data in various ways. The most important reason for using graphs is that the human brain is "wired" for pattern recognition, not numerical processing. A properly constructed graph aids pattern recognition and will quickly supply a considerable amount of information about a data set.[1] The number of distinct graphical displays available is very large. This section discusses only a few important types of graphs.

---

[1]A very useful book discussing various techniques to construct good graphs is Tufte (1983).

Sequence Plots

If the outcomes of a process or a system can be measured repeatedly over time, the resulting series of values is called a *time series*. A first analysis of *any* time series should be done via a sequence plot.

EXAMPLE 3.1

In 1987 and 1988, newsstand sales for North American magazines were declining by an annual average of 10 percent, regardless of magazine category.[2] This decline had an impact on two streams of revenue: newsstand sales and the advertising revenue tied to these sales. In order to arrest this decline, TV Guide magazine conducted a consumer contest from February to April 1988. The purpose of this promotion was to entice new readers to try the product and to encourage infrequent readers to become frequent readers.

A study was undertaken to answer the following question: Was the decline in TV Guide's newsstand sales arrested during the 10–week promotion in the period from February to April 1988? If so, by how much?

Data were collected as follows. TV Guide is a weekly magazine, and newsstand sales were measured for the 50 issues from September 12, 1987 to August 20, 1988. Since the consumer promotion had been run from January 30, 1988 to April 2, 1988, the 50 measurements covered the 20 weeks prior to the contest, the 10 weeks of the contest, and the 20 weeks after the contest. The data are stored in ASCII file NEWSSTAN.DAT. Figure 3.1 gives a sequence plot of the 50 weekly sales values. The Minitab commands used to produce it are given in Section 3.9 (p. 86).

> In a **sequence plot** the individual values are plotted over time, with time usually plotted on the horizontal axis. It is advisable to supplement the plot by a line indicating the general level—for example, a line at the mean—and to connect the successive observations to see more clearly their variability over time.

In the example, time is measured by weekly intervals. Thus the unit is a week. The response variable is newsstand sales. It is clear from the diagram that newsstand sales have been decreasing, in particular during the last 25 weeks for which data are available. The early weeks of the contest, in particular week 23, have higher newsstand sales than previous weeks. It turns out, however, that the third week of the contest coincided with a special editorial (announced on the cover) about the Calgary Olympics, so the effects of this editorial and of the promotion may be confounded. The sequence plot in Figure 3.1 does not suggest that the promotion was effective.

---

[2]The data were kindly supplied by L. A. Nicholson.

FIGURE 3.1
Sequence Plot of
Weekly Newsstand
Sales Data

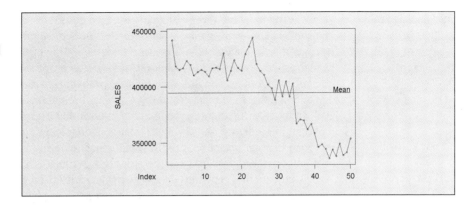

EXAMPLE 3.2

Let us continue Example 2.6: A study was done at a large hospital to examine the waiting time in minutes from booking an operation until the patient's arrival in the operating room. Management considered it important that waiting time not exceed 12 hours (720 minutes). Data were gathered for 47 consecutive bookings in September 1989. The data are stored in ASCII file HOSPITAL.DAT. A sequence plot is given in Figure 3.2.

In this example, the unit is a booking. The response variable is waiting time. After a statistical analysis—examples of which will be discussed in Chapter 5—the somewhat unusual result for the 21st booking was examined further.

outlier

We call observation 21 an *outlier* because it is far away from the rest of the data. Outliers can greatly influence a data analysis. Their treatment depends on the context, and there are no automatic rules about how to deal with them. In this case, treatment of the outlier was easy: After examining the record from which this waiting time (2,900) was obtained, a coding error was discovered—the waiting time should have been 290 minutes.

FIGURE 3.2
Sequence Plot
of Waiting Times

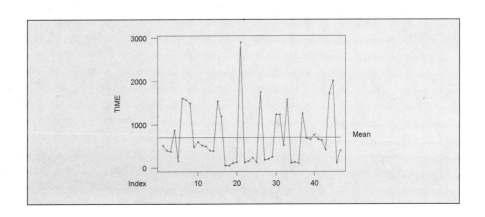

random time series

      The main point this particular sequence illustrates is that this time series seems to be *random over time*. That is, there is no sequential pattern in this time series, and no information would be lost if the order of the observations were arbitrarily rearranged. Chapter 5 expands on this discussion of random time series. For now, such randomness implies that the level of the time series does not change over time and that there is no pattern in the way the observations lie above or below this level. In terms of prediction, randomness implies that every observation is equally important to predicting future values; that is, more recent observations are no more important than earlier observations. Randomness also implies that there is neither deterioration nor improvement in the process over time.

random process

      A process that generates data whose time series is random is said to be a *random process*. We will have more to say about random processes in Chapter 5 and later.

Histograms, Frequency Distributions, and Dotplots

The graphs in the remainder of this section are suitable for cross-sectional data, and for time series data when the order of the observations can be ignored.

FIGURE 3.3 Summaries for Waiting Time Data

```
                                Frequency
               Class       Midpoint  (= Count)

                0 -  240      120       15      ****************
              240 -  480      360        8      ********
              480 -  720      600       10      **********
              720 -  960      840        2      **
              960 - 1200     1080        1      *
             1200 - 1440     1320        3      ***
             1440 - 1680     1560        5      *****
             1680 - 1920     1800        2      **
             1920 - 2160     2040        1      *
                                        ___
                                         47
```

(a) Histogram

Midpoint	Frequency (= Count)	Cumulative Frequency	Relative Frequency	Relative Cumulative Freq.
120	15	15	0.32	0.32
360	8	23	0.17	0.49
600	10	33	0.21	0.70
840	2	35	0.04	0.74
1080	1	36	0.02	0.77
1320	3	39	0.06	0.83
1560	5	44	0.11	0.94
1800	2	46	0.04	0.98
2040	1	47	0.02	1.00

(b) Relative and cumulative frequencies

Histograms, frequency distributions, and **dotplots** convey very similar information. These terms are often used interchangeably, but in this book each term always refers to the corresponding graph as described in this section.

Figure 3.3(a) shows the histogram for the data in Figure 3.2. (The incorrect value for observation 21 was, of course, corrected from 2,900 to 290.) In the process of constructing the histogram, several consecutive classes of values for waiting time and their midpoints were first determined. Then the number of observations falling into each class was counted, and a *bar* (here a row of asterisks) representing the number of observations was drawn. This rearrangement of the data tells us the number of waiting times in a particular class of values. For example, there were 10 waiting times between 480 and 720 minutes, that is, close to the midpoint 600 minutes. In the construction of this histogram, I have followed Minitab's convention of placing a number that occurs at the boundary of two classes with the class of larger values.

It is customary, but not necessary, to turn the histogram by 90° from the view shown in Figure 3.3(a) so that the values of the variable of interest are plotted on the horizontal axis, and the frequency is plotted on the vertical axis. Minitab produces such a histogram, and the result is given in Figure 3.4(b). In this histogram,

FIGURE 3.4 Two Histograms for Waiting Time Data

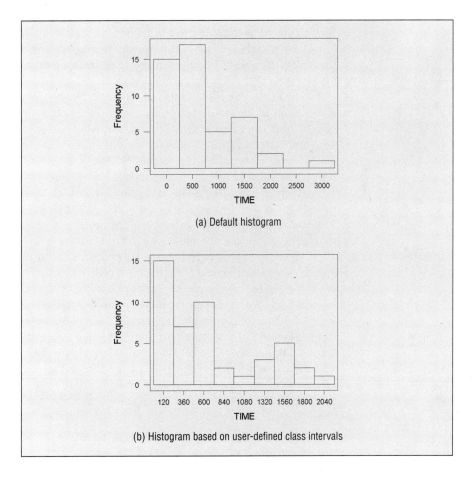

(a) Default histogram

(b) Histogram based on user-defined class intervals

FIGURE 3.5 Dotplot for Waiting Time Data

the midpoints are defined to coincide with the midpoints in Figure 3.3(a). The midpoints in the histogram in Figure 3.4(a) are determined by Minitab. The two histograms give roughly the same message, but the added detail in the lower histogram is preferred.

The **dotplot** is a related graph available in Minitab that shows more detail than the histogram. It is a character-based graph and not a high-resolution graph. Figure 3.5 displays a dotplot for the waiting times data.

In a histogram or dotplot, each value of the variable of interest is associated with the number of observations in the sample that take on that value. When the number of distinct values is very large, several class *intervals* are established. The value for each individual observation is then placed within the appropriate interval, simplifying the picture. In most situations, the intervals should be of equal width. (This may not always be feasible for the two extreme intervals.) A good understanding of the data is usually required to define appropriate class intervals so that the essentials of the data are clearly displayed.

The third vertical bar in the histogram of Figure 3.4(b) implies that there are 10 bookings in the class whose midpoint is 600 minutes. Since midpoints are 240 minutes apart, this class reflects observations whose values are between 480 (inclusive) and 720 (exclusive). The exact waiting times for each of the 10 bookings cannot be obtained from this histogram. We can only deduce that their values were somewhere between 480 and 720 minutes.

Both the two histograms in Figure 3.4 and the dotplot in Figure 3.5 give roughly the same message with respect to the distribution of waiting time values. There was considerable variation in waiting times, and a considerable proportion of the waiting times was 720 minutes (12 hours) or more.

cumulative frequency   Figure 3.3(b) gives additional information about the waiting times. The *cumulative frequencies* count the number of observations whose values are *less than the highest value in that class*.[3] They are easily obtained from the frequencies by summing up the frequencies in all classes up to and including the class of interest. Figure 3.3(b) also lists relative frequencies and relative cumulative frequencies. We can use Figure 3.3(b) to determine that 33 waiting times, or 70%, were less than 12 hours (720 minutes); that is, 30% were 12 hours or more. Management felt that 70% was a surprisingly high percentage. But if the conditions underlying the process were not expected to change in the near future so that there would be neither improvement nor deterioration, then management should expect that roughly

---

[3]Often, cumulative frequencies are defined as the number of observations *equal to or less than* a particular value.

the same percentage of waiting times will be 12 hours or more in the near future as well. Graphs of the histogram and the relative cumulative frequency distribution are given in Figure 3.6.

Stem-and-Leaf Plots

Similar to the histogram, the **stem-and-leaf plot** is another graphical tool that is useful for cross-sectional data, or time series data where the time sequence can be ignored. It provides more information than the histogram. It is easier to show the construction of a stem-and-leaf plot with an example than to describe it.

Consider a small company that surveyed its customers regarding the quality of its service. As part of a questionnaire, customers were asked their ages, and the results for a particular subgroup of 30 customers were as follows:

36	24	77	34	34	43	42	38	40	33
51	51	79	19	18	39	32	27	82	60
48	51	59	63	73	27	22	29	59	69

FIGURE 3.6
Histogram and Cumulative Histogram for Waiting Time Data

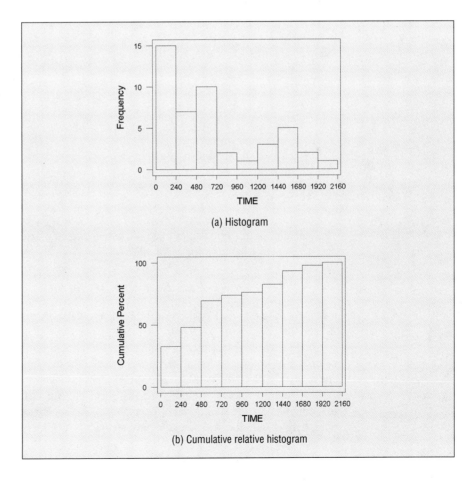

(a) Histogram

(b) Cumulative relative histogram

To construct the stem-and-leaf plot, we proceed as follows: The first digit of each data value is recorded to the left of a vertical line, and the second digit is recorded to the right of the line as we pass through the ages in the order in which they were listed.

```
1 | 9 8
2 | 4 7 7 2 9
3 | 6 4 4 8 3 9 2
4 | 3 2 0 8
5 | 1 1 1 9 9
6 | 0 3 9
7 | 7 9 3
8 | 2
```

Given this display of the data, we now rearrange the digits in each line into ascending order, yielding the following stem-and-leaf plot:

```
1 | 8 9
2 | 2 4 7 7 9
3 | 2 3 4 4 6 8 9
4 | 0 2 3 8
5 | 1 1 1 9 9
6 | 0 3 9
7 | 3 7 9
8 | 2
```

Each line in this display contains a "stem" and one or more "leaves." Consider the first line,

```
1 | 8 9
```

The meaning of this line is that there are two ages in the data set whose first digit is one: 18 and 19. Likewise, the second line

```
2 | 2 4 7 7 9
```

means that there were five ages in the data set whose first digit is two: 22, 24, 27, 27, and 29.

The stem-and-leaf plot is similar to a histogram, but it provides more information. For example, the above stem-and-leaf plot is similar to a histogram with classes 10–20, 20–30, 30–40, etc.

Figure 3.7 shows Minitab's stem-and-leaf plot for the age data. Note that the first column contains additional information: It accumulates the number of observations starting with the lowest and highest stem and working toward the stem contain-

FIGURE 3.7

Minitab Stem-and-Leaf Plot for the Age Data

```
Stem-and-leaf of AGE      N = 30
Leaf Unit = 1.0
    2     1   89
    7     2   24779
   14     3   2344689
   (4)    4   0238
   12     5   11199
    7     6   039
    4     7   379
    1     8   2
```

ing the middle observation(s). It denotes the stem with the middle observation(s) by recording its number of leaves in parentheses.

In the stem-and-leaf plot for the age data, each number was separated into two parts, the stem and the leaf. All ages consisted of two digits only, and thus the stem describes the first (the most significant) digit and the leaf the second.

In many data sets, the numbers consist of more than two digits. In such a case, the stem-and-leaf plot divides the digits into two categories, the more significant digits represented by the stem and the less significant digits represented by the leaf. The less significant digits are always rounded in such a way that at most the most significant digit among them is nonzero.

Suppose that the numbers in some data set have up to four digits. For example, consider the numbers 48, 134, and 1,392. Let the stem represent the two most significant digits and let the leaf represent the two least significant digits. Then,

The stem for 1,392 is 13 and its leaf is 92 rounded to 90.

The stem for 134 is 1 and its leaf is 34 rounded to 30.

The stem for 48 is 0 and its leaf is 48 rounded to 50.

In a stem-and-leaf plot, all digits represented by the stem are recorded, but only the first digit represented by the leaf is. Thus, 1,392 has stem value 13 and recorded leaf value 9. The recorded leaf value is given in units of 10s, that is, 9 represents $9(10) = 90$; here, "10" is called the *leaf unit*.

Consider the surgical waiting time data in the previous section. The waiting times were:

510	400	370	870	150	1,610	1,570	1,490	480	600
520	500	400	390	1,540	1,190	50	50	110	130
290	120	150	230	120	1,750	180	200	250	1,230
1,230	520	1,580	110	130	100	1,260	690	660	770
660	640	420	1,720	2,020	110	400			

The waiting times range from 50 to 2,020 minutes, so they have up to four digits. Figure 3.8 shows two stem-and-leaf plots for them. In the first plot, generated with Minitab's default settings, the stem consists of one digit and the leaf of three. Thus the leaf unit is 100. Consider the fifth line of this plot,

14   0 89

The second number, 0, is the stem value, and the third number, 8, is the most significant digit for one of the leaf values. Since the leaf unit is 100, the leaf value is

FIGURE 3.8 Two Stem-and-Leaf Plots of Waiting Times

```
Stem-and-leaf of TIME          N = 47
Leaf Unit = 100

   10      0  1111111111
   17      0  2222233
  (11)     0  444444455555
   19      0  66777
   14      0  89
   12      1
   12      1  2223
    8      1  55
    6      1  6667
    2      1  8
    1      2  0

              (a) Default plot


Stem-and-leaf of TIME          N = 47
Leaf Unit = 10

    2      0  55
   13      1  01112233558
   17      2  0359
   19      3  79
   (5)     4  00028
   23      5  0122
   19      6  04669
   14      7  7
   13      8  7
   12      9
   12     10
   12     11  9
   11     12  336
    8     13
    8     14  9
    7     15  478
    4     16  1
    3     17  25
    1     18
    1     19
    1     20  2

        (b) Plot with user-defined settings
```

8(100) = 800. Thus the waiting time represented by this stem and leaf is 0800 or 800 minutes. The first number in the line, 14, indicates that there were 14 bookings whose waiting times were 800 minutes or more.

Just as in the case of histograms, there is no correct number of stems in a stem-and-leaf plot. The number depends on the data and the context. In the second plot in Figure 3.8, the stems are defined to be 100 minutes apart. Its first line,

2   0 55

means that there were two waiting times whose stem value is 0. The leaf unit is 10, which differs from Figure 3.8(a); thus the corresponding leaf values were both 5(10) = 50. (Recall that these are possibly rounded values: If, based on the original data, the significant digits for a leaf had been 48, 50, or 53, they would all have been represented by 50.) Thus the two, possibly rounded, waiting times were 050 and 050, that is, 50 and 50 minutes.

Comparing the two stem-and-leaf plots in Figure 3.8, the default plot is preferable because it gives an adequate summary of the distribution of values. The other plot has too many stems; it looks a little cluttered.

Pareto Diagrams

A **Pareto diagram** is another graphical tool useful for cross-sectional data or for time series data that can be treated as if they were cross-sectional. It is useful for *categorical* variables when the relative importance of the various categories is to be conveyed. The construction and interpretation of a Pareto diagram is best illustrated with an example.

EXAMPLE 3.3

For some time, defective products of a manufacturing process were being recorded in a general category as the results of "inadequate operations." It became important for management to investigate the reasons for these defectives, so a more detailed analysis of 2,165 products counted the number of defectives by cause, as shown below:

Cause	Number	% Defective	% of All Defectives
Caulking	198	9.1	(47.6)
Fitting	25	1.2	(6.0)
Connecting	103	4.8	(24.7)
Torque	18	0.8	(4.3)
Gapping	72	3.3	(17.3)
Total	416	19.2	(99.9)

Source: Ishikawa (1976), p. 42.

FIGURE 3.9
Pareto Diagram for
Defects

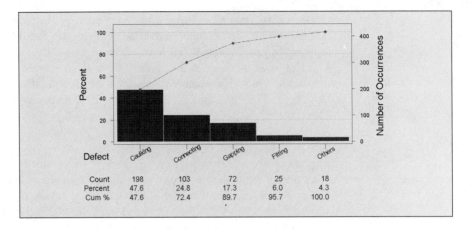

	Caulking	Connecting	Gapping	Fitting	Others
Count	198	103	72	25	18
Percent	47.6	24.8	17.3	6.0	4.3
Cum %	47.6	72.4	89.7	95.7	100.0

In all there were 416 defective products, which is 19.2% of the total number inspected. Of all products inspected, 198 or 9.1% were defective because of caulking problems. Of defective products, 47.6% had caulking problems. The Pareto diagram is shown in Figure 3.9.

> In a **Pareto diagram** the values of the categorical variable are arranged in order of descending importance of the categories, where importance is typically measured by frequency of occurrence. Superimposed on this graph is a line indicating the cumulative percentage for the first two most important categories, the first three, etc.

The Pareto diagram in Figure 3.9 suggests that the caulking and connecting error categories are the most important, accounting for 72% of all defective products. Therefore, it may be advisable for management to concentrate on reducing these two kinds of errors.

A Pareto diagram is useful because the important problems are immediately visible. It can be displayed in an office or on the shop floor, and it is easy to understand. It suggests which problems to tackle first, because it is often easier to reduce a tall bar on the graph by half than to reduce a shorter bar to 0. Sometimes there are many categories to be displayed in a Pareto diagram, and the number of observations in some of them is low. It is then advisable to combine these categories into an "Other" category. This category should always be drawn at the very right hand side of the Pareto diagram, even if it does not have the shortest bar, to remind the reader that it is made up of several very short bars.

Other applications might be a Pareto diagram of the amount of time spent on various tasks in an office or of the causes of equipment failure. In order to see the improvement, it is essential to obtain Pareto diagrams both before and after any improvement effort.

Importance need not be measured by just frequency of occurrence, the number of incidences in the example. This frequency could also be weighted by the amount each incidence costs, so that the vertical axis of the Pareto diagram would express losses in monetary terms.

Scatterplots

Very often managers need to know the extent to which two variables tend to vary together. A convenient graph showing the extent of this covariability or correlation is the **scatterplot.**

To illustrate this plot, consider Example 2.8, which discussed the picking and packing activities of a shipping department. The first question was whether the time taken to pick and pack an order (TIME) was related to certain other characteristics of the order. Let us look at the relationship between TIME and (1) the total number of items in the order (ITEMS) and (2) the number of lines on the order (LINES). The data are stored in ASCII file PICKPACK.DAT. A partial Minitab listing of the relevant data is given in Figure 3.10. Note that each row represents data about one order.

Scatterplots of TIME vs. LINES and TIME vs. ITEMS are given in Figure 3.11. Consider the plot of TIME vs. LINES. Each "." represents one order. For example, the values for TIME and LINES for order 3 are given as 7 and 3 in row 3 of Figure 3.10, and a "." at the intersection of TIME = 7 and LINES = 3 represents this order in Figure 3.11. All other orders were plotted similarly. Note that each "." may represent one or more orders.

The scatterplot of TIME versus LINES in Figure 3.11 suggests that the larger the number of lines in an order, the longer it *tends* to take to prepare the order for shipment. This relationship is not very strong, however. In the second scatterplot of TIME vs. ITEMS, again the relationship is not very strong, but there is one very unusual order—an outlier—for which the values of TIME and ITEMS are 5 and

FIGURE 3.10 Picking and Packing Data

ROW	ITEMS	LINES	TIME	ROW	ITEMS	LINES	TIME
1	10	5	6	62	4	2	4
2	10	10	7	63	2	1	6
3	4	3	7	.			
4	4	4	6	.			
5	20	1	6	.			
6	2	1	4	92	20	9	10
.				93	11	7	7
.				94	6	2	4
.				95	10	10	7
58	27	12	11	96	8	6	6
59	20	7	13	97	2	2	3
60	96	1	5	98	2	2	3
61	10	5	6				

FIGURE 3.11 Scatterplots of Picking and Packing Data

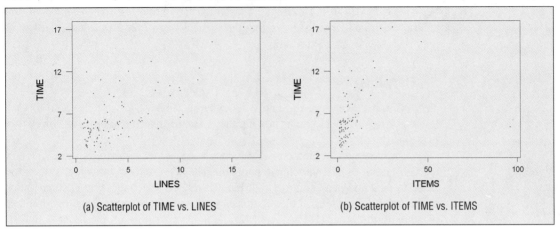

(a) Scatterplot of TIME vs. LINES　　　(b) Scatterplot of TIME vs. ITEMS

close to 100, respectively. Going back to Figure 3.10, we see that the corresponding order is listed in row 60. Before proceeding with an analysis, it would be wise to go back to the original data and examine why this order is so unusual: Were some values coded incorrectly? Was this a special order?

The picking and packing data came from a cross-sectional study. Scatterplots can also be useful for time series data. Consider the following example. Managers keep careful track of price, value, and returns on their companies' stocks. Suppose a manager wants to know whether the returns for Northern Telecom stock are related to the returns from the Toronto Stock Exchange, as measured by the TSE 300 composite index. Figure 3.12 lists the monthly returns for Northern Telecom (NTL) and the TSE 300 in 1977. Returns here are measured as *percentage* changes from 1 month to the next, that is,

$$\frac{\left(\begin{array}{c}\text{Price of stock at end of a particular}\\\text{month plus dividends for that month}\end{array}\right) - \left(\begin{array}{c}\text{Price at end of}\\\text{previous month}\end{array}\right)}{\text{Price of stock at end of previous month}} \times 100$$

FIGURE 3.12
Stock Return Data
for 12 months for
Northern Telecom
and the Toronto
Stock Exchange

ROW	NTL	TSE	ROW	NTL	TSE
1	-6	-1	7	-4	0
2	2	2	8	-5	-3
3	7	3	9	-11	1
4	-2	-2	10	-2	-3
5	-2	-1	11	8	5
6	10	6	12	-7	5

A sample of 12 months was available, and two measurements were made each month, one for NTL and one for the TSE. (In this process, the unit is a month, and the two variables are the returns for NTL and the TSE.) Sequence plots of the two time series did not reveal any time series pattern. This suggested that the time series are random, so that the time order of the observations is not informative. Managers were therefore justified to ignore the time series order. Figure 3.13 gives a scatterplot for the data.

Associating the return for Northern Telecom in a particular month with that of the TSE 300 index in the same month, we get one point on the scatterplot. The scatterplot suggests moderate positive correlation of the two variables, that is, when the return for Northern Telecom is high (or low), that for the TSE 300 index tends to be high (or low) as well. In general, such a positive correlation should *not* be taken to imply an underlying cause-and-effect relationship unless other facts or theory indicate that overall returns on stocks influence a particular stock (or vice versa).

Summary of Graphical Displays

Several graphical displays were discussed in the last few subsections. Each one is useful in a variety of contexts. When the data come from a time series study, you should first do a time series plot of the variables of interest to see what the pattern is over time.

If there is no time series pattern or if the data come from a cross-sectional study, then some of the other plots may be useful. When the variable is categorical, a Pareto diagram will best present the important categories since categories are in descending order of importance. When the variable is ordinal or quantitative, a histogram, frequency distribution, dotplot, or stem-and-leaf plot will display the frequency with which the various values of the variable occur. Finally, a scatterplot is a useful display to show the association between two ordinal or quantitative variables.

FIGURE 3.13
Scatterplot of Stock Data

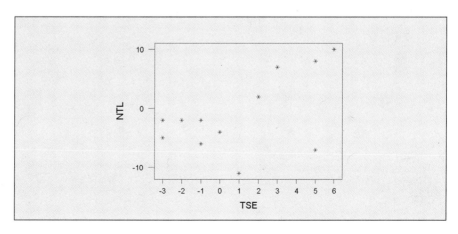

3.3

NUMERICAL SUMMARY MEASURES

The previous section introduced several ways of summarizing data graphically. After studying these graphical summaries, a manager analyzing data should examine some numerical summary measures that are useful for cross-sectional data, and also for time series data *if* the time series is random. These measures are illustrated here with the data on TSE 300 returns given in Figure 3.12. A sequence plot and a histogram of these returns are given in Figure 3.14. The sequence plot suggests randomness; that is, the sequence of values contains no time series information.

We will first discuss how the *center* of the histogram can be described in more detail, and then describe the variability of values around their center. There are many reasons why a manager would want to know the center of a histogram and the variability around it. The center is indicative of a typical value for the data. As a one-number summary, it roughly suggests the magnitude of values to expect in the data set. Variability suggests how representative the center is for the values in the data set. When there is high variability, many values in the data set may not even be close to the center. These and other summary measures are particularly useful when comparing two or more data sets, or when relating a new data set to an old one or a standard.

Measures of Central Location

We will discuss three measures of central location: the **mean** or **average,** the **median,** and the **mode.** We will use the 12 monthly TSE returns from Figure 3.12 to illustrate them:

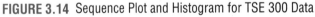

$$-1 \quad 2 \quad 3 \quad -2 \quad -1 \quad 6 \quad 0 \quad -3 \quad 1 \quad -3 \quad 5 \quad 5$$

FIGURE 3.14 Sequence Plot and Histogram for TSE 300 Data

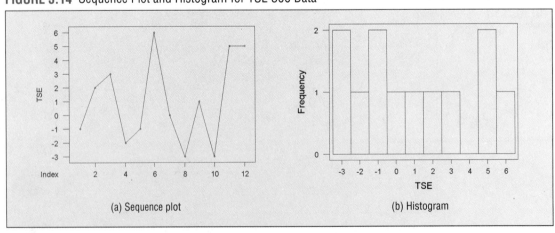

(a) Sequence plot

(b) Histogram

Let us first introduce some notation. The letter y denotes the variable of interest, here the return for the TSE 300 index. The letter n denotes the sample size, here $n = 12$. The individual values in the sample are denoted $y_1, y_2, y_3, \ldots, y_n$, here $y_1 = -1$, $y_2 = 2$, $y_3 = 3, \ldots, y_{12} = 5$.

We are now ready to define the *mean*.

The **mean** or **average** for a variable of interest, y, is the sum of all values divided by the total number of values. We denote this mean $\bar{y}$, and so we have[4]

$$\bar{y} = \frac{\sum_{i=1}^{n} y_i}{n}$$

For the TSE returns, we have

$$\bar{y} = \frac{-1 +2 +3 -2 -1 +6 +0 -3 +1 -3 +5 +5}{12} = \frac{12}{12} = 1$$

As another example, suppose there are $n = 100$ inventory units. The variables recorded for each unit are

- The date it was received

- Its supplier

- Its purchase price

- Whether or not the unit was damaged in inventory.

We therefore have measurements on four variables for all units in the sample. We can readily calculate and interpret the average purchase price. The average date of receipt could tell us how old the inventory is. If the suppliers are coded 1, 2, 3, etc., it does not make sense at all, however, to compute an average for supplier. But if the fourth (categorical) variable is coded 1 for damaged unit and 0 for undamaged unit, then the mean of these codes represents the fraction of damaged units in the sample. As we saw for the categorical variable "supplier," it does not make sense to compute an average for a categorical variable with more than two categories.

---

[4]The summation notation involving the capital Greek letter sigma, Σ, is widely used. It indicates to replace the letter i in the term following Σ with the integer values ranging from 1 to n, and then to sum the resulting n terms. For example, $\sum_{i=1}^{n} y_i$ means to sum up $y_1, y_2, y_3, \ldots, y_n$; that is,

$$\sum_{i=1}^{n} y_i = y_1 + y_2 + y_3 + \cdots + y_n$$

The *mean* is the most frequently used measure of central location. But outliers tend to strongly influence the mean. Consider the following data set:

1   1   1   1   1   1   1   1   1   100

The mean is $\frac{109}{10} = 10.9$. But this figure does not represent the data well, because of the outlying 100. The next measure of central location discussed is not sensitive to outlying values. Let us define the *median:*

The **median** is the value of the central observation when the observations are listed in ascending or descending order. When there is an even number of observations, the median is taken to be the average of the two central observations.

In ascending order, the TSE 300 return data are:

−3   −3   −2   −1   −1   0   1   2   3   5   5   6

and the median equals the average of the 6th and the 7th highest value, $(0 + 1)/2 = 0.5$. This value is quite close to the mean because there are no outlying observations on either side of the mean, as is suggested by the histogram in Figure 3.14.

The median for the data set

1   1   1   1   1   1   1   1   1   100

is 1. Although the value 1 is more representative of this data set than the mean, which is 10.9, a proper reporting of a measure of central location should include the fact that there was one value that is quite different from the bulk of the data.

The final measure of central location to be discussed is the *mode:*

The **mode** is the most frequently occurring value.

The mode for the data set

1   1   1   1   1   1   1   1   1   100

is 1.

Both the mean and the median are unique by definition, but this is not the case for the mode. There can be situations where there is more than one mode. Consider the following data set:

1   2   2   3   3   3   4   6   7   8   8   9   9   9   10   12

FIGURE 3.15

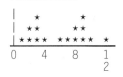

modal range

The histogram for this data set is shown in Figure 3.15. The two modes are seen to be 3 and 9.

When there is a clearly *bimodal* situation, the data may come from two distinct groups, and you should investigate what, if anything, distinguishes them.

In ascending order, the TSE returns are

$$-3 \quad -3 \quad -2 \quad -1 \quad -1 \quad 0 \quad 1 \quad 2 \quad 3 \quad 5 \quad 5 \quad 6$$

and there is also no unique mode.

When data are summarized in a histogram or a frequency distribution, it is often useful to speak of the *modal range,* that is, the range of values that occurs most frequently. For example, consider the two histograms of the waiting time data for operating rooms in Figure 3.4. The first histogram suggests that the modal range has midpoint 500, whereas the second histogram suggests that the modal range has midpoint 120. Both modal ranges tell roughly the same story about the data. The differences are due to the differing detail of the two histograms.

Figure 3.16 displays the shapes of three *idealized* frequency distributions. They are idealized in that not all data distributions look like them. These figures are to show the relative location of the three measures of location. In the distribution with long tail to the left, the mean has the smallest and the mode the largest value, with the median being intermediate. This kind of distribution is said to be *negatively skewed* or *skewed to the left.* When the distribution has a long tail to the right, the ranking of the three measures of location is reversed, and the distribution is said to be *positively skewed* or *skewed to the right.* Finally, when the distribution is symmetrical, the three measures coincide.

One important variable whose distribution often is positively skewed as in Figure 3.16(b) is the distribution of personal income. The distributions of returns for almost all stocks are symmetrical as in Figure 3.16(c). These three idealized shapes are not the only ones that can occur; the relationship among mean, median, and mode may well be different.

Of the three measures of central location, the mean is most frequently used. When the frequency distribution is considerably skewed, it is advisable to report the median, possibly in addition to the mean, since the mean is heavily influenced by long tails. When the frequency distribution has two or more modes that are distinct in value, it is important to report this fact. Otherwise, when there is only one mode, the mean or median are preferred measures of central location.

Measures of Dispersion

This section introduces three measures of dispersion: the **standard deviation,** the **variance,** and the **range.** As indicated in Chapter 1, most practical situations are characterized by variability, and managers need one-number summaries that express variability. In finance, for example, the standard deviation (or variance) is used as a measure of volatility over time—and therefore of risk—for returns on stocks, mutual funds, etc. (See, for instance, the monthly mutual funds performance surveys found in many business papers.) As another example, consider a variable that measures product quality for which management has specified a target level. If

FIGURE 3.16
Mean, Median and
Mode for Three
Idealized Frequency
Distributions

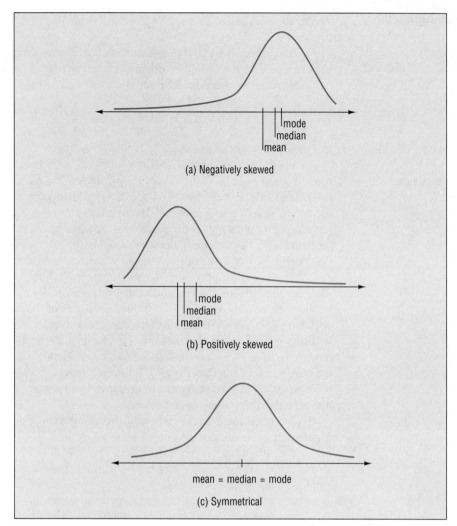

(a) Negatively skewed

(b) Positively skewed

(c) Symmetrical

FIGURE 3.17
Dotplots of
Monthly Returns
for Northern
Telecom and
TSE 300

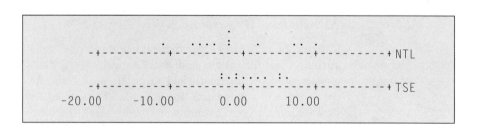

the mean is at the target level, a one-number summary measure of dispersion will tell management the extent to which products meet the target level.

Figure 3.17 gives the dotplots of monthly returns for Northern Telecom and the TSE 300 index, derived from Figure 3.12. The mean returns for Northern Telecom and the TSE 300 are $-12/12 = -1$ and $12/12 = 1$, respectively. Over the entire 12-month period, the average return was higher for the TSE 300 index than for Northern Telecom. Examination of Figure 3.17 suggests that TSE 300 returns tend to be less dispersed around their mean than Northern Telecom returns—in a sense, Northern Telecom was more "risky." Let us now turn to a definition of the standard deviation:

The **standard deviation** of a variable is

$$s = \text{Square root of} \left[\frac{\text{Sum of squared deviations from average}}{(n-1)} \right]$$

or

$$s = \sqrt{\frac{\sum_{i=1}^{n}(y_i - \bar{y})^2}{n-1}}$$

The standard deviation uses the values of all observations and computes the extent to which they vary around their mean.

To compute the standard deviation, the following steps must be carried out:

1. Find the deviations of individual values around the average, $(y_i - \bar{y})$.

2. Square[5] these deviations, $(y_i - \bar{y})^2$.

3. Sum the squared deviations, $\sum (y_i - \bar{y})^2$.

4. Average the resulting sum, $\sum(y_i - \bar{y})^2/(n-1)$. For a technical reason not discussed in this book[6], averaging is done by *dividing the sum by $(n-1)$,* the number of observations minus one, rather than by n.

5. Obtain the square root of the resulting average. The symbol used for the sample standard deviation is s.

---

[5]Squaring each deviation treats positive and negative deviations equally since the result of the squaring operation is a positive number. Treating positive and negative deviations equally could also have been achieved by simply dropping the negative signs and obtaining absolute values. There is no obvious reason for using the squaring operation, other than that its mathematical properties are more easily worked out.

[6]The reason for using the divisor $n - 1$ is related to *unbiasedness,* as discussed in many statistics texts, e.g., Keller, Warrack, and Bartel (1994).

FIGURE 3.18

Computation of the Standard Deviation for the TSE Data

Month	y_i	$y_i - \bar{y}$	$|y_i - \bar{y}|$	$(y_i - \bar{y})^2$
1	-1	-2	2	4
2	2	1	1	1
3	3	2	2	4
4	-2	-3	3	9
5	-1	-2	2	4
6	6	5	5	25
7	0	-1	1	1
8	-3	-4	4	16
9	1	0	0	0
10	-3	-4	4	16
11	5	4	4	16
12	5	4	4	16
			Sum =	112

Steps 1 to 3 of the computation of the standard deviation for the TSE data are illustrated in Figure 3.18. The resulting standard deviation is $s_{TSE} = \sqrt{112/11} = 3.19$. The standard deviation for the Northern Telecom returns is $s_{NTL} = 6.49$.

The following empirical rule should help interpret the standard deviation:

Empirical Rule for Standard Deviation When the histogram for a list of values is approximately symmetrical with shape as in Figure 3.16(c), then

- Roughly 68% of the values are within one standard deviation of the mean.

- Roughly 95% of the values are within two standard deviations of the mean.

- Almost all values are within three standard deviations of the mean.

To get a better idea of how this empirical rule works, consider the 120 monthly returns for the TSE 300 index for the period from 1976 to 1985. A histogram for the data is given in Figure 3.19. The shape of the frequency distribution is roughly symmetrical, and it looks similar to Figure 3.16(c). Selected statistics for the 120 returns are:

n	Mean	Median	Standard Deviation
120	1.434	1.200	5.195

Therefore, an interval extending one standard deviation around the mean will extend from -3.77 ($= 1.43 - 5.20$) to 6.63 ($= 1.43 + 5.20$). This interval contains 86 of the 120 values, or 71.7%, a result close to the result obtained from the empirical rule, that is, 68%. Of the 120 values, 115 (95.8%) are within two standard deviations of the mean, and this also agrees closely with the empirical rule.

FIGURE 3.19
Histogram for
Monthly TSE 300
Returns for 1976
to 1985

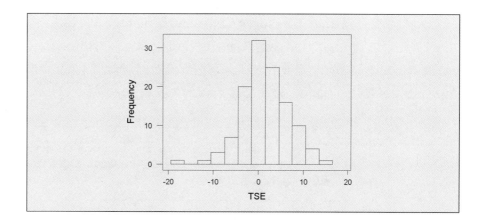

A measure of variability that is closely related to the standard deviation is the variance:

> The **variance** is the square of the standard deviation.

The variance for the 12 TSE 300 returns, listed in Figure 3.12, is $s^2_{TSE} = 3.19^2 = 10.1$. The variance, like the standard deviation, is frequently used in practice. The standard deviation is a better descriptive measure because it is expressed in the original units, while the variance is expressed in those units squared. For example, if the data measure family incomes in dollars, the standard deviation measures the variability in those incomes in dollars, whereas the variance measures that variability in squared dollars.

The standard deviation is useful to compare two data sets. Suppose there are two stocks, A and B. If the standard deviation for the returns on stock A is lower than that for stock B, then the returns for stock A are less volatile, and so stock A is less risky as an investment (all other things being equal).

A final, less useful measure of variability is the range:

> The **range** is the difference between highest and lowest values for a list of numbers.

For the data in Figure 3.12, the range for Northern Telecom returns is $10 - (-11) = 21$, and that for the TSE 300 returns is $6 - (-3) = 9$. Using the range as a measure of dispersion, there is more variation in Northern Telecom returns than in TSE 300 returns. The range is simple to compute, but it takes into consideration only the values of the extreme observations, so it may not adequately reflect the amount of variation in the entire data set.

Other Measures Characterizing One Variable

Figure 3.16, discussed earlier, displayed three idealized shapes for frequency distributions, displaying negative and positive skewness, and symmetry, or lack of skewness. Summary measures of skewness are available in numerical form, but we will not discuss them further, except for noting that:

> A **skewness** value of 0 suggests a symmetrical distribution, and a positive (or negative) skewness suggests a distribution with long tail to the right (or left).

It is often desirable to report the percentage or fraction of observations that fall below a particular value of a variable of interest.

> The xth **percentile** is that value for a variable of interest such that $x\%$ of all observations are equal to it or less than it. A **quantile** is similarly defined in terms of fractions.
>
> When the n observations are sorted in ascending order, the xth percentile corresponds to the value of observation $x(n + 1)/100$.

Percentiles arise by asking one of the following questions:

- Given a particular numerical value for the variable of interest, what percentage of all observations is less than or equal to this value?

- Given a percentage, what is the numerical value for the variable of interest so that the given percentage of all observations is less than or equal to this value?

To answer the first question, we must count the number of observations less than or equal to the given value and express this number as a percentage. Consider Example 3.2 (p. 47), where management considered it important that waiting times not exceed 720 minutes. Using the raw data in ASCII file HOSPITAL.DAT., the dotplot in Figure 3.5, or the stem-and-leaf plot in Figure 3.8(b), we find the waiting times for 33 of the 47 operations (or $33/47 = 70.2\%$) to be less than or equal to 720 minutes. Thus, 720 minutes is the 70th percentile or the 0.70 quantile. As a further example, consider the customer age data displayed in Figure 3.7. Since the age for 24 of the 30 customers is 60 years or less, 60 is the $24/30 = 80$th percentile.

As another instance of the first question, consider the pipeline bonding problem in Section 2.5. It was required that the strength of the bond, as measured by disbondment, be 13 mm or less. If the disbondment value for 98% of the pipelines in a batch is 13 mm or less, then the value 13 mm is the 98th percentile or the 0.98 quantile for the pipelines in that batch.

Let us turn now to the second question. In order to compute the xth percentile for a sample of n observations, the observations must first be sorted in ascending

FIGURE 3.20 Minitab Output: Descriptive Statistics for Stock Return Data

	N	MEAN	MEDIAN	TRMEAN	STDEV	SEMEAN
NTL	12	-1.00	-2.00	-1.10	6.49	1.87
TSE	12	1.000	0.500	0.900	3.191	0.921

	MIN	MAX	Q1	Q3
NTL	-11.00	10.00	-5.75	5.75
TSE	-3.000	6.000	-1.750	4.500

order. The xth percentile then corresponds to the value of observation $x(n + 1)/100$ among the sorted observations.

As an example, consider the monthly return data for the TSE 300 returns in Figure 3.12. In ascending order, the 12 monthly returns are

$$-3 \quad -3 \quad -2 \quad -1 \quad -1 \quad 0 \quad 1 \quad 2 \quad 3 \quad 5 \quad 5 \quad 6$$

The value of the 25th percentile corresponds to sorted observation number $25(12 + 1)/100 = 3.25$. Since this is not a whole number, the value of the 25th percentile is between the third and fourth largest observations, that is, between -2 and -1. Note that the xth percentile, as defined here, does not necessarily have a unique value; it only does when $x(n + 1)/100$ is a whole number.[7] Likewise, the 75th percentile corresponds to observation number $75(12 + 1)/100 = 9.75$, so its value is between 3 and 5. Note that the median equals the 50th percentile, so its value corresponds to observation 6.5—that is, it is halfway between 0 and 1, so it equals 0.5.

In terms of quantiles, the 0.25 quantile for the data of monthly TSE 300 returns is between -2 and -1, the 0.75 quantile is between 3 and 5, and the 0.50 quantile is 0.5.

Some of the summary statistics discussed so far can be found with Minitab. Figure 3.20 lists the Minitab output for such statistics. In addition, Figure 3.20 lists TRMEAN (which won't be covered in this book), and SEMEAN (which will be covered in Chapter 7). Q1 and Q3 refer to the first and third quartiles, that is, the 25th and 75th percentiles.

3.4

MEASURES OF COVARIATION

This section discusses two one-number summaries that describe the linear association between two variables: the *correlation coefficient* and the *covariance*. The correlation coefficient measures the strength of linear association; it is informally described in the first subsection. High correlation does not necessarily imply causation, as is explained in the second subsection. Computation of the correlation

---

[7]To get a unique answer, computer programs typically use interpolation, but we will not discuss the mechanics of this in this text.

coefficient is left to the third subsection, where the covariance is introduced. In addition to being a useful statistic in its own right, the covariance is needed to compute the correlation coefficient.

Correlation

This subsection discusses a one-number summary that describes the extent of linear association between two variables. The question answered is: How well does a line represent a scatterplot? As with all one-number summaries, it is always advisable to look at the full data set via a graph before interpreting the summary, so that unexpected features in the data do not go unnoticed.

The **correlation** coefficient measures the degree of linear association between two variables.

Its value is between -1 and $+1$. A value of $+1$ indicates a perfect positive linear relationship. A value of -1 indicates a perfect negative linear relationship. The closer the coefficient value is to the extremes, the more closely correlated the variables are.

The symbol used for the sample correlation coefficient is r. To avoid ambiguities, subscripts are sometimes used. For example, the correlation between variables x and y might be denoted r_{xy}.

FIGURE 3.21

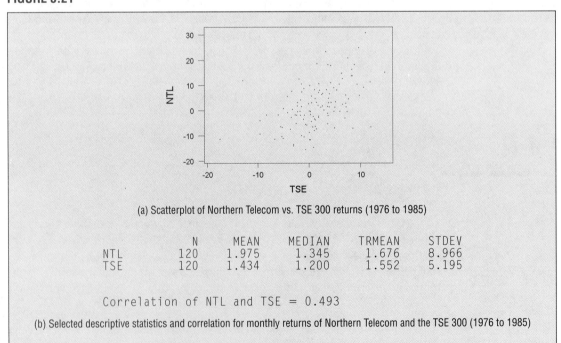

(a) Scatterplot of Northern Telecom vs. TSE 300 returns (1976 to 1985)

	N	MEAN	MEDIAN	TRMEAN	STDEV
NTL	120	1.975	1.345	1.676	8.966
TSE	120	1.434	1.200	1.552	5.195

Correlation of NTL and TSE = 0.493

(b) Selected descriptive statistics and correlation for monthly returns of Northern Telecom and the TSE 300 (1976 to 1985)

The correlation coefficient is usually computed only when both variables are quantitatively scaled. It should be used with great caution when one or both of the variables are ordinal. It should not be used when one or both variables are categorical.

Figure 3.21(a) gives a Minitab scatterplot of monthly returns for the TSE 300 index and Northern Telecom for the period from 1976 to 1985. Figure 3.21(b) gives the correlation between Northern Telecom and TSE 300 returns as $r = 0.493$, and it also lists descriptive statistics. The correlation is quite moderate: Returns of Northern Telecom are not highly related to returns from the market as measured by the TSE 300 index.

The coefficient of correlation measures the strength of association between two variables. It must lie between -1 and $+1$. A value close to $+1$ (or -1) suggests a very high positive (or negative) correlation. A value close to 0 suggests lack of correlation. A few scatterplots and their correlations are given in Figure 3.22.

FIGURE 3.22 Selected Scatterplots and Correlation Coefficients

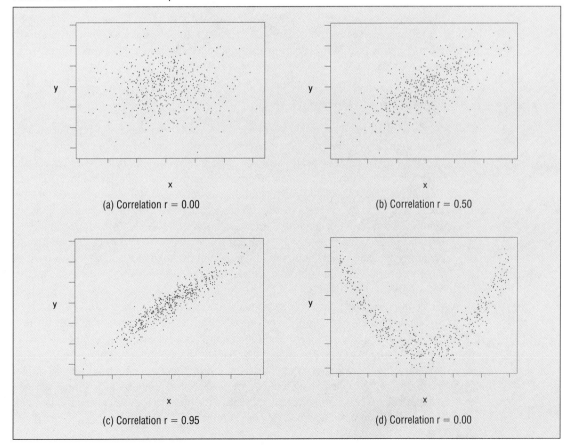

(a) Correlation r = 0.00

(b) Correlation r = 0.50

(c) Correlation r = 0.95

(d) Correlation r = 0.00

Note the correlation coefficient for the last scatterplot, which may come as a little surprise. It is 0 because there is no *linear* (straight line) association between the two variables. The correlation coefficient, as defined here, is incapable of expressing the strength of a *nonlinear* association. When interpreting the coefficient of correlation, bear in mind that it measures the strength of a *linear* association between two variables across a collection of units or subjects—it suggests the extent to which a straight line summarizes the scatterplot well.

In later chapters, we will encounter many uses for the correlation coefficient and ideas related to it. At this point let us briefly consider the use of the correlation coefficient in portfolio selection. A portfolio consists of a number of stocks, bonds, mutual funds, etc., and their mix is determined by the investor's attitude toward risk. Consider a simple portfolio consisting of only two stocks. If the portfolio consists of two highly positively correlated stocks, then the returns from these stocks will tend to move together: when one stock is doing well so is the other, and vice versa. Overall there will be considerable volatility in the return from the portfolio because the returns from the two stocks will tend to move in tandem. If, however, the two stocks are highly negatively correlated, then the two stock returns tend to move in opposite directions: when one stock is doing well, the other tends not to do well. Overall the movement in one stock tends to be offset by that in the other, and the volatility in the combined return from the portfolio tends to be much less than in the case of two highly positively correlated stocks. Thus if you want a portfolio with low risk (that is, low volatility), then you should choose stocks whose returns are negatively correlated. Of course, actual portfolio selection is much more complex.

Causation vs. Correlation

When the values of two characteristics tend to be correlated in a population or a process, in that both characteristics tend to be high, low, or intermediate for a particular unit, we cannot necessarily say that one of the characteristics causes the other one. For example, as mentioned in Section 1.3, church attendance rate and suicide rate have tended to be very highly correlated in the United Kingdom over many years, but this does *not* imply that one causes the other. There may be intervening factors, not yet identified, that explain both of them. Indeed, economic activity appears to be important in explaining this high correlation. In years when the economy is doing well, both suicide and church attendance rates tend to be low; when the economy is doing poorly, both rates tend to be high. As we have stressed before, it is necessary to control for background variables, here possibly the state of the economy, to rule out confounding and to make sense of the data.

In experimental studies, the introduction of randomization usually insures that treatment and control groups are very similar with respect to all factors except for the treatment. Thus, confounding variables should not be present. We may then say that a higher response in the treatment group than in the control group is *caused* by the presence of the treatment. In the TV commercial study, Example 2.1, we may be able to say that higher purchase rate for the dog food is caused by the treatment group having viewed the TV commercial.

In observational studies, it is usually much more difficult to make causal conclusions because of the possible presence of unidentified confounding variables. Just because women had a lower chance of being hired in Example 2.4 did not mean there is a causal relationship between gender and success at being hired. There was another factor—hiring department—whose effect was confounded with the variable under study, gender. Just because the returns from two stocks are highly correlated does not mean that a change of return in one causes a change of return in the other. The two stocks may move in similar directions because they are in the same industry, and the state of that industry may cause the movement in both stocks.

Covariance

A measure of covariation used in some applications, such as the analysis of financial portfolios, is the **covariance.** A positive covariance suggests positive association; a negative covariance suggests negative association. Its numerical value, however, does not suggest the strength of the association, as does the correlation. In order to compute the correlation, the covariance must be computed first.

Denote the two variables measured on the n units in the sample as x and y. We thus have n pairs of values, $(x_1, y_1), (x_2, y_2), (x_3, y_3), \ldots, (x_n, y_n)$. The following steps must be carried out to compute the covariance between two variables, where a measurement on each variable is available for a sample of units.

1. For each unit, obtain the mean-corrected value for each variable by subtracting the mean of a variable from the value for that variable, $(x_i - \bar{x})$ and $(y_i - \bar{y})$.

2. For each unit, multiply the mean-corrected value for one variable by the mean-corrected value for the other variable. These products are called the *mean-corrected cross-products*, $(x_i - \bar{x})(y_i - \bar{y})$.

3. Sum these cross-products for all units, $\sum_{i=1}^{n}(x_i - \bar{x})(y_i - \bar{y})$.

4. Average this sum by dividing it by $(n - 1)$. (Division by $n - 1$ is for the same technical reason alluded to in the discussion of the standard deviation.) Thus, the covariance is

$$Cov(x, y) = \frac{\sum_{i=1}^{n}(x_i - \bar{x})(y_i - \bar{y})}{n - 1}$$

We will illustrate computation of the covariance with the stock return data (first given in Figure 3.12) where there are $n = 12$ pairs of stock returns, each pair consisting of one Northern Telecom (NTL) and one TSE 300 (TSE) value. For simplicity, let Northern Telecom be variable x, and let TSE 300 be variable y. Recall that the mean of the Northern Telecom values is $\bar{x} = -1$ and that of the TSE 300 values is $\bar{y} = 1$. Steps 1 to 3 for computing the covariance are given in Figure 3.23. The sum of the mean-corrected cross-products is 124. Therefore the covariance between NTL and TSE in the sample is $124/(12 - 1) = 11.27$.

FIGURE 3.23
Computation of
Covariance

Month	NTL x_i	TSE y_i	$(x_i - \bar{x})$	$(y_i - \bar{y})$	$(x_i - \bar{x})(y_i - \bar{y})$
1	-6	-1	-5	-2	10
2	2	2	3	1	3
3	7	3	8	2	16
4	-2	-2	-1	-3	3
5	-2	-1	-1	-2	2
6	10	6	11	5	55
7	-4	0	-3	-1	3
8	-5	-3	-4	-4	16
9	-11	1	-10	0	0
10	-2	-3	-1	-4	4
11	8	5	9	4	36
12	-7	5	-6	4	-24
				Sum =	124

Since the covariance is positive, the association between NTL and TSE is also positive. We cannot conclude from the magnitude of the covariance whether the association is strong or weak. There is, however, a simple relationship between the covariance and the correlation, and we can use the covariance and the standard deviations to calculate the correlation coefficient:

Consider two variables, x and y. The relationship between their **covariance,** $Cov(x, y)$, and their correlation, $r_{x,y}$, is:

$$r_{x,y} = \frac{Cov(x,y)}{s_x s_y}$$

where s_x and s_y are the standard deviations of x and y.

The standard deviations of the NTL and the TSE values were given to be 6.49 and 3.191, respectively, in Figure 3.20, and so the correlation between the 12 NTL and TSE values is $11.27/(6.49 \cdot 3.191) = 0.54$. Thus the association between NTL and TSE for this small sample is positive and moderate.

3.5

FAILURE TO UNDERSTAND VARIABILITY

This brief section illustrates instances in which the nature of variability was not properly understood. The examples arise from the failure to understand two facts:

1. Some values in a data set must lie above their mean, and some below.

2. Only rarely will all values equal their mean.

Example 1: An automotive company had three dealers in a particular city, and one of them performed below the mean of the three (!). This performance was obviously inferior, and something had to be done. For example, the company could urge the dealer to sell his business so that a replacement could be found.[8]

Example 2: Union officials said that, despite the increase in incomes, more than half the league's players earned less than the league-wide mean income of $75,000 a year.[9]

Variability was not properly understood here for the following reasons: It is well known that income distributions are positively skewed. As illustrated in Figure 3.16, the mean is then expected to be above the median. Since half the observations lie below the median, we would *expect* more than half of the observations to be below the mean.

Example 3: In a letter to *The Times* of London, someone wrote that he had been studying a report from the Ministry of Health that said that half the children in the United Kingdom were below mean weight. He felt that this was a disgrace to the nation and that something had to be done to improve the nourishment of British children. (The distribution of weight among children is likely to be symmetrical, so we would *expect* half the children to be below mean weight. . .)

3.6

ANALYSIS OF PIPELINE BONDING EXAMPLE

Section 2.5 described the design of a study to compare two raw materials that were used by a company to produce a "fusion bond" coating of pipelines used for the transmission of natural gas. The response variable, disbondment, was to be compared for two raw materials, A and B. Pipe diameter was the one important known background variable, and it was controlled for by choosing only pipes with a 120-cm diameter. Figure 2.7 summarizes the details of the design, and Figure 3.24 gives the data.

Since this was a time series study, the first step in the analysis was a sequence plot for the response variable (disbondment) as shown in Figure 3.25(a). All disbondment values were well within the target range, that is, below 13 mm. The nuisance variables (the unknown background variables) contributed a fair amount to the variation in disbondment. There do not appear to be any time series patterns in Figure 3.25(a), so we can judge the process to be random and carry out analyses that ignore the time series order. If there were a difference due to the two raw materials, however, a time series pattern might be disguised by this difference. It is therefore advisable to plot the time series for the two raw materials separately. It is not clear from Figure 3.25(a), though, whether there is any appreciable difference between the two raw materials.

---

[8]Reported in Deming (1986, p. 58).

[9]From the *Wisconsin State Journal,* 11 March 1983.

FIGURE 3.24 Results for Pipeline Example

Batch	Raw Material	Disbondment	Batch	Raw Material	Disbondment
1	B	7.2	16	A	6.3
2	B	7.2	17	A	5.3
3	A	6.7	18	B	4.6
4	B	5.6	19	B	4.8
5	A	7.2	20	A	6.6
6	A	8.1	21	B	3.3
7	A	5.2	22	B	6.1
8	A	6.5	23	B	4.0
9	B	2.3	24	B	4.6
10	A	6.3	25	B	4.7
11	A	5.8	26	B	4.5
12	A	5.1	27	A	6.8
13	B	4.4	28	A	4.6
14	B	6.3	29	B	7.0
15	A	6.6	30	A	7.2

FIGURE 3.25

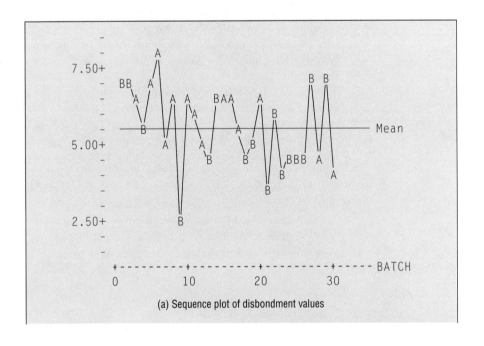

(a) Sequence plot of disbondment values

**FIGURE 3.25
(continued)**

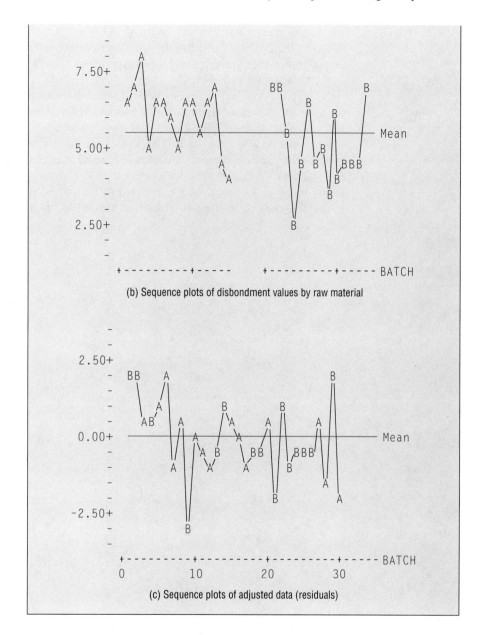

(b) Sequence plots of disbondment values by raw material

(c) Sequence plots of adjusted data (residuals)

Figure 3.25(b) presents separate sequence plots for the two raw materials. Neither sequence is characterized by time series patterns, so it is reasonable to ignore the time series order. Figure 3.25(b) suggests that raw material B is possibly somewhat better since it leads to less disbondment. Note that some of the variation in disbondment values around the overall mean can be accounted for by raw material since the disbondment values for raw material B tend to be slightly lower than the disbondment values for raw material A. When accounting for raw material, however, there is still considerable variation in disbondment values—which must be due to nuisance variables. A further experiment might focus on identifying the important nuisance variables.

Ignoring the time series order, Figure 3.26 gives dotplots and stem-and-leaf plots for the two raw materials, and it lists descriptive statistics, stratified by raw material. Both types of plot suggest that raw material B is somewhat better than raw material A. The mean for B is by almost one disbondment unit lower than the mean for A. Given the means alone, raw material B is clearly better than A. But both standard deviations are a little larger than 1. Thus, there is considerable variability in the disbondment values, reflected by the two overlapping distributions. It is therefore not entirely clear-cut that raw material B is better than A.

FIGURE 3.26

```
RAW_MAT
A                                         .     .   . .: . ::: .  .
                 +---------+---------+---------+---------+-- DISBOND
RAW_MAT                             :
B                    .    .  . :: . ... .:
                 +---------+---------+---------+---------+-- DISBOND
               0.0        2.5       5.0       7.5      10.0
```

(a) Dotplots of disbondment values by raw material

```
Stem-and-leaf of DISBOND
Leaf Unit = 0.10

RAW_MAT = A                          RAW_MAT   = B

    0    2                              1    2   3
    0    3                              2    3   3
    2    4   06                        (7)   4   0456678
    6    5   1238                       6    5   6
   (7)   6   3356678                    5    6   13
    2    7   2                          3    7   022
    1    8   1                          0    8
```

(b) Stem-and-leaf plot

DISBOND	RAW_MAT	N	MEAN	MEDIAN	STDEV
	A	15	6.073	6.300	1.069
	B	15	5.107	4.700	1.439

DISBOND	RAW_MAT	MIN	MAX	Q1	Q3
	A	4.000	8.100	5.200	6.700
	B	2.300	7.200	4.400	6.300

(c) Summary statistics

As noted earlier, Figure 3.25 suggested randomness of the time series. Sometimes nonrandom aspects are not obvious from the sequence plot since their not-yet-identified effects may be hidden by the effects of the factors in the study. A residual analysis is then sometimes useful. In a residual analysis, the original data are first adjusted by subtracting the overall mean. They are then further adjusted by subtracting the factor effect. For this example, the adjusted (or *residual*) values are computed by subtracting mean disbondment for raw material A from every disbondment value for raw material A and doing a similar adjustment for raw material B values. Figure 3.25(c) gives a sequence plot of the resulting residual values. Its message regarding randomness does not differ from Figure 3.25(a)—the series appears to be random.

residual analysis

3.7

EXAMPLES OF DESIGNING STATISTICAL STUDIES

The last chapter discussed some principles of data collection, and this chapter has discussed ways of analyzing and summarizing data. Design of a study and analysis of the collected data, however, cannot be viewed in isolation: A study's design partially depends on how the data will be analyzed. Thus we are now ready to give two detailed examples of how to design a statistical study.

A Study of a Gapping Problem of the Buick Headlamp Lens

Summary

Description of the Problem. In early October 1990, Autosystems Manufacturing was having problems with the Buick Regal headlamp assembly.[10] Rainwater was often entering the lamps through gaps between the lens and the housing. These gaps varied significantly in size. The gapping problem was thought to arise during the injection molding process, in which, after a machine injects the material, the lenses are robotically removed from the machine and then cooled before measurements are made.

Managerial Questions. A study was to be done to answer two managerial questions:

1. Is the injection molding process performing satisfactorily with respect to the part weight of lenses, lens-to-housing gap, and lens length?

2. Is there a relationship among these three variables, and can this relationship be used to improve the process?

_____
[10]I thank Mr. Neil Huff for providing the example.

Statistical Questions.   These two managerial questions were translated into several statistical questions.

1. a. Is the injection molding process random for part weight of lenses? Do part weights vary within industry limits (3% above and below average part weight)? What percentage of part weights fall outside these industry limits?

   b. Is the process random for the lens to housing gap? What proportion of gaps are greater than 2 mm? (Such gaps would be suspect for leaks.)

   c. Is the process random for lens length?

2. What are the correlations among the three variables?

Practical Use of Study.   Answers to these questions were to help management identify the causes of the gapping problem and how they could be removed. In particular, answers to these questions would make it possible to plan experiments for improving the quality of the production process. Since a satisfactory process would have weak relationships among the variables, any strong relationship would point to potential problems.

Current Knowledge about Managerial Questions.   The initial best guess at answers to the managerial questions was as follows. (1) The three processes were expected to be random, and the means of part weight and lens length were expected to be satisfactory. The mean of the lens to housing gap was expected to be too high, and the variability in the variables was expected to be too large. (2) The relationships among the three variables were expected to be strong.

Statistical Details

Description of Process.   The definitions of process and unit were the same for all questions: The injection molding process consisted of the machine injecting the molds, removing them robotically from the machine, and cooling them. The process was located at Autosystems' plant, and it was to be studied during October and November 1990. The unit of the process is an individual left lens. Management's attention was on the left lens since the gapping problem was more pronounced for it.

Variables to be Measured.   Three variables were to be measured for each lens: part weight, part length, and gap from a standard housing unit. Statistical questions 1a–c each use one of these variables; all three are needed to answer statistical question 2. The response variable is the gap from a standard housing unit. Management wanted to know the influence of the other two on the response variable.

Statistical Aspects of Interest.   Each of statistical questions 1a–c relates to the randomness of the process. For question 1a, the process mean and standard deviation of part weight were also needed, as were the shape of its frequency distribution and two selected percentiles. For question 1(b), the process mean and standard deviation of gap were needed, as were the shape of its frequency distribution and the percentile corresponding to 2 mm. The three correlations were needed for question 2. It was expected that all three processes were random. The process mean and standard deviation for part weight were expected to be 303 grams and 1 gram, and for gap they were expected to be 1.5 mm and 0.2 mm. All part weights were expected to be within industry limits. About 0.5% of gaps were expected to exceed 2 mm. All three correlations were expected to exceed 0.5.

Data Collection Plans

Type of Sample.   Data were to be collected by taking a lens from the process at regular intervals until 60 lenses were measured, a number considered to provide sufficient numerical accuracy.

Operational Definitions.   The variable part weight was to be determined by weighing a left lens on a scale accurate enough so that the weight in grams was off by no more than 0.005 grams; the range of values was expected to be 300–306 grams. The variable part length was the length of a left lens, measured in mm to an accuracy of 0.01 mm; its range was expected to be 101–102 mm. The variable lens to housing gap was to be measured in mm to an accuracy of 0.001 mm; the range of values was expected to be 1.0–2.3 mm. All three variables were quantitative.

Sampling Details.   A lens was to be measured every 1.5 hours, yielding 10 lenses per day. This was to be done for 6 consecutive working days, yielding the 60 lenses.

Potential Data Collection Weaknesses.   Since the process was operating smoothly and it was not difficult to measure lenses, no problems were foreseen and the data were expected to be reliable. The greatest weakness of the study was that it was likely to provide preliminary information only, and so a more extensive experiment was considered necessary.

Fictional Data.   Data like the following were expected:

Weight	Length	Gap
303.7	401.40	1.30
302.9	401.36	1.37
303.1	401.42	1.33
302.8	401.39	1.33
303.2	401.25	1.36
:		
:		

Data Analysis Plans

Graphical Summaries.   For each of statistical questions 1(a–c), a sequence plot of the relevant variable was to be plotted to check randomness. Dotplots were needed for weight and gap to examine the shape of their frequency distributions. For question 2, three scatterplots were needed for gap vs. weight, gap vs. length, and weight vs. length.

Numerical Summaries.   Means and standard deviations were to be computed for weight and gap; furthermore, the required percentiles were to be computed.

A Study of a Hospital's Emergency Department

Summary

Description of Problem.   When a patient arrives at the hospital's emergency department[11], a nurse examines the patient to determine whether he or she represents an emergency, an urgent case, or a deferrable case. Since treatment priority was given to critically ill patients, treatment of deferrable and urgent cases could sometimes be delayed. Management was interested in the waiting times between various procedures for these three different cases. For example, a long wait was common between the patient's first contact with a physician and the completion of treatment. This delay could be attributed to waiting for the return of laboratory results and to referrals to specialists. It was more pronounced for emergency patients, since more investigation and treatment were needed and since all such cases were subsequently referred to specialists.

Managerial Questions.   The study was to answer the following managerial questions.

1. Is the time between admittance and first seeing a nurse lowest for emergency cases and highest for deferrable cases?

2. Is the time between admittance and first seeing a physician lowest for emergency cases and highest for deferrable cases?

3. Is the time between seeing a physician and discharge lowest for deferrable cases and highest for emergency cases?

Statistical Questions.   For each of the three "time" variables, the corresponding statistical question compares the population means for the three patient populations.

Practical Use of Study.   The study was to examine the validity of some patients' perception that the time until seeing a nurse and subsequently a physician was not in accordance with the severity of the affliction. It seemed that the majority of complaints came from deferrable patients.

---

[11]The study is real, but the hospital's name is omitted to protect confidentiality.

Current Knowledge about Managerial Questions. The rankings given in the managerial questions were expected in the data.

Statistical Details

Description of Population. The study was to be cross-sectional. The population was to consist of the 5,566 emergency department patients at the hospital in July 1990. For the purposes of this study, this large population was to be divided into three subpopulations, consisting of the 85 true emergency patients, the 3,543 urgent patients, and the 1,938 deferrable patients. A subject was to be an emergency department patient.

Variables to be Measured. In each population, three variables were to be measured on each subject: the time until a patient saw a nurse, the time until seeing a physician, and the time between seeing a physician and discharge. Each variable is the response variable for one of the three questions. In addition to these three response variables, a fourth variable indicated which population the patient was in.

Statistical Aspects of Interest. The population means were needed for each variable, stratified by the three populations. The population means (time in minutes) were expected to be as given in the following table.

	Emergency	Urgent	Deferrable
Time to see nurse	<5	<20	<20
Time to see physician	<5	<60	<60
Time until discharge	>150	>120	>30

Data Collection Plans[12]

Type of Sample. This was a cross-sectional study of the three populations in July 1990. There were three frames with 85, 3,543, and 1,938 subjects, respectively. These frames were stored in the hospital's computer, and random samples could be drawn from them using standard computer software available to the hospital's staff.

Operational Definitions. In addition to other information, each patient's record listed the times when the patient was admitted, first seen by a nurse, first seen by a physician, last seen by a physician, and discharged from the emergency department. The required variables could be computed from these entries. The "time to see a nurse" was the time in minutes from being admitted until first seen by a nurse, the "time to see a physician" was the time in minutes from being admitted until being first seen by a physician, and the "time until discharge" was the time in minutes from last seeing a physician until discharge. The ranges for these three quantitative variables were expected to be 0–60, 0–120, and 0–300 minutes, respectively. The

---

[12]The results from the study as actually carried out are described in Section 7.8.

fourth variable recorded which population the patient was in (1, 2, or 3), and it was categorical.

Sampling Details.   Using available computer software, 50 subjects were to be randomly drawn from each frame, the corresponding records were to be pulled, and the required data were to be downloaded.

Potential Data Collection Weaknesses.   The greatest weakness was expected to be the possible incompleteness of patients' records. It was felt, however, that there was no relationship between the fact that a record was incomplete and the variables under study. Therefore an incomplete record was to be replaced by another randomly drawn record.

Fictional Data.   Data like the following were expected.

Nurse	Physician	Discharge	Population
4	5	179	1
7	17	10	1
7	8	143	1
12	42	85	1
⋮			

Data Analysis Plans

Graphical Summaries.   For each of the three variables, frequency distributions for the samples from the three populations were to be obtained in the form of dot-plots, using the same horizontal axis to simplify comparison. These three sets of dotplots were to give a visual impression of how the three variables were distributed in the three populations.

Numerical Summaries.   Means and standard deviations were to be computed for all nine variables so that appropriate numerical comparisons could be made.

3.8

SUMMARY AND OUTLOOK

In the previous chapter, you learned how collection of data should be planned, and in this chapter you learned how data, once collected, can be summarized. Any data summary should consist of a number of graphs, supplemented by some summary measures—in particular, measures of central location, dispersion, and correlation.

Some of the tools discussed in this chapter are useful for cross-sectional data and some are useful for time series data. In the next chapter, we will examine cross-sectional data in greater detail—in particular, we will discuss a simple *model* for cross-sectional data. In Chapters 5 and 6, we will then turn to time series and how they can be modeled. In particular, we will show the conditions under which time series data can be analyzed with the tools developed for cross-sectional data in Chapter 4.

Throughout the remainder of this book we will emphasize how *models* can be formulated for the way in which data arise. It will turn out that, given certain assumptions, a particular model may be useful for cross-sectional studies and that, given somewhat different assumptions, a similar model may be useful for time series studies. Regardless of the kind of study done, it will always be necessary, however, to check if the model assumptions are approximately met.

Key Terms and Concepts

graphical displays
    sequence plot
    Pareto diagram
    histogram, frequency distribution,
        dotplot
    stem-and-leaf plot
    scatterplot

numerical summary measures
    central location: mean, median,
        mode
    dispersion: standard deviation,
        variance, range
    skewness
    percentile, quantile
    correlation, covariance

References

Deming, W. E. (1986), *Out of the Crisis,* Massachusetts Institute of Technology, Center for Advanced Engineering Study, Cambridge, MA.

Ishikawa, K. (1982), *Guide to Quality Control,* 2nd Revised Edition, Asian Productivity Organization, Tokyo.

    This text is one of the classics in quality control.

Keller, G., Warrack, B., and Bartel, H. (1994), *Statistics for Management and Economics: A Systematic Approach,* 3rd Edition, Duxbury Press, Belmont, CA.

Tufte, E. R. (1983), *The Visual Display of Quantitative Information,* The Graphics Press, Cheshire, CN.

    This beautifully prepared book discusses various techniques to construct good graphs.

USING MINITAB FOR WINDOWS

This section shows how several of the graphs in this chapter were generated with Minitab for Windows.[13]

Figure 3.1

IMPORTING AN ASCII FILE INTO THE MINITAB WORKSHEET

Choose *File* ▸ *Other Files* ▸ *Import ASCII Data*
In the *Import ASCII Data* dialog box,
    Under *Store data in column* type **C1**
    Click *ok*
    In the *Import Text From File* dialog box,
        Choose and click data file *newsstan.dat,* click *ok*
            (File newsstan.dat, which consists of one column only, is now stored in column C1.)

NAMING A COLUMN IN THE MINITAB WORKSHEET

Choose *Window* ▸ *Data*
In the *Data* window,
    Click the box immediately under *C1,* type **SALES**
    Click any empty cell
        (Column C1 is now named SALES. Always, always name your columns!)

OBTAINING THE MEAN FOR A COLUMN OF DATA

Choose *Calc* ▸ *Column Statistics*
In the *Column Statistics* dialog box,
    Under *Statistic* click *Mean*
    Click the box next to *Input variable* and type **SALES**
    Click *ok*
        (The following output will appear in the Session Window. The mean will be used in the sequence plot we will create below.)

Session Window Output

```
MTB > Read 'C:\MTBWIN\DATA\NEWSSTAN.DAT' C1.
Entering data from file: C:\MTBWIN\DATA\NEWSSTAN.DAT
  50 rows read.
MTB > Mean 'SALES'.
MEAN = 394622
```

---

[13]The steps given in this section are appropriate for Minitab Release 10 for Windows. Since Release 10 became available only during the page proof stage, the Minitab graphs and other output in this book are based on Release 9; the differences between the two releases are minor as they relate to this book.

TIME SERIES PLOT

> Choose *Graph* ► *Time Series Plot*
> In the *Time Series Plot* dialog box,
> > Type **SALES** in *Graph variables*, click *ok*

ADDING A TITLE TO A TIME SERIES PLOT

> Choose *Graph* ► *Time Series Plot*
> In the *Time Series Plot* dialog box,
> > Type **SALES** in *Graph variables*
> > Next to the *Annotation* box, click on ▼, click *Title*
> > In the *Title* dialog box.
> > > Type **Sequence Plot of Weekly Newsstand Sales Data**
> > > Click *ok*
> > Click *ok*
> > > (Note that the title produced with Minitab does not actually appear in Figure 3.1.)

ADDING TEXT TO A TIME SERIES PLOT

> Choose *Graph* ► *Time Series Plot*
> In the *Time Series Plot* dialog box,
> > Type **SALES** in *Graph variables*
> > Next to the *Annotation* box, click on ▼, click *Text*
> > In the *Text* dialog box,
> > > Under *Point* type **45 395000**
> > > Click the box under *Text* and type **Mean**
> > > Click *ok*
> > > > (These steps add the word "Mean" at the point (Index = 45, SALES = 395,000) on the graph.)
> > Click *ok*

ADDING A LINE TO A TIME SERIES PLOT

> Choose *Graph* ► *Time Series Plot*
> In the *Time Series Plot* dialog box,
> > Type **SALES** in *Graph variables*
> > In the *Line* dialog box,
> > > Next to the *Annotation* box, click on ▼, click *Line*
> > > Under *Points* type **0 394622 50 394622**
> > > Click *ok*
> > > > (These steps draw a line at the value 394,622 across the graph.)
> > Click *ok*

Figure 3.2

ENTERING DATA DIRECTLY INTO THE MINITAB WORKSHEET

Choose *Window* ▸ *Data*
In the *Data* window,
    Click the box immediately under *C1*, type **TIME**
    Type the following numbers in the first 50 rows of column C1, using the down arrow to move to the next row:

510	400	370	870	150	1610	1570	1490	480	600	520
500	400	390	1540	1190	50	50	110	130	2900	120
150	230	120	1750	180	200	250	1230	1230	520	1580
110	130	100	1260	690	660	770	660	640	420	1720
2020	110	400								

    Click any empty cell

SAVING A MINITAB WORKSHEET AS A MINITAB FILE

Choose *File* ▸ *Save Worksheet As*
In the *Save Worksheet As* dialog box
    Minitab is selected as the default type file
    Type **hospital** under *File Name*
    Click *ok*

OBTAINING THE MEAN FOR A COLUMN OF DATA

Choose *Calc* ▸ *Column Statistics*
In the *Column Statistics* dialog box,
    Under *Statistic* click *Mean*
    Click the box next to *Input variable* and type **TIME**
    Click *ok*
        (The following output will appear in the Session window.)

Session Window Output

MTB > Save 'C:\MTBWIN\DATA\HOSPITAL.MTW';
SUBC> Replace.
Saving worksheet in file: C:\MTBWIN\DATA\HOSPITA.MTW
MTB > Mean 'TIME'.
MEAN = 703.83

The following commands generate Figure 3.2:

Choose *Graph* ► *Time Series Plot*
In the *Time Series Plot* dialog box,
    Type **TIME** in *Graph variables*
    Next to the *Annotation* box, click on ▼, click *Title*
    In the *Title* dialog box,
        Type **Sequence Plot of Waiting Times** and click *ok*
    Next to the *Annotation* box, click on ▼, click *Text*
    In the *Text* dialog box,
        Under *Point* type **50 703.83**
        Click the box under *Text,* type **Mean** and click *ok*
    Next to the *Annotation* box, click on ▼, click *Line*
    In the *Line* dialog box,
        Under *Points* type **0 703.83 47 703.83** and click *ok*
    Click *ok*

Figure 3.4

HISTOGRAM

Choose *Graph* ► *Histogram*
In the *Histogram* dialog box,
    Under *Graph variables,* type **C1**
    Click *ok*
        (These steps generate the default histogram in Figure 3.4.)

HISTOGRAM WITH USER-DEFINED MIDPOINTS

Choose *Graph* ► *Histogram*
In the *Histogram* dialog box,
    Under *Graph variables,* type **C1**
    Click *Options*
    In the *Histogram Options* dialog box,
        Under *Definition of Intervals,* click the circle to left of *midpoint/cutpoint positions*
        In the box to right of *midpoint/cutpoint positions,* type **120:2040/120**
        Click *ok*
            (The last four lines define the class midpoints to range from 120 to 2040 in intervals of 240.)
    Click *ok*
        (Figure 3.4(b) is generated by these steps.)

Figure 3.6(b)

RELATIVE CUMULATIVE HISTOGRAM

> Choose *Graph* ▸ *Histogram*
> In the *Histogram* dialog box,
>> Under *Graph variables*, type **C1**
>> Click *Options*
>>> Under *Type of Histogram*, click the circle next to *Cumulative Percent*
>>> Under *Type of Intervals*, click the circle next to *CutPoint*
>>> Under *Definiton of Intervals*, click circle to left of *midpoint/cutpoint positions*
>>> To right of *midpoint/cutpoint positions*, type **0:2160/240**
>>> Click *ok*
>>>> (These options request a cumulative relative histogram. They define the end-points of the class intervals to extend from 0 to 2160 and the width of the intervals to be 240.)
>> Click *ok*

Figure 3.8

STEM-AND-LEAF PLOT

> Choose *Graph* ▸ *Character Graphs* ▸ *Stem-and-Leaf*
> In the *Stem-and-Leaf* dialog box,
>> Under *Variables*, type **C1**
>> Click *ok*
>>> (These steps generate the stem-and-leaf plot for variable C1 in Figure 3.8(a). Several useful graphs are available in Minitab in the form of low-resolution character graphs. The output is in the Session window.)

STEM-AND-LEAF PLOT WITH USER-DEFINED STEM INTERVALS

> Choose *Graph* ▸ *Character Graphs* ▸ *Stem-and-Leaf*
> In the *Stem-and-Leaf* dialog box,
>> Under *Variables*, type **C1**
>> Next to *Increment*, type **100**
>> Click *ok*
>>> (These steps generate Figure 3.8(b). The stems are to increase in intervals of 100.)

Figure 3.9

ENTERING DATA INTO THE WORKSHEET FOR A PARETO DIAGRAM

> Choose *Window* ▸ *Data*
> In the *Data* window,
>> Click the box immediately under *C1*, type **Defect**
>> Type the following words in the first five rows of column C1, using the down arrow to move to the next row: **Caulking Fitting Connecting Torque Gapping**
>> Click the box immediately under *C2*, type **Number**

Type the following numbers in the first five rows of column C2, using the down arrow to move to the next row: **198 25 103 18 72**

Click any empty cell

      (You may want to save the data at this point.)

PARETO DIAGRAM

Choose *Stat* ▸ *SPC* ▸ *Pareto Chart*

In the *Pareto Chart* dialog box,

    Click the circle to the left of *Chart defects table*

    To the right of *Labels in,* type **C1**

    To the right of *Frequencies in,* type **C2**

    Click *ok*

        (A Pareto diagram is now generated, using the category names in C1 and the corresponding defect count in C2.

Figure 3.10

IMPORTING AN ASCII FILE AND NAMING THE MINITAB COLUMNS

Choose *File* ▸ *Other Files* ▸ *Import ASCII Data*

In the *Import ASCII Data* dialog box,

    Under *Store data in column* type **C1-C6**

    Click *ok*

    In the *Import Text from File* dialog box,

        Choose and click data file *pickpack.dat*

        Click *ok*

Choose *Window* ▸ *Data*

In the *Data* window,

    In the cells immediately below columns C2, C3, and C5, type **ITEMS LINES TIME**

    Click any empty cell

PRINTING COLUMNS FROM THE WORKSHEET INTO THE SESSION WINDOW

Choose *Window* ▸ *Session*

In the *Session* window, type **PRINT C2 C3 C5**

        (The data for columns C2, C3, and C5 now appear in the Session window.)

Figure 3.11

SCATTERPLOT

Choose *Graph* ▸ *Plot*

In the *Plot* dialog box,

    In the *Graph variables* box, type **C5** in row 1 under *Y* and type **C3** in row 1 under *X*

    Click ok

SCATTERPLOT WITH USER-DEFINED PRINTING SYMBOLS

>Choose *Graph* ▸ *Plot*
>In the *Plot* dialog box,
>>In the *Graph variables* box, type **C5** in row 1 under *Y* and type **C3** in row 1 under *X*
>>Click *Edit Attributes*
>>In the *Symbol* dialog box,
>>>Click the down arrow next to *Type,* click *Dot,* click *ok*
>>>>(The last three rows lead to dots being used as printing symbols in the scatterplot.)
>>Click *ok*

SCATTERPLOT WITH JITTER

>Choose *Graph* ▸ *Plot*
>In the *Plot* dialog box,
>>In the *Graph variables* box, type **C5** in row 1 under *Y* and type **C3** in row 1 under *X*
>>Click *Options*
>>In the *Plot Options* dialog box,
>>>Click the box next to *Add Jitter to Direction,* click *ok*
>>>>(The last two rows lead to random offsetting of printing symbols so that overlapping printing symbols can be seen.)
>>Click *ok*

Figure 3.20

>Choose *File* ▸ *Other Files* ▸ *Import ASCII Data*
>In the *Import ASCII Data* dialog box,
>>Under *Store data in column* type **C1 C2**
>>Click *ok*
>>In the *Import Text from File* dialog box,
>>>Choose and click data file *stock.dat*
>>>Click *ok*
>Choose *Window* ▸ *Data*
>In the *Data* window,
>>In the cells immediately below columns C1 and C2, type **NTL** and **TSE**
>>Click any empty cell

DESCRIPTIVE STATISTICS

>Choose *Stat* ▸ *Basic Statistics* ▸ *Descriptive Statistics*
>In the *Descriptive Statistics* dialog box,
>>Under *Variables* type **C1 C2**
>>Click *ok*
>>>(The descriptive statistics appear in the Session window.)

3.10

MINITAB COMMANDS

Appendix A gives a brief introduction to Minitab Release 10 for Windows, and Appendix B gives a brief introduction to earlier releases of Minitab. This section lists the Minitab commands in Release 10 for Windows that were introduced in this chapter. Minitab's main menu consists of the following choices:

File, Edit, Manip, Calc, Stat, Window, Graph, Editor, Help

Each submenu introduced in this chapter is listed under the corresponding main menu. It is briefly explained and a page reference to an explanation in this chapter is given in parentheses.

File
> Save Worksheet As   page 88
>> [save data in ASCII, Minitab, or other formats]
>
> Other Files
>> Import ASCII Data   page 86
>>> [enter data into the Minitab worksheet from an ASCII file]

Calc
> Column Statistics   page 86
>> [compute statistics on columns, such as the mean and standard deviation]

Stat
> Basic Statistics
>> Descriptive Statistics   page 92
>>> [obtain a variety of descriptive statistics for columns]

SPC
> Pareto chart   page 91
>> [yields a Pareto diagram]

Window
> Session   page 91
>> [move to Minitab's Session window]
>
> Data   page 86
>> [move to Minitab's Data window where you can operate on the data worksheet]

Graph

3.11

PROBLEM FOR CLASS DISCUSSION

3.1 Maple Engineering and Construction

Maple Engineering and Construction Canada was interested in examining project margins for those heavy construction projects that were competitively tendered. In particular, the following questions were to be addressed:

- Is there any pattern to the project margins over time?

- How accurate are estimated project margins?

- Is there a relationship between project margin and project size?

- Could the data be used to predict project margins for future projects?

These questions were to be answered with respect to both actual and relative contribution margins. The discussion here will be restricted to actual contribution margins and the first two questions.

Data were gathered for all 51 competitively tendered heavy construction projects that were completed between 1982 and 1988. The data were obtained from company files. For each project, three variables were measured: revenue (in $1,000), actual margin (in $1,000), and estimated margin (in $1,000).

The data, listed in the following table, are stored in ASCII file MAPLE.DAT.

Project Margin Data

ROW	REVENUE	ACTMARG$	ESTMARG$	ROW	REVENUE	ACTMARG$	ESTMARG$
1	1,359	209	156	27	97	24	16
2	1,027	59	100	28	369	58	39
3	1,194	143	78	29	39	7	5
4	193	35	18	30	304	24	20
5	395	69	39	31	537	54	49
6	1,825	173	224	32	2,711	216	240
7	94	26	13	33	371	38	37
8	148	22	18	34	1,875	271	101
9	631	56	57	35	73	19	10
10	42	11	4	36	720	84	55
11	1,081	81	80	37	1,354	104	133

		Project Margin Data					
ROW	REVENUE	ACTMARG$	ESTMARG$	ROW	REVENUE	ACTMARG$	ESTMARG$
12	114	7	10	38	202	52	31
13	854	74	87	39	2,943	199	201
14	85	13	28	40	275	59	46
15	17	5	2	41	342	52	47
16	435	26	30	42	354	25	25
17	863	89	110	43	592	36	30
18	194	22	18	44	183	13	11
19	57	19	5	45	299	32	20
20	975	88	71	46	756	71	72
21	288	3	30	47	136	12	11
22	134	32	19	48	155	20	13
23	694	87	51	49	2,656	206	182
24	648	109	70	50	3,401	314	288
25	276	8	20	51	2,680	223	201
26	639	42	50				

SOURCE: The data were kindly provided by M. Reinders.

The Minitab output in Figure 3.27 is useful for answering the questions. In addition to the three variables listed above, REVENUE, ACTMARG$, and ESTMARG$, a fourth variable, ERROR = ACTMARG$ − ESTMARG$, is created and analyzed.

FIGURE 3.27

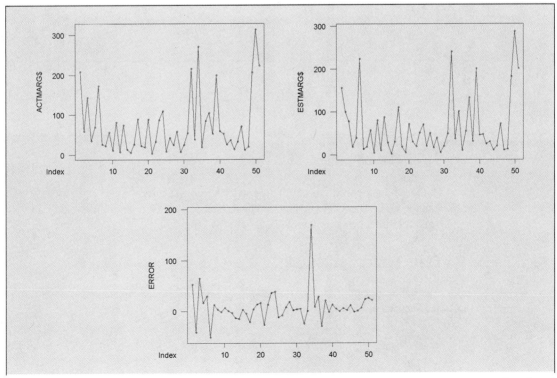

(continues)

FIGURE 3.27 (continued)

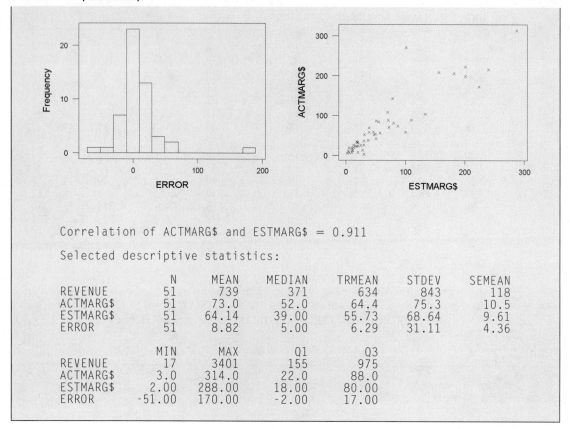

```
Correlation of ACTMARG$ and ESTMARG$ = 0.911

Selected descriptive statistics:

                  N       MEAN     MEDIAN    TRMEAN    STDEV    SEMEAN
REVENUE          51        739        371       634      843       118
ACTMARG$         51       73.0       52.0      64.4     75.3      10.5
ESTMARG$         51      64.14      39.00     55.73    68.64      9.61
ERROR            51       8.82       5.00      6.29    31.11      4.36

                MIN        MAX         Q1        Q3
REVENUE          17       3401        155       975
ACTMARG$        3.0      314.0       22.0      88.0
ESTMARG$       2.00     288.00      18.00     80.00
ERROR        -51.00     170.00      -2.00     17.00
```

3.12

EXERCISES

Although answers are given in Appendix C, do not turn to them right away if you cannot find an answer on your own. Return to the exercise the next day and try again before turning to Appendix C.

Exercises for Section 3.2

3.2   The following table gives the Canadian population (in 1,000s) by country of birth for selected countries in 1961 and 1981.

	1961	1981
Canada	15,394	20,216
United Kingdom	970	885
United States	284	312
Germany	189	198
Italy	258	387
Poland	171	149
Asiatic countries	58	413
Total	18,238	24,083

SOURCE: *Canada Year Book 1985*, p. 61.

Draw Pareto diagrams, excluding Canadians born in Canada, by country of birth in 1961 and 1981. (Don't forget the "Others" entry.) Comment on the differences.

3.3 Consider each situation described below and indicate if a Pareto diagram would be useful. If so, sketch the Pareto diagram, labelling both axes. If not, briefly describe why not.

a To get an overview of the annual incomes of its 1,000 members, an organization found out that 130 members make between $0 and $19,999, 400 between $20,000 and $39,999, 290 between $40,000 and $59,999, 80 between $60,000 and $79,999, and 100 between $80,000 and $99,999.

b A clothing store was interested in the popularity of different colors of shirts. The five colors carried were referred to as colors 1 to 5. In a particular month, colors 1 to 5 were sold 130, 150, 100, 200, and 180 times, respectively.

c On a particular day, 100 customers were surveyed regarding their satisfaction with a particular service, and 40 customers indicated they were very satisfied, 25 were satisfied, 15 were indifferent, 5 were dissatisfied, and 15 were very dissatisfied.

d To get an idea of how busy a car dealership was throughout the week, the number of visits to the dealership was recorded for several weeks. The average number of visits on Mondays was 10, on Tuesdays it was 12, on Wednesdays 18, on Thursdays 15, on Fridays 20, and on Saturdays 30.

3.4 This is a continuation of Problem 2.17 regarding the Ralston Purina Canada Ltd. data. You are to view the data as arising from a population study.

a What is the unit? Is this a sample or a census?

For the remaining questions, use the Minitab output at the end of this question. (The data are stored in ASCII file PURINA.DAT.)

b Answer the second question of the Ralston Purina study: How is market share in 1987 related to that in 1988?

c In answering (b), should you exclude the data for market number 86? What are the pros and cons?

d Looking at the two scatterplots below, can you roughly describe the shape of the distribution of "SHARE_88" values? (For example, is it symmetrical, negatively skewed, bimodal, etc.?)

The following Minitab output should help you answer the above questions:

FIGURE 3.28

ROW	SHARE_87	SHARE_88	ROW	SHARE_87	SHARE_88	ROW	SHARE_87	SHARE_88
1	3.692	4.549	33	7.048	6.530	65	11.182	11.466
2	6.610	6.921	34	20.918	20.967	66	19.707	19.707
3	6.913	5.216	35	6.061	6.269	67	15.538	16.067
4	7.744	7.851	36	0.000	0.000	68	10.872	11.807
5	5.945	5.517	37	6.347	8.797	69	9.514	11.679
6	5.284	5.159	38	6.915	7.232	70	10.409	12.750
7	14.171	13.973	39	20.782	21.536	71	60.128	45.455
8	4.618	6.419	40	7.398	6.461	72	17.825	17.501
9	0.000	0.000	41	0.000	1.791	73	10.211	8.930
10	4.108	5.432	42	11.914	15.425	74	14.975	18.716
11	13.118	14.949	43	7.613	4.355	75	4.639	5.545
12	0.000	0.000	44	12.387	12.436	76	27.672	28.782
13	9.383	7.101	45	0.000	1.867	77	13.718	19.508
14	9.373	12.657	46	11.723	15.044	78	36.674	34.580
15	6.216	6.871	47	11.894	6.474	79	3.817	3.676
16	3.628	3.257	48	0.000	0.000	80	2.700	9.813
17	2.498	5.343	49	6.527	8.090	81	15.047	18.073
18	5.905	5.625	50	26.509	6.792	82	20.634	24.761
19	7.489	6.801	51	9.773	10.545	83	13.804	17.155
20	2.180	2.145	52	15.327	13.704	84	0.000	5.433
21	1.582	1.837	53	7.167	4.746	85	9.405	18.492
22	18.450	16.054	54	11.361	10.733	86	242.436	219.450
23	16.687	17.078	55	5.542	5.752	87	9.567	4.249
24	13.006	11.156	56	7.299	5.234	88	0.000	0.000
25	4.412	4.022	57	6.665	2.801	89	17.693	21.135
26	13.495	11.650	58	21.761	22.131	90	5.346	5.467
27	10.237	3.718	59	9.708	7.545	91	2.830	3.379
28	1.829	2.630	60	3.387	3.301	92	41.017	75.088
29	5.739	5.622	61	10.405	12.622	93	0.365	0.699
30	7.475	5.631	62	14.088	13.352	94	1.183	4.673
31	3.095	2.983	63	19.617	22.755	95	12.426	12.521
32	4.639	7.399	64	18.583	17.759	96	0.000	0.000

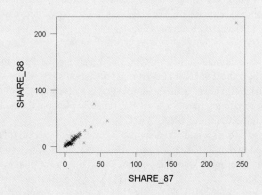

	N	MEAN	MEDIAN	TRMEAN	STDEV	SEMEAN
SHARE_87	96	12.56	7.68	9.27	25.43	2.60
SHARE_88	96	12.76	7.17	9.56	23.68	2.42

Correlation of SHARE_87 and SHARE_88 = 0.978

(For the remainder of the analysis, the "outlying" value, market number 86, was deleted.)

FIGURE 3.28 (continued)

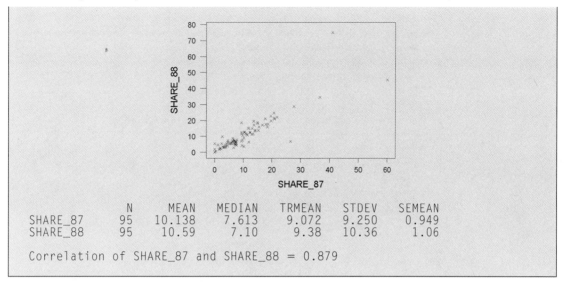

	N	MEAN	MEDIAN	TRMEAN	STDEV	SEMEAN
SHARE_87	95	10.138	7.613	9.072	9.250	0.949
SHARE_88	95	10.59	7.10	9.38	10.36	1.06

Correlation of SHARE_87 and SHARE_88 = 0.879

Exercises for Section 3.3

3.5 Suppose your variable of interest is income of residents in the United States. For residents age 25 and older in 1994, would the average or median be higher for income?

3.6 Both of the following sets of numbers have the same average of 50.

    Data set A: 50   40   60   30   70   25   75

    Data set B: 50   40   60   30   70   25   75   50   50   50

  a Which set has the smaller standard deviation, and why? No computations are necessary. You may want to plot the data.
  b Compute the standard deviation for each set of numbers.

3.7 Compute the mean, median, mode, standard deviation, variance, and range for the following data: 11, 12, 12, 13, 14, 14, 14, 16, and 20. Is the frequency distribution of the data skewed? If so, is it positively or negatively skewed? What are the 10th, 25th, 60th, and 75th percentiles?

3.8 Consider an object whose weight is very difficult to measure so that precise measurements cannot easily be obtained. An imprecise measuring device was used repeatedly (100 times) to measure the object's weight. The mean and standard deviation of the 100 measurements were 6.0 mg and 0.5 mg, respectively. The frequency distribution of the 100 measurements was roughly as in Figure 3.16(c) so the empirical rule for the standard deviation applies.
  a Give an interval that contains roughly 68% of measurements.
  b Roughly what proportion of measurements were between 5.0 mg and 7.0 mg?
  c Roughly what proportion of measurements were less than or equal to 7.0 mg? (In other words, which percentile is 7 mg?)

3.9 Your data consist of measurements on two variables for several respondents: income (in dollars) and the size of the respondent's dwelling (in square meters). In what units are each of the following descriptive statistics measured?

a The mean size of respondents' dwellings
b The variance of the respondents' incomes
c The standard deviation of the respondents' incomes
d The median size of respondents' dwellings
e The correlation coefficient between income and size of dwelling

3.10 Consider the three types of measurement scales for variables—categorical, ordinal, and quantitative. How useful are mean, median, mode, and standard deviation for each?

3.11 This exercise gives you some practice with summation notation. Consider the following set of $n = 3$ numbers: 2, 3, and 7, denoted y_1, y_2, and y_3. Compute

a $\sum y_i$
b $\sum y_i^2$
c $\sum (y_i - \bar{y})$
d $\sum |y_i - \bar{y}|$
e $\sum (y_i - \bar{y})^2$

Exercise for Section 3.4

3.12 The following table lists the average weekly hours worked and hourly earnings of wage earners in manufacturing for nine provinces in 1982.

Province	Average Weekly Hours	Average Hourly Earnings
Newfoundland	36.4	9.27
Nova Scotia	36.7	9.07
New Brunswick	37.0	9.39
Quebec	37.9	9.46
Ontario	38.3	10.16
Manitoba	37.0	9.07
Saskatchewan	35.8	11.14
Alberta	37.1	11.94
British Columbia	34.7	13.89

Source: *Canada Year Book, 1985*, p. 181.

a Does a population or a process underlie this problem? Briefly describe the population or process. What is the unit? What is the response variable?
b Using Minitab, compute the correlation coefficient between the two variables.
c Is such a correlation coefficient an informative statistic? Why or why not?
d If your answer to (c) was yes, are you surprised by the value of the correlation? Why or why not?
e To improve your intuition about the various summary statistics, it is useful to calculate them in detail without a software package. Using a pocket calculator, compute the mean and the standard deviation for the two variables. Compute the covariance and then the correlation. Does the correlation you compute agree with the result in (b)? Reconcile any differences.

Exercises for All Sections in Chapter 3

3.13 The following annual starting salaries (in $1,000) were offered to 16 recently graduated accounting majors:

27.5	24.9	26.2	26.5	26.4	25.4	25.8	25.5
24.6	27.6	26.8	26.0	25.6	26.4	24.4	24.8

To improve your intuition about the various summary statistics, it is useful to calculate them in detail without a software package. Use a pocket calculator to answer the following questions.

  a Is this data set a population or a sample? How do you know? What is the unit? What is the response variable?
  b Find the mean, mode, and median of these 16 values.
  c What is their standard deviation?
  d Use classes of $24,000 \le y < 24,500$, $24,500 \le y < 25,000$, etc., to construct a frequency distribution table. Represent this graphically.
  e Find the 25th and 75th percentiles.

3.14 The dispatch operation at an IBM subsidiary receives and records service calls from customers. It is an important interface with IBM's customers, and it is critical that customers' service calls be taken promptly and efficiently. Customers are placed on hold when placing their service calls, and the length of time customers are on hold is of interest. The target value for time on hold is 16 seconds.

A study was undertaken to determine if the dispatch process was meeting the stated objective for responding to customer calls and if the process was stable. Attempts were to be made to develop a model that could be used for prediction and planning.

It was anticipated that, due to seasonal variation, there would be fewer incoming calls in the summer months. Due to vacation time, operator staffing is below normal as well at this time. Data were collected during July to October 1987, and 70 days of data were obtained from the dispatch operation, some manually and some electronically. In the sampling period, there were few customer complaints.

Three variables were measured each day: the number of operators on duty (STAFF), the number of incoming calls (CALLS), and the waiting time in hours totaled for all customers (WAIT). Two variables were of prime interest: CALLS was important to determine if any pattern or trend existed; WAIT was most important: it was a function of incoming calls and staffing levels. STAFF could be controlled for, but was not during this study, and it was of interest what effect it had on WAIT time. Other variables, such as operator proficiency, may have an effect on the process. A strong relationship between STAFF and WAIT was suspected before the study was carried out.

The data are given in the table on p. 102 and are stored in ASCII file DISPATCH.DAT.

  a Does a population or a process underlie this problem? Briefly describe the population or process. What is the unit? What is the response variable in the following questions?
  b Obtain a sequence plot for the waiting time data. Is there any time series pattern? If so, describe it. Are there any unusual observations?
  c Obtain a dotplot and a histogram for the WAIT data. Describe them.
  d What are the mean, median, and mode for WAIT? How do they differ? If they differ, can you give a rationale for this?
  e What are the range and standard deviation for WAIT?
  f Draw lines to mark the target value for waiting time on the plots in (b) and (c). What implications can you suggest based on the resulting graphs?

g To which percentile of the distribution of WAIT does the target value correspond? For what proportion of days is the target value exceeded by average waiting time?

h Using your answer in (g) and other information given, what proportion of customer waiting times exceed the target value?

i Obtain a scatterplot of WAIT vs. CALLS, WAIT vs. STAFF, and CALLS vs. STAFF. What are the corresponding correlations? Do you find these plots and correlations surprising? What implications do they have for future staffing?

DAY	STAFF	CALLS	WAIT	DAY	STAFF	CALLS	WAIT
1	24	3,142	48	36	27	2,763	17
2	26	2,704	22	37	30	2,610	9
3	24	2,351	31	38	24	2,616	22
4	25	2,834	33	39	26	2,876	23
5	24	2,662	42	40	28	2,830	20
6	25	3,351	30	41	28	2,667	22
7	24	2,605	21	42	30	2,729	12
8	26	2,583	19	43	29	2,407	23
9	24	2,501	17	44	28	2,813	12
10	22	2,424	31	45	28	2,698	15
11	28	2,862	23	46	30	2,848	11
12	27	2,674	22	47	29	2,551	15
13	27	2,636	24	48	27	2,979	22
14	29	2,098	14	49	28	2,741	25
15	22	2,517	35	50	28	2,653	27
16	22	2,749	33	51	28	2,789	28
17	23	2,573	18	52	23	2,792	41
18	23	2,541	26	53	28	3,299	22
19	23	2,368	18	54	28	2,770	27
20	22	1,977	23	55	27	2,837	24
21	20	2,911	39	56	28	2,802	18
22	23	2,698	23	57	26	2,610	28
23	20	2,425	26	58	24	3,031	29
24	23	2,791	24	59	26	3,156	35
25	25	3,029	21	60	23	2,838	28
26	25	2,715	20	61	21	2,893	46
27	23	2,513	11	62	20	2,744	40
28	20	2,417	20	63	25	2,935	22
29	33	2,723	11	64	25	2,994	22
30	31	2,893	14	65	24	3,016	36
31	30	2,673	28	66	25	2,738	26
32	33	2,636	11	67	24	2,625	26
33	27	2,429	16	68	26	3,040	30
34	27	2,977	22	69	28	2,833	19
35	27	2,729	13	70	26	2,916	28

SOURCE: The data were kindly provided by D. Bradford.

3.13

SUPPLEMENTARY EXERCISES

3.15 Data follow for the number of defectives collected during the production process in the month of April at a certain electrical manufacturer (producing mainly stereo equipment). Draw Pareto diagrams by
  a Item (combining all items with less than 60 defectives into "Others")
  b Responsible section (combining all sections with less than 60 defectives into "Others")
  c Item within the sections Purchasing, Electronics subsidiary B, and Coil plant
Briefly summarize the main conclusions.

Item	Number	Responsible Section
Vacuum tube	327	Electronics subsidiary A
Pilot lamp	240	Purchasing section
Transistor	176	Electronics subsidiary B
Neon tube	105	Purchasing section
Speaker	90	Speaker plant
Coil (A)	61	Coil plant
Rotary switch	21	Assembly parts plant
Volume control	15	Volume control maker
Carbon resistance	14	Resistor plant
Diode	14	Electronics subsidiary B
Condenser (C)	12	Purchasing section
Transformer (B)	10	Transformer plant
Condenser (D)	9	Purchasing section
Variable condenser	8	Purchasing section
Condenser (A)	50	Condenser plant
Condenser (B)	45	Condenser plant
Headphone jack	43	Purchasing section
Transformer	36	Coil plant
Coil (B)	33	Coil plant
Six-spool trimmer	31	Purchasing section
Coil (C)	8	Coil plant
Seesaw switch	8	Assembly parts plant
Solid-state resistor	8	Solid-state resistor plant
Transformer (C)	7	Transistor plant
Slide switch	6	Assembly parts plant
Printed circuit	2	Printed circuit plant
Composite parts	1	Ceramic plant
Others	23	

SOURCE: K. Ishikawa, *Guide to Quality Control*, 2nd Revised Edition, Asian Productivity Organization, 1982, p. 175.

3.16 Very often histograms must be based on data summarized in a table that gives several classes for the variable of interest and the number of units falling into each class. When the classes are of equal width, it is easy to draw the histogram: The height of the bar for each class can correspond to the number (or percentage) in the class. When the classes are *not* of equal width, great care must be taken in labelling the two axes and in determining the height for each class.
  The following table gives the income distribution of Canadian families in 1971.

Income Group	% of Families
Under $3,000	9.0
$ 3,000–$ 4,999	11.5
5,000– 6,999	12.2
7,000– 9,999	22.0
10,000– 11,999	14.0
12,000– 14,999	14.2
15,000– 19,999	10.9
20,000 and over	6.2

Source: *Canada Year Book, 1985,* p. 191.

Draw a histogram in bar graph form. The horizontal axis should be labelled in 1,000s of dollars. Note that the class intervals are of *un*equal width. The vertical axis should be labelled "% of Families per $1,000." (Therefore, a class that is $2,000 wide and contains 10% of families should be represented by a bar that reaches up to the "5% per $1,000" mark on the vertical axis.) Assume for simplicity that no income is higher than $30,000, but think about what you would do without this simplifying assumption. (To check the readability of your histogram, show it to a friend who is not in this class, and ask him or her to tell you the proportion of families with incomes under $3,000 and that with incomes between $15,000 and $20,000.)

3.17 Pareto diagrams are useful in many areas where improvement is of interest. Investigate a situation in your department at work where a Pareto diagram may usefully convey information about how to make improvements. Present your results and conclusions for (a) to (g) in a short memorandum (one page or less).

a Define your objectives for using the Pareto diagram. Based on the results, what actions do you anticipate?

b Give a brief description of the categorical variable for which the Pareto diagram is to be constructed.

c How would you make data collection reliable?

d How frequently should data be reported (hourly, daily, monthly, etc.)?

e Should the data be stratified? If so, which variable should be used for stratification purposes? (A "yes" here implies that several Pareto diagrams are required.)

f Can the data be expressed in amounts of money?

g Data collection is *not* necessary, but attach a mock-up Pareto diagram of the results you expect. In your diagram, label the axes.

3.18 The medical records department of the Toronto General Hospital is composed of 10 interdependent sections, each overseen by a front-line supervisor. Its total staffing complement slightly exceeds 110 employees. Because of increasing concern about absenteeism in the department and its impact on departmental efficiency, productivity, and staff morale, a study was done to answer the following questions (among others):

▪ What is the overall incidence of absenteeism in the department and in each section?

▪ What is the average number of days employees are absent per year, both for the department as a whole and for each section?

▪ Is the pattern of absenteeism changing over time?

It was expected that absenteeism would vary considerably across sections. Furthermore, an increase in absenteeism was expected over time since the hospital adopted a more generous sick-time allowance during the period under study.

Data were collected as follows. A retrospective observational study was carried out using department records to collect absenteeism data. Additional information on age, section, and seniority was collected from personnel files. Yearly data were collected for 1986 to 1988 on all employees in the department. (The data for 1988 covered the period from January to September only.) Five variables were measured: Section (1 = assembly, 2 = doctors' study, 3 = coding, 4 = filing room, 5 = transcription, 6 = ward secretaries, 7 = patient registration, 8 = evenings, nights, weekends, 9 = manager's office, and 10 = oncology medical records); Age (in years); Seniority (number of years the employee worked in the department); Number of absences; and Number of days absent. (Note the differences between number of absences and number of days absent: An absence consists of one or more *consecutive* days absent.)

The following tables list the numbers of employees, the numbers of absences, and the *average* number of days employees were absent by section for 1986 and 1987. The table also gives information for the department.

1986

Section	Number of Employees	Number of Absences	Average Days Absent
1. Assembly	14	44	12.64
2. Doctors' Study	7	22	7.00
3. Coding	12	30	11.00
4. Filing Room	15	34	5.20
5. Transcription	17	44	9.94
6. Ward Secretaries	14	12	1.50
7. Patient Registration	13	34	10.46
8. Evenings, etc.	6	13	23.30
9. Manager's Office	3	0	0.00
10. Oncology Records	0	0	0.00
Department Total	101	233	

1987

Section	Number of Employees	Number of Absences	Average Days Absent
1. Assembly	15	48	14.60
2. Doctors' Study	10	37	6.60
3. Coding	16	47	9.62
4. Filing Room	18	35	6.11
5. Transcription	20	39	2.95
6. Ward Secretaries	17	32	3.00
7. Patient Registration	13	52	20.85
8. Evenings, etc.	5	4	1.80
9. Manager's Office	3	3	2.33
10. Oncology Records	3	4	3.00
Department Total	120	301	

The average number of days employees were absent in 1986 was 8.93 for the 101 employees in the department.

a In the department as a whole, what was the average number of days employees were absent in 1987?

b Obtain a Pareto diagram for the number of incidences of absence in 1986 by section. Do the same for 1987. When obtaining these two diagrams, combine sections 8, 9, and 10 into an "Other" section. Compare the two diagrams.

c Obtain a Pareto diagram for the total number of days employees were absent in 1986 by section. Do the same for 1987. When obtaining these two diagrams, combine sections 6, 9, and 10 into an "Other" section. Compare the two diagrams.

d Would it have been better to use the *average* number of days employees were absent in each section, rather than the *total* number? Briefly discuss the pros and cons.

e Why is it not meaningful to draw the cumulative line for the Pareto diagram using the *average* number per section? Why would it be meaningful to draw this line for the Pareto diagram using the *total* number per section?

3.19 In many supermarkets, sales per employee hour (SPEH) are used as a measure of productivity. For a particular store, SPEH figures (in dollars) for 10 successive weeks are 186, 182, 166, 181, 167, 168, 176, 152, 190, and 182.

a Analyze the data without using Minitab.

i Draw a sequence plot. Does there appear to be a pattern in the sequence of values?

ii Draw a histogram, in which the first midpoint is $150 and midpoints are $10 apart.

iii Draw a dotplot. Why is the impression given by this dotplot different from the histogram obtained in (ii)?

iv Draw a stem-and-leaf plot. Contrast it with (ii) and (iii).

v What are the values for the measures of central location and dispersion? Interpret each and compare.

b Use Minitab to do (i) to (v) in (a) above.

3.20 *Business Week* conducts an annual survey of executive compensation. The companies surveyed are asked to report the salary, bonus, and other income (for example, income from exercising stock options) of their top executives. The table contains the total compensation (salary plus bonus plus other income) of the 25 highest-paid executives in the United States in 1982, as reported in the May 9, 1984, edition of *Business Week*. The data are stored in ASCII file SALARY.DAT.

TOTAL COMPENSATION (IN $1,000)

51,544	43,833	15,431	7,929	7,718	3,762	3,582	3,358
3,090	3,014	2,722	2,451	2,371	2,345	2,318	2,204
2,158	2,033	1,967	1,951	1,920	1,909	1,828	1,821
1,806							

a Is this a population or a sample? If it is a sample, (i) what population was it drawn from? (ii) is it a representative sample? (iii) can it be used for generalizations to the population?

b Construct three histograms using class interval widths of 2,000, 3,000, and 4,000. Which one gives the clearest pattern? Why do you suppose the histogram is shaped this way? How do you expect the mean and the median to compare?

c Obtain a dotplot and a stem-and-leaf plot. Do they give about the same picture as the best histogram in (b)?

d Find the mean and the median. Why is there such a large discrepancy between the mean and the median?

e What is the class with most values for each of the three histograms obtained in (b)?

f Find the standard deviation of the compensations. Why is it so large?

g Find the 10th, 50th and 90th percentiles. Interpret them. Are the 10th and 90th percentiles equally far away from the 50th percentile? Comment.

h Excluding the three largest and the three smallest values, recalculate the mean, median, and standard deviation. Contrast these *trimmed* values with the untrimmed values in (d) and (f).

i When might the trimmed mean be preferable to the untrimmed mean?

3.21 A business executes projects on an ongoing basis.[14] The cost of each project is estimated prior to commencing work. The size of the project and the business's ability to complete it on budget are very important to continued success. A study was undertaken to answer the following questions:

- Does project size, as measured by actual costs, change over time?

- Is the difference between estimated and actual project costs related to project size?

- Is there a relationship between the number of staff on a project and completing the project on budget?

It was anticipated that project size was decreasing over time.

The data were collected as follows. Three variables were measured on every 10th project completed between 1986 and 1988: budgeted cost (in dollars), actual cost (in dollars), and number of staff. The data, listed in the following table, are stored in ASCII file COMPLIAN.DAT. Use these data and the tools discussed in this chapter to answer the above questions.

Project Data

Row	Budget	Actual	Staff	Row	Budget	Actual	Staff
1	15,000	14,898	2	16	12,000	11,835	3
2	17,500	18,200	3	17	36,000	41,200	2
3	10,070	9,788	2	18	67,000	81,007	4
4	3,400	3,100	1	19	2,958	2,958	1
5	4,000	4,050	2	20	17,000	11,904	3
6	21,000	20,150	1	21	15,000	15,454	1
7	8,500	8,550	2	22	17,325	17,325	2
8	11,689	11,689	2	23	8,777	8,700	1
9	59,321	69,699	4	24	47,000	55,300	4
10	19,000	18,001	2	25	11,200	10,200	1
11	6,300	5,222	3	26	43,000	42,300	2
12	14,345	13,500	2	27	86,980	98,700	5
13	55,000	67,889	4	28	14,700	15,640	2
14	13,400	15,300	2	29	88,849	101,878	5
15	27,000	28,555	3	30	39,365	38,000	3

3.22 As described in Study 5 of Chapter 1 (p. 7), a division of Abitibi-Price was using two different methods of measuring wood delivered to three pulp and paper mills. Wood was delivered by trucks. The volume of each truckload was physically measured by a government-licensed

---

[14]The name of the company is omitted to protect confidentiality. The data are real.

individual. At the same time, each load was also weighed by a company employee. The purpose of taking both measurements was to obtain information on weight-to-volume ratios for the wood. A study was undertaken to answer two managerial questions:

- Do the government-set weight/volume ratios, used as a basis for collecting charges for the wood harvested by the company, accurately reflect the situation?

- Is it practical to stop the costly practice of measuring each truckload of wood and instead to rely upon a sampling process?

The government-set ratios (measured in kilograms per cubic meter, or kg/m³) for spruce and balsam were 769 and 920, respectively. It was anticipated that the government-set weight/volume ratios would be close to, but below, the average figures for spruce and balsam at Abitibi-Price and that the weight/volume ratios varied randomly over time.

Monthly aggregate data were obtained on two variables for both spruce and balsam: weight of all truckloads in a month (expressed in kilograms), and volume of all truckloads in a month (expressed in solid cubic meters). Data were collected from June 1982 to September 1987.

Different lengths of time elapse between the time wood is cut and the time it is hauled to the weigh scales, which can affect the weight because of air drying. It was assumed, however, that this will not have a systematic effect because there are deliveries from many different sources and from many producers. Furthermore, because of ice breakup, no wood is hauled in April and May each year. (Wood is cut during this time, but it is delivered once the roads firm up.)

The data are given in the table and are stored in ASCII file ABITIBI.DAT. (An asterisk "*" in the table denotes a missing value.) Answer the following questions with respect to the spruce data only.

a Is this a study of a population or a process? What is the unit?
b Obtain a sequence plot for the weight/volume ratios. Is there any time series pattern? If so, describe it. Are there any unusual observations?
c Obtain a dotplot and a histogram for the data. Describe them. How meaningful are these plots in light of your answer to (b)?
d What are mean, median and mode? How do they differ? If they differ, can you give a rationale for this? How meaningful are these summaries in light of your answer to (b)?
e Draw lines to mark the government-set ratio on the plots in (b) and (c). What implications can you suggest based on the resulting graphs? Can you answer the first managerial question above?
f Obtain a scatterplot for the volume and weight values. What is the correlation between volume and weight? Do you think that measurement of only one of volume or weight is reasonable? How meaningful is this scatterplot in light of your answer in (b)?
g Can you answer the second managerial question above?

| | Weight and Volume Data for Spruce and Balsam Wood | | | | | |
| | Spruce | | | Balsam | | |
Month	Volume (m³)	Weight (kg)	kg/m³	Volume (m³)	Weight (kg)	kg/m³
1	13,400	10,170,001	759	13	9,410	724
2	29,000	21,750,000	750	68	56,260	827
3	30,100	22,105,008	734	66	63,320	959
4	16,700	12,735,002	763	13	10,310	793
5	27,400	20,570,000	751	66	56,120	850

| | | Weight and Volume Data for Spruce and Balsam Wood | | | | |
| | Spruce | | | Balsam | | |
Month	Volume (m³)	Weight (kg)	kg/m³	Volume (m³)	Weight (kg)	kg/m³
6	9,000	7,149,999	794	149	130,030	873
7	8,500	6,924,999	815	420	390,400	930
8	30,100	23,204,992	771	286	261,120	913
9	44,700	35,235,008	788	214	186,580	872
10	37,900	31,294,992	826	29	26,230	904
11	30,700	23,834,992	776	32	25,940	811
12	44,700	33,134,992	741	47	44,390	944
13	22,400	17,020,000	760	69	59,130	857
14	35,100	24,654,992	702	116	99,020	854
15	20,700	15,135,000	731	98	95,060	970
16	21,800	16,790,000	770	91	79,070	869
17	35,400	27,870,000	787	148	132,460	895
18	33,800	26,990,000	799	17	14,390	846
19	45,000	37,250,000	828	40	26,500	662
20	46,200	37,910,000	821	17	14,490	852
21	42,400	32,320,000	762	49	43,030	878
22	34,000	24,800,000	729	71	63,970	901
23	45,700	32,985,008	722	208	184,860	889
24	40,200	29,510,000	734	559	524,630	939
25	31,100	23,555,008	757	31	24,870	802
26	26,900	21,344,992	793	589	494,430	839
27	25,900	20,994,992	811	149	124,430	835
28	41,600	35,080,000	843	909	702,230	773
29	59,700	50,884,992	852	1,858	1,612,860	868
30	43,400	35,570,000	820	2,223	1,932,510	869
31	17,100	13,155,002	769	785	665,650	848
32	29,100	21,454,992	737	2,186	1,993,720	912
33	21,700	15,585,002	718	3,956	3,636,120	919
34	18,500	13,325,000	720	1,894	1,602,580	846
35	24,400	17,520,000	718	3,593	2,737,210	762
36	38,400	28,720,000	748	971	798,370	822
37	29,200	22,460,000	769	3,564	2,802,880	786
38	44,400	35,920,000	809	4,824	4,104,780	851
39	42,800	35,040,000	819	5,856	4,840,220	827
40	27,300	22,165,008	812	5,906	5,326,020	902
41	44,200	32,010,000	724	22,414	18,962,672	846
42	15,200	10,960,002	721	13,776	12,378,819	899
43	38,000	26,000,000	684	12,922	11,521,540	892
44	22,400	14,319,998	639	6,192	5,546,139	896
45	30,600	22,930,000	749	3,425	2,774,550	810
46	27,900	22,395,008	803	1,1758	9,033,359	768
47	29,900	24,294,992	813	7,334	6,043,780	824
48	55,500	44,775,008	807	6,657	5,511,590	828
49	77,400	64,970,000	839	*	*	*
50	34,200	28,310,000	828	*	*	*
51	9,000	6,650,000	739	*	*	*
52	52,500	36,725,008	700	*	*	*
53	36,100	25,505,008	707	*	*	*
54	30,100	22,604,992	751	*	*	*

SOURCE: The data were kindly provided by M. Innes. To protect confidentiality, the data were slightly altered.

3.23   Gasoline is blended at a refinery to a number of specifications. Some of the specifications are internal, such as octane number and aromatics content. Other specifications, such as vapor pressure, are legislated. If a specification on a batch is not met, the batch must be reblended. Reblends take time and may result in a missed shipment. Costly components may also be required to make the correction. On the other hand, exceeding the specification costs money because components are not blended optimally. The ideal situation is to meet the specification exactly. A study was done at a Canadian refinery to answer the following questions:

1. Does batch size affect the deviation of vapor pressure from its specification?

2. Does grade of gasoline affect this deviation?

3. The vapor specification changes seasonally. Is the deviation of vapor pressure from its specification affected by seasonality?

It was expected that vapor pressure for larger batches would be closer to specifications. Vapor pressure for the premium grade of gasoline was also expected to be closer to specifications. Finally, no seasonal effect was anticipated.

Data were collected on 119 gasoline batches blended between July 1, 1988 and June 30, 1989.[15] Four variables were measured for each batch: grade of gasoline (1 = regular leaded, 2 = regular unleaded, and 3 = premium), batch size (in cubic kilometers), seasonal specification of Reid vapor pressure (in kilopascals), and Reid vapor pressure as measured by the refinery's laboratory. The data are listed in ASCII file GASOLINE.DAT. Use these data and the tools discussed in this chapter to answer the above questions.

---

[15]The name of the company has been omitted and data have been slightly altered to protect confidentiality.

CROSS-SECTIONAL STUDIES: A BASIC MODEL

This chapter will help you answer the following kinds of questions:

- A manager wants to survey his customers regarding their views about a service provided by his company. How should he sample his large customer base?

- A new supplier had delivered a batch of components. One of the important quality characteristics was an internal dimension of the component that was hard to measure. A sample of 50 components yielded a sample mean deviation from target of 0.06 micrometers and a standard deviation of 3.55 micrometers. Using this information, can the manager estimate the proportion of components in the batch whose internal dimension was within 10 micrometers of target?

4.1

INTRODUCTION

The last two chapters introduced some basic issues related to collecting and summarizing data. This chapter focuses on cross-sectional studies. Recall that underlying a cross-sectional study is a *population* in whose numerical description we are interested. Typically, a population consists of a large number of units that can be listed in a *frame*. A census of all units can be carried out in rare circumstances only, so a sample must be drawn from which generalizations are to be made to the population. The symbols N and n will denote the numbers of units in the population and the sample, respectively. Typically n is much smaller than N.

- In this chapter you will learn more about one important type of cross-sectional study, the *survey,* and how to draw samples from a relevant population.

- You will extend what you learned in Chapter 3 about using histograms and cumulative histograms to describe distributions of values. Specifically, you will study an important distributional pattern called the *normal distribution.* You will learn about its implications and how to judge when it is appropriate to use it.

- Finally, you will learn a simple model, including the assumptions underlying it, that is useful for some cross-sectional studies. In Chapter 5, you will learn that a similar model is useful for time series studies under slightly different assumptions.

4.2

SURVEYS

Section 2.7 gave a brief introduction to **surveys,** and this section adds a little more material. A survey often has its beginnings when an individual or institution has information needs and existing data are not sufficient.

When designing a survey, the manager must first define the objectives of the investigation in a specific and unambiguous manner, including the required accuracy level of the sample. Then the manager must develop the survey methodology. For example, the manager must

- Define and find the population of eligible respondents

- Determine the method of data collection

- Design and pretest the questionnaire

- Select appropriate samples

- Hire and train interviewers, if necessary

- Develop procedures for handling nonresponse

- Determine how the data are to be summarized and analyzed

Design of the questionnaire is critical, and there is extensive literature about it (for example, see Payne, 1980). Concepts must be clearly defined, and questions must be unambiguously phrased. Furthermore, the questionnaire must not be unduly long. It must be designed to minimize response errors and bias. This can be achieved, for instance, by referring to time periods recent enough for the respondent to remember, by asking questions sensitively and not unduly invading the respondent's privacy, and by asking for information that is not too difficult to provide.

Before selecting the sample, the relevant population must be defined. It could consist of individual persons, government agencies, businesses, etc. Once defined, a listing of the members of this population (that is, the frame) must be obtained. Finally, the sample must be selected scientifically, which will involve some form of random sampling. The simplest approach is *simple random sampling,* where any possible subset of the selected size must have the same chance of being selected. (This is discussed in the next section.) Other, more complex forms of random sampling, like stratified and cluster sampling, will not be discussed in this text. (See the text by Scheaffer et al., 1990, for details.)

When conducting the survey, the manager must ensure that interviewers, if used, are properly trained. Once the data have been collected, it is often useful to recheck a subsample of the survey: It is important to check for omissions or obvious mistakes in the data. Missing values are often a problem, and the manager must decide what to do about them. Finally, when a "clean" data file has been obtained, the data can be analyzed.

Many investigators are tempted to use some shortcuts, but it is important to avoid the temptation so that the survey results are not invalidated and the user of the results is not misled. Four shortcuts to avoid are:

1. **Failure to use an appropriate sampling procedure.** For example, choosing a sample based purely on what is convenient can invalidate any generalizations to the population of interest.

2. **No pretest of the field procedures.** A small-scale pilot study of the survey is usually essential to locate possible misunderstandings or biasing effects of different questions and procedures.

3. **Failure to follow up nonrespondents.** It is not uncommon for surveys to have more than 50% nonresponse. A follow-up study of nonrespondents is often needed to see if there are any differences between respondents and nonrespondents.

4. **Inadequate quality control.** It is important, for example, that execution of the survey in the field correspond to its design.

Once the survey has been analyzed, the manager must find out how good it is and determine the margin of error for the various statistics computed. This is necessary so that the manager knows the extent to which the survey results can be generalized to the population from which the sample was selected.

sampling error

There are two sources of errors when generalizing from the sample to the population, sampling and nonsampling errors. *Sampling error* comes about because random sampling was used in the selection of the sample from the population: The difference between the sample and the population is then purely due to chance. The evaluation of sampling error is possible *only* if the sample has been selected scientifically through some form of random sampling. In that case, statements can be made about the likely margin of error. Chapter 7 gives more detail about computation of the margin of error.

nonsampling error

Errors or biases that enter the study because the sampling procedure was not random are called *nonsampling errors* because they are *not* due to the random sampling procedure. There are many possible causes of nonsampling error, and the investigator *must* carefully consider whether any have arisen. The size of nonsampling errors is difficult, if not impossible, to assess. A few examples of nonsampling errors are selected respondents' refusals to respond to the questionnaire, respondents who are not at home, incorrect information, coding errors, and clerical errors. The effect of some nonsampling errors is random in that their effects tend to cancel out in large samples. Biases, induced when the effects of nonsampling errors tend to go in the same direction, can be very serious. Some contributing causes to such biases can be an improper frame, nonresponse, "loaded" questions, and interviewer errors. It is considered good practice to report any of these problems if they may have occurred.

As an example of an inappropriate sampling procedure, consider the *Literary Digest*'s prediction that Alfred E. Landon would defeat Franklin D. Roosevelt in the 1936 U.S. presidential election. Roosevelt, of course, won in a landslide vote. At that time, the *Literary Digest* ran the most widely publicized poll. Its final prediction was based on more than 2,000,000 questionaires by mail, but despite this very large sample, the final prediction was in error by 19 percentage points. Other polls correctly predicted a Roosevelt victory.

The failure of the *Literary Digest*'s prediction is easy to explain. The population in this example consisted of all voters in the 1936 presidential election. The *Digest*'s sample of voters was obtained from lists of automobile and telephone owners. At that time, these voters were among the better off. With the arrival of the New Deal, however, the population of American voters was sharply divided along income lines, with the better off favoring the Republican party and people with below-average incomes tending toward the Democratic party. Thus, the *Literary Digest*'s sampling procedure tended to favor Republicans, so it was certain to exaggerate the strength of the Republican party in the 1936 election.

Our description of surveys is necessarily very brief. If you plan to do a survey, it is important to get additional information or to consult a properly trained professional. There are many books on the subject, such as Scheaffer et al. (1990). Extensively described examples can be found in Tanur et al. (1989). More information can also be obtained from professional organizations, such as the American Statistical Association, the American Marketing Association, the American Association for Public Opinion Research, the Statistical Society of Canada, and the Advertising Research Foundation.

4.3

SAMPLING

In this section, you will learn the basic details for scientifically obtaining a sample from a population. The procedure, **simple random sampling,** uses a chance device to select subjects or units from the frame for the sample. You will also learn about sampling with and without replacement.

Before proceeding, let us review some concepts that will be used in this chapter. They relate to the distinction between a population and a sample.

Cross-sectional studies are ultimately interested in describing populations.

The following box reviews some important concepts related to populations:

> The **population** consists of all units or subjects of interest. The population size (the number of units or subjects) is denoted N.
>
> The **frame** is a list of all N units or subjects in the population.
>
> The **response variable** characterizes each unit or subject, but its values are not typically known for every unit or subject in the population. The response variable will be denoted by the symbol y.
>
> The **population distribution** of the response variable is a histogram or dot-plot of the response variable values for all units or subjects in the population.
>
> The **population average** for the response variable is the average of all N values in the population. It is denoted μ_y (the Greek letter *mu*), and is typically unknown.
>
> The **population standard deviation** is the standard deviation of all N values, it is denoted σ_y (the lowercase Greek letter *sigma*), and is typically unknown.
>
> **Parameters** are summary measures for the population. Examples are μ_y and σ_y.

Sometimes a *census* of all units in the frame can be obtained and can be used to describe the features of the population that are relevant to the managerial questions at hand.

In many practical situations, however, it is impossible to obtain a census: The population size N may be too large, so that it is prohibitively expensive or too time-consuming to carry it out. We must then resort to a *sample* from the population. The following box reviews some important concepts for samples:

> The **sample** is drawn from a population to learn something about the population, and it consists of a typically small subset of all N units or subjects. The sample size is denoted n. The response variable value for each unit or subject in the sample is known.
>
> The **sample distribution** of the response variable is a histogram (or dotplot or stem-and-leaf plot) of the response variable values for all units or subjects in the sample.
>
> The **sample average** is the average of the n response variable values in the sample. It is denoted $\bar{y}$ (said "y bar").
>
> The **sample standard deviation** is the standard deviation of the n response variable values in the sample, and it is denoted s_y.
>
> **Statistics** are summary measures for the sample. Examples are $\bar{y}$ and s_y.

We will want to use sample results to generalize to the corresponding population. We can never hope for the sample to exactly represent the population: We know there will be sampling error. How should we take samples so that we can evaluate this error?

Consider an example:

EXAMPLE 4.1

In Problem 2.2 (p. 35) we discussed Bell Canada's proposal to extend the Toronto local calling area to the Whitby exchange. This proposal would have eliminated long distance toll charges on calls from Whitby to Toronto. The monthly flat rate for Whitby customers would have increased by $10.25, from $8.75 to $19.00. In May 1989 Bell Canada surveyed its Whitby customers, who rejected Bell's proposal. Among the 10,942 respondents, 4,869 were for the proposal and 6,073 were against it. Considering the population of respondents, a study was to be done to look at differences between the two subpopulations of respondents "for" and "against." One variable of interest was the dollar cost of calls to Toronto in May 1989. In particular, it was desired to obtain the proportion of customers in each subpopulation whose dollar costs were less than $10.25, the proposed increase in the monthly flat rate. It was felt that a sample size of $n = 50$ respondents from each subpopulation would provide sufficient information for the purposes of this study.

How should each sample be obtained so that the questions in Problem 2.2 can be answered? To answer the questions, we need to know the distribution of dollar costs for calls to Toronto in each subpopulation and the proportion of subscribers for whom these costs are less than $10.25. Before we decide how to form the samples, some ideas regarding random sampling must be introduced that go beyond those discussed in Section 2.6.

Simple Random Sampling

As was mentioned in Chapter 2, random sampling is possible only when a *frame* exists for the population of interest. Let us continue with Example 4.1, focusing on the subpopulation of $N = 4,869$ "for" respondents. Each "for" respondent is characterized by a value for the response variable, dollar costs of calls to Toronto in May 1989. Since it is not economically feasible to obtain the value of the response variable for all $N = 4,869$ "for" respondents, a simple random sample of size $n = 50$ is to be taken. All the needed data are stored in Bell's computer, so the frame of $N = 4,869$ "for" respondents is readily available. We can assume the "for" respondents to be labeled 0001 to 4869 in the frame. How should a simple random sample be drawn from this frame?

A **simple random sample** of size n is drawn when *every* possible sample of size n from the population of N units or subjects has the *same* chance of being selected. Note that what is *random* about the sample is the *selection procedure*.

Other random sampling procedures exist, where different samples of size n do not necessarily have the same chance of being selected. This book assumes that all random samples are *simple* random samples.

Random samples can be drawn with the help of random numbers. Such random numbers are obtained from a chance device, a simple version of which is a ten-sided fair die whose sides are labelled 0, 1, 2, . . . , 9. This die is tossed many times and the results are recorded. Suppose that the first few tosses yield

13894678391866373918261 4...

If we group these digits in pairs,

13 89 46 78 39 18 66 37 39 18 26 14...

then (1) every number between 00 and 99 will occur equally often in a large table so constructed, and (2) successive numbers are completely unrelated, that is, they are random in sequence. If we group the digits in threes,

138 946 783 918 663 739 182 614...

then (1) every number between 000 and 999 will occur equally often, and (2) again, successive numbers are random. If we group the digits in fours,

1389 4678 3918 6637 3918 2614...

then (1) every number between 0000 and 9999 will occur equally often, and (2) successive numbers are random.

For the purposes of the Bell Canada problem, it is most convenient to group the digits in fours. We can then take enough numbers consisting of four digits and let the random sample of "for" respondents correspond to the "for" respondents in the frame with these numbers. Using our example, the first "for" respondent chosen has number 1389, the second "for" respondent has number 4678, etc. We ignore number 6637 because no such "for" respondent exists, there being only 4,869. Once the $n = 50$ "for" respondents in the random sample have been selected, the exact values for their dollar costs can be determined.

Figure 4.1 shows a list of 500 random digits—the first few in the first line were used above. There are books consisting entirely of random numbers, but their use has decreased in recent years because random numbers can easily be obtained with statistical software packages like Minitab. Thus, it is very simple to determine which subjects should be in a random sample when the frame is stored in a computer.

It is easy to obtain random numbers with Minitab. For example, to obtain 50 random numbers between 0001 and 4869 and store them in variable C1, you can

FIGURE 4.1 500 Random Digits

13894	67839	18663	73918	26149	88554	11670	78488	48512	91824
58967	63647	92585	87845	58315	04230	48341	99020	48541	25014
84707	06997	60520	41975	69794	87242	53916	46466	65167	75888
13434	95659	35777	61994	73677	99397	34218	34886	43288	53927
79298	14808	10498	26986	30431	27860	95100	52924	15274	11499
63165	09654	69268	62999	17222	80298	76702	57480	15461	91783
72173	90340	44072	64804	65609	16394	76992	34773	57527	50193
42410	91488	17982	84755	26412	10725	61962	72215	56945	98086
53650	35275	78626	60330	84951	85075	23539	73444	99618	63480
22218	68790	73865	20332	99689	32428	57084	54901	69044	65204

proceed as follows:

> Choose *Calc* ▸ *Random Data* ▸ *Integer*
> In the *Integer Distribution* dialog box,
>> Click the box next to *Generate,* type **50**
>> Click the box below *Store in column(s),* type **C1**
>> Click the box next to *Minimum value,* type **1**
>> Click the box next to *Maximum value,* type **4869**
>> Click *ok*

For our present purpose of selecting data from a frame, we will use the following approach: Suppose the data for your frame are stored in Minitab in the 4,869 rows of columns C1 to C6, and you want to obtain a simple random sample of 50 units, to be stored in columns C11 to C16. Then you can proceed as follows:

> Choose *Calc* ▸ *Random Data* ▸ *Sample from Columns*
> In the *Sample from Columns* dialog box,
>> Click the box next to *Sample,* type **50**
>> Click the box below *Sample,* type **C1-C6**
>> Click the box below *Store Samples in,* type **C11-C16**
>> Click *ok*

If you want to obtain further help about these Minitab menu items, use the Minitab Help facility.

Before turning to the results for the sample of $n = 50$ "for" respondents, we must discuss sampling with and without replacement.

Sampling with Replacement, Sampling without Replacement

The sequence of four-digit numbers in the previous section refers to the "for" respondents to be included in the sample of $n = 50$ units. Notice, however, that number 3918 occurs twice in this sequence. Should this mean that "for" respondent 3918 be included twice in the sample? This is not desirable; so the second occurrence of the number 3918 should be ignored when drawing the random sample of size $n = 50$. Before proceeding, two definitions are needed.

> Suppose you sample units from a population in sequence. If a unit is drawn from the population to be in the sample, is examined, and is then returned to the population so that it can possibly be drawn again, we have **sampling with replacement.** If a unit is drawn, but is not returned to the population so that no unit can ever be represented more than once in a sample, we have **sampling without replacement.**

In most practical situations, sampling without replacement is preferred. This is also the case in the Bell Canada example.

It turns out, however, that many of the formulas to be discussed later in this book are simpler if sampling is done *with* replacement. But:

> When the sample size n is small in comparison to the population size N, say when n is less than 5% of N, then the formulas for sampling with and without replacement are basically identical.

Since most samples taken in business applications are small in comparison to the population size, we will only discuss sampling *with* replacement from now on, because the formulas for sampling with replacement then apply approximately to sampling *without* replacement as well. In the Bell Canada example, the sample size is $n = 50$ and the population size is $N = 4,869$, so the sample size is small.

Analysis of Two Examples

This section discusses two examples. Let us first continue our discussion of the Bell Canada example. The data are stored in ASCII file EAS.DAT. where the values for five variables are listed: (1) NUMBER of calls to Toronto, (2) COST of calls to Toronto (in dollars), (3) amount of telephone BILL (in dollars), (4) whether the customer subscribes to custom calling features (CCF = 1 = yes, CCF = 0 = no), and (5) vote in EAS survey (survey = 1 = for, survey = 0 = against). Figure 4.2 gives dotplots and descriptive statistics for the "for" and "against" respondents. Figure 4.3

FIGURE 4.2 Dotplots and Descriptive Statistics for Bell Canada Example ("For" Respondents: SURVEY=1, "Against" Respondents: SURVEY=0)

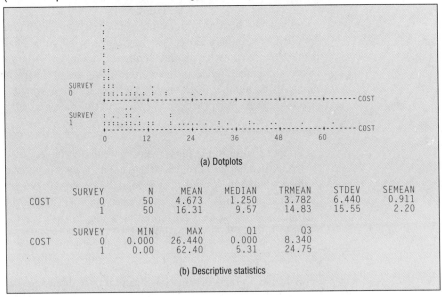

(a) Dotplots

COST	SURVEY	N	MEAN	MEDIAN	TRMEAN	STDEV	SEMEAN
	0	50	4.673	1.250	3.782	6.440	0.911
	1	50	16.31	9.57	14.83	15.55	2.20

COST	SURVEY	MIN	MAX	Q1	Q3
	0	0.000	26.440	0.000	8.340
	1	0.00	62.40	5.31	24.75

(b) Descriptive statistics

FIGURE 4.3 Cumulative Frequency Distributions for Bell Canada Data

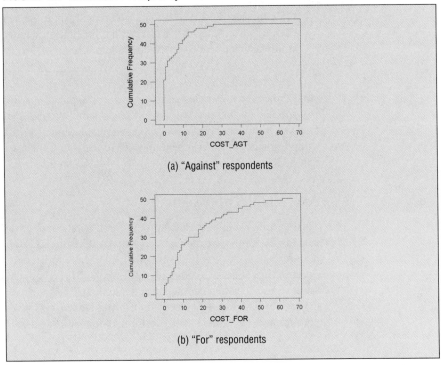

(a) "Against" respondents

(b) "For" respondents

FIGURE 4.4 Raw Data for Bell Canada Example

0.00	0.00	0.00	0.34	0.68	1.20	2.38	2.73	$\frac{26}{50} = 52\%$
2.96	3.34	4.06	4.61	5.54	5.91	6.22	6.46	
6.51	6.82	7.08	7.36	7.50	7.74	8.18	9.22	
9.42	9.72	11.92	12.18	13.22	13.28	18.22	18.25	
18.35	18.41	20.63	21.09	22.29	24.45	25.64	27.27	
30.65	31.33	33.24	39.06	39.73	41.33	45.84	47.34	
53.53	62.40							

(a) "For" respondents

0.00	0.00	0.00	0.00	0.00	0.00	0.00	0.00	$\frac{41}{50} = 82\%$
0.00	0.00	0.00	0.00	0.00	0.00	0.34	0.34	
0.51	0.52	0.52	0.68	0.96	1.04	1.10	1.12	
1.20	1.30	1.35	1.86	2.08	2.32	2.58	3.03	
4.42	5.07	6.46	7.10	7.50	8.31	8.43	8.79	
10.15	10.41	11.38	12.88	13.02	13.12	16.50	17.27	
23.57	26.44							

(b)"Against" respondents

gives the **corresponding cumulative frequency distributions.** From them, we can determine that dollar costs for calls to Toronto were less than $10.25 for about $\frac{27}{50} = 54\%$ of the "for" respondents and about $\frac{40}{50} = 80\%$ of the "against" respondents.

counting method   The actual proportion of dollar costs less than $10.25 was 52% in the "for" sample and 82% in the "against" sample. These two proportions were calculated from the raw data after they were conveniently arranged in ascending order, as shown in Figure 4.4. Surprisingly, a large proportion of "for" respondents had dollar costs for calls to Toronto that were less than the cost of the proposal, and a fair proportion of "against" respondents had dollar costs exceeding that of the proposal. Factors other than dollar costs in May 1989 must have influenced a considerable number of respondents in deciding whether to vote for or against Bell Canada's proposal.

Notice that both the cumulative frequency distributions in Figure 4.3 rise steeply at first and then taper off. As could also be seen from the corresponding dot-plots in Figure 4.2, this shape indicates that both distributions are positively skewed.

The next example involves a variable that is symmetrically distributed.

EXAMPLE 4.2

An automotive parts manufacturer was concerned with the machining of a major component for a windshield wiper system. There had been problems with this component, and a new supplier had promised to supply the component using new production technology. The component is characterized by several dimensions that must be very close to specifications. This example concentrates on height, which should be 30.000 mm. The automotive parts manufacturer considered components to be acceptable if their height was within 0.010 mm of the specification. The new supplier produced a batch of 1,100 components with the new equipment and delivered it to the automotive parts manufacturer, who was interested in the distribution

FIGURE 4.5 Component Height Example

```
0.4     1.1    -0.6    -0.5     1.4    -6.9     3.9     7.3    -0.5     3.3    -2.0
3.6     0.9    -2.5     0.2    -3.5    -5.2     1.1    -4.0    -1.8     5.0     1.7
-1.3    -2.8    -0.3    -0.7     0.3    -0.5     1.8    -4.4     2.4     1.4    -6.0
-6.7     5.9     7.6     0.3    -1.8     2.4     0.9     2.5     2.4     5.1    -8.3
3.0    -2.9     4.5    -0.8    -0.8    -2.5
```
(a) Raw data

	N	MEAN	MEDIAN	TRMEAN	STDEV	SEMEAN
HT_DEV	50	0.062	0.250	0.095	3.554	0.503

	MIN	MAX	Q1	Q3
HT_DEV	-8.300	7.600	-2.125	2.400

(b) Descriptive statistics

FIGURE 4.6 Graphs for Component Height Data

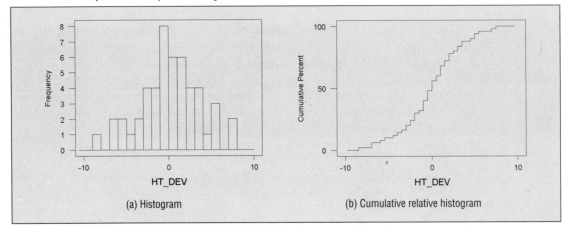

(a) Histogram   (b) Cumulative relative histogram

of height values and, in particular, in the proportion of components that would meet the specification. Since accurate measurement of each component was quite expensive and time-consuming, a random sample of $n = 50$ components had been taken from the batch and measured. The measurements obtained were deviations from 30.000 mm, expressed in micrometers (thousandths of a millimeter). Expressed in micrometers, the height specification required that the deviations be between -10 and $+10$. (Note that 0.010 mm equals 10 micrometers.) The data are stored in ASCII file HEIGHT.DAT.

The raw data and descriptive statistics for the component height data are given in Figure 4.5. A histogram and a cumulative frequency distribution are given in Figure 4.6.

Figure 4.6 shows that all 50 sample deviations were well within specifications. It is, of course, not clear that all 1,100 components in the population have height values within specifications. The distribution of values appears to be symmetrical. This is evident from the histogram, but also from the cumulative frequency distribution, which at first rises gently, then more steeply, and then more gently again.

Section 4.5 (the section after next) discusses a special kind of symmetrical distribution that is of considerable importance, the normal distribution. It can be used to approximate the distribution of height deviation values. First, however, we briefly turn to the notion of standardization.

4.4

STANDARDIZATION

We need to understand the concept of standardization for two purposes: (1) to be able to discuss the normal distribution in the next section, and (2) to point us to observations that are surprisingly far away from the bulk of the data. Standardization consists of a convenient rescaling or reexpression of the data, where actual values on a variable of interest are converted into standardized or z-values.

Standardized values indicate how many standard deviations a value is above or below the mean, that is,

$$\text{Standardized Value} = z = \frac{\text{Actual Value} - \text{Mean}}{\text{Standard Deviation}}$$

If we know the sample mean $\bar{y}$ and the sample standard deviation s_y, then the actual value y is standardized as

$$z = \frac{y - \bar{y}}{s_y}$$

The value of z thus indicates how many standard deviations away from the mean an observation's value can be found. A large negative or positive z value suggests that the corresponding observation is far away from the bulk of the data. (A value of 3 or larger, or -3 or smaller, is typically considered large.) Such an observation might be an outlier and require some attention.

For example, let us find the standardized value for the last height deviation value given in Figure 4.5. The deviation value is $y = -2.5$. The sample mean and standard deviation of the 50 height deviation values are $\bar{y} = 0.062$ and $s_y = 3.554$, so the standardized value for this observation is

$$z = \frac{y - \bar{y}}{s_y} = \frac{-2.5 - 0.062}{3.554} = -0.72$$

In other words, the last height deviation value is 0.72 standard deviations *below* the mean. Using the rule that a z-value above $+3$ or below -3 is considered large, this observation is close to the bulk of the data.

Figure 4.7 shows the frequency distribution of height deviation values in a dotplot. Note the added horizontal line with the standardized (z) values. The shape of the frequency distribution of standardized values, of course, does not differ from the shape of the distribution of unstandardized values.

Knowing the z-value for an observation, and the mean and standard deviation for the sample, we can calculate back to the original deviation value for the observation by rewriting the standardization formula, $z = (y - \bar{y})/s_y$, as $y = \bar{y} + z\,s_y$. For example, the maximum standardized value is 2.121. Thus the maximum height deviation is 2.121 standard deviations above the mean: It is $0.062 + 2.121(3.554) = 7.6$.

One important application of standardization is to place an observation relative to the sample it was drawn from. A height deviation of 5.0 micrometers may at first seem large until we are told that its standardized value is $z = 1.39$. Likewise, if we are told that the largest value in a sample has standardized value $z = 6$, we know that the value is an outlier that requires attention.

Standardized values are useful in many applications, for example, to determine whether or not an observation might be an outlier. They are also useful for the normal distribution, which we discuss next.

FIGURE 4.7 Standardized Values for Height Deviation

	N	MEAN	MEDIAN	TRMEAN	STDEV	SEMEAN
HT_DEV	50	0.062	0.250	0.095	3.554	0.503
Z	50	0.000	0.053	0.009	1.000	0.141

	MIN	MAX	Q1	Q3
HT_DEV	-8.300	7.600	-2.125	2.400
Z	-2.353	2.121	-0.615	0.658

(a) Descriptive statistics

```
                                 :
                    .     :  .:.  :
            .     ...  ....:::.::.:::.:.:...:   .    :
        +----------+----------+----------+----------+--- HT-DEV
      -10.0       -5.0        0.0        5.0       10.0


         +----------+----------+----------+----------+--- z
       -2.83      -1.42      -0.02       1.39       2.80
```

(b) Dotplot

4.5

THE NORMAL DISTRIBUTION

This section and the next introduce an important theoretical distribution, the normal distribution. It is important in many statistical applications.

If we examine the distribution of deviation values in the histogram of Figure 4.6, we note that the values tend to center around the overall mean and that the height of the distribution tends to decrease in a symmetric fashion as we move away from the mean. This pattern is only a rough description of the histogram in Figure 4.6, but if we had drawn a histogram for a much larger number of height deviation values, all obtained by random sampling, then the shape of the histogram would resemble the shape of the superimposed curve in Figure 4.8.

The curve reflects the frequency distribution of a very useful theoretical pattern—the *normal distribution.* It describes variation in many phenomena, including output from many (but not all) business processes, such as weight of products and diameter of units.

> One way for the **normal distribution** to result is for the observed measurements to be the summation of a large number of independent sources of variation, typically not known or identified, and of which none has a dominant influence.

The normal distribution approximates many data histograms well. There are also many phenomena to which the normal distribution does not apply. For example, the distributions of family or personal income are not normal; they tend to be positively skewed.

FIGURE 4.8
Histogram of
Height Deviation
Data with
Superimposed
Normal Distribution

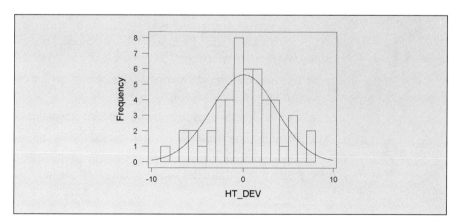

FIGURE 4.9
Percentages for the
Normal Distribution

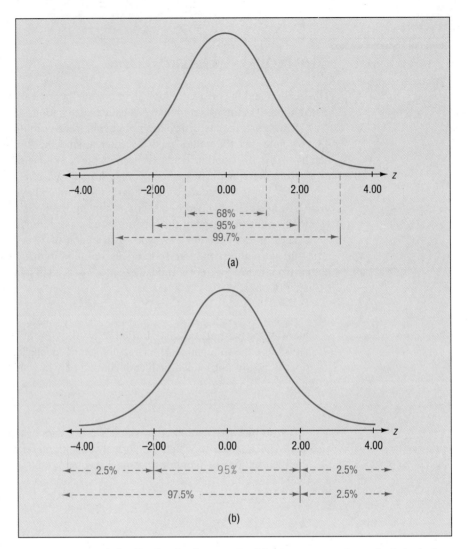

The normal distribution is characterized by its mean and standard deviation. It is symmetrical around its mean and bell-shaped. Furthermore, the following results hold approximately:

- 68% or roughly $\frac{2}{3}$ of the observations lie in an interval extending 1 standard deviation around the mean.

- 95% of the observations lie within 2 standard deviations of the mean.

- 99.7% of the observations lie within 3 standard deviations of the mean.[1]

Figure 4.9 gives two graphs of the normal distribution for standardized values. Figure 4.9(a) illustrates some of these facts about the normal distribution. Fig-

---

[1]The *empirical rule* for the standard deviation, discussed in Chapter 3, is based on the fact that many symmetrical distributions are roughly normal in shape.

ure 4.9(b) shows that, because of the symmetry of the normal distribution, 97.5% of the observations lie to the left of a value that is 2 standard deviations above the mean. For this reason, the standardized value 2 corresponds to the 97.5th percentile when a variable follows the normal distribution pattern. Because of symmetry, the standardized value -2 corresponds to the 2.5th percentile of a normal distribution. Furthermore, since 68% of the observations lie within 1 standard deviation of the mean, the standardized value -1 corresponds to the 16th percentile of the normal distribution, and +1 corresponds to the 84th percentile of the normal distribution.

To illustrate these results further, consider intelligence quotient (IQ), which is defined as normally distributed in the adult population, with mean 100 and standard deviation 15. Thus about 68% of all IQs are within 1 standard deviation of the mean, that is, within the interval from $100 - 15$ to $100 + 15$, or from 85 to 115. Furthermore, 2.5% of all IQs exceed 130. This latter figure follows from the fact that 95% of all values are within 2 standard deviations of the mean, that is, within the interval from 70 to 130. Furthermore, 5% of all values are outside this interval in a symmetric fashion, so 2.5% are above the interval (above 130). These results are graphically illustrated in Figure 4.9(b).

The normal distribution is symmetrical and bell-shaped. Let us also examine the shape of the cumulative normal distribution. Figure 4.6 gave the histogram and cumulative histogram of the height deviation data. Since that histogram is well approximated by a normal distribution, we can expect the cumulative normal distribution to have a shape similar to the shape of the cumulative in Figure 4.6. Figure 4.10 displays the normal distribution and its cumulative. Note that the cumulative value at any z, denoted $F(z)$, is equivalent to the proportion of values at z and below for the normal distribution. Thus the proportion of values less than or equal to $z = 2$ is 0.975, so the value of the cumulative normal distribution at $z = 2$ is $F(2) = 0.975$. The cumulative normal distribution at first rises gently, then more steeply, most steeply at the mean, after which it rises more and more gently.

Percentiles and **quantiles** for these and other standardized values—that is, values for $F(z)$,—and thus percentage values for other intervals can easily be obtained with statistical software packages and also from appropriate tables. The following Minitab commands obtain the quantile for the standardized value $z = 2$:

> Choose *Calc* ▸ *Probability Distributions* ▸ *Normal*
> In the *Normal Distribution* dialog box,
>> Click the circle next to *Cumulative Probability*
>> Click the box next to *Mean*, replace its contents with **0**
>> Click the box next to *Standard deviation,* replace its contents with **1**
>> Click the box to the left of *Input constant*
>> Click the box to the right of *Input constant,* type **2**
>> Click *ok*

The following output then appears in the Minitab Session window:

```
MTB > CDF 2;
SUBC>   Normal 0.0 1.0.
    2.0000    0.9772
```

FIGURE 4.10
Correspondence Between the Curve of a Distribution of Normal Values and the Curve of the Cumulative Values of the Same Distribution.

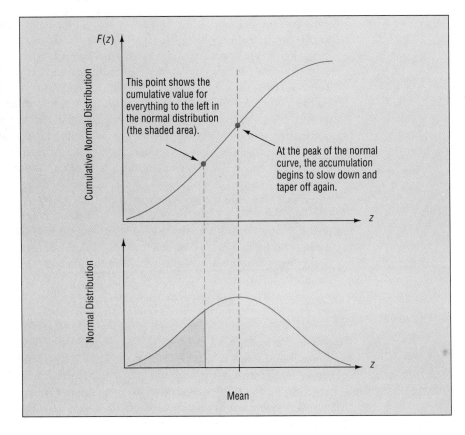

As another example, the following Minitab commands obtain the quantile for the value $y = 130$ from a normal distribution with mean 100 and standard deviation 15:

Choose *Calc* ▸ *Probability Distributions* ▸ *Normal*
In the *Normal Distribution* dialog box,
    Click the circle next to *Cumulative Probability*
    Click the box next to *Mean,* replace its contents with **100**
    Click the box next to *Standard deviation,* replace its contents with **15**
    Click the box to the left of *Input constant*
    Click the box to the right of *Input constant,* type **130**
    Click *ok*

The following output then appears in the Minitab Session window:

```
MTB > CDF 130;
SUBC>   Normal 100 15.
  130.0000    0.9772
```

Minitab gives numerical results accurate to four decimal digits: The quantile corresponding to the standardized value $z = 2$ equals $F(2) = 0.9772$; that is, the

FIGURE 4.11

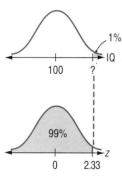

proportion of observations less than or equal to a value that is 2 standard deviations above the mean is 0.9772. This value, 0.9772 or 97.72%, is slightly different from the value given in Figure 4.9 (97.5%), which is only an approximation.

Instead of using Minitab, you can use a normal distribution table to obtain quantiles, denoted $F(z)$, from the normal distribution. Table 4.1 gives numerical results accurate to four decimal digits. For example, the quantile corresponding to the standardized value $z = 2$ is $F(2) = 0.9772$.

Consider one more example: At least how large must an IQ be so that it is among the top 1%? Both Table 4.1 and Minitab allow us to find quantiles. We must first convert "top 1%" into a quantile: We are looking for the 0.99 quantile. The z-value corresponding to the 0.99 quantile is such that $F(z) = 0.99$. Using Table 4.1, the desired z-value is 2.33. Thus, the 0.99 quantile of a normal distribution corresponds to a value that is 2.33 standard deviations above the mean. Since IQ values are normally distributed with mean $\mu_{IQ} = 100$ and standard deviation $\sigma_{IQ} = 15$, the 0.99 quantile for the IQ distribution is

$$\mu_{IQ} + z\,\sigma_{IQ} = 100 + 2.33(15) = 135$$

Thus an IQ must be at least 135 to be among the top 1%.

prediction interval

A 2-standard-deviation interval around the mean is called a 95% **prediction interval.**[2] This terminology is used since the interval predicts, with probability 95%, where another value randomly drawn from the population will fall. With respect to the IQ example, we say that chances are 95% that a randomly chosen person's IQ will be within the interval from 70 to 130.

FIGURE 4.12
95% Prediction Interval

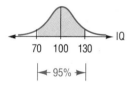

In general, a prediction interval is obtained as

Population Mean $\pm z$ (Population Standard Deviation)

or

$$\mu_y \pm z\,\sigma_y$$

where z, which determines the proportion of values in the interval, is obtained from the normal distribution. Typically, the population parameters μ_y and σ_y are unknown and must be estimated from the corresponding sample statistics, $\bar{y}$ and s_y. The approximate formula for the prediction interval is thus

FIGURE 4.13

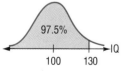

FIGURE 4.14

$$\bar{y} - zs_y \qquad \bar{y} \qquad \bar{y} + zs_y \qquad y \qquad \bar{y} \pm z\,s_y$$

one-sided prediction interval

Since chances are 97.5% that a randomly selected person's IQ value is 130 or less, the interval of IQ values up to and including 130 is called a *one-sided 97.5% prediction interval.* Another 97.5% prediction interval consist of IQ values of 70 and up.

---

[2]Here and elsewhere in this book, we associate $z = 2$ with a 95% interval. Of course, the exact z-value for a 95% interval is $z = 1.96$. But the value $z = 2$ is easier to remember, and it is sufficiently accurate for most applications.

TABLE 4.1   The Cumulative Normal Distribution

For a normal distribution, this table lists the probability $F(z)$ that an observation is less than or equal to a value that is z standard deviations away from the mean

z	F(z)	z	F(z)	z	F(z)	z	F(z)	z	F(z)
−4.00	0.0000	−2.19	0.0143	−1.64	0.0505	−1.09	0.1379	−0.54	0.2946
−3.50	0.0002	−2.18	0.0146	−1.63	0.0516	−1.08	0.1401	−0.53	0.2981
−3.00	0.0013	−2.17	0.0150	−1.62	0.0526	−1.07	0.1423	−0.52	0.3015
−2.80	0.0026	−2.16	0.0154	−1.61	0.0537	−1.06	0.1446	−0.51	0.3050
−2.70	0.0035	−2.15	0.0158	−1.60	0.0548	−1.05	0.1469	−0.50	0.3085
−2.69	0.0036	−2.14	0.0162	−1.59	0.0559	−1.04	0.1492	−0.49	0.3121
−2.68	0.0037	−2.13	0.0166	−1.58	0.0571	−1.03	0.1515	−0.48	0.3156
−2.67	0.0038	−2.12	0.0170	−1.57	0.0582	−1.02	0.1539	−0.47	0.3192
−2.66	0.0039	−2.11	0.0174	−1.56	0.0594	−1.01	0.1562	−0.46	0.3228
−2.65	0.0040	−2.10	0.0179	−1.55	0.0606	−1.00	0.1587	−0.45	0.3264
−2.64	0.0041	−2.09	0.0183	−1.54	0.0618	−0.99	0.1611	−0.44	0.3300
−2.63	0.0043	−2.08	0.0188	−1.53	0.0630	−0.98	0.1635	−0.43	0.3336
−2.62	0.0044	−2.07	0.0192	−1.52	0.0643	−0.97	0.1660	−0.42	0.3372
−2.61	0.0045	−2.06	0.0197	−1.51	0.0655	−0.96	0.1685	−0.41	0.3409
−2.60	0.0047	−2.05	0.0202	−1.50	0.0668	−0.95	0.1711	−0.40	0.3446
−2.59	0.0048	−2.04	0.0207	−1.49	0.0681	−0.94	0.1736	−0.39	0.3483
−2.58	0.0049	−2.03	0.0212	−1.48	0.0694	−0.93	0.1762	−0.38	0.3520
−2.57	0.0051	−2.02	0.0217	−1.47	0.0708	−0.92	0.1788	−0.37	0.3557
−2.56	0.0052	−2.01	0.0222	−1.46	0.0721	−0.91	0.1814	−0.36	0.3594
−2.55	0.0054	−2.00	0.0228	−1.45	0.0735	−0.90	0.1841	−0.35	0.3632
−2.54	0.0055	−1.99	0.0233	−1.44	0.0749	−0.89	0.1867	−0.34	0.3669
−2.53	0.0057	−1.98	0.0239	−1.43	0.0764	−0.88	0.1894	−0.33	0.3707
−2.52	0.0059	−1.97	0.0244	−1.42	0.0778	−0.87	0.1922	−0.32	0.3745
−2.51	0.0060	−1.96	0.0250	−1.41	0.0793	−0.86	0.1949	−0.31	0.3783
−2.50	0.0062	−1.95	0.0256	−1.40	0.0808	−0.85	0.1977	−0.30	0.3821
−2.49	0.0064	−1.94	0.0262	−1.39	0.0823	−0.84	0.2005	−0.29	0.3859
−2.48	0.0066	−1.93	0.0268	−1.38	0.0838	−0.83	0.2033	−0.28	0.3897
−2.47	0.0068	−1.92	0.0274	−1.37	0.0853	−0.82	0.2061	−0.27	0.3936
−2.46	0.0069	−1.91	0.0281	−1.36	0.0869	−0.81	0.2090	−0.26	0.3974
−2.45	0.0071	−1.90	0.0287	−1.35	0.0885	−0.80	0.2119	−0.25	0.4013
−2.44	0.0073	−1.89	0.0294	−1.34	0.0901	−0.79	0.2148	−0.24	0.4052
−2.43	0.0075	−1.88	0.0301	−1.33	0.0918	−0.78	0.2177	−0.23	0.4090
−2.42	0.0078	−1.87	0.0307	−1.32	0.0934	−0.77	0.2206	−0.22	0.4129
−2.41	0.0080	−1.86	0.0314	−1.31	0.0951	−0.76	0.2236	−0.21	0.4168
−2.40	0.0082	−1.85	0.0322	−1.30	0.0968	−0.75	0.2266	−0.20	0.4207
−2.39	0.0084	−1.84	0.0329	−1.29	0.0985	−0.74	0.2297	−0.19	0.4247
−2.38	0.0087	−1.83	0.0336	−1.28	0.1003	−0.73	0.2327	−0.18	0.4286
−2.37	0.0089	−1.82	0.0344	−1.27	0.1020	−0.72	0.2358	−0.17	0.4325
−2.36	0.0091	−1.81	0.0351	−1.26	0.1038	−0.71	0.2389	−0.16	0.4364
−2.35	0.0094	−1.80	0.0359	−1.25	0.1056	−0.70	0.2420	−0.15	0.4404
−2.34	0.0096	−1.79	0.0367	−1.24	0.1075	−0.69	0.2451	−0.14	0.4443
−2.33	0.0099	−1.78	0.0375	−1.23	0.1093	−0.68	0.2483	−0.13	0.4483
−2.32	0.0102	−1.77	0.0384	−1.22	0.1112	−0.67	0.2514	−0.12	0.4522
−2.31	0.0104	−1.76	0.0392	−1.21	0.1131	−0.66	0.2546	−0.11	0.4562
−2.30	0.0107	−1.75	0.0401	−1.20	0.1151	−0.65	0.2578	−0.10	0.4602
−2.29	0.0110	−1.74	0.0409	−1.19	0.1170	−0.64	0.2611	−0.09	0.4641
−2.28	0.0113	−1.73	0.0418	−1.18	0.1190	−0.63	0.2643	−0.08	0.4681
−2.27	0.0116	−1.72	0.0427	−1.17	0.1210	−0.62	0.2676	−0.07	0.4721
−2.26	0.0119	−1.71	0.0436	−1.16	0.1230	−0.61	0.2709	−0.06	0.4761
−2.25	0.0122	−1.70	0.0446	−1.15	0.1251	−0.60	0.2743	−0.05	0.4801
−2.24	0.0125	−1.69	0.0455	−1.14	0.1271	−0.59	0.2776	−0.04	0.4840
−2.23	0.0129	−1.68	0.0465	−1.13	0.1292	−0.58	0.2810	−0.03	0.4880
−2.22	0.0132	−1.67	0.0475	−1.12	0.1314	−0.57	0.2843	−0.02	0.4920
−2.21	0.0136	−1.66	0.0485	−1.11	0.1335	−0.56	0.2877	−0.01	0.4960
−2.20	0.0139	−1.65	0.0495	−1.10	0.1357	−0.55	0.2912		

z	F(z)	z	F(z)	z	F(z)	z	F(z)	z	F(z)
0.00	0.5000	0.55	0.7088	1.10	0.8643	1.65	0.9505	2.20	0.9861
0.01	0.5040	0.56	0.7123	1.11	0.8665	1.66	0.9515	2.21	0.9864
0.02	0.5080	0.57	0.7157	1.12	0.8686	1.67	0.9525	2.22	0.9868
0.03	0.5120	0.58	0.7190	1.13	0.8708	1.68	0.9535	2.23	0.9871
0.04	0.5160	0.59	0.7224	1.14	0.8729	1.69	0.9545	2.24	0.9875
0.05	0.5199	0.60	0.7257	1.15	0.8749	1.70	0.9554	2.25	0.9878
0.06	0.5239	0.61	0.7291	1.16	0.8770	1.71	0.9564	2.26	0.9881
0.07	0.5279	0.62	0.7324	1.17	0.8790	1.72	0.9573	2.27	0.9884
0.08	0.5319	0.63	0.7357	1.18	0.8810	1.73	0.9582	2.28	0.9887
0.09	0.5359	0.64	0.7389	1.19	0.8830	1.74	0.9591	2.29	0.9890
0.10	0.5398	0.65	0.7422	1.20	0.8849	1.75	0.9599	2.30	0.9893
0.11	0.5438	0.66	0.7454	1.21	0.8869	1.76	0.9608	2.31	0.9896
0.12	0.5478	0.67	0.7486	1.22	0.8888	1.77	0.9616	2.32	0.9898
0.13	0.5517	0.68	0.7517	1.23	0.8907	1.78	0.9625	2.33	0.9901
0.14	0.5557	0.69	0.7549	1.24	0.8925	1.79	0.9633	2.34	0.9904
0.15	0.5596	0.70	0.7580	1.25	0.8944	1.80	0.9641	2.35	0.9906
0.16	0.5636	0.71	0.7611	1.26	0.8962	1.81	0.9649	2.36	0.9909
0.17	0.5675	0.72	0.7642	1.27	0.8980	1.82	0.9656	2.37	0.9911
0.18	0.5714	0.73	0.7673	1.28	0.8997	1.83	0.9664	2.38	0.9913
0.19	0.5753	0.74	0.7704	1.29	0.9015	1.84	0.9671	2.39	0.9916
0.20	0.5793	0.75	0.7734	1.30	0.9032	1.85	0.9678	2.40	0.9918
0.21	0.5832	0.76	0.7764	1.31	0.9049	1.86	0.9686	2.41	0.9920
0.22	0.5871	0.77	0.7794	1.32	0.9066	1.87	0.9693	2.42	0.9922
0.23	0.5910	0.78	0.7823	1.33	0.9082	1.88	0.9699	2.43	0.9925
0.24	0.5948	0.79	0.7852	1.34	0.9099	1.89	0.9706	2.44	0.9927
0.25	0.5987	0.80	0.7881	1.35	0.9115	1.90	0.9713	2.45	0.9929
0.26	0.6026	0.81	0.7910	1.36	0.9131	1.91	0.9719	2.46	0.9931
0.27	0.6064	0.82	0.7939	1.37	0.9147	1.92	0.9726	2.47	0.9932
0.28	0.6103	0.83	0.7967	1.38	0.9162	1.93	0.9732	2.48	0.9934
0.29	0.6141	0.84	0.7995	1.39	0.9177	1.94	0.9738	2.49	0.9936
0.30	0.6179	0.85	0.8023	1.40	0.9192	1.95	0.9744	2.50	0.9938
0.31	0.6217	0.86	0.8051	1.41	0.9207	1.96	0.9750	2.51	0.9940
0.32	0.6255	0.87	0.8079	1.42	0.9222	1.97	0.9756	2.52	0.9941
0.33	0.6293	0.88	0.8106	1.43	0.9236	1.98	0.9761	2.53	0.9943
0.34	0.6331	0.89	0.8133	1.44	0.9251	1.99	0.9767	2.54	0.9945
0.35	0.6368	0.90	0.8159	1.45	0.9265	2.00	0.9773	2.55	0.9946
0.36	0.6406	0.91	0.8186	1.46	0.9279	2.01	0.9778	2.56	0.9948
0.37	0.6443	0.92	0.8212	1.47	0.9292	2.02	0.9783	2.57	0.9949
0.38	0.6480	0.93	0.8238	1.48	0.9306	2.03	0.9788	2.58	0.9951
0.39	0.6517	0.94	0.8264	1.49	0.9319	2.04	0.9793	2.59	0.9952
0.40	0.6554	0.95	0.8289	1.50	0.9332	2.05	0.9798	2.60	0.9953
0.41	0.6591	0.96	0.8315	1.51	0.9345	2.06	0.9803	2.61	0.9955
0.42	0.6628	0.97	0.8340	1.52	0.9357	2.07	0.9808	2.62	0.9956
0.43	0.6664	0.98	0.8365	1.53	0.9370	2.08	0.9812	2.63	0.9957
0.44	0.6700	0.99	0.8389	1.54	0.9382	2.09	0.9817	2.64	0.9959
0.45	0.6736	1.00	0.8413	1.55	0.9394	2.10	0.9821	2.65	0.9960
0.46	0.6772	1.01	0.8438	1.56	0.9406	2.11	0.9826	2.66	0.9961
0.47	0.6808	1.02	0.8461	1.57	0.9418	2.12	0.9830	2.67	0.9962
0.48	0.6844	1.03	0.8485	1.58	0.9429	2.13	0.9834	2.68	0.9963
0.49	0.6879	1.04	0.8508	1.59	0.9441	2.14	0.9838	2.69	0.9964
0.50	0.6915	1.05	0.8531	1.60	0.9452	2.15	0.9842	2.70	0.9965
0.51	0.6950	1.06	0.8554	1.61	0.9463	2.16	0.9846	2.80	0.9974
0.52	0.6985	1.07	0.8577	1.62	0.9474	2.17	0.9850	3.00	0.9987
0.53	0.7019	1.08	0.8599	1.63	0.9484	2.18	0.9854	3.50	0.9998
0.54	0.7054	1.09	0.8621	1.64	0.9495	2.19	0.9857	4.00	1.0000

Let us return to the 50 height deviation values given in Figure 4.5. Figure 4.8 showed their histogram and a superimposed normal distribution; it suggests that a normal distribution well describes the distribution of height deviations. Since the histogram is well described by a normal distribution, we would also expect the *cumulative* histogram to be well described by a *cumulative* normal distribution.

In Figure 4.15, the cumulative normal distribution with mean and standard deviation equal to that for the 50 height deviation values is superimposed on the cumulative histogram for the height deviations. Its shape is a stylized "S" shape, increasing gradually at first, then more and more steeply, and finally tapering off again. Inspection of Figure 4.15 suggests that the cumulative normal distribution is quite close to the actual cumulative distribution of the height diameter data. Thus these data vary in normal distribution fashion.

Let us illustrate the fact that a normal distribution accurately describes the distribution of height deviations by finding the quantile corresponding to 2.0 micrometers. Using Figure 4.15, we can use the cumulative distribution for the height **counting method** deviations to find that approximately 70% of the height deviations, or about 35 in 50, are less than or equal to 2.0 micrometers. Using the raw data in Figure 4.5, we find the exact proportion to be $\frac{36}{50} = 72\%$. Thus, 2.0 micrometers equals the 0.72 quantile.

Since the normal distribution approximates the height deviation values well, we can also derive the quantile for 2.0 micrometers by using Table 4.1 or the *Calc ▸ Probability Distributions ▸ Normal* menu in Minitab. For these data, the sample mean is $\bar{y} = 0.062$ and the standard deviation is $s_y = 3.554$. Thus, the standardized value for $y = 2.0$ micrometers is

$$z = \frac{y - \bar{y}}{s_y} = \frac{2.0 - 0.062}{3.554} = 0.55$$

Using Table 4.1 or the *Calc ▸ Probability Distributions ▸ Normal* menu in Minitab, the proportion of values less than $z = 0.55$ is about 0.71, so $z = 0.55$ equals the 0.71 quantile (the 71st percentile) of the normal distribution. This result agrees closely with the direct computation in the previous paragraph, where we ob-

FIGURE 4.15
Cumulative
Frequency
Distribution of
Height Deviation
Data (Cumulative
Normal Distribution
Superimposed)

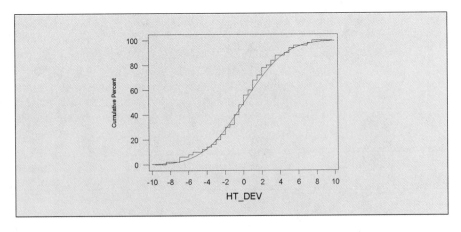

tained 2.0 micrometers to correspond to the 72nd percentile. This supports our visual impression in Figure 4.15 that the normal distribution closely approximates the distribution of height deviations.

In Example 4.2 (p. 121), it was mentioned that height deviation values had to be between -10 and 10 micrometers for components to meet the tight specifications. Since the sample of $n = 50$ components was randomly drawn from the population of $N = 1,100$ components, the sample can be used to generalize to the population, subject to sampling error. We expect the normal distribution with mean $\bar{y} = 0.062$ and standard deviation $s_y = 3.554$ to closely describe the data distribution of all 1,100 components. We can thus use Minitab (or Table 4.1) to find that the standardized value for -10 micrometers is

$$z = \frac{-10 - \bar{y}}{s_y} = \frac{-10 - 0.062}{3.554} = -2.83$$

which equals the 0.0023 quantile of the normal distribution. Likewise, the standardized value for 10 micrometers is 2.80, which equals the 0.9974 quantile. Overall then, a fraction of

$$0.9974 - 0.0023 = 0.9951$$

or 99.51% of the height deviation values can be expected to meet the specifications in the population.

Summarizing, the normal distribution describes a distinct pattern for a distribution of data values. Using the mean and standard deviation of these values alone, a normal distribution pattern allows us to easily find the proportion of data values falling in any particular interval: We must first standardize the limits of the interval, and then use the standardized values in a table of the normal distribution, such as Table 4.1. Alternatively, we can use the *Calc* ▸ *Probability Distributions* ▸ *Normal* menu in Minitab.

In general, the normal distribution describes variation for a very large number of values, and its outline is then very smooth. When data are available from a sample only, the outline of the sample frequency distribution (as represented, for example, in a histogram) is not necessarily smooth but may be somewhat jagged, even if this sample was drawn from a much larger set of values whose distributional shape is normal. The reason for such jaggedness is that a small sample can never be expected to fully represent the larger population from which it was drawn. For this reason, it is often useful to smooth the outline of a sample frequency distribution and then to check if the smoothed curve is of normal shape.

Judging the closeness of the actual cumulative frequency distribution to a cumulative normal distribution is difficult for the human eye, because it involves checking the extent to which a particular graph of some data can be approximated by the cumulative normal *curve*. In general, the eye has a much easier time checking the extent to which a particular graph of data can be approximated by a *line*. A slight redrawing of the normal cumulative distribution achieves such a comparison. This graph is called a *normal probability plot,* discussed in the next section.

4.6

THE NORMAL PROBABILITY PLOT

In the last section we saw how to make use of the normal distribution when it is applicable. The normal distribution pattern does not describe all data distributions well. For example, consider the variable Costs of Calls to Toronto, discussed for the "for" respondents in Example 4.1. The dotplot in Figure 4.2 is quite positively skewed, so use of the normal distribution is not appropriate. In order to compute the proportion of "for" respondents for whom the costs were $10.25 or less in Section 4.3, we used the raw data in Figure 4.4. We *counted* the number of "for" respondents in the sample whose costs were $10.25 or less and used the result to estimate the corresponding proportion of "for" respondents in the population to be $\frac{26}{50} = 0.52$.

If we could have used the normal distribution in this case, we would have standardized $10.25, using the mean (16.31) and standard deviation (15.55) from Figure 4.2. The resulting standardized value is $z = (10.25 - 16.31)/15.55 = -0.39$. Using the table of the normal distribution, the estimate of the proportion of "for" respondents whose costs are $10.25 or less would have been 0.35. This differs, of course, from the estimate obtained in the previous paragraph (0.52) because it was *wrong* to use the normal distribution in this example.

The remainder of this section discusses a graphical tool that helps assess the appropriateness of the normal distribution for a particular application.

The Normal Probability Plot: Interpretation

The normal probability plot is a convenient tool for judging the normality of the distribution of data values. It is easily derived with Minitab. For every observation in the sample, Minitab computes a corresponding normal score (NSCORE), to be expected *if* the sample had come from a normal distribution. (The details of how this "expected normal score" is obtained should not concern you here. They are explained later in this section.) The distribution of observed values in the sample is well approximated by a normal distribution if a plot of the expected normal scores versus the observed values is well approximated by a straight line. Figure 4.16 gives the normal probability plot for the height deviation data. There is an added horizontal axis for the standardized observed (z) values, which facilitates drawing the line expected if the data were normal.

line expected under normality

The *line expected under normality* is drawn such that

$$\text{NSCORE} = z$$

or such that

$$\text{NSCORE} = \frac{y - \bar{y}}{s_y}$$

where y refers to the variable in whose normality we are interested. Here $y =$ HT_DEV. Regardless of whether the horizontal line is expressed in standardized

FIGURE 4.16 Height Deviation Example

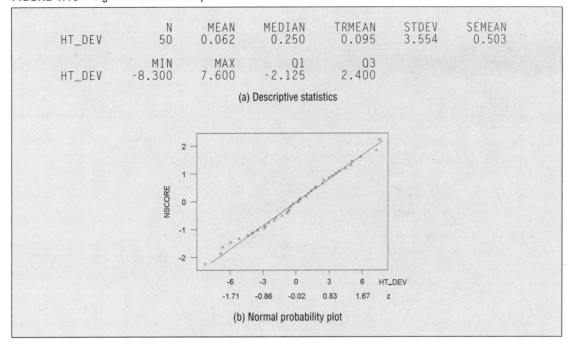

	N	MEAN	MEDIAN	TRMEAN	STDEV	SEMEAN
HT_DEV	50	0.062	0.250	0.095	3.554	0.503

	MIN	MAX	Q1	Q3
HT_DEV	-8.300	7.600	-2.125	2.400

(a) Descriptive statistics

(b) Normal probability plot

units (z) or unstandardized units (y), we can readily draw the line expected under normality.

If the horizontal axis is labeled by standardized values, then we must find any two points for which NSCORE $= z$ and draw the line through them. For example, we could pick the points $(-1, -1)$ and $(1, 1)$, where each pair of numbers is given in the format:

(Horizontal axis, Vertical axis)

That is, the first number in each pair refers to the standardized observed score (z) and the second number refers to the expected normal score (NSCORE).

If the horizontal axis is labeled by unstandardized values (y), then we must find any two points for which NSCORE $= (y - \bar{y})/s_y$, or for which $y = \bar{y} + $ NSCORE (s_y). Since the mean and standard deviation for HT_DEV are $\bar{y} = 0.062$ and $s_y = 3.554$, respectively, we could choose the two points $(0.062 - 1(3.554), -1)$ or $(-3.492, -1)$ and $(0.062 + 1(3.554), 1)$ or $(3.616, 1)$.

In Figure 4.16, the line expected under normality suggests that the distribution of height deviation values is well approximated by a normal distribution.

Let us now look at normal probability plots for nonnormal data. In Figures 4.17 and 4.18, data distributions are shown that considerably deviate from normality. Deviations from the line expected under normality suggest that the normal distribution is *not* a good approximation for the data distribution.

FIGURE 4.17

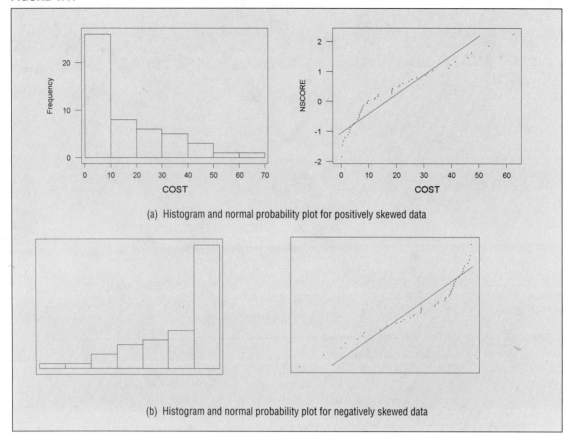

(a) Histogram and normal probability plot for positively skewed data

(b) Histogram and normal probability plot for negatively skewed data

FIGURE 4.18 Graphs for Thin-Tailed Data

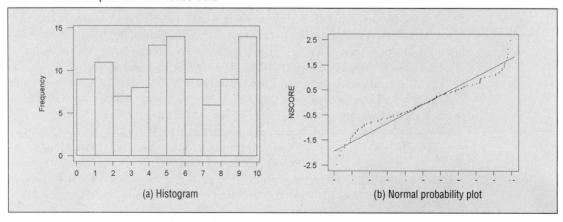

(a) Histogram

(b) Normal probability plot

Figure 4.17(a) describes the data on costs of calls to Toronto of the "for" respondents, introduced in Example 4.1. The distribution of cost values is quite positively skewed. Consequently, the normal probability plot does not follow a straight line as would be expected if the data distribution were closely approximated by a normal distribution. The actual normal probability plot is bow-shaped, starting below the superimposed line, rising above it, and ending up below it again. The deviation from normality is quite pronounced. What is important here is that there is a strong *pattern* to the deviation from normality. Figure 4.17(b) shows the normal probability plot for a negatively skewed distribution; it has a similarly bow-shaped pattern, but the bow starts and ends *above* the line expected under normality.

The histogram in Figure 4.18 is somewhat flat, and there are not really any tails. In comparison with the normal distribution, this kind of a distribution is said to be *thin-tailed*. Its normal probability plot shows a *pattern* to the deviation from the expected line under normality that can be described as *reverse* S-shaped: It starts below the superimposed line, crosses it, crosses below again, and finally ends up above the line.

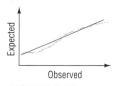

FIGURE 4.19

A distribution with a few observations far into each tail is called *thick-tailed* in comparison to the normal distribution. Its normal probability plot has an S-shape similar to Figure 4.18, but one in which the S starts *above* the line and ends *below* the line.

In this section we have seen how we can check if a normal distribution is a reasonable approximation to a data distribution.

> When a normal distribution fits the data well, all we need from the data are the mean and standard deviation to describe *any* feature of interest in the data, such as, for example, percentiles. The only additional tool that is needed is a table of the normal distribution, like Table 4.1.

By far, not all data distributions can be approximated by a normal distribution. When the normal distribution is not a good approximation, we must keep all the data to describe various features of interest. Sometimes an intermediate tool—a data transformation, introduced in Section 4.7—can be helpful to re-express the data in different units that then follow a normal distribution.

Let us briefly summarize our approach to making probabilistic statements in cross-sectional studies. The flowchart in Figure 4.20 shows the steps involved. Unless you are taking a census, be sure to obtain a random sample. When the distribution is approximately normal, quantiles and prediction intervals are readily found with the normal table or Minitab. When it is not, we must use the "counting method" for the data to get approximate quantiles and prediction intervals.

The Normal Probability Plot: Technical Details

This section is for *technically interested* readers only. If you are not interested in the technical details of obtaining normal probability plots, you can skip this subsection without loss of continuity.

FIGURE 4.20
Flowchart for
Making
Probabilistic
Statements in a
Cross-Sectional
Study

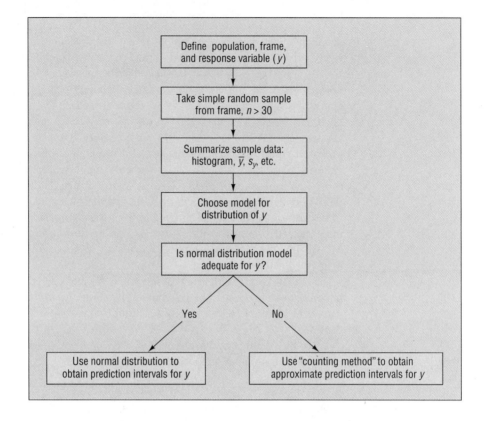

In order to illustrate the normal probability plot, let us work with a small sample of $n = 20$ income values drawn randomly from a population. The income values (in $1,000), y, sorted in ascending order, are as follows:

9	10	11	20	21	22	23	24	28	41
47	48	50	62	71	111	128	169	197	351

The sample mean and standard deviation are $\bar{y} = 72.2$ and $s_y = 84.7$. Using the standardization formula, $z = (y - \bar{y})/s_y$, we can standardize the income values, yielding:

−0.75	−0.73	−0.72	−0.62	−0.60	−0.59	−0.58	−0.57	−0.52	−0.37
−0.30	−0.29	−0.26	−0.12	−0.01	0.46	0.66	1.14	1.47	3.29

Judging the normality of the income values can be done with the standardized data (z), or with the raw data (y). It is easier to use the standardized data to explain how to obtain a normal probability plot. This plot answers the question of whether a normal distribution adequately describes the distribution of incomes. If it does, then subject to sampling error alone, we will need only the sample mean and sample standard deviation (and a table of the normal distribution, such as Table 4.1) to estimate quantiles and related quantities for the population of income values. If it does not, then we will have to use the raw data to get such estimates.

To obtain the normal probability plot for the $n = 20$ standardized income values (z), we first answer the following question:

> If a random sample of $n = 20$ observations were drawn from a normal distribution, what would we expect the standardized value to be for the smallest observation? For the second smallest observation? The third smallest, etc.?

Let us call these values the *expected normal scores* for the smallest observation, for the second smallest observation, etc. We would, of course, expect the smallest observations in a sample to be in the lower tail of the normal distribution.

When there are $n = 20$ observations, each observation makes up $\frac{1}{20} = 5\%$ of the sample size. We should therefore expect the smallest observation to be among the bottom 5% of values from a normal distribution, that is, between the 0th percentile and the 5th percentile. Since the 0th percentile for a normal distribution is at $-\infty$ and the 5th percentile is at -1.65, we would expect the smallest observation to be between $-\infty$ and -1.65. It turns out that the expected normal score for the smallest observation in $n = 20$ approximately equals -1.87.

We should expect the second smallest observation to be among the next 5% of values from a normal distribution, that is, between the 5th and 10th percentiles, or between -1.65 and -1.28. In fact, the expected normal score for the second smallest observation in $n = 20$ approximately equals -1.40.

We can derive the expected normal scores for the third smallest through the largest observation in the same way. The resulting $n = 20$ expected normal scores are:

-1.87	-1.40	-1.12	-0.91	-0.74	-0.58	-0.44	-0.31	-0.18	-0.06
0.06	0.18	0.31	0.44	0.58	0.74	0.91	1.12	1.40	1.87

Having derived the expected normal scores for the $n = 20$ observations in our sample, we now must answer a second question:

> How close are the expected normal scores to the observed standardized values (z)?

Only if all $n = 20$ expected normal scores are reasonably close to the corresponding observed standardized values would it be reasonable for us to conclude that a normal distribution adequately describes the distribution of standardized values. To judge this, we just plot the expected normal scores (NSCORE) against the observed standardized values (z) and check how well this plot is approximated by the line NSCORE $= z$. For the $n = 20$ income values, the plot is given in Figure 4.21. The line does not describe this scatterplot well at all: The distribution of incomes is positively skewed, so a normal distribution is a poor description of the distribution of income values. Note that the horizontal axis is labeled both by stan-

FIGURE 4.21

Illustrative Income Data ($n = 20$): Normal Probability Plot

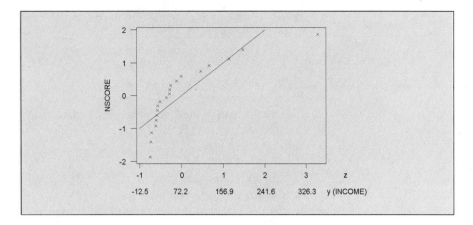

dardized values and by income values (in $1,000). It does not much matter which one is used, as long as the line expected under normality is drawn in such a way that NSCORE equals z.

As was shown in the beginning of this section, the expected normal scores (NSCORE) are easily derived with Minitab, whether the raw data are in ascending order or not.

4.7

TRANSFORMATIONS TO NORMALITY

In this section we discuss how some data can be transformed so that the transformed values are well described by a normal distribution.

Consider the 1989 income figures for a sample of $n = 60$ families described in Figure 4.22. The data are stored in ASCII file INCOMES.DAT. The histogram of the data (Figure 4.23) is positively skewed, as supported by the normal probability plot. This distributional shape is quite common for distributions of income.

There is considerable evidence that, if the income values are transformed into their natural (or any other) logarithms, the distribution of transformed values will follow a normal distribution. The 60 income figures were re-expressed with a logarithmic transformation, and the results are shown in Figure 4.24.

The normal probability plot in Figure 4.24 shows that the logarithmically transformed income data are well described by a normal distribution. In general, the following observation holds.

> **Logarithmically transformed** measurements follow a *normal distribution* when the untransformed measurements are the *product* of a large number of independent sources of variation, typically not known or identified, and none of which is of dominant influence.

FIGURE 4.22 Data on Family Incomes

50446	2969	50792	41406	43819	106597	46523	46959
102667	11179	69138	6849	72868	9968	7816	21347
62288	8919	33230	41735	22368	97097	7909	350787
11985	4360	27555	15109	74358	127730	36363	110882
11670	47744	49589	197090	5934	20403	46948	65638
31367	44237	10485	27535	19911	24026	37588	70761
24142	38206	19666	10233	169132	13364	27233	21198
28581	49056	22628	35703				

(a) Raw income data

	N	MEAN	MEDIAN	TRMEAN	STDEV	SEMEAN
INCOME	60	48235	34466	40071	55569	7174

	MIN	MAX	Q1	Q3
INCOME	2969	350787	16248	50706

(b) Descriptive statistics

FIGURE 4.23
Graphs for Family
Incomes (in $1,000)

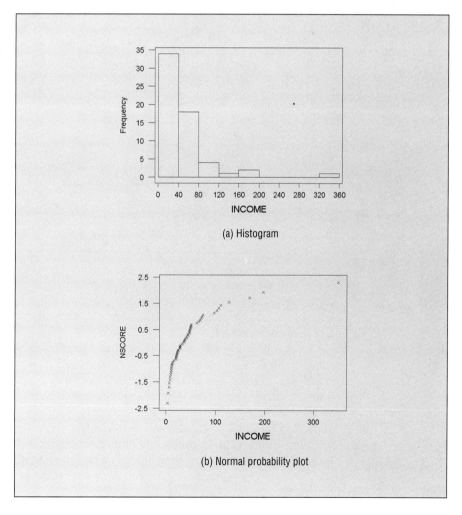

(a) Histogram

(b) Normal probability plot

FIGURE 4.24 Logarithmic Transformation of Income Data

ROW	INCOME	LOG(INC)
1	50446	10.8287
2	2969	7.9960
3	50792	10.8355
...		
58	49056	10.8007
59	22628	10.0269
60	35703	10.4830

(a) Income data and its logarithmic transformation

	N	MEAN	MEDIAN	TRMEAN	STDEV	SEMEAN
LOG(INC)	60	10.337	10.447	10.337	0.964	0.124

	MIN	MAX	Q1	Q3
LOG(INC)	7.996	12.768	9.689	10.834

(b) Descriptive Statistics

(c) Graphs

Over the years, incomes typically develop by percentage changes that are compounded, and this compounding is mathematically expressed by a product. Hence it is not surprising that distributions of logarithmically transformed income figures are often normal.

Let us see how we can use the fact that the logarithmically transformed income data follow a normal distribution. The sample of $n = 60$ families was randomly selected from a much larger population of families, and so we can generalize from the sample to the population, subject to sampling error. Let us try to estimate the proportion of families in this population whose incomes are less than $50,000. Since the logarithmically transformed incomes approximately follow a normal distribution, we must also logarithmically transform the $50,000 figure so that we can locate it on a normal distribution whose mean and standard deviation are 10.337 and 0.964, as given for the logarithmically transformed income values in Figure

4.24. The logs used there were actually natural logs, and the natural log of 50,000 is 10.820. This value can be standardized to

$$z = \frac{10.820 - 10.337}{0.964} = 0.50$$

and from Table 4.1, or the *Calc ▸ Probability Distributions ▸ Normal* menu in Minitab, we find that $z = 0.50$ corresponds to the 69th percentile of a normal distribution. Therefore, the proportion of families in the population whose incomes are less than $50,000 can be estimated at 69%.

To obtain this result, all we needed was

- Evidence that the logarithmically transformed data follow a normal distribution

- The mean and standard deviation of the logarithmically transformed data

- A table of the normal distribution

Not all nonnormal data distributions can be transformed to normality. In particular, the logarithmic transformation does not necessarily lead to normality. When all data values are positive and their distribution has considerable positive skewness, the logarithmic transformation sometimes works and can be used as a starting point. When the logarithmic transformation does not work, other simple transformations sometimes do, but you should be judicious in your choice of transformation. In this book, we consider only one other transformation, the **square root transformation.** It sometimes works for data distributions that have moderate positive skewness.

To illustrate the use of a square root transformation, consider Figure 4.25, where the income data from Figure 4.22 are re-expressed with a square root transformation. The normal probability plot shows that the data so transformed do not follow a normal distribution: They are still somewhat positively skewed. The

FIGURE 4.25 Square-Root Transformation of Income Data

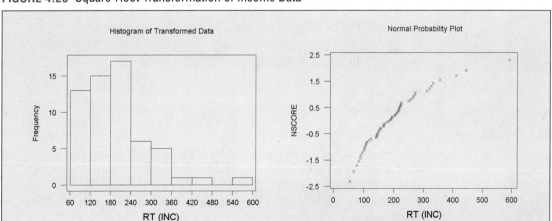

square root transformation can be expected to work when the data are somewhat less positively skewed than when the logarithmic transformation would work. Once again, there will be many situations when the untransformed data do not follow a normal distribution and when neither the logarithmic nor the square-root transformations lead to normality.

4.8

MODELING

In the last few sections, the statistical **model of a random variable** was implicitly developed. A *model* is a conceptualization that tries to capture the salient aspects of a real-life phenomenon. A model's usefulness depends on the degree to which the important characteristics of a situation have been incorporated. A model is *always* a simplification of the real-life situation and cannot capture all its aspects. The degree of detail depends on the problem for whose solution the model is formulated. A variable is called *random* when its values are randomly drawn from a population of values.

The model of a random variable is as follows:

The **model of a random variable** is based on the assumption that simple random sampling is used to draw observations from the population. The model consists of two premises:

1. There is a constant level around which observations vary

2. The observations vary randomly around the constant level.

This model can be simply represented by the following equation:

Actual Observation = Mean + Random Deviation

or

$$y \quad = \quad \mu_y \quad + \quad \epsilon$$

where the random deviation ϵ (the Greek letter *epsilon*) has mean 0 and standard deviation σ_y. (Since the mean of all actual observations is μ_y, the mean random deviation must be 0.)

In many, but not all, applications the random deviation ϵ follows a normal distribution.

---

residual

The random deviation from the mean is often called the **residual.** Thus we write the equation representing the model of a random variable as

Actual Observation = Mean + Residual,

or

$$y \quad = \quad \mu_y \quad + \quad \epsilon$$

In many applications, this model usefully describes sampling from a population. Since it is usually not possible to take a census, a sample must be taken that can be used to estimate the parameters, μ_y and σ_y, and other features of the population. For example, in Example 4.2 (p. 121) a simple random sample of 50 height deviation values was taken from the population of 1,100 height deviations. This sample was used to estimate the population mean μ_y by the sample mean, $\bar{y} = 0.062$, and the population standard deviation σ_y by the sample standard deviation, $s_y = 3.554$.

The histogram of values from a random sample sometimes follows a normal distribution. Sometimes the transformed values follow a normal distribution. Often no transformation to normality can be found.

The flowchart in Figure 4.20 showed the approach to obtaining probabilistic statements in a cross-sectional study. We can now slightly expand it to include the possibility of using transformations. The result is in Figure 4.26.

FIGURE 4.26 Expanded Flowchart for Making Probabilistic Statements in a Cross-Sectional Study

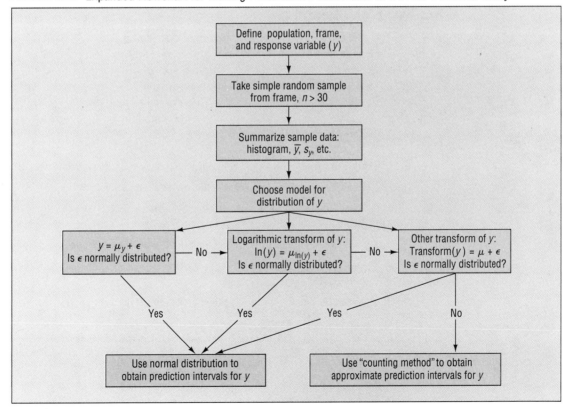

4.9

SUMMARY AND OUTLOOK

This chapter introduced some basic tools that are useful for learning about a population through a cross-sectional study. When it is not possible to take a census, a simple random sample must be taken from the population frame. The histogram of values in the sample can be obtained, and this histogram is sometimes well approximated by a normal distribution. When this is not the case, a transformation to normality can sometimes be found.

When normality applies, the data can be summarized by their mean and standard deviation. In addition to the normal table, this mean and standard deviation are all that is needed to obtain any percentile of the distribution of data values. Likewise, prediction intervals for the response variable y can be found from a simple formula, $\mu_y \pm z\,\sigma_y$.

When normality does not apply, use of the normal table is inappropriate, and the raw data and counting must be used to obtain prediction intervals and percentiles of the distribution of data values.

The next chapter discusses how to analyze a time series study of a process. It will turn out there that, under certain assumptions, the cross-sectional tools discussed in this chapter can again be usefully employed.

Key Terms and Concepts

survey	normal distribution
simple random sampling	*prediction interval*
population, frame	normal probability plot
cumulative frequency distribution	transformation
percentile, quantile	*logarithmic, square root*
standardization	model of a random variable *residual*

References

Payne, S. L. (1980), *The Art of Asking Questions,* Princeton University Press, Princeton, NJ.

This book gives detailed information about how to phrase questions properly.

Scheaffer, R. L., Mendenhall, W., and Ott, L. (1990), *Elementary Survey Sampling,* 4th edition, PWS-Kent, Boston.

This is a good introductory text to survey sampling. It gives many necessary details.

Sheatsley, P., Turner, A., and Waksberg, J. (n. d.), *What Is a Survey?,* American Statistical Association, Washington, DC.

This little booklet provides a useful overview of surveys. It does not provide technical details.

Tanur, J. M., Mosteller, F., Kruskal, W. H., Lehmann, E. L., Link, R. F., Pieters, R. S., and Rising, G. R., editors (1989), *Statistics: A Guide to the Unknown,* 3rd edition, Wadsworth Inc., Belmont, CA.

This book presents statistical applications from a variety of contexts. Some of them are surveys.

4.10

USING MINITAB FOR WINDOWS

This section shows how several of the graphs in this chapter were generated with Minitab for Windows.

Figure 4.2
Choose *File ▶ Other Files ▶ Import ASCII Data*
In the *Import ASCII Data* dialog box,
      Under *Store data in column* type **C1-C5** and click *ok*
      In the *Import Text From File* dialog box,
         Choose and click data file *eas.dat*, click *ok*
Choose *Window ▶ Data*
In the *Data* window,
      In the boxes immediately under *C1* to *C5*, type **NUMBER, COST, BILL, CCF, SURVEY**
      Click any empty cell

MULTIPLE DOTPLOTS WITH A STRATIFICATION VARIABLE

Choose *Graph ▶ Character Graphs ▶ Dotplot*
In the *Dotplot* dialog box,
      Click the box under *Variables*, type **C2**
      Click the box to the left of *By variable*
      Click the box to the right of *By variable*, type **C5**
      Click the box to the left of *Same scale for all variables*
      Click *ok*

DESCRIPTIVE STATISTICS WITH A STRATIFICATION VARIABLE

Choose *Stat ▶ Basic Statistics ▶ Descriptive Statistics*
In the *Descriptive Statistics* dialog box,
      Click the box under *Variables*, type **C2**
      Click the box to the left of *By variable*
      Click the box to the right of *By variable*, type **C5**
      Click *ok*

Figure 4.3

UNSTACKING DATA

Choose *Manip* ▸ *Unstack*

In the *Unstack* dialog box,

    Click the box under *Unstack,* type **C1-C4**

    Click the box next to *Using subscripts in,* type **C5**

    Click the first box under *Store results in blocks,* type **C11-C14**

    Click the second box under *Store results in blocks,* type **C21-C24**

    Click *ok*

> (These commands unstack the data in columns C1–C4 by variable C5, which denotes the "against" respondents, C5 = 0, and the "for" respondents, C5 = 1. The data for the "against" respondents are stored in columns C11–C14, for the "for" respondents in columns C21–C24.)

Choose *Window* ▸ *Data*

In the *Data* window,

    Use the cursor to move to the box immediately under *C12,* type **COST_AGT**

    Use the cursor to move to the box immediately under *C22,* type **COST_FOR**

    Click an empty cell

CUMULATIVE RELATIVE HISTOGRAM AS A STEP FUNCTION

Choose *Graph* ▸ *Histogram*

In the *Histogram* dialog box,

    Under *Graph variables,* type **C12**

    Click *Options*

    In the *Histogram Options* dialog box,

        Under *Type of Histogram,* click the circle next to *Cumulative Frequency*

        Under *Type of Intervals,* click the circle next to *CutPoint*

        Under *Definition of Intervals,* click the circle to the left of *midpoint/cutpoint positions*

        To the right of *midpoint/cutpoint positions,* type $-1{:}68/1$

        Click *ok*

    Under *Data display,* click the down arrow next to *Display,* click *Connect*

    Click *Edit Attributes*

    In the *Connect* dialog box,

        Click the circle next to *Step,* click *ok*

    Click *ok*

        (These commands generate Figure 4.3(a).)

Figure 4.7

Choose *File* ▸ *Other Files* ▸ *Import ASCII Data*

In the *Import ASCII Data* dialog box,

    Under *Store data in column,* type **C1**

    Click *ok*

    In the *Import Text from File* dialog box,

        Choose and click data file *height.dat,* click *ok*

Choose *Window ▸ Data*
In the *Data* window,
    In the box immediately under *C1,* type **HT_DEV**
    Click any empty cell

MATHEMATICAL EXPRESSIONS

Choose *Calc ▸ Mathematical Expressions*
In the *Mathematical Expressions* dialog box,
    Click the box next to *Variable (new or modified),* type **C2**
    Click the box under *Expression,* type **(C1-0.062)/3.54**
    Click *ok*
        (These commands compute the standardized values for C1 and store them in C2. The mean and standard deviations of C1 were obtained in Figure 4.5.)

Figure 4.16

NORMAL SCORES

Choose *Calc ▸ Functions*
In the *Functions* dialog box,
    Click the circle left of *Input Column*
    Click the box right of *Input Column,* type **C1**
    Click the box right of *Result in,* type **C2**
    Click the circle left of *Normal scores*
    Click *ok*
        (These commands compute the expected normal scores values for C1 and store them in C2.)
Choose *Window ▸ Data*
In the *Data* window,
    Click the cell immediately under *C2,* type **NSCORE**
    Click any empty cell
Choose *Graph ▸ Plot*
In the *Plot* dialog box,
    In the *Graph variables* box, type **C2** in row 1 under *Y* and type **C1** in row 1 under *X*
    Under *Data display,* click the down arrow next to *Display,* click *Symbol*
    Click *Edit Attributes*
    In the *Symbol* dialog box,
        Click the down arrow next to *Type,* click *Cross,* click *ok*
            (The last two rows lead to crosses being used as printing symbols in the scatterplot.)
    Click the down arrow next to *Annotation,* click *Line*
    In the *Line* dialog box,
        Click the first box under *Points,* type **-7.76 -2.2 7.88 2.2**
        Click *ok*
    Click *ok*
        (The line annotation command instructs Minitab to draw a line connecting the points $(-7.76, -2.2)$ and $(7.88, 2.2)$, where the first number in each pair refers to the horizontal axis and the second to the vertical axis.)

Figure 4.24

Choose *File* ▸ *Other Files* ▸ *Import ASCII Data*
In the *Import ASCII Data* dialog box,
    Under *Store data in column*, type **C1**
    Click *ok*
    In the *Import Text From File* dialog box,
        Choose and click data file *incomes.dat,* click *ok*
Choose *Window* ▸ *Data*
In the *Data* window,
    In the box immediately under *C1*, type **INCOME**
    Click any empty cell

LOGARITHMS

Choose *Calc* ▸ *Mathematical Expressions*
In the *Mathematical Expressions* dialog box,
    Click the box next to *Variable (new or modified)*, type **C2**
    Click the box under *Expression*, type **LOGE(C1)**
    Click *ok*
        (These commands compute the natural logarithms for C1 and store them in C2.)
Choose *Window* ▸ *Data*
In the *Data* window,
    Click the cell immediately under *C2*, type **LOG(INC)**
    Click any empty cell
Choose *Calc* ▸ *Functions*
In the *Functions* dialog box,
    Click the circle left of *Input Column*
    Click the box right of *Input Column*, type **C2**
    Click the box right of *Result in*, type **C3**
    Click the circle left of *Normal scores*
    Click *ok*
Choose *Window* ▸ *Data*
In the *Data* window,
    Click the cell immediately under *C3*, type **NSCORE**
    Click any empty cell
Choose *Graph* ▸ *Plot*
In the *Plot* dialog box,
    In the *Graph variables* box, type **C3** in row 1 under *Y* and type **C2** in row 1 under *X*
    Under *Data display*, click the down arrow next to *Display*
    Click *Symbol*
    Click *Edit Attributes*
    In the *Symbol* dialog box,
        Click the down arrow next to *Type*, click *Cross*, click *ok*
    Click *ok*

4.11

PROBLEMS FOR CLASS DISCUSSION

4.1   Frame for an Election Poll

Suppose that you want to carry out a poll in the city you live in to find out what proportion of voters would vote for the party in power if the next election were to be held within 2 weeks. What is the population of interest, and how would you get a frame?

4.2   A Road Authority

A road authority is responsible for planning and supervising the construction of highways.[3] As part of a new highway, a bridge had to be constructed for which the estimated amount of concrete needed was 5,650 m³. This study was conducted to determine the strength of concrete used in the bridge. The first question to be addressed was

1. Is the strength of the concrete used in the bridge up to the road authority's standards? (If not, a penalty was to be imposed on the contractor for failing to meet the required standards.)

    Data collection proceeded as follows. The process of delivering concrete was subdivided into successive sublots of 100 m³. Each sublot was delivered by several trucks, and one truck was selected at random from each sublot. When the selected truck arrived at the construction site, three buckets of concrete were collected, one from the first third of the truck's load, one from the middle third, and one from the last third. These buckets were mixed together, and a set of two cylinders were labelled and prepared for the laboratory. For each cylinder, the compression strength (in megapascals, MPa) was measured after 28 days. Finally, the variable of interest was "Mean 28-day compression strength for the two cylinders." This variable was to be used for further analysis.

    The road authority required that the mean of the variable of interest be at least 1.4 standard deviations above 30 MPa. (The standard deviation in question refers to the variable of interest.) Furthermore, no mean 28-day compression strength was to be lower than 26 MPa. It was expected that the mean 28-day compression strength values would be between 26 and 45 MPa. A second question was to be answered:

2. What is the overall proportion of values of the variable of interest for the construction site that fall below 26 MPa?

    The data are stored in ASCII file CONCRETE.DAT. The output in Figure 4.27, generated in the Minitab Session window, will be useful in answering the two questions. One further question: Was simple random sampling used to collect the data?

---

[3]The name of this authority is omitted to protect confidentiality. The data are real. The concrete in the one truck for which the variable of interest value is less than 26 MPa was used in the construction of curbs and gutters, and not in the structure itself, and so the contractor was not required to remove and replace the concrete.

FIGURE 4.27

```
MTB > Read 'C:\MTBWIN\DATA\CONCRETE.DAT' C1 C2.
Entering data from file: C:\MTBWIN\DATA\CONCRETE.DAT
    55 rows read.
MTB > Let C3 = (C1+C2)/2.
MTB > NAME C3 'VALUE'
MTB > PRINT C3

VALUE
   36.80    40.10    31.85    37.05    35.75    29.05    32.45    30.25    39.65
   33.75    34.00    34.80    31.55    36.45    32.65    38.45    28.15    30.30
   33.30    35.50    35.70    37.15    35.65    37.20    32.80    30.10    34.50
   33.40    35.00    32.80    33.15    39.50    38.75    36.45    30.25    25.85
   28.30    41.35    36.00    37.20    39.25    36.00    34.25    32.30    43.75
   47.80    40.85    41.05    45.15    34.25    38.70    31.75    33.75    42.70
   38.75

MTB > Describe C3.

                     N       MEAN     MEDIAN     TRMEAN      STDEV     SEMEAN
VALUE               55     35.514     35.500     35.393      4.403      0.594

                   MIN        MAX         Q1         Q3
VALUE           25.850     47.800     32.650     38.700

MTB > Histogram C3
```

(a) Histogram

```
MTB > NScores C3 C4.
MTB > NAME C4 'NSCORE'
MTB > Plot C4*C3
```

FIGURE 4.27 (continued)

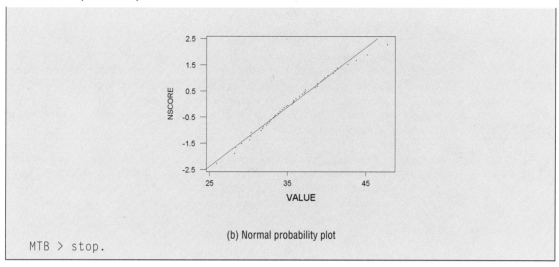

(b) Normal probability plot

MTB > stop.

4.12

EXERCISES

Although answers are given in Appendix C, do not turn to them right away if you cannot find an answer on your own. Return to the exercise the next day and try again before turning to Appendix C.

Exercises for Section 4.5

4.3 A bank reports the mean monthly account balance for its Mastercard accounts to be $450 with a standard deviation of $90. Assuming that the distribution of account balances is normal, what proportion of account balances:
   a Exceeds $540?
   b Is greater than or equal to $540?
   c Is between $495 and $585?
   d Is between $405 and $585?

4.4 Daily demand for a perishable item follows a normal distribution with mean 100 and standard deviation 15.
   a If 120 items were stocked on a particular day, what would be the probability of running out of stock?
   b The manager wants the probability of running out of stock to be 1%. How many items should be stocked?

4.5 Eleanor scores 700 on the mathematics part of the Scholastic Aptitude Test (SAT). Scores on the SAT follow the normal distribution with mean 500 and standard deviation 100. Gerald takes the American College Testing Program test of mathematical ability, which has mean 18 and standard deviation 6. He scores 24.
   a If both tests measure the same kind and levels of ability, who has the higher score?
   b What is the proportion of scores on the mathematics part of the SAT (i) over 800 and (ii) between 400 and 500?

c What is the cut-off point for scores on the mathematics part of the SAT so that 5% of students score above it?

4.6 A manufacturer needs washers that have a thickness of between 0.45 and 0.55 cm; any other thickness is unusable. Machine shop A will sell washers at $1.00 per thousand; the thickness of their washers is normally distributed with a mean of 0.5 cm and a standard deviation of 0.025 cm. Machine shop B will sell washers at $0.90 per thousand; the thickness of their washers is normally distributed with a mean of 0.5 cm and a standard deviation of 0.028 cm. Which shop offers a better deal? Why?

4.7 Consider variables that cannot take on negative values, such as income. Many such variables have a distribution that is positively skewed, but some have a distribution well approximated by a normal distribution. What must be true of the numerical relationship between the mean and standard deviation of such a variable for normality to be definitely *not* appropriate?

Exercise for Section 4.6

4.8 File NPP.DAT contains artificially generated data on 10 variables. Obtain the normal probability plot for each variable, and judge its normality. In each case, describe any pattern that suggests a deviation from normality (negative skewness, thin-tailedness, etc), and judge how serious this deviation is. Be sure to use columns other than C1–C10 for any variables you create.

Exercises for Section 4.7

4.9 Continue your analysis of the 10 variables in file NPP.DAT.
a Use a logarithmic transformation on the variables in columns 3, 4, 5, 6, and 8 in file NPP.DAT. For each transformed variable, obtain the normal probability plot and judge its normality. In each case, describe any pattern that suggests a deviation from normality (negative skewness, thin-tailedness, etc.), and judge how serious this deviation is.
b Do (a) using a square-root transformation.

4.10 After a square-root transformation, the values of a certain variable have a normal distribution with mean 50 and a standard deviation 10.
a What is the 10th percentile of the distribution of *untransformed* values?
b What proportion of untransformed values exceeds 3,000?

4.13

SUPPLEMENTARY EXERCISES

4.11 Suppose that the residential telephone numbers in the phone book for a large city are the frame for the population of interest in a study. A simple random sample of size $n = 100$ is to be drawn from this frame.
a What is the population? What is the unit?
b Why does the following procedure *not* lead to a simple random sample?

Pick 10 different pages at random from the phone book, and then pick 10 numbers at random from each of these 10 pages.

c Why does the following procedure possibly *not* lead to a simple random sample?

Pick 100 pages at random from the phone book (with replacement), and then pick one number at random from each of these 100 pages.

d Can you design a simple procedure to draw a simple random sample from the telephone book? What seems to be the major difficulty in doing so?

4.12 For a particular brand of automobile battery, the distribution of the amount of time from its installation in a car until it fails and must be replaced is a normal distribution with mean of 3.2 years and standard deviation of 0.6 years.
a What is the probability that a battery of this type will last at least 3 years?
b In a very large group of batteries, how long would a battery have to last before failing in order to be in the top 10% of all batteries in terms of time until failure?

4.13 Most graduate schools of business require applicants to submit a score on the GMAT, which is administered by the Educational Testing Service. Since 1965, GMAT scores have mean 480, with standard deviation 100. Past evidence shows the distribution of GMAT scores to be normally distributed.
a What fraction of scores would you expect to find in the interval from 400 to 580?
b Suppose that a graduate business school automatically accepts all applicants whose GMAT score exceeds 650. Approximately what fraction of all those taking the GMAT would qualify for admission under this criterion?
c The business school in (b) has a policy of considering applications only from applicants with GMAT score above 550. What proportion of applications considered will be automatically accepted because the applicant has a GMAT score exceeding 650? What additional assumption(s), if any, did you make to obtain a numerical answer?

4.14 Suppose that a business student in a class presentation on small businesses cites the census data on dollar sales volume as follows:

Mean = $1.5 million

Standard deviation = $1.1 million

Distribution of dollar sales volume figures: normal

What would your reaction be?

4.15 A builder requires her electrical subcontractor to finish the electrical wiring in a renovated office building in 28 days or less. To provide an incentive to finish on time, she specifies a $1,000 penalty if the electrical work takes longer than 28 days. The subcontractor feels that he is most likely to finish in about 20 days, but because of unforeseen events, he guesses it might take him several days more or less than this. More precisely, suppose that he has assessed the required time to have a normal distribution with mean 20 days and standard deviation 5 days. What is the chance of the subcontractor incurring the penalty implied by this assessment?

4.16 An instructor in a university department teaches two daytime sections of the same course. Since the midterm dates are not the same, she decides to give two different exams. The distributions of points in the two sections are as follows:

Marks	Section 1	Section 2
0	0	0
1	0	0
2	0	1
3	2	1
4	4	4
5	4	6
6	6	8
7	10	5
8	8	3
9	2	2
10	4	0

Number of Students	40	30
Mean	6.75	5.87
Standard Deviation	1.87	1.65

The instructor feels that the differences in the two distributions are due to differences in test difficulty. She feels that the two sections are comparable with respect to the students' ability.

A student from section 1 could not attend the exam for his section, and so the instructor asked him to attend the exam for section 2. He got 5 points on that exam. (His results are included in the summary for section 2, given above.)

The instructor has to put a grade for this student on the grade sheet for section 1, but hesitates to use the value 5. Is there any foundation for her hesitation? Can you think of a better option? What numerical value would this option lead to? What would you do in the instructor's place?

4.17 A real estate company operating in a midsize North American city conducted a study to determine whether market values of residential properties could be accurately predicted from the assessed values and other characteristics of the property. From the houses sold in 1990 in a certain area of the city, a random sample of 60 houses was obtained and the following characteristics were measured on each house: MARKET (the sales value of the house in $1,000), ASSESS (the assessed value of the house in $1,000), and AREA (the size of the living area in square feet).

The data are listed at the end of this problem, and they are also stored in ASCII file REAL.DAT. (Note that the houses are listed in order of the size of their living areas.) Answer the following questions.

a According to the data collection procedure outlined above, is this a time series or a cross-sectional study? If it is a time series study, describe the process; otherwise describe the population. Do you think this design is appropriate for this situation? Briefly state your reasons. What is the unit? What is the response variable?

b Describe the nature and the strength of the relationship between MARKET and AREA. For the purposes of the study, what would you like this relationship to be? What are the implications of the actual relationship for the study? Be brief.

c Describe the nature and the strength of the relationship between ASSESS and AREA. For the purposes of the study, what would you like this relationship to be? Are there differences between this relationship and the one in (b)? If yes, what are the practical implications of these differences? Be brief.

d The variable ERROR represents the difference between the market and assessed values. What do the mean, median, standard deviation, and distribution shape of ERROR tell you about the differences between market and assessed values, in particular, the usefulness of using the assessed value to predict the market value?

e Assuming normality if necessary, calculate the 90% prediction interval for ERROR and interpret it in the context of the study.

f Did you have to make any assumptions to calculate the answer in (e)? If yes, what are they and how reasonable are they? What effect do these assumptions have on the accuracy of your answer in (e)? What measures, if any, could be taken to improve the accuracy of the prediction interval in (e)?

g Noting that the average MARKET value is 56.43 higher than the average ASSESS value—that is, the average ERROR is 56.43—the following procedure is proposed to estimate market value:

Estimated Market Value = Assessed value + Mean(ERROR)

= ASSESS + 56.43

Calculate the probability that the estimated market value is within $30,000 of the actual market value for a randomly drawn property. Do *not* make any assumptions not warranted by the data.

ROW	MARKET	ASSESS	AREA	ROW	MARKET	ASSESS	AREA
1	104.0	31.20	521	31	149.6	72.88	926
2	77.6	112.80	538	32	152.0	98.40	931
3	100.8	128.80	544	33	148.8	58.40	965
4	104.8	88.80	577	34	176.0	120.80	966
5	124.0	95.20	661	35	176.8	104.00	967
6	138.4	78.40	662	36	174.4	112.00	1011
7	145.6	91.20	677	37	153.6	104.00	1011
8	132.0	90.40	691	38	168.8	108.00	1024
9	149.6	112.00	694	39	161.6	100.80	1033
10	169.6	84.80	712	40	161.6	89.60	1040
11	131.2	86.40	721	41	174.4	120.00	1047
12	102.4	29.60	722	42	165.6	105.60	1051
13	139.2	104.80	743	43	158.4	80.80	1052
14	143.2	106.40	760	44	167.2	103.20	1056
15	134.4	88.80	767	45	179.2	116.80	1060
16	124.0	90.40	780	46	153.6	96.00	1060
17	156.8	89.60	787	47	174.4	91.20	1070
18	144.0	101.60	802	48	171.2	121.60	1075
19	139.2	59.20	814	49	162.4	96.80	1079
20	137.6	57.60	815	50	166.4	120.00	1100
21	156.0	112.80	825	51	171.2	126.40	1106
22	138.4	72.00	834	52	156.0	102.40	1138
23	142.4	102.40	838	53	167.2	117.60	1164
24	143.2	89.60	858	54	193.6	128.80	1171
25	158.4	103.20	883	55	159.2	68.00	1237
26	140.0	80.80	890	56	188.8	88.00	1249
27	150.4	92.80	899	57	180.8	94.40	1298
28	164.8	128.80	918	58	155.2	85.60	1435
29	124.8	83.20	920	59	189.6	124.00	1602
30	120.0	18.40	923	60	181.6	122.40	1804

PROCESSES AND STATISTICAL PROCESS CONTROL

This chapter will help you solve the following types of problems:

- The manager of a small printing company wants to know if the ratio of the cost of printing an order to the revenue from it has remained roughly stable in the recent past. How can she use the ratios for the last 119 orders to answer this question?

- Complaints had arisen at a walk-in clinic about increasing waiting times, especially in the afternoon. How can the office manager find out whether these complaints are well-founded?

5.1

INTRODUCTION

In the last chapter, you learned about cross-sectional studies, the normal distribution, and the model of a random variable. In this chapter, you will learn about simple time series models, the processes generating the data, and their statistical analyses. You will learn

- The method to determine if a time series and the process generating it are random

- How to use a *control chart,* a very useful tool for monitoring process quality

- A new tool for experimental design, *blocking*

- Some implications these statistical tools and methods have for management

You will see that the tools for cross-sectional analyses discussed in the previous chapter can be used to aid in the analysis of time series data if the time series is random.

5.2

THE DEFINITION OF A PROCESS

Although the terms *process* and *system* are often used interchangeably in this book, the term *process* is the more commonly used term in relation to the ideas described in this chapter. As introduced in Chapters 1 and 2, the definition of a process suggests that it is the role of managers to work *on* the process and of workers to work *in* it (Deming 1986). So it becomes the manager's job to guide and improve the process. In Chapter 2, you saw that a time series study (also called an *analytic* study) is often concerned with predicting the future behavior of a process. This chapter introduces some statistical tools for time series studies.

A process is a particular configuration to achieve an objective. It usually involves a series of steps. One process might be the production of wheels. Another might involve truck drivers picking up shipments, moving them through one or more truck terminals, and finally delivering them to the customer. The process is the whole combination of people, equipment, input materials, methods, and environment that work together to produce output (services or products). The total performance of the process—the quality of its output and its productive efficiency—depends on the way the process has been designed and built, and on the way it is operated.

Processes go on repeatedly. Both intermediate and final outcomes can be measured. In the trucking example, an intermediate result might be the amount of time a truck driver has to wait for loading or unloading at a terminal, and a final result might be the proportion of incomplete shipments. If information on the ongoing behavior of the process in its current state (the *state of the process*, for short) is gathered and analyzed correctly, it can also show if action is needed to improve the process.

When studying a process, we measure the variable of interest through time. The unit in a process may be defined in various ways. For example, when we are interested in the loading aspect of the trucking process, the units are successive trucks, and the variable of interest is "Waiting time for loading or unloading." Another aspect of interest might be the daily number of trucks waiting more than 30 minutes for loading and unloading. In this case, the units are successive days of the loading and unloading operation, and the variable of interest is "Number of trucks waiting more than 30 minutes."

Action on the process is directed toward the *future* and is taken to *prevent* the future production of a service or product that is out-of-specification. In the trucking example, the aim is to reduce the proportion of incomplete shipments.

On the other hand, **action on the output** is directed toward the *past* because it attempts to *detect* and correct problems after output already exists. In the trucking example, detecting and completing incomplete shipments would be action on the output of the system. Action on the output is a poor substitute for effective first-time process performance. Action should always be taken to improve the process itself.

5.3

THE SEQUENCE PLOT CONSIDERED FURTHER

This section examines simple time series with the sequence plot. It introduces the notion of a **random time series.** Let us consider an example of analyzing a process.[1]

EXAMPLE 5.1

A particular bendclip used in the automotive industry must have a diameter between 0.55 and 0.90 millimeter (mm). On a number of successive days, one clip was taken from the production line every half hour during production and its diameter was measured. Data for 40 bendclips are stored in ASCII file BENDCLIP.DAT.

Let us study the performance of the production process over time. This process consists of the people working on the line and the training they receive, the raw material used for the bendclips, the equipment available for production, the working environment (light conditions, noise level, cleanliness of the work site, etc.), and other factors. All these factors working together result in the output as measured by the bendclip diameter. In this example, the units are the bendclips, measured every half hour, and the response variable is diameter, a quantitative variable.

Figure 5.1 shows the raw data in time-series order, and Figure 5.2 gives a sequence plot of the 40 bendclip diameter values. Such a time series plot is useful both for improving the process and for predicting future values.

FIGURE 5.1 Bendclip Diameter Values: Raw Data (read row by row)

0.70	0.71	0.68	0.66	0.84	0.73	0.84	0.76	0.74	0.63	0.77
0.80	0.78	0.70	0.75	0.62	0.72	0.67	0.77	0.67	0.72	0.77
0.65	0.86	0.81	0.60	0.76	0.73	0.73	0.72	0.75	0.81	0.67
0.75	0.69	0.72	0.74	0.74	0.72	0.79				

---

[1]This is a modified example from *Continuing Process Control and Process Capability Improvement,* published by the Statistical Methods Office, Operations Support Staffs, Ford Motor Company, September 1985.

FIGURE 5.2 Bendclip Diameter Values: Sequence Plot

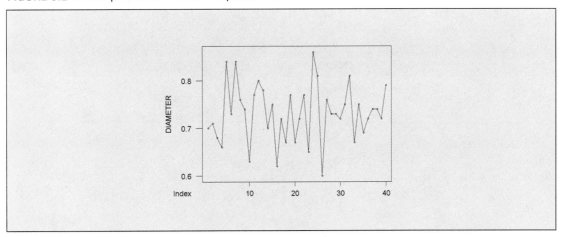

random series

The main point of displaying the diameter values in time-series order is to illustrate that this time series is a *random* sequence *over time;* that is, there is no pattern in this time series, and no information would be lost if the order of the observations were arbitrarily rearranged. For now, such randomness implies that the level of the time series does not change over time and that there is no pattern in the way the observations lie above or below this level. As you examine sequence plots in the future, your eye will improve in judging the randomness of a series. We will present some statistical summaries and other graphs to aid you in determining if a particular time series is random.

Consider first the sequence plots of some decidedly nonrandom time series in Figure 5.3. In the top two sequences, there is no general level and the sequence is either moving up or down. In a *level shift,* the left (earlier) and right (later) parts of the sequence fluctuate around different averages. A cycle may be due to a seasonal effect, such as a monthly one, where values for the same month tend to be close together across different years. Increasing dispersion can arise when more *noise* or imprecision is gradually introduced into the system. *Meandering* occurs when observations close together in time also tend to be close together in value. Meandering differs from a cycle in several ways; for instance, in a cycle the high point is reached at constant intervals, whereas a meandering sequence may exhibit its high points at varying intervals. Finally, in an *oscillating* sequence, observations close together in time tend to be far apart in value. To identify this kind of sequence, draw a line representing the mean on the sequence plot. For an oscillating sequence, the line connecting successive observations crosses the mean much more frequently than would happen in a random series.

When encountering random time series for the first time, many people think that randomness implies "many fluctuations." This is not the case. The next section gives a more precise idea of how many fluctuations to expect from a random series.

FIGURE 5.3 Some Sequence Plots for Nonrandom Time Series

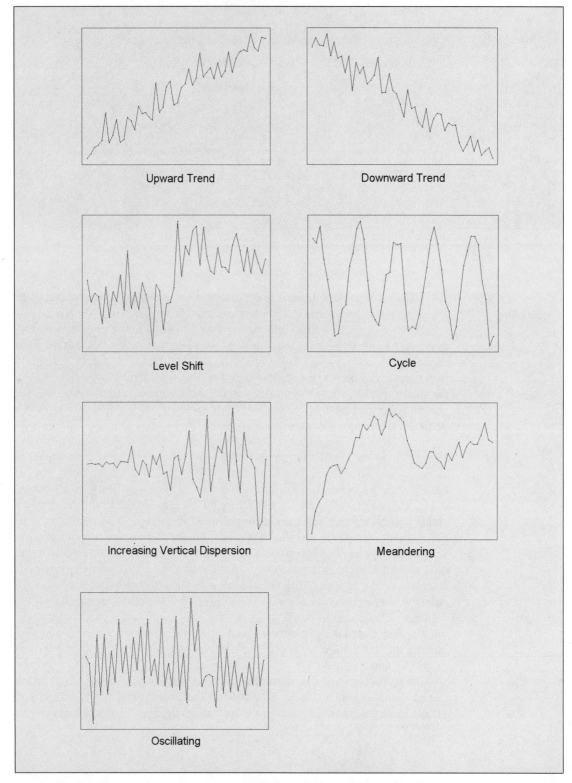

Upward Trend

Downward Trend

Level Shift

Cycle

Increasing Vertical Dispersion

Meandering

Oscillating

If you add a line representing the mean level to any graph in Figure 5.3, you will notice that the deviations from this line follow a definite pattern. For example, for an upward trend, these deviations tend at first to be negative, then get closer to 0, and finally become positive. Unless it is known that the process generating the data has undergone a change, we will forecast the next observation to follow the pattern of the sequence in question.

randomness

For the time being, we define *randomness* to consist of absence of any of these and other nonrandom patterns. It implies that the time sequence of values could be arbitrarily rearranged without losing any information. Figure 5.4 presents a few random sequences. Covering up all but 10 to 15 observations of any series, you will note that short random sequences often suggest deterministic patterns. As you uncover more observations, randomness becomes apparent as it becomes clear that there is in fact no deterministic pattern underlying the process.

FIGURE 5.4
Sequence Plots for
Random Sequences

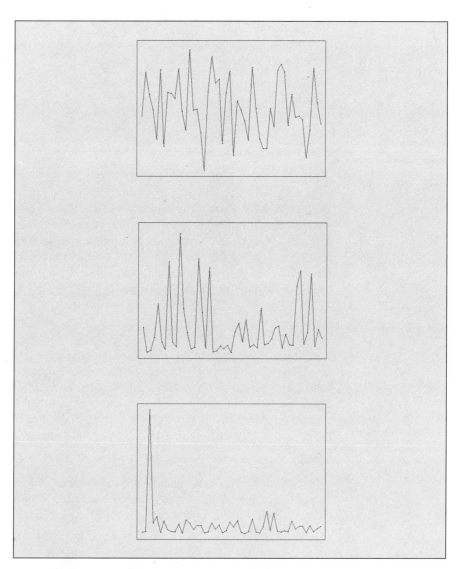

Many time series we observe are just short segments taken from much longer sequences. In principle, many more observations could have been observed before the one with which the observed sequence begins, and many observations could be observed after the one with which the observed sequence ends. We are typically interested in the process generating the overall sequence (of which the observed sequence is just a short segment). When we judge the observed sequence to be random, it is often reasonable to also judge the overall sequence to be random if we

random process   expect unchanged process conditions. We will then say that the *process* generating the data is *random*. For example, if we say that the process generating the bendclip diameters is random, we imply that, *over time,*

- The diameter values tend to vary around their mean value.

- The deviations from the mean value follow no deterministic pattern: they vary randomly around the mean.

The next section introduces the *runs test,* which provides supplementary information about the randomness of a time series.

5.4

THE RUNS TEST FOR RANDOMNESS

The *runs count* is a statistical summary measure that we use in the runs test, which gives additional information about the randomness of a series. To compute it, we first note whether each observation in a series is above (+) or below (−) a reference level, such as the mean (which is the default in Minitab). Then we create a new series consisting only of the plus and minus signs. A *run* is a string of consecutive pluses or minuses. A simple example is

$$+ + - + + + - - +$$

where there are five runs: $++$, $-$, $+++$, $--$, and $+$.

Figure 5.5 illustrates the runs count for the sequence of bendclip diameter values. The sequence plot in Figure 5.5 includes the center line at the mean, 0.732. Below the sequence plot you will see a string of plus and minus signs, indicating whether an observation is above (+) or below (−) the mean. The symbol "^" marks the beginning of each new run. Finally, note the cumulative count of the runs, in which $\frac{1}{6}$ means 16 and $\frac{2}{4}$ means 24.

In a **runs test,** it is the number of *runs* that is of primary interest, not the numbers of values that fall above and below the mean. But if the number of observations above and below the mean is about equal, and if we are looking at a truly random se-

FIGURE 5.5 Sequence Plot of Bendclip Data Illustrating the Runs Count

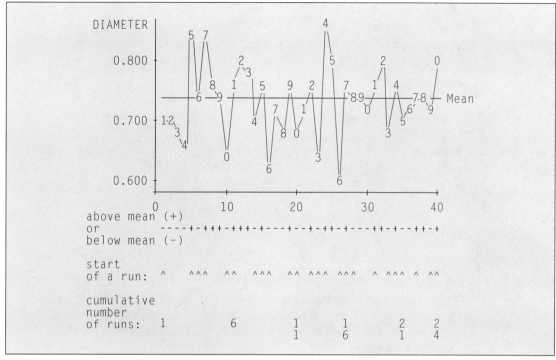

quence, then the expected run length is about 2.[2] Thus, if the bendclip diameter series is random, the **expected number of runs** is about $\frac{40}{2} = 20$. Recall from the runs count in Figure 5.5 that the **observed number of runs** is 24.

Figure 5.6 shows the Minitab output for the runs test: The *observed number of runs* around the mean, denoted "K" in Figure 5.6, is also 24, and the *expected number of runs* is 20.95 (using an exact formula for the case when the numbers of observations above and below the mean are not equal). For this application, we can judge the observed and expected numbers of runs to be "fairly close," so we can conclude that the runs test supports a visual impression of randomness for the bendclip diameter time series. This judgment is based on the *p*-value (also called the **statistical significance**) of the runs test, which Minitab reports to be 0.3275. *Note:* We will ignore the last line

p-value, statistical significance

Cannot reject at alpha = 0.05

whenever it appears in this book.

---

[2]Strictly speaking, the expected number of runs is 2 only if the numbers of observations above and below the mean are equal. When the numbers of observations above and below the mean are not equal, then computation of the expected number of runs is somewhat more complicated, but this computation need not concern us here.

FIGURE 5.6 Runs Test for Bendclip Diameter Data

```
DIAMETER

K = 0.7318

The observed no. of runs = 24
The expected no. of runs = 20.9500
19 Observations above K  21 below
          The test is significant at 0.3275
          Cannot reject at alpha = 0.05
```

Note: **This book will ignore this last line of the Minitab output for a runs test whenever it appears. We use the rule of thumb on this page instead.**

We use the following rule of thumb for the *p*-value:

> The ***p*-value** (or **statistical significance**) is a statistical measure of how close the observed number of runs is to the number of runs expected for a random series; it is always between 0 and 1. For sample sizes above 20, use the following rule of thumb:
> If the *p*-value is
>
> - **Greater than 0.10:** The runs test does not call the series' randomness into question (in this case, we say that the runs test is *not significant*),
> - **Less than 0.01:** The runs test suggests a *non*random time series pattern (we say that the runs test is *significant*)
> - **Between 0.01 and 0.10:** The runs test is *inconclusive.*

When the sample size is 20 or less, the results from the runs test are unreliable. We must then exclusively rely on visual inspection of the sequence plot. If the sample size is greater than 20 and the runs test is inconclusive, then we must rely on other diagnostic information, including visual inspection and some other diagnostic tools described in Chapters 11 and 12.

In Figure 5.6, the *statistical significance* is 0.3275, so the runs test *does not call into question* the randomness of this time series: We can attribute the difference between the observed number of runs and the number of runs expected under randomness to chance variation alone. When this is so, we also say that "the runs test is *not* significant" because it does *not* call randomness into question. We conclude that the bendclip data come from a random process.

Before proceeding, a few remarks are in order to clarify why the observed number of runs does not have to *equal* the expected number of runs for a random time series. Consider a fair coin, for which the probability of heads is 50%. If you were to flip a fair coin 20 times, you would expect 10 heads. If you were to observe 8 heads only in 20 flips of a coin, you probably would not question your belief that the coin is fair. But if you were to observe 2 heads only in 20 flips, you would question the fairness of the coin. As long as the observed number of heads is close to the expected number, a prior belief of the coin's fairness is not called into question.

Fairness of a coin can be judged by the number of heads. One way to judge the randomness of a time series is by the number of runs. If the observed number of runs is *close* to the expected number, given randomness, the randomness of a time series is not called into question. A statistical measure of this closeness is the *p*-value, whose computation will not be discussed in this book, but whose interpretation is simple with the above rule of thumb.

When examining a time series of a process, we use the runs test to choose between two possible *states* for the process: (1) the process is random, and (2) the process is not random. One of these states *must* be true, but it is typically not possible to know for sure—the runs test and all other sample data can give only an incomplete answer. When there is a difference between the expected number of runs for a random process and the observed number of runs, this difference can either be due to chance (if the process is random) or due to the process not being random. Our judgment of randomness or nonrandomness is always subject to error, but the rule of thumb regarding the *p*-value tries to keep the possibility of error small. The following table summarizes these observations:

		State of the process is. . .	
		Random	Nonrandom
Decision based on runs test	Do not call randomness into question.	Correct decision	Erroneous decision
	Call randomness into question.	Erroneous decision	Correct decision
	Result is inconclusive.	—	—

Let us briefly mention two of the nonrandom sequences displayed in Figure 5.3. In a meandering sequence, where observations close together in time tend to be close in value, the sequence tends to persist above or below the center line longer than a random sequence would. So, for a meandering sequence, the number of runs would be less (or, equivalently, the average run length would be longer). For an oscillating sequence, the reverse would be true.

It may be tempting to base your analysis of randomness on the runs test alone, but it is dangerous to do so. Your judgment of randomness or nonrandomness should primarily be informed by visual inspection of the sequence plot for the time series. The runs test can only *supplement* this visual impression. A single number like the runs count can capture only limited aspects of the data; it never tells the whole story. For example, the runs test is not good at detecting increasing dispersion around a constant level (see Figure 5.3). It can also happen that a particular nonrandom series displays offsetting patterns of nonrandomness that lead to a runs count suggesting randomness. In addition to the runs test, you should always investigate the actual sequence plot for shifts in level, increasing dispersion, and other nonrandom patterns. In your judgment, you should use other information you may have about the process.

stable process   A random process is often called a **stable process.** In this book we use the terms *random process* and *stable process* interchangeably.

Figures 4.20 and 4.26 presented flow charts for cross-sectional studies. Figure 5.7 presents a corresponding flow chart for time series studies and relates it to cross-sectional studies. Note that, when a random process model is adequate, its analysis is the same as the analysis of a cross-sectional study. When the random

FIGURE 5.7 Flow Chart for Making Probabilistic Statements

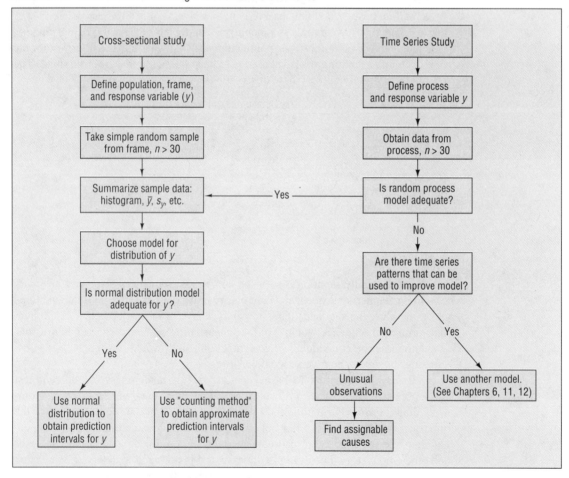

model is not appropriate, an alternative time series model has to be found. When unusual observations are present, any assignable causes for them should be identified.

5.5

NORMALITY VS. RANDOM PROCESS

A *random* process can be analyzed with statistical tools that are similar to the tools for cross-sectional studies introduced in Chapter 4. Data from a *nonrandom* process should *never* be treated as cross-sectional; it is essential that the nature of the non-randomness be described.

Since a random sequence contains no information in its time order, we can ignore the time order and treat the data from a random process *as if* they came from a cross-sectional study.

We concluded in the last section that the bendclip diameter data were generated by a random process. Ignoring the time series order of the observations, we can summarize them in a histogram (see Figure 5.8). We can summarize the 40 observations by computing their mean (0.732), standard deviation (0.060), and range (0.26). Note that the distribution of values in the histogram centers around the mean

FIGURE 5.8 Analysis of Bendclip Diameter Data, continued

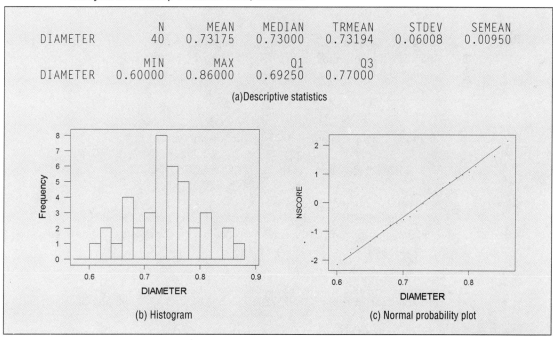

	N	MEAN	MEDIAN	TRMEAN	STDEV	SEMEAN
DIAMETER	40	0.73175	0.73000	0.73194	0.06008	0.00950

	MIN	MAX	Q1	Q3
DIAMETER	0.60000	0.86000	0.69250	0.77000

(a) Descriptive statistics

(b) Histogram

(c) Normal probability plot

FIGURE 5.9

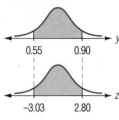

and falls off quickly as we move away from the mean. All observations are well within an interval extending 3 standard deviations around the mean. A normal distribution appears to well approximate the data, and this is supported by the normal probability plot, also given in Figure 5.8.

In Example 5.1 (p. 160), it was mentioned that bendclip diameters must be between 0.55 mm and 0.90 mm. Since the normal distribution approximates their data distribution well, we can use their mean and standard deviation, 0.732 mm and 0.060 mm, to standardize 0.55 mm and 0.90 mm. The corresponding standardized values are $(0.55 - 0.732)/0.06 = -3.03$ and $(0.90 - 0.732)/0.060 = 2.80$. Using Table 4.1 or the *Calc ▸ Probability Distributions ▸ Normal* menu in Minitab, we find that the corresponding quantiles of the normal distribution are 0.0013 and 0.9974, so a fraction of

$$0.9974 - 0.0013 = 0.9961$$

or 99.61% of the bendclip diameters can be expected to meet the specifications, as long as the conditions underlying the presently random process remain unchanged.

prediction interval

We can also obtain a *prediction interval* within which a given percentage of future bendclip diameters can be expected to fall. In general, the prediction interval formula for a *random* process is the same as in Section 4.5 (p. 129),

$$(\text{Process Mean}) \pm z(\text{Process Standard Deviation})$$

or

$$\mu_y \pm z\, \sigma_y$$

FIGURE 5.10

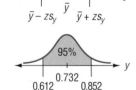

where z, which determines the proportion of values in the interval, is obtained from the normal distribution, and μ_y and σ_y must be estimated from the corresponding sample statistics. Thus, the approximate formula for the prediction interval is

$$\bar{y} \pm z\, s_y$$

For the bendclip example, a 95% prediction interval is[3]

$$0.732 \pm 2(0.060) \qquad \text{or} \qquad 0.732 \pm 0.120$$

or from 0.612 to 0.852.

Thus, 95% of bendclip diameters can be expected to fall between 0.61 mm and 0.85 mm, as long as the conditions underlying the process remain unchanged.

---

[3]Here and elsewhere in this book, we associate $z = 2$ with a 95% interval. Of course, the exact z-value for a 95% interval is $z = 1.96$. But the value $z = 2$ is easier to remember, and it is sufficiently accurate for most applications.

Our approach to finding the prediction interval and the percentage of diameters within specifications was justified after carrying out two consecutive steps:

1. We examined the process for randomness, and judged it to be random, so the data could be treated as if they were cross-sectional.

2. We examined the histogram and judged it to be normal.

When the process is judged random and the histogram of the sample is normal with a given mean and standard deviation, then each future bendclip diameter can be thought of being randomly drawn from a normal distribution with that mean and standard deviation—as long as the process remains unchanged.

Randomness is a feature of time series in which there is random variation *over time* around the center line. If a time series is random, then the time series order of the observations can be ignored for further analysis, in particular, for prediction purposes. Normality describes some frequency distributions when data are cross-sectional or can be treated as such.

There are many random processes whose histograms are *not* normal. Consider the following example.

EXAMPLE 5.2

A printing company in a large metropolitan area has been serving the advertising industry for more than 30 years.[4] The company mainly produces specialty items, such as promotion materials and manuals. A study was done to examine the ratio of paper costs to the total selling price. Three questions were addressed by the study:

1. Has there been a change recently in the ratio of paper costs to total selling price?

2. Is this ratio close to the industry rule of thumb of 1:3?

3. To what extent do this ratio and the total selling price correlate?

It was expected that the ratio was stable over time. It was also expected that the median ratio was less than the 1:3 rule and that there was considerable variation in the ratio from one order to another. Finally, the relationship between the ratio and the total selling price was expected to be weak.

Data on two variables were collected on all 119 printing orders produced from September 1988 to August 1989: (1) selling price for the order, and (2) cost of paper (both given in dollars). The data are stored in ASCII file PAPER.DAT.

Let us concentrate on the first two questions. Figure 5.11 gives a sequence plot of the variable RATIO, the ratio of paper cost to selling price. Visual inspection of the sequence plot suggests randomness, which is also supported by the runs test.

Since the process yielding the ratio of paper cost to selling price can be judged to be random, the ratio data can be treated as cross-sectional. Figure 5.12 displays a histogram and a normal probability plot; the ratio data are positively skewed. Although we can say that the ratios vary randomly around their sample

---

[4]The name of the company has been omitted to protect confidentiality. The data are real.

FIGURE 5.11 Printing Company Data

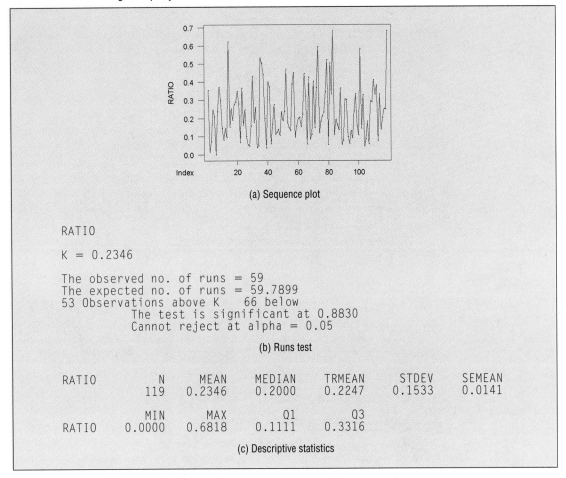

```
RATIO

K = 0.2346

The observed no. of runs = 59
The expected no. of runs = 59.7899
53 Observations above K    66 below
         The test is significant at 0.8830
         Cannot reject at alpha = 0.05
```

(b) Runs test

RATIO	N	MEAN	MEDIAN	TRMEAN	STDEV	SEMEAN
	119	0.2346	0.2000	0.2247	0.1533	0.0141

RATIO	MIN	MAX	Q1	Q3
	0.0000	0.6818	0.1111	0.3316

(c) Descriptive statistics

FIGURE 5.12 Printing Company Data, continued

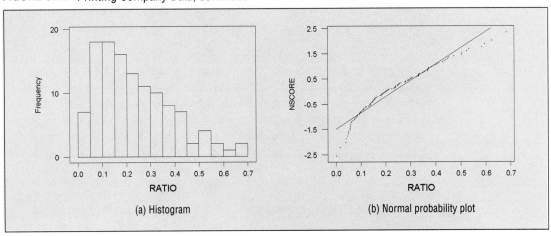

(a) Histogram   (b) Normal probability plot

FIGURE 5.13 Printing Company Data Listed in Ascending Order of Magnitude (Read Row by Row)

0.000	0.014	0.037	0.038	0.045	0.047	0.049	0.054	0.054	0.055
0.057	0.057	0.058	0.060	0.065	0.073	0.074	0.078	0.080	0.084
0.085	0.090	0.094	0.095	0.097	0.100	0.106	0.106	0.110	0.111
0.111	0.118	0.121	0.130	0.133	0.136	0.137	0.137	0.142	0.142
0.145	0.147	0.147	0.151	0.153	0.155	0.156	0.156	0.160	0.166
0.166	0.177	0.180	0.183	0.184	0.187	0.190	0.194	0.198	0.200
0.202	0.206	0.210	0.213	0.224	0.233	0.235	0.237	0.238	0.239
0.246	0.247	0.250	0.252	0.253	0.260	0.276	0.278	0.280	0.288
0.289	0.294	0.298	0.301	0.305	0.322	0.329	0.330	0.331	0.331
0.333	0.345	0.348	0.355	0.365	0.367	0.368	0.371	0.371	0.381
0.388	0.400	0.404	0.411	0.426	0.432	0.440	0.445	0.451	0.471
0.503	0.503	0.522	0.531	0.583	0.595	0.623	0.682	0.682	

$\frac{91}{119} = 76\%$

mean, given to be 0.23 in Figure 5.11, with sample standard deviation 0.15, we *cannot* use the normal table in conjunction with this sample mean and standard deviation to compute the proportion of ratios less than 1:3.

counting method

To obtain the proportion of ratios less than 1:3, we must use a cruder approach and obtain the proportion of ratios less than 1:3 by counting the data sorted by size of RATIO, given in Figure 5.13. This proportion is 91 in 119 or 76%. If the process remains unchanged, we can expect about 76% of ratios to be less than the industry rule of thumb in the future.

We can now answer the first two questions given in Example 5.2.

1. The process is random (stable), so there has not been a recent change in the ratio.

2. The ratio is not close to the 1:3 rule of thumb. There is considerable variation. Furthermore, about 76% of ratios are less than 1:3.

When a process is *not* judged to be random, the time series order of the observations cannot be ignored and the data cannot be treated as if they were cross-sectional. The meaning of a histogram is then unclear.

> When we judge a process to be *nonrandom,* it is pointless to obtain a histogram to check for normality. We must then describe the nature of the non-randomness.

Chapters 6, 11 and 12 will be helpful in analyzing a nonrandom process.

5.6

THE CONTROL CHART

The **control chart,** an important tool for statistical process control, derives its name from Shewhart (1931), who states that a process "will be said to be controlled when, through the use of past experience, we can predict, at least within limits, how the [process] may be expected to vary in the future." A controlled process is said to be *in statistical control.* Using the terminology introduced earlier, we say that such a process is *random* or *stable,* which are the terms used in the remainder of this book. Management implications of a stable process are discussed in greater detail in Section 5.9.

i chart

Control charts are used for *monitoring* a process. Ideally, you should monitor any process with a control chart for one or more quality characteristics. There are many types of control chart. This section introduces the *i* **chart,** the control chart for individual observations. Chapter 8 discusses other control charts.

The *i* chart, a slight variation on the sequence plot, makes use of some properties of frequency distributions. The *i* chart for the bendclip diameter data is given in Figure 5.14. It is only slightly different from the sequence plot in Figure 5.2: In addition to the center line at the mean (which Minitab labels $\overline{\overline{X}}$), there are two other lines, the *upper control limit* (**UCL**) and the *lower control limit* (**LCL**). The UCL is at a value 3 standard deviations above the mean, and the LCL is at a value 3 standard deviations below the mean. The 3-standard-deviation limits are widely used in practice since the bulk of the data can be expected to be within 3 standard deviations of the mean regardless of the shape of the frequency distribution. In some applications, limits based on multiples other than 3 may be preferred, but the consequences should be studied carefully. In Figure 5.14, the UCL is drawn at $0.73 + 3(0.06) = 0.91$, and the LCL is drawn at $0.73 - 3(0.06) = 0.55$.

A **random process** exhibits a control chart in which the bulk of the observations lie between the lower control limit (LCL) and the upper control limit (UCL). Furthermore, the way in which successive measurements vary around the center line is completely patternless (that is, random).

The histogram of data from a random process may or may not resemble a normal distribution. If it does, and if the estimates of the process mean and standard deviation are accurate, then about 99.7% of the observations should fall between the UCL and the LCL on a control chart based on 3-standard-deviation limits.

The *i* chart in Figure 5.14 suggests that the process generating the bendclip data is stable.

Summarizing, a process is judged to be stable if

- Visual inspection of the sequence plot suggests randomness
- The visual impression of randomness is supported by the runs test
- *All* observations are within the upper and lower control limits

Often the histogram of observations from a random process is approximately normal. This can be checked with a normal probability plot.

We say that a stable process implies the operation of a stable set of chance causes. As long as the process continues to be stable, there is no reason for management to tinker with the process in the hope of making it better. In fact, tinkering with a stable process is likely to be counterproductive: Benign neglect is called for. A stable process can, of course, be improved, but improvement requires more than

FIGURE 5.14
i Chart for Bendclip
Diameter Data

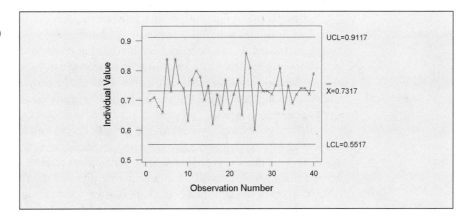

superficial observation of the current results of the process: Planned experimentation is needed.

If a process is deemed to be stable and likely to remain so, we can extrapolate
the UCL, mean $\overline{\overline{X}}$, and LCL into the future for prediction: The observations will
continue to vary randomly about the past mean level and will almost always stay
within the control limits, just as they have in the past. This type of prediction can
be made for the process generating the bendclip diameter values.

5.7

MODELING

The last few sections developed the statistical *model* of a stable process. As indicated in Section 4.8 (p. 144), a model is *always* a simplification of the real-life situation; the degree of detail in the model depends on the problem to be solved. We
can summarize the model of a stable process as follows:

The **model of a stable process** has two premises:

1. There is a constant level around which observations vary over time.

2. The observations vary randomly around the constant level.

This model can be simply represented by the following equation:

Actual Observation = Mean + Random Deviation

= Mean + Residual

or

$$y \qquad = \quad \mu_y \; + \quad \epsilon$$

where ϵ has mean 0 and standard deviation σ_y. Just as in Section 4.8, the term
residual is usually used instead of "random deviation."

In many, but not all, applications the residual ϵ follows a normal distribution.

---

process parameter

The parameters μ_y and σ_y characterize the process, and therefore they are called *process parameters*. These process parameters are typically not known. They can be estimated by the mean and standard deviation obtained from a sample from a *random* process. This estimation step is similar to estimating *population* parameters for cross-sectional studies in Chapter 4: Obtain a simple random sample from the population frame, and estimate the population parameters from the corresponding sample statistics.

You should carefully contrast the model of a random (or stable) process with the model of a random variable, discussed in Section 4.8. One of the major differences is that a process is *judged* random if it appears random after careful study (for instance, after the examination of a sequence plot and the runs test). When such a process appears random, however, there is always the possibility that a *nonrandom* time series pattern was not revealed by the statistical tools employed. In the model of a random variable, on the other hand, the sequence of observations is chosen by simple random sampling from the population frame. Therefore the observations are random *by design,* and the order in which the observations were drawn is immaterial and can be ignored.

Saying that a process is random is the same as saying that a stable system of chance causes is at work generating units over time. If this stable system of chance causes can be expected to persist, then we can use the model of a random process for prediction:

> Each future unit's value can be predicted to be the mean plus or minus random variation due to chance causes.

stable process

We cannot predict the actual amount of random variation—that is, the size of the residual—for each unit. But we can describe our uncertainty regarding its size by the *same* frequency distribution for *each* future unit; that is, *the process is called* **stable** *since the distribution of values remains unchanged over time.* This distribution is often well described by a normal distribution, but it need not be. (For an illustration of a stable process when a normal distribution describes the random variation around the mean, see Figure 5.16 on page 180.)

In many applications, the model of a stable process is a useful way to conceptually describe the process. We can never observe a process for the entire length of its life. Thus, we must take a sample from the process to estimate its parameters, μ_y and σ_y, and other features. For example, we took a sample of 40 bendclip diameters from the process producing bendclip diameters. We used the control chart and judged the process from which the sample was taken to be stable. Finally, we used the sample to estimate the process mean μ_y by the sample mean, 0.73, and the process standard deviation σ_y by the sample standard deviation, 0.06.

We judge a process to be random if

- Visual inspection of the sequence plot suggests constant level and random variation around it

- The visual impression is supported by the runs test

- *All* observations are within the upper and lower control limits

As we discuss further examples throughout this book, your ability to visually judge randomness will improve. We will discuss additional diagnostic statistical tools to help with this judgment.

If *any* observation is outside the control limits, it is important that you carefully check whether there was any special cause at work that might explain why

treatment of outliers

this observation was an *outlier*. If you can find such a special cause for an outlier, perhaps you can prevent the special cause from happening again. In that case, you might be able to discard or correct the outlier before proceeding with further analysis. After a special cause has been removed, however, it is generally advisable to collect new information to ensure that the modified process is stable.

If, after careful study, you cannot find a special cause for an outlier, then it *might* be reasonable for you to judge the outlier to be due to the stable system of chance causes: Once in a while, a large deviation is to be expected from a process in which only a stable system of chance causes is at work. For example, suppose the data are random *and* come from a normal distribution: In the long run, 99.7% of the observations will be within the control limits, but 0.3% will fall outside.

If you judge the process to be stable, you should retain the outlier and proceed with the analysis. You should keep in mind, however, that, particularly in small samples, outliers can seriously affect the sample statistics, such as $\bar{y}$ and s.

Many processes are not quite stable in that there may be a very slight time series pattern at work. Nevertheless, the process may be usefully described as stable in that its future behavior can be successfully predicted with this model.

The notion of random variation is important for the model of a stable process. Some people argue that there is no random variation in principle and that all variation is caused[5], but that the variation can be treated as if it were random when there is a large number of relatively independent small causes at work. Regardless of one's philosophical position here, the model of a random process is often useful when it serves descriptive purposes or leads to reliable predictions.

5.8

USE OF THE TERM *RANDOM*

Section 2.8 (p. 33) reviewed two other uses of the term *random*—*random sampling* and *randomization*. We noted that both random sampling and randomization try to achieve the same goal: to ensure the absence of biases by impartial selection of units. In this chapter we have encountered the term "random" in a third way: in a *random process*. In a random process, successive measurements of variables are generated as if they were obtained from a particular frequency distribution by random sampling.

---

[5]In other words, "God does not roll dice." —A. Einstein.

5.9

STATISTICAL PROCESS CONTROL: IMPLICATIONS FOR MANAGEMENT

The last few sections introduced the model of a stable process. This section discusses some of the implications this model has for management. As Deming (1986) points out, it is management's job to work *on* the process and ensure that the process is stable and continually improved. Deming's text is an excellent source for more information on the material discussed in this section.

If the conditions underlying a process do not change, a stable process can be expected to behave in the future as it did in the past. If these conditions *do* change, changes are likely to become apparent on the control chart. For example, one or more points may fall outside the control limits or a nonrandom pattern may develop. Either case signals the need for attention, perhaps to locate a special or "assignable" cause that can be corrected.

When the control chart indicates that the process is stable, it gives an indication of the capabilities of the process because the mean, standard deviation, and distributional shape have *predictive* value. The upper and lower control limits are roughly the limits within which the measurements are likely to fall in the future.

process capability vs. specification limit

These control limits are to be distinguished from the *specification* or *tolerance* limits, which indicate what we would *like* the process to be doing. The control limits are computed from the data. In a sense, the control chart is the process speaking to us. Specification limits, on the other hand, are set by judgment and come from outside the process. If the control limits are wider than what we would like them to be, the underlying process must be improved. Improvement requires a thorough understanding of the process; this can be obtained only by careful study of the process and the factors that influence it. If the process is stable, simple exhortations to improve its capability are usually futile. Merely tinkering with the process is likely to do more harm than good. Planned experimentation is needed to improve a stable process.

When a process is not stable, substantial effort, guided by examination and analysis of sequence plots, may be needed to make it stable.

common, special, and structural causes

In dealing with the causes underlying variation in a process, it is useful to distinguish among *common, special,* and *structural* causes. **Common** causes are the myriad of ever-present sources of variation that contribute in varying degrees to relatively small, random deviations in a unit's value from the process mean. Process variation is the collective effect of all common causes, since it defines the amount of variation inherent in the process. When only common causes of variation are present, the process is said to be random or stable; a one-number summary for the magnitude of their combined effect is the process standard deviation, σ_y. The common causes behave like a constant system of chance causes; they operate on every unit and are attributable to the process, not to one person or a special event. A few examples of common causes are given in Figure 5.15.

Special causes are any factors that sporadically cause variation over and above that caused by the constant system of common chance causes. Often, special

FIGURE 5.15
Some Examples of
Common Causes

Poor design of product or of service.

Poor training and instruction, and poor supervision.

Incoming materials not suited to the requirements.

Procedures not suited to the requirements.

Machines out of order or not suited to the requirements.

Uncomfortable working conditions, e.g., poor lighting and ventilation, unnecessary dirt, awkward handling of materials.

Humidity not suited to the process, vibration.

Shift of management's emphasis from quantity to quality, back and forth, without understanding how to achieve quality.

Failure to measure the effects of common causes, and to reduce them.
SOURCE: Deming (1986), p. 336f.

causes lead to an extreme point in the data. Special causes are also called *assignable,* because the variation they induce can be tracked down and assigned to an identifiable source. Until all special causes of variation are identified and corrected, they will continue to affect the process output in unpredictable ways so that the process *cannot* be considered stable. Special causes are specific to, for instance, a particular worker, local condition, or machine. They can be discovered by examining control charts. Some quality control practitioners prefer the term *special cause charts* for control charts because they are useful for "identifying instances where a special cause has occurred and trying to prevent its reoccurrence" (B. Joiner, *Quality Progress,* January 1988, p. 31). Points outside the control limits *and* points within the control limits that are not in random sequence are good starting points for identifying special causes. A few examples of special causes are malfunctioning machinery, use of the wrong raw material, and accidents.

Finally, **structural** causes lead to regular, systematic changes in output. Long-term trends and seasonal variation are examples. Chapters 9 through 12 discuss how to incorporate structural causes into the model.

Figure 5.16 depicts the effects of common causes and special causes, and it shows that prediction is not possible in the presence of special causes.

When special causes are present (so that the process is not stable), or when the control limits of a stable process are too wide (so that the process is not capable of meeting the specification limits), actions are required to remove variation due to special or common causes. Two types of actions typically are required: *local actions* and *actions on the process.*

local action

action on process

Local actions ("tinkering") are usually required to eliminate special causes of variation. They can usually be taken by people close to the process (that is, those who work *in* the process). **Actions on the process** are usually required to reduce variation due to common causes. They almost always require management action for correction because a particular worker can do nothing about causes common to everybody. Although management is usually responsible for correcting common

FIGURE 5.16 Effects of Common and Special Causes

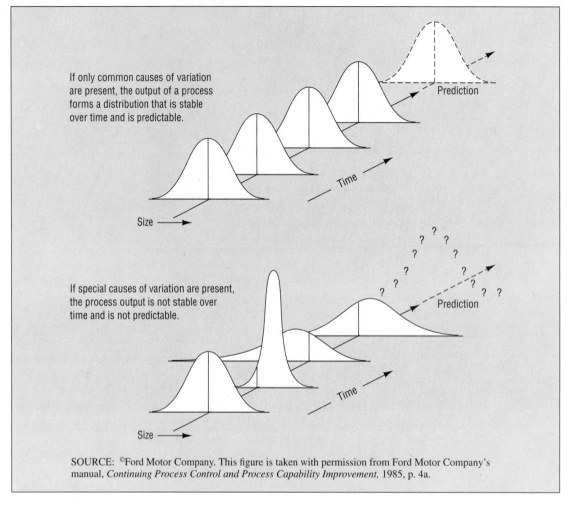

If only common causes of variation are present, the output of a process forms a distribution that is stable over time and is predictable.

Prediction

Time

Size

If special causes of variation are present, the process output is not stable over time and is not predictable.

? ? ?
? ?
? ?
? ?
? Prediction
? ? ?

Time

Size

SOURCE: ©Ford Motor Company. This figure is taken with permission from Ford Motor Company's manual, *Continuing Process Control and Process Capability Improvement,* 1985, p. 4a.

local action ↔ **special cause**

action on process ↔ **common cause**

causes, other people directly connected with the process are sometimes in a better position to identify these causes and pass them on to management for correction. It has been estimated that about 10% of all process problems can be corrected by local actions, but that the remaining 90% require actions on the process; that is, they require action by management.[6]

Two types of mistakes can be made with respect to common and special causes:

1. Ascribing a variation or a mistake to a special cause, when in fact it is due to common causes

---

[6]These estimates are given, e.g., by J. M. Juran and W. E. Deming.

2. Ascribing a variation or a mistake to common causes, when in fact it is due to a special cause

The first mistake usually results in overadjustment. A common example of the second mistake is not to look for a special cause. There is, of course, no hope of avoiding both mistakes all the time. The control chart with control limits set 3 standard deviations from the mean is a reasonable guide to balancing both mistakes in many circumstances.

We cannot predict the performance of a process that is not stable. We do not know its capability and, in particular, whether it can meet the specifications. We must first stabilize the process by detecting and eliminating special causes of variation.

When a process is stable, its future behavior is predictable in that the distribution of values is known. Common causes are then the only sources of variation. "But a [stable state] is not a natural state for a. . . process. It is a state of achievement, arrived at by elimination, one by one, by determined effort, of special causes of excessive variation" (Deming, *Interfaces,* August 1975, p. 5). Of course, a stable process does not imply that there are no defectives. Process capability is determined by the total variation that comes from common causes, and it can be used to assess whether customer expectations can be met. As long as the process remains stable, it will continue to produce the same proportion of out-of-specification output. Only a stable process can be the basis for continuing improvement, with output becoming more and more uniform.

When a system is stable, as evidenced by a satisfactory control chart, there is danger in tinkering with the system and overcontrolling it by acting on the remaining ups and downs. This usually leads to worse performance than if the stable process were left alone.

Control charts can be used in many processes throughout service and manufacturing organizations. Figure 5.17 lists a few situations for which control charts would be appropriate.

Summarizing, there are many benefits to using control charts:

- Operators or clerks at the job station can use control charts for monitoring a process to decide when action should or should not be taken.

- The capability of a stable process is predictable—the distributions of quality characteristics remain nearly constant hour after hour, day after day. Control charts can be used to determine whether customer specifications can be met.

- Control charts provide a common language for discussing process performance, such as between different stations in the process, or between supplier and user.

- Control charts can be used to distinguish between common and special causes of variation in order to suggest whether local or management action is needed.

- When a control chart indicates that a process is stable, the performance of the process can be improved by reducing common cause variation. This can lead to higher quality, lower unit costs, and higher effective capacity.

FIGURE 5.17
Examples of
Characteristics for
Which a Control
Chart Can Be Used

Daily number of personnel out sick or otherwise absent

Time taken for supplier to notify automotive company of failure of power train or chassis engineering, number of such failures per month

Daily number of errors in filling parts orders for dealers in an automotive company's parts and service division

Time to process travel expense in an accounting division

Number of computer sign-on calls in a product engineering office that give busy signals

Number of times incorrect dosages of drugs are given to patients in a hospital

Number of toxic reactions observed to drugs given

Number of surgical complications per day

Number of adverse patient outcomes per day

Elapsed time from completion of laboratory tests until results are recorded in the patient's chart

Number of standbys taken per flight of an airline

Number of passengers bumped per flight

Distribution of time for delivery of baggage

Number of pieces of luggage either lost or delayed

Daily costs of laundry in a hotel

Number of errors in reservations in a hotel

Frequency of overbooking in a hotel

Turnover of managers or of other people

Deviation of actual delivery time from the agreed-upon target date

5.10

QUALITY AND SPECIFICATION LIMITS

Whereas the ideas of process control as described in the previous sections are relevant to both the service and the manufacturing industries, the comments in this section may be more pertinent to the manufacturing sector. Consider first an example. A few years ago, Ford Motor Co. found itself in the following situation.

EXAMPLE 5.3

This example was reported by B. Gunter in "A Perspective on the Taguchi Methods," *Quality Progress,* June 1987, pp. 44–52. [© 1987 American Society of Quality Control. Used with permission.]

A major subassembly had been simultaneously outsourced for manufacture to a Japanese firm and to one of Ford's own U.S. plants. Both sources were required to produce the same product to the same specifications. However, it turned out that customers could detect a difference. Over time, it became clear that warranty complaints about the U.S.-built product far exceeded complaints about the Japanese product. In particular, customers complained of noisiness for the U.S. subassembly, while there were practically no such complaints for the Japanese one.

To investigate, Ford collected a sample of Japanese and American subassemblies and completely disassembled and measured every part. What they found was comparable to the situation shown in Figure 5.18. In fact, both the Japanese [Figure 5.18(a)] and American [Figure 5.18(b)] factories made the product within specifications—both had zero defects. However, the American plant had not recognized the importance of reducing variability even when specifications were being met. Their product therefore varied widely within the specifications. The Japanese, on the other hand, had made extensive process control efforts to reduce variability. As a result, their product was much more consistent. Consequently, gears and bearings fitted better, worked more smoothly, and made significantly less noise than the American-made product. Moreover, because they had worked to reduce variability through their system—and not just to get parts within specs and eliminate defects—they had less scrap and rework and less inventory, and thus incurred both lower costs and higher quality. In short, their system loss was far less than that of the American plant's.

Figure 5.18(c) contains the major message of this section: A quality loss is sustained whenever the quality characteristic for any product is not on target. The further away the quality characteristic is from the target, the larger is the quality loss. In other words, we must define quality loss as *deviation from target,* not as lack of conformance to certain specifications. The further a measurement is from the target, the higher the quality loss, regardless of whether the measurement is within specifications. Quality loss function 1 in Figure 5.18(c) illustrates this idea, whereas quality loss function 2—for which the quality loss is the same low value as long as the output meets the specifications—does not. If the concept of "zero defects" means that no output must be outside specifications, then "zero defects" is not good enough.

Quality loss must be measured by systems-wide costs, not local costs at points of defect detection, implying that variability in output must be continually reduced. This is difficult to achieve by trying to "inspect quality into the product" (that is, by checking conformance to specifications). It is best done by designing quality into the product itself and into the process of production, and by continual improvement of both product and process.

FIGURE 5.18 Why Zero Defects Is Not Good Enough

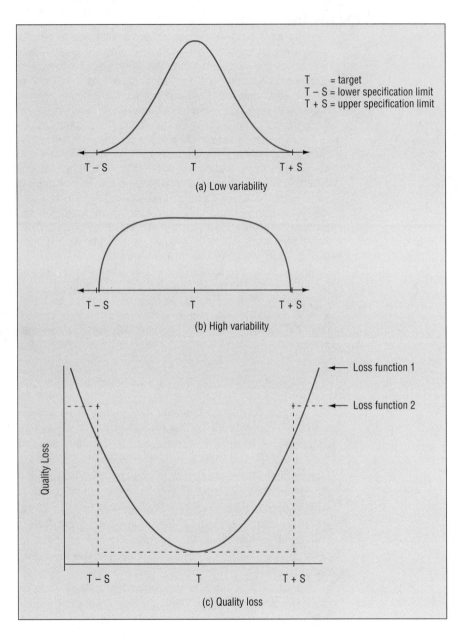

T = target
T − S = lower specification limit
T + S = upper specification limit

(a) Low variability

(b) High variability

(c) Quality loss

5.11

EXAMPLE: ESTIMATING HARVEST COMPLETION TIME

The following example serves as a vehicle to summarize many of the ideas discussed so far in this chapter.

Description of Problem

In 1988, a Campbell Soup Company mushroom farm produced about 160,000 pounds of mushrooms per week.[7] Each day, between 100 and 200 employees were needed to complete the task of harvesting the mushrooms from the bed. Because of the size of this manual task, it had been quite easy to misjudge the number of people required to finish the job on time. When this happened often, the employees became demoralized and angry since they were asked to work through supper. Furthermore, the product lost value if left unpicked overnight, since a viral disease could result, causing yield reductions of 50% and revenue losses of $15,000 per day.

To improve this situation, a model was developed that was used each morning to estimate harvest completion time that day. This estimate could be used to take appropriate action if estimated completion time was longer than 10 hours. The estimate was based on the estimated size of the harvest, the number of harvesters who had been scheduled 1 week earlier for that day, the harvesting group's average speed, and any factors that might affect that speed.

Summary

Managerial Questions. As part of a larger study, the following two questions were to be answered:

1. Is the prediction process stable over time?

2. How well does the model predict harvest completion time?

Process. This was a time series study of the process of estimating harvest completion times. The process was studied in the fall of 1988. It was located at Campbell Soup Company's mushroom farm.

Findings. The prediction process was stable over time. On average, harvest completion times were overestimated by about 20 minutes. About one-quarter of harvests took more than an hour longer than estimated.

---

[7]The data were kindly supplied by T. Adlington.

Recommendations. The prediction model needed refinement to improve the accuracy of prediction.

Statistical Details

Statistical Questions. The following statistical questions were studied.

1. Is the prediction process stable?

2. a What are the process mean and standard deviation for prediction errors?
   b On what proportion of days do actual harvest completion times exceed estimated harvest completion times by 1 hour or more?

Statistical Unit. The process unit was a day or a harvest.

Description of Process. The process consisted of mushroom harvesting at Campbell Soup Company's mushroom farm. Management was particularly interested in the performance of the model estimating harvest completion times.

Sampling Scheme. Data were collected each day during the 49-day period from September 19, 1988 to November 6, 1988.

Description of Variables. Four variables were measured for the overall study:

1. Estimated harvest completion time (time of day given as a decimal; for example, 4:30 P.M. is 16.5)

2. Actual harvest completion time (time of day given as a decimal)

3. Estimated size of the harvest (in pounds)

4. Actual size of the harvest (in pounds)

To answer the questions of concern in this section, only two variables were needed: estimated harvest completion time and actual harvest completion time. The response variable, prediction error (TIME_ERR), was the difference between these two variables: TIME_ERR equals actual minus estimated completion times. All three variables were quantitative and measured in hours.

Process Characteristics of Interest. Statistical question 1 could be answered by checking the randomness of the process generating the prediction errors. Question 2 could be answered only if the process were random; to answer it, the distribution of prediction errors was needed, in particular, its mean and standard deviation.

Data. A listing of the data is given in Figure 5.19; the data are stored in ASCII file MUSHROOM.DAT. TIME_ERR, the response variable, is the difference between actual and estimated times. Descriptive statistics are given in Figure 5.20. The number of hours by which actual and estimated completion times differed was between -5.5 and 4.2 hours.

FIGURE 5.19
Harvest Completion
Time Data

ROW	TIME_EST	TIME_BACT	SIZE_EST	SIZE_ACT
1	18.4	18.0	12000	23350
2	17.8	17.0	20000	23900
3	16.8	14.5	18500	14220
4	14.1	13.7	12500	8680
5	18.9	18.9	6250	6200
6	13.9	15.6	4650	8430
7	15.3	14.3	7750	11200
8	18.1	18.1	16750	14320
9	23.4	17.9	24500	19510
10	21.4	18.0	22000	15670
11	18.1	14.8	21000	13850
12	18.7	17.6	15800	9080
13	13.5	15.8	7890	7890
14	16.0	16.4	11780	11780
15	18.7	18.0	16000	18200
16	15.2	16.0	12000	11920
17	15.7	17.4	12000	10310
18	16.9	18.1	23000	19310
19	19.7	18.1	23000	15840
20	19.1	17.8	11750	11520
21	18.7	17.6	17750	14280
22	17.4	17.4	17750	16890
23	16.1	14.6	16000	13690
24	17.5	17.2	13750	12150
25	16.4	16.2	11500	9820
26	16.0	16.6	11250	11460
27	20.2	18.2	17000	18160
28	20.9	21.0	25000	28590
29	17.1	17.5	19500	22840
30	16.8	21.0	21000	25710
31	19.2	18.1	29000	26380
32	15.0	13.4	16000	11240
33	21.8	21.1	10750	7150
34	24.3	21.1	18000	17710
35	19.4	21.1	21000	19450
36	15.6	18.0	17000	12080
37	16.0	14.4	13000	12090
38	15.8	16.2	15000	14690
39	15.7	16.1	17000	14240
40	17.4	18.0	18000	19570
41	18.5	21.0	17000	19250
42	20.9	18.0	24000	23050
43	17.3	16.0	16500	15710
44	19.8	18.0	14500	12290
45	15.5	15.1	12500	11240
46	15.6	15.1	21000	19180
47	18.0	19.3	17000	15190
48	14.5	16.1	10000	9710
49	15.5	17.4	15500	17430

FIGURE 5.20 Summary Statistics for Harvest Completion Times

	N	MEAN	MEDIAN	TRMEAN	STDEV	STEMEAN
TIME_EST	49	17.604	17.400	17.500	2.393	0.342
TIME_ACT	49	17.282	17.500	17.278	1.992	0.285
SIZE_EST	49	16171	16500	16166	5130	733
SIZE_ACT	49	15233	14280	15069	5332	762
TIME_ERR	49	-0.322	-0.400	-0.302	1.792	0.256

	MIN	MAX	Q1	Q3
TIME_EST	13.500	24.300	15.700	19.000
TIME_ACT	13.400	21.100	16.000	18.100
SIZE_EST	4650	29000	12000	19750
SIZE_ACT	6200	28590	11350	19215
TIME_ERR	-5.500	4.200	-1.400	0.700

Data Analysis. The analysis proceeded as follows: To answer question 1, a control chart of prediction errors was obtained (see Figure 5.21). Using the sample mean and standard deviation of TIME_ERR from Figure 5.20, the value for the UCL was $(-0.322) + 3(1.792) = 5.1$ and that for the LCL was -5.7. Figure 5.21 also lists results from a runs test. To answer question 2, a histogram and a normal probability plot of the prediction errors were obtained (see Figure 5.22).

FIGURE 5.21
Harvest Completion
Times

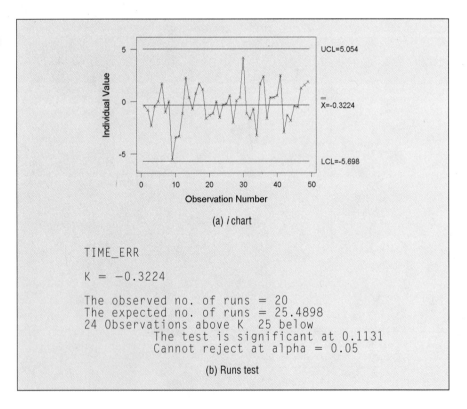

(a) *i* chart

```
TIME_ERR

K = -0.3224

The observed no. of runs = 20
The expected no. of runs = 25.4898
24 Observations above K   25 below
           The test is significant at 0.1131
           Cannot reject at alpha = 0.05
```

(b) Runs test

FIGURE 5.22
Graphs for Harvest
Completion Times

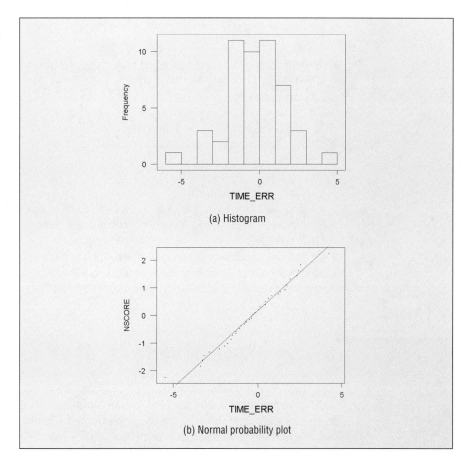

(a) Histogram

(b) Normal probability plot

Conclusions. Visual inspection of Figure 5.21 did not reveal any time series pattern; in particular, there was no weekly pattern (a week consisting of seven harvests). This visual impression of randomness was supported by the runs test, whose p-value was 0.1131. None of the observations was outside the control limits. Question 1 could thus be answered: The process was judged to be random and thus stable.

Given that the prediction process was judged to be random, question 2 could also be addressed with the data at hand. The sample mean and standard deviation of the prediction errors, -0.322 and 1.792, could be used to estimate the process mean and process standard deviation. The histogram and normal probability plot in Figure 5.22 suggested that the distribution of prediction error was normal, although there was a little cause for concern at the two extremes. With respect to the mushroom farm's prediction process for harvest completion times, we can now say that

- On average, completion times were overestimated by 0.32 hours (about 20 minutes).

- The standard deviation of the error in estimating completion times was 1.79 hours.

- Roughly 23% of all harvests took at least an hour longer to complete than estimated. More precisely, 22.79%, calculated as follows: For a time error of 1 hour, the standardized value is

$$z = \frac{\text{Time error—Mean Time error}}{\text{Standard deviation}}$$

$$= \frac{1-(-0.322)}{1.792} = 0.74$$

According to Table 4.1 or the *Calc* ▶ *Probability Distributions* ▶ *Normal* menu in Minitab, $F(z = 0.74) = 0.7703$. The answer we seek is the percentage $1 - 0.7703 = 0.2297$.

As long as current conditions underlying the harvesting process and the estimation procedure remained unchanged, these results could be expected to hold.

5.12

DESIGNING AN EXPERIMENT

Chapter 2, in particular, Sections 2.2 (p. 12) and 2.5 (p. 22), introduced basic notions of **experimental design.** This section builds on that material. We have a response variable, and we need to know the effect of a factor of interest on it. There are several known background variables that may influence the response, and we must control for them. In Section 2.5, we controlled for the one known background variable (pipe diameter) by holding it constant. This section introduces **blocking,** a useful way of controlling for a known background variable that is not held constant. There are also unknown background variables that may influence the response; randomization is used so that the response does not confound the effects of the factor and these nuisance variables. Consider an example:

EXAMPLE 5.4

The owner of a chain of retail stores was interested in the effectiveness of various in-store display alternatives for a high-volume product. As part of a larger study, an experiment was run to compare the effectiveness of expanding the display space allocated to a particular brand of soap. Thus there was one factor in this experiment, Size of display space. This factor was to be studied at two levels: (1) regular display space determined as the number of shelf facings recommended by the stock manager, and (2) expanded display space, twice the regular display space. Data were gathered for weekly periods, so the unit was 1 week. There was one response variable, sales per week.

Several important background variables were known to influence sales: price, time of year (seasonality), advertising by competing supermarkets and manufacturers, store loyalty, and stability of surrounding population. Some of these background variables could be influenced by the owner of the retail chain. For example, only one store was selected for the experiment to eliminate the difference among store policies. Furthermore, this store's clientele was considered loyal, and it was located in an area that was not changing much (for instance, due to student population movements). The owner promised not to change display and advertising for competing brands during the term of the study. Furthermore, the price of the product under study was to be kept constant throughout the study period.

It was known, however, that the product had a modest seasonal sales pattern. To control for this background variable, a *paired comparison* design was created. Figure 5.23 documents the study. Each 2-week period was designated a *block* since the effect of seasonality was felt to be negligible in such a short period. The two display sizes, regular and expanded, were paired for each 2-week period, and each

FIGURE 5.23
Documentation
Form for
Example 5.4

1. **Objective:** Compare the effectiveness of two display alternatives for a high-volume product.

2. **Background information:** The retail store was interested in its display and advertising activities and was conducting a large-scale study. This experiment was part of the study.

3. **Experimental variables:**

   A. Response variable   Measurement technique

        1. Sales   Number of units sold per week

   B. Factor   Levels

        1. Display   Regular (R), expanded (E)

   C. Background variables   Method of control

        1. Seasonality of sales   Blocking on 2-week periods

        2. Several others   Held constant

4. **Replication:** The experiment was to be run for 32 weeks, so 16 comparisons were available for the two display alternatives.

5. **Methods of randomization:** Flip of a coin to determine the display alternative for the first week of each 2-week period.

6. **Design matrix:** See Figure 5.24.

7. **Data collection forms:** (attach copy) Data will be recorded and plotted on a control chart.

8. **Planned methods of statistical analysis:** Sequence plot of unit sales; sequence plot of differences in sales in each block; dotplot of differences.

9. **Estimated cost, schedule, and other resource considerations:** The study can be done during the next 8 months.

FIGURE 5.24 Results of Paired-Comparison Experiment

2-week Period(block)	First week Display	Sales	Second week Display	Sales	Difference in Sales (Expanded − Regular)
1	Expanded	29	Regular	19	10
2	Regular	24	Expanded	30	6
3	Regular	7	Expanded	16	9
4	Expanded	16	Regular	18	−2
5	Regular	14	Expanded	24	10
6	Expanded	32	Regular	18	14
7	Regular	19	Expanded	31	12
8	Expanded	44	Regular	38	6
9	Expanded	28	Regular	27	1
10	Expanded	35	Regular	29	6
11	Expanded	33	Regular	23	10
12	Regular	34	Expanded	49	15
13	Regular	41	Expanded	55	14
14	Expanded	43	Regular	36	7
15	Expanded	37	Regular	24	13
16	Expanded	46	Regular	44	2

size was to be used for 1 week. The assignment of a size to one of the 2 weeks was done by flipping a coin. The experiment was run for 32 weeks, thus creating 16 blocks. The data are stored in ASCII file DISPLAY.DAT. The results are given in Figure 5.24.

---

paired comparison design

In a *paired comparison design,* the factor of interest has two levels. *Blocks* are created by pairing up experimental units that have the same value of the background variable to be controlled for. In each block, the response variable thus does not confound the effect of the factor and the background variable. The two units in each block are randomly assigned to the two levels of the factor. The experiment is **blocking** *replicated* by using several blocks for the experiment. The purpose of blocking is thus to have several experimental units that are similar with respect to the background variable to be controlled for; each unit is assigned to one of the levels of the factor.

In the example, the factor, size of display space, has two levels, regular and expanded. The experimental unit is a week, and two adjacent weeks make up a block. The effect of seasonality on sales is negligible in each block. The experiment is replicated 16 times.

The first step in any paired-comparison experiment is the sequence plot of the response data. The results for the sales data are given in Figure 5.25(a). By examining the sequence plot, the variation in the sales data can be partitioned as follows:

- A large component of the overall variation is due to the background variable captured by blocking—seasonality. In other words, sales vary considerably across blocks.

FIGURE 5.25

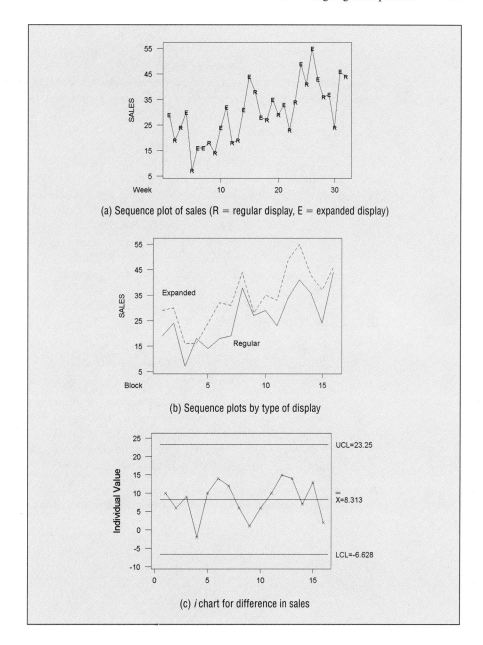

(a) Sequence plot of sales (R = regular display, E = expanded display)

(b) Sequence plots by type of display

(c) *i* chart for difference in sales

- Separating the effects of the factor under study from those of nuisance variables is not easy because of the variation across blocks. Sales are higher, however, for expanded display during many 2-week periods.

Our analysis proceeds with overlaid sequence plots for the two display alternatives. Refer to Figure 5.25(b). Sales for the regular display tend to be less than sales for the expanded display, but the data are still dominated by the seasonal effect of the blocking variable.

In a paired-comparison design, the block effect for each pair is removed by obtaining the *difference* between the two response variable values for each block. The differences for the 16 blocks are given in Figure 5.24. Note that the differences are always computed as Expanded − Regular, regardless of the order of display size in any 2-week period.

Figure 5.25(c) displays the control chart for these differences, which appear to be random. All differences are within the control limits. Since there are only 16 differences, the runs test would be unreliable. All the evidence supports that the process generating the differences is stable. We can thus treat the differences as if they were from a cross-sectional study. Figure 5.26 gives a dotplot and descriptive statistics for the differences. Differences tend to be positive: After removing the effect of seasonality, we see that the expanded display tends to lead to higher sales than the regular display. The average difference in the sample is 8.31, and the standard deviation is 4.98. On average, there is a pronounced positive effect on sales attributable to doubling the display space.

Why is there still variation in these differences? There may be two sources for this variation:

1. The added sales in each block (that is, in each 2-week period) due to the larger display size may not be exactly the same, even if *all other things* remain constant.

2. Sales can be affected by nuisance variables. Randomization does not eliminate nuisance variables; it just ensures that *in the long run* their effects on the response variable (sales) average out at the different levels of the factor of interest. If the variable sales is affected in this way, then the difference in sales at the two factor levels in each block is affected in a similar way.

These two sources contribute moderately to overall variation. They are not negligible in comparison to the factor (display alternative) and the blocking variable (seasonality).

FIGURE 5.26 Dotplot and Descriptive Statistics for the Difference in Sales

```
                          .    .
            .    . .    :.  .:  ...:.
  --+---------+---------+---------+-- Difference
  -10        0        10        20
```

(a) Dotplot

	N	MEAN	MEDIAN	TRMEAN	STDEV	SEMEAN
Difference	16	8.31	9.50	8.57	4.98	1.24

	MIN	MAX	Q1	Q3	
Difference	-2.00	15.00	6.00	12.75	

(b) Descriptive statistics

The analysis for this experiment is typical for many paired-comparison experiments, in which the effect of a blocking variable on the response is expected to be large. The effect of a blocking variable is removed, making it possible to study the effect of the factor under a wide range of conditions for the blocking variable that might be expected in the future.

In general the analysis proceeds as follows:

- Obtain a sequence plot for the original data.

- Compute the difference between the two responses in each block, and obtain a sequence plot for these differences. The purpose of computing these differences is to keep the effect of the blocking variable from interfering with the factor of interest.

- If the differences are judged to come from a random process, they can be analyzed as if they were cross-sectional.

We have discussed blocking when the variable to be blocked has only two levels, here Regular and Expanded display. The resulting experimental design is a *paired-comparison* design. It is also possible to design blocked experiments for factors with more than two levels. For details, see, for example, Moen, Nolan, and Provost (1991).

This section discussed some aspects of experimental design that are important in the context of time series studies. Judgment is needed in the analysis of such studies. In particular, we must judge whether the current conditions underlying the process will remain unchanged in the future. If changes occur, we may not be able to project the results from the experiment into the future.

5.13

SUMMARY AND OUTLOOK

This chapter introduced several statistical tools in the context of statistical process control. It also discussed management implications for stable processes and processes that are not stable. A process was defined to be stable if it is random—that is, if observations vary randomly around a constant level. Tools discussed for assessing randomness were (1) the sequence plot and its close relative the control chart, which are graphical tools helpful in judging the randomness of a series, and (2) the runs test, a statistical procedure that can give supplementary information about a series' randomness. These tools are also useful in many other applications involving time series, and some of them will be discussed in later chapters.

We saw that, when a process is stable, the time series data can be treated as if they are cross-sectional, and the tools from Chapter 4 can be applied to summarize the data further.

Many stable processes are characterized by normal data histograms. In such cases, 99.7% of the observations can be expected to fall within 3-standard-deviation control limits. Other stable processes are characterized by nonnormal data histograms. In these cases, it is not clear what percentage of the observations will fall within specific control limits. This is often the situation when the variable of interest represents counts or proportions. For example, the variables "Number of errors in reservations in a hotel" or "Proportion of errors in reservations in a hotel," measured daily, may not display approximately normal data histograms. Another example could be the daily number of accidents in a plant.

To learn about the effect of a factor on a response variable in the presence of an important background variable, the background variable must be controlled for. This can be done with blocking.

Data generated by processes constitute a time series. The random process model is the simplest model for a time series. Of course, not all time series can be modeled successfully this way. The next chapter and Chapters 11 and 12 introduce other models for time series. The next chapter introduces the *random walk* model for a time series; it has applications in, for example, finance and economics.

Key Terms and Concepts

random time series
runs test for randomness
   observed vs. expected number of
   runs
   p-value, statistical significance
random process
   stable process
control chart
   i chart
   $\overline{\overline{X}}$, *UCL, LCL*

common, special, and structural causes
  of variation
local action, action on process
experimental design
  blocking

References

Deming, W. E. (1986), *Out of the Crisis,* Massachusetts Institute of Technology, Center for Advanced Engineering Study, Cambridge, MA.

   This text is an important contribution to quality control and the statistical ideas underlying it.

Moen, R. D., Nolan, T. W., and Provost, L. P. (1991), *Improving Quality Through Planned Experimentation,* McGraw-Hill, New York.

   This book gives an excellent introduction to the design of experiments at an elementary level.

Shewhart, W. A. (1931), *The Economic Control of Quality of Manufactured Product,* reprinted 1980 by the American Society for Quality Control, Milwaukee, WI.

   This is one of the classics of statistical quality control. It is still a font of good ideas.

5.14

USING MINITAB FOR WINDOWS

This section shows how several of the graphs in this chapter were generated with Minitab for Windows.

Figure 5.6

Choose *File* ▸ *Other Files* ▸ *Import ASCII Data*
In the *Import ASCII Data* dialog box,
    Under *Store data in column*, type **C1**
    Click *ok*
    In the *Import Text From File* dialog box,
        Choose and click data file *bendclip.dat*, click *ok*
Choose *Window* ▸ *Data*
In the *Data* window,
    In the box immediately under *C1*, type **DIAMETER**
    Click any empty cell

RUNS TEST

Choose *Stat* ▸ *Nonparametrics* ▸ *Runs Test*
In the *Runs Test* dialog box,
    Type **DIAMETER** under *Variables*, click *ok*

Figure 5.13

Choose *File* ▸ *Other Files* ▸ *Import ASCII Data*
In the *Import ASCII Data* dialog box,
    Under *Store data in column*, type **C1 C2**
    Click *ok*
    In the *Import Text From File* dialog box,
        Choose and click data file *paper.dat*, click *ok*
Choose *Window* ▸ *Data*
In the *Data* window,
    In the boxes immediately under *C1* to *C3*, type **ORDER$ PAPER$ RATIO**
    Click any empty cell
Choose *Calc* ▸ *Mathematical Expressions*
In the *Mathematical Expressions* dialog box,
    Click the box next to *Variable (new or modified)*, type **C3**
    Click the box under *Expression*, type **C2/C1**
    Click *ok*

SORTING A COLUMN OF DATA IN ASCENDING ORDER

Choose *Manip* ▸ *Sort*
In the *Sort* dialog box,
    Click the box under *Sort column(s)*, type **C3**
    Click the box under *Store sorted column(s) in*, type **C5**
    Click the box next to *Sort by column*, type **C3**
    Click *ok*

Choose *Window ▸ Data*
In the *Data* window,
    In the box immediately under *C5*, type **SORTED**
    Click any empty cell
Choose *Window ▸ Session*
In the *Session* window,
    Type **PRINT C5**

Figure 5.14

Choose *File ▸ Other Files ▸ Import ASCII Data*
In the *Import ASCII Data* dialog box,
    Under *Store data in column*, type **C1**
    Click *ok*
    In the *Import Text from File* dialog box,
        Choose and click data file *bendclip.dat*, click *ok*
Choose *Window ▸ Data*
In the *Data* window,
    In the box immediately under *C1*, type **DIAMETER**
    Click any empty cell

i CHART

Choose *Stat ▸ Control Charts ▸ Individuals*
In the *Individuals Chart* window,
    Click the box next to *Variable*, type **C1**
    Under *Sigma*, click circle to left of *Historical*
    Under *Sigma*, click box to right of *Historical*, type **0.06**
    Click ok

        (These commands request an *i* chart for column C1, and they tell Minitab to use the sample standard deviation 0.06 as an estimate of the process standard deviation Sigma, when computing the control limits.)

5.15

MINITAB COMMANDS

This section lists the Minitab Release 10 for Windows menu commands that have been introduced so far. Each submenu introduced in this and earlier chapters is listed under the corresponding main menu. It is briefly explained and a page reference to an explanation in the text is given.

File

Save Worksheet As   page 88
  [save data in ASCII, Minitab, or other formats]
Other Files
  Import ASCII Data   page 86
   [enter data into the Minitab worksheet from an ASCII file]

Manip

Sort   page 197
  [sort the data in a column and rearrange the rows in other columns
  accordingly]
Unstack   page 148
  [unstack columns into several smaller columns]

Calc

Mathematical Expressions   page 149
  [carry out algebraic expressions, natural logs, etc., on columns]
Functions   page 149
  [compute various functions on columns, for example, normal
  scores]
Column Statistics   page 86
  [compute statistics on columns, such as mean and standard deviation]

Stat

Basic Statistics
  Descriptive Statistics   pages 92, 147
   [compute a variety of descriptive statistics for columns]
Control Charts
  Individuals   page 198
   [create a control chart for individual observations]
SPC
  Pareto Chart   page 91
   [create a Pareto chart]
Nonparametrics
  Runs Test   page 197
   [carry out the runs test for data in a column. Note: There must be no
   missing data]

Graph

Plot   page 91
  [obtain high-resolution scatterplots]
Time Series Plot   page 87
  [obtain high-resolution time series plots]
Histogram   page 89
  [obtain high-resolution histograms, cumulative histograms, etc.]
Character Graphs
  [obtain low-resolution plots based on characters]

5.16

PROBLEMS FOR CLASS DISCUSSION

5.1 Signing of Office Leases

A company owns several office buildings, and wished to study the lease-signing process for tenants at one of its office buildings, in particular, the *turnaround time* for leases—the length of time between entering the original agreement and executing the final lease document.[8] Lease turnaround times should be reasonably short since the potential for deals falling apart increases with the turnaround time.

This study was undertaken to address the following managerial questions:

1. Is the turnaround process stable?

2. Is there a relationship between turnaround times and (a) the size of the leased premises, and (b) the number of other locations the tenant leases from the Company?

3. Can turnaround time be predicted for future leases?

4. Is it feasible to implement a new policy of not allowing occupancy until a lease is executed?

It was expected that the average turnaround time would be 8 weeks. (At the time of the initial agreement, tenants were promised occupancy within 8 to 10 weeks.) Negative relationships were expected in the second question.

Data were collected by consecutively examining all 30 leases signed between September 1987 and September 1988. Three variables were measured on each lease: turnaround TIME (in weeks), SIZE of tenant (in hundreds of square feet), and number of other LOCATIONS the tenant leases from the Company (1 = no other location, 2 = one other location, 3 = two to five other locations, 4 = five to ten other locations, and 5 = more than ten other locations). [Note that some tenants have hundreds of other locations.] The data are stored in ASCII file LEASES.DAT.

This discussion will focus on managerial questions 1, 3, and 4. The Minitab commands produced the following output in the Session window. (High-resolution graphs are included where generated. Annotation commands are not given.)

---

[8]The name of the company is omitted to protect confidentiality. The data are real.

FIGURE 5.27

```
MTB > Read 'C:\MTBWIN\DATA\LEASES.DAT' C1-C3.
Entering data from file: C:\MTBWIN\DATA\LEASES.DAT
    30 rows read.
MTB > NAME C1 'TIME' C2 'SIZE' C3 'LOCATNS'
MTB > PRINT C1-C3

  ROW     TIME     SIZE    LOCATNS       ROW     TIME     SIZE    LOCATNS

    1        5       46        3          16        2       15        1
    2        3       28        1          17        3       15        1
    3        3       13        2          18        1       15        1
    4        5       18        1          19       21        9        1
    5        8       21        4          20        3       13        1
    6        9       31        1          21        8       13        3
    7       16       25        5          22       11       25        1
    8        7       17        1          23        4       15        1
    9        2        8        5          24        7       17        2
   10        5       26        4          25        5       13        3
   11        4       58        5          26        3       13        1
   12        6       23        5          27        6       13        1
   13        7       13        1          28        4       13        1
   14       13       34        5          29        4       13        1
   15        6       71        5          30        2       13        1

MTB > Describe C1.

               N       MEAN     MEDIAN    •TRMEAN      STDEV     SEMEAN
TIME          30      6.100      5.000      5.500      4.381      0.800

             MIN        MAX         Q1         Q3
TIME       1.000     21.000      3.000      7.250

MTB > IChart C1;
SUBC>   Sigma 4.381.
```

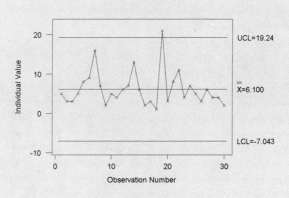

i Chart for TIME

```
MTB > Runs C1.

    TIME

    K = 6.1000

    The observed no. of runs =  11
    The expected no. of runs =  14.3333
    10 Observations above K    20 below
              The test is significant at  0.1619
              Cannot reject at alpha = 0.05


MTB > Delete 19 C1-C3
MTB > Describe C1.

              N       MEAN     MEDIAN     TRMEAN      STDEV     SEMEAN
TIME         29      5.586      5.000      5.370      3.418      0.635

            MIN        MAX         Q1         Q3
TIME      1.000     16.000      3.000      7.000

MTB > IChart C1;
SUBC>   Sigma 3.418.
```

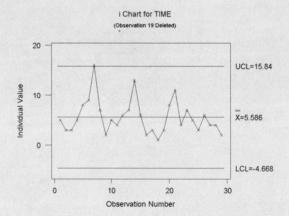

i Chart for TIME
(Observation 19 Deleted)

```
MTB > Runs C1.

    TIME

    K = 5.5862


    The observed no. of runs =  11
    The expected no. of runs =  15.0690
    12 Observations above K    17 below
              The test is significant at  0.1126
              Cannot reject at alpha = 0.05
```

```
MTB > Delete 7 C1-C3
MTB > Describe C1.
```

	N	MEAN	MEDIAN	TRMEAN	STDEV	SEMEAN
TIME	28	5.214	5.000	5.077	2.820	0.533

	MIN	MAX	Q1	Q3
TIME	1.000	13.000	3.000	7.000

```
MTB > IChart C1;
SUBC>   Sigma 2.82.
```

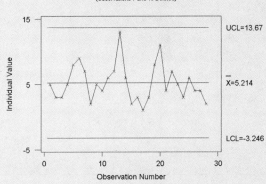

i Chart for TIME
(Observations 7 and 19 Deleted)

```
MTB > Runs C1.

TIME

K = 5.2143


The observed no. of runs =   11
The expected no. of runs =   14.3571
11 Observations above K    17 below
        The test is significant at  0.1748
        Cannot reject at alpha = 0.05

MTB > Histogram C1;
SUBC>   CutPoint 0:14/2;
SUBC>   Bar.
```

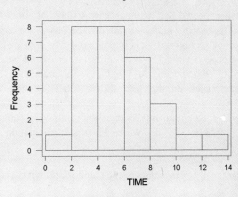

Histogram for TIME

```
MTB > NScores C1 C4
MTB > NAME C4 'NSCORE'
MTB > Plot C4*C1;
SUBC>   Symbol;
SUBC>     Type 5;
SUBC>   Jitter 0.025 0.025.
```

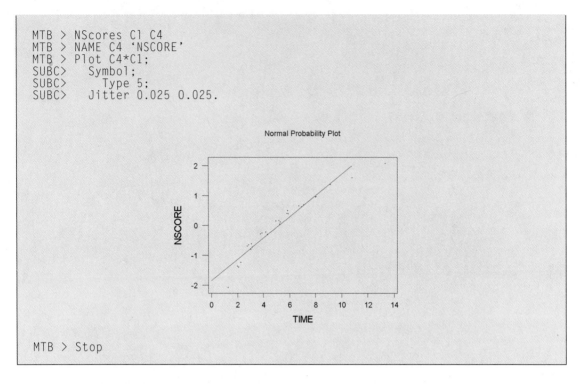

```
MTB > Stop
```

5.2 Attendance at a Medical Clinic

A medical walk-in clinic provides urgent medical care equivalent to that provided by most family physicians' offices.[9] Appointments are not required. Patients tend to utilize this clinic when their own family physicians are unavailable. One of the duties of the clinic management is to attempt to match the number of clinic staff to the anticipated workload. Overstaffing results in unnecessary expenditures, and understaffing results in poor service. There have been occasional complaints recently by patients, regarding long waiting times, and by the staff, regarding increased workload. A study was done to address three questions:

1. Is weekday attendance at the clinic stable, or changing over time?

2. What is the variation in attendance, and is it getting smaller or larger over time?

3. Is attendance on the first shift of value in predicting total daily attendance?

It was expected that attendance was stable at about 65 patients per day, with 30 patients in the first shift. Variation in attendance was expected to be increasing over time and to be higher in the second shift than in the first.

Data on two variables were collected for the 64 week days (excluding holidays) between May 1, 1989 and July 31, 1989: (1) total attendance for the two daily shifts (TOTAL), and (2) attendance on the first shift (SHIFT_1). The data are stored in ASCII file CLINIC.DAT.

The Minitab commands produced the following output in the Session window. (High-resolution graphs are included where generated. Annotation commands are not given.)

---

[9]The data are real, but the name of the clinic is omitted to protect confidentiality.

FIGURE 5.28

```
MTB > Read 'C:\MTBWIN\DATA\CLINIC.DAT' C1 C2.
Entering data from file:  C:\MTBWIN\DATA\CLINIC.DAT
     64 rows read.
MTB > NAME C1 'TOTAL' C2 'SHIFT_1' C3 'SHIFT_2'
MTB > PRINT C1 C2
```

ROW	TIME	SIZE	ROW	TIME	SIZE	ROW	TIME	SIZE
1	76	37	23	53	24	45	68	38
2	70	35	24	76	36	46	79	40
3	53	27	25	67	30	47	77	36
4	71	29	26	60	24	48	70	28
5	66	33	27	65	31	49	80	34
6	67	38	28	75	29	50	82	45
7	71	31	29	75	34	51	79	49
8	77	40	30	76	42	52	75	38
9	76	38	31	68	33	53	80	42
10	76	41	32	61	30	54	77	37
11	76	34	33	37	28	55	73	36
12	63	33	34	66	22	56	83	43
13	78	48	35	78	44	57	86	37
14	72	27	36	83	35	58	77	30
15	87	39	37	70	32	59	80	38
16	86	40	38	76	37	60	66	33
17	87	43	39	77	35	61	64	32
18	76	38	40	87	38	62	81	35
19	76	34	41	87	46	63	84	41
20	75	31	42	64	31	64	96	47
21	63	25	43	89	45			
22	82	44	44	88	40			

```
MTB > Describe C1.
```

	N	MEAN	MEDIAN	TRMEAN	STDEV	SEMEAN
TIME	64	74.36	76.00	74.88	9.88	1.23

	MIN	MAX	Q1	Q3
TIME	37.00	96.00	68.00	80.00

```
MTB > IChart C1;
SUBC>  Sigma=9.88.
```

I Chart for TOTAL

```
MTB > Let C1(33)=67        # Note:  Error Correction!
MTB > Describe C1.

              N      MEAN    MEDIAN    TRMEAN     STDEV    SEMEAN
TIME         64     74.83     76.00     75.00      8.72      1.09

            MIN       MAX        Q1        Q3
TIME      53.00     96.00     68.00     80.00


MTB > IChart C1;
SUBC>    Sigma=8.82.
```

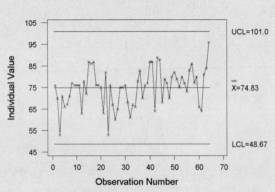

```
MTB > Runs C1.

    TIME

    K = 74.8281


    The observed no. of runs =  27
    The expected no. of runs =  31.0000
    40 Observations above K    24 below
            The test is significant at  0.2820
            Cannot reject at alpha = 0.05

MTB > Let C3 = C1-C2.
MTB > Describe C1 C2.

              N      MEAN    MEDIAN    TRMEAN     STDEV    SEMEAN
TIME         64     74.83     76.00     75.00      8.72      1.09
SHIFT_1      64    35.781    36.000    35.793     6.217     0.777
```

```
                 MIN          MAX            Q1           Q3
TIME            53.00        96.00         68.00         80.00
SHIFT_1         22.000       49.000        31.000        40.000

MTB > IChart C2;
SUBC>    Sigma 6.217.
```

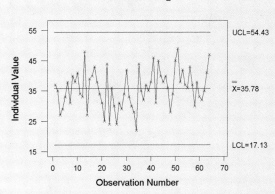

```
MTB > Runs C2.

    SHIFT_1

    K = 35.7813


    The observed no. of runs =  29
    The expected no. of runs =  32.9687
    33 Observations above K   31 below
            The test is significant at   0.3170
            Cannot reject at alpha = 0.05

MTB > Plot C1*C2.
```

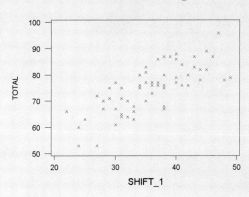

```
MTB > Correlation C1 C2.
Correlation of TOTAL and SHIFT_1 = 0.751
MTB > Plot C2*C3.
```

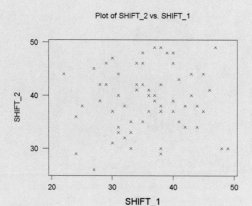

Plot of SHIFT_2 vs. SHIFT_1

```
MTB > Correlation C2 C3.
Correlation of SHIFT_1 and SHIFT_2 = 0.057
MTB > NScores C1 C4.
MTB > NAME C4 'NSCORE'.
MTB > Plot C4*C1.
```

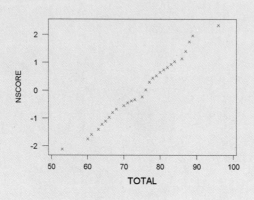

Normal Probability Plot

```
MTB > Stop
```

5.17

EXERCISES

Although answers are given in Appendix D, do not turn to them right away if you cannot find an answer on your own. Return to the exercise the next day and try again before turning to Appendix D.

Exercises for Section 5.4

5.3 In the following sequences, count the number of runs.
  a $+ + - - - + - + -$
  b $+ - + - +$
  c $+ + + - - - +$
  d T T H H H T H

5.4 Consider the following sequence of numbers: 186, 182, 166, 181, 167, 168, 176, 152, 190, and 182. The mean of the sequence is 175. What is the number of runs around the mean?

5.5 What is the relationship between the expected number of runs in an oscillating time series and the expected numbers of runs for a random series? Justify your answer.

5.6 The data analyzed in this problem relate to quarterly net sales and net income for Marshall Field & Company, a Chicago-based retail department chain. The data are stored in ASCII file MFIELD.DAT. They cover the period from the first quarter in 1961 to the fourth quarter in 1975. The variable of interest here is a quarterly financial ratio, net income to net sales (RATIO).

Is the time series of RATIO values random? If yes, justify your answer. If no, what time series pattern do you see? Use the following Minitab output from the Session window to answer this question.

FIGURE 5.29

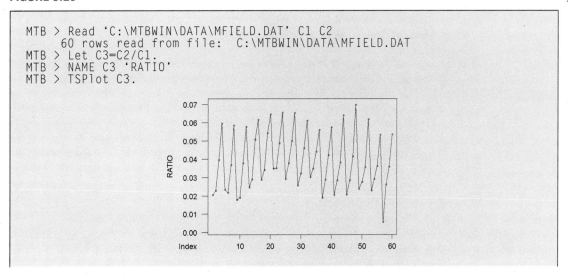

```
MTB > Runs C3.

   RATIO

   K = 0.0388

   The observed no. of runs =  30
   The expected no. of runs =  29.8000
   24 Observations above K    36 below
            The test is significant at  0.9567
            Cannot reject at alpha = 0.05

MTB > Describe C3.

                   N      MEAN    MEDIAN    TRMEAN     STDEV    SEMEAN
   RATIO          60   0.03884   0.03577   0.03866   0.01561   0.00202

                 MIN       MAX        Q1        Q3
   RATIO     0.00569   0.06989   0.02654   0.05357

MTB > Stop
```

Exercises for Section 5.5

5.7 An automotive lathe is shut down for corrective maintenance whenever a part it produces has a diameter greater than 2.01 cm or smaller than 1.99 cm. The lathe is designed to produce parts that are normally distributed with a mean diameter of 2.00 cm and standard deviation of 0.005 cm. Suppose that the production process is random.

a When the lathe is operating as designed, what is the probability that the lathe will be stopped?

b Suppose that a component within the lathe wore out and that the lathe has begun producing parts that are too wide on average, with mean diameter of 2.015 cm, but with unchanged standard deviation. What is the chance that the next diameter is between 1.99 and 2.01 cm, so that the lathe is not shut down?

5.8 Companies bottling soft drinks monitor their filling machines very closely since underfilled bottles are easily spotted by consumers and government penalties for underfilling can be severe. On the other hand, overfilling is an expensive waste of money. The soda water filling process at a particular plant is known to be stable and to fill bottles with an average of 500.0 ml (milliliter) and a standard deviation of 1.2 ml.

a What proportion of bottles are filled with 499.0 ml or more of soda water?

b Do you have to make any assumptions to compute the result in (a)? If so, what are they and how reasonable are they?

Exercises for Section 5.6

5.9 Consider the 10 variables stored in ASCII file NPP.DAT. Based on your visual impression from a control chart and the results from a runs test, was each variable generated by a random process?

5.10 The data to be analyzed in this problem relate to monthly returns from

1. A stock portfolio based on a trading plan devised prior to 1978

2. The Value Line Composite index, a broadly based stock index based on 1700 stocks

The data refer to the 46 months from January 1978 to October 1981. They are stored in ASCII file PORTFOLI.DAT. The main variable of interest is the difference (DIFFRNCE) between the monthly return of the stock portfolio, PORTFOLI in column 1, and the monthly return of the Value Line Composite index, VALUELIN in column 2.

  a Is a random process model appropriate for the variable DIFFRNCE? Justify your answer.
  b Does a normal distribution describe the distribution of the variable DIFFRNCE well? Justify your answer. If no, describe the shape of the distribution.
  c What is the probability that the value of DIFFRNCE is 0 or more in the next month (November 1981)? (Note that a DIFFRNCE value of 0 or more in any month implies that the return on the stock portfolio is at least as high as the return on the Value Line index in that month.)

The following Minitab commands typed in the Session window generate the output necessary for this problem:

```
Read 'C:\MTBWIN\DATA\PORTFOLI' C1 C2
NAME C1 'PORTFOLI' C2 'VALUELIN'
Let C3=C1-C2
NAME C3 'DIFFRNCE'
TSPlot C3
Runs C3
Describe C3
NScores C3 C4
NAME C4 'NSCORE'
Plot C4*C3
Stop
```

5.11 Refer to Exercise 3.14 (data for the dispatch function at IBM). The data are stored in ASCII file DISPATCH.DAT. Consider the WAIT sequence in column 3.

  a Is the sequence random? Are there any unusual values? When do they occur?
  b Is the distribution normal? Are there any unusual values? When do they occur?
  c Draw the control chart. What managerial implications does it have? Based on your answers in (a) and (b), can you use the control limits for prediction purposes?
  d Do (a) to (c) for the CALLS sequence.
  e Do (a) to (c) for the STAFF sequence. Remembering that STAFF, the number of operators on duty, can be influenced by management, what implications do your conclusions have for management?

Exercise for Section 5.12

5.12 The manager responsible for an accounts payable department wanted to improve the process of paying invoices. The team responsible for improving the process developed an alternative payment procedure that was to be compared with the existing procedure. The procedure to be chosen was to have the lowest number of errors and the highest number of invoices paid.

  The team was concerned that day-to-day variation in the process could affect the comparison. A block design was carried out for the comparison. For 25 days, the two procedures were used by two different clerks. On half of the days, clerk 1 was to use the new procedure, and on the other half of the days, clerk 1 was to use the existing procedure. For each clerk, daily data were recorded for (1) process used (0 = old, 1 = new), (2) number of invoices paid, and (3) number of errors. The data are stored in ASCII file ACC_PAY.DAT.

Using the number of invoices paid as the response variable, which procedure should be chosen? Prepare appropriate graphs and summary measures.

Exercises for All Sections in Chapter 5

5.13   A rental car franchise is interested in the number of economy rental cars rented on a daily basis. Data for 52 successive days in late June and July 1985 are available. The owner of the franchise is interested in whether the data can be used for predicting the demand for rental cars in the near future. Correct prediction of demand will make it easy to have an adequate number of cars on hand every day. The data for variable RENTED, the number of rented cars, are as follows. (Read the data row by row.) They are stored in the ASCII file RENTAL.DAT.

```
24  22  21  17  19  19  16  13  16  16  19  19  23  19

23  20  21  24  23  22  19  22  23  18  18  19  20  20

22  22  19  19  22  24  24  24  23  21  19  22  24  23

20  21  23  22  21  19  20  21  24  22
```

a   Describe the unit in this process study.

b   At which values of RENTED should the three control lines be drawn in the time series plot? Draw these lines.

c   Were the RENTED data generated by a random process? Justify your answer.

d   In order to draw the line expected under normality in the normal probability plot for RENTED, you must obtain two points first and then draw the line through these two points.

     i) Suppose that the value of NSCORE is -1.2 for the first of these two points. What should the associated value for RENTED be for this point?

     ii) Suppose that the value of NSCORE is 1.2 for the second point. What should the associated value for RENTED be for this point?

     Using these two points, draw the line expected under normality in the normal probability plot.

e   If you were to assume that the process generating the RENTED data is random, what would be your best guess for the next day's number of economy cars rented? In light of your answer to (c), is this best guess reliable? Is it too high, too low, or just about right?

f   If you were to assume that the process generating the RENTED data is random and that the distribution of RENTED is normal, what is an approximate 95% prediction interval for the next day's number of economy cars rented? In light of your answer to (d), is this interval forecast reliable? Is the interval too wide, too narrow, or just about right?

The following Minitab commands typed in the Session window generate the output necessary for answering the above questions:

```
Read 'C:\MTBWIN\DATA\RENTAL' C1
NAME C1 'RENTED'
PRINT C1
TSPlot C1
Runs C1
Describe C1
NScores C1 C2
NAME C2 'NSCORE'
Plot C2*C1
Stop
```

5.14 In late 1983, Firestone ran advertisements with the headline "Pay no dough if it doesn't snow!", followed by

> We all know it's going to snow—but what we don't know is how much. Isn't it nice to know that Firestone takes the guesswork out of buying snow tires in our unpredictable Canadian winter?

> Buy Firestone Snow Biter Radials or 721 All Season Steel-Belted Radials between October 17 and December 31, 1983. And we'll refund all or part of your money if the snowfall is below average between June 1, 1983 and May 31, 1984.

Finally, the following promise was made, clarifying what was meant by "below average":

> If it snows less than 20% of average snowfall, you keep the tires and you receive 100% refund of your purchase price.

> If it snows less than 40% of average snowfall, you keep the tires and you receive 50% of your purchase price.

For Toronto customers, snowfall was to be measured at the international airport, and Environment Canada data were to be used.

Annual snowfall (in cm) at Toronto's international airport for 1940 to 1982 is stored in ASCII file SNOWFALL.DAT. The following data should be read row by row:

168.2	111.3	125.2	139.7	206.3	121.3	153.1	182.3	144.4	119.6
204.9	178.5	84.2	66.7	131.3	149.8	152.7	115.3	120.8	149.0
190.7	132.8	124.7	121.8	119.2	174.6	153.5	161.1	156.7	89.2
136.5	163.9	195.0	112.2	102.4	157.8	149.8	174.9	131.5	177.5
103.2	141.1	139.2							

a Describe the unit in this process study.
b Is the annual snowfall data generated by a random process? Justify your answer. If the data did come from a random process, what implications would this have for predicting the next year's snowfall? What if the data did not come from a random process?
c Does annual snowfall follow a normal distribution?
d Assume now that (1) annual snowfall data are generated by a random process and follow a normal distribution, and (2) the sample mean and standard deviation for the 43 annual values can be used as the known mean and standard deviation for the process. What is the chance that a Toronto purchaser of Firestone tires will get a 100% refund? A 50% refund? Do you have to make additional assumptions to answer these questions?
e How reasonable are the two assumptions made in (d) and your additional assumptions? Discuss.

The following Minitab commands typed in the Session window generate the output necessary to do this problem.

```
Read 'C:\MTBWIN\DATA\SNOWFALL' C1
NAME C1 'SNOW'
TSPlot C1
Runs C1
Describe C1
NScores C1 C2
NAME C2 'NSCORE'
Plot C2*C1
Stop
```

5.15   In an effort to understand the patterns of attendance at a museum in a large metropolitan city, the monthly general public attendance figures were collected for the main building and the planetarium from July 1985 to June 1989. The data are stored in ASCII file MUSEUM.DAT. The attendance figures are stored in variables MAIN and PLANET respectively. Some relevant Minitab output is presented in Figure 5.30.

a   Is the attendance process stable at the main building? Explicitly describe the reasons for your answer.

b   Can you compute the probability that July 1989 attendance at the main building will be 40,000 or above? If yes, compute it; if no, explain why this computation cannot be done.

c   Suppose that, in an effort to improve attendance at the main building, the museum's management institutes the following policy: If the attendance figure for a particular month dips below 40,000, then a staff meeting is to be held to analyze the reasons for poor attendance that month, and appropriate adjustments are made. Do you think this policy is likely to result in improved attendance? State your reasons.

d   Is the process of attendance stable at the planetarium?

e   Is there a relationship between main building and planetarium attendance? If yes, describe the shape and the strength of the relationship.

FIGURE 5.30

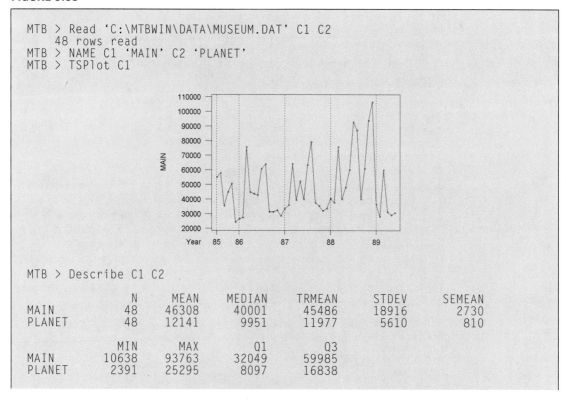

```
MTB > Read 'C:\MTBWIN\DATA\MUSEUM.DAT' C1 C2
      48 rows read
MTB > NAME C1 'MAIN' C2 'PLANET'
MTB > TSPlot C1
```

```
MTB > Describe C1 C2

                 N        MEAN      MEDIAN      TRMEAN       STDEV      SEMEAN
MAIN            48       46308       40001       45486       18916        2730
PLANET          48       12141        9951       11977        5610         810

               MIN         MAX          Q1          Q3
MAIN         10638       93763       32049       59985
PLANET        2391       25295        8097       16838
```

```
MTB > Runs C1
MAIN
    K = 46308.2305
    The observed no. of runs =   22
    The expected no. of runs =   23.5000
    18 Observations above K    30 below
            The test is significant at 0.6402
            Cannot reject at alpha = 0.05

MTB > NScores C1 C3
MTB > Plot C3*C1
```

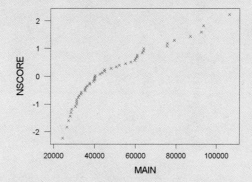

```
MTB > Histogram C1
```

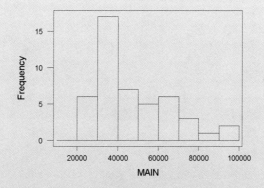

```
MTB > TSPlot C2
```

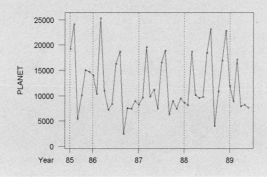

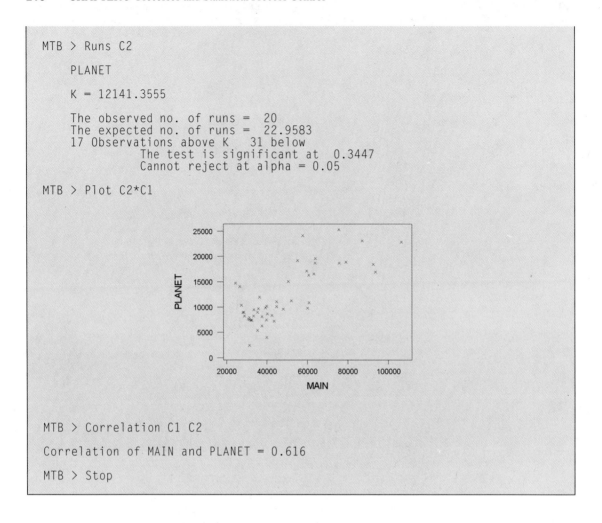

```
MTB > Runs C2

    PLANET

    K = 12141.3555

    The observed no. of runs =  20
    The expected no. of runs =  22.9583
    17 Observations above K    31 below
              The test is significant at  0.3447
              Cannot reject at alpha = 0.05

MTB > Plot C2*C1
```

```
MTB > Correlation C1 C2

Correlation of MAIN and PLANET = 0.616

MTB > Stop
```

5.16 For the purposes of this exercise, monthly stock returns are defined to be the percentage change in the price of a stock from one month to the next, after some financial adjustment in the stock price to account for stock splits, dividends, etc. The following list of 60 returns is for Northern Telecom Limited (NTL). The period covered extends from January 1981 to December 1985. (The data are stored in the ASCII file RETURNS.DAT as the last 60 observations for NTL.)

−1.82	−.37	20.89	8.69	23.42	−11.57	5.52	−13.96
11.88	12.50	6.01	1.74	−1.72	−1.75	−.89	−.45
−10.45	−4.06	−5.31	15.16	2.69	30.78	17.88	6.05
6.58	8.24	−1.97	18.18	4.76	18.61	3.19	3.04
8.27	−6.71	13.84	−14.62	−13.55	4.14	−3.46	3.24

−7.42	9.81	7.60	11.20	−6.60	1.51	−7.96	−2.21
16.34	−1.66	−6.29	−3.36	10.99	−5.79	6.68	−2.40
−10.37	−2.76	2.84	8.01				

a Describe the unit in this process study.

b Obtain a time series plot for the data and add the control chart limits to it. Do the data behave like a random process? Do a runs test to check your visual impression. Can you think of some implications for forecasting stock prices, if the data did behave like a random process?

c If the stock returns followed a normal distribution, about 68% of the 60 values would be expected to fall within 1 standard deviation of the mean and about 95% of the 60 values would be expected to fall within 2 standard deviations of the mean. What is the actual proportion of values falling within 1 and 2 standard deviations of the mean?

d Obtain a normal probability plot of the data. Is the normality assumption reasonable for these stock return data? Are there any unusual observations? If so, for which months?

The following Minitab commands typed in the Session window yield output you can use to answer the above questions.

```
Read 'C:\MTBWIN\DATA\RETURNS' C1 C2
NAME C1 'NTL'
Delete 1:60 C1
Describe C1
TSPlot C1
Runs C1
Sort C1 C2 # Note: The data will be sorted in ascending order in C2.
NAME C2 'SORTED'
PRINT C2
NScores C1 C3
NAME C3 'NSCORE'
Plot C3*C1
Stop
```

5.17 A company's computer maintenance department has a telephone number for all service or trouble calls related to computer maintenance. It is critical to respond to these calls promptly so that customers build up a favorable image of the information services division. A study was undertaken to determine current performance levels and to develop an improvement strategy for the coming year. Two questions were to be addressed:

1. What is the response time to service calls?

2. Given unchanged service conditions, can the average daily number of service calls be predicted for the near future?

The data to be analyzed relate to 60 consecutive service calls received in late August and in September 1989. The response time—defined as the number of business hours elapsed between registering the call and beginning repair work—was measured for each call. The data are stored in ASCII file RESPONSE.DAT.

The following questions relate to Minitab output given in Figure 5.31.

a Is the process of responding to service calls random? Briefly justify your answer.

b Assuming the process to be random, but making no further assumptions that are not warranted by the data, estimate the proportion of service calls in the near future for which the response time will be longer than 10 hours.

c Using only the information given in the statement of this problem and the Minitab output, can you answer question 2? If yes, provide a brief answer. If no, why not?

FIGURE 5.31

```
MTB > Read 'C:\MTBWIN\DATA\RESPONSE' C1
    60 rows read from file C:\MTBWIN\DATA\RESPONSE.DAT
MTB > NAME C1 'RESPTIME'
MTB > TSPlot C1
```

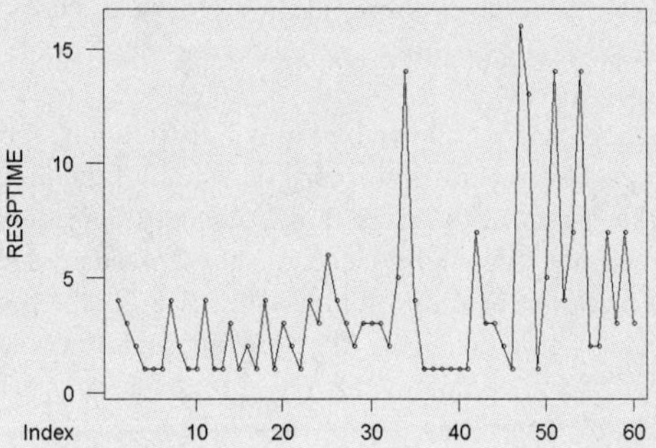


```
MTB > Runs C1

    RESPTIME

    K = 3.6667

    The observed no. of runs = 24
    The expected no. of runs = 27.6667
    20 Observations above K  40 below
              The test is significant at 0.2819
              Cannot reject at alpha = 0.05

MTB > Describe C1

                    N      MEAN    MEDIAN    TRMEAN     STDEV    SEMEAN
RESPTIME           60     3.667     3.000     3.204     3.634     0.469

                  MIN       MAX        Q1        Q3
RESPTIME        1.000    16.000     1.000     4.000

MTB > DotPlot C1

     .
     :
     :
     :
     :
     :      :
     :   .  :
     :   :  :  :
     :   :  :  :
     :   :  :  :        :                       .
     :   :  :  :   :  .  :                   .   :     .
  +---------+---------+---------+---------+---------+------- RESPTIME
0.0       3.0       6.0       9.0      12.0      15.0

MTB > Stop
```

5.18 A 500 gram (g) can of cocoa powder is filled in a production line by automatic equipment. The filling process is known to be stable, and the process standard deviation is 2 g. Suppose that the process mean weight has been set at 505 g since consumer protection regulations require that no more than 0.5% of all cans contain less than 500 g cocoa powder.

   a What are the unit and the response variable?

   b Is the consumer protection regulation being met?

   c To the nearest 0.1 g, what should the process average be to just meet the regulation?

   d Do you have to make any assumptions to compute the results in (b) and (c)? If so, what are they and how reasonable are they?

5.18

SUPPLEMENTARY EXERCISES

5.19 Consider a process whose unit is a day. Each day you measure two variables. Supposing that the time series of each variable is random, does it make sense to compute the correlation between the two variables? If no, why not? If yes, do you expect the correlation to be 0, or are other values between -1 and $+1$ possible as well? Briefly discuss your answer, citing examples. No calculations are necessary.

5.20 Refer to Problem 3.22 (data for Abitibi-Price). The data are stored in ASCII file ABITIBI.DAT. Consider the sequence of weight/volume ratios for spruce.

   a Is the sequence random? Are there any unusual ratios? In which periods do they occur?

   b Is the distribution normal? Are there any unusual ratios? In which periods do they occur? Given your answer in (a), how meaningful is this plot?

   c Draw the control chart. Based on your answers in (a) and (b), can you use the control limits for prediction purposes?

5.21 Describe a situation at work (preferably in a system you are responsible for) or another organization you are familiar with, in which a control chart may be useful, but is not currently used. Do not collect any data. Briefly describe

   a The context and variable to be plotted

   b How the variable is monitored currently

   c Why monitoring is important, and the potential benefits from a control chart

   d The factors (that is, common causes of variation that are operative at all times, and special causes) that may influence the data

   e The sampling period (hourly, daily, etc.)

   f How the data are to be gathered, who is to collect them, and who is to update the chart

   g Who should see the chart

   h Who is responsible for taking corrective action

   i What problems you foresee in implementing this chart.

Finally, give a mock-up of the proposed control chart, fully labelling both axes.

5.22 Answer the following questions.

   a How can you learn whether, with respect to some quality characteristic, a system is stable?

   b If a system is stable, where lies the main responsibility for further improvement? Why is it futile in this circumstance to plead with the manager, superintendents, division chiefs, and the work force for better quality?

    c If a system is not stable, what would your answers be to the questions in (b)? What would be different about your attempt to accomplish improvement?

5.23 Answer the following questions.
    a Is absenteeism a stable process in your company?
    b How about fires? Accidents?
    c If yes, where lies the responsibility for improvement?

5.24 The data analyzed in this problem are *the changes from the previous year* (CHANGE) in the U.S. civilian unemployment rate from 1890 to 1974. Data on the unemployment rate are stored in Column 2 of ASCII file US_ANN.DAT. Using the Minitab output in Figure 5.32, answer the following questions:
        Is the time series for CHANGE random? If *yes,* describe your reasoning and provide a rough interval prediction for the value of CHANGE in 1975. If *no,* describe the nature of the pattern. What model might be appropriate for CHANGE?

FIGURE 5.32

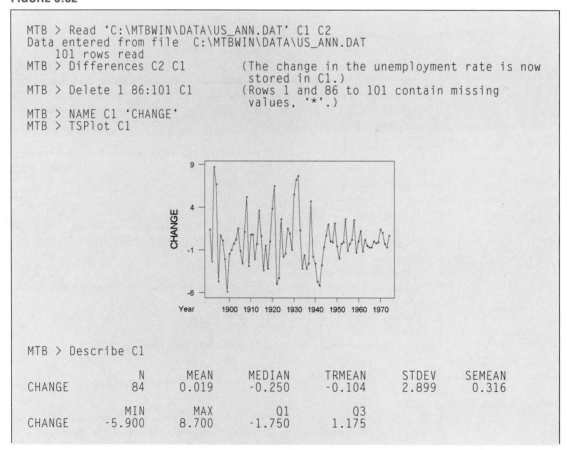

```
MTB > Runs C1

    CHANGE

    K = 0.0190

    The observed no. of runs =  39
    The expected no. of runs =  41.4762
    34 Observations above K    50 below
            The test is significant at   0.5726
            Cannot reject at alpha = 0.05

MTB > Stop
```

5.25   Suppose that a manager is responsible for the production of a part that is supplied to an important customer. The manager must report estimates of the costs of manufactured goods on a monthly basis several months in advance. To gain some understanding of these costs, the manager decided to examine the costs of goods manufactured for 30 recent *weeks*. He used the following three variables in the analysis:

$$C1 = COST = \text{Cost in dollars of goods manufactured for the week}$$

$$C2 = NUMBER = \text{Number of units produced during the week}$$

$$C3 = UNITCOST = \text{Unit cost for the week (C1/C2).}$$

The data are stored in ASCII file SINGLEPT.DAT.

a   Does the time series of NUMBER come from a random process? Be specific.

b   Does a normal distribution describe the distribution of NUMBER well? Be specific. Draw the line expected under normality on the appropriate plot.

c   Does the time series for UNITCOST come from a random process? Be specific.

d   Does a normal distribution describe the distribution of UNITCOST well? Be specific. Draw the line expected under normality on the appropriate plot.

e   Assume now that

1. The process generating UNITCOST is random.

2. The distribution of UNITCOST is normal.

3. The process mean level and process standard deviation equal the sample mean and sample standard deviation given in the output.

What unit cost figure should the manager use for 1 week's production in order to be 90% sure that the actual unit cost figure is below his prediction?

f   Given your conclusions in (a) to (d) and other available information, do you think that the assumptions made in (e) and thus the results derived there are reliable? Briefly justify your answer for each of the three assumptions made in (e).

g   Suppose the assumptions made in (e) are adequate. Can you use the results in (e) to derive an estimate of costs of goods manufactured for next week if weekly production is to be 4,000 units and the manager wants to be 90% sure that the actual figure is below his prediction? If yes, derive the prediction. If no, what additional information do you need?

5.26   Martin Marietta Manned Space Systems in New Orleans produces the external tank for NASA's space shuttle. One measure of overall manufacturing performance for this tank is the number of major hardware nonconformances. For 35 space shuttles produced between 1983 and 1986, the number of nonconformances is stored in the file MARTIN.DAT. Reading row by row, the data are as follows.

500	445	395	340	320	230	180	180	195
180	160	145	135	125	125	250	95	90
105	100	105	70	105	90	55	90	70
135	70	65	125	195	215	90	180	

SOURCE: J. Ryan, "High Tech, High Touch," *Quality Progress,* September 1987, p. 20.

a   Obtain a sequence plot for the data. Is the production process stable with respect to number of nonconformances? Does the runs test support your visual impression? Draw the 3-standard-deviation control limits on the sequence plot. Comment.

b   Is the data distribution normal?

c   Delete the data for the first 15 space shuttles. Repeat (a) and (b) for the remainder of the observations. (What rationale might there be for deleting the first few observations?)

5.27   The Transportation Systems Office in the Ontario Ministry of Transportation provides systems development services to clients within the Ministry on a request basis.[10] The Office has four distinct sections that specialize in different types of engineering work: Sections 11 (structural design systems), 12 (engineering materials and research), 13 (transportation planning systems), and 14 (highway engineering systems). When a request is received by a section, it is evaluated, and completion time and cost are estimated. Once an evaluated request is approved for cost expenditure and completion date by the client, appropriate systems professionals apply their skills and talents to produce an acceptable set of deliverables that, when combined and implemented, produce a working system. A study was undertaken to answer the following questions.

- Is the estimation process stable?

- How do the approved cost and time figures compare with the actual figures? (It was considered acceptable for the difference between actual and approved costs to be 10% of actual cost or less and for the approved completion time to be within 30 days of actual completion time.)

- Is there a relationship between cost and time deviations?

- Are there differences across the four sections?

It was anticipated that cost and time deviations are within acceptable limits and that the process is stable. It was thought that there would not necessarily be a relationship between cost and time deviations, since elapsed times are influenced more by scheduling considerations than by the specific time that staff are assigned to projects.

---

[10]The data were kindly supplied by B. P. Vervenne.

Data were collected for the 148 projects completed in the period from April 1984 to March 1988. Six variables were measured on each project: (1) project number, (2) section number, (3) approved completion date, (4) actual completion date, (5) approved cost (in dollars), and (6) actual cost (in dollars). (Variables 3 and 4 are counted in days from January 1, 1984: day 1 = January 1, 1984, day 366 = December 31, 1984, day 367 = January 1, 1985, etc.) The data are stored in ASCII file TRANSMIN.DAT.

Use the data to answer the questions above plus an additional question:

- Are any of the projects outlying on any of the variables? If so, remove these projects from the analysis and redo it. Is there any justification for such removal? Do your answers to the above four questions change?

5.28 A Canadian waste management company experienced significant growth over the past few years.[11] In particular, cash requirements were growing rapidly, making cash management ever more important. Some concerns had arisen regarding the bad debt experience. A study was done to examine three managerial questions:

1. Is there a relationship between bad debt experience and the size of the accounts receivable (AR) balance?

2. Is there a relationship between bad debt experience and the three other variables, gross revenue, gross margin, and AR turnover?

3. Is the bad debt experience changing over time?

It was expected that bad debt as a percentage of total AR would be fairly constant. The relationship of bad debt with both AR turnover and gross revenue was expected to be strong, that with gross margin to be moderate.

Four variables were measured in each of the 35 months between January 1987 and November 1989: (1) bad debt, (2) the total outstanding AR balance, (3) gross revenue (in millions), and (4) gross margin, i.e., gross revenue minus direct selling costs (in millions). The data are stored in ASCII file ACC_REC.DAT.

The variable bad debt experience was defined as the ratio of bad debt to total outstanding AR balance (RATIO). It was expected that this ratio would be fairly constant. The relationship between this ratio and sales was expected to be strong.

a Obtain the control limits for RATIO.

b Is the process generating the RATIO values stable? Briefly justify your answer. If no, what are your concerns?

c Is the distribution of RATIO values normal? Briefly justify your answer. If no, describe the shape of the distribution.

d Is there a relationship between RATIO and total sales? Briefly describe the nature of this relationship.

In questions (e) to (g), assume that the process generating RATIO is stable and that the distribution of RATIO values is normal.

e Obtain a 90% prediction interval for the RATIO values. Interpret.

f Give a value for RATIO that will be exceeded with probability 1% only.

g If you knew that the total outstanding AR balance in December 1989 were $60,000, could you give an estimate of bad debt in December 1989 that would be exceeded with

---

[11]The data were slightly altered to protect confidentiality.

probability 1% only? If yes, provide a numerical answer. If no, what additional information do you need?

h Given your assessment in (b) regarding the stability of the process, how reliable is your answer in (e)?

i Assuming the process to be stable, but given your assessment regarding normality in (c), how reliable is your answer in (f)? Briefly discuss your concerns, if any, about the numerical answer in (f).

5.29 A pharmaceutical company's marketing department prepares monthly sales forecasts for many pharmaceutical products. The forecast quality has been a continuing issue in discussions between several departments concerned, particularly in marketing and finance. A study was done to identify the best forecasting method out of the available forecasting tool-kit. This study used the forecasts for a major product. Three questions were to be answered:

1. Are the deviations between sales and forecast random for the forecasting methods used?

2. Which method predicts sales most accurately?

3. Using the best method identified in (2), what level of safety stocks shall the company provide for the next month (July 1989) to have a 95% probability that sales will not be higher than the forecast?

Data were collected for the 42 months from January 1986 to June 1989. Four variables were measured in each month: the actual unit sales for the pharmaceutical product, and the forecasts of sales for the month in question using models A, B, and C. (Note that models A, B, and C have been in use for some time.) The data are stored in ASCII file FORECAST.DAT.

In this problem, you will analyze the quality of forecasting model C. Note that, in file FORECAST.DAT, the actual SALES are stored in C1 and the forecasts using MODEL_C in C4. You should create another variable measuring the forecast error for model C (ERROR_C), that is, the difference between actual sales and the forecasts from model C.

a Obtain the UCL and the LCL for ERROR_C.

b Is the process generating the ERROR_C values random? Be specific and justify your answer.

c What does the SALES vs. MODEL_C plot and the accompanying correlation tell you about the quality of forecasting model C?

d What does the ERROR_C vs. SALES plot and the accompanying correlation tell you about the quality of forecasting model C? Be specific.

e If forecasting model C were good, what would you expect the ERROR_C vs. SALES plot to look like? What would you expect the correlation between ERROR_C and SALES to be?

f Is the distribution of ERROR_C values approximately normal? Briefly justify your answer. If no, describe the shape of the distribution.

For questions (g) and (h), assume that the process generating forecasting errors is random, that the distribution of ERROR_C is normal, and that none of the concerns you may have raised in (c) and (d) is important.

g What is the 95th percentile for the distribution of forecasting errors?

h Suppose that the model C forecast for July 1989 was 120,000 items. How many items would have to be available to have 95% probability that sales will not exceed the number of available items?

i Given the concerns you had in (b) to (d), and (f), how reliable are your answers in (g) and (h)?

j Overall, give your brief evaluation of forecasting model C.

5.30 This problem analyzes a situation first described in Section 3.7. In early October 1990, Autosystems Manufacturing was having problems with the Buick Regal headlamp assembly. Rainwater was often leaking into the lamps because of gaps between the lens and the housing. These gaps varied significantly in size. The process of interest was injection molding of the lenses. After a machine injects the mold, the lenses are robotically removed from the machine and then cooled before measurements are made. The gapping problem was thought to stem from the injection molding process. A study was done to answer several questions:

1. **a** Is the injection molding process random for part weight of lenses? Do part weights vary within industry limits, which are set 3% above and below average part weight? What percentage of part weights falls outside these industry limits?

   b Is the process random for the lens to housing gap? What proportion of gaps is greater than 2 mm? (Such gaps would be suspect for leaks.)

   c Is the process random for lens length?

2. What is the relationship among lens weight, lens length, and the size of the gap?

   Data were collected by taking one lens from the process every 1.5 hours, yielding 10 lenses per day. This was done for 6 days, so the sample consisted of 60 lenses. Three variables were measured on each lens: part WEIGHT (in grams), part LENGTH (in mm), and GAP from a standard housing unit (in mm). The data are stored in ASCII file HEADLAMP.DAT.

   a Is the "lens to housing gap" process stable?

   b Assuming the process to be stable and making any necessary additional assumptions, what proportion of parts will be produced in the near future for which the gap is larger than 1.35 mm?

   c Assuming the process to be stable and making any necessary additional assumptions, what is the probability that the gap for the next part produced will be larger than 1.35 mm?

   d Assuming the process to be stable and making any necessary additional assumptions, what is the probability that the gap for the next part produced will not exceed the gap for the last part for which data are available?

   e Did you have to make any *additional* assumptions in (b–d)? If so, briefly describe what they were and how reasonable they were.

   f In light of your answer to (a), is the numerical answer to (b) reliable? If you had expressed concerns in (a), how would you revise your numerical answer to (b)?

   g Answer managerial questions 1(a–c).

   h Answer managerial question 2.

5.31 The Department of National Defense (DND) procures many items in order to maintain the operational readiness of the Canadian Forces.[12] Some of these items flow directly from the suppliers or contractors to the DND units requiring them. The balance are subject to periodic reviews to assure that all contractual requirements have been met before the materiel is delivered. These contract reviews are carried out by a number of regional Canadian Forces

---

[12]Thanks to A. Hofmann for making the data available.

Technical Services Detachments (CFTSD) established specifically for this purpose. A study was undertaken at one of these detachments to answer the following question:

What is the time required to perform a contract review?

During the period from February 1, 1991 to July 31, 1991, 165 review files were closed. Two variables were recorded for each: type of contract (1, 4, or 9), and the time taken to perform the review in hours (TIME). The data are stored in ASCII file CFTSD.DAT. The following questions relate to the 104 contracts of type 9, which is for items of basic design.

a Is the review process stable?

b In order to draw the line expected under normality on the normal probability plot, you must first find two points through which you can then draw the line. If one of these points has an NSCORE value of 1.6, what is the corresponding value for TIME? If the other point has an NSCORE value of −1.6, what is the corresponding value for TIME?

c Is the distribution of TIME normal? If it is not normal, what shape does it have?

d Assuming the process to be stable, but making no other assumptions unwarranted by the data, estimate the chances that the next contract for an item of basic design will be reviewed in 40 hours or less.

e In light of your analysis of the data, is the numerical answer to (d) reliable? If you had expressed concerns earlier, briefly describe their likely effect on your answer in (d).

5.32 The engineering department of a certain company was responsible for the design of construction and maintenance contracts for office buildings and other facilities. These design projects were regularly late as measured by their scheduled completion dates. The company's policy was that all design projects should be completed within 50 days of their scheduled completion date. It was felt that this policy was not always complied with. A related issue was whether delays could be linked to the project manager in charge of a particular project or to the magnitude of the project (as measured by the construction costs).

Data were collected for all 47 design projects consecutively completed between January 1, 1990 and December 31, 1990. Three variables were measured on each project: MNGR (1, 2, or 3), an identifier for the project manager who handled the project; COST (in dollars), the construction cost; and DELAY (in days), the difference between the actual and the scheduled completion dates. The data are stored in ASCII file DESIGN.DAT.

a Is this a cross-sectional or a time series study? What is the unit? If it is a cross-sectional study, what is the population? If it is a time series study, what is the process? What is the response variable?

b Is the process for DELAY random?

c A subsequent investigation showed that the extreme delays for projects 43, 44, and 47 were because they were placed on hold at the customers' requests, a circumstance that is both unusual and not under the company's control. These observations were dropped from the data. How does this change your answer to (b)?

For parts (d) to (l) assume that the process for DELAY is random and that observations 43, 44, and 47 have been dropped.

d In order to draw the line expected under normality on the normal probability plot for DELAY, you must first find two points through which you can then draw the line. If one of these points has an NSCORE value of 1.5, what is the corresponding value for DELAY? If the other point has an NSCORE value of −1.5, what is the corresponding value for DELAY?

e Is the distribution of DELAY normal? If it is not normal, what shape does it have?

f Assuming that the distribution for DELAY is normal, calculate the probability that the next project's delay will exceed 50 days.

g Would the assumption of normality be appropriate for the square root of DELAY, R_DELAY? *Assuming* this assumption to be appropriate, calculate the probability that the next project's delay will exceed 50 days.

h Calculate the probability that the next project's delay will exceed 50 days without making *any* assumptions about normality.

i Rank the accuracy of the probabilistic estimates in (f) to (h) (based on *your* opinion of their accuracy). Briefly state your reasons.

j If the company wanted to compute a bound for DELAY that would be exceeded no more than 1% of the time, what should it be? You should use the most appropriate model in (f) to (h) here.

k Do the delays appear to be related to the project costs?

l Do the delays appear to be related to the project manager in charge?

5.33 This exercise is a continuation of Exercise 5.12.

a Using the number of errors as the response variable, which procedure should be chosen? Prepare appropriate graphs and summary measures.

b In the above analysis and in Exercise 5.12, you ignored any differences between the two clerks. What speaks for and what against this assumption?

5.34 A gauging instrument was to be chosen for plant use. Two instrument brands were available. The chosen brand was to have the best repeatability, where repeatability was measured by the standard deviation of 10 measurements on the same part. The chosen brand was to be used by more than 100 operators in the plant. An operator's level of skill was known to influence repeatability.

It took about 1 hour to take the 10 measurements on a part. The plant manager said that about 60 hours of operator time would be available for the study.

Thirty operators were chosen at random from all the operators in the plant. Each selected operator tested each brand. The order in which the two brands were tested by an operator was randomized. For each operator, data were recorded on (1) brand tested first (1 or 2), (2) repeatability for brand 1 (standard deviation of 10 measurements on a part), and (3) repeatability for brand 2. The data are stored in ASCII file GAUGE.DAT.

a What is the purpose of randomizing the order in which each operator tests the two brands?

b Which brand should be chosen? Prepare appropriate graphs and summary measures.

6

TIME SERIES ANALYSIS: RANDOM WALKS

This chapter will help you solve the following types of problems:

- You want to predict the closing value for the price of a stock at the end of the next month. How can you use the stock's month-end closing prices for the last 5 years to do this?

- Your company has been in a phase of rapid growth that you expect to persist. How can you use monthly sales for the last few years to predict sales in the near future?

6.1

INTRODUCTION

In Chapter 5, you learned a simple time series model, the model of a random process. A process is random if there is no information whatsoever contained in the sequence of values generated by the process. The sequential order of the observations is then not important in the sense that the order could be changed without loss of information, so the time series values can be treated as if they were cross-sectional data. Summaries of the observations that ignore the sequential order—such as histograms, dotplots, means, standard deviations—are then useful. Often, but not always, a random process is accompanied by a normal distribution of values.

If the conditions underlying a stable process will remain unchanged in the near future, then it is possible to predict the behavior of the process. In particular,

- Observations will tend to fall around the center line, which is at the mean, in a random pattern.

- If the distribution of values is normal, 99.7% of all observations will be within 3 standard deviations of the mean.

In this chapter, you will learn another simple time series model, the *random walk model,* which is closely related to the model of a random process. We will check the appropriateness of this new model for two time series: (1) Standard & Poor's Composite Stock Index (SP), and (2) quarterly gross national product (GNP) data. Again you will see the usefulness of transformations that were introduced in Chapter 4.

6.2

RANDOM WALKS

The random walk is a time series of values for which successive changes from one value to the next are generated by a random process. Let us turn to an example to illustrate.

Standard & Poor's Composite Stock Index

Suppose you want to predict the closing value for Standard & Poor's composite index, SP, for January 1985. You have available 60 monthly closing values for SP for the period from January 1980 to December 1984. The data, stored in ASCII file SP_MONTH.DAT, are listed in Figure 6.1. *Any* analysis of a time series should start with a sequence plot. This is also given in Figure 6.1: The sequence of SP values does *not* conform to our model of a random process. The control chart in Figure 6.2 underlines this. Since the mean and standard deviation of the 60 SP values are 137.8 and 20.85, the upper and lower control limits in Figure 6.2 are at $137.8 + 3(20.85) = 200.4$ and $137.8 - 3(20.85) = 75.25$, respectively.

Although all values of the time series are well within 3 standard deviations of the mean, the behavior of the time series is *definitely not random* over time. There seems to be a *meandering* pattern, where observations close together in time tend to be close in value. The runs test for randomness in Figure 6.3 confirms the visual impression from Figure 6.2: Since the *p*-value is 0.0000, the runs test is significant, that is, the series is *not* random.

If you had just observed the 60th value (which is 167.24), and if you had to base a prediction of the 61st month's closing value on the time series plot in Figure 6.2, your prediction would *not* be at the mean of SP, 137.8, but closer to the most recently observed values—that is, around 167.24. Your prediction interval would *not* extend 3 standard deviations around the mean or even 3 standard deviations around 167.24. It would be much narrower because of the small variability in the

FIGURE 6.1 Listing and Time Series Plot for the SP Data

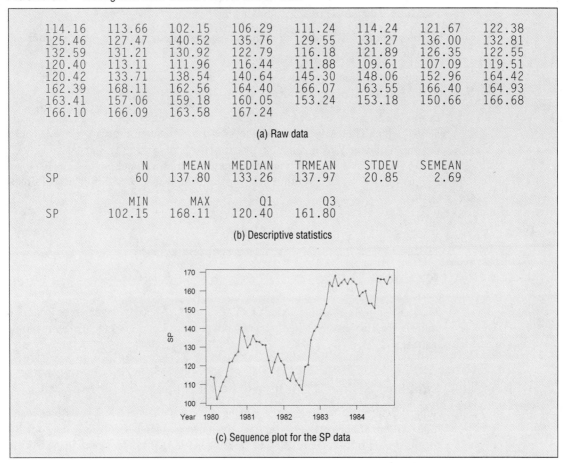

```
114.16   113.66   102.15   106.29   111.24   114.24   121.67   122.38
125.46   127.47   140.52   135.76   129.55   131.27   136.00   132.81
132.59   131.21   130.92   122.79   116.18   121.89   126.35   122.55
120.40   113.11   111.96   116.44   111.88   109.61   107.09   119.51
120.42   133.71   138.54   140.64   145.30   148.06   152.96   164.42
162.39   168.11   162.56   164.40   166.07   163.55   166.40   164.93
163.41   157.06   159.18   160.05   153.24   153.18   150.66   166.68
166.10   166.09   163.58   167.24
```

(a) Raw data

```
              N      MEAN    MEDIAN   TRMEAN    STDEV    SEMEAN
SP           60     137.80   133.26   137.97    20.85     2.69

            MIN      MAX       Q1       Q3
SP        102.15   168.11   120.40   161.80
```

(b) Descriptive statistics

(c) Sequence plot for the SP data

FIGURE 6.2
i Chart of SP Data

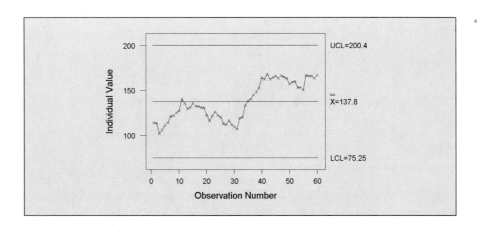

FIGURE 6.3
Runs Test for
SP Data

```
SP

  K =    137.8007

  The observed no. of runs =   4
  The expected no. of runs =  30.7000
  27 Observations above K   33 below
            The test is significant at 0.0000
```

most recent observations as compared to the overall variability in the 60 values. Thus, a random model is *totally* inappropriate for the data at hand.

The remarks in the last paragraph, relating to the prediction of the 61st month's closing value (that is, the closing value in January 1985), hinge on using the most recent values more heavily for prediction than earlier values. Putting this another way, what seems to be important to predict the *change* from the (known) 60th value to the (unknown) 61st value is the *difference* between successive values in the past. The details of the appropriate statistical technique, *differencing,* are described in the next subsection.

Differencing

Let us look at differences of successive values of the SP series. Such differences are called differences of *lag 1,* or "lag 1 differences," because they measure the change between observations *one* period apart. (If interest had focused on observations one year or *twelve* periods apart, *lag 12* differences would have been computed.) For example, the first two values are 114.16 and 113.66, and so the change to the second value from the first is 113.66 − 114.16 = −0.50; that is, there is a decline to the second value.

Figure 6.4 shows the lag 1 differences for the SP data. The time series plot in Figure 6.5(a) does not display the meandering nature of the original SP values. There is much less of a time series pattern to these lag 1 differences, if there is a time series pattern at all. Figure 6.5(a) thus suggests that lag 1 differences in SP values may be random. In Figure 6.5(a), the control limits are at UCL = 17.5 and LCL = −15.7; they are determined by the magnitude of the standard deviation, which is much larger than the mean. All lag 1 differences are between the upper and lower control limits, and they appear to be randomly distributed around the center line. The runs test in Figure 6.5(b) is somewhat inconclusive, but it does not suggest nonrandomness.

A **random walk** is a time series whose lag 1 differences are a random series.

In a random walk, the standard deviation of the lag 1 differences is typically less than the standard deviation of the undifferenced series.

FIGURE 6.4 Lag 1 Differences for the SP Data

```
ROW       SP        D_SP

  1    114.16          *      (The lag 1 difference is not defined for row 1
                              because there is no value for row 0 of SP.)
  2    113.66    -0.5000      (The difference for row 2 is SP in row 2 minus
                              SP in row 1, 113.66 - 114.16 = -0.50
  3    102.15   -11.5100
  4    106.29     4.1400
  5    111.24     4.9500
...

 57    166.10    -0.5800
 58    166.09    -0.0100
 59    163.58    -2.5100
 60    167.24     3.6600
```

(a) Partial listing of SP and lag 1 differences

```
            N        N*      MEAN     MEDIAN    TRMEAN     STDEV    SEMEAN
SP         60         0    137.80     133.26    137.97     20.85      2.69
D_SP       59         1     0.900      0.710     0.710      5.530     0.720

          MIN       MAX        Q1         Q3
SP     102.15    168.11    120.40     161.80
D_SP   -11.510   16.020    -2.520      4.460
```

(b) Descriptive statistics

FIGURE 6.5
Lag 1 Differences
of SP Data: Checks
of Randomness

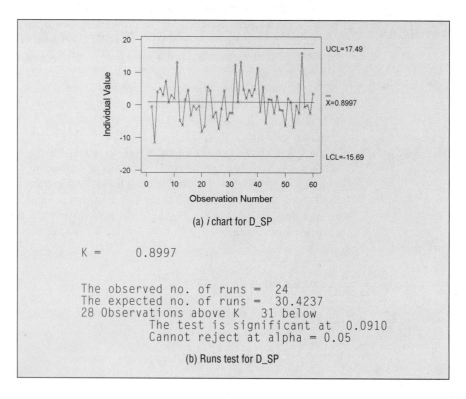

(a) *i* chart for D_SP

```
K =      0.8997


The observed no. of runs =   24
The expected no. of runs =   30.4237
28 Observations above K    31 below
        The test is significant at  0.0910
        Cannot reject at alpha = 0.05
```

(b) Runs test for D_SP

In a random walk, the *un*differenced series is, of course, *not* random; see, for example, the SP values in Figure 6.2.

Using this definition of a random walk, we can conclude that the 60 SP values come from a process that is a random walk. The discussion here only used elementary time series concepts to check if the randomness assumption holds for the lag 1 differences, the visual check of their sequence plot, the control chart limits, and the runs test. But more advanced techniques, some of which will be discussed in Chapters 11 and 12, essentially lead to the same conclusion. In fact, there is considerable evidence in the financial literature that the stock market follows a random walk.

Further Discussion of the SP Series as a Random Walk

What is essential in the definition of a random walk is that the lag 1 differences of the series be random. Nothing whatsoever is assumed about the histogram of lag 1 differences. They may or may not follow a normal distribution. Let us check the histograms of both the original 60 SP values and their 59 lag 1 differences, given in Figure 6.6.

FIGURE 6.6
Graphs for SP Data

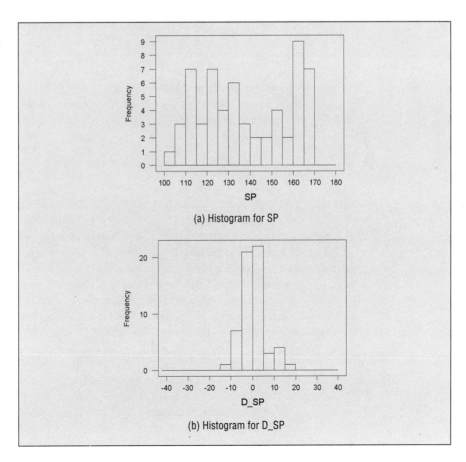

(a) Histogram for SP

(b) Histogram for D_SP

FIGURE 6.7
Normal Probability
Plot of Lag 1
Differences of
SP Data

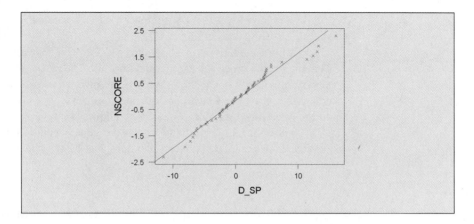

The histogram of SP values, in fact, is quite *useless* since the underlying time series is not random. A normal distribution superimposed on the histogram for the lag 1 differences may be a crude approximation, and a further visual check, the normal probability plot displayed in Figure 6.7, confirms this. Figure 6.7 suggests possible deviations from the line expected under normality: Several points at the upper end of the scale are somewhat below the line. These deviations are serious enough so that the normal distribution is at best a crude approximation for the lag 1 differences.

As was suggested in the discussion of Figure 6.2 when motivating the lag 1 differences, the local variation in SP values, as measured by the variation in the changes, is much less than the overall variation in SP values, as measured by the variation of SP values around their mean. A comparison of the standard deviation of the SP values and that of their lag 1 differences is instructive now. Part of Figure 6.4 is reproduced here:

	N	N*	MEAN	MEDIAN	STDEV
SP	60	0	137.80	133.26	20.85
D_SP	59	1	0.900	0.710	5.530

The standard deviation of lag 1 differences, 5.53, is much lower than the standard deviation of SP values, 20.85. Such a drop is necessary for a random walk to be a useful model for the time series. Of course, even when there is such a drop, the random walk model may not be appropriate.

To show that lag 1 differences will not always have a lower standard deviation than the original time series, Figure 6.8 gives some statistics for the bendclip diameter data, discussed in Chapter 5. See Figure 5.2, p. 161. Here the standard deviation of the bendclip diameter values, 0.06, is *smaller* than the standard deviation of their lag 1 differences, 0.09, and a random walk model would be inappropriate. In fact, in Chapter 5 we had seen that the bendclip diameter values themselves are random. It turns out that the lag 1 differences of a random series are *not* a random series and that their standard deviation is larger than that for the undifferenced series. The lag 1 differences will tend to oscillate—that is, the line connecting successive values will cross the mean more frequently than would be expected of a ran-

FIGURE 6.8 Bendclip Diameter Data (DIAMETER) and Their Lag 1 Differences (D_DIAMTR)

	N	MEAN	MEDIAN	TRMEAN	STDEV	SEMEAN
DIAMETER	40	0.73175	0.73000	0.73194	0.06008	0.00950
D_DIAMTR	39	0.0023	0.0000	0.0014	0.0937	0.0150

	MIN	MAX	Q1	Q3
DIAMETER	0.60000	0.86000	0.69250	0.77000
D_DIAMTR	-0.2100	0.2100	-0.0600	0.0600

(a) Descriptive statistics

```
K =      0.7318

The observed no. of runs =   24
The expected no. of runs =   20.9500
19 Observations above K    21 below
          The test is significant at   0.3275
          Cannot reject at alpha = 0.05
```

(b) Runs test for DIAMETER

```
K =      0.0023

The observed no. of runs =   27
The expected no. of runs =   20.3846
18 Observations above K    21 below
          The test is significant at    0.0310
```

(c) Runs test for D_DIAMTR

dom series. Hence there will be too many runs, and the time series plot will have a saw-tooth appearance.

Prediction for the SP Series

Let us now obtain a prediction for the closing value in January 1985 (the 61st value of the SP series). The 60th value is *known* to be 167.24 (see Figure 6.1). We need to predict the change to the 61st value. If conditions underlying the series in the recent past can be expected to persist into the near future, then the change to the 61st value will be similar to the changes between successive values (that is, lag 1 differences) in the past. Since these lag 1 differences are random for the SP series, their time order is not important in predicting the next lag 1 difference. What is important is the *distribution* of lag 1 differences, which Figure 6.7 showed to be approximately normal with mean and standard deviation as given in Figure 6.4, 0.90 and 5.53, respectively. So we can predict the next lag 1 difference—the change from the 60th to the 61st value—to be a random draw from the same distribution from which the previous lag 1 differences were drawn. A good estimate for this change is the mean of that distribution, which is approximately 0.90. Thus the prediction for the 61st observation is

$$167.24 + 0.90 = 168.14$$

This is an application of the following prediction model:

Predicted Next Value = Current Level + Mean Change

Of course, there is considerable uncertainty about this prediction. This uncertainty comes about because we had to predict the change in the presence of considerable variation in past changes, as indicated by their standard deviation, 5.53. The usual 3-standard-deviation limits around the prediction are $3(5.53) = 16.59$ units away from the predicted level. The resulting 99.7% prediction interval is

$$168.14 \pm 16.59 \qquad \text{or} \qquad 151.55 \text{ to } 184.73.$$

The "99.7%" comes about since (1) the lag 1 differences of the SP values approximately follow a normal distribution, and (2) we used a multiple of 3 standard deviations around the point prediction, 168.14. Other multiples could be used, and they would lead to different prediction intervals. The general formula for a prediction interval is

prediction interval   Predicted Value $\pm z$(Standard Deviation of Changes)

The value of z is chosen from the normal distribution, Table 4.1 or the *Calc* ▸ *Probability Distributions* ▸ *Normal* menu in Minitab, in accordance with the level of uncertainty that is acceptable in a given case. Using this table is, of course, only reasonable if the distribution of changes is approximately normal.

The amount of uncertainty expressed by the width of the 3-standard-deviation interval for the SP example may be considered "too high," but it is *irreducible* given the current data. Since we had concluded that the lag 1 differences are random, predictability cannot be improved by further pondering the *available* data. In principle, it may be possible to obtain additional information. Studies of stock price behavior, however, have shown that additional information would not help much. In this application, the *high uncertainty is a fact of life*.

Before turning to the next application, a few comments on modeling are in order.

6.3

MODELING OF A PROCESS

In Chapter 5, we defined a stable or random process in which only common causes of variation are present. Such a process will generate data with constant level and random variation around it. The distribution of values around the constant level is sometimes normal. When this model adequately describes a particular process and when the conditions underlying the process are not expected to change, then the model can be used for prediction. In particular,

- It is expected that the process will continue to generate values around the center line, representing the mean of the recent observations.

- There is no time series pattern to the way the values will fall around the center line.

- Practically all observations will fall between the upper and lower control limits, UCL and LCL, which characterize the capability of the process.

Since any process generates output that can be measured, resulting in data, we often talk of a **data-generating process.**

data-generating process

A **model** of many data-generating processes can be represented conceptually by the equation

Actual = Systematic Part + Residual

or

y = Systematic Part + ϵ

where

Actual or y refers to an actual observation generated according to the model

Systematic Part refers to a predictable feature of the model that is common to *all* observations

Residual or ϵ describes the amount by which an Actual observation differs from the Systematic Part, and it captures the random aspect. The process mean of residuals equals 0, and their standard deviation is denoted σ.

The model can be used for prediction purposes. For example, to get a *point prediction* (that is, a one-number prediction or best guess), the Systematic Part of the model can be used, and to get an *interval prediction,* a 3-standard-deviation (3σ) interval can be constructed around it.

The Residual is due to the fact that a chance system of common causes operates in any process. This leads to variability among the individual observations generated by the process. The numerical value of the residual for an individual observation cannot be predicted or explained using information presently available. Thus, the residual reflects the uncertainty in the model due to imperfect information that is expected to persist until more complete information is obtained. In this sense, the residual can be interpreted as if it were unpredictable or random, and we say that the Residual captures the random aspect of the model. A one-number summary for this uncertainty is the residual's standard deviation, σ. Given the currently available information used to build the model, this uncertainty is irreducible. If we used additional information, we could possibly find an improved model, which accounts for some of this uncertainty.

In the random process model, the basis for prediction—that is, the Systematic Part—is the process mean. In the random walk model, the basis for prediction is the most recent observation.

Modeling a Random Process

Section 5.7 (p. 175) discussed the model of a random process. In this model, the Systematic Part is the mean of the process, μ_y. The Residual, ϵ, is the deviation of an actual observation from the process mean. Often the Residuals are normally distributed. In symbolic form, we can write this as

$$y = \mu_y + \epsilon$$

We can view the generation of an Actual value, y, as a two-stage process:

1. y is set at the mean μ_y, the Systematic Part

2. The chance system of common causes draws a value from the distribution of Residuals (ϵ) and adds this to the Systematic Part.

Models are useful devices for communicating how we think data are generated. A model attempts to capture the salient aspects of the data-generating process, leaving out seemingly unimportant details. Since not all aspects of the process are captured, the model is only an approximation. But it may be useful if the salient aspects modeled allow a sufficiently accurate understanding of the data-generating process and sufficiently accurate predictions into the near future.

Modeling a Random Walk

The major business use for the random walk model is in describing the movement of the stock market, such as stock market indexes, stock prices, and mutual fund prices. There is considerable evidence that the random walk model is an adequate model for such time series. Variations on the random walk model are appropriate for other financial time series, such as interest rates and exchange rates. The appropriateness of the random walk model has important implications for finance that are discussed in elementary finance texts.

The random walk model also fits the modeling framework outlined at the beginning of this section. In a random walk, the lag 1 differences (that is, the changes) are random, so the *model for the lag 1 differences* is

Actual = Systematic Part + Residual

or

Change = Mean Change + Residual

where the Residuals (that is, the deviations of actual changes from the mean change) constitute a random series. The model for the random walk (which is the *un*differenced series) is

Observed Value = Previous Value + Change

Combining this with the model for Change, we get

Observed Value = Previous Value + (Mean Change + Residual)

or

Observed Value = (Previous Value + Mean Change) + Residual

model of a random walk

It is common notation to let y_{-1} represent the previous value of the variable of interest. Here the subscript "-1" in y_{-1} is to denote the value of y "one period before." In symbolic notation, we thus have the model of a random walk:

$$y = (y_{-1} + \mu) + \epsilon$$

or

Actual = Systematic Part + Residual

Thus the model for a random walk fits the general model of a data-generating process, where

Actual or y refers to an actually observed value generated by the random walk.

Systematic Part, or $y_{-1} + \mu$, is the prediction for a particular observation, which is obtained by adding the mean change, μ, to the previous value, y_{-1}.

Residual or ϵ describes by how much an actual value differs from the predicted value. The mean of the Residuals is 0, and their standard deviation is denoted σ.

The **random walk model** can be represented by two simple equations:

1. Observed Value = Previous Value + Change

2. Change = Mean Change + Residual.

These two equations can be combined to read

Observed Value = (Previous Value + Mean Change) + Residual

or

$$y = (y_{-1} + \mu) + \epsilon$$

and so the random walk model fits the basic model equation,

Actual = Systematic Part + Residual

The process parameters μ and σ are typically unknown and must be estimated by the sample mean change and the sample standard deviation of changes.[1]

We can view the generation of an Actual value y from a random walk as a three-stage process:

1. y is set at the previous value.

2. The mean change μ is added to the previous value.

3. A chance system draws a value from the distribution of Residuals (ϵ) and adds this to the Systematic Part, which equals the previous value plus the predicted change.

With respect to the SP series, we can write the random walk model as

$$SP = SP_{-1} + \text{Mean D\_SP} + \epsilon$$

where SP_{-1} is the previous SP value, D_SP is the lag 1 Differences of SP, and the residual ϵ is a random observation from an approximately normal distribution with mean 0 and standard deviation equal to the standard deviation σ of lag 1 differences, estimated by 5.53.

When getting a point prediction for the next SP value, a point prediction for the residual ϵ is its mean, 0. So the point prediction is

$$SP_{-1} + 0.90$$

where Mean D_SP = 0.90 is an estimate of the process mean change μ. In order to get an interval prediction for the next value of SP, we must construct an interval around this point prediction using a suitable multiple from the normal distribution. A 95% prediction interval extends 2 standard deviations around the point prediction, or

$$(SP_{-1} + 0.90) \pm 2(5.53) \qquad \text{or} \qquad (SP_{-1} + 0.90) \pm 11.06$$

prediction interval   In general, the prediction interval for the next unit is

$$(y_{-1} + \mu) \pm z\,\sigma$$

where the previous value, y_{-1}, is known, and the process parameters must be estimated from the sample. Finally the multiple z comes from the normal distribution

---

[1]Notice that

$$\text{Residual} = (\text{Observed Value} - \text{Previous Value}) - \text{Mean Change}$$

or

$$\text{Residual} = \qquad \text{Change} \qquad - \text{Mean Change}$$

In other words, the Residual differs from the lag 1 difference (change) by a constant only (the Mean Change, which equals the mean of the lag 1 differences). It can be shown that the standard deviation of Residuals is exactly the same as the standard deviation of changes.

table, but it must have been ascertained that the normal distribution describes the distribution of changes well.

The appropriateness of a random walk model can be examined with suitable *diagnostic checks*. The model is adequate if

- Visual inspection of the sequence plot of lag 1 differences suggests randomness.

- This visual impression of randomness is supported by the runs test.

- All lag 1 differences are within the control limits.

(If the runs test is inconclusive, you must rely on the other diagnostics.) Furthermore, probabilities can be attached to prediction intervals computed from the random walk model, if

- The normal probability plot of lag 1 differences suggests normality.

Figure 5.7 presented a flow chart for modeling a random process. Figure 6.9 expands this flow chart to incorporate the modeling approach discussed in this chapter.

Simulation of a Random Walk

The random walk model is used for planning in many business situations that depend on any of the time series mentioned on page 238. Sometimes it is necessary to get an idea of how a particular time series might develop in the future. Using the random walk model, it is possible to simulate the development of such time series.

Consider the evaluation of a proposed investment strategy. Since the movement of many stock market indexes is well described by a random walk model, the future development of the stocks considered for investment can be simulated suitably far into the future, and the investment strategy can be evaluated. This simulation and evaluation step can be carried out repeatedly to see how the proposed investment strategy would do for many possible future scenarios. It can then be compared with other investment strategies.

As an example, consider the SP monthly closing values discussed in previous sections. The most recent value available was the closing value in December 1984, 167.24. Using the random walk model implies that successive changes can be simulated using a normal distribution with mean 0.90 and standard deviation 5.53.

In Figure 6.10, 36 values are randomly drawn from a normal distribution with mean 0.90 and standard deviation 5.53. The resulting sample mean (0.561) and standard deviation (5.282) for the 36 values are not far from 0.90 and 5.53. These changes are then accumulated and the accumulations are added to the most recently available closing value, 167.24. The resulting simulated time series covers 36 months and is plotted in Figure 6.11. This simulated time series is, of course, only *one* plausible way the SP series will develop in the next 36 months. Using another 36 randomly drawn values from a normal distribution with mean 0.90 and standard deviation 5.53, a second plausible realization is plotted in Figure 6.12.

Such simulations are useful since many more plausible realizations can be simulated and used to evaluate the consequences of a planned action. It is then possible to modify the planned action in such a way that its consequences will be satis-

FIGURE 6.9 Flow Chart for Time Series Modeling

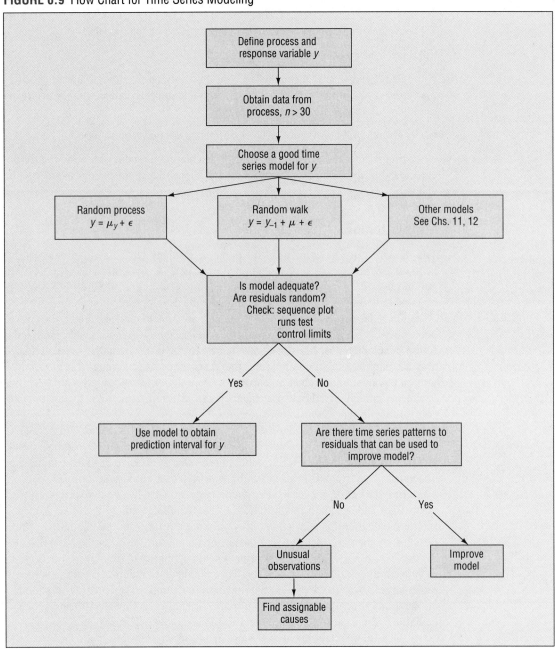

FIGURE 6.10
Simulated Changes for the SP Series

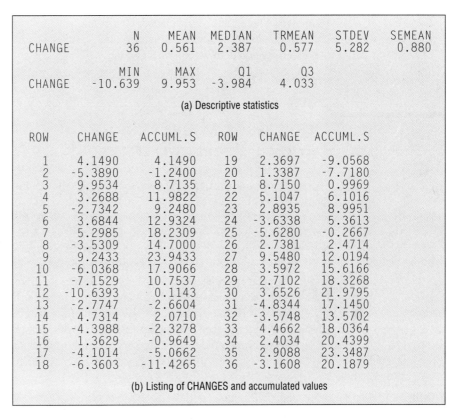

	N	MEAN	MEDIAN	TRMEAN	STDEV	SEMEAN
CHANGE	36	0.561	2.387	0.577	5.282	0.880

	MIN	MAX	Q1	Q3
CHANGE	-10.639	9.953	-3.984	4.033

(a) Descriptive statistics

ROW	CHANGE	ACCUML.S	ROW	CHANGE	ACCUML.S
1	4.1490	4.1490	19	2.3697	-9.0568
2	-5.3890	-1.2400	20	1.3387	-7.7180
3	9.9534	8.7135	21	8.7150	0.9969
4	3.2688	11.9822	22	5.1047	6.1016
5	-2.7342	9.2480	23	2.8935	8.9951
6	3.6844	12.9324	24	-3.6338	5.3613
7	5.2985	18.2309	25	-5.6280	-0.2667
8	-3.5309	14.7000	26	2.7381	2.4714
9	9.2433	23.9433	27	9.5480	12.0194
10	-6.0368	17.9066	28	3.5972	15.6166
11	-7.1529	10.7537	29	2.7102	18.3268
12	-10.6393	0.1143	30	3.6526	21.9795
13	-2.7747	-2.6604	31	-4.8344	17.1450
14	4.7314	2.0710	32	-3.5748	13.5702
15	-4.3988	-2.3278	33	4.4662	18.0364
16	1.3629	-0.9649	34	2.4034	20.4399
17	-4.1014	-5.0662	35	2.9088	23.3487
18	-6.3603	-11.4265	36	-3.1608	20.1879

(b) Listing of CHANGES and accumulated values

FIGURE 6.11
Sequence Plot of the Simulated SP Series

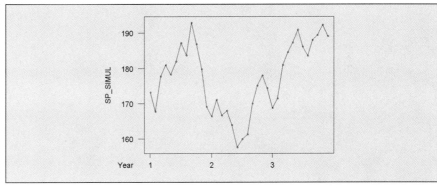

FIGURE 6.12
Another Simulated SP Series

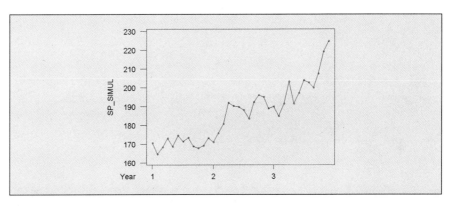

factory for a large number of plausible realizations that were simulated from an appropriate random walk model. Of course, the simulated realizations are only good if the underlying random walk model is good.

6.4

QUARTERLY CANADIAN GROSS NATIONAL PRODUCT DATA

This section examines quarterly Canadian gross national product data from the first quarter in 1971 to the last quarter in 1983, stored in Column 3 of ASCII file CND_QRT.DAT. This time series is not a random walk, but a simple preliminary step, called the *square root transformations*, leads to a series that is close to a random walk. (Transformation were already discussed in Section 4.7, p. 140.)

The 52 quarterly values are in billions of dollars. They are seasonally adjusted at annual rates. The data were obtained from the Bank of Canada Review. A listing of the data and a sequence plot are given in Figure 6.13.

The GNP data, of course, do not constitute a random series. There is a very strong and slightly accelerating upward drift, with variability around a smooth curve drawn through the data being very small. Using a random process model for

FIGURE 6.13 Quarterly Canadian GNP Data

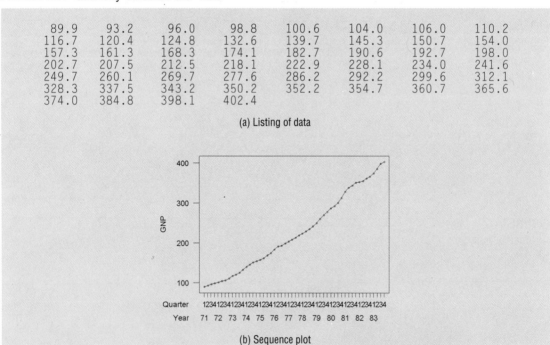

(a) Listing of data

(b) Sequence plot

FIGURE 6.14 Lag 1 Differences of Quarterly GNP Data

	N	N*	MEAN	MEDIAN	TRMEAN	STDEV	SEMEAN
GNP	52	0	224.5	210.0	222.0	96.3	13.4
D_GNP	51	1	6.127	5.600	5.882	3.031	0.424

	MIN	MAX	Q1	Q3
GNP	89.9	402.4	141.1	309.0
D_GNP	1.800	16.200	4.000	7.900

(a) Descriptive statistics

(b) *i* chart for D_GNP

the GNP series as a basis for predicting future GNP values, say of the 53rd value corresponding to the first quarter of 1984, would be totally inappropriate. This is so, for example, because the mean of the 52 GNP values, 224.5, is not useful at all to predict the 53rd value. Since we expect the 53rd value to be closer to the most recent values, a random walk specification for the GNP data may be a good starting point. The lag 1 differences of the GNP data are described in Figure 6.14.

The sequence of lag 1 differences does not appear to be random. The more recent lag 1 differences are more variable than earlier lag 1 differences. This should be taken into consideration in predicting the next lag 1 difference. Furthermore, one lag 1 difference is outside the control limits. Comparing Figures 6.13 and 6.14, notice that the variation in lag 1 differences tends to increase as GNP increases.

transformation

When variation in the lag 1 differences tends to increase with the size of the undifferenced values, as in the GNP example, one simple preliminary step often helps: a **transformation** of the undifferenced values. Many transformations are available, as discussed in Section 4.7. Two very important ones are the square root transformation and the logarithmic transformation. In the case of the GNP data, we use the square root transformation, and we let R_GNP be the variable containing the transformed GNP values. The first few values for GNP (GNP), lag 1 differences of GNP (D_GNP), square root of GNP (R_GNP), and lag 1 differences of R_GNP (DR_GNP) are given in Figure 6.15.

FIGURE 6.15

```
ROW       GNP       D_GNP      R_GNP       DR_GNP

  1       89.9         *       9.4816          *
  2       93.2      3.3000     9.6540       0.172454
  3       96.0      2.8000     9.7980       0.143945
  4       98.8      2.8000     9.9398       0.141860
  5      100.6      1.8000    10.0300       0.090136
  6      104.0      3.4000    10.1980       0.168084
  7      106.0      2.0000    10.2956       0.097591
  8      110.2      4.2000    10.4976       0.201988
  9      116.7      6.5000    10.8028       0.305159
 10      120.4      3.7000    10.9727       0.169916
  .
  .
  .
```

(a) Partial listing of GNP data, lag 1 differences (D_GNP),
square root of GNP data (R_GNP), and
lag 1 differences of R_GNP (DR_GNP)

	N	N*	MEAN	MEDIAN	TRMEAN	STDEV	SEMEAN
R_GNP	52	0	14.632	14.491	14.615	3.257	0.452
DR_GNP	51	1	0.2074	0.1908	0.2051	0.0827	0.0116

	MIN	MAX	Q1	Q3
R_GNP	9.482	20.060	11.878	17.577
DR_GNP	0.0534	0.4527	0.1585	0.2584

(b) Descriptive statistics

A sequence plot of the values contained in R_GNP is given in Figure 6.16. The sequence plot of lag 1 differences of R_GNP, given as a control chart, is in Figure 6.17.

The sequence plot of DR_GNP does not display the increasing variability of the sequence plot for D_GNP. This is due to the square root transformation[2]. Further visual examination of Figure 6.17 suggests that the DR_GNP series may be random. All values are within the 3-standard-deviation limits, though observation 41, corresponding to the first quarter of 1981, is close to the upper control limit.

However, examine the runs test for DR_GNP shown in Figure 6.18. The fact that there are too few runs shows that our judgment of randomness based on visual examination of Figure 6.17 was not quite satisfactory. The runs test forces us to conclude that the random walk model for R_GNP is not really appropriate. The random walk model for the square root of GNP is much better, however, than the random walk model for GNP. Subsequent chapters will introduce further refinements for analyses of time series data.

------

[2]A logarithmic transformation was also tried. It was too extreme, however, and led to decreasing dispersion in the lag 1 differences.

FIGURE 6.16
Sequence Plot of
R_GNP

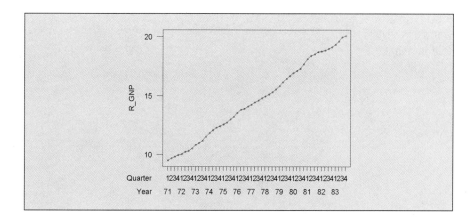

FIGURE 6.17
Sequence Plot of
Lag 1 Differences
of R_GNP

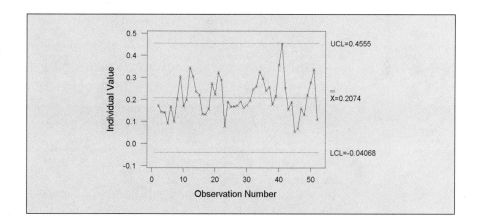

FIGURE 6.18
Runs Test for
DR_GNP

```
K = 0.2074

The observed no. of runs =  13
The expected no. of runs =  26.0196
22 Observations above K   29 below
          The test is significant at  0.0002
```

Even though further refinements are necessary, let us assume for purposes of illustration that the random walk model can be used for prediction.

Figure 6.19 gives a normal probability plot for the lag 1 differences of the square root of GNP, and there is some deviation from normality. (You should draw in the line expected under normality.) The slightly bow-shaped pattern suggests a very mild degree of positive skewness. Note the outlying value at the top of the graph.

FIGURE 6.19
Normal Probability
Plot for the
DR_GNP Data

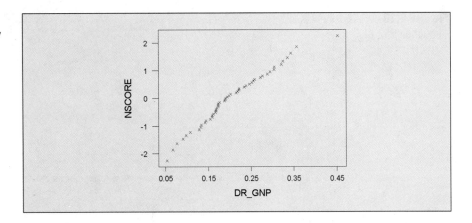

Let us summarize our findings about the GNP series:

- A square root transformation of the GNP series is useful, resulting in R_GNP.

- R_GNP does not quite follow a random walk. The lag 1 differences (DR_GNP) are not quite random, since their sequence plot displays too few runs.

- The distribution of lag 1 differences can only approximately be described by a normal distribution. It displays a mild amount of positive skewness.

It is thus clear that the random walk model for the square root of GNP is not as successful as the random walk model for the SP data. A more refined model of the GNP data is needed.

In using the square root transformation, no information has been lost. After modeling the transformed data, we can go back to the original data by reversing the transformation process. For example, we could obtain a predicted value for the change in the square root of GNP. From this a predicted value for the square root of GNP can be obtained, and by squaring that value we can get a prediction for GNP.

In spite of our reservations about the adequacy of a random walk model for the quarterly square rooted GNP data, let us obtain a prediction for the first quarter in 1984 with this model *to show the mechanics.*

The random walk model is

$$\sqrt{GNP} = \left[\sqrt{GNP_{-1}} + \text{Mean of DR\_GNP} \right] + \epsilon$$

where

$\sqrt{GNP_{-1}}$ is the square root of GNP in the last quarter 1983, $\sqrt{402.4} = 20.1$

Mean of DR_GNP is the mean of the lag 1 differences of the square root of GNP (DR_GNP), 0.2074 (see Figure 6.15)

ϵ measures the residual variation that is irreducible given the information available. Here the appropriate standard deviation applicable to Residual for prediction purposes is the standard deviation for DR_GNP, 0.0827 (see Figure 6.15) and the mean of Residual equals 0.

Therefore, a *point prediction* for the square root of GNP in the first quarter 1984 is

$$\sqrt{\text{GNP}_{-1}} + \text{Mean of DR\_GNP} \qquad \text{or} \qquad \sqrt{402.4} + 0.2074 = 20.27$$

so a prediction for GNP in the first quarter 1984 is

$$(20.27)^2 = 410.8$$

A 3-standard-deviation *prediction interval* for the square root of GNP in the first quarter 1984 is

$$\text{Point Prediction} \pm 3(\text{Standard Deviation})$$

or

$$20.27 \pm 3(0.0827) \qquad \text{or} \qquad 20.02 \text{ to } 20.52$$

and so the corresponding 99.7% prediction interval for GNP in the first quarter 1984 is

$$(20.02)^2 \text{ to } (20.52)^2 \qquad \text{or} \qquad 400.8 \text{ to } 420.9$$

Once again, we had reservations about the adequacy of the random walk model, and so this prediction derived from it is not adequate.

There is an important warning about data following a random walk. As seen in the SP data, random walks often display meandering behavior that might suggest cyclical behavior. One may be tempted to use this cyclical pattern for prediction purposes. But the meandering behavior is *not* cyclical (as this book defines the term). A true cyclical time series pattern displays *constant* time periods from peak to peak or from trough to trough. When a random walk suggests a cyclical pattern, it is an optical illusion. Peaks or troughs cannot be expected to be a constant number of periods apart. The fact that changes are random defeats any attempt to exploit such "cyclical" patterns.

6.5

SUMMARY AND OUTLOOK

Both applications in this chapter suggest the usefulness of differencing, or examining the changes between successive observations. When these changes are random, the original time series is said to be a random walk. The SP data closely followed a random walk, whereas the square roots of the GNP data only very approximately followed one. An interesting book on the financial implications of the random walk model is Malkiel (1990).

The GNP application suggested a further simple technique for modeling data, a transformation. Here a square root transformation was useful to achieve constance of standard deviation for the lag 1 differences of the transformed series.

In order to check the adequacy of models, several diagnostic checks must be carried out

- To check the randomness of a time series, use a control chart and the runs test

- To check the normality of a distribution, use a normal probability plot

In a random walk we again find randomness, but in disguise. It is the lag 1 differences that are random. As in Chapter 5, we used control charts to visually determine the randomness of the lag 1 differences, and so control charts have important applications outside the quality control applications discussed in Chapter 5.

We will have more to say about random walks in Chapter 11. The next chapter examines cross-sectional data in more detail. In particular, it discusses how the margin of error can be estimated when generalizing from a sample to the population it was randomly drawn from. Once estimation of the margin of error will have been discussed for cross-sectional data, we will be able to apply these ideas to some time series data in Chapter 8, where we will also introduce a few more types of control charts.

Key Terms and Concepts

differencing	random walk
data-generating process	transformation

Reference

Malkiel, B. G. (1990), *A Random Walk Down Wall Street: Including a Life-Cycle Guide to Personal Investing*, Norton, NY.

6.6

USING MINITAB FOR WINDOWS

This section shows how several of the graphs in this chapter were generated with Minitab for Windows.

Figure 6.1(c)

Choose *File* ▸ *Other Files* ▸ *Import ASCII Data*
In the *Import ASCII Data* dialog box,
    Under *Store data in column,* type **C1**
    Click *ok*
    In the *Import Text From File* dialog box,
        Choose and click data file *sp_month.dat,* click *ok*

DELETING ROWS FROM THE WORKSHEET

> Choose *Window* ► *Data*
> In the *Data* window,
>> Highlight rows 61 to 144 in column *C1*
>> Choose *Edit* ► *Cut Cells*
>>> (These commands delete rows 61 to 144. They are not used in the analysis.)
>> In the box immediately under *C1*, type **SP**
>> Click any empty cell

LABELING THE TIME AXIS OF A TIME SERIES PLOT

> Choose *Graph* ► *Time Series Plot*
> In the *Time Series Plot* dialog box,
>> Under *Graph variables* in the first box under *Y*, type **SP**
>> Click the circle left of *Calendar*
>> Click down arrow in box right of *Calendar*, click *Month Year*
>>> (These commands label the horizontal axis by month and year.)
>> Click *Options*
>> In the *Time Series Plot Options* dialog box,
>>> Click the first box under *Month*, type **1**
>>> Click the first box under *Year*, type **1980**
>>>> (These commands label the horizontal axis starting with January 1980.)
>>> Click the first box under *Display* so that the cross disappears.
>>>> (This command keeps the months from being printed under the horizontal axis so that the labeling is not too cluttered.)
>>> Click *ok*
>> Click *ok*

> **Figure 6.4(a)**

LAG 1 DIFFERENCES

> Choose *Stat* ► *Time Series* ► *Differences*
> In the *Differences* dialog box,
>> Click box to the right of *Series*, type **C1**
>> Click box to the right of *Store differences in*, type **C2**
>> Click *ok*
>>> (The lag 1 differences are now stored in column C2.)
> Choose *Window* ► *Data*
> In the *Data* window,
>> Click the cell immediately under *C2*, type **D_SP**
>> Click any empty cell
> Choose *Window* ► *Session*
> In the *Session* window, type **PRINT C1 C2**

Figure 6.5(b)

Choose *File* ▸ *Other Files* ▸ *Import ASCII Data*
In the *Import ASCII Data* dialog box,
    Under *Store data in column,* type **C1**
    Click *ok*
    In the *Import Data From File* dialog box,
        Choose and click data file *sp_month.dat,* click *ok*
Choose *Window* ▸ *Data*
In the *Data* window,
    Highlight rows 61 to 144 in column *C1*
    Choose the *Edit* menu, click *Cut Cells*
    In the box immediately under *C1,* type **SP**
    Click any empty cell
Choose *Stat* ▸ *Time Series* ▸ *Differences*
In the *Differences* dialog box,
    Click box to the right of *Series,* type **C1**
    Click box to the right of *Store differences in,* type **C2**
    Click *ok*
Choose *Window* ▸ *Data*
In the *Data* window,
    Click the cell immediately under *C2,* type **D_SP**
    Click any empty cell

COPYING COLUMNS, USING OR DELETING SPECIFIED ROWS

Choose *Manip* ▸ *Copy Columns*
In the *Copy* dialog box,
    In the box under *Copy from columns,* type **C2**
    In the box under *To columns,* type **C3**
    Click *Use Rows*
    In the *Copy-Use Rows* dialog box,
        Click circle to the left of *Use rows*
        Click box under *Use rows,* type **2:60** and click *ok*
    Click *ok*

        (Column C2 contains a missing value, but the runs command only works with columns that contain no missing values. So this copy command is needed. The runs test can be done for column C3.)

Choose *Stat* ▸ *Nonparametrics* ▸ *Runs Test*
In the *Runs Test* dialog box,
    Type **C3** under *Variables,* click *ok*

Figure 6.10

RANDOM DATA FROM A NORMAL DISTRIBUTION

Choose *Calc* ▸ *Random Data* ▸ *Normal*
In the *Normal Distribution* dialog box,
   Click the box next to *Generate,* type **36**
   Click the box under *Store in column(s),* type **C5**
   Click the box next to *Mean,* replace with **0.90**
   Click the box next to *Standard deviation,* replace with **5.53**
   Click *ok*
      (This generates 36 observations from a normal distribution with mean 0.90 and standard deviation 5.53 in column C5.)
Choose *Window* ▸ *Data*
In the *Data* window,
   Click the cell immediately under *C5,* type **CHANGE**
   Click any empty cell
Choose *Stat* ▸ *Basic Statistics* ▸ *Descriptive Statistics*
In the *Descriptive Statistics* dialog box,
   Under *Variables,* type **C5**
   Click *ok*

PARTIAL SUMS

Choose *Calc* ▸ *Functions*
In the *Functions* dialog box,
   Click the box to the right of *Input column,* type **C5**
   Click the box to the right of *Result in,* type **C6**
   Click the circle next to *Partial sums,* click *ok*
      (This accumulates successive rows of C5 and stores the resulting Partial Sums in C6. Note that ROW 2 for C6 is the sum of the first two rows of C5.)
Choose *Window* ▸ *Session*
In the *Data* window,
   In the cell under *C6,* type **ACCUML.S ,** click any other cell
Choose *Calc* ▸ *Mathematical Expressions*
In the *Mathematical Expressions* dialog box,
   Click the box next to *Variable (new or modified),* type **C7**
   Click the box under *Expression,* type **167.24+C6**
   Click *ok*
      (This adds the accumulated changes to the most recently available closing value, 167.14.)
Choose *Window* ▸ *Data*
In the *Data* window, type **SP_SIMUL** in the cell under *C7* and click any other cell

Figure 6.15

Choose *File* ▸ *Other Files* ▸ *Import ASCII Data*
In the *Import ASCII Data* dialog box,
    Under *Store data in column,* type **C1-C3,**
    Click *ok*
    In the *Import Text From File* dialog box,
        Choose and click data file *cnd_qrt.dat,* click *ok*
Choose *Window* ▸ *Data*
In the *Data* window,
    Highlight rows 1 to 96 in column *C3*
    Choose *Edit* ▸ *Cut Cells*
        (These commands delete rows 1 to 96, which contain missing values.)
    Highlight rows 53 to 91 in column *C3*
    Choose *Edit* ▸ *Cut Cells*
    In the box immediately under *C3,* type **GNP**
    Click any empty cell
Choose *Stat* ▸ *Time Series* ▸ *Differences*
In the *Differences* dialog box,
    Click box to the right of *Series,* type **C3**
    Click box to the right of *Store differences in,* type **C4**
    Click *ok*
Choose *Window* ▸ *Data*
In the *Data* window,
    Click the cell immediately under *C3,* type **D_GNP**
    Click any empty cell

SQUARE ROOTS OF THE VALUES IN A COLUMN

Choose *Calc* ▸ *Mathematical Expressions*
In the *Mathematical Expressions* dialog box,
    Click the box next to *Variable (new or modified),* type **C5**
    Click the box under *Expression,* type **Sqrt(C3)**
    Click *ok*
        (C5 contains the square roots of C3.)
Choose *Window* ▸ *Data*
In the *Data* window,
    In the cell under *C5,* type **R_GNP**
    Click any empty cell
        ("R" is a convenient way to suggest the square *root* of a variable.)
Choose *Stat* ▸ *Time Series* ▸ *Differences*
In the dialog box,
    Click box to the right of *Series,* type **C5**
    Click box to the right of *Store differences in,* type **C6**
    Click *ok*
Choose *Window* ▸ *Data*

In the Data window,
    In the cell under *C6*, type **DR_GNP**
Choose *Stat ▸ Basic Statistics ▸ Descriptive Statistics*
In the *Descriptive Statistics* dialog box,
    Under *Variables* type **C5 C6**
    Click *ok*

6.7

EXERCISES

Although answers are given in Appendix C, do not turn to them right away if you cannot find an answer on your own. Return to the exercise the next day and try again before turning to Appendix C.

6.1 This problem deals with the mechanics of random walks. You need neither a calculator nor a software package for this problem. Suppose that you are given a company's sales (in 1,000s of units) for the 10 months from September 1993 to June 1994:

| 134 | 99 | 130 | 166 | 168 | 267 | 314 | 432 | 355 | 385 |

Let SALES be the variable containing these 10 figures.
a   What is the statistical unit?
b   Draw a sequence plot of SALES. Describe it. What is the mean of SALES? The standard deviation is 120.6. [Verify this.]
c   Draw a sequence plot of the lag 1 differences of SALES, D_SALES. Describe it. What is the mean of D_SALES? The standard deviation is 60.5.
d   If you were to treat the SALES data as a random process, what would be a point prediction and a 3-standard-deviation prediction interval for SALES in July 1994?
e   If you were to treat the SALES data as a random walk, what would be a point prediction and a 3-standard-deviation prediction interval for SALES in July 1994?
f   Using differently colored pens, plot the point and interval predictions obtained in (d) and (e) on the sequence plot obtained in (b). Which set of predictions looks more reasonable?

6.2 Refer to the Minitab output in Figure 6.20, which relates to real Gross Domestic Product (GDP) in billions of dollars in the United States for the years 1948 to 1990. The data are stored in ASCII file US_ANN.DAT.
a   Is the random walk model appropriate for GDP? Justify your answer.
b   What does the standard deviation of D_GDP tell you about the random walk model?
c   Calculate (i) the 95% prediction interval for the value of GDP in 1991, and (ii) the probability that GDP in 1991 will exceed $5,500 billion. Assume here that the random walk model is appropriate and that any additional assumptions needed for these calculations hold.
d   In addition to assuming that the random walk model is appropriate, what other assumptions had to be made in (c)? How reasonable are they?
e   Given your answers to (a) and (d), how confident are you in your numerical answers in (c)?
f   Consider now a random walk model for the natural logarithm of GDP, L_GDP. Answer the questions in (a) to (e). Do you prefer the random walk model for GDP or that for L_GDP? Why?

FIGURE 6.20

```
MTB > Read 'C:\MTBWIN\DATA\US_ANN.DAT' C1-C4
Entering data from file: C:\MTBWIN\DATA\US_ANN.DAT
    101 rows read.
MTB > Delete 1:58 C4     #Note: There are missing data in these rows.
MTB > NAME C4 'GDP'
MTB > PRINT C4

GDP
    260.2     259.0     286.7     331.3     349.4     369.5     370.2     403.2
    425.1     447.7     453.9     492.7     511.8     530.0     570.1     602.0
    644.4     699.3     766.4     810.4     885.9     957.1    1008.2    1093.4
   1201.6    1343.1    1453.3    1580.9    1761.7    1965.1    2219.2    2464.3
   2684.3    3000.5    3114.8    3355.9    3724.8    3974.1    4205.3    4497.2
   4840.2    5163.2    5423.4

MTB > TSPlot C4
```

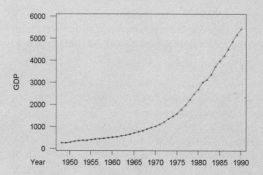

```
MTB > Differences 1 C4 C5
MTB > NAME C5 'D_GDP'
MTB > TSPlot C5
```

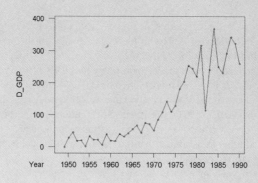

```
MTB > Copy C5 C6;
SUBC>    Omit 1.
MTB > Runs C6


    C6


    K = 122.9333



    The observed no. of runs =   6
    The expected no. of runs =  20.8095
    16 Observations above K   26 below
            The test is significant at  0.0000


MTB > Describe C4 C5


                N       N*      MEAN     MEDIAN    TRMEAN    STDEV    SEMEAN
GDP            43        0      1663        957      1549     1544       236
D_GDP          42        1     122.9       73.3     117.2    111.8      17.3

               MIN      MAX        Q1         Q3
GDP            259     5423       454       2684
D_GDP         -1.2    368.9      30.9      233.7

MTB > NScores C5 C12
MTB > NAME C12 'NSCORE'
MTB > Plot C12*C5
```

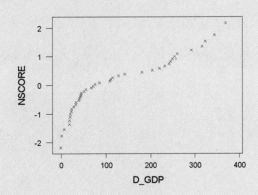

```
MTB > Let C6=Loge(C4)
MTB > NAME C6 'L_GDP'
MTB > PRINT C6
```

```
L_GDP

5.56145    5.55683    5.65844    5.80302    5.85622    5.91215    5.91404
5.99943    6.05232    6.10412    6.11788    6.19990    6.23793    6.27288
6.34581    6.40026    6.46832    6.55008    6.64170    6.69753    6.78660
6.86391    6.91592    6.99705    7.09141    7.20274    7.28159    7.36575
7.47403    7.58330    7.70490    7.80966    7.89518    8.00653    8.04392
8.11847    8.22277    8.28755    8.34410    8.41121    8.48471    8.54931
8.59848

MTB > TSPlot C6
```

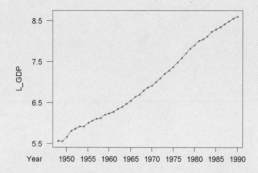

```
MTB > Differences 1 C6 C7
MTB > NAME C7 'DL_GDP'
MTB > TSPlot C7
```

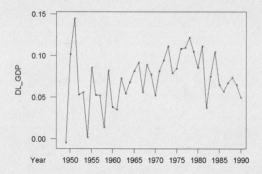

```
MTB > Copy C7 C8;
SUBC>    Omit 1.
MTB > Runs C8


    C8


    K =  0.0723



    The observed no. of runs =  19
    The expected no. of runs =  21.8095
    23 Observations above K     19 below
            The test is significant at  0.3758
            Cannot reject at alpha = 0.05


MTB > Describe C6 C7


                    N       N*      MEAN     MEDIAN    TRMEAN     STDEV     SEMEAN
L_GDP              43        0      6.986      6.864     6.978     0.952     0.145
DL_GDP             42        1    0.07231    0.07403   0.07299   0.03113   0.00480

                  MIN      MAX         Q1         Q3
L_GDP           5.557    8.598      6.118      7.895
DL_GDP       -0.00462  0.14459    0.05312    0.09231

MTB > NScores C7 C12
MTB > Plot C12*C7
```

```
MTB > Stop
```

6.3 This problem concerns sales of motor homes by Winnebago Industries during a time period in which the value of the company's common stock went from virtually nothing to nearly a billion dollars, at the price level of the early 1970s. The data are monthly unit sales from November 1966 to February 1972. The data, stored in ASCII file WINNEBAG.DAT, are as follows (read row by row):

61	48	53	78	75	58	146	193	124	120	134	99
130	166	168	267	314	432	355	384	232	235	293	242
248	236	209	358	352	406	562	389	416	493	409	328
222	195	156	439	671	874	558	621	628	652	495	344
405	586	403	700	837	1,224	1,117	1,214	762	846	1,228	937
1,396	1,174	628	1,753								

a Do the untransformed data follow a random walk? (Don't forget to carry out the diagnostic checks.)

b Perform a square root transformation. Do the resulting transformed data follow a random walk?

c Perform a natural log transformation. Do the resulting transformed data follow a random walk?

d Using your most satisfactory model from (a), (b), and (c), find a prediction for sales in March 1972. Get both a point prediction and a "3-standard-deviations around the mean" interval prediction. How reliable is this prediction in light of the diagnostic checks?

6.8

SUPPLEMENTARY EXERCISES

6.4 In Section 6.2 we analyzed the SP monthly closing values for 1980 to 1984. The monthly closing values for January 1985 to December 1991 are stored in rows 61 to 144 of column C1 of ASCII file SP_MONTH.DAT.

a Do the data for 1985 to 1991 follow a random walk? Describe any unusual features you see.

b Drop the three outlying values from the series of lag 1 differences. Is the resulting series of revised lag 1 differences suggestive of a random walk? Describe any unusual features you see.

c Assume the random walk model is appropriate. Use the parameter estimates based on the revised lag 1 difference series in (b) to get a point prediction and a 95% prediction interval for the closing value in January 1992. In light of your answers to (a) and (b), comment on the validity of using these predictions.

d Contrast your process parameter estimates obtained from the data in (b) with those obtained in Section 6.2. Are you surprised by the differences? Justify your answer.

6.5 ASCII file EXCHANGE.DAT contains 75 exchange rates for Canadian dollars per U.S. dollar. The rates are closing values for the months from December 1983 to February 1990, and they were taken from the Bank of Canada Review.

a Do the rates data follow a random walk? Describe any concerns you might have.

b Is normality an appropriate assumption for the lag 1 differences?

c Assuming that the rates data follow a random walk and that normality is appropriate, obtain a point prediction and a 95% prediction interval for the exchange rate in March 1990.

d Given your concerns in (a) and (b), are the point and interval predictions obtained in (c) reasonable?

e Use a logarithmic transformation of the exchange rate data, and repeat (a) through (d) for the transformed data.

f Do you prefer the random walk model for the exchange rate or for the logarithmically transformed values? Why?

6.6 This problem relates to the number of telex terminals in the CNCP Telex Network. The data are quarterly from the first quarter in 1971 to the fourth quarter in 1981; that is, there are 44 quarters. In this analysis, it is of interest to understand how the number of terminals develops over time and to get a prediction of that number for the first quarter in 1982.

The data, stored in ASCII file TELEX.DAT, are as follows:

1,000	1,022	1,041	1,071	1,093	1,123	1,139	1,169
1,204	1,225	1,255	1,293	1,339	1,388	1,411	1,440
1,469	1,502	1,531	1,586	1,621	1,644	1,675	1,705
1,733	1,760	1,774	1,791	1,823	1,853	1,882	1,918
1,967	2,005	2,036	2,065	2,109	2,149	2,181	2,219
2,273	2,304	2,353	2,365				

Note the definition of some of the variables used in the analysis: NUMBER is the number of telex terminals connected at the end of a quarter, D_NUMBER is the lag 1 difference of NUMBER, R_NUMB is the square root of NUMBER, and DR_NUMB is the lag 1 difference of R_NUMB.

In your answers to the following questions, be concise.

a At which values should the center line, the upper control limit, and the lower control limit be drawn on the time sequence plot for D_NUMBER? Draw these three lines. What speaks against treating the process generating NUMBER as a random walk?

b What speaks for treating the process generating NUMBER as a random walk?

c Balancing your answers in (a) and (b), is it reasonable to treat the process generating NUMBER as a random walk?

d What does the normal probability plot for D_NUMBER tell you?

e Draw the center line, the upper control limit, and the lower control limit on the sequence plot for DR_NUMB. Is it reasonable to treat the process generating R_NUMB as a random walk? Briefly justify your answer.

f If a choice had to be made between using the random walk model for NUMBER and that for R_NUMB, which one should be used for predicting the number of telex terminals in the system in the first quarter in 1982? Briefly justify your answer.

g Using a random walk model for R_NUMB, get a point prediction and a 95% interval for the number of connected telex terminals in the first quarter 1982. In light of your answer to (e), how reliable are this best guess and this 95% interval?

6.7 Suppose that the time series pattern for monthly sales of a particular product is well described by a random walk. In particular, assume that it is the *square root of sales* that follows a random walk. The current sales value is 3,600.

a Assume that the relevant changes have a normal distribution with mean 5 and standard deviation 15. What is a 90% prediction interval for sales in the next month?

FIGURE 6.21

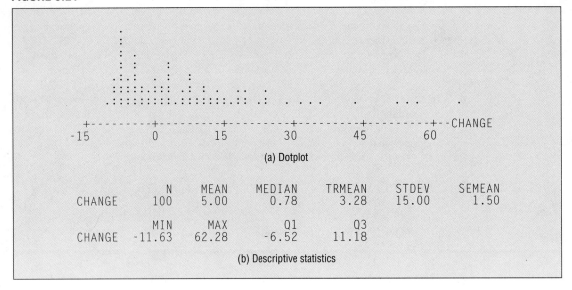

(a) Dotplot

	N	MEAN	MEDIAN	TRMEAN	STDEV	SEMEAN
CHANGE	100	5.00	0.78	3.28	15.00	1.50

	MIN	MAX	Q1	Q3
CHANGE	-11.63	62.28	-6.52	11.18

(b) Descriptive statistics

   b Assume that the relevant changes have a normal distribution with mean 5 and standard deviation 15. What is the probability that sales next month will more than double, that is, exceed 7,200?

   c Assume that the distribution of the relevant changes is as shown in Figure 6.21. What is the probability that sales next month will more than double, that is, exceed 7,200?

Making Inferences In Cross-Sectional Studies

This chapter will help you solve the following kinds of problems:

- A TV manufacturer wants to know how many people own color TVs. A survey reports that 60% of TV owners have color sets. Is it likely that the actual percentage might be a lot higher?

- In a poll of 1,000 voters, 270 (27%) say that they support the incumbent governor. If this is a random sample, what is the chance that the correct proportion is actually 35%?

- In a large hospital, the mean number of sick days taken by a sample of employees in a particular year was 10 days. In the following year, the mean for another sample was 12 days. Could the difference in these sample means be due to chance, or is it suggestive of an overall increase in the mean number of sick days?

7.1

Introduction

In Chapter 4, you learned some basic facts about cross-sectional studies. The main aim in many cross-sectional studies is to describe the population of values for the variable of interest, y, in particular, to obtain several population parameters of y,

FIGURE 7.1

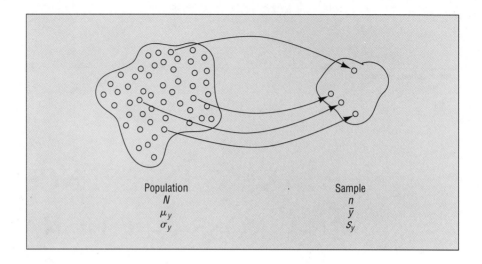

such as the population mean μ_y and standard deviation σ_y. Typically, however, the size of the population frame, N, is large, and we cannot obtain information about the population via a census. Therefore, we cannot compute the population parameters. But we can take a *random* sample of size n from the population frame and use the sample statistics to *estimate* the corresponding population parameters. For example, we can use the sample mean and standard deviation, $\bar{y}$ and s_y, to estimate the corresponding population mean and standard deviation, μ_y and σ_y. (See Figure 7.1.) Generalizing from the sample to the population is what we call *inference*.

In Chapter 4, we also formulated the *model of a random variable,* which is based on the fact that simple random sampling is used to draw observations from the population. The model consists of two premises:

1. There is a constant level around which observations vary.

2. The observations vary randomly around the constant level.

This model can be simply represented by the following equation:

Actual Observation = Mean + Residual

or

$$ y \quad = \quad \mu_y + \quad \epsilon $$

where ϵ has mean 0 and standard deviation σ_y. In many, but not all, applications the distribution of the residual ϵ is normal.

In Chapter 4, we ignored the potential sampling error and treated the sample-based *estimates* of the population parameters as if they were the *exact* values. The main objective of this chapter is to describe the likely size of the sampling error.

You will

- Learn how far away a statistic can be from the parameter it is used to estimate

- Learn more about how to estimate population parameters from sample statistics

- Learn how to obtain point and interval estimates for a

  Population mean

  Difference between two population means

  Population proportion

  Difference between two population proportions

- Learn how to carry out hypothesis tests

In Chapter 8, you will learn how to use these cross-sectional tools for random time series.

7.2

RANDOM SAMPLING

Ideally, a census should be used to obtain the population distribution of values and the parameters for the variable of interest, y. In most cross-sectional studies, however, it will not be practical nor possible for you to carry out a census: You will have to rely on sample results instead and generalize from the sample to the population. In order to describe the likely size of the margin of error in this generalization, you must have taken a *random* sample. In this section, you will learn how much a **population vs. sample** statistic (such as a sample mean) can differ from the corresponding parameter (such as the population mean).

EXAMPLE 7.1

Suppose that you are a safety officer responsible for the specifications for a new elevator. You know that the elevator may carry a maximum of nine persons, and you are considering the adequacy of a total maximum weight of 693 kg. Since the elevator is to be used only by the employees of the office building where this elevator is to be installed, you investigated the distribution of weights for the population of 950 employees. Here, weight is your variable of interest, y. You found that the distribution of y was approximately normal with mean $\mu_y = 65$ kg and standard deviation $\sigma_y = 12$ kg. This distribution is illustrated in Figure 7.2.

The question you want to address is:

What is the chance that the maximum weight of 693 kg will be exceeded when nine persons are on the elevator?

FIGURE 7.2
Distribution of
Weight Values

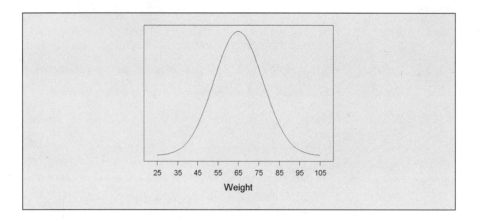

In this problem, you are taking a sample of size $n = 9$ from a population for which the response variable, y = weight, is normally distributed with population mean $\mu_y = 65$ kg and population standard deviation $\sigma_y = 12$ kg. You want to find out the chance that the *total* weight for the sample exceeds 693 kg or that the *average* weight for the sample exceeds $\bar{y} = \frac{693}{9} = 77$ kg.

In order to answer the elevator example question, we will proceed as follows: We can assume that the $N = 950$ employees in the population frame are labelled from 001 to 950. Each employee has a value for the response variable, y = weight. The distribution of weight values was given in Figure 7.2. Since the elevator will be used repeatedly, the safety officer wants to know what proportion of the times, when nine persons are on it, their average weight exceeds 77 kg. This can be obtained by *simulating* elevator rides in the following way:

1. Draw 9 persons randomly from the frame of $N = 950$ employees and compute their average weight, $\bar{y}$. Record the average weight as a summary for this simulated elevator ride.

2. Repeat (1) a large number of times, each time only recording the average weight as a summary for each simulated elevator ride.

3. Compute the proportion of average weights recorded in (2) that exceed 77 kg.

The remainder of this section is as follows: We discuss the simulation approach in greater detail. We then describe the important statistical concept underlying these simulations, the sampling distribution of the mean. We then apply the sampling distribution of the mean to answer the main question for the elevator example. Finally, we report some additional simulations that illustrate an important property of the sampling distribution of the mean.

Some Simulations

The main reason for the simulations in this section is to lay the groundwork for the results in Section 7.3, where we discuss how to estimate a population mean from a sample mean.

Recall the statistical question of the elevator study:

What is the chance that the average weight of 9 employees exceeds 77 kg, where the sample of 9 employees is drawn by simple random sampling without replacement from the frame of 950 employees?

To answer this question, we must consider what the results would be if the safety officer were to repeatedly sample 9 employees from the frame and record their average weight each time. Each such average would characterize one simulated elevator ride. The safety officer, who knows the exact weight for each subject in the frame, could do this, in principle at least, for *all possible* samples of size 9. The number of such samples, drawn from the frame and each consisting of 9 employees, is enormous. Few computers, if any, could list them all. Therefore the safety officer decided to list only a large number of the many possible samples of size 9 by simulating a large number of elevator rides. The first few *sample means* so obtained were

62.2   64.2   62.8   61.4   63.0   68.0   59.4   . . .

As you can see, these sample means vary.

To get a better idea of what the safety officer has done so far, look at the *left* side of Figure 7.3. At the top you see Figure 7.2, redrawn with the horizontal axis somewhat condensed. Remember that this is the population distribution of $y =$ weight from which simple random samples of size $n = 9$ were repeatedly drawn.

Below this population distribution, look at the dotplot for the first simple random sample, and notice that it resembles the population distribution somewhat. We would like the sample dotplot to be identical to the population distribution, but this is too much to hope for since there are only 9 employees in the sample, whereas there are 950 in the population. All we can hope for is that the sample dotplot is reasonably close to the population distribution.

In the right half of Figure 7.3, the population mean (μ_y) is, of course, at 65 kg, and the asterisk (*) on the line for the first random sample marks the sample mean, $\bar{y} = 62.2$ kg. Just as we expected the dotplot for the first sample to be close to the population distribution, so the sample mean for the first sample should be close to the population mean. (Note the expanded horizontal axis for this half of the graph.)

Figure 7.3 also shows the results for a few additional samples: The dotplots are given on the left side and the sample means on the right side. All these samples were, of course, randomly drawn from the population of 950 employees.

All the sample dotplots in Figure 7.3 are "close" to the population distribution. Furthermore, the resulting sample means are "close" to the population mean, $\mu_y = 65$. To get a better idea of how close sample means are to the population mean, the approach depicted in Figure 7.3 can be continued until a very large number of samples of size $n = 9$ has been randomly drawn from the population distribution. The distribution of the resulting sample means, called the *sampling distribu-*

FIGURE 7.3 Sampling (*see text*)

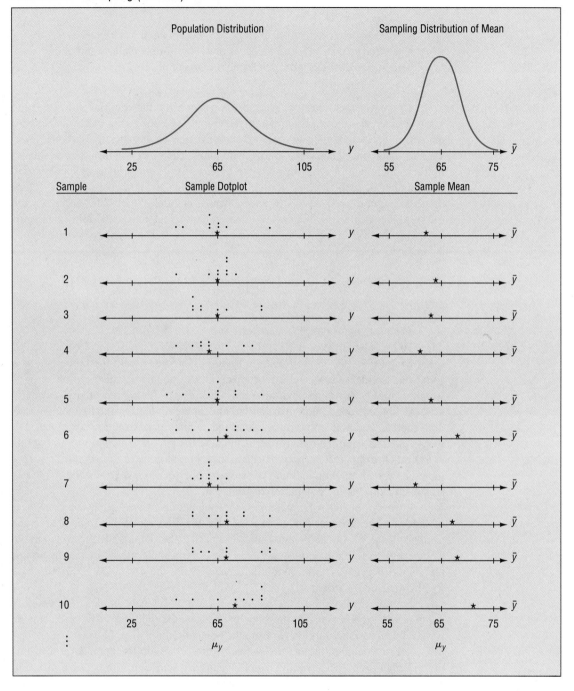

tion of the mean, is depicted in the top right part of Figure 7.3. An enlarged version is also given in Figure 7.4.

The resulting $\bar{y}$ values vary around the population mean $\mu_y = 65$. Some of them differ from the population mean by more than 10 kg, but most of them are within 5 kg of the population mean. It turns out that the average of the large number of $\bar{y}$ values is 65 kg, and that their standard deviation is 4 kg. Remember that each $\bar{y}$ value was based on 9 observations and note that

1. The mean of the very large number of sample means equals the population mean, $\mu_y = 65$ kg.

2. The standard deviation of the sample means equals $\sigma_y/\sqrt{n} = 12/\sqrt{9} = 4$ kg.

3. The shape of the distribution of the sample means is very close to normal.

These three results are no coincidence and will be generalized in the next subsection. From now on, we will call the distribution of all possible sample means the **sampling distribution of the mean.** Given the large number of simulated samples, we can expect the distribution of the sample means in Figure 7.4 to well approximate this sampling distribution of the mean.

(Before continuing, consider the shape of the sampling distribution of the mean if a sample of size $n = 1$ were drawn. To derive its shape, you should draw a graph similar to Figure 7.3.)

The Sampling Distribution of the Mean

The reason for discussing the simulations in the last section was to introduce the following important general result regarding the sampling distribution of the mean. This result, called the *Central Limit Theorem,* can be proved mathematically (proof omitted). There are many uses for this general result, the most important one being to estimate a population mean.

FIGURE 7.4
Distribution of a Very Large Number of Sample Means, $\bar{y}$, Each Based on 9 Observations Randomly Drawn from the Employee Population

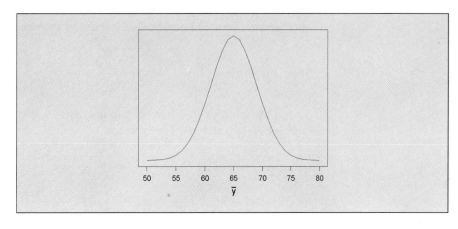

Suppose that

- Simple random samples of size n are drawn *repeatedly* from a large population of N units whose *population mean, μ_y,* and *population standard deviation, σ_y,* are *known.*

- The sample mean $\bar{y}$ is computed for each sample.

Then the resulting distribution of sample means—that is, of $\bar{y}$ values—is called the **sampling distribution of the mean.**

The sampling distribution of the mean is important because it can be used to estimate the *margin of error* when generalizing from a sample mean $\bar{y}$ to the population mean μ_y. It is characterized by the following three properties:

Property 1.   The average of all sample means equals the population mean:

$$\text{Average of all } \bar{y} \text{ values} = \mu_y$$

Property 2.   The standard deviation of all sample means equals (Population Standard Deviation)$/n$:

$$\text{Standard Deviation of all } \bar{y} \text{ values} = \frac{\sigma_y}{\sqrt{n}}$$

This standard deviation is called the **standard error of the mean.**

In the elevator example, the standard error of the mean measures the standard deviation of the sample averages based on 9 employee weights, where each sample average characterizes one elevator ride. Symbolically, we can write this as

$$\text{Standard Error} = \sqrt{\frac{\sum (\bar{y} - \mu_y)^2}{\text{Number of possible } \bar{y} \text{ values}}}$$

It is a mathematical fact (but we will not derive it in this book) that the right hand side is equal to $\sigma_y/\sqrt{n}$. In other words,

$$\text{Standard Error of the Mean} = \frac{\sigma_y}{\sqrt{n}}$$

Property 3. The shape of the distribution of sample means is close to normal for large *n, regardless* of the shape of the distribution of unit values in the population.[1]

If the population distribution of values is close to normal, then the sampling distribution of $\bar{y}$ is approximately normal even if *n* is very small, as in the elevator example. The less normal the population distribution of *y* values, the larger *n* must be for the sampling distribution of $\bar{y}$ to be normal. In many situations, the sampling distribution is normal, even if $\bar{y}$ is based on only *n* = 20 observations.

Before proceeding, note the following distinction:

The **population distribution**—that is, the distribution of values in the population for the response variable *y*—describes the distribution of **unit values** when units are randomly drawn from the population.

The **sampling distribution of the mean** describes the distribution of sample means $\bar{y}$ when **samples** of size *n* are randomly drawn from the population.

Application to the Elevator Example

Let us now apply the general results from the last subsection to the elevator example. The managerial question is:

What is the chance that the maximum weight of 693 kg will be exceeded when 9 persons are on the elevator?

The resulting statistical question is:

What is the chance that the average weight, $\bar{y}$, of *n* = 9 employees exceeds 77 kg, where the sample of *n* = 9 employees is drawn by simple random sampling without replacement from the frame of *N* = 950 employees?

Since the sample mean $\bar{y}$ is the only number that is needed to determine whether the maximum weight is exceeded for an elevator ride, this statistical ques-

FIGURE 7.5

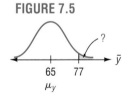

65   77

μ_y

---

[1]Another illustration of this will be given in Example 7.2.

tion is about the distribution of sample means. The safety officer will take a *random* sample. Thus, the distribution of these sample means is *known*.

- Using property 1 of the sampling distribution of the mean, discussed in the previous subsection, the safety officer's sample mean is expected to be close to $\mu_y = 65$ kg.

- How close a sample mean can be expected to be to 65 kg depends on the variability in sample means. Using property 2, this variability is described by the standard error of the mean, $\sigma_y/\sqrt{n} = 12/\sqrt{9} = 4$ kg.

- Finally, property 3 implies that the distribution of sample means is approximately normal.

FIGURE 7.6

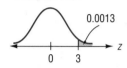

0.0013

The chance that a sample mean $\bar{y}$ exceeds 77 kg can thus be computed by standardizing the value 77 kg:

$$z = \frac{\bar{y} - \mu}{\sigma_y/\sqrt{n}} = \frac{77 - 65}{4} = 3$$

From Table 4.1 or the *Calc ▶ Probability Distributions ▶ Normal* menu in Minitab, chances are 99.87% that a sample mean will *not* exceed 77 kg, so chances are 0.13% that a sample mean *will* exceed 77 kg. We have thus answered the safety officer's statistical question.

Does the statistical question answer the original managerial question? The crucial assumption was that the 9 employees are randomly drawn from the population. Whenever 9 employees use the elevator, a random numbers table is, of course, not used to draw them from the population frame. But it *may* be reasonable to assume that the way employees enter the elevator is virtually random with respect to their weight; that is, their decision to enter the elevator is entirely unrelated to their weight. *If* this is a reasonable assumption, then the answer to the statistical question is also the answer to the managerial question.

We have computed the chance to be 0.13% that the sample mean weight for $n = 9$ employees, $\bar{y}$, exceeds 77 kg. Be sure that you see why this probability is different from the probability that the weight for *one* randomly chosen employee exceeds 77 kg. To compute the latter probability, note that the subject is an employee and the relevant distribution of values is the population distribution of y = weight, given in Figure 7.2, whose mean is $\mu_y = 65$ kg and whose standard deviation is $\sigma_y = 12$ kg. Standardizing the value 77 kg, we get

FIGURE 7.7

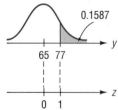

0.1587

$$z = \frac{\bar{y} - \mu}{\sigma_y} = \frac{77 - 65}{12} = 1$$

From Table 4.1 or the *Calc ▶ Probability Distributions ▶ Normal* menu in Minitab, chances are 84.13% that the employee's weight will *not* exceed 77 kg, and so chances are 15.87% that the employee's weight *will* exceed 77 kg. We used the population distribution of weight values to compute this probability, whereas we used the sampling distribution of the mean to answer the statistical question for the elevator example.

An Application to Auditing

This section illustrates the conditions under which the sampling distribution of $\bar{y}$ is normal. Consider an example.

EXAMPLE 7.2

Suppose you are an auditor who must audit an inventory population consisting of $N = 9{,}000$ inventory items. You want to know the total value of this inventory. In order to compute the total, you would need to take a census, auditing every one of the 9,000 inventory items and then computing their total. But let us assume that you cannot take a census due to budgetary and time constraints. Therefore you decide to take a sample of n inventory items and audit them.

Let us formulate the auditor's problem in terms of means so that we can relate it to earlier results in this section. The variable of interest is y, audit value. Since the population total audit value is just $N \cdot \mu_y$, where μ_y is the population mean audit value, all the auditor needs to know is this population mean. Since a census is not possible, the population mean can be estimated by the sample mean, $\bar{y}$. The following question now arises:

How good is the sample mean $\bar{y}$ as an estimate of μ_y? That is, how close can $\bar{y}$ be expected to be to μ_y?[2]

Section 7.3 will answer this question. First, let us illustrate once more the sampling distribution of the mean, in particular, the conditions under which it is approximately normal. In the elevator example, the population distribution of weight values was normal, and so the sampling distribution of the mean was normal, regardless of the sample size n used to compute a sample mean $\bar{y}$. When the population distribution is not normal, what happens to the shape of the sampling distribution of the mean? Earlier, the answer to this question was that the sampling distribution is nevertheless normal, provided that the sample size n is large enough ($n > 20$ being a common operationalization of "large enough").

In order to be justified to use the results regarding the sampling distribution of the mean, it is *essential* that you use random sampling. To draw a random sample, you must obtain the frame for the $N = 9{,}000$ inventory units, numbered from 0001 to 9000. Let us also introduce two individuals:

1. The *auditor* who would like to take a census of all $N = 9{,}000$ units in order to compute their exact total value, but only has a limited budget. So the auditor must resort to a *sample,* knowing that the results cannot be expected to be exact because of sampling error.

---

[2]Note that, when $\bar{y}$ and μ_y differ, the discrepancies in the estimated total ($N \cdot \bar{y}$) and true total ($N \cdot \mu_y$) are accentuated by a factor of N.

FIGURE 7.8
Frequency
Distribution of
Inventory Values

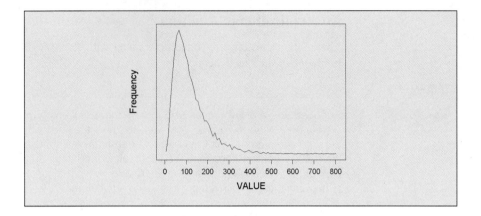

2. The auditor's guardian angel, who already has taken a census of all N = 9,000 units, has recorded their exact values, and has computed the mean and standard deviation as μ_y = \$120.60 and σ_y = \$83.50, respectively. The guardian angel has also obtained a frequency distribution of the 9,000 values, given in Figure 7.8. Alas, however, the guardian angel is completely disinterested in the auditor's concerns, and just watches.

Let us discuss a few more simulations to illustrate the shape of the sampling distribution of the mean. We use the population of N = 9,000 inventory values from Example 7.2, whose distribution is graphed in Figure 7.8. This population distribution is clearly not normal; it is positively skewed. First, we take a simple random sample of size n = 4 from the population and retain the sample mean $\bar{y}$. Furthermore, we do this repeatedly, yielding a large number of sample means drawn from the inventory population, each based on 4 observations. The resulting sample means were stored as Minitab variable FOUR. Their distribution should well approximate the sampling distribution of the mean for samples of size n = 4 from the inventory population, as shown in the top graph of Figure 7.9. Note that the distribution is positively skewed, but less so than the distribution of inventory values in Figure 7.8.

Second, we take a simple random sample of size n = 9 and again only retain the sample mean $\bar{y}$. We also do this repeatedly and store the resulting sample means in Minitab variable NINE. The resulting sampling distribution of the mean is given in the middle graph of Figure 7.9. It is less skewed than the top distribution in Figure 7.9.

Third, we obtain the sampling distribution for a large number of sample means, each based on 16 observations, as shown at the bottom of Figure 7.9.

In all three graphs, the center of the distribution remains unchanged. As we move from the top to the bottom graph in Figure 7.9, the variability in the distributions decreases, and the degree of skewness becomes less pronounced. The standard deviation of FOUR—that is, the standard error of the mean for samples of size n = 4—is $83.5/\sqrt{4}$ = 41.75; that of NINE is $83.5/\sqrt{9}$ = 27.83; and that of SIXTEEN is $83.5/\sqrt{16}$ = 20.88.

FIGURE 7.9
Selected Sampling
Distributions

The mean and standard deviation of VALUE, and the theoretical means and
standard deviations of FOUR, NINE, and SIXTEEN are:

```
              Mean        St.Dev
VALUE        120.60        83.50
FOUR         120.60        41.75
NINE         120.60        27.83
SIXTEEN      120.60        20.88
```

The means and standard deviations for the sampling distributions graphed
below were close to these theoretical values.

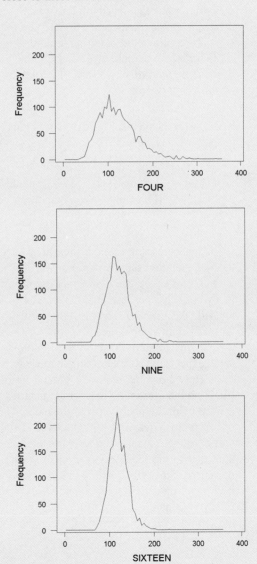

The larger the sample size each sample mean is based on, the closer the resulting sampling distribution is to a normal distribution. The generalization of this is property 3 about the sampling distribution of the mean.

Note the distinction between *population distribution* and *sampling distribution of the mean*. In the elevator example, the population distribution describes the distribution of the response variable weight for the $N = 950$ employees. The sampling distribution of the mean describes the distribution of all possible sample means, where each sample mean characterizes one elevator ride. In the auditing example, the population distribution describes the distribution of the response variable audit value for the $N = 9,000$ inventory units. The sampling distribution of the mean describes the distribution of sample means if the auditor were to repeatedly sample from the population and to record the sample mean each time.

To continue the auditing example, let us now assume that the auditor has taken a random sample of $n = 100$ units, computed the sample average to be $\bar{y} = \$134$, multiplied this by 9,000, and used the result as an estimate of the total value of all inventory units.

- How good is the resulting estimate? (This question will be addressed in Section 7.3.)

- Given that the guardian angel *knows* the population mean and standard deviation to be $\mu_y = \$120.6$ and $\sigma_y = \$83.5$, should he be surprised that a random sample of size $n = 100$ results in a sample mean $\bar{y} = \$134$, $\$13.4$ above the correct mean?

To address this second question, let us assume that the auditor has *not yet* taken the random sample of size $n = 100$.

As far as the guardian angel is concerned, the auditor's sample will be one of many possible ones, each characterized by a different sample mean. Since the auditor will take a *random* sample, the guardian angel *knows* what the distribution of all these different sample means is.

Using property 1 about the sampling distribution of the mean, the guardian angel expects the auditor's sample mean to be about $120.6.

How close the auditor's sample mean can be expected to be to $120.6 depends on the variability in sample means. Using property 2, this variability is described by the standard error of the mean, $\$83.5/\sqrt{100} = \$8.35$.

Finally, since $n = 100$ is a large sample, property 3 implies that the distribution of sample means is approximately normal, and so the probability is roughly 95% that an individual sample mean is within 2 standard deviations of the population mean. Since the quantity whose variation we are describing here is the sample mean, the standard deviation here refers to the standard deviation of sample means (that is, the standard error of the mean), which is $8.35. Thus chances are 95% that the auditor's sample mean $\bar{y}$ will be in the interval

Population Mean $\pm$ 2 (Standard Error of Mean)

which is

$$120.6 \pm 2(8.35) \qquad \text{or} \qquad 120.6 \pm 16.7$$

or between \$103.9 and \$137.3.

FIGURE 7.10

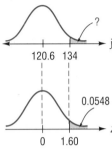

The auditor's sample mean was \$134, which is well within this interval. So the guardian angel should *not* be surprised by the auditor obtaining a sample mean of \$134, which is \$13.40 above the actual population mean.

Another way of gauging the guardian angel's degree of surprise is to compute the probability that the auditor would observe $\bar{y} = 134$ or higher. This is the probability of getting the observed sample result ($\bar{y} = 134$) or a more unusual one. We must standardize \$134 by computing $z = (134 - 120.6)/8.35 = 1.60$. Using Table 4.1 or Minitab, the probability of observing $z = 1.60$ or higher is $1 - 0.9452 = 0.0548$. So the guardian angel's surprise should at most be moderate.

If the auditor, however, were *not* to take a random sample, then the guardian angel would have no way of computing such an interval since the three properties discussed apply *only* when samples are drawn by simple random sampling. Nor could we address the guardian angel's degree of surprise.

Now, what about the auditor? How should the auditor use the sample mean $\bar{y}$ to make an inference about the unknown population mean μ_y? The next section addresses this question.

7.3

INFERENCES ABOUT A POPULATION MEAN

We will now use the sampling distribution of the mean to estimate a population mean from the results of a simple random sample.

Let us review the inventory example discussed in the previous section. The auditor needs the total value for the $N = 9{,}000$ inventory units in the population. The auditor does not know the population total, nor the population mean μ_y (which is the total divided by 9,000), nor the variability of individual unit values throughout the population, as measured by the population standard deviation σ_y. The auditor took a simple random sample of size $n = 100$ from the population, and computed the sample mean and standard deviation as $\bar{y} = \$134$ and $s_y = \$80$.

The managerial question is:

What is a reasonable estimate of the population mean μ_y, and how reliable is this estimate?

This question relates only to the *center* of the population distribution depicted in Figure 7.8, as measured by the mean μ_y. It relates to *no* other feature of this population distribution.

Since the population mean μ_y is unknown, the auditor uses the corresponding sample quantity, the sample mean $\bar{y}$, to estimate it. Likewise, since the population standard deviation σ_y is unknown, the auditor uses the sample standard deviation s_y to estimate it. One-number estimates such as $\overline{y}$ and s_y are called *point estimates*.

Point estimation: If we randomly draw a sample from a population, we can use the sample means $\overline{y}$ as the point estimate of the population mean μ_y and the sample standard deviation s_y as the point estimate of the population standard deviation σ_y.

When the sample is not drawn randomly, there is no basis for such estimates.

Using the point estimate alone, it is not clear how good the estimate is. We next discuss a way of establishing the reliability of point estimates of the mean μ_y.

Interval Estimation for the Population Mean Based on Large Samples

In order to express how far the population mean μ_y can be from its point estimate, the sample mean, we now introduce the *confidence interval*. We again start with the sampling distribution of the mean. Figure 7.11 illustrates the idea. If the sample size n is large enough, we know that the extent to which a sample mean $\overline{y}$ differs from the population mean μ_y is well described by a normal distribution. Chances are 95% that a sample mean is no more than $2\sigma_y/\sqrt{n}$ from the population mean μ_y.

When the population mean is unknown, the sample mean $\overline{y}$ is a point estimate for it. Furthermore, a confidence interval for the population mean is constructed as $2\sigma_y/\sqrt{n}$ around the sample mean. For 95% of the samples, the sample means are within $2\sigma_y/\sqrt{n}$ of the population mean μ_y, and the corresponding confidence intervals constructed around these sample means cover the population mean (see the results for samples 1, 2, and 4 in Figure 7.11). Note, however, that 5% of sample means are more than $2\sigma_y/\sqrt{n}$ away from the population mean, and the corresponding confidence intervals constructed around these sample means do *not* cover the population mean (see the result for sample 3 in Figure 7.11).

If we take one simple random sample of size n from a population whose unknown population mean is μ_y, then a point estimate for the population mean is the sample mean $\overline{y}$ and an interval estimate is the confidence interval

$$\overline{y} \pm 2\frac{\sigma_y}{\sqrt{n}}$$

This is called a 95% confidence interval for the population mean μ_y.[3]

---

[3]Here and elsewhere in this book, we associate $z = 2$ with a 95% interval. Of course, the exact z-value for a 95% interval is $z = 1.96$. But the value $z = 2$ is easier to remember, and it is sufficiently accurate for most applications.

FIGURE 7.11   Interpretation of a Confidence Interval for μ_y

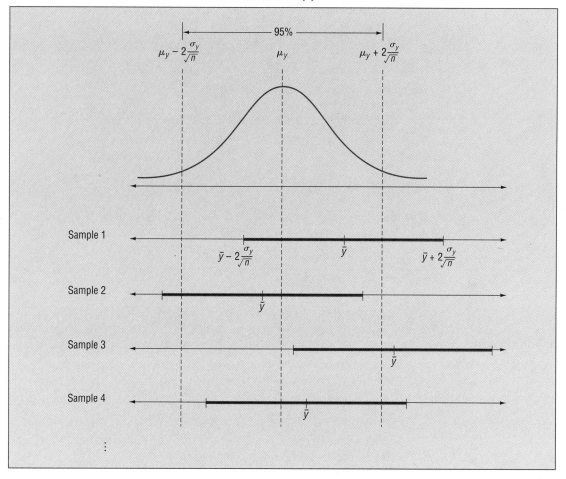

In most practical applications, when taking a simple random sample, we do not know the population standard deviation σ_y, and so we also do not know the standard error of the mean, $\sigma_y/\sqrt{n}$, which we need to construct a confidence interval. The sample standard deviation s_y, however, is a point estimate for the population standard deviation σ_y. So we can get a *point estimate for the standard error of the mean*, which we call the *estimated standard error of the mean,*

$$\frac{\text{Sample Standard Deviation}}{\sqrt{n}} = \frac{s_y}{\sqrt{n}}$$

We can use this estimated standard error of the mean to obtain a confidence interval for the population mean.

Interval estimation: A 95% *confidence interval* for the population mean μ_y, based on a large random sample, is[4]

$$\text{Point Estimate} \pm 2(\text{Estimated Standard Error})$$

or

$$\bar{y} \pm 2\frac{s_y}{\sqrt{n}}$$

The interpretation of the interval is: If we repeatedly use this confidence interval procedure, then 95% of the intervals so constructed will cover the true—but unknown—population mean μ_y, and 5% will not.

FIGURE 7.12

95%CI

118 134 150

The data for the inventory example are stored in ASCII file AUD_INV.DAT. The summaries for the $n = 100$ values are $\bar{y} = \$134$ and $s_y = \$80$. The estimated standard error is $\$80/\sqrt{100} = \$8$, so the 95% confidence interval is

$$134 \pm 2(8) \quad \text{or} \quad 134 \pm 16,$$

or from 118 to 150.

Intervals with different degrees of confidence can be constructed, too. For example a 99.7% confidence interval is computed as

$$\bar{y} \pm 3\frac{s_y}{\sqrt{n}}$$

The only difference is that the multiple 3 is used instead of 2.

Note once again that both the point and interval estimates relate to the center of the population distribution as measured by the population mean μ_y. They relate to *no* other feature of this population distribution.

---

[4]This is only approximate. Because the standard error is estimated from a sample, the appropriate multiple for a 95% confidence interval is slightly higher than 2. The appropriate multiple comes from tables of the t-distribution (see Section 7.6). For the case of large sample sizes considered here, where n > 30, the approximation is excellent.

> **Interval estimation:** A **confidence interval** for the population mean μ_y, based on a large random sample, is
>
> Point Estimate $\pm\ z$ (Estimated Standard Error)
>
> or
>
> $$\bar{y} \pm z\frac{s_y}{\sqrt{n}}$$
>
> where z is an appropriate multiple from the normal distribution (Table 4.1 or the *Calc ▸ Probability Distributions ▸ Normal* menu in Minitab), which determines the degree of confidence in the interval.

interpretation of confidence interval

Large here typically means that n exceeds 30. When n is between 20 and 30, the confidence intervals obtained are still useful, but they are a little too tight.[5]

From the perspective of what is called *classical* or *sampling theory,* the term "95% confidence" can be interpreted as follows: If we could draw a large number of samples and if we computed a 95% confidence interval each time, then about 95% of all intervals so constructed would contain the true population mean.

From the *Bayesian* perspective, the interpretation would be: The probability is 95% that the population mean lies in the interval from $(\bar{y} - 2s_y/\sqrt{n})$ to $(\bar{y} + 2s_y/\sqrt{n})$, or from 118 to 150 in the inventory example.

(If these two perspectives seem the same to you, don't worry about it. The differences are not really important for this course.)

As a final example, suppose the auditor wanted an 80% confidence interval for the population mean. Let us first discuss how to find the appropriate multiple from the normal distribution. Since the auditor wants an 80% interval, the auditor wants a z value such that it is exceeded with probability *10%* (this is one-half of 20% since there are two tails). Therefore, the auditor needs the 90th percentile from a normal distribution. Table 4.1 or the *Calc ▸ Probability Distributions ▸ Normal* menu in Minitab gives the appropriate z value to be $z = 1.28$. So the 80% confi-

---

[5]The reason why a *large* sample is required is that the z-multiple used in the confidence interval formula should be used only when the standard error of the mean ($\sigma_y/\sqrt{n}$) is *known.* When the standard error is *unknown* and must be estimated by $s_y/\sqrt{n}$, the appropriate multiple for a confidence interval is somewhat larger than the z-multiple, but when $n > 30$, z is an adequate approximation of the correct multiple.

We had used the cutoff $n > 20$ in a different context on p. 271: When $n > \mathbf{20}$, the sampling distribution of the mean is approximately normal regardless of the shape of the population distribution, so z-multiples can be used to characterize various aspects of the sampling distribution of the mean. The results for the sampling distribution of the mean, however, were phrased in terms of *known* standard errors ($\sigma_y/\sqrt{n}$). When the standard error is not known and must be *estimated* by $s_y/\sqrt{n}$, the z-multiple can be used only if $n > \mathbf{30}$.

FIGURE 7.13 Confidence Intervals with Minitab

Choose the *Stat* ▸ *Basic Statistics* ▸ *1-Sample t* menu and fill in the dialog box. The following output will appear in the Session window:

```
MTB > TInterval 95.0 C1.
                 N       MEAN      STDEV    SE MEAN    95.0 PERCENT C.I.
VALUE          100     134.00      80.00       8.00    ( 118.12,  149.88)
```

FIGURE 7.14

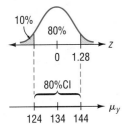

dence interval for μ_y is

$$134 \pm 1.28(8) \quad \text{or} \quad 134 \pm 10$$

or from 124 to 144.

Confidence intervals can also be obtained with Minitab. Figure 7.13 gives the Minitab results for a 95% confidence interval for the mean audit value. Note that the Minitab name for the response variable is VALUE.

We can now answer the managerial question for the auditing example, given at the beginning of this section: How close can the sample mean $\bar{y}$ be expected to be to the population mean μ_y? A reasonable estimate for the population mean is the sample mean, $\bar{y} = \$134$. An estimate for the *margin of error* is the estimated standard error of the mean, $8. Chances are 95% that the point estimate of the population mean μ_y, $\bar{y} = \$134$, is no further than $16 from the correct, but unknown, population mean. Since there were $N = 9{,}000$ items in inventory, a point estimate for the inventory total is $134(9{,}000) = \$1{,}206{,}000$. With 95% degree of confidence, this point estimate is no more than $16(9{,}000) = \$144{,}000$ away from the total.

Sometimes a *one-sided confidence interval* is useful. In the auditing example, the 80% confidence interval extended from $124 to $144. We can thus say that chances are 90% that the population mean is covered by the interval consisting of values less than or equal to $144. We can also say that chances are 90% that the population mean is covered by the interval consisting of values greater than or equal to $124. (See Figure 7.15.)

one-sided confidence interval

FIGURE 7.15

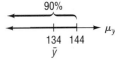

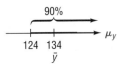

The Standard Deviation vs. the Standard Error

So far, we have introduced several concepts regarding standard deviations among which there might appear to be only very subtle differences, i.e.,

1. The population standard deviation, σ_y, which measures the extent to which the response variable value y for an individual unit may differ from the population mean, μ_y

2. The sample standard deviation, s_y, which measures the extent to which the response variable value y for an individual unit in the sample may differ from the sample mean, $\bar{y}$; s_y can be used as a point estimate of σ_y when σ_y is unknown

3. The standard error of the mean, $\sigma_y/\sqrt{n}$, which measures the extent to which the sample mean, $\bar{y}$, may differ from the population mean, μ_y

4. The estimated standard error of the mean, $s_y/\sqrt{n}$, which can be used to estimate the standard error of the mean when σ_y and thus $\sigma_y/\sqrt{n}$ are unknown

The population standard deviation characterizes the degree of dispersion in the population distribution. It is a one-number summary for how far values for the response variable tend to be away from the population mean. It can only be computed when a census is available for the population of interest.

When only a random sample is available from the population, the population distribution is, of course, not available, and so the population mean μ_y and the population standard deviation σ_y are unknown. The random sample can be used to obtain a histogram that gives a rough idea of the shape of the population distribution. The center of this sample histogram, as measured by the sample mean $\bar{y}$, provides an estimate of the center of the population distribution, μ_y, and the dispersion in the histogram, as measured by the sample standard deviation, s_y, provides an estimate of the dispersion of the population distribution, as measured by σ_y. We have called $\bar{y}$ and s_y point estimates of μ_y and σ_y.

We must indicate by how much the point estimate $\bar{y}$ can differ from the population mean μ_y, that is, by how much the center of the sample histogram can differ from the center of the population distribution. The standard error of the mean, $\sigma_y/\sqrt{n}$, is a useful yardstick for this margin of error. Since σ_y is typically unknown, so is $\sigma_y/\sqrt{n}$. But since s_y provides a point estimate for σ_y, so $s_y/\sqrt{n}$ provides a point estimate for $\sigma_y/\sqrt{n}$, the margin of error.

The larger the sample size n—that is, the closer the sample is to a census—the closer we expect the sample histogram to be to the population distribution, and the closer we expect the point estimates $\bar{y}$ and s_y to be to the population parameters μ_y and σ_y. Finally, the larger the sample size, the closer the standard error of the mean, $\sigma_y/\sqrt{n}$, and its estimate, $s_y/\sqrt{n}$, are to 0.

prediction interval

At this point, we should contrast a prediction interval (PI) with a confidence interval (CI). As we had seen in previous chapters, a *prediction interval* refers to the response variable value for an *individual* unit from the population of interest. Its general form is

$$\mu_y \pm z\,\sigma_y$$

where z comes from a normal table. Since μ_y and σ_y are typically unknown, they must be estimated from a simple random sample. We use the point estimates $\bar{y}$ and s_y for μ_y and σ_y, so the estimated prediction interval is

$$\bar{y} \pm z\,s_y$$

In order to use this prediction interval formula, we must have used a normal probability plot for the sample to show that the underlying population distribution is well approximated by a normal distribution.

confidence interval

The *confidence interval* relates to the unknown population *mean* of the response variable values, μ_y. Its general form is

$$\bar{y} \pm z \frac{\sigma_y}{\sqrt{n}}$$

Since σ_y is typically unknown, we must estimate it from the sample by s_y, and so the confidence interval is

$$\bar{y} \pm z \frac{s_y}{\sqrt{n}}$$

This confidence interval formula is valid, regardless of the shape of the underlying population distribution, as long as the sample size n is reasonably large.

EXAMPLE 7.3

Let us contrast these two types of intervals by revisiting Example 4.2. A new supplier has just shipped a batch of $N = 1{,}100$ components to an automotive parts manufacturer. The response variable y is the deviation of an important internal height dimension from specifications; y is measured in micrometers. A simple random sample of $n = 50$ components is taken, and the response variable is measured on each, yielding a sample mean and standard deviation of $\bar{y} = 0.062$ and $s_y = 3.554$, respectively. A histogram of the 50 measurements suggests normality.

FIGURE 7.16

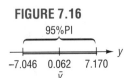

Using the sample statistics as point estimates of the population parameters, and thus ignoring sampling uncertainty, a 95% prediction interval for y is

$$0.062 \pm 2(3.554) \qquad \text{or} \qquad 0.062 \pm 7.108$$

This prediction interval extends from -7.046 to 7.170 micrometers, and we can expect the height deviation for about 95% of the components in the batch to fall within this interval.

Let us concentrate on the unknown population mean μ_y for the $N = 1{,}100$ components. A point estimate for it is $\bar{y} = 0.062$, and a 95% confidence interval is

FIGURE 7.17

95%CI

$-0.943 \mid 1.067$ → μ_y

0.062

$\bar{y}$

$$0.062 \pm 2\left(\frac{3.554}{\sqrt{50}}\right) \qquad \text{or} \qquad 0.062 \pm 1.005$$

This confidence interval extends from -0.943 to 1.067 micrometers, and we have 95% confidence that the population mean height deviation is covered by this interval. Note again that this confidence interval refers exclusively to the *center* of the distribution of y.

7.4

INFERENCES ABOUT THE DIFFERENCE BETWEEN TWO MEANS

In this section we examine the difference between the means of two populations. We take a simple random sample from the first population and another simple random sample from the second. We use these *independently* obtained results from the two populations to estimate the difference in their means.

EXAMPLE 7.4

Friden Neopost is one of the largest suppliers of mailing equipment in the world. In 1991, its customer base in a large North American city consisted of approximately 3,500 installations. A study was done to quantify the prevalence of maintenance agreements and to determine equipment reliability and age.

Data were collected for the period of October 1990 to October 1991.[6] Data on each of the machines is recorded on "tub cards," which are used for dispatching service technicians. A random sample of 239 tub cards was obtained from the customer base. Three variables were measured for each mailing machine: (1) maintenance contract (0 = no, 1 = yes), (2) number of service calls, and (3) age in the field (in months). The data are stored in ASCII file MAILEQUP.DAT.

One of the questions to be addressed was:

What is the difference in the mean number of service calls between mailing machines for which there is a maintenance contract and those for which there is not?

We can view this study as comparing two populations: Population 1 consists of mailing machines for which there was a maintenance contract, and population 2 of machines for which there was not. The response variable is y, the number of service calls between October 1990 and October 1991. Let us define the following notation:

n_1 and n_2 are the sample sizes from each population

$\bar{y}_1$ and $\bar{y}_2$ are the sample means

s_1 and s_2 are the sample standard deviations

A simple random sample of $n_1 = 183$ units was taken from population 1, yielding sample mean and sample standard deviation $\bar{y}_1 = 0.88$ and $s_1 = 1.85$, re-

---

[6]The data were kindly supplied by R. B. Douglas.

spectively. The corresponding results for population 2 were $n_2 = 56$, $\bar{y}_2 = 0.57$, and $s_2 = 1.57$.

The information available can be conveniently laid out in the following table.

	Population 1	Population 2
Population mean	$\mu_1 = ?$	$\mu_2 = ?$
Sample size	$n_1 = 183$	$n_2 = 56$
Sample mean	$\bar{y}_1 = 0.88$	$\bar{y}_2 = 0.57$
Sample std. dev.	$s_1 = 1.85$	$s_2 = 1.57$

The objective is to estimate the difference between the two population means

Population Mean 2 $-$ Population Mean 1   or $\mu_2 - \mu_1$

If this difference equals 0, the two population means are identical. If this difference is positive (or negative), population mean 2 is greater (less) than population mean 1.

point estimate for difference

A point estimate for the difference is

$$\bar{y}_2 - \bar{y}_1 \quad \text{or} \quad 0.57 - 0.88 = -0.31.$$

The average number of service calls for population 1 (mailing machines with a maintenance contract) seems to considerably exceed that in population 2. But we must not interpret this figure as if it were based on completely accurate results for each population. Since the value -0.31 is a sample result and not from a census, we must consider the possibility of inaccuracies due to using sample means rather than population means. For $\bar{y}_1$, the estimated mean for population 1, the estimated standard error is

$$\frac{s_1}{\sqrt{n_1}} = \frac{1.85}{\sqrt{183}} = 0.137$$

Similarly, for $\bar{y}_2$, the estimated mean in population 2, the estimated standard error is

$$\frac{s_2}{\sqrt{n_2}} = \frac{1.57}{\sqrt{56}} = 0.210$$

standard error of the difference

To get the estimated standard error of the difference $\bar{y}_2 - \bar{y}_1$, we combine the two estimated standard errors obtained above. This is done by computing the square root of the sum of squares of the two individual estimated standard errors for $\bar{y}_1$ and $\bar{y}_2$:

$$\sqrt{0.210^2 + 0.137^2} = 0.25$$

A 95% confidence interval for the difference between two population means, based on results from two *large* independent random samples, is obtained analogously to the 95% confidence interval for a mean in Section 7.3:

Point Estimate ± 2(Estimated Standard Error)

confidence interval for difference

Here the point estimate is the difference between the two sample means, −0.31, and the estimated standard error of this difference is 0.25. So a 95% confidence interval for the difference in mean number of service calls between populations 2 and 1 is

$$-0.31 \pm 2(0.25) \quad \text{or} \quad -0.31 \pm 0.50 \quad \text{or} \quad -0.81 \text{ to } 0.19$$

FIGURE 7.18

95%CI

$\bar{y}_2 - \bar{y}_1$

The interval is rather wide. It covers the value 0, where the two *population* means would be equal. Given the available sample information, we conclude that the estimate for the difference, −0.31, is imprecise. Values somewhat far from it, in particular 0, are plausible for the difference between the two population means. The value 0 is important since $\mu_2 - \mu_1 = 0$ implies that $\mu_2 = \mu_1$; that is, the two population means are equal. Since 0 is plausible, the sample results do not rule out the possibility of no difference between the *population* means.

Summarizing, we have the following:

Inference about the **difference between two population means** based on two large random samples that were independently obtained:

Point estimate: $\quad \bar{y}_2 - \bar{y}_1$

Standard error: $\quad \sqrt{\dfrac{s_2^2}{n_2} + \dfrac{s_1^2}{n_1}}$

Confidence Interval: $\quad (\bar{y}_2 - \bar{y}_1) \pm z\sqrt{\dfrac{s_2^2}{n_2} + \dfrac{s_1^2}{n_1}}$

The sample sizes are large if both n_1 and n_2 are 20 or greater.

Figure 7.19 shows how to use Minitab to obtain a 95% confidence interval for the difference between two means. Minitab's interval agrees with the interval we found.

one-sided confidence interval for difference

We can also find one-sided confidence intervals for the difference. Since the 95% confidence interval for the difference between the two population means extends from −0.81 to 0.19, a 97.5% one-sided confidence interval covers values that are less than or equal to 0.19.

Let us find the degree of confidence in an interval that consists of negative values only. Such an interval would suggest that population mean 2 is less than population mean 1. Since the normal table is applicable to find confidence intervals

FIGURE 7.19
Confidence
Intervals with
Minitab: Difference
Between Two
Means

Choose the *Stat* ▸ *Basic Statistics* ▸ *2-Sample t* menu and fill in the dialog box. The following output will appear in the Session window:

```
MTB > TwoT 95.0 c3 c1:
SUBC>   Alternative 0.

TWOSAMPLE T FOR CALLS

TYPE    N        MEAN     STDEV     SE MEAN
1       183      0.88     1.85      0.14
0       56       0.57     1.57      0.21

95 PCT CI FOR MU 1 - MU 0: ( -0.19,  0.81)

TTEST MU 1 = MU 0 (VS NE): T= 1.23 P=0.22 DF= 106
```

in this case, all we need to do is standardize the value 0:

$$z = \frac{0 - \text{Point Estimate}}{\text{Estimated Standard Error}} \quad \text{or} \quad z = \frac{0 - (-0.31)}{0.25} = 1.24$$

FIGURE 7.20

89%CI

$\mu_2 - \mu_1$

$-0.31 \quad 0$

$\bar{y}_2 - \bar{y}_1$

Using Table 4.1, the corresponding probability is 0.8925. The degree of confidence is about 89% that the difference between populations means 2 and 1 is negative or that population mean 2 is less than population mean 1. Likewise, the degree of confidence is about 11% that population mean 2 is greater than population mean 1. Thus, the data at hand do not provide overwhelming evidence that one of the population means is larger than the other.

7.5

INFERENCES ABOUT POPULATION PROPORTIONS

This section applies the results from Sections 7.3 and 7.4 to inferences about population *proportions*. This is possible since a proportion can be viewed as a very simple kind of mean.

Inferences About a Population Proportion

Let us first discuss inferences about a single population proportion.

EXAMPLE 7.5

Consider the following quote from the *American Banker,* October 5, 1987, page 1:

> Last year, 10% of the public quit patronizing their most important financial institution and took their business elsewhere, according to *American Banker's* latest consumer opinion survey.

Later on in the article, we are told that the "survey . . . is based on 1,130 telephone interviews of a random cross section of the American public."

The important question is: What does this 10% figure estimate, and how reliable is this estimate?

Let us assume that the $n = 1,130$ subjects whose opinions were elicited were indeed randomly drawn from the population of interest and that 10% of them or 113 changed their most important financial institution.

Before proceeding, let us phrase this example in our terminology and then show that a proportion is indeed a mean. The response variable of interest is y, Change of financial institution, and for every subject in the population it can take on one of two values, yes or no. This dichotomy represents the simplest kind of categorical variable. There are many other such dichotomous variables, such as sex, whose two values are female and male; quality, whose values could be defective and effective; or the variable outcome, whose two values could be success and failure. We can conveniently code the values for all these dichotomous variables as "1" and "0", where the assignment of 1 and 0 is arbitrary:

dichotomous variable

1	0
success	failure
female	male
defective	effective
yes	no

When the response variable is dichotomous, the proportion of 1's—that is, the proportion of successes or yes answers in the population—is the population parameter of interest. Typically we do not know the value of the dichotomous variable for all subjects or units in the population, so we have to estimate this proportion from a sample for which we have obtained the sample proportion. Let us summarize these definitions:

When the response variable y is dichotomous, its value for every subject or unit in the population is 1 (success) or 0 (failure).

The *population* proportion of successes is denoted π (the Greek letter pi).

The *sample* proportion of successes is denoted p.

Note that π is a population parameter and p is a sample statistic that is used as a point estimate for π.

In Example 7.5 (the banking example), $p = 0.10$. We want to use p to make an inference about π.

We will first show that a proportion is indeed a mean. Let us use the coding 1/0 for yes/no in the example. In the sample of 1,130 subjects, there were 113 changes of financial institution; that is, there were 113 1's and $1{,}130 - 113 = 1{,}017$ 0's. The average of all these 1's and 0's is

$$\bar{y} = \frac{1(113) + 0(1{,}017)}{1{,}130} \qquad \text{or} \qquad \bar{y} = \frac{113}{1{,}130} = 0.10 = p$$

This average equals the proportion of changes of financial institution. A proportion is thus a mean when the response variable is dichotomous, and we can apply the results about means from Section 7.3 to proportions.

> **Point estimation:** When the sample is drawn randomly from the population, the sample proportion p is a point estimate of the population proportion π.

In the example, $p = 0.10$ is a point estimate of the population proportion π of people who changed their financial institution. How good is this estimate? What is the margin of error? To answer these questions, let us obtain a confidence interval. When estimating a population mean or the difference between two population means, we used the following formula for a confidence interval:

Point Estimate $\pm$ Multiple(Estimated Standard Error)

When estimating a proportion, the formula for the standard error is very simple. This simplicity is due to the fact that the dichotomous variable of interest takes on only one of two values. It is known that

$$\text{Standard Error of Proportion} = \sqrt{\frac{\pi(1 - \pi)}{n}}$$

(For a derivation, see, for example, Keller, Warrack, and Bartel, 1994.) As before, the larger the sample size, the lower the standard error. This formula is not very useful for obtaining a confidence interval since it requires that the population proportion π be known. This proportion, however, is what we are trying to estimate. So we must resort to an estimated standard error of the proportion, where we use the point estimate p for π:

$$\text{Estimated Standard Error of Proportion} = \sqrt{\frac{p(1 - p)}{n}}$$

The standard error of the proportion is

$$\sqrt{\frac{\pi(1-\pi)}{n}}$$

and it can be estimated by

$$\sqrt{\frac{p(1-p)}{n}}$$

The estimated standard error for the banking example is $\sqrt{[0.1(1-0.1)/1,130]} = 0.00892$. Using this we can now find a confidence interval.

Interval estimation: A **confidence interval** for the population proportion π, based on a large random sample, is

$$p \pm z \sqrt{\frac{p(1-p)}{n}}$$

where z is an appropriate multiple from the normal distribution, and determines the degree of confidence in the interval.

The sample can be considered large if both the sample number of successes, np, and failures, $n(1-p)$, are greater than or equal to 5.

FIGURE 7.21

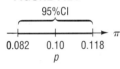

In the banking example, $np = 113$ and $n(1-p) = 1,017$, so the sample is large. A 95% confidence interval for the population proportion of changes in financial institution is

$$0.10 \pm 2(0.00892) \qquad \text{or} \qquad 0.10 \pm 0.018$$

Chances are 95% that the population proportion of changes in financial institution is within 0.018 of 0.10.

EXAMPLE 7.6

Consider a pre-election poll. In a random sample of $n = 1,000$ voters, 45% said they would vote for the incumbent. How accurate is this estimate?

The estimated standard error is

$$\sqrt{\frac{0.45(1-0.45)}{1,000}} = 0.0157$$

A 95% confidence interval is

$$0.45 \pm 2(0.0157) \qquad \text{or} \qquad 0.45 \pm 0.03$$

The point estimate of the population proportion who would vote for the incumbent is 0.45. Chances are 95% that this estimate is within 3 percentage points of the correct value. This statement is often rendered in the media as: "45% of respondents would vote for the incumbent. This percentage is accurate within 3 percentage points 19 times out of 20." Since $\frac{19}{20} = 0.95$, the "19 times out of 20" refers to a 95% confidence interval.

Inferences about the Difference Between Two Population Proportions

The results from Section 7.4 can be used to make inferences about the difference between two population proportions.

EXAMPLE 7.7 _____

As part of the study described in Example 7.4 (p. 285), a further question asked how the proportion of mailing machines with maintenance contracts differed between two models, say, models 1 and 2.

_____

Let the model 1 mailing machines comprise population 1 and the model 2 machines comprise population 2. Independent random samples were obtained from both populations, and the information available can be conveniently laid out in the following table:

	Population 1	Population 2
Population proportion	$\pi_1 = ?$	$\pi_2 = ?$
Sample size	$n_1 = 86$	$n_2 = 52$
Sample proportion	$p_1 = 0.78$	$p_2 = 0.85$

We want to estimate the difference between the two population proportions,

$$\pi_2 - \pi_1$$

A point estimate for this difference is the corresponding difference in sample proportions,

$$p_2 - p_1 \qquad \text{or} \qquad 0.85 - 0.78 = 0.07$$

The estimated standard error of this difference equals the square root of the sum of the squared standard errors for the two sample proportions,

$$\sqrt{\frac{p_2(1-p_2)}{n_2} + \frac{p_1(1-p_1)}{n_1}} \quad \text{or} \quad \sqrt{\frac{0.85(0.15)}{52} + \frac{0.78(0.22)}{86}} = 0.067$$

Thus, a 95% confidence interval for the difference between the two population proportions is

$$0.07 \pm 2(0.067) \quad \text{or} \quad 0.07 \pm 0.13$$

FIGURE 7.22

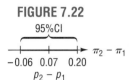

This interval extends from -0.06 to 0.20. It is rather wide, and it includes the value 0. Since the value 0 implies that the two population proportions are equal, the sample data do not provide much evidence for the population proportion of mailing machines with maintenance contracts being different between the two models.

Summarizing, we have the following:

Inference about the *difference between two population proportions* based on two large independent random samples:

Point estimate: $p_2 - p_1$

Standard error: $\sqrt{\dfrac{p_2(1-p_2)}{n_2} + \dfrac{p_1(1-p_1)}{n_1}}$

Confidence Interval: $(p_2 - p_1) \pm z \sqrt{\dfrac{p_2(1-p_2)}{n_2} + \dfrac{p_1(1-p_1)}{n_1}}$

The sample sizes are large if each of n_1p_1, $n_1(1-p_1)$, n_2p_2, and $n_2(1-p_2)$ is 5 or greater.

Flowchart for Inferences Regarding Population Parameters

In the last few sections, we have discussed inferences regarding four parameters:

1. A population mean, μ

2. A difference between two population means, $\mu_2 - \mu_1$

3. A population proportion, π

4. A difference between two population proportions, $\pi_2 - \pi_1$

The approach to finding point estimates, standard errors, and interval estimates is similar for all four parameters. The flowchart in Figure 7.23 summarizes the results.

FIGURE 7.23   Flowchart for Estimating Population Parameters

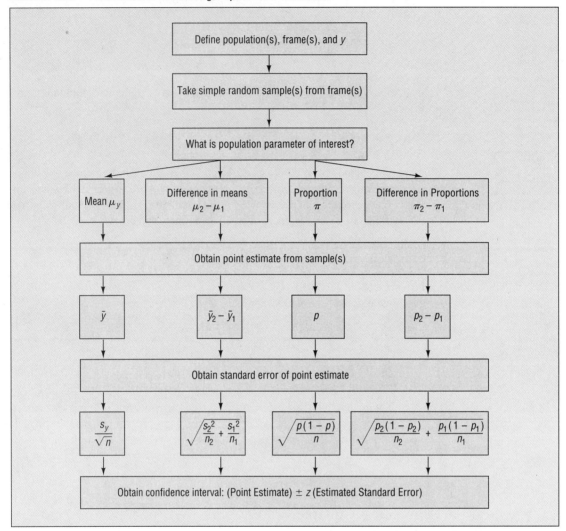

7.6

INTERVAL ESTIMATION FOR A POPULATION MEAN BASED ON SMALL SAMPLES

This section discusses the estimation of a population mean from the results of a small sample. For the results in this section to be reliable, the distribution of the population under study must be approximately normal. Consider an example.

EXAMPLE 7.8

A marketing manager is interested in average product usage in a particular market segment. Here, product usage is defined to be the number of units a customer purchased in a year. Suppose that $n = 16$ customers were randomly drawn from the population. Their product usage values were

25	21	17	22	21	24	21	21
22	17	23	20	24	21	16	18

The manager wants an estimate of average product usage in the market segment and a measure of how reliable this estimate is.

The normal probability plot for these 16 values suggests that they were drawn from a population distribution that is approximately normal. The mean and standard deviation of the 16 product usage values are $\bar{y} = 20.81$ and $s_y = 2.66$. What would be a 95% confidence interval for average product usage μ_y in the market segment?

Earlier, we estimated the standard error of the mean

$$\frac{\text{Population Standard Deviation}}{\sqrt{n}} = \frac{\sigma_y}{\sqrt{n}}$$

by

$$\frac{\text{Sample Standard Deviation}}{\sqrt{n}} = \frac{s_y}{\sqrt{n}}$$

or $2.66/\sqrt{16} = 0.67$ for the product usage example.

We ignored the fact that we used s_y as an estimate of σ_y when obtaining interval estimates. This was justified in the large sample case discussed in Section 7.3, but it is not justified when interval estimates are to be based on small samples, say, when $n < 30$.

When the sample size n is small, the fact that σ_y has to be estimated by s_y leads to *added* uncertainty in the estimation procedure. This is incorporated by using *multiples* in the confidence interval formula that are *somewhat larger* than the corresponding multiples from the normal distribution.

Interval estimation: A **confidence interval** for the population mean μ_y, based on a **small** random sample from an approximately *normal* population distribution, is

$$\text{Point Estimate} \pm t \ \ (\text{Estimated Standard Error}) \quad \text{or} \quad \bar{y} \pm t\frac{s_y}{\sqrt{n}}$$

where t is an appropriate multiple from the **t-distribution** with $n - 1$ **degrees of freedom**. This multiple determines the degree of confidence in the interval. It can be found in Figure 7.24.

FIGURE 7.24
t-Multiples for
Selected Intervals

Degrees of Freedom	Multiple					
	80%	90%	95%	97%	99%	99.5%
2	1.386	2.920	4.303	5.643	9.925	14.089
3	1.250	2.353	3.182	3.896	5.841	7.453
4	1.190	2.132	2.776	3.298	4.604	5.598
5	1.156	2.015	2.571	3.003	4.032	4.773
6	1.134	1.943	2.447	2.829	3.707	4.317
7	1.119	1.895	2.365	2.715	3.499	4.029
8	1.108	1.860	2.306	2.634	3.355	3.833
9	1.100	1.833	2.262	2.574	3.250	3.690
10	1.093	1.812	2.228	2.527	3.169	3.581
11	1.088	1.796	2.201	2.491	3.106	3.497
12	1.083	1.782	2.179	2.461	3.055	3.428
13	1.079	1.771	2.160	2.436	3.012	3.372
14	1.076	1.761	2.145	2.415	2.977	3.326
15	1.074	1.753	2.131	2.397	2.947	3.286
16	1.071	1.746	2.120	2.382	2.921	3.252
17	1.069	1.740	2.110	2.368	2.898	3.222
18	1.067	1.734	2.101	2.356	2.878	3.197
19	1.066	1.729	2.093	2.346	2.861	3.174
20	1.064	1.725	2.086	2.336	2.845	3.153
21	1.063	1.721	2.080	2.328	2.831	3.135
22	1.061	1.717	2.074	2.320	2.819	3.119
23	1.060	1.714	2.069	2.313	2.807	3.104
24	1.059	1.711	2.064	2.307	2.797	3.091
25	1.058	1.708	2.060	2.301	2.787	3.078
26	1.058	1.706	2.056	2.296	2.779	3.067
27	1.057	1.703	2.052	2.291	2.771	3.057
28	1.056	1.701	2.048	2.286	2.763	3.047
29	1.055	1.699	2.045	2.282	2.756	3.038
30	1.055	1.697	2.042	2.278	2.750	3.030
35	1.052	1.690	2.030	2.262	2.724	2.996
40	1.050	1.684	2.021	2.250	2.704	2.971
∞	1.036	1.645	1.960	2.170	2.576	2.808

t-multiples

For 80%, 90%, 95%, 97%, 99%, and 99.5% confidence intervals and selected degrees of freedom, Figure 7.24 lists appropriate multiples from the *t*-distribution. The size of the *t*-multiple decreases as the sample size *n* (and the degrees of freedom, *n* − 1) increases. For very large degrees of freedom, the appropriate *t*-multiple is very close to the appropriate multiple from the normal distribution.

The degrees of freedom figure is used to identify in which row of the *t*-table the appropriate multiple can be found. The reason for calling this figure *degrees of freedom* involves technical statistical considerations that we will not discuss.

Regardless of the degree of confidence, the multiple based on the normal distribution is usually a good approximation for the corresponding t-multiple when the degrees of freedom exceed 30.

For the product usage example, the degrees of freedom are $n - 1 = 15$, so the appropriate t-multiple for a 95% confidence interval for the mean is 2.131. Therefore, the 95% confidence interval for mean product usage in the market segment is

$$20.81 \pm 2.131\left(\frac{2.66}{\sqrt{16}}\right) \quad \text{or} \quad 20.81 \pm 1.42$$

Figure 7.25 illustrates how t-multiples not given in Figure 7.24 can be found with Minitab.

The following table summarizes when to use a z- (i.e., a normal) or a t-multiple in the confidence interval formula,

$$\bar{y} \pm (t\text{- or } z\text{-multiple})\frac{s_y}{\sqrt{n}}$$

		Population Distribution	
		Approximately Normal	Not Normal
Degrees of Freedom ($n - 1$)	≤ 20	t	no method
	21–30	t	t
	>30	t or z	t or z

FIGURE 7.25
Finding t-Multiples with Minitab

Choose the *Calc ▸ Probability Distributions ▸ T* menu
In the *T-distribution* dialog box,
  Click *Inverse cumulative probability*
  In the *Degrees of freedom* box, type **15**
  Click *Input constant,* type **0.975** in the box to its right
  Click *ok*

The following output will appear in the Minitab Session window:

```
MTB > InvCDF .975;
SUBC>   T 15.
       0.9750 2.1315
```

When the sample size is large—that is, when the degrees of freedom exceed 30—then either the z- or the t-multiple can be used. It is best to use the t-multiple, but the z-multiple is then a good approximation to the t-multiple. For large sample sizes, it does not matter what the shape of the population distribution is, since the sampling distribution of $\bar{y}$ is then approximately normal and the estimated standard error, $s_y/\sqrt{n}$, approximates the exact standard error, $\sigma_y/\sqrt{n}$, very well. When the sample size is intermediate (roughly between 20 and 30), however, it is advisable to use the t-tables in order to incorporate the uncertainty added by using the estimated standard error rather than the exact standard error. For small sample sizes—that is, when the degrees of freedom are 20 or less—the population distribution must be approximately normal, and the t-multiple must then be used in the confidence interval formula (rather than the z-multiple). When a small random sample is drawn from a *nonnormal* population distribution, a general formula for the confidence interval is *not* available.

7.7

HYPOTHESIS TESTING

Note: This section can be skipped without loss of continuity.

The topic of hypothesis testing has been very important in statistics and its applications.[7] Briefly, a **hypothesis test** consists of checking to what extent a given data set supports a hypothesized value for some parameter of interest, such as a population mean or a population proportion. Hypothesis testing is a complex topic, and there are many subtleties. This section presents a very rudimentary introduction to hypothesis tests. Overall, their use is de-emphasized in this text, and other, typically more informal, tools are used to replace them. We will illustrate the use of hypothesis tests for a mean, a difference between two means, and a proportion.

Hypothesis Test for a Population Mean

Let us first illustrate a hypothesis test for a population mean. As an example consider a modified version of Example 7.2 (p. 273).

EXAMPLE 7.9

Management had reported the book value for the inventory account to be $1,305,000. Since there were $N = 9,000$ inventory items, this implied that the reported average book value was $1,305,000/9,000 = \$145$. It was the auditor's task to ascertain that the reported book value accurately reflected the actual book value.

---

[7]The reader will find a more detailed description of hypothesis tests in many introductory statistics texts, e.g., D. R. Anderson, D. J. Sweeney and T. A. Williams, *Statistics for Business and Economics,* 4th Edition, West Publishing Company, 1990.

To do so, the auditor took a simple random sample of size $n = 100$ from the population of $N = 9,000$ inventory items, and the resulting sample mean and standard deviation were $\bar{y} = \$134$ and $s_y = \$80$, respectively. Should the auditor be surprised by the difference between management's reported average, \$145, and the sample average, \$134?

Let us phrase the auditor's problem in terms of a hypothesis test. The auditor wants to check if management's claim is true or not. So the auditor postulates the hypothesis that the population mean inventory value is $\mu_0 = 145$, where the subscript "0" is to emphasize that this is not necessarily the actual population mean, but the hypothesized mean.[8] In this book we define a hypothesis test as a method of checking to what extent the data support the hypothesis.

The hypothesis is either true (the population mean equals 145) or it is not true (the population mean is different from 145). Furthermore, the data either support the hypothesis or they do not. If the data support the hypothesis *and* it is true, or if the data do not support the hypothesis *and* it is not true, then a correct conclusion has been drawn from the data. Otherwise, the conclusion is incorrect. Since, however, we do not know if the hypothesis is true, we can also not know for sure if the conclusion we draw from the data is correct.

The hypothesis testing problem, as described in the previous paragraph, can be summarized by the following table:

Has the Correct Conclusion Been Drawn from the Data?

		Hypothesis is	
		True	Not true
Is hypothesis supported by the data?	Yes	correct	incorrect
	No	incorrect	correct

Even though we cannot know whether the conclusion drawn from the data is correct or incorrect, we do know that simple random sampling was used to obtain the data. To measure the extent to which the data support the hypothesis, we will ask the question:

To what extent could the difference between the hypothesized value μ_0 and the sample mean $\bar{y}$ be due to chance?

---

[8] In hypothesis testing, the above hypothesis ($\mu_0 = 145$) is typically called the *null hypothesis,* and there is an alternate hypothesis. There are many subtleties in the approach with two hypotheses, and we will not pursue it further in this book.

We will operationalize this question by asking:

> Given that the hypothesis is true and that simple random sampling was used, what is the probability of obtaining a sample mean that is as far away from the hypothesized value for the population mean as the observed sample mean or further away?

If simple random sampling is used, then the sampling distribution of the mean, discussed on p. 269, tells us how far away from the hypothesized population mean the sample mean is likely to be:

1. When the hypothesis is true, the sample mean $\bar{y}$ is likely to be close to the hypothesized value μ_0.

2. When the hypothesis is true, the standard error of the mean, $\sigma_y/\sqrt{n}$ is a measure of the extent to which a sample mean can differ from μ_0. Here, σ_y is the standard deviation of the population from which we are drawing the sample and n is the sample size.

3. When the hypothesis is true, the extent to which the sample mean can differ from the hypothesized population mean is well described by a normal distribution, as long as n is large enough.

The graph in Figure 7.26 illustrates these facts. Note that $\bar{y}_{obs}$ denotes the observed sample mean. The portion of the curve to the left of $\bar{y}_{obs}$ corresponds to sample mean values that are further away from the hypothesized value than the observed sample mean. If we standardize the observed value, we get one measure of how unusual the observed sample mean is under the hypothesis. If the hypothesis is true, the standardized observed sample mean is

$$z_{obs} = \frac{\bar{y}_{obs} - \mu_0}{\sigma_y/\sqrt{n}}$$

FIGURE 7.26
Sampling Distribution of the Mean When the Hypothesis Is True

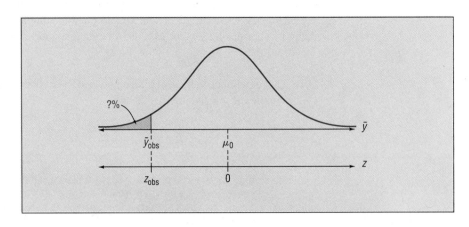

When the data support the hypothesis, $\bar{y}_{obs}$ is close to μ_0, and then z_{obs} is close to 0. A standardized value between roughly -2 (or -3) and $+2$ (or $+3$) would not be surprising in light of the hypothesis. If such a value is obtained, the data do not contradict the hypothesized value.

In order to apply these results to the auditing example, we must know the hypothesized value ($\mu_0 = \$145$), the sample size ($n = 100$), the observed sample mean ($\bar{y}_{obs} = \$134$), and the *population* standard deviation σ_y. We do not know the latter, but we can estimate it from the sample by the usual sample standard deviation, s_y. The standardized observed sample mean is

$$z_{obs} = \frac{\bar{y} - \mu_0}{s_y/\sqrt{n}}$$

Since the sample standard deviation for this example is $s_y = 80$, the standardized observed sample mean is

$$z_{obs} = \frac{134 - 145}{80/\sqrt{100}} = -1.38$$

indicating that the sample mean ($\bar{y} = \$134$) is not surprisingly far away from the hypothesized value ($\mu_0 = \$145$). Thus the sample data would not really contradict the value of the hypothesized population mean, and the auditor could accept management's claim about the book value.

We had asked above:

> Given that the hypothesis is true and that simple random sampling was used, what is the probability of obtaining a sample mean that is as far away from the hypothesized value as the observed sample mean or further away?

FIGURE 7.27

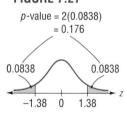

p-value = 2(0.0838)
= 0.176

0.0838   0.0838

−1.38 0 1.38

p-value

This question can now easily be answered with the normal table. Using the observed standardized sample mean, $z = -1.38$, we find in Table 4.1 or with the *Calc ▸ Probability Distributions ▸ Normal* menu in Minitab that the answer is 0.0838 or 8.38%. Thus, if the hypothesis is true—if $\mu_0 = \$145$—the probability is a little over 8% that we will observe a value less than or equal to the sample mean ($\$134$). Again, the sample mean value of $\$134$ is not really surprising in light of management's claim.

In many applications, the probability reported above, 0.0838, is *doubled* since it is the absolute size of the discrepancy that matters, and not its direction. The result is called the *statistical significance* or the *p-value*, where p stands for "probability." Here, the p-value is 2(0.0838) = 0.1676. In general, if the p-value is close to 1, the observed data support the hypothesis, and if the p-value is close to 0, the observed data do not support the hypothesis. In applications, a cut-off value will have to be chosen for the p-value. The cut-off value typically ranges between 0.01 and 0.10, a very common value being 0.05. Alternatively, if it is difficult to choose a definite cut-off for the p-value, then we could consider the data to be inconclusive regarding the hypothesis when the p-value is in the range from 0.01 to 0.10.

Let us summarize these comments regarding the *p*-value.

When the hypothesis is true, the ***p*-value** (or statistical significance) measures the probability of observing a sample result at least as unusual as the observed sample result.

The *p*-value (or statistical significance) is always between 0 and 1. To interpret it, we use the following rule of thumb[9]

If the *p*-value is

Greater than 0.10, the observed data do not call the hypothesis into question (in this case, we say that the test result is *not* significant)

Less than 0.01, the observed data call the hypothesis into question (we say that the test result is significant)

Between 0.01 and 0.10, the observed test result is inconclusive regarding the hypothesis.

---

hypothesis testing procedure

Overall, a hypothesis test consists of the following steps:

1. State the hypothesis.

2. Collect the data.

3. Compute the standardized observed sample mean, z_{obs}, and the *p*-value. Note that

$$z_{obs} = \frac{\text{Observed Sample Mean} - \text{Hypothesized Population Mean}}{\text{Standard Error of Mean}}$$

4. Draw a conclusion using the rule of thumb given above.

Let us consider another example illustrating a hypothesis test for a population mean.

EXAMPLE 7.10

In 1971, a business asked a survey organization to survey Canadian families with respect to their attitudes regarding a particular product group. One of the questions was to ask for family income. The *Canada Year Book 1985* indicated that the average income of families in Canada in 1971 was $10,400. The survey organization was to take a random sample from the Canadian population of families, and one of the uses of the income question was to check if the resulting sample average in-

---

[9]This rule of thumb was discussed in Section 5.4, p. 166.

come $\bar{y}$ was not surprisingly different from the population average μ_y. A surprisingly large difference would, of course, cast some doubt on the sampling procedure. Thus the hypothesized mean for the population from which the sample was drawn was $\mu_0 = 10,400$. A simple random sample of $n = 100$ families was obtained, the resulting sample mean income was $\bar{y} = \$8,000$ and the sample standard deviation was $s_y = \$5,000$.

Do the sample data support the hypothesis? We can follow the hypothesis testing procedure outlined above:

1. The hypothesis was that the population mean is $\mu_0 = 10,400$.

2. The random sample of size $n = 100$ yielded the sample mean $\bar{y} = 8,000$ and the sample standard deviation $s_y = 5,000$.

3. The standardized observed sample mean was

FIGURE 7.28

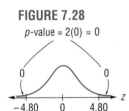

p-value $= 2(0) = 0$

$$z_{obs} = \frac{8,000 - 10,400}{5,000 \,/\, \sqrt{100}} = -4.80$$

Using Table 4.1 or the *Calc ▸ Probability Distributions ▸ Normal* menu in Minitab, we find the probability to be close to 0 that a z-value is less than or equal to -4.80. Given that the hypothesis is true, the probability is very close to 0 that an observed sample mean would be $\$8,000$ or less. The p-value is also close to 0.

4. We can use either $z_{obs} = -4.80$ or p-value $= 0$ to conclude that the hypothesis is definitely called into question.

What are the possible reasons for this conclusion? Of course, just due to chance a simple random sample from the Canadian population of families could have yielded a sample mean far away from the population mean; this happens very rarely, but it *can* happen. Another reason could be that the wrong population was sampled: There are millions of Canadian families, and they are spread over a large country; so it was difficult to obtain a simple random sample. After further investigation, it was learned that, in fact, a simple random sample of $n = 200$ families had been attempted, but the response rate was only 50% and the resulting 100 responses were treated as if they were a random sample. We know, of course, that ignoring nonresponse can lead to serious biases.

Hypothesis Test for the Difference Between Two Population Means

Hypothesis tests can also be carried out when we are interested in the difference between two populations. Consider Example 7.4 to illustrate the approach for a difference between two population means. In Example 7.4, Friden Neopost was interested in the reliability of its mailing machines in a large North American city. One of the questions that needed to be addressed can be reformulated as a hypothesis test:

> Is it reasonable to conclude that there is no difference in the mean number of service calls between mailing machines for which there is a maintenance contract and those for which there is not?

Denoting the population mean number of service calls for the two populations by μ_1 (maintenance contract) and μ_2 (no maintenance contract), the hypothesis is that the difference between these two population means is $\mu_2 - \mu_1 = 0$.

One random sample each was available from the two populations. The sample of $n_1 = 183$ units from population 1 had sample mean and sample standard deviation $\bar{y}_1 = 0.88$ and $s_1 = 1.85$, respectively. The corresponding results for population 2 were $n_2 = 56$, $\bar{y}_2 = 0.57$, and $s_2 = 1.57$.

We again use the four steps for hypothesis testing outlined in the last subsection.

1. The hypothesis here refers to the difference between the two population means, which is hypothesized to be $\mu_2 - \mu_1 = 0$. The difference value 0 corresponds to no difference in mean reliability of the two populations, where reliability is measured by the number of service calls.

2. The sample results were $n_1 = 183$, $\bar{y}_1 = 0.88$, $s_1 = 1.85$, $n_2 = 56$, $\bar{y}_2 = 0.57$, and $s_2 = 1.57$.

3. We need to obtain the standardized difference between sample means. We obtain the difference by a method like the one we used to obtain the standardized sample mean,

$$z_{obs} = \frac{\begin{array}{c}\text{Observed Difference} \\ \text{Between Sample Means}\end{array} - \begin{array}{c}\text{Hypothesized Difference} \\ \text{Between Population Means}\end{array}}{\text{Standard Error of Difference}}$$

The standard error of the difference was derived in Section 7.4 (p. 287) as

$$\sqrt{\frac{s_2^2}{n_2} + \frac{s_1^2}{n_1}}$$

For the mail equipment example, we have

$$\sqrt{\frac{1.57^2}{56} + \frac{1.85^2}{183}} = 0.25$$

Therefore, the standardized observed difference is

$$z_{obs} = \frac{(0.57 - 0.88) - 0}{0.25} = -1.24$$

FIGURE 7.29

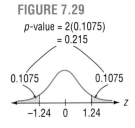

p-value = 2(0.1075)
= 0.215

The *p-value* measures the probability of observing a sample result at least as unusual as the observed sample result. In order to compute the *p*-value, note that observing a sample difference more unusual than the observed difference implies that the corresponding standardized difference would be *less* than $z_{obs} = -1.24$ in this case. Using Minitab or Table 4.1, the resulting probability is 0.1075 to observe a difference in sample means at least as unusual as the observed difference, -0.31. To compute the *p*-value, we must double this probability. Thus the *p*-value is $2(0.1075) = 0.215$.

4. Given the result for z_{obs}, the sample data do not contradict the hypothesis of no difference between the population means; that is, the observed difference between sample means is not surprisingly large. We conclude that the average reliability of mailing machines with a maintenance contract and those without is about the same. We, of course, reach the same conclusion with the *p*-value (0.215).

Hypothesis Test for a Population Proportion

Let us also use an example to illustrate hypothesis tests about a population proportion.

EXAMPLE 7.11

A new supplier delivered a large number of simple components and promised that the proportion of defectives was no larger than 5%. A simple random sample of size $n = 150$ was taken from this population of components to check if the 5% promise was kept.

We use the same four steps taken above to test a hypothesis regarding a proportion π:

1. The hypothesis is that the population proportion is $\pi_0 = 0.05$.

2. The simple random sample of $n = 150$ components resulted in 9 defectives: the sample proportion was $p = \frac{9}{150} = 0.06$.

3. The standardized sample proportion is

$$z_{obs} = \frac{\text{Observed Sample Proportion} - \text{Hypothesized Population Proportion}}{\text{Standard Error of Proportion}}$$

If the hypothesis ($\pi_0 = 0.05$) is true, then the standard error of the sample proportion is

$$\sqrt{\frac{\pi_0(1 - \pi_0)}{n}}$$

as given in Section 7.5 (p. 290). So, the standardized sample proportion is

$$z_{obs} = \frac{p - \pi_0}{\sqrt{\pi_0(1 - \pi_0)/n}}$$

For the example, the standard error of the sample proportion is

$$\sqrt{\frac{0.05(1 - 0.05)}{150}} = 0.0178$$

and so

$$z_{obs} = \frac{0.06 - 0.05}{0.0178} = 0.56$$

FIGURE 7.30

p-value = 2(0.2877)
= 0.5754

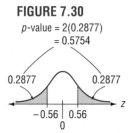

The *p-value* measures the probability of observing a sample result at least as unusual as the observed sample result. In order to compute the *p*-value, note that observing a sample proportion more unusual than the observed proportion implies that the corresponding standardized proportion would be *larger* than $z_{obs} = 0.56$ in this case. Using Table 4.1 or the *Calc* ▸ *Probability Distributions* ▸ *Normal* menu in Minitab, the probability is $1 - 0.7123 = 0.2877$ of observing a sample proportion equal to the one observed or more unusual. The *p*-value doubles this probability since it is the absolute size of the discrepancy that matters, not its direction. Thus the *p*-value is $2(0.2877) = 0.5754$.

4. The sample result thus does not call into question the hypothesized value: If indeed the population proportion of defectives were 5%, it should not surprise us to find 6% defectives in a simple random sample of $n = 150$ components.

7.8

EXAMPLE: A STUDY OF A HOSPITAL'S EMERGENCY DEPARTMENT

In this section, we analyze data about a hospital's emergency department. As part of the analysis, we use estimation of the difference between means, discussed in this chapter. The data were first introduced in Section 3.7 (p. 82) which also describes some background for the study.

Summary

Managerial Questions. When a patient arrives at the hospital's emergency department, a nurse examines the patient to determine if the case is an emergency, if it is urgent, or if it is deferrable.[10] Since treatment priority was given to critically ill

---

[10]The study is real, but the hospital's name is omitted to protect confidentiality.

patients, treatment of deferrable and urgent cases could sometimes be delayed. The study examined the validity of some patients' perception that the time until seeing a nurse and subsequently a physician was not in accordance with the severity of the affliction. The study answered the following managerial questions:

1. Is the time between admittance and first seeing a nurse lowest for emergency cases and highest for deferrable cases?

2. Is the time between admittance and first seeing a physician lowest for emergency cases and highest for deferrable cases?

3. Is the time after seeing a physician until discharge lowest for deferrable cases and highest for emergency cases?

Data Collection.   Samples of size 50 each were taken from the emergency, urgent, and deferrable patients seen by the emergency department in July 1990. For each patient, data were collected on the three time variables mentioned in the three managerial questions.

Findings.   The results were as follows. (1) The mean time between admittance and first seeing a nurse was lowest for emergency cases, and about the same for the other two cases. (2) The mean time between admittance and first seeing a physician was lowest for emergency cases, intermediate for urgent cases, and highest for deferrable cases. (3) The mean time until discharge was about the same for emergency and urgent cases and lowest for deferrable cases. For the emergency patients, the numerical values anticipated for the means on the first two variables were lower than actually observed.

Recommendations.   Overall the results do not support the concerns expressed by some of the deferrable patients about dangerously long waiting times. Some of the waiting times, however, are very long, and the waiting times for emergency cases were higher than expected. Procedures in the emergency department should be examined to see how these waiting times can be reduced.

Detailed Results

Statistical Questions.   The statistical questions were:

1. Is the mean time between admittance and first seeing a nurse lowest for emergency cases and highest for deferrable cases?

2. Is the mean time between admittance and first seeing a physician lowest for emergency cases and highest for deferrable cases?

3. Is the mean time after seeing a physician until discharge lowest for deferrable cases and highest for emergency cases?

Statistical Unit.   The subject (unit) in the study was a patient who was seen by the emergency department.

Description of Population. The population in this cross-sectional study consisted of all patients who were seen by the emergency department in July 1990. This population was divided into three subpopulations, consisting of 85 emergency, 3,543 urgent, and 1,938 deferrable patients, respectively. The three frames consisted of a listing of all patients, which was stored in the department's computer.

Sampling Scheme. Using computer software, a simple random sample of size 50 was drawn without replacement from each of the three subpopulations. This sampling scheme resulted in 50 of the 85 emergency patients being in the sample, and so the sample size is a large fraction of this (sub)population size.

Description of Variables. Four variables were measured on each patient: (1) the time between admittance and first seeing a nurse, (2) the time between admittance and first seeing a physician, (3) the time until discharge after seeing a physician, and (4) the subpopulation the patient was in (1=emergency, 2=urgent, 3=deferrable). The three time variables were measured in minutes and were of main interest. The fourth variable was used for stratification.

FIGURE 7.31 Emergency Department Data

ROW	NURSE	DOCTOR	DISCHRGE	URGENCY
1	4	5	179	1
2	7	17	10	1
3	7	8	143	1
4	12	42	85	1
5	2	32	320	1
.				
.				
.				
51	25	25	50	2
52	8	8	360	2
53	0	23	198	2
54	16	21	330	2
55	10	30	165	2
.				
.				
.				
100	2	12	20	2
101	2	2	10	3
102	13	13	15	3
103	8	18	105	3
104	0	20	55	3
105	8	108	20	3
.				
.				
.				

(a) Partial listing

	URGENCY	N	MEAN	MEDIAN	TRMEAN	STDEV	SEMEAN
NURSE	1	50	8.32	7.00	7.59	7.31	1.03
	2	50	13.60	9.00	11.77	13.64	1.93
	3	50	12.00	8.50	10.57	11.97	1.69
DOCTOR	1	50	25.20	20.00	23.32	22.35	3.16
	2	50	36.10	26.50	33.09	28.37	4.01
	3	50	45.56	37.50	42.91	36.26	5.13
DISCHRGE	1	50	164.1	140.0	154.5	117.2	16.6
	2	50	135.9	92.5	111.5	155.7	22.0
	3	50	48.90	25.00	43.82	48.91	6.92

	URGENCY	MIN	MAX	Q1	Q3
NURSE	1	0.00	36.00	4.00	12.00
	2	0.00	64.00	4.00	18.25
	3	0.00	49.00	3.75	13.25
DOCTOR	1	0.00	81.00	8.75	32.75
	2	2.00	116.00	17.75	48.00
	3	1.00	153.00	16.50	77.50
DISCHRGE	1	10.0	535.0	82.0	209.7
	2	5.0	645.0	30.0	167.5
	3	0.00	200.00	10.00	86.25

(b) Descriptive statistics

Population Characteristics of Interest. For each time variable, the parameters of interest were the means, stratified by the categorical variable indicating urgency. Furthermore, differences between these means were needed. The corresponding standard deviations and the frequency distributions were of secondary interest.

Data. There were 150 subjects in the sample. A partial listing of the data and the descriptive statistics are given in Figure 7.31. The data are stored in ASCII file EMERGNCY.DAT. All 150 subjects were used for the analysis.

Data Analysis. Figure 7.32 presents dotplots of the time until first seeing a nurse for each of the three subpopulations. It appears that the mean of this variable is a little lower for the emergency cases (8.32 minutes) than for the other two whose means appear similar (13.60 for urgent cases, 12.00 for deferrable cases). Figure 7.33 gives similiar dotplots for the time between admittance and first seeing a physician. The sample mean for this variable seems to be lowest for emergency (25.2 minutes), intermediate for urgent (36.1), and highest for deferrable cases (45.6). Finally Figure 7.34 gives similar dotplots for the time until discharge, and its mean seems to be lowest for deferrable cases (48.9 minutes), the other two cases being similar (164 minutes for emergency, 136 for urgent). Figure 7.35 lists numerical comparisons between the means of the three subpopulations for each variable. These comparisons support the visual impressions based on Figures 7.32–7.34.

FIGURE 7.32   Emergency Department Data: Waiting Time Until Nurse

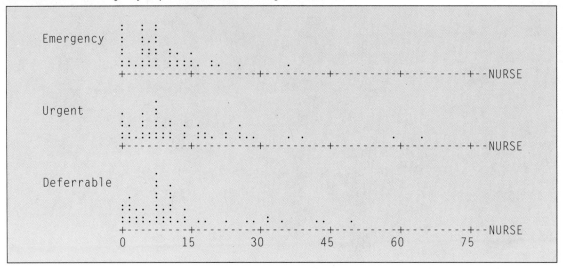

FIGURE 7.33   Emergency Department Data: Waiting Time Until Doctor

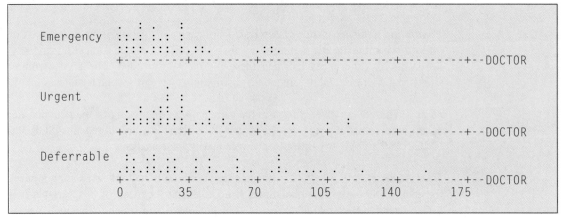

FIGURE 7.34 Emergency Department Data: Waiting Time Until Discharge

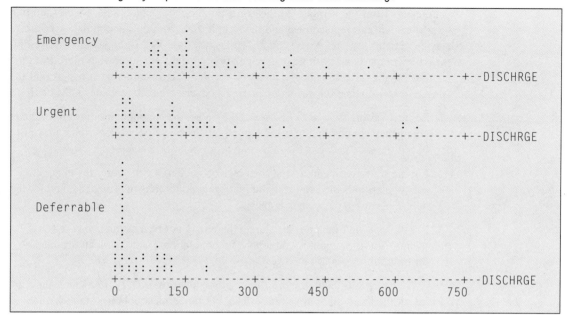

FIGURE 7.35 Emergency Department Data: Comparison of Means

	Emergency vs. Urgent	Emergency vs. Deferrable	Urgent vs. Deferrable
Variable: NURSE			
Point estimate	-5.28	-3.68	1.60
Standard error	2.19	1.98	2.56
95% CI	(-9.66, -0.90)	(-7.64, 0.28)	(-3.53, 6.73)
P(Diff < 0)	0.008	0.032	0.735
Variable: DOCTOR			
Point estimate	-10.90	-20.36	-9.46
Standard error	5.11	6.03	6.51
95% CI	(-21.11, -0.68)	(-32.44, -8.30)	(-22.48, 3.56)
P(Diff < 0)	0.017	0.001	0.074
Variable: DISCHRGE			
Point estimate	28.2	115.2	87.0
Standard error	27.6	18.0	23.1
95% CI	(-27.0, 83.4)	(79.2, 151.2)	(40.8, 133.2)
P(Diff < 0)	0.846	1.000	0.9999

Conclusions.   The confidence intervals reported in Figure 7.35 allow us to make inferences from the samples to the corresponding subpopulations. Since sampling was done without replacement and the sample size from the subpopulation of emergency patients was relatively large (50 out of 85 or 59%), the standard errors involving comparisons with this subpopulation's means are somewhat high. Both the ranges for the 95% confidence intervals for the difference between means and the degree of confidence for one-sided intervals covering negative values indicate that

1. For the waiting time until first seen by a nurse, the subpopulation mean for the emergency subpopulation is lowest and, given the standard error, there may not be a difference between the other two subpopulation means.

2. For the waiting time until first seen by a physician, the mean for the emergency subpopulation is lowest, for the urgent subpopulation is intermediate, and for the deferrable subpopulation is highest.

3. For the waiting time until discharge, there may not be a difference between the means for the emergency and urgent subpopulations, and the mean for the deferrable subpopulation is lowest.

These results hold for the three subpopulations in July 1990, and they are based on the three random samples. It is, of course, desirable to establish such results for other months as well. This, however, is not possible given the current data since a cross-sectional study was done for July 1990 only. In order to check if these results are stable over time, the study would have to be repeated for several months. Any generalizations to future months must come from judgment; they are neither confirmed nor contradicted by these data.

7.9

SUMMARY AND OUTLOOK

This chapter discussed how random samples can be used to make inferences about population parameters, in particular, a population mean, a difference between the means of two populations, a population proportion, and a difference between two population proportions. Since a random sample can be obtained only when a frame of the population exists, the results of this chapter apply only to cross-sectional studies.

We used simulations to illustrate the size of the sampling error—that is, the margin of error—when using a statistic computed from a randomly drawn sample to estimate the corresponding population parameter. These simulations lead to the important concepts of the sampling distribution of a statistic and its standard error.

Having obtained a description of the sampling error, we introduced point estimates and confidence intervals. The confidence intervals discussed in this chapter have the general form

$$\text{Point Estimate} \pm \text{Multiple(Estimated Standard Error)}$$

where the multiple determines the degree of confidence. No assumption is needed about the shape of the population distribution of values, as long as the sample size is large enough. What is "large enough" depends on the particular parameter at hand: (1) The sample size should exceed 20 for a population mean, (2) both sample sizes should exceed 20 for the difference between two population means, and (3) both np and $n(1-p)$ should exceed 5 for a population proportion or the difference between two population proportions.

This chapter also briefly discussed hypothesis tests.

In many studies, comparison is needed between the mean of a control population and the mean of a treatment population, which can be viewed as the comparison of two means and analyzed using the results from this chapter.

The next chapter discusses what additional assumptions and judgments are necessary to apply some of the ideas discussed in this chapter to time series studies, where the idea of a random sample is elusive.

Key Terms and Concepts

sampling distribution of the mean
    standard error of the mean
population distribution
    parameter
        mean, difference between two
        means, proportion, difference
        between two proportions

inference about a parameter
    point estimation
    interval estimation
        confidence interval: Point
        Estimate ± Multiple
        (Estimated Standard Error)
        one-sided confidence interval
    hypothesis test
t-distribution
    degrees of freedom

References

Cryer, J. D., and Miller, R. B. (1994), *Statistics for Business: Data Analysis and Modeling,* 2nd Edition, Duxbury Press, Belmont, CA.

Keller, G., Warrack, B., and Bartel, H. (1994), *Statistics for Management and Economics,* 3rd Edition, Duxbury Press, Belmont, CA.

Mendenhall, W., Reinmuth, J. E., and Beaver, R. (1989) *Statistics for Management and Economics,* 6th Edition, Duxbury Press, Belmont, CA.

    This is one of the classics of statistics texts for business students. It provides an excellent introduction to statistics using a traditional approach.

7.10

USING MINITAB FOR WINDOWS

This section shows how several of the graphs in this chapter were generated with Minitab for Windows.

Figure 7.14

Choose *File ▸ Other Files ▸ Import ASCII Data*
In the *Import ASCII Data* dialog box,
    Under *Store data in column*, type **C1**
    Click *ok*
    In the *Import Text From File* dialog box,
        Choose and click data file *aud_inv.dat*, click *ok*
Choose *Window ▸ Data*
In the *Data* window,
    In the box immediately under *C1*, type **VALUE**
    Click any empty cell

CONFIDENCE INTERVAL FOR A POPULATION MEAN

    Choose *Stat ▸ Basic Statistics ▸ 1-Sample t*
    In the *1-Sample t* dialog box,
        Click the box under *Variables*, type **C1**
        Click the circle to the left of *Confidence interval*
        Click the box to the right of *Level*, type **95.0**
        Click *ok*

Figure 7.19

Choose *File ▸ Other Files ▸ Import ASCII Data*
In the *Import ASCII Data* dialog box,
    Under *Store data in column*, type **C1-C4**
    Click *ok*
    In the *Import Text From File* dialog box,
        Choose and click data file *mailequp.dat*, click *ok*
Choose *Window ▸ Data*
In the *Data* window,
    In the boxes immediately under *C1* and *C3*, type **TYPE** and **CALLS**
    Click any empty cell

CONFIDENCE INTERVAL FOR THE DIFFERENCE BETWEEN TWO POPULATION MEANS

    Choose *Stat ▸ Basic Statistics ▸ 2-Sample t*
    In the *2-Sample t* dialog box,
        Click the circle next to *Samples in one column*

Click the box next to *Samples,* type **C3**
Click the box next to *Subscripts,* type **C1**
Click the box next to *Confidence level,* type **95.0**
Click *ok*

Figure 7.25

Choose *Calc* ▸ *Probability Distributions* ▸ *T*
In the *T distribution* dialog box,
   Click *Inverse cumulative probability*
   In the *Degrees of freedom* box, type **15**
   Click *Input constant,* type **0.975** in box to its right
   Click *ok*

7.11

PROBLEM FOR CLASS DISCUSSION

7.1 Bell Canada

Consider the study of voting results regarding extended area service between Whitby and Toronto, described in Section 2.11 (p. 35).[11] Data were collected as follows: The 10,942 customers who responded to the May 1989 survey were split into two groups consisting of the 4,869 "for" and the 6,073 "against" voters, and from each group a simple random sample of 50 customers was drawn. Four variables were measured for each of the 100 customers in the sample regarding their May 1989 telephone bill: (1) the number of calls to Toronto, (2) the dollar cost of calls to Toronto, (3) the total telephone bill, and (4) whether or not the customer subscribed to Custom Calling Features, such as call forwarding (1 = yes, 0 = no). A fifth variable recorded their voting in the survey (1 = for, 0 = against).

The study's main questions were: Do "for" voters differ from "against" voters in

- The number of calls to Toronto?

- The monthly dollars spent on calls to Toronto?

- The total monthly telephone bill?

- The extent to which they subscribe to Custom Calling Features?

The Minitab output from the Session window (Figure 7.36) should be useful in answering these questions.

---

[11] The data were kindly provided by G. Duffy. Before the study was done, it was expected that more than 20% of "for" respondents would subscribe to premium services.

FIGURE 7.36

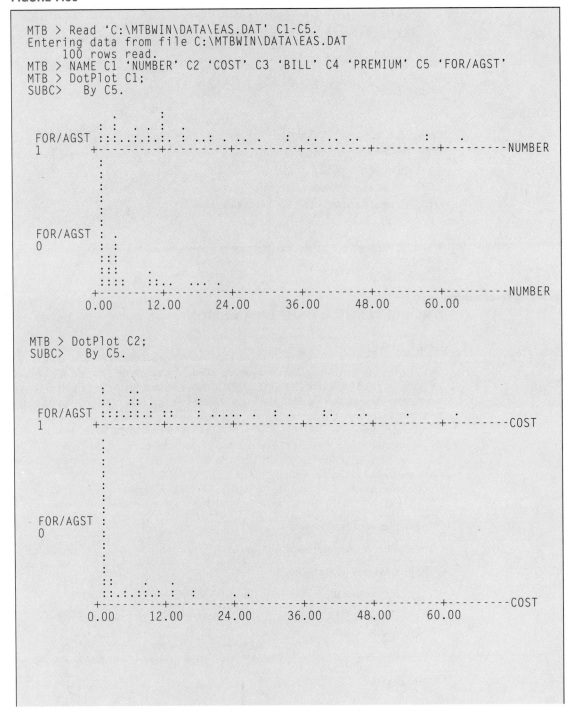

```
MTB > DotPlot C3;
SUBC>   By C5.


  FOR/AGST        :   :.::: :.:.   :    .   .
  1             :  ::.:::.:. ::::. ..: :::  :.  .  :      .
                +---------+---------+---------+---------+---------+---------BILL
                        :.
                        :.
  FOR/AGST        ::::    :     .
  0             ::::::::::::::... :.    . :    .   .               .
                +---------+---------+---------+---------+---------+---------BILL
            0.00       40.00      80.00     120.00     160.00     200.00

MTB > Describe C1-C4;
SUBC>   By C5.

              FOR/AGST        N      MEAN    MEDIAN    TRMEAN    STDEV    SEMEAN
NUMBER           0           50     4.260     2.000     3.523    5.609     0.793
                 1           50    18.14     12.00     16.55    16.49      2.33
COST             0           50     4.673     1.250     3.782    6.440     0.911
                 1           50    16.31      9.57     14.83    15.55      2.20
Bill             0           50    47.20     34.22     42.27    36.83      5.21
                 1           50    62.76     56.49     60.65    35.88      5.07
PREMIUM          0           50     0.1400    0.0000    0.0909   0.3505    0.0496
                 1           50     0.1800    0.0000    0.1364   0.3881    0.0549

              FOR/AGST      MIN       MAX        Q1        Q3
NUMBER           0        0.000    21.000     0.000     5.000
                 1        0.00     63.00      5.75     26.75
COST             0        0.000    26.440     0.000     8.340
                 1        0.00     62.40      5.31     24.75
Bill             0       12.19    211.00     23.00     55.90
                 1       11.34    160.64     33.85     89.63
PREMIUM          0        0.0000    1.0000    0.0000    0.0000
                 1        0.0000    1.0000    0.0000    0.0000

MTB > TwoT C4 C5.

TWOSAMPLE T FOR PREMIUM
FOR/AGST     N       MEAN      STEV     SE MEAN
1           50      0.180     0.388      0.055
0           50      0.140     0.351      0.050

95 PCT CI FOR MU 1 - MU 0:  (-0.107, 0.187)

TTEST MU 1 = MU 0 (VS NE): T=0.54 P=0.59 DF+ 97

MTB > Stop
```

7.12

EXERCISES

Although answers are given in Appendix C, do not turn to them right away if you cannot find an answer on your own. Return to the exercise the next day and try again before turning to Appendix C.

Exercises for Section 7.2

7.2   This exercise guides you through the steps for finding the exact sampling distribution of the mean in a very simple situation: A population consists of $N = 3$ units, and their values on the response variable are 6, 4, and 10. A random sample of size $n = 2$ is to be taken with replacement.

   a   List all possible samples and the probability of obtaining each.

   b   Determine the value of $\bar{y}$ for these samples.

   c   Find the sampling distribution of $\bar{y}$ and graph it. What is the mean of this sampling distribution?

   d   Determine the population mean μ_y. How does this compare with the mean computed in (c)?

   e   What is the probability that the sample mean to be taken will exceed the population mean?

   f   Assume that a random sample of size $n = 2$ is to be taken without replacement. Repeat (a) to (e) above and contrast your results.

7.3   The average income of families in Canada in 1971 was $10,400 and the standard deviation of incomes was approximately $6,800. (Source : *Canada Year Book 1985*, p. 191.)

   a   What is the unit? Using this information alone, could you determine if the distribution of family incomes was normal? Why or why not?

   b   Suppose that a simple random sample of 400 families is to be chosen from the Canadian population in 1971 and that the sample mean of the 400 income values will be computed.

     i   What is the probability that the sample mean will be less than $11,000? What is the probability that it will be between $9,000 and $11,000? (If you cannot compute these probabilities reliably, explain why not.)

     ii   Construct an interval around the population mean into which the sample mean will fall with probability 95%. (If you cannot do this, explain why not.)

     iii   Find a value for the sample mean that will be exceeded with probability 1% only.

7.4   A new supplier of a part used in assembly claims that the population mean and standard deviation of the parts' diameters in a very large batch are 100 mm and 6 mm, respectively.

   a   Suppose that specifications call for diameters to be between 88 mm and 104 mm. What proportion of diameters meet the specifications if the supplier's claim is correct? What additional assumptions do you have to make so that the numerical answer is justified?

   b   Suppose that specifications call for diameters to be between 88 mm and 112 mm. Answer the questions in (a).

   c   If the supplier's claim is correct, what is the probability that the diameter of a randomly picked part is between 98 mm and 102 mm?

   d   Suppose that a random sample of $n = 36$ parts is to be taken from the batch upon receipt and that the batch is to be accepted if the sample mean diameter is between 98 mm and 102 mm. If the supplier's claim is correct, what is the probability of accepting the batch? What additional assumptions do you have to make so that the numerical answer is justified?

   e   Why are the probabilities in (c) and (d) not the same?

   f   Suppose that the supplier's claim is not correct and that the mean and standard deviation are 102 mm and 8 mm. Answer the first question in (d).

Exercises for Section 7.3

7.5 Suppose that the mean and standard deviation of the after-tax profit for a sample of 100 retail stores in metropolitan Toronto were 4.8 and 1.6 cents per dollar revenue, respectively.
  a What are the population, the unit, and the response variable?
  b Give a point estimate for the population mean. Discuss the merits of solely using this estimate.
  c Give a 95% interval estimate for the population mean. In order to compute this, is it necessary to assume that response variable values are normally distributed throughout the population? Why or why not?
  d Suppose another retail store was to be drawn randomly from the population. Can you give an approximate 95% interval for this store's value on the response variable? In order to compute this, is it necessary to assume that response variable values are normally distributed throughout the population? Why or why not?
  e Are the intervals computed in (c) and (d) different? Should they be? Why or why not?

7.6 Use the information from the *Canada Year Book,* given in Exercise 7.3. Suppose you carried out a survey in 1971. One of the questions in it asks for family income. The survey was sent to 200 households chosen by simple random sampling from the Canadian population, and 100 replies were received. The sample mean income was $8,000 and the sample standard deviation was $5,000.
  a Assuming that these results came from a random sample, do you find them to be surprisingly different from what you'd expect given what you know about the population? Why or why not? What are the consequences of your conclusion with respect to the overall survey results?
  b In (a), was it reasonable to treat the 100 replies as a simple random sample? Justify your answer. If your answer is no, what are the consequences for interpretation of the survey results?

7.7 In 1982, the liabilities of bankruptcies and insolvencies in the 10 Canadian provinces were (in millions of dollars, provinces listed from east to west) 13, 54, 3, 25, 836, 665, 66, 33, 206, and 414. (Source: *Canada Year Book 1985,* p. 583.)
    Note that in this example, the population of interest consists of the provinces, so the unit of observation is a province. The response variable is "liabilities in millions of dollars." You want to obtain the population average for the response variable. Would a confidence interval be useful here? Why or why not? If yes, give a 95% confidence interval.

7.8 Children's Toys Company plans to introduce a new toy to the market. The company distributes its existing products through a large number of retail stores. In order to assess the potential success of the new toy, Children's Toys plans to introduce the toy into a random sample of retail stores for 1 month. Because sampling is expensive, the marketing managers of Children's Toys want to select no more stores than are necessary to obtain an accurate estimate. The managers estimate that the initiation of the sample design would cost $1,000 and that the cost of the sample would increase from that amount by $500 for every store included in the sample. From past studies with similar products, the managers estimate the variance of monthly sales for this product to be 10,000 in each store. If the budget limitation for sampling is set at $19,000, what is the greatest confidence level that could be achieved for a symmetric confidence interval, $76 in *total* width, for the mean monthly sales per store?

7.9   Oxygen Inc. produces oxygen for medical uses and injects it into 244 cu.ft. cylinders. The filling operation consists of transferring the oxygen from storage into cylinders. One of the important variables characterizing a cylinder is the percentage of oxygen by volume. The acceptable limits for this variable were set by management to be from 99.6% to 100%.

A random sample of 35 cylinders filled recently was checked for oxygen content, and the sample mean and standard deviation were 99.68% and 0.06%, respectively.

a   Obtain a point estimate and 95% confidence interval for the mean oxygen content of all cylinders recently filled.

b   Obtain a 95% prediction interval for the oxygen content of another cylinder selected randomly from all those recently filled.

c   Why do the results in (a) and (b) differ?

d   What is the probability that the oxygen content for another randomly chosen cylinder is within acceptable limits?

e   What is the proportion of cylinders whose oxygen content is within acceptable limits?

f   For which of (a), (b), (d), and (e) do you have to assume that oxygen content is normally distributed? Briefly justify your answer.

Exercises for Section 7.4

7.10   GMAT scores among the people taking the test are known to be normally distributed.

a   What are the population, the unit, and the response variable?

b   Do you think that GMAT scores are approximately normally distributed for the roughly 120 students in the first year of one of the top 20 North American MBA programs in the 1993/94 academic year? Why or why not? If not, what do you think is the shape of this distribution?

c   A random sample of size 25 was drawn from the applicants at a business school. GMAT score mean and standard deviation were 580 and 80. What is a 90% confidence interval for the population mean? Briefly describe the population of interest here.

d   At another business school, a random sample of size 36 was drawn from the applicants. GMAT score mean and standard deviation were 600 and 100. What is a 90% confidence interval for the population mean?

e   What is a 90% confidence interval for the difference between the population means of the two business schools in (c) and (d)? Interpret.

f   What degree of confidence do you have in a one-sided interval for the difference between the population means that covers all positive values (that is, that extends from 0 to infinity)? What about an interval that covers all negative values? Interpret these results.

7.11   One of the pioneering controlled randomized experiments in medicine was carried out in 1948 to evaluate the new antibiotic drug streptomycin (Medical Research Council, 1948). A total of 107 tubercular patients were randomly assigned: 52 to be given bed rest only (control), and 55 to be also given streptomycin (treatment). The degree of improvement after 6 months was measured for each patient; if we code this improvement between $+2$ (considerable improvement) and -3 (death), the results were as follows:

Improvement After 6 Months	Treated Patients	Control Patients
+2	28	4
+1	10	13
0	2	3
−1	5	12
−2	6	6
−3	4	14
	55	52

a Is this a study of a population, or a process? Briefly describe the population or process. What is the unit? What is the response variable?

b How well do the data establish the effectiveness of streptomycin? Ánswer this question with the help of a 99% confidence interval and a one-sided confidence interval that covers all positive values.

c If your coding for death was changed from −3 to −10, but the other codings remained unchanged, would your answer in (b) change?

To get the means and standard deviations for the improvement score in the treatment and control groups, you may want to use Minitab. If you do so, it is easy to input the data for the treated patients into a column, say, C1, by using the following SET command in the Session window:

```
MTB > SET C1
DATA> 28(2) 10(1) 2(0) 5(-1) 6(-2) 4(-3)
DATA> END
MTB > DESCRIBE C1
```

A similar command could be used for the control patients.

Exercises for Section 7.5

7.12 Suppose that, in a recent poll of 900 eligible voters, 380 respondents indicated that they would vote for the party currently in power.

a Define the population of interest. Should there be a geographical component to your definition? Should there be a time component to your definition? What is the response variable? What are the possible values for the response variable? What is the scale of measurement for the response variable?

b Does the population sampled from match the population of interest? If it does not, what are the consequences?

c Can you think of an easy way of ensuring that the respondents are a random sample from the population sampled from? Discuss the features of your procedure that would preclude the sample from being a perfect simple random sample.

d Treating the poll as a random sample from the population, find a point estimate and a 95% confidence interval for the population proportion. Find a 90% confidence interval. Interpret the results.

7.13 A television manufacturer would like to know what proportion of television set owners have color sets. In a sample of 100 randomly selected owners, 60% were found to own color sets. Construct a 95% confidence interval for the population proportion of television owners who have color sets. Interpret the results.

7.14 The billing department of a company processes a large number of billings every day. The company wanted to estimate the proportion of incorrect billings on a particular day. In a simple random sample of 100 billings from a day's work, 12 are found to be incorrect.
  a Is this a study of a population or a process? What are the unit and the response variable?
  b Obtain a 95% confidence interval for that day's overall proportion of incorrect billings. Interpret.

7.15 Each of two suppliers of small components delivered a large batch of components, and their proportions of defectives were to be compared. One random sample was taken from each batch. For supplier 1, there were 5 defectives among the 110 sampled; for supplier 2, there were 7 defectives among the 90 sampled.
  a Obtain a 90% confidence interval for the difference between the two batch proportions of defectives. Interpret the result.
  b What is the degree of confidence in an interval for the difference between the two batch proportions that covers positive values only? Interpret.

Exercises for Section 7.7

7.16 Restate the rule of thumb regarding the p-value in terms of z_{obs}. In doing so, carefully retrace the steps we went through to obtain the p-value from z_{obs}.

7.17 Refer to Exercise 7.11 (evaluation of streptomycin). Test the hypothesis that the mean improvement for treated patients is the same as that for control patients.

7.18 Refer to Exercise 7.14 (incorrect billings). Based on past experience, the manager in charge feels that the proportion of incorrect billings is 5%. Do the data, 12 incorrect billings in a sample of $n = 100$, contradict the manager's experience? Test the hypothesis that $\pi_0 = 0.05$. Interpret.

Exercises for All Sections in Chapter 7

7.19 Suppose that a manufacturer has just marketed a new industrial appliance with a 1-year warranty. The product development plan estimates that the cost of meeting the warranty terms will be $50 per appliance, on average, with an estimated standard deviation of $40. As the warranty period expires for the first appliances sold, the manufacturer will note the actual costs of warranty servicing. The following approach has been suggested for determining whether average warranty costs are exceeding the $50 target:

  Wait for warranty data on the first 100 appliances sold and conclude that the average cost will exceed the target if the sample mean exceeds $58.

  A timely conclusion about actual warranty costs is desirable because the manufacturer wishes to reduce the warranty terms if they are proving too generous to be profitable. On the other hand, an unnecessary reduction of warranty terms would adversely affect future sales of the industrial appliance. Assume that the warranty data on the initial sales will constitute random sample observations.

a Suppose that warranty costs (y) are right on target; that is, $\mu_y = \$50$ and $\sigma_y = \$40$. What is the probability that the sample mean for the 100 appliances will exceed $58 (so that the manufacturer will conclude average cost to exceed the target)?

b Suppose that warranty costs are *not* on target and that average costs are in fact $10 higher than the target; that is, $\mu_y = \$60$ and $\sigma_y = \$40$. What is the probability that the sample mean for the 100 appliances will exceed $58 (so that the manufacturer will conclude average cost to exceed the target)?

c A second approach was finally chosen. After warranty data had been received from 16 appliances, it was felt that a decision had to be made. Sample mean and sample standard deviation for these 16 observations were found to be $58 and $24. What can be concluded?

7.20 A company that specializes in sales and installation of home heating equipment is considering opening a new sales office to target a particular neighborhood. The management feels that the office should be opened only if the average yearly heating expenditures in the neighborhood are at least $2,000 per house. A random sample of 60 houses was taken to find out yearly heating expenditures. The results are stored in ASCII file HOMEHEAT.DAT. The heating expenditures for the last year are recorded in the variable HEAT. Descriptive statistics for the sample along with some other Minitab output are given in Figure 7.37.

a What are the population, the unit, and the response variable in this study?

b Calculate the 98% confidence interval for the population mean of HEAT. Interpret it in the context of this study.

c Did you have to make any assumptions to compute the interval in (b)? If yes, what are they and how reasonable are they? Be specific.

d Given your answers to (b) and (c) above, should the new office be opened? Give reasons for your decision.

e Consider a house picked at random from the neighborhood, and compute the probability that this house's heating expenditures for last year exceeded $2,000, stating explicitly any assumptions that have to be made for this computation. (For this part, you should *assume* that these assumptions hold.)

f How reasonable are the assumptions made in (e)? Be specific. In view of the adequacy of these assumptions, how believable are the results in (e)?

Now suppose that another unit of the company specializes in refurbishing old kitchens. One idea for an advertising campaign is to target the older houses in the neighborhood since they are more likely to have older kitchens. In the random sample of 60 houses, it was found that 35 houses had modern kitchens and 25 did not. For the houses *with* modern kitchens, the average house age was 34 years with a standard deviation of 8 years. For the houses *without* modern kitchens, the average age was 36 years with a standard deviation of 7 years.

g Compute a 90% confidence interval for the difference in mean age between houses with modern kitchens and those without modern kitchens. Compute a one-sided confidence interval for this difference that covers all negative values.

h Did you have to make any assumptions for your computation in (g)? If yes, what are they and how reasonable are they? Be specific.

i What would be the implications of the 90% confidence interval in (g) containing 0?

j What would be the implications of the 90% confidence interval in (g) *not* containing 0?

k Do you think targeting older houses for the advertising campaign is a good idea? State your reasons.

FIGURE 7.37

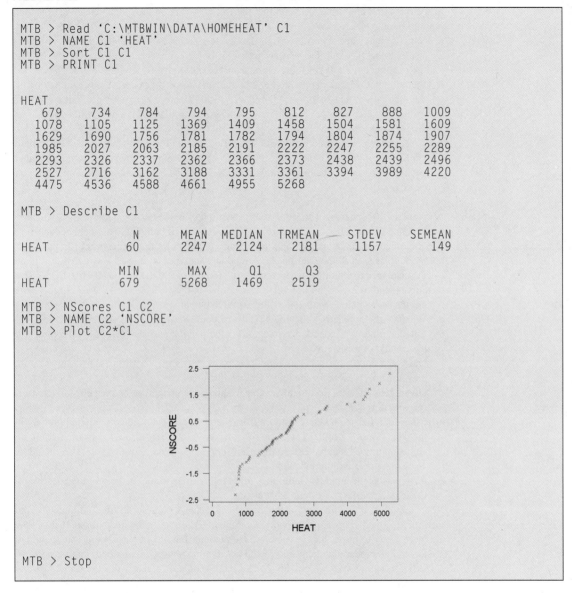

```
MTB > Read 'C:\MTBWIN\DATA\HOMEHEAT' C1
MTB > NAME C1 'HEAT'
MTB > Sort C1 C1
MTB > PRINT C1


HEAT
    679     734     784     794     795     812     827     888    1009
   1078    1105    1125    1369    1409    1458    1504    1581    1609
   1629    1690    1756    1781    1782    1794    1804    1874    1907
   1985    2027    2063    2185    2191    2222    2247    2255    2289
   2293    2326    2337    2362    2366    2373    2438    2439    2496
   2527    2716    3162    3188    3331    3361    3394    3989    4220
   4475    4536    4588    4661    4955    5268

MTB > Describe C1

                   N     MEAN   MEDIAN   TRMEAN      STDEV    SEMEAN
HEAT              60     2247     2124     2181       1157       149

                 MIN      MAX       Q1       Q3
HEAT             679     5268     1469     2519

MTB > NScores C1 C2
MTB > NAME C2 'NSCORE'
MTB > Plot C2*C1
```

```
MTB > Stop
```

7.21   A manufacturing company received a large shipment of components needed in the assembly of a product. The supplier for this component was new, so the company decided to measure an internal dimension (in mm) that was important for proper functioning of the final assembly. In a simple random sample of 36 components from the large shipment, the sample mean and standard deviation were 40 mm and 3 mm, respectively.

a   What are the population, unit, and response variable?

b Making any necessary assumptions, obtain a 98% confidence interval for the mean value of the internal dimension in the large shipment. Interpret this interval.

c What assumptions did you have to make for the confidence interval in (b) to be reliable? Briefly justify your answer.

d The sampling procedure used was described as follows: Since storage space at the company was tight, the supplier had delivered the components to two storage locations, and about half the shipment was stored in each location. The company then took a random sample of 18 components from each location to get its sample of size 36. Was this simple random sampling? Briefly justify your answer.

7.13

SUPPLEMENTARY EXERCISES

7.22 In 1984, there were about 60 million cards in the United States issued by MasterCard, and the average billing amount for that year was approximately $820. Assume that the standard deviation of billing amounts was $400, and assume that little is known about the shape of the distribution of billing amounts. A random sample of size 64 is to be taken from the population.

a What are the population and the unit?

b Given that little is known about the shape of the distribution of billing amounts, can you compute the probability that the sample mean exceeds $940? If yes, compute it. If no, why not?

c What is the probability that the sample mean is between $700 and $800?

7.23 A small U.S. county bank reported that its 6,000 savings accounts have a mean balance of $1,000 and a standard deviation of $1,200. Auditors for the federal government have decided to randomly sample 100 of the bank's accounts in order to assess the accuracy of the mean balance reported by the bank. They will certify the bank's reported figure only if the sample mean balance is within $150 of the reported mean balance.

a Assuming that the small bank's reported figures are correct, what is the probability that the auditors will not certify the bank's report?

b Do you have to make any assumptions to answer the question given in (a)?

7.24 Mr. Bill Smith needs to estimate the average monthly telephone bill in a small city. He wants to have 90% confidence in the estimate. (The corresponding z-value will be used for computation of the confidence interval.) Furthermore, he wants the estimate to be accurate to within $0.75 of the true average telephone bill. You have been retained by Mr. Smith to perform the desired survey. As a first step he wants to know what sample size should be taken to obtain the required accuracy in the estimate. The results from a preliminary sample should be useful in estimating the sample size required. The telephone bills for this preliminary sample were (in dollars)

24   25   23   22   17   14   21   19   27   22

Suggest an appropriate sample size.

7.25 Suppose there are two researchers, Smith and Jones, each of whom takes a simple random sample from a population, without knowing the other's work. Suppose further that both get the *same* sample standard deviation and that they compute 95% confidence intervals for the population mean.

a If Smith's confidence interval is one-third as wide as Jones', what is the relationship between Smith's and Jones' sample sizes?

b Would the answer in (a) change if each had computed a 99% confidence interval? An 80% confidence interval?

c What are the implications of your answer in (a)?

7.26   Companies bottling soft drinks monitor their filling machines very closely, since underfilled bottles are easily spotted by consumers and government penalties for underfilling can be severe. On the other hand, overfilling is an expensive waste of money. The soda water filling machine at a particular plant is known to fill bottles with an average of 500.0 ml (milliliter) and a standard deviation of 1.2 ml.

a What proportion of bottles are filled with 499.0 ml or more of soda water?

b Do you have to make any assumptions to compute the result in (a)? If so, what are they and how reasonable are they?

c If an inspector were to draw 50 bottles at random from the end of the filling line, what would be the probability that the inspector's sample mean amount of soda water is 499.6 or less?

d Do you have to make any assumptions to compute the result in (c)? If so, what are they and how reasonable are they?

7.27   In a large hospital, concerns arose about the number of sick days taken by employees. Before considering what action to take, the hospital wanted to estimate the mean number of days of sick leave taken by all its employees in 1988. A simple random sample of size 60 was taken from the hospital's personnel files, and the number of sick days taken by each employee in 1988 was recorded. The sample mean and standard deviation were computed to be 12 days and 10 days, respectively.

a Estimate the population mean using a 90% confidence interval.

b How many personnel files would the statistician have to select in order to estimate the population mean to within 2 days with 99% confidence?

c Based on the information given above, can you estimate approximately what proportion of all employees take more than 7 days of sick leave? Briefly justify your answer.

7.28   A bank was interested in differences regarding the number of the bank's services used by businesses between its downtown and suburban branches. As a preliminary step, two representative bank branches were chosen in a large city, one downtown and the other in a suburban area. From each branch's files, a random sample of business accounts was selected, and the number of the bank's services (loans, investment counselling, checking, etc.) used by each account was recorded. The number of accounts chosen in the downtown and suburban branches were 70 and 40, respectively, the resulting sample means were 3.0 and 2.6, and the sample standard deviations were 1.3 and 1.2.

a Briefly describe the populations and the unit.

b Obtain a 98% confidence interval for the difference between the two means. What degree of confidence do you have in an interval that covers all positive values? All negative values?

c Based on the data, would you say that there is a difference between the two means? How would you judge whether this is an important difference?

7.29   In order to examine the effect of oiling on the shelf life of eggs, a study was carried out using eggs laid by a homogeneous strain of hens. The effect of oiling was considered satisfactory only if the mean shelf life increased by at least 5 days on average. Many different ways of applying the oil were studied, but this problem will concentrate on only one of them, immediate oiling after the eggs have been washed. The shelf life was recorded for 100 eggs that were washed but not oiled, and for 60 eggs that were washed and oiled. All eggs were stored under identical conditions.

The frequency distributions for shelf life were approximately normal for both the control and treatment groups, the respective sample means were 20 and 24 days, and the sample standard deviations were 8 and 9 days.

a   Do the data support the contention that oiling is effective *at all*? To answer this question, obtain a 99% confidence interval and a one-sided confidence interval that covers all positive values.

b   Do the data suggest that the effect of oiling is satisfactory?

7.30   Suppose that you are the polling consultant to a legislator. A simple random sample of 400 voters showed that 38% listed energy problems as the most important issue facing the nation.

a   Define the population of interest. What is the unit? Should there be a geographical component to your definition? Should there be a time component to your definition? What is the response variable? What are the possible values for the response variable? What is the scale of measurement for the response variable?

b   Give a 90% confidence interval for the proportion of all voters who hold this opinion. Interpret.

c   Give a 90% confidence interval, assuming that a simple random sample of 100 voters was taken. Interpret.

7.31   The accounting system of a company is used to provide financial and other information for managerial decision-making. To ensure that the data used in the accounting system are reliable, auditors perform various checks on a regular basis. Suppose an auditor is interested in the 10,000 sales invoices issued in the last quarter; in particular, the auditor wishes to estimate the proportion of sales invoices on which the sales figure is incorrectly stated. An estimate of this proportion will be obtained from a random sample of 100 sales invoice.

a   Assume that the sales invoices are numbered 0000 to 9999 and that every invoice ending in a "9" is in error, (that is, 10% are in error). Use Figure 4.1 (p. 118) to draw a sample of 100 sales invoices from the population by using consecutive groupings of four digits, and list the numbers of the invoices that are in error.

b   Based on your sample results in (a), obtain 80%, 90%, and 95% confidence intervals for the proportion of sales invoices in error.

c   Do any of the intervals in (b) contain the true proportion in error?

7.32   Durham College enrolled approximately 38,000 registrants in the 1989/90 fiscal year. Of these, the part-time enrollment in the fall of 1989 was approximately 9,000 students, 3,000 of which were enrolled by the Economic Development Unit. Analyzing its economic and demographic environment, the College determined that there will be considerable opportunities for increased enrollment in part-time programs. In order to ensure that Durham College's system is responsive to the needs and perceptions of its customers, a survey was undertaken asking registrants to answer the following five questions:

1   How did you find out about the program? (Answers: 1 = Continuing Education calendar, 2 = from a teacher or staff member, 3 = from your employer, 4 = from friends or relatives, 5 = other)

2 How easy or difficult was it to get additional information about the courses? (Answers: 1 = very difficult, 2 = difficult, 3 = not easy or difficult, 4 = easy, 5 = very easy)

3 How easy or difficult was it to register for courses? (Answers: 1–5 as in Question 2, 6 = someone else registered for me)

4 In your opinion, how close does the course description fit your actual experience? (Answers: 1 = not at all, 2 = not too close, 3 = so-so, 4 = close, 5 = exact)

5 Would you recommend Durham College courses to others? (Answers: 1 = yes, 2 = maybe, 3 = no)

It was expected that

1 75% of registrants would find the information from the calendar

2 80% would find it easy or very easy to get additional information

3 15% would find it difficult or very difficult to register

4 90% would find the course descriptions to be close to or exactly the same as the actual experience

5 90% would recommend Durham courses to others

Data were gathered by randomly sampling 110 registrants from the 3,000 part-time students in the Economic Development Unit's Management and Productivity centers. The results for the 101 responses received were as follows:

			Question		
Answer	1	2	3	4	5
1	55	3	2	2	95
2	5	6	8	3	6
3	23	22	8	16	0
4	11	41	30	64	
5	7	29	46	16	
6			7		

The data were kindly provided by G. Gagliardi.

a Consider the population parameters for which expectations were given. Use the data to find 95% confidence intervals for each parameter. Which expectations are not supported by the data?

b What are the implications of nonresponse in this study?

7.33 A manufacturing company received a large shipment of components needed in the assembly of a product. The supplier for this component was new, and so the company decided to test the quality of the components using an expensive testing procedure. In a simple random sample of size 400, 10 components failed the test.

a Making any necessary assumptions, obtain a 98% confidence interval for the proportion of components in the large shipment that fail the test. Interpret this interval.

b What assumptions did you have to make for the confidence interval in (a) to be reliable? Briefly justify your answer.

7.34 An IQ test is given to a randomly selected group of 20 first-year students at a given university and also to a randomly selected group of 25 fourth-year students at the same university. For the first-year students, the sample mean is 120 and the sample *variance* is 196. For the fourth-year students, the sample mean is 128 and the sample *variance* is 121.

a Obtain a 99% confidence interval for the difference between the corresponding population means. Comment about the difference.

b Test the hypothesis that the two population means are equal. Comment.

7.35 In the mid-1970s, Canada Post implemented a coding system in order to facilitate the management of mail sorting and delivery. A study was done to analyze the effect of adding the postal code (zip code) on delivery times. An equal number of letters was sent to Toronto from two dropping points, one in Vancouver, B.C., and one in Whistler, B.C. These two locations were chosen because their sizes are very different and because delivery times were expected to be long enough to provide meaningful variation. Half the letters from each dropping point had postal codes. The following questions were to be addressed.

1 Does the inclusion of the postal code have an effect on delivery time?
2 Does point of origin have an effect on delivery time? Is this influenced by inclusion of the postal code?

Twenty letters with postal code and 20 letters without postal code were sent from each point of origin. Thus there were 80 letters in all. At each point of origin, the 40 letters were mailed at 9 A.M. on 22 October 1990 by putting them into one mailbox. Three variables were recorded for each letter: (1) delivery time (in number of days when Canada Post delivers mail), (2) presence of postal code (1 = yes, 0 = no), and (3) origin (1 = Vancouver, 2 = Whistler).

The following table summarizes the data:

		Origin	
		Vancouver	Whistler
Postal code	No	Mean = 5.47 SD = 1.00	Mean = 4.93 SD = 0.26
	Yes	Mean = 3.67 SD = 0.82	Mean = 4.47 SD = 0.64

a Does usage of the postal code seem to make a difference for letters sent from Vancouver? Base your conclusion on a 95% confidence interval. Briefly interpret this interval.
b Base your conclusion in (a) on a one-sided confidence interval.
c Base your conclusion in (a) on a hypothesis test.
d Does usage of the postal code seem to make a difference for letters sent from Whistler? Base your conclusion on a one-sided confidence interval.
e Using your answers in (a), (b), and (d), contrast your conclusions regarding usage of the postal code for the two points of origin. Be specific.
f Part of the description of how data were collected reads: "At each point of origin, the 40 letters were mailed... by putting them into one mailbox." Do you think *several* mailboxes should have been chosen at each location? Briefly discuss the pros and cons with respect to (i) evaluating the effectiveness of using postal codes, and (ii) estimating delivery times.

7.36 A large retail organization wanted to evaluate the quality of its sales forecasts. A random sample of 35 items was taken from all items offered for sale in 1991. The actual and the forecasted sales were recorded (in number of units). From these two variables, the difference between actual and forecasted sales was computed as ERROR. The sample of 35 items was ordered in increasing order of actual sales. The data are stored in ASCII file RETAILER.DAT.[12]

---
[12]The data were kindly provided by D. Krass.

a Was this study done as a cross-sectional study or a time series study? If it was a cross-sectional study, briefly describe the population; otherwise, briefly describe the process. Describe the unit. What is the response variable?

b Obtain a 90% confidence interval for the mean of ERROR. Interpret this interval in the context of this study.

c Test the hypothesis that the population mean of ERROR equals 0. Interpret.

d Overall, what is your opinion of the accuracy of the forecasting procedure? Briefly state your reasons.

e Use the counting approach to estimate the probability that forecasted sales for an item are within 150 units of actual sales.

f Calculate a 95% confidence interval for the probability estimate in (e). [*Hint:* Think of defining a new variable with value 1 if the forecast is within 150 of actual sales and 0 otherwise.] Interpret the confidence interval in the context of this application.

8

MAKING INFERENCES IN TIME SERIES STUDIES

This chapter will help you solve the following kinds of problems:

- Management of a retail chain wants to know the effectiveness of a productivity improvement program. Average weekly sales per employee hour were $164 during the 20 weeks before and $174 during the 20 weeks after implementing the program in one store. Is this evidence that the program is effective?

- A manufacturer of electroplating parts samples the production process at regular intervals and records the sample proportion of defective parts. How can the sequence of sample proportions be analyzed to check if the process is stable?

8.1

INTRODUCTION

Let us briefly summarize the results from the last chapter as they relate to a confidence interval for a single mean. In a *cross-sectional* study there is a well-defined population and a frame of *all N* units belonging to this population. When the number of units in the population is large, and a census is not feasible, a sample of size *n* must be taken to *estimate* the population mean μ_y. In order to make quantitative generalizations from the sample to the population, the sample must be randomly drawn from the population. When the random sample has been taken from the population, a 95% confidence interval for the population mean can be computed by the usual formula,

Point Estimate $\pm$ 2(Estimated Standard Error)

The interpretation of this confidence interval, which is based on *sample* results, is that we are 95% sure that it covers the *population* mean μ_y.

In this chapter, we will extend the tools introduced in the last chapter for making inferences regarding population parameters to making inferences regarding the parameters of a random time series process. You will also learn how to obtain control charts for a variety of contexts.

8.2

INFERENCES FOR TIME SERIES STUDIES

Let us first discuss what additional judgments and assumptions are required so that confidence intervals can be reliably computed in a time series study.

In a *time series* study there is no frame because the data are evolving over time. Interest focuses on the *process* that generates the data, in particular, on how data will be generated in the future, and on whether the process is stable. In a stable process, the observations unpredictably vary around the process mean μ_y, where the extent of variation can be summarized by the process standard deviation σ_y. Typically, it is unknown (1) whether the process is random, and (2) what the process mean and standard deviation are if the process is random. But a sample containing recently generated observations is often available. In this case, a visual examination of the sequence plot, in conjunction with the control limits and the runs test, may lead to a *judgment* that the process generating the data is random. If this judgment is justified, then the sample can be treated as random and a confidence interval can be computed for the process mean μ_y. The interpretation of this confidence interval is then as for the case of a cross-sectional study. But remember that this judgment implies the important assumption that the process generating the data was random. Furthermore, we must assume that the process conditions will remain unchanged so that the sample gives a reasonable idea of the values to be generated by the process in the near future. The conclusions based on these assumptions are reliable only if the assumptions are reasonable.

The flow chart in Figure 8.1 outlines our approach to estimating the parameters of a random process. This flow chart is, of course, quite similar to the flow chart for estimating population parameters, Figure 7.23. In this section, two examples will be discussed illustrating how the tools introduced in Chapter 7 can be used in time series studies. The first example involves the fee-setting process at the Mortgage Department Corporation. The second example continues the problem introduced in Section 5.12 (p. 190), in which an experiment tested the effect of shelf display area on sales of a high-volume product in a retail store.

FIGURE 8.1 Flow Chart for Estimating Process Parameters

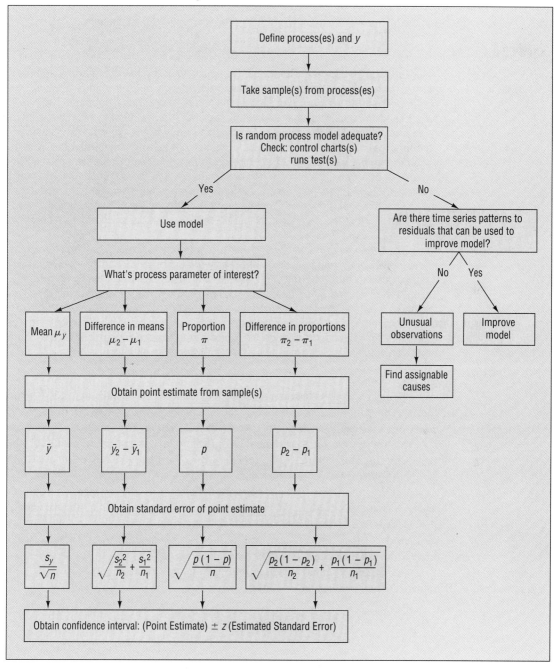

Inference About a Process Mean

Let us illustrate inferences regarding a process mean with an example.

EXAMPLE 8.1

The Mortgage Department Corporation specialized in the mortgage brokerage business in which borrowers are charged fees based on what the market and the borrower will bear at the particular time of the request for funds.[1] Fees may vary over time based on uncontrollable variables, such as the aggregate demand for mortgage money, the available supply of mortgage money from both institutional and private lenders, the volume of transactions in the real estate market, and the trend in prices in the real estate market. In addition to these uncontrollable variables affecting fees, there are also a number of *transaction-specific factors,* such as the amount of the loan, term of the loan, interest rate for the loan, loan-to-value ratio, and gross debt service ratio. Management wanted to identify the types of transaction that generate the greatest fee revenues so that marketing efforts and work allocation could be targeted toward them.

The fee-setting process was somewhat arbitrary in that it was left in the hands of the individual mortgage consultant. Fees were set on a transaction-by-transaction basis according to the borrower's financial circumstances. After obtaining an application that disclosed all pertinent financial details regarding the borrower's request for funds, the consultant determined the fee to be charged for successfully providing the requested loan. This determination came from the consultant's knowledge of how difficult it would be to arrange the funds for the client. Some negotiation with the borrower would also take place until mutual agreement was reached.

A study was done to examine to what extent the fees charged depended on the transaction-specific factors mentioned above. For 51 consecutive weeks in 1989 and 1990, one mortgage transaction per week was selected for the sample and data were collected on several variables. The data are stored in ASCII file FEESET.DAT, the fees being listed in column 1. No relationship could be found between the fee and any of the other variables on which data were collected.

Furthermore, management needed an estimate of the average fee charged. There was no pattern to the time series plot of the 51 fee values, so the fee setting process was considered stable. The runs test and control chart limits supported this assessment. Since the process was judged to be random, the cross-sectional tools from Chapter 7 are available to estimate the process mean, μ_y (see Section 7.3, p. 277). In particular, a 95% confidence interval for this process mean could be obtained from the formula

confidence interval for process mean

$$\bar{y} \pm z \frac{s_y}{\sqrt{n}}$$

---

[1] Many thanks to Robert W. Panasiuk for making the data available.

where $z = 2$. The sample mean and standard deviation for the $n = 51$ fee values were $\overline{y} = \$1,052$ and $s_y = \$548$, respectively, so the 95% confidence interval was

FIGURE 8.2

899 1,052 1,205

├── 95%CI ──┤

$$1,052 \pm 2\left(\frac{548}{\sqrt{51}}\right) \qquad \text{or} \qquad 1,052 \pm 153$$

so chances were 95% that the point estimate, $\overline{y} = \$1,052$, was no more than $153 away from the process mean μ_y. There was thus moderate uncertainty about the numerical value of the process mean.

Analysis of the Shelf Display Experiment

Section 5.12 described an experiment to determine the effect of display area on sales of a high-volume product. This experiment was carried out at one of the stores of a retail chain. Each week, sales per week (in number of units) were measured, and the factor, size of display space, was set at one of two levels, regular and expanded. Figure 5.23 (p. 191) documents the details of the experiment. Because of seasonality, blocks of 2 weeks were used for the two levels of the factor. To remove the effects of the background variable seasonality from the study, the difference between sales under the two display alternatives was computed for each block. This difference was computed as sales for expanded display minus sales for regular display. Figure 5.24 lists the data and the derived response variable, y, the difference between sales under the two display alternatives. The sales difference values for the 16 blocks were:

| 10 | 6 | 9 | −2 | 10 | 14 | 12 | 6 | 1 | 6 | 10 | 15 | 14 | 7 | 13 | 12 |

The sequence plot for the 16 differences suggested a random process for the differences. The distribution of differences was approximately normal. The relevant statistics from Figure 5.26 (p. 194) are:

	N	MEAN	MEDIAN	TRMEAN	STDEV	SEMEAN
Difference	16	8.31	9.50	8.57	4.98	1.24

Let us obtain a 99% confidence interval for the process mean of the differences, μ_y. Given that the process remains stable under unchanged conditions, this mean measures the long-run average for incremental sales due to increasing the display size from regular to expanded. We can use the causal term *due to* here since the experiment was properly designed and randomization was used to deal with any unknown background variables. Since the sample size is $n = 16$, we must use the results for small samples in Section 7.6. The degrees of freedom are $n - 1 = 15$, and the appropriate t-multiple is 2.95. The 99% confidence interval for the process mean μ_y is:

FIGURE 8.3

4.64 8.31 11.98

├── 99%CI ──┤

$$8.31 \pm 2.95\left(\frac{4.98}{\sqrt{16}}\right) \qquad \text{or} \qquad 8.31 \pm 3.67$$

Chances are 99% that the point estimate 8.31 is no more than 3.67 away from the process mean. There is some uncertainty about the exact value of the process mean, but there is no doubt that it is positive. Thus expanded display definitely increases average sales for the high-volume product.

If we had used the large sample results from Section 7.3 instead, we would have used the multiple 2.57 for a 99% confidence interval, yielding

$$8.31 \pm 2.57\left(\frac{4.98}{\sqrt{16}}\right) \quad \text{or} \quad 8.31 \pm 3.20$$

This confidence interval would have been somewhat tight.

This experiment was carried out as a time series study. Blocks were used to control for seasonality, an important background variable. To prevent confounding between the factor of interest and any nuisance variables, each of the two levels of the factor, display size, were randomly assigned to one of the 2 weeks in each block.

In our analysis, since we wanted to project the results from the experiment into the future, we checked the sequence plot of the differences. Only common chance causes seemed to be at work.

What judgments did we have to make to project the results from the experiment into the future? We had to assume that the same set of common chance causes will continue to operate in the future!

8.3

A REMINDER ABOUT RANDOM SAMPLING

In Sections 7.3 and 7.4, we discussed how to assess the accuracy of sample averages and the difference between two sample averages when the averages were computed from *simple random* samples. The measures of accuracy are the standard errors, and they make it possible to estimate the margin of error when generalizing from the sample statistics to the population parameters.

> The formulas for standard errors are valid only when the **sample is drawn randomly** from the population or when it comes from a **random process.** They should not be used for other kinds of samples. If the sample was not drawn by random sampling or did not come from a random process, there is no way of assessing the accuracy of the sample results.

Random sampling is an ideal sampling procedure that is difficult to carry out in its pure form. There are often other sources of variability in addition to the sampling variability due to random sampling. (We called these other errors *nonsam-*

pling errors in Chapters 2 and 4.) In this sense then, the standard errors may underestimate the uncertainty inherent in making generalizations from the sample to the population. The real uncertainty is often much larger.

8.4

HYPOTHESIS TESTS

In Section 7.7, we introduced **hypothesis testing,** and we applied it to cross-sectional studies when simple random samples were drawn. We can also apply hypothesis testing to time series studies when the process under study is random (that is, stable). Given that we can take the process generating the data to be random, the steps are no different from those outlined in Section 7.7:

1. State the hypothesis.

2. Collect the data.

3. Compute the standardized observed sample result, z_{obs}, and the *p*-value.

4. Draw a conclusion using the rule of thumb regarding the *p*-value, given in Section 7.7 (p. 302).

Consider the following example to illustrate the approach for a difference between two process means.

EXAMPLE 8.2

Management of a retail chain was interested in studying increases in average weekly sales per employee hour (SPEH) in order to evaluate the effectiveness of a productivity improvement program. The productivity improvement program would be judged ineffective if the average sales increase was $0. In this study of a process, the unit is a week and the response variable is *y*, Sales per employee hour. Two samples were taken, one before implementation of the improvement program and one after. The data suggested that the "before" and "after" processes were random. The resulting sample data were $n_1 = 20$, $\bar{y}_1 = \$163.60$, and $s_1 = \$9.84$ (where the subscript 1 refers to the "before" measurements), $n_2 = 20$, $\bar{y}_2 = \$174.00$, and $s_2 = \$10.41$ (where the subscript 2 refers to the "after" measurements).

hypothesis test for difference of means

We again use the four steps for hypothesis testing.

1. The hypothesis here refers to the difference between the two process means, $\mu_2 - \mu_1 = \$0$. A difference value $0 corresponds to an ineffective improvement program.

2. The sample results were $n_1 = 20$, $\bar{y}_1 = \$163.60$, $s_1 = \$9.84$, $n_2 = 20$, $\bar{y}_2 = \$174.00$, and $s_2 = \$10.41$.

3. We need to obtain the standardized difference between sample means,

$$z_{obs} = \frac{\begin{array}{c}\text{Observed Difference} \\ \text{Between Sample Means}\end{array} - \begin{array}{c}\text{Hypothesized Difference} \\ \text{Between Process Means}\end{array}}{\text{Standard Error of Difference}}$$

The observed difference between the two sample means is $\bar{y}_2 - \bar{y}_1 = \$174.00 - \$163.60 = \$10.40$. The estimated standard error of the difference was derived in Section 7.4 as

$$\sqrt{\frac{s_2^2}{n_2} + \frac{s_1^2}{n_1}}$$

For the productivity improvement program, we have

$$\sqrt{\frac{10.41^2}{20} + \frac{9.84^2}{20}} = 3.20$$

Therefore, the standardized observed difference is

$$z_{obs} = \frac{(174.00 - 163.60) - 0}{3.20} = 3.25$$

p-value

FIGURE 8.4

p-value = 2(0.0006) = 0.0012

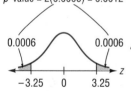

The **p-value** measures the probability of observing a sample result at least as unusual as the observed sample result. In order to compute the p-value, note that observing a sample difference more unusual than the observed difference implies that the corresponding standardized difference would be *larger* than $z_{obs} = 3.25$ in this case. Using Minitab (or interpolating in Table 4.1), the resulting probability is 0.0006. To compute the p-value, we must double this probability. Thus the p-value is $2(0.0006) = 0.0012$.

4. Given the result for z_{obs}, the sample data do not support the hypothesis that there was no difference between the two population means. The observed difference between sample means is surprisingly large. We conclude that the productivity improvement program indeed resulted in improvement on average. We, of course, reach the same conclusion with the p-value (0.0012).

hypothesis test for randomness

Let us also examine use of a hypothesis test in the context of checking for the randomness of a process. In Section 5.4, we had used the runs test as one tool for checking the randomness of a process, and we can easily fit those ideas into the present framework of a hypothesis test.

1. The hypothesis is that the process is random. Randomness has many implications, and one of them has to do with the number of runs, as defined in Section 5.4 (p. 164).

2. For any time series, we can easily count the number of runs above and below the mean, or we can use Minitab to do this for us.

3. Using Minitab, we can get the *p*-value (that is, the statistical significance). Minitab uses appropriate formulas to standardize the observed number of runs and then to compute the *p*-value.

4. Depending on the size of the *p*-value, the runs test does not call the randomness of the series into question, does call randomness into question, or is inconclusive.

8.5

CONTROL CHARTS

Chapter 5 introduced the control chart for individual observations (*i* chart) to check the randomness (stability) of a process. Control charts are applied in many business settings. Whenever the quality of the output from a process can be measured, a control chart can be used to *continuously* monitor the process.

stable process

Before introducing several more control charts frequently used in practice, let us quote W. E. Deming about *stability* of a process.

> There is no such thing as constancy in real life. There is, however, such a thing as a constant-cause system. The results produced by a constant-cause system vary, and in fact may vary over a wide band or a narrow band. They vary, but they exhibit an important feature called stability. Why apply the terms constant and stability to a cause system that produces results that vary? Because the same percentage of these varying results continues to fall between any given pair of limits hour after hour, day after day, so long as the constant-cause system continues to operate. It is the distribution of results that is constant or stable. . . The control chart will tell you whether your process is [stable].[2]

***i*-chart**

The control chart for individual observations is most useful when measurements on all consecutive observations should be included on the control chart. This will often be the case when the rate at which services are rendered or products are produced is not high. The *i* chart is used to check whether the process generating the measurements is stable. Only common causes of variation are at work in a stable process. If the level of variation is too high, the process must be improved, and careful experimentation and analysis are necessary to do so. Management is responsible for such process improvement. If the process is not stable, then special causes of variation are also at work and must be identified so that they can be eliminated or prevented from occurring again. You may want to review Sections 5.6, 5.7, and 5.9 at this point.

When the rate at which services are rendered or products are produced is high, including every observation on the control chart may not be feasible or desir-

---

[2] W. E. Deming, "Some Principles of the Shewhart Methods of Quality Control," *Mechanical Engineering* 66 (1944), 173–177.

able. An observation could then be taken at regular intervals and included on the control chart. In many such situations, however, small samples (often called *subgroups*) are taken consecutively from the process at regular intervals. Control charts have been developed to monitor the results from such samples. In the remainder of this section, we first discuss how to obtain the small samples or subgroups. We then discuss several additional control charts:

- The $\bar{y}$ **chart (or YBAR chart)** for sample means (this is often called an XBAR chart since sample means are often denoted $\bar{x}$)

- The *s* **chart** for sample standard deviations

- The combined $\bar{y}$ **and** *s* **chart**

- The *p* **chart** for sample proportions

Rational Subgrouping

The main purpose for using a control chart is to monitor a process. If only a common set of chance causes is at work, the process is stable, as the control chart should indicate. If special causes are at work in addition to the common chance causes, the process is not stable, and the control chart should immediately show that a change has occurred. For the control charts discussed in this section, samples or *subgroups* are taken at regular intervals and selected statistics for the subgroups are recorded on the control chart. These subgroups should be taken in such a way that only common causes are at work in the delivery or production of the units within each subgroup, and that special causes of variation, if any, occur only between subgroups.

Most commonly, time defines subgroups since special causes usually occur infrequently. It is expected that only common causes are at work for output produced at the same time. Therefore, a subgroup consists of output produced at roughly the same time: Output produced at different times is in different subgroups. Using time as a basis for subgrouping enables the detection of special causes over time. Sometimes, other factors determine a good way to form subgroups, such as customers, suppliers, or operators. Developing rational subgroups depends on the context of the application and requires knowledge about the process being monitored.

Once subgroups have been defined, one or more statistics describing each subgroup, such as the mean, range, standard deviation, or percent defective, can be monitored on a control chart.

Control Charts for Means: $\bar{y}$ or YBAR Charts

In many practical applications, a small sample (subgroup) is taken from the process at regular intervals in order to monitor the process. Consecutive subgroup means are plotted on a control chart. The question now is: Where should the control limits be drawn?

FIGURE 8.5 Pitch Diameter Data

ROW	READG 1	READG 2	READG 3	READG 4	READG 5	YBAR	ST.DEV
1	36	35	34	33	32	34.0	1.58114
2	31	31	34	32	30	31.6	1.51658
3	30	30	32	30	32	30.8	1.09545
4	32	33	33	32	35	33.0	1.22474
5	32	34	37	37	35	35.0	2.12132
6	32	32	31	33	33	32.2	0.83666
7	33	33	36	32	31	33.0	1.87083
8	23	33	36	35	36	32.6	5.50454
9	43	36	35	24	31	33.8	6.97854
10	36	35	36	41	41	37.8	2.94958
11	34	38	35	34	38	35.8	2.04939
12	36	38	39	39	40	38.4	1.51658
13	36	40	35	26	33	34.0	5.14782
14	36	35	37	34	33	35.0	1.58114
15	30	37	33	34	35	33.8	2.58844
16	28	31	33	33	33	31.6	2.19089
17	33	30	34	33	35	33.0	1.87083
18	27	28	29	27	30	28.2	1.30384
19	35	36	29	27	32	31.8	3.83406
20	33	35	35	39	36	35.6	2.19089

Consider the following example:

EXAMPLE 8.3

The data in Figure 8.5 are 100 measurements of pitch diameter of threads on aircraft fittings stored in ASCII file GRANT.DAT.[3] Values are expressed in units of 0.0001 inch in excess of 0.4000 inches. Specifications call for "37 ± 13." Each successive subgroup of $n = 5$ readings consists of items *consecutively* produced at times about 1 hour apart. Note that the data are not equally spaced in time, since five consecutive observations were taken about every hour. The managerial question is:

Is the pitch diameter process stable?

The 100 measurements are plotted in Figure 8.6. It is not appropriate to analyze the 100 measurements as a time series, ignoring the fact that the data are not equally spaced. It is better to analyze the data by looking at the means of each subgroup of $n = 5$ readings, which are labeled YBAR in Figure 8.5. The sequence plot of subgroup means is plotted in Figure 8.7(a). Where should the control limits be drawn?

---

[3] The data are taken from E. L. Grant, *Statistical Quality Control,* McGraw-Hill, 1946.

FIGURE 8.6
Sequence Plot of
Pitch Diameter Data

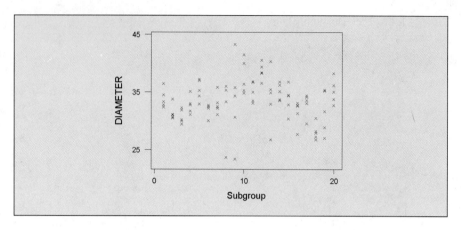

FIGURE 8.7
Pitch Diameter Data

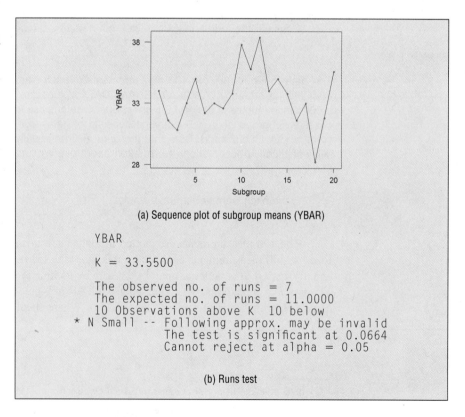

(a) Sequence plot of subgroup means (YBAR)

```
YBAR

K = 33.5500

The observed no. of runs = 7
The expected no. of runs = 11.0000
10 Observations above K   10 below
* N Small -- Following approx. may be invalid
            The test is significant at 0.0664
            Cannot reject at alpha = 0.05
```

(b) Runs test

Our approach to finding upper and lower control limits is similar to what we did in Section 5.6:

- First, we assume the process to be stable so that we can compute the control limits.

- Then, we check how reasonable this assumption is by examining whether all observations lie within the control limits. (Of course, we also use our visual impression of a sequence plot and the runs test to assess the randomness of the process.)

The process generates units over time, and each unit is characterized by a value for the quantitatively scaled response variable, y. At regular intervals, subgroups of size n are taken from the process and subgroup statistics are computed, in particular, the mean $\bar{y}$ and the standard deviation s_y. Let us assume that we have the results from r subgroups and that we want to obtain the $\bar{y}$ control chart. Let us number the consecutive subgroups from 1 to r, and let us use subscripts to denote the corresponding subgroup statistics: For the subgroup means, we have $\bar{y}_1, \bar{y}_2, ..., \bar{y}_r$, and for the subgroup standard deviations, we have $s_1, s_2, ..., s_r$.

In the aircraft fittings example, the response variable is y, pitch diameter (in units of 0.0001 inch in excess of 0.4000 inch). We have $r = 20$ subgroups with $n = 5$ observations each, so we have $nr = 100$ observations in all. The mean and standard deviation for the first subgroup are $\bar{y}_1 = 34.0$ and $s_1 = 1.58114$ (see Figure 8.5).

Let us first derive the control limits for the control chart by assuming that the process is stable and then check this assumption of process stability.

If the process were random with process mean μ_y and process standard deviation σ_y, then the size of the standard error of the mean, $\sigma_y/\sqrt{n}$, would indicate how far a subgroup mean $\bar{y}$ could differ from the process mean μ_y. We do not usually know process mean and standard deviation, and so we must estimate them from the data. Our data consist of the results for r subgroups, each consisting of the *same* number of observations n. We could pool the r subgroup means to estimate the process mean by computing their average. Denote this pooled average by $\bar{\bar{y}}$.

pooled average

Thus the pooled average is

$$\bar{\bar{y}} = \frac{\sum_{j=1}^{r} \bar{y}_j}{r}$$

where $\bar{y}_j$ is the mean for subgroup j, $j = 1, ..., r$; $\bar{\bar{y}}$ serves as a point estimate for the process mean μ_y.

We can also pool the r subgroup standard deviations to get an estimate of the process standard deviation σ_y. When all subgroup sample sizes are equal, the appropriate statistical way to compute the pooled standard deviation is to take the square root of the average of squared standard deviations. Denoting the pooled standard deviation s_{pool}, we have

pooled standard deviation

$$s_{\text{pool}} = \sqrt{\frac{\sum_{j=1}^{r} s_j^2}{r}}$$

where s_j^2 is the squared standard deviation for subgroup j, $j = 1, ..., r$; s_{pool} serves as a point estimate for the process standard deviation σ_y.

For the aircraft fitting example, the pooled average is

$$\bar{\bar{y}} = \frac{34.0 + 31.6 + \cdots + 35.6}{20} = 33.55$$

and the pooled standard deviation is

$$s_{pool} = \sqrt{\frac{1.581^2 + 1.516^2 + \cdots + 2.191^2}{20}} = \sqrt{8.780} = 2.963$$

Thus, estimates for the process mean μ_y and standard deviation σ_y are 33.55 and 2.963, respectively. If the process were stable, we would expect the process to continue at this mean, 33.55, with random variation around it with standard deviation 2.963. If we now took a sample of $n = 5$ units from this stable process, we would expect the variation in the sample mean around the process mean to be described by the standard error of the mean, $\sigma_y/\sqrt{n}$, where $n = 5$. Thus the standard error of the mean would be estimated to be $2.963/\sqrt{5} = 1.325$. The lower and upper control limits for sample means based on $n = 5$ observations from this process are then

$$33.55 \pm 3(1.325) \quad \text{or} \quad 29.57 \text{ and } 37.53$$

Figure 8.8 is the resulting $\bar{\bar{y}}$ control chart, obtained with Minitab, which uses slightly different notation, and denotes this as an XBAR chart, rather than a YBAR chart.

We have now obtained the control limits for a $\bar{y}$ chart. In general, the control limits for such a chart are obtained as follows:

$\bar{y}$ (or YBAR) Control Chart: Suppose r successive subgroups are available from a process. The subgroups are of the *same* size, n. The subgroup means are $\bar{y}_1, \bar{y}_2, ..., \bar{y}_r$, and the subgroup standard deviations are $s_1, s_2, ..., s_r$. The pooled average is

$$\bar{\bar{y}} = \frac{\sum_{j=1}^{r} \bar{y}_j}{r}$$

and the pooled standard deviation is

$$s_{pool} = \sqrt{\frac{\sum_{j=1}^{r} s^2_j}{r}}$$

Then the upper and lower control limits for a $\bar{y}$ control chart are:

$$\bar{\bar{y}} \pm 3\frac{s_{pool}}{\sqrt{n}}$$

FIGURE 8.8
Pitch Diameter Data:
YBAR (=XBAR)
Control Chart

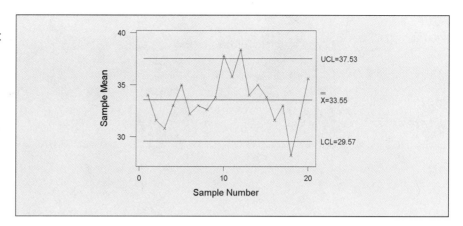

Having obtained the control limits for the $\bar{y}$ chart, let us now check if the process is stable. If the process were stable, then the sequence of $\bar{y}$ values would also be stable. When checking if a process is stable, we use (1) visual impression of the sequence plot, (2) the runs test, and (3) the control limits.

Visual inspection of Figure 8.7(a) suggests a slightly meandering pattern to the sequence of $\bar{y}$ values. This visual impression is not supported by the runs test, shown in Figure 8.7(b). The results from the runs test are not quite reliable, however, since there are only $r = 20$ values for $\bar{y}$. The $\bar{y}$ control chart in Figure 8.8 indicates that the 10th, 12th, and 18th $\bar{y}$ values are outside the control limits. Thus, we conclude that the pitch diameter process is not stable. The three outliers are a good starting point for determining why the process might not be stable. We may be able to identify special causes.

It may appear at first that we should not base the control limits on the standard error of the mean computed from the pooled standard deviation, s_{pool}, but that we should use the standard deviation of all 100 measurements, s_y instead. If we had used the standard deviation of all 100 measurements, $s_y = 3.529$, then the upper and lower control limits would have been UCL $= 33.55 + 3(3.529)/\sqrt{5} = 38.29$ and LCL $= 28.81$, respectively: The control limits would have been wider. The reason for this is easy to see: The pooled standard deviation is based on the variation within the subgroups that were selected in such a way that only common cause variation would be at work. In the example, consecutive values were chosen for each subgroup. Special causes, if any, are more likely to occur between the times at which subgroups were taken. Thus, any special causes of variation would have an effect on the standard deviation based on all 100 measurements: This standard deviation would not only measure common cause variation, but also the additional variation due to special causes. The control limits based on the standard deviation of the 100 measurements would then be *wider*. This might prevent us from concluding that the process is not stable. For this reason, it is advisable to use the pooled standard deviation as a basis for the appropriate standard error of the mean. [See Burr (1976) for further information.]

FIGURE 8.9
Pitch Diameter
Data: Control Chart
Generated Using
the Minitab Default
for Estimating the
Process Standard
Deviation

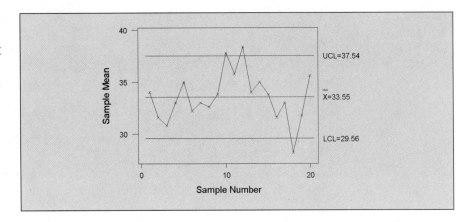

Pooling the standard deviations is one method of estimating the process standard deviation. Other methods exist, one of them being Minitab's default. Figure 8.9 is the control chart generated by default in Minitab. The control limits are quite similar to Figure 8.8. Since this will often be the case, using the Minitab default is a reasonable substitute for using the pooled standard deviation.

Control Charts for Standard Deviations: *s* Charts

In most applications, the $\bar{y}$ chart discussed in the previous section should be accompanied by an *s* chart, a control chart for standard deviations, since a stable process implies stability of not just the means of successive subgroups but also of the standard deviations of successive subgroups. The *s* chart for Example 8.3 is given in Figure 8.10.

Minitab uses the pooled standard deviation, s_{pool}, discussed in the last subsection, to compute the control limits for an *s* chart. Details for the computation of

FIGURE 8.10
Pitch Diameter
Data: *s* Chart for
DIAMETER

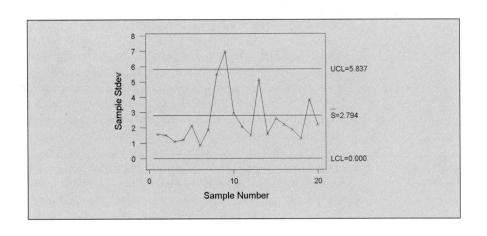

FIGURE 8.11
Pitch Diameter Data:
Combined $\bar{\bar{y}}$ and s
Chart

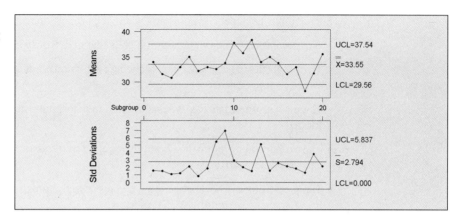

control limits are given in Burr (1976). The center line in Figure 8.10 is denoted $\bar{s} = 2.794$. The upper control limit is UCL $= 5.837$, and the lower control limit is LCL $= 0$. The standard deviation for subgroup 9 is above the upper control limit, suggesting that the subgroup standard deviations are not stable. Visual inspection of Figure 8.10 does not reveal any other problems. Thus, subgroup 9 would be a good starting point for a search for special causes.

Both the $\bar{y}$ chart and the s chart suggest that the process generating the diameters of the aircraft fittings is not stable. These two charts should be interpreted together. For this reason, a combined chart is available in Minitab Release 10 for Windows, as shown in Figure 8.11.

Control Charts for Proportions: p Charts

In the i chart, the $\bar{y}$ chart, and the s chart, the response variable was quantitative. In many processes, however, the variable of interest is dichotomous: Every unit of output is either a success or a failure—it is either effective or defective. We can use some of the results from Section 7.5 (p. 288) to deal with this case.

When the response variable y is dichotomous, random samples (subgroups) of size n are typically taken from the process at regular intervals. For each subgroup, the proportion of successes is computed and recorded in a control chart. Note the same approach we used to obtain $\bar{y}$ and s charts, and note the difference from the i charts discussed in Chapter 5, where the response variable value for *one* individual unit was measured at a particular point in time and entered on the control chart: We take a subgroup of n units, compute the subgroup proportion of successes, p, and enter it on the control chart. This step is repeated at regular intervals. The resulting control chart for proportions is called a *p chart*. The general remarks about rational subgrouping apply to p charts as well.

There are many areas where p charts give useful information about the process.

For example, consider control charts where the proportion recorded is

- The proportion of computer sign-on calls that give a busy signal
- The proportion of accounts payable where errors result in late payment of invoices to suppliers
- The proportion of laboratory tests ordered in a hospital ward that are not performed
- The proportion of rooms in a hotel that are put into satisfactory order before registration of new arrivals
- The proportion of checks rejected when processed through high-speed magnetic ink character recognition (MICR) sorters.

To illustrate how to draw a control chart for proportions, consider the following example.[4]

EXAMPLE 8.4

At regular intervals, samples of 100 electroplating parts are taken, and the proportion of defective parts is recorded. Figure 8.12(b) graphs these proportions for 30 subgroups. The data are stored in ASCII file PLATING.DAT. The question is:

Is the electroplating process stable?

To answer this question, we first discuss how to obtain the control chart limits on Figure 8.12. In terms of statistical notation, we have the following: The response variable y can take on one of two values, 0 or 1. At regular intervals, we take subgroups of size n and record the proportion of ones. We thus have the proportions for r subgroups, $p_1, p_2, p_3, ..., p_r$.

In the electroplating example, we have the results for $r = 30$ subgroups, each based on $n = 100$ units. As given in Figure 8.12, the proportion of defective units for subgroup 1 is $p_1 = 0.01$, for subgroup 30 it is $p_{30} = 0.04$.

If the process were stable, the process proportion of defectives π would be the same in each period. In order to estimate this proportion, we can pool the r subgroup results. Denoting the resulting pooled estimate of π by $\bar{p}$, we have

pooled sample proportion

$$\bar{p} = \frac{\sum_{j=1}^{r} p_j}{r}$$

This estimate is based on rn observations from the process.

---

[4] This example is taken from K. Ishikawa, *Guide to Quality Control,* Second Revised Edition, Asian Productivity Organization, Tokyo, 1982, p. 81.

FIGURE 8.12 Electroplating Data

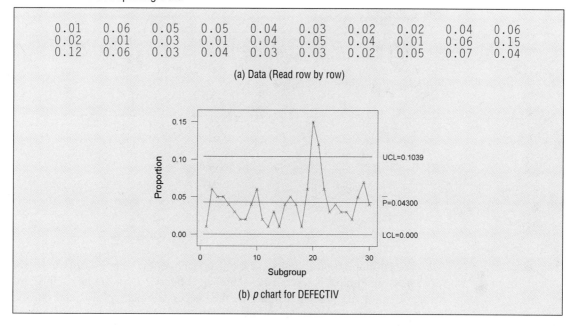

0.01	0.06	0.05	0.05	0.04	0.03	0.02	0.02	0.04	0.06
0.02	0.01	0.03	0.01	0.04	0.05	0.04	0.01	0.06	0.15
0.12	0.06	0.03	0.04	0.03	0.03	0.02	0.05	0.07	0.04

(a) Data (Read row by row)

(b) *p* chart for DEFECTIV

In the electroplating example, the estimate of the process proportion of defectives, π, is

$$\bar{p} = \frac{0.01 + 0.06 + \cdots + 0.04}{30} = 0.043.$$

This estimate represents the center line in Figure 8.12(b). It is based on $rn = 30(100) = 3,000$ observations.

Let us now determine the control limits. To do so, we assume that the process is stable with process proportion π. If we took a subgroup of size n from this process, the subgroup proportion p would not necessarily equal π because of sampling error. A measure of the potential deviation of p from π is the standard error of the proportion (see Section 7.5):

$$\sqrt{\frac{\pi(1 - \pi)}{n}}$$

Since we do not know π, we use the pooled estimate $\bar{p}$ for it. Thus the estimated standard error is

estimated standard error

$$\sqrt{\frac{\bar{p}(1 - \bar{p})}{n}}$$

The upper and lower control limits are computed as usual. The result is summarized in the following box:

Control Chart for Proportions (p Chart):   Suppose r subgroups of the *same* size n are available, and the subgroup proportions are $p_1, p_2, ..., p_r$. Let the pooled proportion of successes be

$$\bar{p} = \frac{\sum_{j=1}^{r} p_j}{r}$$

Then the upper and lower control limits for a p chart are

$$\bar{p} \pm 3 \sqrt{\frac{\bar{p}(1 - \bar{p})}{n}}$$

To obtain the control limits using this procedure, the sample size n must not vary across subgroups: If consecutive subgroups of varying size are taken, this procedure does not apply. Modifications are then necessary that will not be discussed in this book. [See Burr (1976) for further details.]

In the electroplating example, the estimate of the process proportion π was $\bar{p} = 0.043$. The estimated standard error of a proportion based on $n = 100$ observations is

$$\sqrt{\frac{\bar{p}(1 - \bar{p})}{n}} = \sqrt{\frac{0.043(1 - 0.043)}{100}} = 0.0203$$

Thus, the control limits are

$$0.043 \pm 3(0.0203) \qquad \text{or} \qquad -0.018 \text{ and } 0.104$$

In this example, a negative lower control limit would be meaningless, so we move it up to zero (no defectives). These control limits are drawn in Figure 8.12 (with slight differences due to rounding). Thus, if the process were stable, we would expect successive sample proportions, each based on $n = 100$ units, to be between 0 and 0.104.

Except for the two outlying values, visual impression of Figure 8.12 suggests that the process is stable. A runs test, not reported here, supported this visual impression. The two proportions in periods 20 and 21, however, are seen to fall outside the control limits. We thus conclude that the electroplating process was not stable. A search for potential special causes of variation is in order, a good starting point for their identification being periods 20 and 21. If special causes of variation are indeed found, their reoccurrence may be prevented in the future.

It may appear at first that we should not base the control limits on the standard error of the proportion as computed above, but that we should use the standard deviation of the 30 sample proportions directly in the computation of control limits.

If we had used the standard deviation of the 30 proportions, which is 0.030, then the upper and lower control limits would have been UCL = 0.043 + 3(0.030) = 0.133 and LCL = −0.053, respectively—that is, the control limits would have been wider. In many situations when there is a special cause at work, this behavior of the control limits is to be expected, and use of the *wider* control limits based on the standard deviation of the 30 proportions might prevent us from concluding that the process is not stable. For this reason, it is advisable not to use this approach to computing the control limits.

8.6

AN ANALYSIS OF MAINTENANCE RESPONSE TIMES

Over the past three years, Ontario Housing Corporation has made a shift in orientation from being a "bricks and mortar" landlord to concerning itself with overall quality of the housing environments for which it is responsible.[5] This shift has resulted in emphasis on safety and security, anti-drug initiatives, and access to services for tenants. Another important aspect of this shift in emphasis has been the recognition of the importance of providing quality property management with a client-service orientation, since the quality of life of Ontario Housing Corporation's residents is greatly affected by the condition of their physical environment and the way they are treated by their landlord. As part of an ongoing process to improve service quality, a study of response times to maintenance requests was done at one of the large family housing projects owned by one of the largest regional Housing Authorities in Ontario.

Work orders were processed as follows. After a tenant phoned the regional Housing Authority's central maintenance request line, a work order was made out. Work orders were sent to the appropriate area office twice a day, where they were sorted by housing project. The maintenance supervisor for each housing project took the work orders to the project site and assigned the work to onsite staff. When work was completed, the work order was sent back to the head office.

Summary:

Managerial Questions. The following managerial questions were addressed:

1. Should improved maintenance response time be a priority for quality improvement at the housing project? If yes, what improvement targets should be established?

2. Are there types of maintenance requests that occur frequently? Could their number be reduced through property management activities, such as education and project upgrading?

---

[5] Many thanks to M. Tate for making the data available.

Data Collection. All 167 work orders received for the housing project from May to July 1990 were examined. Data were collected on the maintenance response time, the type of request, and the urgency of the request.

Findings. The mean response time—almost 8 days—was high but stable throughout the period under study. There appeared to be an informal system of determining the urgency of a maintenance request: Urgent requests were responded to 5 days faster on average than less urgent requests. The proportion of requests that were responded to in 3 days or less was far lower than the 90% figure expected before the study was done. Some types of requests occurred much more frequently than others. The most numerous type was plumbing requests, which amounted to about a third of all requests.

Recommendations. Management must improve the response process so that 90% of all work orders are responded to within 3 days. Plumbing requests were most numerous, and their cause should be examined in greater detail.

Statistical Details:

Statistical Questions. The statistical questions were as follows:

1. a Is the maintenance response process stable?

  b What is mean response time? What is mean response time stratified by the apparent urgency of the request? What is the difference in mean response times for urgent and less ugent requests?

  c What proportion of response times are 3 days or less?

2. Which types of requests occur most frequently? Is there a difference to this pattern depending on the urgency of request?

Statistical Unit. The unit in this time series study was a maintenance request.

Description of Process. The process consisted of the maintenance department's response to maintenance requests at a large housing project owned by the Ontario Housing Corporation.

Sampling Scheme. All work orders received for the housing project from May to July 1990 were examined. The researcher examined photocopies of all 167 work orders and recorded measurements on four variables.

Description of Variables. For each maintenance request, four variables were measured: (1) the day when the phone call requesting maintenance was received (BEGIN): (2) the day when the work order was completed (END), (3) the TYPE of request, and (4) the URGENCY of the request (1 = urgent, 2 = less urgent). The two variables measuring "day" were recorded by letting 1 August 1990 be day 1, 1 September 1990 be day 32, etc. There were 14 types of request: 1 = plumbing, 2 = electrical, 3 = security, 4 = other, 5 = aluminum door, 6 = bugs, 7 = screens,

8 = smoke detectors, 9 = tiles, 10 = clothes washing machines, 11 = drywall, 12 = dry vent, 13 = fixtures, and 14 = no heat. The designation of urgency was determined by the researcher after the data were collected, assigning a value of 1 if tenants' health and safety might be affected, if there might be a risk of significant property damage, or if a major service was not functioning. The main variable of interest was RESPONSE time, which was obtained by computing the difference between variables END and BEGIN, so it measured the number of days from reception to completion of a work order. Type and urgency of request were used for stratification.

Process Characteristics of Interest.   Was the process stable? If it was, the process mean for response time was needed, both overall and stratified by type and urgency of request. Finally, the proportion of response times less than or equal to 3 days was needed.

Data.   A partial listing of the values on the four variables and on RESPONSE for the 167 work orders is given in Figure 8.13, and descriptive statistics are given in Figure 8.14. The data are stored in ASCII file HOUSING.DAT.

Data Analysis.   After creating the response variable as RESPONSE = END − BEGIN, a time series plot (not shown) was obtained to determine whether the process was stable. Since the mean and standard deviation for the 167 response times were 8.37 and 10.41, UCL was 8.37 + 3(10.41) = 39.6. There was nothing

FIGURE 8.13
Partial Listing of
Housing Project
Data

ROW	BEGIN	END	TYPE	URGENCY	RESPONSE
1	1	2	2	1	1
2	1	3	1	2	2
3	1	1	5	2	0
4	1	31	1	1	30
5	2	24	5	2	22
6	3	22	4	2	19
7	3	7	3	1	4
8	3	3	14	2	0
9	3	3	14	2	0
10	4	10	1	2	6
11	7	7	14	2	0
12	7	22	1	2	15
13	7	9	2	1	2
14	7	10	4	2	3
15	7	7	1	1	0
16	7	29	9	2	22
17	8	9	1	1	1
18	8	9	3	1	1
19	9	10	1	1	1
20	10	32	1	1	22
.					
.					
.					

FIGURE 8.14 Housing Project Data: Descriptive Statistics (One Work Order Removed)

	N	MEAN	MEDIAN	TRMEAN	STDEV	SEMEAN
RESPONSE	166	7.946	4.000	7.147	8.870	0.688

	MIN	MAX	Q1	Q3
RESPONSE	0.000	34.000	1.000	12.250

TYPE	COUNT	URGENCY	COUNT
1	49	1	58
2	21	2	108
3	16	N=	166
4	21		
5	21		
6	4		
7	8		
8	3		
9	4		
10	4		
11	2		
12	4		
13	5		
14	4		
N=	166		

surprising on this plot, except that observation 26 was 79 days, far above the upper control limit. A search for a special cause revealed that work order 26 was not cleared for 79 days due to the unavailability of a required door; it was felt that this outlier could be safely excluded from the analysis. The analysis proceeded with the remaining 166 work orders.

A time series plot for response times is given in Figure 8.15. A visual impression suggested randomness. All observations were within the upper and lower control limits, which are UCL = 7.946+3(8.87) = 34.56 and LCL < 0, respectively.

FIGURE 8.15
Housing Project
Data: Sequence
Plot of Response
Times

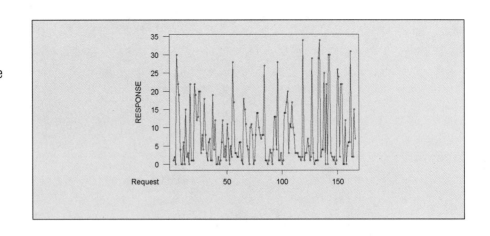

FIGURE 8.16
Housing Project
Data: Runs Test

```
RESPONSE

K =      7.9458

THE OBSERVED NO. OF RUNS =  61
THE EXPECTED NO. OF RUNS =  78.1687
61 OBSERVATIONS ABOVE K  105 BELOW
          THE TEST IS SIGNIFICANT AT   0.0041
```

Note, however, that there were either high or low response times after about work order 120. Furthermore, there appeared to be consecutive sequences of work orders for which the response times were 0 days. The runs test, given in Figure 8.16, reflects this observation: The observed number of runs was less than the number of runs expected for a stable process, and the p-value was low at 0.0041. Since the sample size was large, however, the cutoff values for the rule of thumb about the p-value should be lowered somewhat. A search for special causes did not reveal any assignable variation, so the process was judged to be stable.

Figure 8.17 gives summary information on the variable RESPONSE time, stratified by URGENCY of request. Urgent requests are responded to somewhat faster than less urgent requests. A large proportion of requests was not responded to within three days. Among the 58 urgent requests, only 38 or 66% were responded to within three days, and this figure was $\frac{41}{108}$ or 38% for the less urgent requests. Figure 8.18 lists the number of requests received by type, both overall and stratified by urgency of request.

Conclusions. As described in the data analysis, the process generating response times was deemed to be stable after one outlier was removed. There was a very slight tendency for a consecutive sequence of work orders to have 0 response times. A search for special causes revealed that a work order was completed quickly when a maintenance worker was on site or soon to go to the site; when maintenance staff were deployed at other housing projects, then the time to clear a work order was longer. This tendency was so slight, however, that the process was considered approximately stable.

Given that the process was judged to be stable, the questions regarding mean response time and proportion of requests with 3 days response time or less can be answered. The mean and standard deviation of response times for the 166 work orders were 7.95 and 8.87, respectively. A 95% confidence interval for the process mean was $7.95 \pm 2(8.87)/\sqrt{166}$, or 7.95 ± 1.38. Therefore, the process mean could not be estimated very accurately from the data. Stratifying by urgency of request, Figure 8.17 could be used to obtain a point estimate for the difference between the process means for less urgent and urgent requests: $9.69 - 4.69 = 5.00$ days; its standard error was $\sqrt{6.692^2/58 + 9.415^2/108} = 1.26$, so a 95% confidence interval was $5.00 \pm 2(1.26)$ or 5.00 ± 2.52. Since this interval covers positive values only, the mean response time for less urgent requests was definitely

FIGURE 8.17 Housing Project Data: Stratification by Urgency of Request

	N	MEAN	MEDIAN	TRMEAN	STDEV	SEMEAN
RESPONSE	166	7.946	4.000	7.147	8.870	0.688

	MIN	MAX	Q1	Q3
RESPONSE	0.000	34.000	1.000	12.250

	URGENCY	N	MEAN	MEDIAN	TRMEAN	STDEV	SEMEAN
RESPONSE	1	58	4.690	2.000	3.846	6.692	0.879
	2	108	9.694	6.500	9.061	9.415	0.906

	URGENCY	MIN	MAX	Q1	Q3
RESPONSE	1	0.000	30.000	0.750	6.000
	2	0.000	34.000	2.000	15.000

(a) Descriptive statistics

(b) Dotplots

larger than that for urgent requests, with the point estimate for the difference being 5 days.

The comparison of mean response times for less urgent and urgent requests can also be done with a one-sided confidence interval for the difference in process means that covers positive values only. Positive difference values imply that the process mean for less urgent requests is higher than the process mean for urgent requests. In order to find the degree of confidence in such an interval, the difference value 0 must be standardized, $z = (0 - 5.00)/1.26 = -3.97$. This value is quite far away from 0. Using Minitab or Table 4.1, the cumulative probability at $z = -3.97$ is found to be close to 0. Thus, the degree of confidence in an interval for the difference between these means that covers only positive values was almost 100%, again supporting the conclusion that the mean response time for less urgent requests is higher than that for urgent requests.

FIGURE 8.18
Housing Project
Data: Stratification
by Type of Request

Type	Overall Count	Overall %	Urgent Count	Urgent %	Less Urgent Count	Less Urgent %
1	49	29.5	27	46.6	22	20.4
2	21	12.7	10	17.2	11	10.2
3	16	9.6	11	19.0	5	4.6
4	21	12.7	5	8.6	16	14.8
5	21	12.7	0	0	21	18.5
6	4	2.4	2	3.4	2	1.9
7	8	4.8	0	0	8	7.4
8	3	1.8	2	3.4	1	0.9
9	4	2.4	0	0	4	3.7
10	4	2.4	0	0	4	3.7
11	2	1.2	0	0	2	1.9
12	4	2.4	0	0	4	3.7
13	5	3.0	0	0	5	4.6
14	4	2.4	1	1.7	3	2.8
Total	166		58		108	

The proportions of urgent and less urgent requests completed in 3 days or less were 66% and 38%, respectively. It had been expected that more than 90% of maintenance requests would be completed within 3 days. The data definitely did not support this expectation.

Finally, the relative frequencies of the various types of request were somewhat different when they were stratified by the researcher's perception of urgency of request. As given in Figure 8.18, about 83% of the urgent requests related to types 1–3 (plumbing, electrical, or security problems), and about 64% of less urgent requests related to types 1, 2, 4, and 5 (plumbing, electrical, other, or aluminum door problems).

Surprises. It was surprising that repair requests that appear to have greater urgency were receiving higher priority, despite the fact that there was no formal system in place to set priorities. The variable URGENCY had been created by the researcher as data were collected—*after* the work orders were completed.

8.7

SUMMARY AND OUTLOOK

This chapter applied the methods for cross-sectional studies introduced in Chapter 7 to time series studies. The sample was random by design in Chapter 7, since a random-number table was used to select units from the frame of the population. In time series studies, it is not possible to draw random samples since no frame exists. If the process generating the time series is random, however, the methods from Chapter 7 can be used for time series studies as well. Determining if a process is random requires judgment, and we reviewed several methods introduced in Chapter 5 to determine what conclusions can be drawn about the randomness of the process.

In addition to covering point and interval estimation of process parameters, this chapter also described hypothesis testing for processes. Furthermore, several control charts were introduced:

- The $\bar{y}$ chart

- The s chart

- The combined $\bar{y}$ and s chart

- The p chart

The next two chapters introduce the *regression model,* which can be used in both time series and cross-sectional studies to relate the response variable to other variables that influence it. Once the relationship has been established, it may shed light on the mechanism that links the response variable to the other variables, or it may be used to predict the response variable based on known values for the other variables.

Key Terms and Concepts

estimation
   process mean, difference between
   two process means
hypothesis testing

control chart
   means, standard deviations,
   proportions

References

Burr, I. W. (1976), *Statistical Quality Control Methods,* Marcel Dekker, New York.

This text gives a comprehensive treatment of statistical quality control methods.

Ishikawa, K. (1982), *Guide to Quality Control,* 2nd Revised Edition, Asian Productivity Organization, Tokyo.

This text is one of the classics in quality control.

8.8

USING MINITAB FOR WINDOWS

This section shows how several of the graphs in this chapter were generated with Minitab for Windows.

Figure 8.7

Choose *File ▸ Other Files ▸ Import ASCII Data*
In the *Import ASCII Data* dialog box,
> Under *Store data in column,* type **C1**
> Click *ok*
> In the *Import Text From File* dialog box,
> > Choose and click data file *grant.dat,* click *ok*
Choose *Window ▸ Data*
In the *Data* window,
> In the box immediately under *C1,* type **DIAMETER**
> Click any empty cell

PATTERNED DATA

Choose *Calc ▸ Set Patterned Data*
In the *Set Patterned Data* dialog box,
> Click the box next to *Store results in column,* type **C2**
> Click circle next to *Patterned Sequence*
> Click box to the right of *Start at,* type **1**
> Click box to the right of *End at,* type **5**
> Click box to the right of *Repeat the whole list,* replace box with **20**
> Click *ok*

UNSTACKING DATA COLUMNS

Choose *Manip ▸ Unstack*
In the *Unstack* dialog box,
> Under *Unstack,* type **C1**
> Next to *Using subscripts in,* type **C2**
> Under *Store results in blocks,*
> > Type **C3** in first box
> > Type **C4** in second box
> > Type **C5** in third box
> > Type **C6** in fourth box
> > Type **C7** in fifth box
> Click *ok*

ROW STATISTICS

Choose *Calc ▸ Row Statistics*
In the *Row Statistics* dialog box,
> Click *Mean*
> Under *Input variables,* type **C3-C7**
> Next to *Store result in,* type **C8**
> Click *ok*

Choose *Window ▸ Data*
In the *Data* window,
    In the box immediately under *C8*, type **YBAR**
    Click any empty cell

Choose *Graph ▸ Time Series Plot*
In the *Time Series Plot* dialog box,
    Under *Graph variables*, type **C8** in the box under *Y*
    Click *ok*
Choose *Stat ▸ Nonparametrics ▸ Runs Test*
In the *Runs Test* dialog box,
    Under *Variables*, type **C8**
    Click *ok*

Figure 8.8

YBAR CONTROL CHART

Choose *Stat ▸ Control Charts ▸ Xbar*
In the *Xbar Chart* dialog box,
    Next to *Variable*, type **C1**
    Click *Subgroup size*, type **5** next to it
    Under *Sigma*, click *Historical*, type **2.963** in box next to it
    Click *ok*

Figure 8.9

Choose *Stat ▸ Control Charts ▸ Xbar*
In the *Xbar Chart* dialog box,
    Next to *Variable*, type **C1**
    Click *Subgroup size*, type **5** next to it
    Under *Sigma*, click *Pooled std. dev.*
    Click *ok*

Figure 8.10

s CONTROL CHART

Choose *Stat ▸ Control Charts ▸ S*
In the *S Chart* dialog box,
    Next to *Variable*, type **C1**
    Click *Subgroup size*, type **5** next to it
    Under *Sigma*, click *Pooled std. dev.*
    Click *ok*

Figure 8.11

YBAR AND s CHART

Choose *Stat* ▸ *Control Charts* ▸ *Xbar-S*
In the *Xbar-S Chart* dialog box,
    Next to *Variable,* type **C1**
    Click *Subgroup size,* type **5** next to it
    Under *Sigma,* click *Pooled std. dev.*
    Click *ok*

Figure 8.12

Choose *File* ▸ *Other Files* ▸ *Import ASCII Data*
In the *Import ASCII Data* dialog box,
    Under *Store data in column,* type **C1**
    Click *ok*
    In the *Import Text From File* dialog box,
        Choose and click data file *plating.dat,* click *ok*
Choose *Window* ▸ *Data*
In the *Data* window,
    In the box immediately under *C1,* type **DEFECTIV**
    Click any empty cell
Choose *Calc* ▸ *Mathematical Expressions*
In the *Mathematical Expressions* dialog box,
    In the box next to *Variable (new or modified),* type **C1**
    In the box under *Expression,* type **100*C1**
    Click *ok*

P CHART

Choose *Stat* ▸ *Control Charts* ▸ *P*
In the *P Chart* dialog box,
    Next to *Variable,* type **C1**
    Click *Subgroup size,* type **100** next to it
    Click *ok*
        (Note that Minitab assumes that the specified column contains the *number* of defectives, *not* the proportion of defectives.)

8.9

New Minitab Commands

This section lists the Minitab Release 10 for Windows menu commands that have been introduced so far. Each submenu introduced in this and earlier chapters is listed under the corresponding main menu. It is briefly explained and a page reference to an explanation in the text is given in parentheses.

File

Save Worksheet As   page 88

[save data in ASCII, Minitab, or other formats]

Other Files   page 86

Import ASCII Data

[enter data into the Minitab worksheet from an ASCII file]

Manip

Sort   page 197

[sort the data in a column and rearrange the rows in other
columns accordingly]

Copy Columns   page 252
[copy columns to other columns. You can specify which rows to copy or
which rows to omit, if necessary]

Unstack   page 148

[unstack columns into several smaller columns]

Calc

Random Data   page 253

[generate random data from a variety of probability distributions]

Normal   page 253

[generate random data from any normal distribution]

Probability Distributions

Normal   page 128
[compute cumulative distribution values, inverse cumulative
distribution values, etc., for a normal distribution]

T   page 315

[compute cumulative distribution values, inverse cumulative
distribution values, etc., for a t-distribution]

Mathematical Expressions   page 149

[carry out algebraic expressions, natural logs, etc., on columns]

Function   page 149

[compute various functions on columns; for example, normal scores]

Column Statistics   page 86

[compute statistics on columns; for example, mean and standard deviation]

Row Statistics   page 359

[compute statistics on rows]

Set Patterned Data   page 359

[input patterned data]

Stat

Basic Statistics

Descriptive Statistics   pages 92, 147

[compute a variety of descriptive statistics for columns]

1-Sample t   page 314

[obtain a confidence interval for a mean]

2-Sample t   page 314

[obtain a confidence interval for the difference between two means]

Correlation

> [obtain correlations]

Control Charts

Xbar-S   page 361

> [create two control charts, one for means and one for standard deviations]

Xbar   page 360

> [create a control chart for means]

S   page 360

> [create a control chart for standard deviations]

Individuals   page 198

> [create a control chart for individual observations]

P   page 361

> [create a control chart for proportions]

Time Series

Differences   page 251

> [obtain differences of any lag]

Tables

Tally

> [summarize categorical variables]

Nonparametrics

Runs Test   page 197
> [carry out the runs test for data in a column. Note: none of the data must be missing.]

Graph

Plot   page 91

> [obtain high-resolution scatterplots]

Time Series Plot   page 87

> [obtain high-resolution time series plots]

Histogram   page 89

> [obtain high-resolution histograms, cumulative histograms, etc.]

Character Graphs

> [obtain low-resolution plots based on characters]

Dotplot   page 147

Stem-and-Leaf   page 90

Window

Session   page 91

> [move to Minitab's Session window]

PRINT   page 198

> [print out columns on your worksheet onto the screen]

Data

> [move to Minitab's Data window where you can operate on the data worksheet]

8.10

PROBLEMS FOR CLASS DISCUSSION

8.1 A Small Bakery

The owners of a small bakery of fresh bread have decided to start a home delivery service in order to get an advantage over stores selling factory-made bread. They approached a loan officer at their bank for a small loan to purchase a used car. The loan officer required an estimate of mean daily sales and a 98% confidence interval for this estimate.

The owners have kept sales data for some time. The process of daily sales has been stable recently, and the mean and standard deviation of daily sales for the last 40 days were 120 and 20 loaves, respectively.

a What are the point and interval estimates required by the loan officer? Do you have to make any assumptions to compute these estimates? If so, what are they and how reasonable are they?

b Obtain a 98% prediction interval for daily sales. Interpret this interval and contrast it with the interval obtained in (a).

c After obtaining the loan, the owners advertised their service outside their store and in a local newspaper. The mean and standard deviation of daily sales on the 50 days following the introduction of the home delivery service were 133 and 22. What are the point estimate and the 95% confidence interval for the change in mean sales from the period before to that after introduction of home delivery? Do you have confidence that the mean of daily sales has improved?

d Suppose now that the sequence plot for the daily sales data mentioned in (c) is shown in Figure 8.19. What does this plot tell you? Given this additional information, how useful are the estimate of change and the confidence interval you derived in (b)?

d The owners want to determine the proportion of customers who buy rye bread from them. Of the last 120 customers, 30 bought rye bread. What are the point estimate and a 90% confidence interval for the proportion of all their customers who buy rye bread? Do you have to make any assumptions to compute these estimates? If so, what are they and how reasonable are they?

FIGURE 8.19

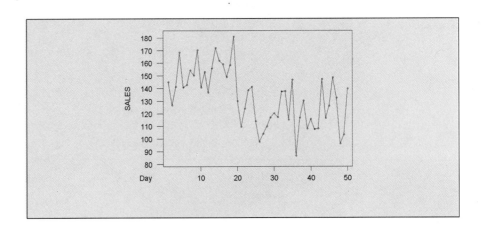

8.2   Control Data[6]

Control Data is a manufacturer of several computer series, including the CYBER 930 Series. Whenever changes to the series are made, documentation must be revised. Such revisions are initiated by *change orders*.

A study was undertaken in late 1988 to answer the following questions:

1. How do change order processing times vary over time?
2. How long does it take for change orders to be approved?
3. Can change-order processing time be predicted?

Data were collected as follows. Ninety-nine change orders were examined during the period from 6 December 1986 to 17 November 1988. The time (in working days) it took for each change order to be approved (that is, the processing time) was recorded. The data are stored in ASCII file CDC.DAT.

After an analysis of the sequence plot of the data, it was realized that two administrators had been responsible for the approval process. The first was responsible for the first 34 change orders and the second for the remaining 65.

FIGURE 8.20

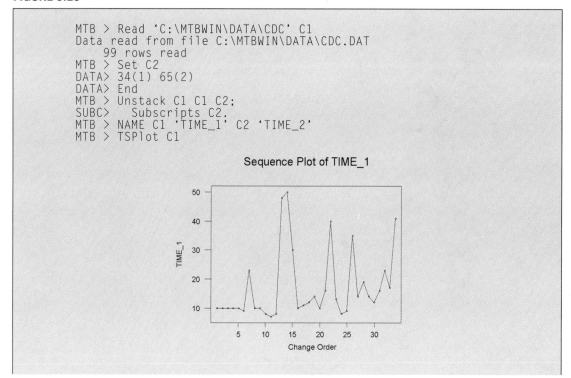

```
MTB > Read 'C:\MTBWIN\DATA\CDC' C1
Data read from file C:\MTBWIN\DATA\CDC.DAT
     99 rows read
MTB > Set C2
DATA> 34(1) 65(2)
DATA> End
MTB > Unstack C1 C1 C2;
SUBC>    Subscripts C2.
MTB > NAME C1 'TIME_1' C2 'TIME_2'
MTB > TSPlot C1
```

Sequence Plot of TIME_1

---

[6] The data were kindly provided by R. Nelson.

```
MTB > Runs C1

    TIME_1

    K =     17.2647

    The observed no. of runs =  14
    The expected no. of runs =  14.2353
      9 Observations above K   25 below
              The test is significant at  0.9154
              Cannot reject at alpha = 0.05

MTB > IChart C2
```

i Chart for Time_2

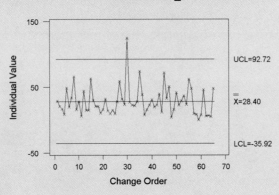

```
MTB > Runs C2

    TIME_2

    K = 28.4000

    The observed no. of runs =  33
    The expected no. of runs =  31.7692
    25 Observations above K    40 below
              The test is significant at  0.7450
              Cannot reject at alpha = 0.05

MTB > Describe C1-C2
```

	N	MEAN	MEDIAN	TRMEAN	STDEV	SEMEAN
TIME_1	34	17.26	12.00	15.80	12.02	2.06
TIME_2	65	28.40	23.00	26.54	21.44	2.66

	MIN	MAX	Q1	Q3
TIME_1	7.00	50.00	10.00	20.00
TIME_2	0.00	125.00	14.50	38.00

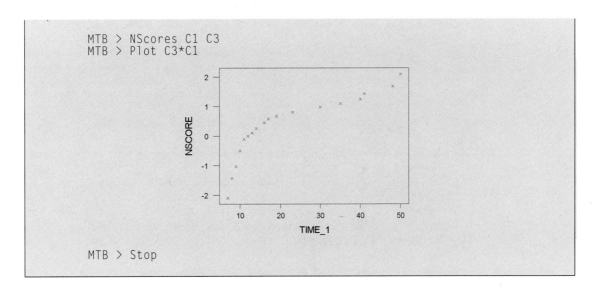

```
MTB > NScores C1 C3
MTB > Plot C3*C1
```

```
MTB > Stop
```

The following questions relate to the Minitab output given in Figure 8.20. The 34 processing times for the first administrator are stored as variable TIME_1 in C1, and the 65 processing times for the second administrator are stored as variable TIME_2 in C2.

a Was the approval process stable under the first administrator? Under the second administrator? If not, describe your concerns.

For questions (b) to (d), assume the approval process was stable under each administrator.

b Making any additional assumptions necessary, what are your point estimate of and a 90% confidence interval for the difference in the mean processing times?

c In addition to assuming a stable approval process under each administrator, did you have to make additional assumptions for your answers in (b)? If yes, list what they are and give your judgment of how reasonable they are.

d For the process under administrator 1, can you obtain the probability that another change order would be processed in 20 working days or less? If yes, provide your numerical answer. If no, why not?

e Given your answers to (a), how reasonable was it to assume a stable approval process under each administrator? If you had concerns in (a), what is their likely effect on the quantitative answers in (b)?

8.11

EXERCISES

Although answers are given in Appendix C, do not turn to them right away if you cannot find an answer on your own. Return to the exercise the next day and try again before turning to Appendix C.

Exercises for Section 8.2

8.3 The chemical industry has been a leader in the application of experimentation to business. The application to be reported here illustrates an experimental evaluation of a modification in a batch chemical process. Yields were obtained for 20 consecutive batches of a chemical process. The first 10 batches were run under a standard process and the second 10 under a modified process aimed at increasing mean yield. The resulting yields, stored in ASCII file CHEMICAL.DAT, were

Standard:	89.7	81.4	84.5	84.8	87.3	79.7	85.1	81.7	83.7	84.5
Modified:	84.7	86.1	83.2	91.9	86.3	79.3	82.6	89.1	83.7	88.5

Source: G. E. P. Box, W. G. Hunter, and J. S. Hunter, *Statistics for Experimenters,* Wiley, 1978.

  a Is the experimental design satisfactory? If not, what improvements do you suggest? Comment.

  b Treating the two samples as simple random samples, find a 95% confidence interval for the difference between mean yields from the modified and the standard process. (Use Minitab first to get a description of the two samples from which you should compute the confidence interval with a calculator. Then use the Minitab menu *Stat* ▸ *Basic Statistics* ▸ *2-Sample t* to get the confidence interval. Are the results the same? If not, explain why there are differences.)

  c Discuss the assumption of having taken simple random samples, made in (b). What speaks for it? What speaks against it?

  d If you could change from the standard to the modified process at no expense in time or money, would you recommend doing so? Why or why not?

Exercise for Section 8.4

8.4 Use the data in Exercise 8.3 to test the hypothesis of a zero difference between mean yields from the modified and the standard processes.

Exercises for Section 8.5

8.5 In May to July 1987, a project was carried out at a 3M plant in St. Paul, Minnesota, to determine current process capability of adhesive coater with respect to adhesion values.[7] The product variable measured was "adhesion number" expressed in ounces per inch. Historical data were available on a monthly basis from March 1985 to February 1987 in the form of a sample of size 4 for which adhesion numbers were recorded. These 96 historical measurements are stored in the first column of ASCII file ADHESION.DAT. Each consecutive set of four measurements makes up one subgroup. The mean and standard deviation for all 96 measurements were 55.124 and 6.466, respectively. The pooled standard deviation was 5.686. Minitab is not needed to answer (a) and (b).

  a Why are the standard deviations for all the data, 6.466, and the pooled standard deviation, 5.686, different?

  b What are the control limits for the $\bar{y}$ control chart? Plot the $\bar{y}$ control chart. Is there any pattern to the sequence plot of $\bar{y}$ values? If so, describe it.

  Use Minitab, if necessary, to answer the remainder of this problem.

  c Does the runs test for the $\bar{y}$ values support your impressions described in (a) and (b)?

  d Obtain the *s* chart. Is the sequence of standard deviations stable?

---

[7] The project and some of the data were described in M. J. Bolduc and K. S. DeGolier, "The Expanding Role of Quality in Specialized Training," *Quality Progress,* July 1988, 34–38. The paper also discusses implementation of statistical process control at a 3M plant.

  e Was the process stable from March 1985 to February 1987? If not, describe what seems to have been the problem.

  f Can you use the 24 $\bar{y}$ values to determine if the adhesion values are normally distributed? What are your conclusions?

8.6 Suppose that 150 billings are randomly selected from a large number each working day and that the proportions of incorrect billings are to be recorded. The resulting numbers of incorrect billings for a 20-day period are as follows:

8	8	10	5	9	6	8	7	16	9
11	5	4	9	9	2	5	6	6	9

Do not use Minitab for this problem.

  a What are the unit and the response variable?

  b Obtain a control chart for the proportions of incorrect billings. Is the process stable? If not, which days should be checked for special causes of variation?

  c Suppose the process is stable. Then you can treat the 20 samples of 150 billings each as one random sample of 3,000 billings. Obtain a 95% confidence interval for the process proportion of incorrect billings. Interpret the interval.

  d If any days are flagged for special causes in (b), remove them from your analysis, and repeat (c) with the appropriate changes. Contrast any differences.

8.7 Suppose a company ships merchandise by parcel. Complaints about incomplete shipments have been received, so 75 shipments are checked in detail on every day of a 6-week period. The number of incomplete shipments are stored in ASCII file SHIPMENT.DAT. The data are as follows.

5	7	8	5	9	4	7	11	7	9	8	7	8	10	10
6	9	9	11	13	12	12	10	9	13	13	7	10	9	13

  a What are the unit and the response variable? If the shipment process were stable, what would be your estimate of the proportion of incomplete shipments? What would be the control limits? Draw the control chart. Carry out the runs test.

  b Based on the results in (a) and a visual inspection of the sequence plot of proportions, does the shipment process seem to be stable? If not, describe any patterns you see.

Exercises for All Sections in Chapter 8

8.8 A weighing procedure is known to make chance errors that follow the normal distribution. Thirty-six weighings of the same object gave a sample average of 250 micrograms with a sample standard deviation of 18 micrograms. Based on these results, the following confidence interval for the exact weight (in micrograms) is proposed: 250 ± 5.

  a What is the approximate level of confidence?

  b Do you have to make any assumptions in order to compute your answer in (a)? If yes, what are they and how reasonable are they?

8.9 This is a continuation of Exercise 5.10 (p. 211), relating to monthly returns from

  1. A stock portfolio based on a trading plan devised prior to 1978

  2. The Value Line Composite index, a broadly based stock index based on 1,700 stocks.

To answer (a) to (c), assume that both a random process model and a normal distribution are appropriate. The data are stored in ASCII file PORTFOLI.DAT.

a What is a 95% confidence interval for the process mean of DIFFRNCE? Interpret this interval.

b Does the confidence interval computed in (a) contain 0? What implications would a "yes" answer have? What implications would a "no" answer have?

c Test the hypothesis that the process mean of DIFFRNCE equals 0.

8.10 Company X specializes in printing various types of labels. Since new printing orders require allocation of considerably more resources (such as for equipment set-up) than the repeat orders, the management was interested in determining the proportion of new orders among all printing orders processed by the company. A recent study collected data for the last 50 orders processed. For each order, 0 was recorded if it was a new order and 1 if it was a repeat order. Altogether, there were 24 new orders and 26 repeat orders. Some relevant Minitab output is given in Figure 8.21.

a Name the type of study (cross-sectional or time series), population or process, unit, the response variable, and the type of the response variable (categorical, ordinal, or quantitative).

FIGURE 8.21

```
MTB > NAME C1 'ORDERS'
MTB > PRINT C1
ORDERS
    0   0   0   1   1   1   0   0   0   1   1   1
    1   0   1   0   0   0   0   1   0   0   1   0
    1   1   1   1   0   1   0   1   1   0   1   1
    0   0   0   1   0   1   1   1   0   1   1   1
    0   0

MTB > TSPlot C1

ORDERS  -
        -
  1.000-     456    0123 5    0  3 5678 0 23 56    0 234 678
        -
        -
  0.500-
        -
        -
  0.000+  123    789      4 6789 12 4     9 1  4  789 1    5    90
        +---------+---------+---------+---------+---------+
        0        10        20        30        40        50

MTB > Runs C1

  ORDERS

  K = 0.5200

  The observed no. of runs =   25
  The expected no. of runs =   25.9600
  26 Observations above K    24 below
           The test is significant at   0.7835
           Cannot reject at ALPHA = 0.05
```

b Calculate the 98% confidence interval for the proportion of new orders. Interpret the meaning of this interval in the context of this study. Did you have to make any assumptions to compute this interval? If so, what are they and how reasonable are they? Be specific.

c The management feels that while the confidence level attached to the interval in (b) is reasonable, the interval itself is much too wide. You are asked to collect a new sample in such a way that the error margin of the 98% confidence interval for the proportion of new orders is no more than ±1% (that is, the width of the interval should not exceed 2%). How large a sample must you collect? Will the new study necessarily produce the accuracy desired by the management? If not, what conditions will have to hold for the desired results to be obtained?

8.12

SUPPLEMENTARY EXERCISES

8.11 This is a continuation of Exercise 8.5. The $\bar{y}$ control chart for the historical data from March 1985 to February 1987 does not describe a stable process. In particular, it shows that there was a problem during the summer. After some investigation, it was determined that the "constant-temperature" test room actually was 5°F cooler in the summer, which could lead to different adhesion numbers. The problem was corrected. Specifications for the process were that adhesion numbers be between 40 and 60 ounces per inch. A study was then carried out to determine process capability during May to July 1987. At regular intervals, eight times for each month, samples of size 4 were taken, and the resulting adhesion values were recorded. The data are listed in column 2 in ASCII file ADHESION.DAT. (Note that you *must* read in both columns first. You will then only use column 2.)

a Obtain the $\bar{y}$ chart, using a pooled standard deviation. Visually inspect it. Carry out the runs test for $\bar{y}$ values. Is the process stable?

b Obtain the $\bar{y}$ control chart with Minitab, using the default estimating method for the process standard deviation. Are the control limits much different from (a)?

c Obtain the s chart. Is the process stable?

d Do the adhesion numbers follow a normal distribution?

e Do the $\bar{y}$ values follow a normal distribution?

f Must the answers to (d) and (e) be the same? Briefly justify your answer.

g In terms of adhesion numbers, what is process capability? Is the process capable of meeting specifications?

8.12 Assurance Ltd., a property and casualty insurer, competes by offering above-average service to its brokers and clients.[8] Service level and customer satisfaction can be measured by the number of inquiry and complaint calls coming in and handled by the consumer service department. These calls vary in length and complexity, and they can be stratified by type: claims-related, direct-billing–related, or underwriting-related. Timely and courteous response to these calls is essential to providing a satisfactory service. A study was undertaken to answer the following questions.

1. How do response times vary for each type of call? What is the average response time for each type?

2. Is there any pattern to the number of calls by type?

_____

[8] The name of the company is fictitious to protect confidentiality. The data are real.

It was expected that response time for claims-related and underwriting-related calls would be less than 8 hours and that it would be less than 4 hours for direct-billing–related calls. Furthermore, no time series pattern was expected for the number of calls, regardless of type.

Data were collected during the 30-day period from 3 October to 14 November 1988. Each day, the number of incoming calls was recorded by type. Furthermore, on each day a random sample of five calls was monitored for each type and the sample mean was recorded for each type.[9] Overall then, there were six variables: the number of incoming calls for each type (CL#, DB#, and UW#), and the average length for each type (CL_TIME, DB_TIME, and UW_TIME). The data, listed in the following table, are stored in ASCII file ASSURANC.DAT.

			Calls Data			
Row	CL#	CL_TIME	UW#	UW_TIME	DB#	DB_TIME
1	0	0.0	8	7.0	6	3.0
2	0	0.0	3	9.0	3	3.3
3	4	3.3	0	0.0	21	4.2
4	8	15.8	2	10.0	16	7.0
5	1	15.0	4	8.0	3	8.3
6	1	3.0	7	8.8	21	3.0
7	0	0.0	1	3.0	24	4.5
8	0	0.0	1	3.0	23	4.6
9	1	2.0	2	15.0	37	4.0
10	3	2.3	3	6.7	61	2.8
11	2	4.0	3	11.3	37	4.2
12	3	6.7	4	8.3	48	3.4
13	1	15.0	7	5.5	49	3.6
14	3	5.7	13	3.4	33	3.2
15	3	4.3	11	8.4	42	4.8
16	6	4.4	10	4.5	49	6.0
17	5	5.4	11	5.7	38	5.0
18	6	5.4	12	7.2	56	6.2
19	3	3.7	2	3.0	38	4.8
20	1	35.0	6	8.0	47	9.2
21	0	0.0	4	4.3	37	7.0
22	1	10.0	3	5.0	33	4.6
23	8	4.6	11	5.0	60	4.6
24	2	10.0	5	11.3	16	5.0
25	2	3.5	16	5.2	36	4.6
26	1	5.0	5	9.2	49	4.8
27	3	4.7	3	3.7	44	3.0
28	3	6.0	10	8.6	42	4.6
29	3	3.7	7	7.8	33	5.0
30	7	7.6	14	7.0	34	4.4

---

[9] The five individual numbers entering each sample mean were discarded so that only the sample mean was recorded.

In answering the following questions, restrict your analysis to the variable DB_TIME.

a   What is the unit here? (What does DB_TIME measure? Remember that the available data determine the unit.)

b   Is the process generating DB_TIME stable?

c   Does the variable DB_TIME follow a normal distribution?

d   Do the available data enable you to answer managerial question 1, listed above, with respect to direct billing calls? If yes, provide an answer. If no, what additional information would you need?

e   Assume that a stable process generated DB_TIME. Can you determine the probability that the response time for a direct-billing-related call is less than 4 hours? If yes, provide an answer. If no, why not, and what additional information do you need?

8.13   This is a continuation of the study described in Section 2.11 (PC security at Northern Telecom, p. 36).

The data were collected as follows. After working hours, audits were conducted on 20 days in October and November 1988. For each audit, a different random sample of 60 offices was selected from the 284 offices, and the selected offices were examined. In addition, proper mailing and handling of proprietary information was monitored in the mailroom on these days. Three variables were measured for each audit: (1) DESKS, the number of offices with desks and related furniture not properly secured after regular hours; (2) PCs, the number of offices with personal computers that were left unlocked or where floppy and hard disks containing proprietary information were left unsecured; and (3) MAILING, the number of proprietary documents improperly mailed, classified, or left unsecured in the mailroom. The data, given in the following table, are stored in ASCII file SECURITY.DAT.

Data on Security Auditss							
Audit	DESKS	PCs	MAILING	Audit	DESKS	PCs	MAILING
1	23	12	0	11	27	19	0
2	14	8	0	12	27	11	0
3	26	19	0	13	35	15	0
4	31	4	0	14	23	7	0
5	18	29	0	15	11	4	0
6	37	13	1	16	14	9	0
7	25	17	0	17	19	13	0
8	19	7	0	18	22	7	0
9	37	12	0	19	17	16	0
10	32	15	0	20	28	20	0

a   Consider the number of offices with desks and related furniture not properly secured after regular hours.

i.   What is the unit? If the process were stable, what would be your estimate of the proportion of offices with desks and related furniture not properly secured after regular hours? What would be the control limits? Obtain the control chart.

ii.   Carry out the runs test and comment on the results.

iii.   Based on the results in (i) and (ii), and a visual inspection of the sequence plot of proportions, does the process seem to be stable? If not, describe any patterns you see.

b   Repeat (a) for the number of offices with personal computers that were left unlocked or where floppy and hard disks containing proprietary information were left unsecured.

8.14   A manufacturer of steel products produces steel coils in a process that operates 24 hours each day. One of the critical qualities of these steel coils is their hardness value, which is measured with the widely used Rockwell hardness test. For quite some time now, the process has been stable with respect to the hardness values. The process mean and standard deviation of hardness values are 80 and 4. In order to monitor the process, hourly random samples of size 25 are taken, and the sample mean is calculated. The process is said to need adjustment if the sample mean hardness value is less than 78 or if it is greater than 82.2.

    a Suppose that the process is stable. Making any additional assumptions necessary, what is the probability that the process will need adjustment in any particular hour?

    b Suppose that, unknown to the manufacturer, the process mean hardness has changed to 83, but that the process standard deviation is unchanged. Making the same necessary additional assumptions as in (a), what is the probability that the process will need adjustment in any particular hour?

    c Did you have to make any assumptions to compute the results required in (a) and (b)? If so, what are they, and how reasonable are they?

    d The sample mean for a particular hour is 85, so the process needs adjustment. A search for a cause reveals that the wrong kind of steel was inadvertently used for this hour's production of steel coils. This kind of steel was the reason for the higher hardness values. If another steel coil were to be taken at random from this hour's production, what would be the probability that its hardness value is less than 83? (Discuss any assumptions you had to make in your calculations.)

8.15   Garage Door Inc. produces metal slats that are assembled to produce automatic garage doors that roll up to open. Each slat should have dimension 300 cm by 10 cm, and one garage door consists of 25 slats so that an assembled garage door should be 300 cm wide and 250 cm high. In recent months, the process producing slats has been stable, with the smaller dimension being 10 cm on average and having a standard deviation of 0.5 cm.

    a A garage door that is less than 246 cm high is considered unacceptable. Given the process capability described above, what proportion of garage doors is considered unacceptable?

    b Suppose that the proportion described in (a) should be 1%. Without changing the process average, what must be done to achieve this?

8.16   A further description of the study partly analyzed in Exercise 7.9 (p. 320) is as follows.

       Oxygen Inc. produces oxygen for medical uses and injects it into 244 cu.ft. cylinders.[10] The filling operation consists of transferring the medical oxygen from storage into 64 cylinders at a time. On average three such batches of 64 cylinders are produced each week.

       A study was done to examine the filling process. Data collection proceeded as follows. Each month during the period from August 1985 to June 1988, one batch of 64 cylinders was picked at random, and from this batch one cylinder was then chosen randomly. Three variables were measured on each selected cylinder: (1) O_2, the percentage of oxygen by volume, (2) CH_4, parts per million (ppm) of methane, and (3) H_2O, ppm of water. The acceptable limits for each variable were set by management as follows: (1) 99.6% to 100% for oxygen, (2) 0 to 25 ppm for methane, and (3) 0 to 6.5 ppm for water.

       The study was conducted to answer the following questions:

1. For each variable, is the filling process stable?
2. For each variable, does the content of a cylinder fall within acceptable limits?
3. For each variable, what is the percentage of units that are within acceptable limits?

---

[10] The name of the company was disguised to protect confidentiality. The data are real.

4. What is the percentage of units that fall within acceptable limits on all three variables?

5. What is the percentage of units that fall within acceptable limits on none of the three variables?

It was anticipated that the answers to questions 1 and 2 would be in the affirmative. The data, listed in the following table, are stored in ASCII file OXYGEN.DAT.

Oxygen Data							
Row	O_2	CH_4	H_2O	Row	O_2	CH_4	H_2O
1	0.9969	25.0	0.15	19	0.9964	24.0	1.90
2	0.9980	30.0	0.70	20	0.9960	20.5	0.10
3	0.9975	23.0	0.20	21	0.9960	23.2	0.40
4	0.9976	24.0	0.10	22	0.9968	24.0	0.80
5	0.9973	24.0	0.50	23	0.9970	23.1	0.40
6	0.9973	26.0	0.40	24	0.9970	20.0	0.50
7	0.9974	27.0	0.30	25	0.9970	22.0	0.80
8	0.9972	24.0	0.50	26	0.9970	22.5	0.15
9	0.9973	23.0	0.20	27	0.9960	17.0	0.50
10	0.9970	25.0	0.40	28	0.9965	22.5	0.10
11	0.9976	24.0	0.50	29	0.9966	20.5	0.40
12	0.9972	25.0	0.20	30	0.9966	19.9	0.70
13	0.9960	25.0	0.20	31	0.9961	20.0	0.50
14	0.9960	25.0	0.30	32	0.9961	21.0	0.50
15	0.9972	22.0	0.10	33	0.9967	22.0	1.40
16	0.9960	25.2	0.40	34	0.9969	21.1	1.40
17	0.9960	20.0	0.70	35	0.9965	21.2	0.70
18	0.9960	24.5	0.40				

a Answer questions 1 and 2, if possible, for the variable O_2. If either answer cannot be provided, briefly justify why.

b In light of your answers in (a), was it reasonable to treat the sample of 35 cylinders as a random sample in Exercise 7.9?

c In light of your answers in (a), how reliable are the confidence and prediction intervals computed in Exercise 7.9?

d Answer questions 1 and 2 with respect to the other two variables, if possible.

e Answer questions 3 to 5, if possible.

8.17 A chemical company developed a new and more efficient process to produce a certain type of plastic. With the old process, they had been producing 1,000 kg of this plastic each day on average for many months. Using control charts and other statistical tools, the company closely monitored production levels for the new process. After overcoming some start-up problems, the company decided to do a process capability study. During the next 40 days, the mean yield for the plastic was 1,020 kg with a standard deviation of 70 kg. Visual inspection and a runs test suggested a stable process.

a What are the unit and response variable in this process study?

b Obtain a 95% confidence interval for the new process mean. Do the data strongly suggest that the new process has a higher mean yield than the old?

c Test the hypothesis that the old process mean (1,000 kg) has not changed.

   d Answer (b), but assume that the new process was monitored for 100 days, yielding the same statistics.

   e What assumptions must you make for the confidence intervals in (b) and (d) to be reliable?

8.18 A company producing pharmaceuticals can tolerate 0.06 milligrams per kilogram (mg/kg) of impurities in a raw material needed for one of its products. A laboratory test for impurities exists, but it is subject to experimental error, so the company tests each batch of the pharmaceutical product 10 times. Suppose that the laboratory testing process is stable and that the process mean experimental error is 0.

   The mean of 10 test readings on a particular batch of the raw material is 0.051 mg/kg, with a standard deviation of 0.015 mg/kg.

   a What are the unit and the response variable in this process study?

   b Suppose the company obtained a confidence interval for the process mean amount of impurities that just extends to the "tolerable" amount (0.06 mg/kg). What was the degree of confidence used? What is the degree of confidence in a one-sided interval for the process mean that extends from 0.06 mg/kg to infinity?

   c Using your results in (b), how would you address the question if the data provide sufficient evidence to indicate that the amount of impurities in the batch exceeds 0.06 mg/kg?

   d In carrying out the computations in (b), did you have to make any assumptions?

8.19 A company manufactures and distributes electrical and electronic connectors and components, and it offers more than 10,000 part numbers to a large number of customers. As inventory is shipped from the company's warehouse, each part number is given a separate line on the invoice. Given the wide variety of part numbers and the large customer base, the dollar value per order is often relatively small. It was suspected that the time consumed to pick (count or weigh) an order with a small dollar value was the same as or higher than the time taken to pick an order with a large dollar value. If this suspicion was correct, a change in pricing policy might be needed. A study was undertaken to answer the following question:

   How does the time required to ship orders less than $200 in value differ from the time required to ship orders exceeding $200 in value?

   Data were collected as follows: On each of the 20 working days between 16 October and 17 November 1989, one order less than $200 in value and one order exceeding $200 in value were randomly picked. The picking time (in minutes) was measured for each order, the picking times for orders less than $200 and orders exceeding $200 in value being stored in T_SMALL and T_LARGE, respectively.

   The following questions relate to the Minitab output given in Figure 8.22.

   a Making any necessary assumptions, obtain a 95% confidence interval for the difference between the process means of picking times for large and small orders.

   b Using your answer in (a), do you think that "the time consumed to pick an order with a small dollar value was the same as or higher than the time taken to pick an order with a large dollar value," as was suspected? Briefly justify your answer.

   c Comparing the two dotplots, answer the question in (b).

   d Did you have to make any assumptions for your answers in (a) to (c) to be reliable? Briefly discuss them. How would you use the data to check if these assumptions are reasonable?

   e Assuming that the picking times for large orders are well approximated by a normal distribution, what is the probability that another large order will be picked within 60 minutes?

FIGURE 8.22

```
MTB > NAME C1 'T_SMALL' C3 'T_LARGE'
MTB > DotPlot C1 C3;
SUBC>   Same.


              .   .    .      :.    .:: :.:.    .
         +---------+---------+---------+---------+---------+--T_SMALL


                    .         :. ...: . .:   ..    .    .... .
         +---------+---------+---------+---------+---------+--T_LARGE
      24.0      32.0      40.0      48.0      56.0      64.0

MTB > Describe C1 C3

                    N     MEAN   MEDIAN   TRMEAN    STDEV
T_SMALL            20    39.35    41.00    39.56     5.56
T_LARGE            20    48.30    47.00    48.33     7.87

                  MIN      MAX       Q1       Q3
T_SMALL         27.00    48.00    35.25    43.75
T_LARGE         34.00    62.00    42.25    54.25

MTB > Stop
```

8.20 A company deals in sales and service of a durable consumer good.[11] The company has been in operation for about 1 year, and the management would like to project sales trends into the near future. A study was conducted to answer four questions:

1. What is the average number of consumer goods sold on a given day of the week?
2. Does customer traffic vary according to the day of the week?
3. How does customer traffic affect the number of consumer goods sold?
4. At what time of the month are sales the greatest and the least?

It was expected that average sales would be lowest on Mondays, Tuesdays, Thursdays, and Fridays, highest on Saturdays, and intermediate on Wednesdays. Customer traffic was expected to be level throughout the week, but higher on Saturdays. Sales were expected to increase throughout the month.

   Data were collected for the 101 business days between 1 May 1989 and 31 August 1989. (There were 27 business days in May, 25 in June, 25 in July, and 24 in August.) Each day three variables were measured: (1) SALES (in units), (2) DAY of the week (1 = Monday, 7 = Sunday), and (3) TRAFFIC (the number of potential purchasers visiting the business). The data are stored in ASCII file SALES_DU.DAT.

a How reasonable was the expectation that sales were expected to increase throughout the month?

b How reasonable was the expectation that average sales would be lowest on Mondays, Tuesdays, Thursdays, and Fridays, highest on Saturdays, and intermediate on Wednesdays?

---
[11] The name of the company and the type of product are disguised to protect confidentiality. The data are real.

   c Can the process generating sales be considered to be stable? Briefly discuss your conclusions.

   d Is the distribution of sales values normal? If not, briefly describe its shape.

For questions (e) to (j) assume the process generating sales to be stable, with process mean and standard deviation equalling 2.02 and 1.66.

   e If the process were stable with mean and standard deviation 2.02 and 1.66, what would you expect average sales to be for Fridays? For Saturdays?

   f Consider the data for the 17 Fridays. Since the process is assumed to be stable, the 17 sales values for Fridays can be analyzed as a simple random sample from it. Consider the sample mean sales (1.29) for the 17 Fridays. Making any further necessary assumptions, what is the probability that a simple random sample of size $n = 17$ from a distribution whose mean and standard deviation are 2.02 and 1.66, respectively, results in a sample mean that is 1.29 or less?

   g In light of your answer to (f), do the data for the 17 Fridays contradict the assumption that the sales process is stable? Briefly justify your answer.

   h In addition to assuming that the process is stable, did you have to make further assumptions to compute the answer in (f)?

   i Consider the data for the 15 Saturdays. Since the process is assumed to be stable, the 15 sales values for Saturdays can be analyzed as a simple random sample from it. Consider the sample mean sales (2.67) for the 15 Saturdays. Making any further necessary assumptions, what is the probability that a simple random sample of size $n = 15$ from a distribution whose mean and standard deviation are 2.02 and 1.66, respectively, results in a sample mean that is 2.67 or more?

   j In light of your answer to (i), do the data for the 15 Saturdays contradict the assumption that the sales process is stable? Briefly justify your answer.

   k How does customer traffic affect the number of consumer goods sold?

8.21 In Canada, respiratory therapists are paramedical staff who carry out treatment procedures and tests ordered by physicians on a routine basis 24 hours per day. They are required to keep a log of the type and number of procedures performed in a normal working day. Associated with each specific test is a value called the *productivity unit* that represents the estimated time required to complete the procedure. These productivity unit values are published by Health and Welfare Canada.

     At a hospital in the Greater Toronto Area, a study was done to examine the respiratory therapists' daily workload, their hours worked, and their productivity.[12] Productivity was measured by the Paid Activity Index (PAI), which is the ratio of total productivity units and paid hours. The following questions were to be answered:

  1. What is the productivity of the respiratory department as measured by the PAI?
  2. Can future productivity be predicted?

The average for the PAI was expected to be 36.

     Daily data were gathered for the 61 days in September and October 1990. Values for five variables were recorded each day: productivity units for (1) pulmonary diagnostics, (2) other diagnostics, (3) routine therapeutics, (4) critical care therapeutics, and (5) paid hours.

---

[12] The name of the hospital is disguised to protect confidentiality. The data are real.

The PAI is computed by summing the productivity units for categories (1) to (4) and dividing this sum by the paid hours. The data are stored in ASCII file RESPIRAT.DAT.

a Is the productivity process stable?

b Suppose the data for September came from one random process and the data for October from another. What is a 95% confidence interval for the difference between the respective process means?

c What light does the interval obtained in (b) shed on the question in (a)?

For the remainder of this exercise, assume that the productivity process is stable.

d Do daily PAI values follow a normal distribution? Briefly justify your answer. If no, briefly describe the shape of the distribution.

e Using your assessment in (d), estimate the probability that the PAI on another day exceeds 50.

f Obtain a 92% confidence interval for the process mean of PAI. Briefly interpret this interval in the context of this application.

8.22 Dufferin Aggregates' Milton operation is the largest commercial limestone quarry in Canada, producing some 40 different products. The quarry has been in operation since 1962. The current plant was designed and built during the early 1970s. Due to recent trends toward tighter specifications and severe penalties associated with nonconformance, plant modifications were undertaken in early 1991 to increase plant efficiency and to create a more consistent crushed stone.

A study was done to evaluate the goal of increased consistency by concentrating on product HL3 (9.5 mm clear stone) because of its sensitivity to product specifications and penalties. The method of evaluating a sample of crushed stone is called the *sieve analysis test:* samples are taken and then split into standard sieve sizes by means of controlled vibrating equipment. The weight of material that passes through each sieve is recorded and then expressed as a percentage of the total sample weight. According to Ontario Provinical Standard Specifications, the allowable ranges for these percentages passing standard sieve sizes were as follows:

Standard Sieve Size	% Passing
13.2 mm	96–100
9.5 mm	50–73
6.7 mm	not given
4.75 mm	0–10

The following managerial question was to be answered by the study.

Have the plant alterations resulted in an increase in quality of the HL3 stone as measured by standard government specifications?

There were three screening lines, and it was expected that the results would be consistent across these lines.

Results for HL3 were analyzed for 70 daily samples taken between August and November 1990 (before the alterations) and for 66 daily samples taken between July and November 1991 (after the alterations). Values for several variables were recorded for each sample. The data are stored in ASCII file AGGREGAT.DAT.[13] The following four variables are

---

[13] The data were kindly provided by B. Simpson.

relevant for the present analysis:

Percent of crushed stone passing through a 9.5 mm sieve:

PASS_BEF for the data taken before the alterations

PASS_AFT for the data taken after the alterations

Screening line (1, 2, or 3),

LINE_BEF and LINE_AFT for the data taken before and after the alterations, respectively.

a Was this a population or a process study? Describe the population (or process). What is the unit?

b Is the process generating the percentage of stone passing the 9.5 mm sieve stable *after* the alterations? Justify your answer.

For the remaining questions, assume that the relevant processes were stable.

c Obtain a 98% confidence interval for the change in process means of percentage passing. Interpret this interval in the context of the application. Using this interval, do you think that the observed change was due to chance alone?

d Obtain a 90% confidence interval for the process mean percentage passing *after* the alterations. Using this interval, are you confident that the government specifications are met for the 9.5 mm sieve?

e What information does an examination and comparison of the standard deviations of the percentage passing yield in the context of this study?

f Is the assumption of normality appropriate for the distribution of PASS_AFT? Briefly justify your answer. If not, describe the shape of the distribution.

g Assuming normality, estimate the proportion of samples that would fall within the allowable ranges set by the provincial government both before and after the alterations.

h Using all available information, answer the managerial question. Justify your answer.

SIMPLE REGRESSION ANALYSIS

This chapter will help you solve the following kinds of problems:

- A manager wants to describe the relationship between the sales of a high-volume product and its price.

- You have data on production time and cost for several industrial molds that were recently produced. What is the predicted cost for another mold for which production time is 400 hours?

9.1

INTRODUCTION

In Chapters 4 to 8, you learned how to analyze data on one response variable; you learned a few simple models, their underlying assumptions, how to check these asumptions, and how to use them for estimation and prediction. In Chapters 4 and 7, you learned about cross-sectional studies, and in Chapters 5, 6, and 8, about time series studies.

In this chapter you will learn the *simple regression model*. A regression model shows how the values of one variable are associated with the values of another variable. In particular, you will learn:

- How to model the relationship between a quantitative *response variable* and a *predictor* variable

- Four assumptions underlying the model, and four diagnostic checks to determine whether the assumptions hold

- How to use the model to improve your understanding of the system of which the variables are a part

- How to predict values of the response variable based on the general model

- How to use the predictor variable to predict new values for the response variable

The last ability is particularly useful when the predictor variable is readily available and inexpensive to measure—but the response variable is not. For example, consider the strength of a weld in a car assembly. Its value can be obtained only by destructive sampling. Yet it may be possible to take X-ray measurements, which can be used to predict the weld's strength.

You will learn to apply the regression model both to cross-sectional data and to time series data. The next section introduces an example that is used throughout the chapter. This will be followed by a statement of the regression model and the assumptions underlying it. Some graphical aids will be discussed that are useful in checking the extent to which the assumptions are met. Finally, use of the regression model for estimation and prediction will be discussed.

9.2

AN EXAMPLE OF SIMPLE REGRESSION

Let us start with a problem that arises in auditing.

EXAMPLE 9.1

Gamma Co., a computer software company, provides services related to computer programming projects.[1] Three categories of personnel are employed by Gamma: programmers, senior programmers, and analysts. The company bills clients on the basis of programming time, other services, and expenses. The revenue from a client's project is expected to be related to the cost of programming time. Management made available data on a sample of recently completed projects in order to answer the following questions:

1. What is the revenue from a typical project?

2. What is the relationship between revenue for a project and cost of programming time?

3. Is revenue out of line for any of the projects based on the cost for programming time?

---

[1]This example is adapted from K. W. Stringer and T. R. Stewart, *Statistical Techniques for Analytical Review in Auditing,* Wiley, 1986, pp. 19–22.

FIGURE 9.1
Data for Gamma Co.

ROW	REVENUE	PROGRAM	ROW	REVENUE	PROGRAM
1	2100	1570	19	2510	1980
2	1910	1500	20	2530	2050
3	1870	1640	21	2950	1950
4	1980	1380	22	2560	1830
5	2010	1580	23	2310	2000
6	1960	1570	24	2920	2160
7	2220	1750	25	2750	1780
8	2150	1540	26	2670	2050
9	2430	1650	27	3180	2260
10	2310	1650	28	3060	2110
11	2240	1490	29	2730	1950
12	2350	1670	30	3020	2050
13	2100	1670	31	2530	2060
14	2450	1780	32	2760	2090
15	2600	1650	33	3070	2200
16	2490	1750	34	2650	2010
17	2260	1550	35	3050	2190
18	2050	1620	36	3150	2080

The third question can be answered only if there is a relationship between revenue and programming cost. Since programming cost makes up a substantial portion of the revenue for a project, any out-of-line project should be examined to identify any reasons for the cost.

Figure 9.1 lists the data for a sample of 36 recently completed projects. The data are stored in ASCII file AUDIT.DAT. Variables REVENUE and PROGRAM contain the revenue and the cost of programming time, respectively, for each project in dollars.

Generally, we use the symbol y to denote the response variable in regression analysis, and so y = revenue in this example. Using the summary information on revenue given in Figure 9.2, we can answer question 1 regarding a typical project. Based on the 36 revenue values alone, the sample mean, $\bar{y}$ = $2,497, estimates revenue from a typical project. Since the sample standard deviation for revenue, denoted s_y, is s_y = $386, a 3-standard-deviation limit around the mean extends from $1,339 to $3,655. There is considerable variability in the project revenue values. No project, however, seems to be out of line. Since the 36 projects are a random sample from the population of projects recently undertaken by Gamma Co., prediction of the revenue from another project can be based on the model discussed in Section 4.8:

$$y = \mu_y + \epsilon$$

The sample mean for the 36 revenue values, $\bar{y}$ = $2,497, estimates the population mean μ_y, and their sample standard deviation, s_y = $386, estimates the standard deviation of the residual ϵ. Predicting the revenue value for another one of the company's recently completed projects is thus subject to considerable uncertainty. Since

FIGURE 9.2 Descriptive Statistics and Histogram for REVENUE Values

	N	MEAN	MEDIAN	TRMEAN	STDEV	SEMEAN
REVENUE	36	2496.7	2500.0	2492.8	386.3	64.4

	MIN	MAX	Q1	Q3
REVENUE	1870.0	3180.0	2167.5	2757.5

(a) Descriptive statistics

(b) Histogram

the sample histogram in Figure 9.2 is roughly normal, an approximate prediction interval for another project's revenue is

$$2{,}497 \pm z(386)$$

(For a review of prediction intervals, see Section 7.3, p. 283)

One reason for the variability among project revenues is that the projects do not require an equal amount of programming time. Thus some of this variation can be accounted for by knowing the cost of programming. A scatterplot of revenue versus cost of programming time is given in Figure 9.3. It suggests a moderate relationship between revenue and cost of programming time for the sample of projects. The sample correlation coefficient is a convenient summary for such a scatterplot. Here it is 0.86 (computation omitted). (You may want to review Section 3.4 on correlation.)

If the sample of 36 projects is representative of the population of projects from which it was drawn, it may be possible to generalize from the scatterplot. In particular,

- As cost of programming time for a project increases, so does its revenue.

- The relationship between cost of programming time and revenue is linear; that is, as cost of programming time increases by $1, revenue tends to increase by a given amount.

FIGURE 9.3

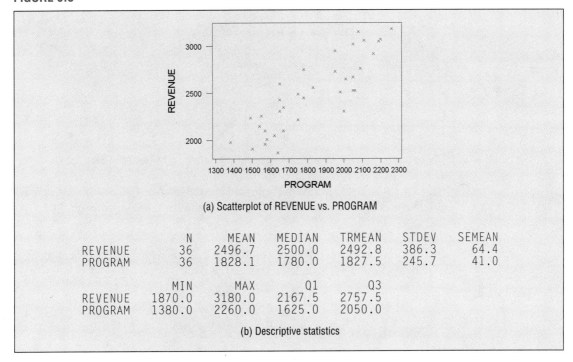

(a) Scatterplot of REVENUE vs. PROGRAM

	N	MEAN	MEDIAN	TRMEAN	STDEV	SEMEAN
REVENUE	36	2496.7	2500.0	2492.8	386.3	64.4
PROGRAM	36	1828.1	1780.0	1827.5	245.7	41.0

	MIN	MAX	Q1	Q3
REVENUE	1870.0	3180.0	2167.5	2757.5
PROGRAM	1380.0	2260.0	1625.0	2050.0

(b) Descriptive statistics

- The relationship is not perfect. For projects with the same given cost of programming time, there is a range of revenue values.

If cost of programming time were known for another project drawn randomly from the same population as the random sample of 36 projects, it might be possible to obtain a reasonably accurate prediction of the project's revenue based on the relationship suggested by Figure 9.3(a).

In the next section, we will introduce the regression model and its assumptions, and we will use another example to illustrate them. Section 9.4 returns us to the Gamma Co. example and discusses how to use regression for its solution.

9.3

THE SIMPLE REGRESSION MODEL AND ITS ASSUMPTIONS

Previous chapters introduced some general notions related to modeling. In particular, Sections 4.8, 5.7, and 6.3 introduced several models. A model is a useful conceptual summary of how we think data are generated. If it adequately describes the data-generating mechanism, then it may shed light on underlying relationships and help explain them. If the data-generating mechanism is expected to remain unchanged for some time, it may also be used for prediction.

All the models discussed so far are of the form,

Actual = Systematic Part + Residual

or

y = Systematic Part + ϵ

where the Residual ϵ represents variation around the Systematic Part that is unpredictable given the *currently* used information.

As we will see shortly, the regression model also fits into this framework. Let us introduce some notation and terminology useful for simple regression.

The **simple regression model** postulates a linear relationship between two variables, x and y. This relationship can be written as

$$y = \beta_0 + \beta_1 x + \epsilon$$

where

y is the **response** variable to be predicted or explained (it is often called the *dependent* variable)

x is the **predictor** or *auxiliary* or *regressor* or *background* variable (it is often called the *independent* variable, an unfortunate terminology)

intercept β_0 is called the *intercept, y-intercept,* or the **constant coefficient**

slope β_1 is the *slope* or the **coefficient of x**

residual ϵ is the **residual** or *error term*. Presence of this term implies that the relationship between x and y is not exact. The average value for ϵ is 0, and its standard deviation is σ. The distribution of ϵ is often normal.

The relationship

$$y = \beta_0 + \beta_1 x + \epsilon$$

fits into our general modeling framework. In the regression model,

Actual = y corresponds to an actual observation on the response variable.

Systematic Part = $\beta_0 + \beta_1 x$ suggests that y systematically varies with x; when $x = 0$, y tends to equal β_0; as x increases by 1 unit, y tends to change by β_1 units.

Residual $= \epsilon$ measures the discrepancy between the Actual value and the Systematic Part. In a good model, the residual is very close to 0 for all units in the population.

Assuming that β_0 and β_1 are known, the following assumptions regarding ϵ are made in the regression model:

Regression Assumptions

Assumption 1: Linearity   For any given value of x, the expected value (that is, the mean) of the residual ϵ is 0.

Assumption 2: Constant Standard Deviation or Homoskedasticity   For any given value of x, the standard deviation of the residual ϵ is σ, a constant that does *not* depend on the value of x.

Assumption 3: Randomness   Knowing the value of the residual for one unit is totally uninformative for predicting the value of the residual of another unit. (In a time series context, we would say that successive residuals are random.)

Assumption 4: Normality   For any given value of x, the distribution of residual values around the regression equation is normal.

In these assumptions, the expression *for any given value of x* is best understood as "in any narrow vertical strip of x values."

Assumption 1 restates, in terms of residuals, the obvious requirement that the regression equation, $\beta_0 + \beta_1 x$, should pass through the center of the scatterplot and capture the Systematic Part of the relationship between x and y.

Assumption 2 says that the variability around the regression equation is the same for *any* value of x. In other words, the uncertainty associated with using $\beta_0 + \beta_1 x$ to predict y is the same, regardless of the x value for which we obtain a prediction. This assumption is also called the assumption of *homoskedasticity*, which means equal variability.

The regression model fits into our usual modelling framework,

Actual = Systematic Part + Residual

where

$$y \quad = \quad \beta_0 + \beta_1 x \quad + \quad \epsilon$$

and assumption 3 captures the requirement that all systematic information, including any time series pattern, should be captured in the Systematic Part. Only *unpre-*

dictable or *random* variability should remain in the Residual part. Given the *currently* used information, this variability is irreducible; some of this variability can possibly be accounted for by considering *additional* information.

Finally, assumption 4 states that the prediction for y given a particular x value, $\beta_0 + \beta_1 x$, is only a best guess and that the uncertainty associated with this guess can be described by a normal distribution. Using assumptions 1 and 2, this normal distribution has mean 0 and standard deviations σ.

These assumptions are checked by the corresponding diagnostic checks, discussed in Section 9.5.

Let us illustrate these assumptions with another example.

EXAMPLE 9.2

Consider a large neighborhood in a North American city. A real estate agent is interested in the relationship between the market value of the homes and their living area.

We define

y = market value of a home (in dollars)

x = living area (in square meters, m²)

The regression model is

$$y = \beta_0 + \beta_1 x + \epsilon$$

where the residual ϵ has mean 0 and standard deviation σ. Its parameters are β_0, β_1, and σ. Let us suppose for now that we *know* the numerical values for β_0, β_1, and σ. (In later sections, we will discuss in great detail how to estimate such a relationship.) In particular, suppose that

$$\beta_0 = 20{,}000 \qquad \beta_1 = 500 \qquad \sigma = 15{,}000$$

The four regression assumptions have several implications for the relationship between the market value, y, and the living area, x:

Assumption 1: Linearity

The Systematic Part of the regression model equals

$$\beta_0 + \beta_1 x = 20{,}000 + 500x$$

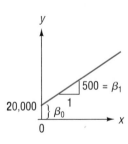

Given the linearity assumption we can interpret the slope parameter $\beta_1 = 500$: A 1-m² difference in the living area (x) between two homes in this neighborhood is associated with an average difference in market value (y) between the two homes of $500.

We can interpret the y-intercept $\beta_0 = 20,000$: Suppose the living area, x, were 0. Then we would expect the market value to equal $20,000 on average. In the context of this example, the interpretation of the y-intercept clearly does not make sense. It reminds us that the living area of homes will always far exceed 0 m².

For homes whose living area is $x = 150$ m², the average market value y is

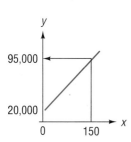

$$20,000 + 500(150) = \$95,000$$

For homes whose living area is $x = 100$ m², the average market value y is

$$20,000 + 500(100) = \$70,000$$

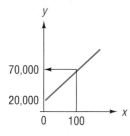

Assumption 2: Constant Standard Deviation

Consider again homes whose living area is $x = 150$; their average market value y is $95,000. The *actual* market value for any one of these homes may differ from $95,000, and the standard deviation $\sigma = \$15,000$ is an indication of how large the difference might be. Thus a 3-standard-deviation prediction interval would extend $3(15,000) = \$45,000$ around the mean, $95,000.

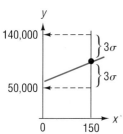

The *same* standard deviation, $\sigma = 15,000$, applies to describe the uncertainty in the regression equation, $20,000 + 500x$, at *any other* value for x. For example, consider again the homes for which $x = 100$; their mean market value y was $70,000. A 3-standard-deviation prediction interval would again extend $45,000 around this mean, $70,000.

It is clear from the size of the standard deviation, $\sigma = 15,000$, that the relationship between market value, y, and living area, x, is quite imprecise.

Assumption 3: Randomness

Suppose that the living area for a particular home was $x = 100$ m². Thus the regression model would predict a market value of $20,000 + 500(100) = \$70,000$. Suppose that the actual market value for this home was $y = \$75,000$. Thus the actual value exceeded the prediction based on the model by the amount of the residual,

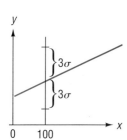

$$\epsilon = y - (\beta_0 + \beta_1 x) = 75,000 - 70,000 = 5,000$$

The randomness assumption implies that the size of the residual for this home has no predictive power at all as to the size of the residual for any other home. The best guess is again that the market value y for any other home is on the regression equation—that is, the best guess for the residual is still 0.

Assumption 4: Normality

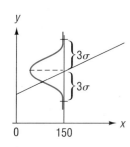

The normality assumption allows us to associate probabilities with prediction intervals. Thus the 3-standard-deviation intervals found above are 0.997 intervals. In other words, chances are 99.7% that the market value is within $45,000 of $70,000 for homes whose living area is 100 m².

Without the normality assumption, we could not associate a probability with any prediction interval found with the regression model.

If we restrict ourselves to homes whose living area was approximately $x = 150$ m², then we can also obtain their proportion of market values y that exceed $100,000. Their average market value is $95,000, the standard deviation of market values is $15,000, and their distribution is normal. Standardizing the value $100,000,

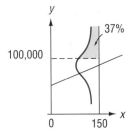

$$z = \frac{100,000 - 95,000}{15,000} = 0.33$$

From Table 4.1 or with Minitab, we find $F(0.33) = 0.63$. Thus the proportion of homes with 150 m² living area whose market value exceeds $100,000 is $1 - 0.63$ or 37%.

Assumptions 1, 2, and 4 imply that, for homes whose living area (x) takes on a given value, the distribution of market values (y) is normal, centered on the regression equation with standard deviation σ. This is true regardless of what the value of x might be. Figure 9.4 illustrates this. Note that the normal distribution of y at any given x value has been turned on its side.

In the discussion of Example 9.2, we have assumed that we know the parameters of the model, β_0, β_1, and σ. This is typically not true, and we must then estimate the parameters from sample data. We have also assumed the assumptions to hold. This may or may not be true in any particular application: We must check the appropriateness of the assumptions with the available data!

Estimation and model checking will be discussed in the next two sections.

FIGURE 9.4
Implications of the Regression Assumptions

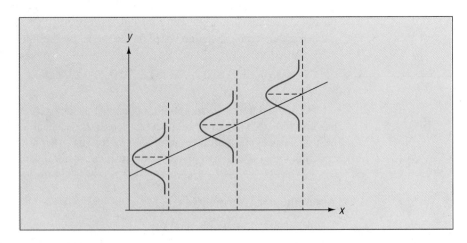

9.4

ESTIMATION OF THE SIMPLE REGRESSION MODEL

In the Gamma Co. example, the population of units consists of all projects recently completed, the response variable y is REVENUE for a project, and the predictor variable x is PROGRAM, the cost of programming time for a project. The simple regression model applied to Gamma Co. implies that

$$\text{Systematic Part} = \beta_0 + \beta_1(\text{PROGRAM})$$

in particular, if two projects differ only in that the programming cost for one is \$1 higher than the programming cost for the other, then the revenues from these two projects are expected to differ by β_1 units.

The residual ϵ implies that the relationship between PROGRAM and REVENUE is not perfect. There are other (possibly unidentifiable) variables that also have an effect on revenue. If PROGRAM is a good predictor of REVENUE, then the residual is small for all projects in the population.

When only sample data are available, the postulated relationship between x and y must be estimated.

The **estimated model** is

$$y = b_0 + b_1 x + e$$

where

b_0 is the estimate from the sample of the intercept β_0

b_1 is the estimate from the sample of the slope β_1

e is the estimate from the sample of the residual ϵ; that is, $e = y - (b_0 + b_1 x)$.

---

fitted value, $\hat{y}$

The estimated systematic part $(b_0 + b_1 x)$ is called the fitted value for y. We use the symbol $\hat{y}$ (said "y hat") to denote the fitted value for y. Thus,

$$\hat{y} = b_0 + b_1 x$$

so the estimated model is

$$y = \hat{y} + e$$

or

Actual = Fitted + Estimated Residual

Having postulated a linear model to relate y to x, we must next obtain numerical values for b_0 and b_1. Values for b_0 and b_1 should be chosen in such a way that the line

$$\hat{y} = b_0 + b_1 x$$

"best" represents the relationship in the scatterplot.

Going back to the scatterplot in Figure 9.3, there are many ways we might draw lines to represent the data, some good and some not. Figure 9.5 gives two such lines. Clearly, line (i) is better than line (ii), but there may be an even better fitted line than (i). What is needed is a criterion to choose a "best" line that can then be obtained by computer.

In some sense, the best line is closest to the data in the scatterplot. The most common criterion for "best" concentrates on *vertical* distances between individual data points and the chosen line. In particular, the *least squares* criterion chooses a line that minimizes the sum of the *squares* of the vertical distances. Figure 9.6 illustrates the vertical distances. (You may want to draw some of the vertical deviations from each line in Figure 9.5 to see which line is better.)

least squares criterion

Minitab easily obtains the best-fitting line based on the least squares criterion. Figure 9.7 displays Minitab regression output. In addition to the values of the estimated intercept and slope, much additional information is given. Most of it is discussed in the remainder of this chapter and the next chapter.

The best fitting line is

$$\hat{y} = 16.6 + 1.357(\text{PROGRAM})$$

and it is superimposed on the scatterplot in Figure 9.8. (You should make sure you know how to draw this line. To practice, draw the line on Figure 9.3 and compare

FIGURE 9.5
Two Possible
Regression Lines
for the Gamma Co.
Data

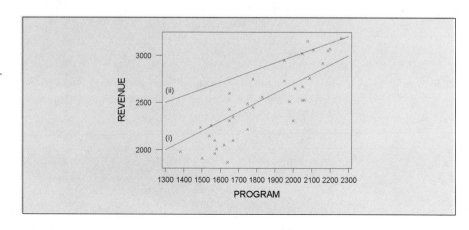

FIGURE 9.6
How to Choose a
Good Line to
Represent a
Scatterplot

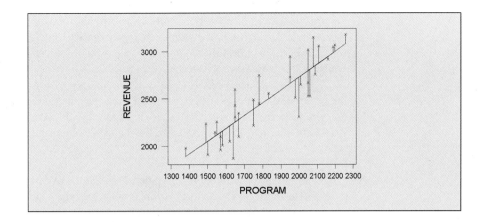

FIGURE 9.7 Regression Output for the Gamma Co. Example

```
The regression equation is
REVENUE = 17 + 1.36 PROGRAM

Predictor        Coef       Stdev      t-ratio          p
Constant         16.6       251.2         0.07      0.948
PROGRAM        1.3567      0.1362         9.96      0.000

s = 198.1       R-sq = 74.5%        R-sq(adj) = 73.7%

Analysis of Variance

SOURCE        DF            SS            MS          F          p
Regression     1       3888947       3888947      99.14      0.000
Error         34       1333653         39225
Total         35       5222600

Unusual Observations
Obs. PROGRAM   REVENUE        Fit  Stdev.Fit   Residual    St.Resid
  23     2000    2310.0     2729.9       40.5     -419.9      -2.17R

R denotes an obs. with a large st. resid.
```

FIGURE 9.8
Regression Line for
the Gamma Co.
Data

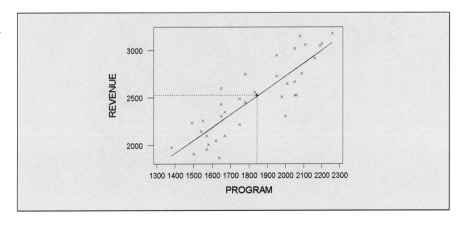

your result with Figure 9.8.) This fitted line is at least a partial answer to question 2 of Example 9.1: What is the relationship between REVENUE and PROGRAM? A full answer to this question requires an evaluation of how strong the relationship is, which will be addressed in the next few sections.

The least squares criterion ensures that the regression equation goes through the center of the data, as measured by the means of the predictor and response variables. This center is marked by a "+" in Figure 9.8. Figure 9.3(b) gives the means for REVENUE and PROGRAM as $2,497 and $1,828, respectively.

> The regression equation is to a scatterplot what the average is to a list of values. The regression equation estimates the average value for the response variable corresponding to each value of the predictor variable.

interpretation of coefficients

The coefficient of the predictor variable x, cost of programming time, 1.357, also called the *slope of x*, can be interpreted as follows: If the costs of programming time for two projects in the sample differed by $1, then the *estimated* revenue for the project with the larger cost of programming time would be $1.36 higher.

Since the data for the Gamma Co. are from an observational study, we must be careful *not* to use a causal interpretation here. For example, we are not justified to conclude that an increase in a project's programming time by $1 would have increased that project's revenue by an estimated amount of $1.36. Such a causal conclusion is justified only for data from an experimental study, controlling for any other variables that might have an influence on the response variable.

extrapolation

If PROGRAM = 0, then $\hat{y} = 16.6$. This value of y is called the *y-intercept*. It has the following interpretation: If no programming time is charged, revenue is estimated to be $16.60. This interpretation may or may not make sense. In this application, it is *very* unreliable because it implies considerable **extrapolation** from the range of values for PROGRAM observed in the sample. To see the dangers of extrapolating beyond the range for which sample data are available, consider Figure 9.9.

FIGURE 9.9
Dangers of Extrapolation

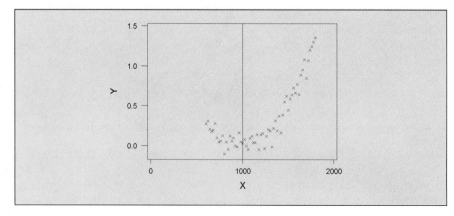

The scatterplot in Figure 9.9 suggests a curvilinear relationship between x and y. If the sample on which the regression equation is based contains data only for x-values between 1,000 and 2,000, a *line* adequately fits the data. It would be entirely inappropriate, however, to extrapolate beyond this range because the linear relationship is only approximately correct and does *not* hold outside the range from 1,000 to 2,000. In particular, it does not hold for values of x below 1,000. If you decide to extrapolate, you must have considerable experience with the context of your data so that you are comfortable with the assumption that the linear relationship is valid outside the range of sample experience.

Figure 9.7 contained a fair amount of regression output. So far, we have only interpreted the values of the coefficients, 16.6 and 1.3567. Before completing our interpretation of Figure 9.7, we must check the adequacy of the assumptions underlying the regression model.

9.5

DIAGNOSTIC CHECKS OF RESIDUALS

The four diagnostic checks discussed in this section are visual aids to judge the adequacy of the four assumptions underlying the regression equation. Their use is essential, in particular, in multiple regression settings with more than one predictor variable. (Multiple regression is discussed in Chapter 10.) Some of these diagnostic checks may seem to be superfluous for simple linear regression, where there is only one predictor variable, x. Although they will be most useful later on, they are most readily explained in the simplest setting.

The four regression model assumptions and the accompanying diagnostic checks are:

Assumption	Diagnostic Check
1. Linearity	Plot of residual vs. x
2. Constant standard deviation	Plot of residual vs. x
3. Randomness of residuals	Control chart, Runs test
4. Normality of residuals	Normal probability plot

These diagnostic checks and their relationship to the assumptions will be discussed shortly. All four checks rely heavily on the residuals. Before turning to the checks, let us briefly discuss the residuals and how they relate to x (PROGRAM) and y (REVENUE). Figure 9.10 lists the following variables for several projects:

REVENUE y, the project revenue

PROGRAM x, the cost of programming time

FITTED $\hat{y}$, the fitted value

RESIDUAL e, the estimated residual

FIGURE 9.17 List of Data Related to the Gamma Co. Example

ROW	REVENUE	PROGRAM	FITTED	RESIDUAL
1	2100	1570	2146.57	46.574
2	1910	1500	2051.61	141.608
3	1870	1640	2241.54	371.540
4	1980	1380	1888.81	91.191
5	2010	1580	2160.14	-150.140
6	1960	1570	2146.57	-186.574
7	2220	1750	2390.77	-170.772
8	2150	1540	2105.87	44.126

	N	MEAN	MEDIAN	TRMEAN	STDEV	SEMEAN
REVENUE	36	2496.7	2500.0	2492.8	386.3	64.4
PROGRAM	36	1828.1	1780.0	1827.5	245.7	41.0
FITTED	36	2496.7	2431.5	2495.9	333.3	55.6
RESIDUAL	36	0.0	49.5	4.0	195.2	32.5

	MIN	MAX	Q1	Q3
REVENUE	1870.0	3180.0	2167.5	2757.5
PROGRAM	1380.0	2260.0	1625.0	2050.0
FITTED	1888.8	3082.7	2221.2	2797.8
RESIDUAL	-419.9	344.9	-160.8	130.2

It also shows some summary statistics for these variables.

To see how the values are related, consider project 1 (ROW 1), for which PROGRAM (x) is \$1,570 and REVENUE (y) is \$2,100. Applying the PROGRAM value in the regression equation,

$$\hat{y} = 16.6 + 1.3567(\text{PROGRAM})$$

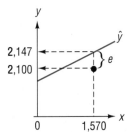

the FITTED value ($\hat{y}$) for project 1 is

$$\hat{y} = 16.6 + 1.3567(1{,}570) = 2{,}146.57$$

The actual revenue is lower than the fitted revenue, and the discrepancy is the estimated residual, RESIDUAL (e),

$$\text{RESIDUAL} = e = y - \hat{y}$$

$$= 2{,}100 - 2{,}146.6 = -46.6$$

Checking the estimated residuals for the first eight projects, you find that some are positive and some are negative. The mean of all 36 estimated residual values is 0, so the regression equation is right on target *on average*. In fact, the least squares criterion ensures that the average of *all* residuals in the sample is always 0.

The standard deviation of estimated RESIDUALs is 195.2, so the actual revenue can be quite discrepant from the fitted revenue. This standard deviation is one useful summary of the goodness of the regression equation. Ideally the standard deviation of residuals should be close to 0.

The four diagnostic checks rely heavily on examining various graphs and statistics related to the residuals, *e*. Let us now discuss them.

Diagnostic Check 1: Adequacy of the Fitted Model to Summarize the Scatterplot

This diagnostic check examines the appropriateness of regression assumption 1, *Linearity:*

> For any given value of *x*, the expected value (that is, the mean) of the residual *ε* is 0.

The phrase "for any given value of *x*" can be operationalized as "in a narrow vertical strip of *x* values."

We need to judge the adequacy of the fitted line, $\hat{y} = b_0 + b_1 x$, for summarizing the data. When the $\hat{y}$ line represents the data, the line goes through the scatterplot and data points lie on both sides of the line. Look at the scatterplot of *y* vs. *x* in Figure 9.11(a). What, if any, pattern do you see with regard to the residuals (the vertical deviations of data points from the line)? Notice that the size of the residuals is not systematically related to the predictor variable value, *x*, or, alternatively, to the $\hat{y}$ value, represented by the line. From this we can conclude that the fitted model passes diagnostic check 1.

When judging whether there is any pattern to the residuals with respect to *x*, or alternatively to $\hat{y}$, our eye must judge the residuals against an upward sloping line in Figure 9.11(a). A slight redrawing of this scatterplot makes the judgment

FIGURE 9.11 Diagnostic Checks 1 and 2 for the Gamma Co. Data

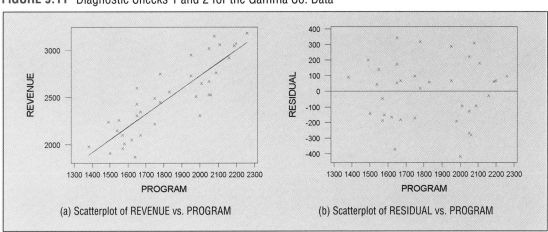

(a) Scatterplot of REVENUE vs. PROGRAM   (b) Scatterplot of RESIDUAL vs. PROGRAM

easier for us, the plot of e (the residual) vs. x in Figure 9.11(b). This plot was obtained from 9.11(a) by rotating the regression line so that it is horizontal: When a residual equals 0, we know that the corresponding point in the scatterplot of y vs. x is on the regression line. Our conclusion from Figure 9.11(b) is the same as before: The fitted model passes diagnostic check 1.

Diagnostic check 1 is passed when the residuals average to 0 in any "small" vertical strip on the scatterplot of y vs. x (or, alternatively, in the scatterplot of residual vs. x). In Figure 9.12(a), the scatterplot of e vs. x in Figure 9.11(b) is subdivided into three vertical strips of *roughly equal numbers of data points,* corresponding to low, intermediate, and high values of x. For practical purposes the number of points in a vertical strip must not be too small. Three vertical strips were used here. But with more data, we would have used more vertical strips. In Figure 9.12(a), the average of the residuals is approximately 0 in each of the vertical strips, and so diagnostic check 1 is passed. The descriptive statistics for each strip, given in Figure 9.12(b), support the visual impression: The means are all close to 0. One way of judging closeness to 0 is by comparing the mean of the residuals in each strip with the overall variability of the residuals. If the strip means are relatively small in comparison to this variability, then, practically speaking, the means are virtually 0. In Figure 9.12(b), the means are no larger than about 13 in absolute value and the magnitude of the variability is about 200; so the means are virtually 0.

Let us look at a situation where diagnostic check 1 would not be passed. Figure 9.13(a) presents a scatterplot whose main feature is that the relationship between x and y is not linear. Thus a line fitted to the data is not a good description. Judging from the y vs. x plot, when $\hat{y}$ values are low or high, the actual y values

FIGURE 9.12 Diagnostic Checks 1 and 2 for the Gamma Co. Data, Continued

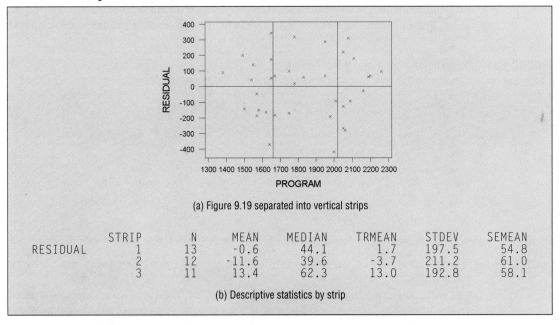

(a) Figure 9.19 separated into vertical strips

	STRIP	N	MEAN	MEDIAN	TRMEAN	STDEV	SEMEAN
RESIDUAL	1	13	-0.6	44.1	1.7	197.5	54.8
	2	12	-11.6	39.6	-3.7	211.2	61.0
	3	11	13.4	62.3	13.0	192.8	58.1

(b) Descriptive statistics by strip

FIGURE 9.13 Example in Which the Linearity Check Is Failed

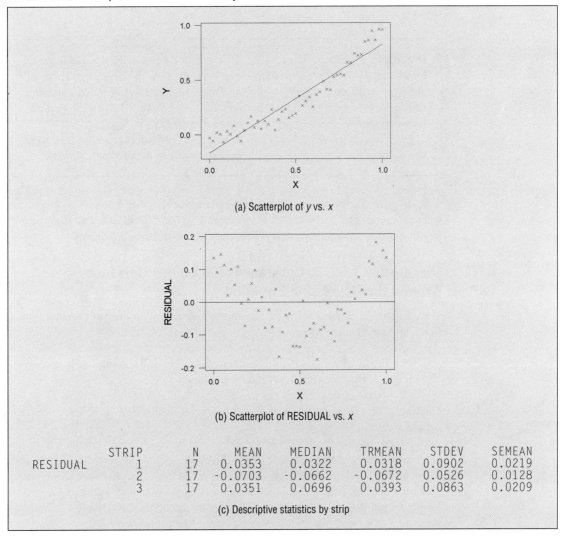

(a) Scatterplot of *y* vs. *x*

(b) Scatterplot of RESIDUAL vs. *x*

	STRIP	N	MEAN	MEDIAN	TRMEAN	STDEV	SEMEAN
RESIDUAL	1	17	0.0353	0.0322	0.0318	0.0902	0.0219
	2	17	-0.0703	-0.0662	-0.0672	0.0526	0.0128
	3	17	0.0351	0.0696	0.0393	0.0863	0.0209

(c) Descriptive statistics by strip

tend to be above the line, and the corresponding residuals tend to be positive. But when $\hat{y}$ values are intermediate, the actual *y* values tend to be below the line, and so the corresponding residuals tend to be negative. The scatterplot of *e* vs. *x* in 9.13(b) represents the failure of diagnostic check 1 very clearly: There is a clear pattern to the way the residuals vary around the line at 0. For low and high values of *x*, the residuals tend to be positive, for intermediate values, they tend to be negative. The descriptive statistics for each of three strips, given in Figure 9.13(c), support the visual impression: The means are large in comparison to the variability in the residuals, particularly in the second strip.

Since a model postulating a linear relationship between *x* and *y* is not adequate, diagnostic check 1 is not passed and a different model should be tried. (In

Chapter 10, we discuss how to model a nonlinear relationship with multiple regression.)

Diagnostic Check 1: Linearity   To carry out this check, we use three to five vertical strips on the scatterplot of e versus x, with the same number of about 15 or more data points in each. Diagnostic check 1 is failed when the residuals do not approximately average to 0 in each vertical strip, in particular when there is a pattern to these nonzero averages.

When diagnostic check 1 is passed, the regression equation is a good summary of the scatterplot, regardless of the value of the predictor variable x.

In general, use at least three vertical strips. The strip boundaries are somewhat arbitrary: The strips are an aid to seeing a potential pattern, and it is the pattern that is important, not exactly where the strip boundaries are drawn.

Diagnostic Check 2: Constancy of Standard Deviation Around the Regression Equation

This diagnostic check examines the appropriateness of regression assumption 2, *Constant Standard Deviation:*

> For any given value of x, the standard deviation of the residual ϵ is σ, a constant that does *not* depend on the value of x.

The term "for any given value of x" can be operationalized as "in a narrow vertical strip of x values."

When diagnostic check 1 is passed, as in the case of the Gamma Co. example, we can proceed to diagnostic check 2. It examines if the *vertical dispersion* of data points around the regression equation is about the *same anywhere* along the regression equation. When this is so, the uncertainty associated with using a $\hat{y}$ value for prediction does not depend on the value of the predictor variable x. The same scatterplot of e vs. x, used for diagnostic check 1, is useful here.

If the dispersion around the regression equation does not depend on the value of x, then the e vs. x scatterplot would show roughly the same amount of dispersion, regardless of the fitted value. Just as in Figure 9.12, it is again advisable to use three vertical strips with about the same number of data points. If the variability of the data points is roughly the same in all three segments, then diagnostic check 2 is passed. Examining Figure 9.12 and the accompanying descriptive statistics, we can pass diagnostic check 2 for the Gamma Co. example.

Diagnostic check 2 would not be passed, for example, if the variability in the residuals increased or decreased with x. An example of such a situation is given in Figure 9.14. The visual impression is very strong that the variability in the residuals increases with x. The descriptive statistics for four vertical strips support this impression: The standard deviations of the residuals steadily increase from 0.036 in strip 1 to 0.31 in strip 4. Thus, diagnostic check 2 fails for the data shown in this figure.

FIGURE 9.14 Data that Fail Diagnostic Check 2: Constancy of Standard Deviation

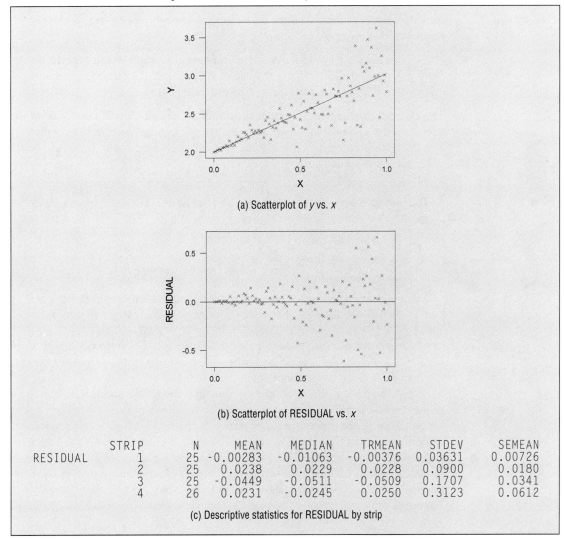

(a) Scatterplot of *y* vs. *x*

(b) Scatterplot of RESIDUAL vs. *x*

	STRIP	N	MEAN	MEDIAN	TRMEAN	STDEV	SEMEAN
RESIDUAL	1	25	-0.00283	-0.01063	-0.00376	0.03631	0.00726
	2	25	0.0238	0.0229	0.0228	0.0900	0.0180
	3	25	-0.0449	-0.0511	-0.0509	0.1707	0.0341
	4	26	0.0231	-0.0245	0.0250	0.3123	0.0612

(c) Descriptive statistics for RESIDUAL by strip

Diagnostic Check 2: Constancy of Standard Deviation To carry out this check, we use three to five vertical strips on the *e* vs. *x* scatterplot, with the same number of about 15 or more data points in each. Diagnostic check 2 is failed when the standard deviation of the residuals is not approximately the same in each vertical strip, in particular when there is a pattern to the changing variability.

When diagnostic check 2 is passed, the uncertainty about the adequacy of the regression equation is the same regardless of the value of the predictor variable *x*.

Diagnostic Check 3: Randomness of Residuals

This diagnostic check examines the appropriateness of regression assumption 3, *Randomness of Residuals:*

> Knowing the value of the residual for one unit is totally uninformative for predicting the value of the residual of another unit. (In a time series context, we would say that successive residuals are random.)

The check of randomness is important for time series data. It is not necessary if the data are cross-sectional and if we are sure that the sample was a random sample. It is still advisable to carry out this check in a cross-sectional study: It just might uncover some surprising features of the data.

Diagnostic Check 3: Randomness of Residuals   The randomness check for the series of residuals consists of

- Visual impression of their sequence plot
- The control limits
- The runs test

When the randomness check is passed, there is no information in the time series of residuals that could be used to improve the simple regression model.

Results for the randomness check in the Gamma Co. example are given in Figure 9.15. The results support randomness. This is not surprising since the Gamma Co. data are from a cross-sectional study.

Figure 9.16 shows an example that fails the randomness check. The scatterplot of the response variable y versus the predictor variable x in Figure 9.16(a) suggests that the linearity and constant standard deviation checks are adequate for these data. A scatterplot does not typically give information about the order in which the units were collected. In this scatterplot, the points representing the units have been labeled A through Z to indicate their time series order. Earlier observations tended to be below the line and later observations above the line. The sequence plot of the residuals in Figure 9.16(b) confirms this: The first 13 residuals tended to be negative, and the last

FIGURE 9.15 Gamma Co. Example: Randomness Check

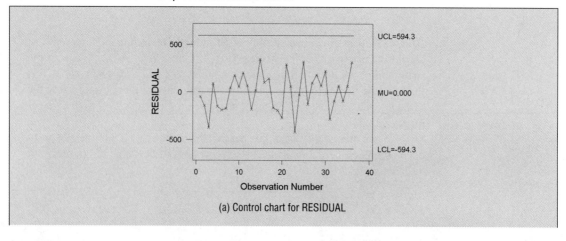

(a) Control chart for RESIDUAL

```
RESIDUAL

K = -0.0000

The observed no. of runs =  16
The expected no. of runs =  18.7778
20 Observations above K   16 below
          The test is significant at   0.3416
          Cannot reject at alpha = 0.05
```

(b) Runs test

FIGURE 9.16 Data That Fail Diagnostic Check 3: Randomness

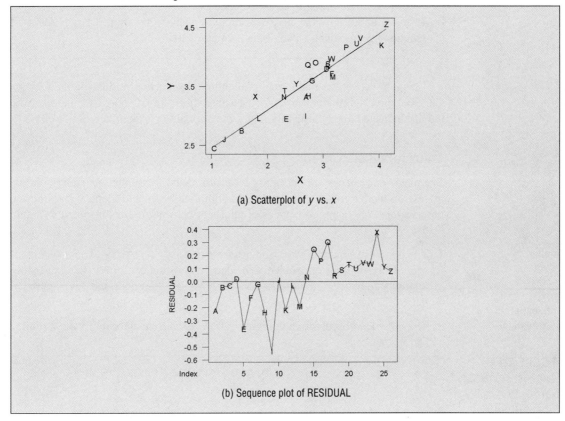

(a) Scatterplot of *y* vs. *x*

(b) Sequence plot of RESIDUAL

13 tended to be positive. There was a pronounced shift upward in the regression equation in the middle of the time series. It would be important to find a reason for this.

When successive residuals are related over time, the model specification is not entirely satisfactory. The model must be refined so that the time series aspect is captured in the Systematic Part and not in the Residual part.

Diagnostic Check 4: Normality of Residuals

This diagnostic check examines the appropriateness of regression assumption 4, *Normality of Residuals:*

404   CHAPTER 9 Simple Regression Analysis

For any given value of x, the distribution of residual values around the
regression equation is normal.

Once diagnostic checks 1, 2, and 3 are passed, normality of the residuals should be
checked. If residuals follow a normal distribution, then prediction intervals for the
response variable can be obtained. The visual tool for diagnostic check 4 is the normal probability plot of residuals. (Section 4.6, page 134, discussed the normal
probability plot. You should review that section before reading on.)

Diagnostic Check 4: Normality of Residuals   To carry out this check, obtain a normal probability plot for the residuals.

    When the normality check is passed, probabilistic statements are read-
ily made about how far an observation is likely to be from the regression
equation for any given value of the predictor variable x.

    Figure 9.17 gives the normal probability plot for the residuals in the Gamma
Co. example. The plot is satisfactory because there are no serious deviations from
the line expected under normality. Thus, the normality check is passed as well.

Unusual Observations

The diagnostic checks are necessary to ensure that all assumptions underlying the
regression model are adequately met. In addition, we should identify any unusual
observations. There are three types of unusual observations, as illustrated in Figure
9.18.

outlier

1. The *outlier* in Figure 9.18(a) is unusual since its value on the y variable is not in
   accordance with the remainder of the data: It does not conform to the regression
   relationship between x and y. Its x value, however, does not stand out from the
   rest of the data.

**influential
observation**

2. The *influential* observation in Figure 9.18(b) is unusual since its x value is quite

FIGURE 9.17
Diagnostic Check 4:
Normal Probability
Plot of RESIDUAL
for the Gamma Co.
Example

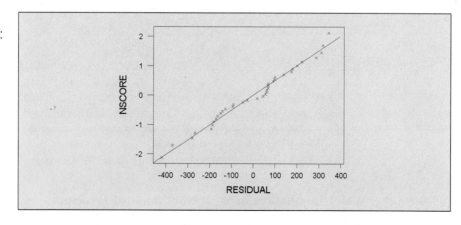

FIGURE 9.18
Unusual Observations

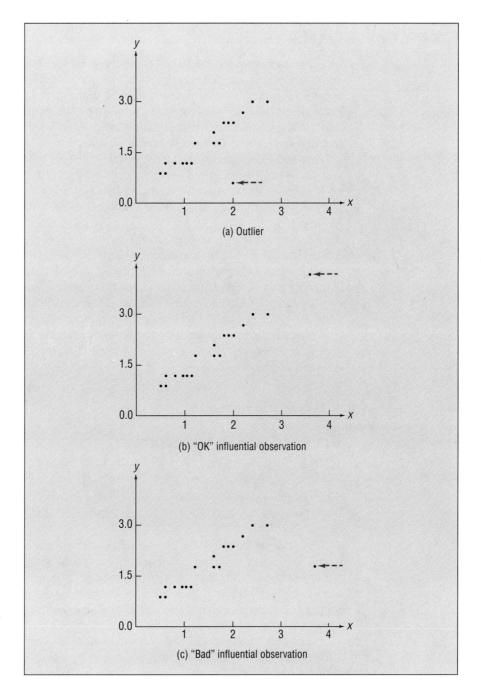

(a) Outlier

(b) "OK" influential observation

(c) "Bad" influential observation

different from the x values in the remainder of the data. Its y value conforms to the regression relationship between x and y.

3. Finally, the *influential* observation in Figure 9.18(c) is unusual since its x value is quite different from the x values in the remainder of the data *and* its y value does not conform to the regression relationship between x and y.

It is important for you to be able to recognize an unusual observation and to describe how it is unusual. You can then look for possible assignable causes as to why the observation is different from the bulk of the data. Apart from this, an influential observation as in Figure 9.18(b) does not affect the regression equation much, whereas an influential observation as in Figure 9.18(c) can seriously distort the regression output. Minitab flags unusual observations at the end of the regression output: Outliers are marked by the symbol "R" and influential observations by the symbol "X." When there is more than one influential observation, it is often difficult for Minitab (or any other software package) to identify influential observations automatically: Various graphical tools like the diagnostic checks are needed to identify them.

For example, at the bottom of Figure 9.7 (page 393), observation 23 is flagged because of its large standardized residual, St. Resid = -2.17. Minitab flags outlying observations when the absolute standardized residual is above 2. When discussing control charts, we had indicated that an observation more than 3 standard deviations from the mean warrants detailed examination for unusualness. Thus, we will not examine observation 23 more closely in this example.

Since none of the observations is unusual in the Gamma Co. example, the answer to question 3 of Example 9.1 is that none of the projects have programming costs that are out of line.

9.6

FURTHER EVALUATION OF THE REGRESSION MODEL

When all four diagnostic checks are satisfactory, the postulated model is adequate. It can then be evaluated further, and the results can be used for estimation and prediction.

If some of the diagnostic checks are failed, causes for the violations must be found. The causes often point to improvements of the model. If no improvements can be made, some or all of the regression output is unreliable, depending on the severity of the violation. If there are unusual observations, it is important to search for possible assignable causes that make these observations different from the bulk of the data.

Figure 9.19 reproduces the regression output for Gamma Co. in Figure 9.7. Various pointers were added to the figure, indicating where the particular part of the output is discussed. Some of the output [t-ratio, p, R-sq(adj), and St.Resid] will be discussed only in Chapter 10; some of it will not be discussed in this book. The values for PROGRAM and REVENUE for the unusual observation were, of course,

FIGURE 9.19 Regression Output for the Gamma Co. Example

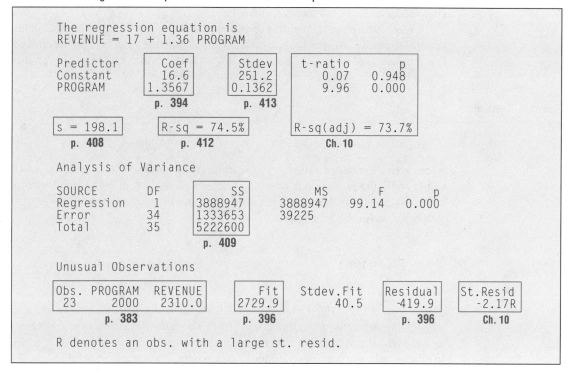

listed in Figure 9.1, the fitted value can be obtained by using these values in the regression equation, and the residual can then be computed.

Overall Evaluation

When we first introduced the Gamma Co. example in Section 9.2, we discussed prediction of revenue for another project drawn from the same population as the sample of 36 projects, but *without* using the relationship between revenue (y) and cost of programming time (x). A reasonable point estimate for its revenue was the sample mean $\bar{y} = \$2,497$, and a measure of uncertainty for this estimate was the sample standard deviation of revenues, $s_y = \$386$. This prediction is based on using the prediction model

$$\text{Actual} = \text{Sample Mean} + \text{Estimated Residual}$$

or

$$y \quad = \quad \bar{y} \quad + \quad e$$

where e is the deviation of y from $\bar{y}$: $e = y - \bar{y}$. The larger the sample variability in these deviations, the more uncertainty there is in using $\bar{y}$ for prediction. A convenient measure for this sample variability is the sample standard deviation of revenue values around their mean, $s_y = \$386$.

When using the relationship between revenue (y) and cost of programming time (x) to predict another project's revenue, the predicted value, which depends on that project's cost of programming time, is on the regression equation. This prediction is based on using the estimated prediction model

standard deviation of residuals, s_e

$$y = \hat{y} + e$$

where e (the estimated residual) is the difference between y (the unknown actual value) and $\hat{y}$ (the prediction from the regression equation). A measure of uncertainty for the value of e is the sample standard deviation of *residuals* around the regression equation for the 36 projects:

$$s = s_e = 198.1$$

(see Figure 9.19).[2] The variability around the estimate is considerably reduced when going from the model that does not use the regression equation to the regression model—the sample standard deviation decreases from $s_y = \$386$ to $s_e = \$198$. In other words, the predictor variable cost of programming time is useful.

---

[2]You may wonder at this point why the standard deviation of residuals reported by Minitab is 198.1 and not 195.2, the standard deviation of RESIDUALs obtained from the *Stat* ▶ *Basic Statistics* ▶ *Descriptive statistics* menu in Figure 9.10. The relationship between the two figures is as follows.
The first number was obtained from the formula

$$s_e = \sqrt{\frac{\Sigma(y_i - \hat{y}_i)^2}{n-2}} = \sqrt{\frac{1{,}333{,}653}{36-2}} = 198.05$$

The second number was obtained from the formula

$$\sqrt{\frac{\Sigma(y_i - \hat{y}_i)^2}{n-1}} = \sqrt{\frac{1{,}333{,}653}{36-1}} = 195.2$$

The difference between the two formulas is the denominator, which is $n-2$ for the first formula and $n-1$ for the second. The first formula is preferable in simple regression where there are 2 variables (the predictor and response variables). A complete explanation of the reason for this is given, for example, in Kleinbaum, Kupper, and Muller (1988). It is related to prediction with the regression equation. This prediction is best based on the sample standard deviation as computed from the first formula. This is why Minitab reports $s = 198.1$.

> The **standard deviation of residuals** (s_e) is to the regression equation ($\hat{y}$) what the standard deviation of a variable (s_y) is to the mean ($\bar{y}$).

Figure 9.20 graphically depicts how regression reduces variation. Figure 20(a) shows the variation in y when the predictor variable x is *not* used for prediction. In that case, prediction of another response variable value is based on the histogram of y, shown in Figure 9.20(a). The sample mean $\bar{y}$ is a reasonable point estimate for prediction. The right panel of Figure 9.20(a) was obtained from the histogram of y values. It shows the deviation of each individual y-value from the sample mean $\bar{y}$. When the regression equation is *not* used for prediction, deviations from the sample mean are indicative of the size of prediction error. An overall summary for these deviations is the sum of squared deviations around the mean, often **total sum of squares** called the "total sum of squares" (Total SS), where

$$\text{Total SS} = \sum_{i=1}^{n}(y_i - \bar{y})^2$$

The right panel of Figure 9.20(a) was plotted as a y vs. x plot (for convenience only) so that comparison with Figure 9.20(b) is easier. If the y-values had been displayed in ascending order or in any other order, their deviations from $\bar{y}$, and thus the total sum of squares, would have been the same. Another convenient summary measure for these deviations is the standard deviation of y, s_y, where

$$s_y = \sqrt{\dfrac{\sum\limits_{i=1}^{n}(y_i - \bar{y})^2}{n-1}}$$

Figure 9.20(b) shows variation when the predictor variable x *is* used for prediction. The left panel displays the sample mean $\bar{y}$ [as a horizontal line just as in part (a)] and the regression equation $\hat{y}$. When using the predictor variable x for prediction, the regression equation is used to get point predictions. The right panel displays the regression equation and the deviations of the actual y values from it ($y - \hat{y}$). They are much smaller than the deviations in Figure 9.20(a), where x was *not* used to obtain predictions. An overall summary for these deviations is the sum of squared de- **error sum of squares** viations around the regression equation, often called the "error sum of squares" (Error SS):

$$\text{Error SS} = \sum_{i=1}^{n}(y_i - \hat{y}_i)^2$$

FIGURE 9.20 Reduction of Variation When Using Regression

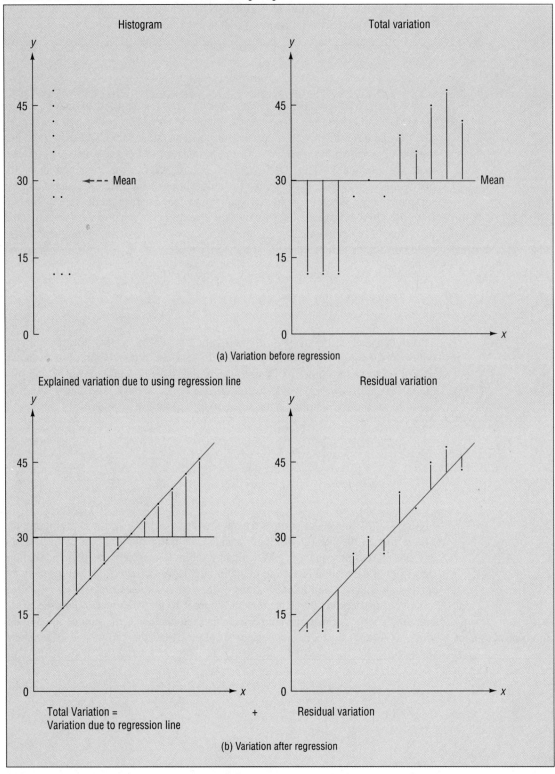

In fact, the deviations of the y values from the regression equation ($e = y - \hat{y}$) are smaller than the deviations of the y values from the mean ($y - \bar{y}$) by an amount that is the difference between the regression equation and the mean ($\hat{y} - \bar{y}$). [These deviations are accounted for because the regression equation uses the predictor variable x. They are displayed in the left panel of Figure 9.20(b).] A convenient summary for the deviations of y values from the regression equation ($e = y - \hat{y}$) is the standard deviation around the regression equation, s_e,

standard deviation of residuals

$$s_e = \sqrt{\frac{\sum_{i=1}^{n}(y_i - \hat{y}_i)^2}{n - 2}}$$

The smaller s_e is than the standard deviation of y, s_y, the more useful x is for prediction.

Another useful measure for evaluating the goodness of the regression equation is how well the actual values for the response variable y in the sample would have been predicted from the regression equation (that is, from the $\hat{y}$ values). Figure 9.21 gives a plot of actual values y (REVENUE) versus $\hat{y}$ (FITTED) for the Gamma Co. example. It also suggests that the predictor variable is useful in the Gamma Co. example.

The correlation between REVENUE (y) and FITTED ($\hat{y}$),

$$R_{y,\hat{y}} = 0.863$$

FIGURE 9.21 Gamma Co. Example, Continued

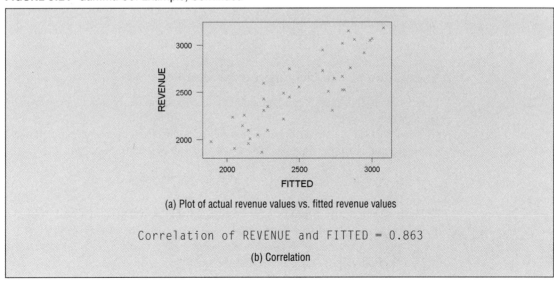

(a) Plot of actual revenue values vs. fitted revenue values

Correlation of REVENUE and FITTED = 0.863

(b) Correlation

is also given in Figure 9.21. The square of this correlation is $R^2 = (0.863)^2 = 0.745$, which is given in the Minitab output in Figure 9.19 in percentage form, R-sq $= R^2 = 74.5\%$. The closer the correlation is to 1—and thus R^2 to 100%—the better the regression model is for prediction.

---

coefficient of determination

The **coefficient of determination** equals R^2, which in turn is the square of the correlation between fitted and actual values of the response variable, $R_{y,\,\hat{y}}$. It turns out that

$$R^2 = 1 - \frac{\displaystyle\sum_{i=1}^{n}(y_i - \hat{y}_i)^2}{\displaystyle\sum_{i=1}^{n}(y_i - \bar{y})^2}$$

$$= 1 - \frac{\text{Error SS}}{\text{Total SS}}$$

Thus, R^2 measures the proportion of the variation in the response variable y that is accounted for by the predictor variable x.

Let us defer discussion of R-sq(adj), also given in Figure 9.19, to the chapter on multiple regression. In this book, we will not discuss the "Analysis of Variance" regression output shown in Figure 9.19.

Estimation of Coefficients: Large Samples

The results in this section are applicable when the sample size n is large. It usually suffices that $n > 30$.

In Section 9.2, we had postulated the relationship between revenue and cost of programming time to be linear for the population of Gamma Co. projects,

$$\text{REVENUE} = \beta_0 + \beta_1(\text{PROGRAM}) + \epsilon$$

Using the sample of 36 projects, we estimated this postulated relationship by the method of least squares (see Section 9.4) as

$$\text{REVENUE} = b_0 + b_1(\text{PROGRAM}) + e$$

The values for b_0 and b_1 are given in Figure 9.19, and the relevant portion of Figure 9.19 is reproduced here:

```
Predictor        Coef        Stdev        t-ratio           p
Constant         16.6        251.2           0.07       0.948
PROGRAM        1.3567       0.1362           9.96       0.000

s = 198.1      R-sq = 74.5%       R-sq(adj) = 73.7%
```

The constant coefficient is b_0 and its value, 16.6, was obtained from the sample of 36 projects. The value of b_0 is a point estimate of the unknown constant coefficient in the population, β_0.

The coefficient of PROGRAM is b_1 and is used as a point estimate of the unknown coefficient of PROGRAM in the population, β_1. In Section 9.4, $b_1 = 1.357$ was interpreted as follows: If the costs of programming time for two projects in the sample differed by \$1, then the *estimated* revenue for the project with the larger cost of programming time would be \$1.36 higher.

Let us now discuss the two columns headed "Coef" and "Stdev." (The columns headed "t-ratio" and "p" will be discussed in Chapter 10.)

The entries under "Coef" are the values for b_0 and b_1. So we have the estimated regression model,

REVENUE = 16.6 + 1.36(PROGRAM) + e

or

$\hat{y} = 16.6 + 1.36(\text{PROGRAM})$

standard error of coefficient

The entries under "Stdev" are estimated standard errors referring to the coefficients immediately to the left.[3] When estimating the coefficients β_0 and β_1 in the postulated regression model from the corresponding sample values, b_0 and b_1, there is uncertainty and the standard error is a measure of this uncertainty. With respect to the Gamma Co. example, the estimate of β_1, the coefficient of PROGRAM, is $b_1 = 1.356$, and its standard error is 0.136.

When the diagnostic checks of the regression assumptions in Section 9.5 are acceptable, the standard error can be used to compute confidence intervals for the coefficient.

The general formula for finding confidence intervals is:

confidence interval for coefficient

$$\begin{pmatrix} \text{Point} \\ \text{Estimate for} \\ \text{Coefficient} \end{pmatrix} \pm (\text{Multiple}) \begin{pmatrix} \text{Estimated} \\ \text{Standard Error} \\ \text{for Coefficient} \end{pmatrix}$$

---

[3]It may be useful here to review the standard error of the mean, discussed in Chapter 7, in particular, Sections 7.2 and 7.3.

The multiple is chosen so that we can have a given degree of confidence in the interval. When the sample size is large ($n > 30$), the appropriate multiple comes from a normal distribution table (see Table 4.1 or use the *Calc ▸ Probability Distributions ▸ Normal* menu in Minitab). When the sample size is less than 30, the resulting intervals are somewhat too tight. The exact results for small sample sizes are given in Section 10.11.

For a 68% confidence interval, the appropriate z-value is 1, and for a 95% confidence interval, it is 2. These multiples are used in the following two statements:

1. The probability is 68% (or, we have 68% confidence) that β_1, the true value of the coefficient of PROGRAM, lies within limits $1.356 \pm 1(0.136)$, or between 1.220 and 1.492.

2. The probability is 95% that β_1 lies within limits $1.356 \pm 2(0.136)$, or between 1.084 and 1.628.

Similar statements could also be made about the constant coefficient, β_0, estimated by $b_0 = 16.6$ with standard error 251.3.

Note that the statements in (1) and (2) above refer to the unknown regression coefficients β_0 and β_1, not to inferences or predictions regarding individual observations. For the most part, managers are more often concerned with inferences about observations, such as the revenue from another project with a given cost of programming time, rather than inferences about the unknown regression coefficients β_0 and β_1. Such inferences will be discussed in Section 9.7.

violations of the regression assumptions

Let us mention the influence of violations of the regression assumptions. Violation of an assumption is, of course, a matter of degree. Judgment is needed to determine the seriousness of the violation, and this book should help you improve your judgment skills.

Let us first mention the randomness assumption. When it is not reasonable, the reliability of the statistics in the regression output depends on the type of time series pattern in the residuals. For example, Figure 9.16(b) showed a sequence plot in which the residuals are not random, and the regression equation is shifting over time. In this case, none of the regression statistics would be appropriate when applying the regression results to the behavior of the process in the near future, even if the other three assumptions appear reasonable.

When the randomness assumption is reasonable, the following comments apply:

- If the linearity assumption is inadequate, then all regression output is useless. In particular, the sample regression equation,

$$\hat{y} = b_0 + b_1 x$$

is then meaningless.

- If the linearity assumption is reasonable, then the coefficients and the regression equation can be safely interpreted as described earlier and used.

Margin figure:

β_1

1.220 1.356 1.492

b_1

├── 68% CI ──┤

- If both the linearity and the constant standard deviation assumptions are reasonable, then we can also safely use the standard errors of the coefficients and obtain confidence intervals. Furthermore, we can use the standard deviation around the regression equation (s_e) and the coefficient of determination (R^2) to evaluate the overall goodness of the model.

- If the linearity, constant standard deviation, and normality assumptions are reasonable, then we can also safely obtain prediction intervals, as outlined in the next section.

9.7

PREDICTION FOR INDIVIDUAL OBSERVATIONS: LARGE SAMPLES

This section introduces prediction of individual observations. These results are correct only for large samples (when $n > 30$). Small-sample results are given in Section 10.11.

To illustrate the ideas, suppose that programming for another project has just been completed and that the cost of programming time was $2,000. The following question has been raised:

> What is a **point prediction** of this project's revenue, and what is a **prediction interval** for it?

The new project was completed in the same system as the previously discussed sample of 36 projects. Thus, the results from this sample may serve as a reasonable guide to predict revenue for this project. The predictor variable value $2,000 does not require extrapolation, as can be seen by locating it in Figure 9.3, so

point prediction

we can use the estimated regression equation to get a point prediction for revenue,

$$\hat{y} = 16.6 + 1.356(\text{PROGRAM})$$

$$= 16.6 + 1.356(2,000)$$

$$= \$2,730$$

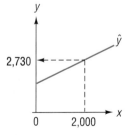

If the predictor variable value had required extrapolation, then we should have satisfied ourselves with additional contextual information that the regression equation is valid at that point.

The actual value for this project's revenue will not necessarily equal $2,730, and there is uncertainty about how close the actual value will be to this estimate. The measure of how far an actual value can deviate from the regression equation is

standard error of prediction

called the **standard error of prediction.** When the sample size is large, a rough estimate for it is given by the standard deviation of residuals, $s = s_e = 198.1$.

Having obtained a point prediction for the new project's revenue, $2,730, and for the standard error of prediction, 198.1, we can get interval predictions. All four regression assumptions must be met for these interval predictions to be reliable.

prediction interval

When the sample size is large, the multiples needed in prediction intervals for individual observations are obtained from Table 4.1 or from the *Calc* ► *Probability Distributions* ► *Normal* menu in Minitab. Thus, we can make the following statements:

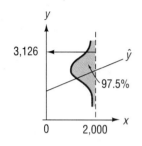

The probability is 68% that the new project's revenue falls within the limits 2,730 ± 1(198.1), or between $2,532 and $2,928.

The probability is 95% that the new project's revenue falls within the limits 2,730 ± 2(198.1), or between $2,334 and $3,126.

The probability is 97.5% that the new project's revenue is below 2,730 + 2(198.1) = $3,126.

Thus, there is considerable uncertainty associated with the point prediction $2,730 for the new project's revenue.

Predictive information about new observations can also be obtained with Minitab. Figure 9.22 gives the details for the new project whose cost of programming time was $2,000.

The last two lines,

```
     Fit   Stdev.Fit        95% C.I.              95% P.I.
    2729.9      40.5    ( 2647.7, 2812.2)   ( 2319.0, 3140.8)
```

FIGURE 9.22 Prediction of Another Project's Revenue (PROGRAM = 2,000)

```
The regression equation is
REVENUE = 17 + 1.36 PROGRAM

Predictor        Coef        Stdev       t-ratio          p
Constant         16.6        251.2          0.07      0.948
PROGRAM        1.3567       0.1362          9.96      0.000

s = 198.1        R-sq = 74.5%        R-sq(adj) = 73.7%

Analysis of Variance

SOURCE          DF          SS            MS           F          p
Regression       1     3888947       3888947       99.14      0.000
Error           34     1333653         39225
Total           35     5222600

Unusual Observations
Obs.   PROGRAM   REVENUE        Fit  Stdev.Fit   Residual    St.Resid
 23       2000    2310.0     2729.9       40.5     -419.9       -2.17R
R denotes an obs. with a large st. resid.

     Fit   Stdev.Fit        95% C.I.              95% P.I.
    2729.9      40.5    ( 2647.7, 2812.2)   ( 2319.0, 3140.8)
```

contain the predictive information: Using Minitab, the point prediction for revenue is Fit = $\hat{y}$ = 2,729.9, and the 95% prediction interval (95% P.I.) extends from 2,319.0 to 3,140.8. This prediction interval is slightly wider than the 95% prediction interval we computed earlier (from $2,334 to $3,126), since Minitab uses the exact formulas, discussed in Section 10.11. For a discussion of the entry under "95% C.I.," also see Section 10.11.

Prediction intervals were discussed in earlier sections; see Sections 4.5, 5.5 and 7.3. The formula for obtaining approximate prediction intervals in the regression context is similar:

$$\hat{y} \pm z\, s$$

It leads to intervals that are slightly tight. If only small samples are available for obtaining the sample regression equation, this formula leads to intervals that are quite a bit too tight. Then the results in Section 10.11 must be used.

confidence interval vs. prediction interval

Section 9.6 discussed how to estimate the parameters β_0 and β_1 of the regression model. We used the term *confidence interval* for an interval expressing the uncertainty in the estimate of such a *parameter.* In this section, we discussed how to predict the response variable value y of another observation for which we know the value on the predictor variable x. We used the term *prediction interval* for an interval expressing the uncertainty in the prediction of this *response variable value.* In general, the term confidence interval denotes uncertainty about a model parameter, and the term prediction interval denotes uncertainty about an individual observation's response variable value.

9.8

STANDARD DEVIATIONS AND STANDARD ERRORS

In this and previous chapters, we have discussed models for how individual observations are generated and the parameters useful for these models. Typically, there was uncertainty about the actual values of both individual observations and parameters. A quantitative measure for this uncertainty was the standard deviation. This section distinguishes among the various standard deviations that have been mentioned so far.

Standard deviation of the response variable: When we do not know an individual value y, we can predict it at the population mean μ_y (or, if μ_y is unavailable, at the sample mean $\bar{y}$). A summary measure for the uncertainty in this estimate is the standard deviation of y values around their population mean, σ_y. If unavailable, this standard deviation can be estimated by the sample standard deviation, denoted s_y.

Standard deviation of residuals: Sometimes auxiliary information is available regarding individual units in the form of a predictor variable x and a regression model can be built, linking y and x. Knowing the predictor variable x for a particular unit, we can predict that unit's reponse variable value using the regression equa-

tion. A summary measure for the uncertainty in this prediction is the standard devi-
ation of y values around the regression equation, denoted $\sigma = \sigma_\epsilon = \sigma_{\text{residual}}$. This
standard deviation can be estimated by the sample standard deviation of residuals,
$s = s_e$.

Standard error: We can estimate a parameter by a corresponding sample statistic; for example, we can estimate the population mean μ_y by the sample mean $\bar{y}$. A
summary measure for the error incurred when using the sample statistic to estimate
the unknown parameter is the standard deviation of the statistic; this standard deviation is usually called standard error. When estimating the mean μ_y, we need the
standard deviation of $\bar{y}$, discussed in Section 7.3, which we called the *standard
error of the mean.* To express uncertainty regarding the parameters of a regression
equation (β_0 or β_1), we use the standard deviation of the corresponding sample regression coefficient, given in the Stdev column of the Minitab output (see Figure
9.19). We call it the *standard error of the regression coefficient.*

9.9

AN APPLICATION TO FINANCE

This section illustrates some statistical aspects of an important model in finance, the
market model. Its financial applications are described in most introductory finance
texts; for example, see Brealey and Myers (1991). The market model relates the returns on a stock to the returns of a stock market index to see how the particular
stock performs differently from the market. In this application, we use monthly
stock returns, which we define as follows:

stock return   The monthly stock return equals the percentage change in the stock's price
from the previous month after some financial adjustments. These adjustments are
made to account for dividend payments, stock splitting, etc. Letting P_i be the adjusted price of a particular stock at the end of month i, the stock return for month i,
y_i, is

$$y_i = 100 \frac{P_i - P_{i-1}}{P_{i-1}}$$

The return on the stock market index is similarly defined. Denote it x. Much
empirical and theoretical work has been done on the market model. One elementary
treatment consists of regressing the return for a particular stock on the market return,

$$y_i = \beta_0 + \beta_1 x_i + \epsilon_i$$

We shall investigate this model here.

Consider the returns for Amdahl Corporation (y), as traded on the New York
Stock Exchange, and the returns for Standard & Poor's Composite Index (x). Val-

ues of *y* and *x* for the 84 months from January 1985 to December 1991 are stored in columns 1 and 4 of ASCII file STCKRTRN.DAT. Figure 9.23 gives a listing of the data and descriptive statistics. Figure 9.24 displays a sequence plot of the Amdahl returns and the runs test: There is no time series pattern to these data. Thus the monthly Amdahl returns are well described by a random process. This is true for the Standard & Poor (SP) returns as well. (No graphs are given.) Indeed, there is considerable empirical evidence that monthly returns are well modeled by a random process. A scatterplot for the Amdahl and SP returns is given in Figure 9.25.

FIGURE 9.23 Market Model: Amdahl vs. Standard & Poor (SP)

ROW	AMDAHL	SP	ROW	AMDAHL	SP	ROW	AMDAHL	SP
1	17.76	7.41	29	-8.56	0.60	57	-14.52	-0.65
2	5.09	0.87	30	-4.75	4.79	58	-10.38	-2.52
3	-13.64	-0.29	31	3.56	4.82	59	7.61	1.65
4	-10.53	-0.46	32	20.08	3.50	60	12.75	2.14
5	8.24	5.41	33	8.02	-2.42	61	9.75	-6.88
6	-5.45	1.21	34	-34.75	-21.76	62	-11.11	0.85
7	7.69	-0.48	35	-10.00	-8.53	63	4.46	2.43
8	-0.53	-1.20	36	27.60	7.29	64	-8.55	-2.69
9	-12.61	-3.47	37	-7.45	4.04	65	19.84	9.20
10	-11.34	4.25	38	3.99	4.18	66	1.56	-0.89
11	16.79	6.51	39	-1.48	-3.33	67	-6.92	-0.52
12	17.00	4.51	40	18.73	0.94	68	-18.02	-9.43
13	6.34	0.24	41	16.22	0.32	69	-13.13	-5.12
14	3.23	7.15	42	17.39	4.33	70	6.05	-0.67
15	-3.13	5.28	43	-8.33	-0.54	71	21.98	5.99
16	3.23	-1.41	44	-18.31	-3.86	72	1.80	2.48
17	2.67	5.02	45	0.00	3.97	73	12.58	4.15
18	6.87	1.41	46	-0.63	2.60	74	-7.09	6.73
19	-3.57	-5.87	47	-11.83	-1.89	75	5.93	2.22
20	24.79	7.12	48	15.71	1.47	76	0.00	0.03
21	-4.17	-8.54	49	-2.96	7.11	77	6.58	3.86
22	11.80	5.47	50	-4.46	-2.89	78	-12.03	-4.79
23	-2.00	2.15	51	-11.33	2.08	79	2.56	4.49
24	6.25	-2.83	52	15.79	5.01	80	-9.01	1.96
25	29.10	13.18	53	18.99	3.51	81	-2.75	-1.91
26	25.73	3.69	54	-26.78	-0.79	82	16.98	1.19
27	-5.94	2.64	55	-11.94	8.84	83	-19.22	-4.39
28	13.33	-1.15	56	5.25	1.55	84	26.00	11.16

(a) Listing of data

	N	MEAN	MEDIAN	TRMEAN	STDEV	SEMEAN
AMDAHL	84	1.96	2.18	2.04	13.11	1.43
SP	84	1.224	1.510	1.430	5.043	0.550

	MIN	MAX	Q1	Q3
AMDAHL	-34.75	29.10	-8.49	12.39
SP	-21.760	13.180	-1.187	4.450

(b) Descriptive statistics

FIGURE 9.24
Amdahl Returns

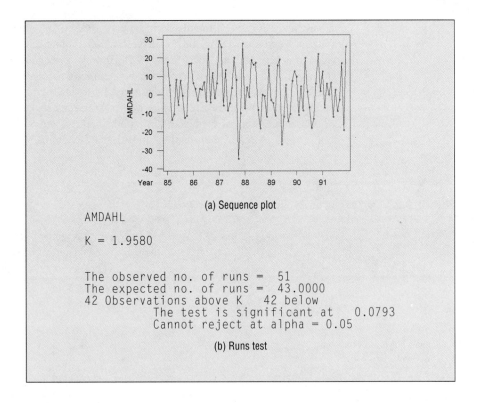

AMDAHL

K = 1.9580

The observed no. of runs = 51
The expected no. of runs = 43.0000
42 Observations above K   42 below
         The test is significant at   0.0793
         Cannot reject at alpha = 0.05

(b) Runs test

FIGURE 9.25
Market Model:
Amdahl vs. SP

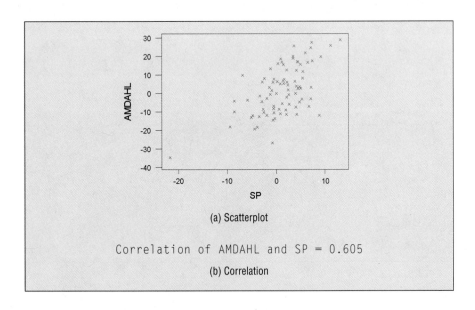

(a) Scatterplot

Correlation of AMDAHL and SP = 0.605

(b) Correlation

There is a moderate positive relationship, with a correlation of 0.605. Note the one unusual observation with very low values on both Amdahl and SP returns.

Results for a regression of the Amdahl returns on the SP returns are given in Figure 9.26. Figures 9.27 to 9.29 display the diagnostic checks. You should study them carefully. All four assumptions are reasonable; note the very moderate departure from normality. We can now safely interpret the regression output. The estimated regression is:

$$\hat{y} = 0.03 + 1.57x$$

Let us interpret the coefficients. Consider first the interpretation of $b_1 = 1.57$: On average, a 1% monthly return on SP is associated with a 1.57% monthly Amdahl return. In other words, if the SP return is 1% higher in 1 month than in another, then the Amdahl return is expected to be 1.57% higher. Also, if the SP return is 1% lower in 1 month than in another, then the Amdahl return is expected to be 1.57% lower.

In general, if $b_1 > 1$, an improvement in the market is accompanied by a more pronounced improvement of the stock in question, on average; likewise, on average a deterioration in the market is accompanied by a more pronounced deteri-

FIGURE 9.26 Market Model: Regression Output

```
The regression equation is
AMDAHL = 0.03 + 1.57 SP

Predictor      Coef        Stdev      t-ratio         p
Constant      0.032        1.179         0.03      0.978
SP            1.5731       0.2285        6.88      0.000

s = 10.50     R-sq = 36.6%      R-sq(adj) = 35.8%

Analysis of Variance

SOURCE          DF          SS         MS          F          p
Regression       1      5222.9     5222.9      47.38      0.000
Error           82      9039.4      110.2
Total           83     14262.4

Unusual Observations
Obs.       SP      AMDAHL       Fit   Stdev.Fit    Residual    St.Resid
 25      13.2       29.10     20.77        2.96        8.33       0.83 X
 34     -21.8      -34.75    -34.20        5.38       -0.55      -0.06 X
 54      -0.8      -26.78     -1.21        1.23      -25.57      -2.45R
 55       8.8      -11.94     13.94        2.08      -25.88      -2.51R

R denotes an obs. with a large st. resid.
X denotes an obs. whose X value gives it large influence.
```

FIGURE 9.27 Market Model: Diagnostic Checks 1 and 2 (Linearity and Constancy of Standard Deviation)

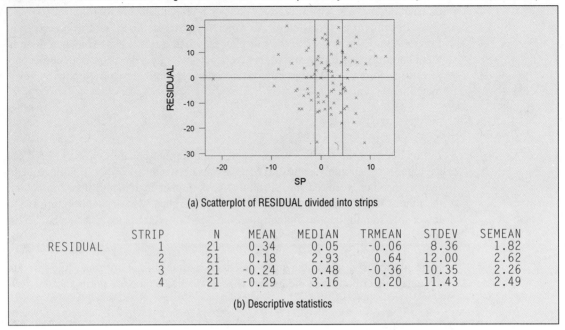

(a) Scatterplot of RESIDUAL divided into strips

RESIDUAL	STRIP	N	MEAN	MEDIAN	TRMEAN	STDEV	SEMEAN
	1	21	0.34	0.05	-0.06	8.36	1.82
	2	21	0.18	2.93	0.64	12.00	2.62
	3	21	-0.24	0.48	-0.36	10.35	2.26
	4	21	-0.29	3.16	0.20	11.43	2.49

(b) Descriptive statistics

FIGURE 9.28
Market Model:
Diagnostic Check 3
(Randomness)

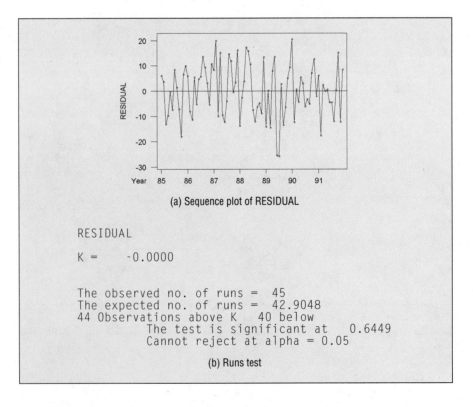

(a) Sequence plot of RESIDUAL

RESIDUAL

K =   -0.0000

The observed no. of runs = 45
The expected no. of runs = 42.9048
44 Observations above K   40 below
        The test is significant at   0.6449
        Cannot reject at alpha = 0.05

(b) Runs test

FIGURE 9.29
Market Model:
Diagnostic Check 4
(Normality of
RESIDUAL)

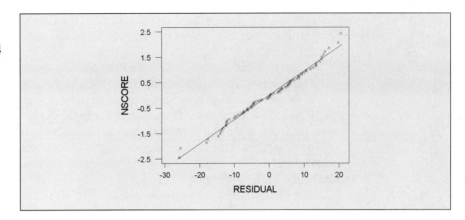

oration of the stock. If $b_1 < 1$, an improvement (or deterioration) in the market is accompanied by a less pronounced improvement (or deterioration) of the stock on average. In the financial literature, the value of b_1 is often called the stock's *beta*.

Consider now the interpretation of $b_0 = 0.03$. In those months when the SP return was 0%, the Amdahl returns averaged to 0.03. In months when the market remained unchanged, the stock price increased very slightly on average.

So far we have ignored entirely the fact that the coefficients b_0 and b_1 were obtained from a sample of $n = 84$ monthly stock returns. When generalizing from this sample to the process from which the sample was drawn, we must not ignore sampling uncertainty. The standard errors of the regression coefficients, stored in the column titled Stdev in Figure 9.26, give an indication of this. The relevant part of the regression output follows:

```
Predictor      Coef      Stdev
Constant      0.032      1.179
SP            1.5731     0.2285
```

The standard error for b_0, 1.179, is quite large, suggesting that the process intercept, β_0, is *very* imprecisely estimated by $b_0 = 0.032$. There is also a fair amount of uncertainty regarding β_1—the standard error of b_1 is 0.2285. A 95% confidence interval for β_1 is

$$1.5731 \pm 2(0.2285) \qquad \text{or} \qquad 1.57 \pm 0.46$$

It thus extends from 1.11 to 2.03. We can be quite sure, however, that $\beta_1 > 1$. To obtain the degree of confidence in a one-sided confidence interval for β_1 that covers values larger than 1, we must standardize the value 1:

$$z = \frac{1 - 1.5731}{0.2285} = -2.51$$

Using Minitab or Table 4.1, we find that $F(-2.51) = 0.0060$. Thus the required degree of confidence is $1 - 0.0060 = 99.4\%$: We can be virtually certain that β_1 exceeds 1.

Finally, let us interpret the standard deviation of the residuals, $s_e = 10.5$, and the coefficient of determination, $R^2 = 0.366$. The value of R^2 means that only 36.6% of the total variation in Amdahl returns can be accounted for by the variation in SP returns. A large share of the movement in the Amdahl returns is associated with forces other than those reflected by the movement in the market as measured by the SP returns. This is also reflected by the value of the standard deviation of residuals, $s_e = 10.5$, which is not much lower than the standard deviation of Amdahl returns (13.11 in Figure 9.23).

In this section we have touched upon some statistical aspects of the market model, a simple regression model. There are many profound financial implications that we have not touched upon here. Most introductory finance textbooks, such as Brealey and Myers (1991), deal with them in detail.

9.10

SUMMARY AND OUTLOOK

This chapter examined the relationship between a response variable y and another variable, the predictor variable x. For example, in the production of batches of steel products, the time it takes to produce a batch, y, may be related to the size of the batch, x. Since the relationship is statistical rather than exact, a value for the predictor variable does not imply a unique value for the response variable. This imprecision may be due to a number of reasons. For example, the values of other possibly influential variables cannot be obtained nor controlled for. Often, a large number of such background variables may each have a small influence on the value that the response variable takes on for a given value of the one predictor variable considered. Their joint influence, however, may be substantial. Continuing the steel batch example, if the statistical relationship between production time and batch size is good, it may be possible for the manager to predict how long an order of a given size is likely to take.

A regression equation is used for explanation or prediction. The fact that the response variable y is related to the predictor variable x, however, does not mean that x causes y (or vice versa). To prove causality from x to y usually requires careful observation and experimentation. The discussion of correlation vs. causation (Chapter 3) and of randomization for experiments is relevant here. Although the question of causality can be an important research issue, it is often not important in the managerial use of regression and correlation. If there is a relationship between x and y, and the value of x is *known* whereas that of y is *unknown*, then x may be useful for predicting y, whether x causes y or y causes x, or an unspecified variable causes both.

The next chapter covers multiple regression, where the response variable is related to several predictor variables. (Again, there might be other background variables whose values cannot be obtained or controlled for.) It is important to model the way in which the response variable is related to these predictor variables and to identify which variables are important and which ones are not.

Key Terms and Concepts

simple regression model
  regression coefficients, residual
regression assumptions
  1. linearity
  2. constant standard deviation
     (homoscedasticity)
  3. randomness of residuals
  4. normality of residuals
diagnostic checks of the assumptions
unusual observations
  outlier, influential observation

estimated regression equation
  least squares line, standard deviation
  of residuals, coefficient of
  determination
estimation of regression coefficients
  point estimate, standard error,
  confidence interval
prediction of response variable
  point prediction, standard error of
  prediction, prediction interval
extrapolation

References

Brealey, R., and Myers, S. (1991), *Principles of Corporate Finance,* 4th Edition, McGraw-Hill, New York.

Kleinbaum, D. G., Kupper, L. L., and Muller, K. E. (1988), *Applied Regression and Other Multivariable Methods,* 2nd Edition, Duxbury Press, Belmont, CA.

  This is an introductory text to regression and some other techniques with an emphasis on applications.

9.11

USING MINITAB FOR WINDOWS

This section shows how several of the graphs in this chapter were generated with Minitab for Windows.

Figure 9.7

Choose *File* ► *Other Files* ► *Import ASCII Data*
In the *Import ASCII Data* dialog box,
    Under *Store data in column,* type **C1 C2**
    Click *ok*
    In the *Import Text From File* dialog box,
        Choose and click data file *audit.dat,* click *ok*
Choose *Window* ► *Data*
In the *Data* window,
    In the boxes immediately under *C1* and *C2,* type **REVENUE** and **PROGRAM**
    Click any empty cell

REGRESSION OUTPUT

Choose *Stat* ▸ *Regression* ▸ *Regression*
In the *Regression* dialog box,
 Click the box next to *Response*, type **C1**
 Click the box next to *Predictors*, type **C2**
 Under *Storage*, click the boxes next to *Residuals* and *Fits*
 Click *ok*
  (The residuals are now stored in C4 as RESI1, and the fitted values are stored in C3 as FITS1.)
Choose *Window* ▸ *Data*
In the *Data* window,
 In the boxes immediately under *C3* and *C4*, type **FITTED** and **RESIDUAL**
 Click any empty cell
  (The residuals are renamed RESIDUAL and the fitted values FITTED.)

Figure 9.8

SUPERIMPOSING THE REGRESSION LINE ON A *y* VS. *x* SCATTERPLOT

Choose *Graph* ▸ *Plot*
In the *Plot* dialog box,
 Under *Graph variables*, type **C1** under *Y* and type **C2** under *X*
 Click the box to the right of *Annotation*, click *Line*
 In the *Line* dialog box,
  Under *Points*, type **PROGRAM FITTED** in the first line
  Click *ok*
   (The points specified will be connected on the plot.)
 Click *ok*

Figure 9.12

SUPERIMPOSING VERTICAL OR HORIZONTAL REFERENCE LINES ON A GRAPH

Choose *Graph* ▸ *Plot*
In the *Plot* dialog box,
 Under *Graph variables*, type **C4** under *Y* and type **C2** under *X*
 Click the box to the right of *Frame*, click *Reference*
 In the *Reference* dialog box,
  Under *Direction*, click the first box, type **1**
  Under *Positions*, click the first box, type **1660**
  Under *Direction*, click the second box, type **1**
  Under *Positions*, click the second box, type **2010**
  Under *Direction*, click the second box, type **2**
  Under *Positions*, click the second box, type **0**
  Click *ok*
   (Direction = 1 specifies a vertical line. Position = 1660 specifies the line to be drawn at 1660. Several lines can be specified. Direction = 2 yields horizontal lines.)
 Click *ok*

"STRIP" STATISTICS FOR THE RESIDUALS

Choose *Manip* ▸ *Sort*

In the *Sort* dialog box,

Under *Sort column(s)*, type **C2**

Under *Store sorted column(s) in*, type **C13**

In the box to the right of *Sort by column*, type **C2**

Click *ok*

(This sorts the values in C2 in ascending order and stores the values in C13.)

Choose *Window* ▸ *Session*

In the *Session* window,

Type **PRINT C13** and press *Enter*

(The sorted values of C2, stored in C13, are now printed, and we can find cutoff values for C2 so that the number of observations in each strip is about the same. We use these values in the following coding command to indicate which observations fall into which strips.)

Choose *Manip* ▸ *Code Data Values*

In the *Code Data Values* dialog box,

Under *Code data from columns*, type **C2**

Under *Into columns*, type **C13**

In the first row under *Original values*, type **0:1660**

In the first row under *New*, type **1**

In the second row under *Original values*, type **1660:2020**

In the second row under *New*, type **2**

In the third row under *Original values*, type **2020:2400**

In the third row under *New*, type **3**

Click *ok*

Choose *Window* ▸ *Data*

In the *Data* window,

In the box immediately under *C13*, type **STRIP**

Click any empty cell

(There are three strips. Each observation has a value for C13, STRIP, based on column C2.)

Choose *Stat* ▸ *Basic Statistics* ▸ *Descriptive statistics*

In the *Descriptive statistics* dialog box,

Under *Variables*, type **RESIDUAL**

Click the box to the left of *By variable*, click the box to the right of *By variable*, type **STRIP**

Click *ok*

(The "STRIP" statistics now appear in the Session window.)

Figure 9.22

PREDICTION WITH A REGRESSION MODEL

Choose *Stat* ▸ *Regression* ▸ *Regression*
In the *Regression* dialog box,
 Click the box next to *Response,* type **C1**
 Click the box next to *Predictors,* type **C2**
 Click the *Options* box
 In the *Regression Options* dialog box,
  Under *Prediction intervals for new observations,* type **2000**
  Click *ok*
 Click *ok*
  (Predictive information is requested for another observation for which the predictor variable value is 2000.)

9.12

PROBLEM FOR CLASS DISCUSSION

9.1   Production Times for Molds

In this example, we will analyze the relationship between production time and cost for a medium-size mold at a mold maker.[4] The process of manufacturing molds is very labor intensive. First, product designers initiate an idea for a product through making a prototype with wood or wax. This prototype is then given to potential customers and marketing agents for approval. Then a production mold is designed and manufactured using modern manufacturing technologies, such as Computer-Aided Design/Computer-Aided Manufacturing (CAD/CAM). The manufacturing lead time for a mold greatly affects the production schedule for the product, so the production time for a mold is a major concern for both mold maker and customer.

A study was carried out to examine production time and cost for a medium-size mold at Mold Maker. The following questions are to be addressed in this section:

> How well can the cost of a medium-size mold be predicted from the time it takes to carry out the major operations? What is the predicted cost for a mold for which total hours are 4,000?

Data were collected on 38 medium-size molds produced between March 1987 and April 1989. Seven variables were measured for each mold: (1) CAD/CAM programming hours, (2) design hours, (3) CNC machining hours, (4) conventional machining hours, (5) handwork hours, (6) total hours, and (7) mold manufacturing costs (in $1,000). The data for the 38 molds are stored in ASCII file MOLDS.DAT. Only variables C6 = HOURS and C7 = COST are used in this example.

The Minitab session output in Figure 9.30 is useful to answer the questions.

---

[4]To protect confidentiality, the name of the company has been withheld, and the data have been slightly altered.

FIGURE 9.30

```
MTB > Read 'C:\MTBWIN\DATA\MOLDS' C1-C7
      38 rows read from file C:\MTBWIN\DATA\MOLDS.DAT
MTB > NAME C6 'HOURS' C7 'COST'
MTB > PRINT C6 C7
```

ROW	HOURS	COST	ROW	HOURS	COST
1	3770	168	20	3491	155
2	3700	165	21	4465	197
3	3081	138	22	2895	129
4	4824	215	23	3692	162
5	4838	215	24	3969	177
6	3306	145	25	3740	168
7	3738	164	26	3645	163
8	3076	133	27	3895	173
9	3474	154	28	3699	165
10	3976	174	29	4312	193
11	2523	115	30	3449	150
12	3620	163	31	3910	173
13	2482	110	32	3414	151
14	3019	135	33	3393	152
15	2048	92	34	3350	147
16	3930	175	35	3871	173
17	3345	150	36	3887	175
18	3615	163	37	3469	156
19	3077	138	38	3899	173

```
MTB > Plot C7*C6
```

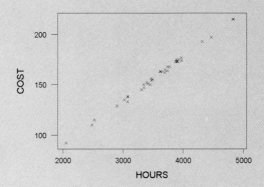

```
MTB > Describe C6 C7
```

	N	MEAN	MEDIAN	TRMEAN	STDEV	SEMEAN
HOURS	38	3576.0	3632.5	3579.3	569.7	92.4
COST	38	159.05	163.00	159.18	25.23	4.09

	MIN	MAX	Q1	Q3
HOURS	2048.0	4838.0	3335.3	3896.0
COST	92.00	215.00	146.50	173.00

```
MTB > Regress C7 1 C6 C10 C11;
SUBC>    Residuals C12;
SUBC>    Predict 3000;
SUBC>    Predict 4000.

The regression equation is
COST = 0.97 + 0.0442 HOURS

Predictor       Coef        Stdev     t-ratio       p
Constant       0.970        1.681        0.58    0.568
HOURS       0.0442068    0.0004645       95.17    0.000

s = 1.610       R-sq = 99.6%    R-sq(adj) = 99.6%

Unusual Observations
Obs.    HOURS      COST      Fit  Stdev.Fit  Residual   St.Resid
  5      4838   215.000   214.843     0.642     0.157      0.11 X
  8      3076   133.000   136.950     0.349    -3.950     -2.51R
 15      2048    92.000    91.506     0.756     0.494      0.35 X
 30      3449   150.000   153.440     0.268    -3.440     -2.17R

R denotes an obs. with a large st. resid.
X denotes an obs. whose X value gives it large influence.

    Fit  Stdev.Fit          95% C.I.             95% P.I.
133.591     0.374   (132.832,134.349)   (130.239,136.943)
177.797     0.327   (177.134,178.461)   (174.466,181.129)

MTB > NAME C11 'FITTED' C12 'RESIDUAL'
MTB > Plot C12*C6
```

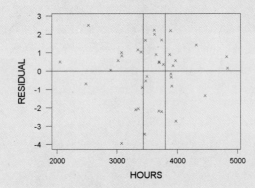

```
MTB > Code (2000:3440) 1 (3440:3800) 2 (3800:5000) 3 C6 C13
MTB > NAME C13 'STRIP'
MTB > Describe C12;
SUBC>    By C13.

                STRIP    N    MEAN   MEDIAN   TRMEAN   STDEV   SEMEAN
RESIDUAL            1   13  -0.160    0.494   -0.057   1.737    0.482
                    2   13   0.089    0.465    0.216   1.775    0.492
                    3   12   0.077    0.227    0.146   1.305    0.377
```

```
MTB > TSPlot C12
```
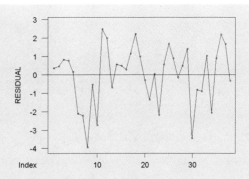

```
MTB > Runs C12

     RESIDUAL

     K =      0.0000

     The observed no. of runs =  16
     The expected no. of runs =  19.1579
     23 Observations above K    15 below
             The test is significant at   0.2767
             Cannot reject at alpha = 0.05

MTB > NScores C12 C13
MTB > NAME C13 'NSCORE'
MTB > Plot C13*C12
```
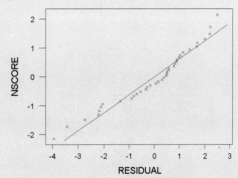

```
MTB > Let C14=C7/C6
MTB > NAME C14 'RATIO'
MTB > TSPlot C14
```
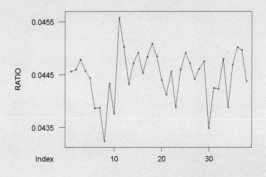

```
MTB > Runs C14

    RATIO

    K =  0.0445

    The observed no. of runs =  16
    The expected no. of runs =  19.5263
    22 Observations above K   16 below
            The test is significant at   0.2342
            Cannot reject at alpha = 0.05

MTB > Describe C14

                  N     MEAN   MEDIAN   TRMEAN    STDEV   SEMEAN
    RATIO        38  0.04449  0.04457  0.04450  0.00048  0.00008

                MIN      MAX       Q1       Q3
    RATIO   0.04324  0.04558  0.04424  0.04481

MTB > NScores C14 C12
MTB > Plot C12*C14
```

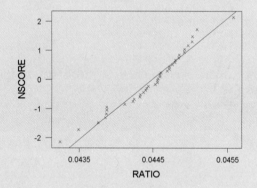

```
MTB > Plot C14*C6
```

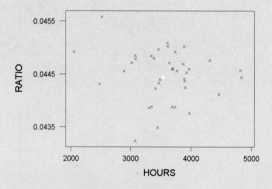

```
MTB > Stop
```

9.13

EXERCISES

Although answers are given in Appendix C, do not turn to them right away if you cannot find an answer on your own. Return to the exercise the next day and try again before turning to Appendix C.

Exercise for Section 9.3

9.2 Consider a product whose main quality characteristic, y, is expensive to measure. Let x be a proxy variable for y that is inexpensive to measure. For a large batch of products, suppose that the relationship between y and x is

$$y = \beta_0 + \beta_1 x + \epsilon$$

with $\beta_0 = 5.0$ and $\beta_1 = 0.9$, and standard deviation of ϵ equal to $\sigma = 10.0$.
a Draw the regression equation.
b Suppose the value of the proxy variable is $x = 50$ for a product. What is a point prediction for the quality characteristic? What is a 95% prediction interval? What is the probability that the quality characteristic exceeds 55?
c Consider a large number of products for which the proxy variable value is 50. What proportion of these products have a value on the quality characteristic that exceeds 55?
d Suppose the proxy variable value is 60 for another product. Answer the questions in (b).
e What must the proxy variable value be for a product so that the probability is 99% that its quality characteristic exceeds 55?

Exercise for Section 9.4

9.3 Consider the following data on the response variable y and the predictor variable x:

y:	110	114	113	116	111
x:	5	7	6	8	6

Draw a scatterplot and add a straight line to the plot that best fits the relationship. What is the slope of this "eyeball" line? What is the intercept? Use Minitab to check the accuracy of your line.

Exercises for All Sections in Chapter 9

9.4 The data analyzed in this problem arose in connection with an investigation into the effectiveness of a detergent. The response variable y was washing performance, as measured by the percentage reflectance in terms of white standards, and the predictor variable x was detergent level, coded to three values (-1, 0, and $+1$). The data were given in A. J. Feuell and R. E. Wagg, "Statistical methods in detergency investigations," *Research*, Vol. 2, 1949, pp. 334–337. An experiment was run nine times at each of the three levels. Use the output from the Minitab session window (Figure 9.31) to answer the following questions.

a Describe the relationship between y and x, as given in the scatterplot. Does a linear model linking y and x seem reasonable?

b Carry out the diagnostic checks of the four assumptions for the regression model. What are your concerns?

For questions (c) to (e), assume that the four assumptions are satisfied.

c Interpret the constant coefficient and the slope coefficient in the context of this example.

d Give 95% confidence intervals for both β_0 and β_1. Interpret them. Does the latter interval cover 0? What are the implications if it does? If it does not?

e If a detergent level of 0.5 were chosen, what would be a point prediction for washing performance? What would be a 90% prediction interval? Interpret it.

f In light of your answers to (b), how reliable are your answers in (c) to (e)?

FIGURE 9.31

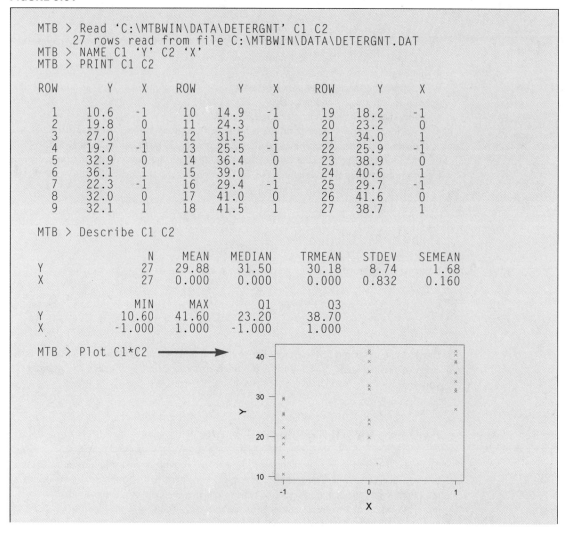

```
MTB > Regress C1 1 C2 C10 C11;
SUBC>    Residuals C12.

The regression equation is
Y = 29.9 + 6.91 X

Predictor        Coef        Stdev     t-ratio        p
Constant       29.881        1.293       23.11    0.000
X               6.906        1.584        4.36    0.000

s = 6.720      R-sq = 43.2%    R-sq(adj) = 40.9%

Analysis of Variance

SOURCE          DF          SS          MS          F        p
Regression       1      858.36      858.36      19.01    0.000
Error           25     1128.84       45.15
Total           26     1987.20

MTB > NAME C11 'FITTED' C12 'RESIDUAL'
MTB > Plot C12*C2
```

```
MTB > Describe C12;
SUBC>    By C2.

                X        N      MEAN    MEDIAN    TRMEAN    STDEV    SEMEAN
RESIDUAL       -1        9     -1.18     -0.68     -1.18     6.53      2.18
                0        9      2.35      3.02      2.35     8.11      2.70
                1        9     -1.18     -0.69     -1.18     4.83      1.61

                X      MIN       MAX        Q1        Q3
RESIDUAL       -1    -12.38      6.72     -6.43      4.67
                0    -10.08     11.72     -6.13     10.07
                1     -9.79      4.71     -4.99      3.01

MTB > TSPlot C12
```

```
MTB > Runs C12

RESIDUAL

K =     0.0000

The observed no. of runs =    8
The expected no. of runs =   14.4815
14 observations above K    13 below
          The test is significant at   0.0110

MTB > NScores C12 C13
MTB > NAME C13 'NSCORE'
MTB > Plot C13*C12
```

```
MTB > Stop
```

9.5 Refer to Exercise 3.14 (Dispatch function at IBM, p. 101) and to Exercise 5.11 (p. 211). Investigate the problem with regression analysis, using WAIT as response variable and STAFF as predictor variable. The data are stored in ASCII file DISPATCH.DAT.

a Obtain sequence plots for WAIT and STAFF. What do you see? Find a 98% confidence interval for the mean of WAIT. Given that the data come from a process, what does this mean represent? Are you justified to compute confidence intervals? Does a normal distribution well describe the sample histogram of WAIT values? How can this histogram be used for prediction purposes?

b Obtain a scatterplot of WAIT vs. STAFF. Describe any relationship you see.

c Find the least squares regression equation and plot it on the scatterplot obtained in (b). Interpret the coefficients in the context of this application.

d Carry out the four diagnostic checks. Are any of the four assumptions violated? If so, describe the nature of these violations.

e What is the standard deviation of the WAIT measurements? What is the standard deviation of residuals? Based on the regression output alone, what is the correlation between WAIT values and FITTED WAIT values?

In parts (f) to (h), assume that the diagnostic checks are satisfactory.

f   Find an approximate 95% interval for β_1. Interpret this.

g   Using the regression equation, find the predicted value for WAIT on a day when STAFF is (i) 30 and (ii) 50. Are either of these predictions extrapolations?

h   What are the 95% prediction intervals for the predictions in (g)?

i   If any of the diagnostic checks done in (d) were not satisfactory, what implications do these violations have for your answers in (f) to (h)?

j   Remembering that STAFF, the number of operators on duty, can be influenced by management, what implications do your conclusions have for management?

9.6   Refer to Exercise 3.22 (Abitibi-Price p. 107) and to Exercise 5.20 (p. 210). Analyze the spruce data, using VOLUME as response variable and WEIGHT as predictor variable. The data are stored in ASCII file ABITIBI.DAT.

a   Obtain sequence plots for volume and weight. What do you see?

b   Obtain a scatterplot of volume vs. weight. Describe any relationship you see.

c   Find the least squares regression equation and plot it on the scatterplot obtained in (b). Interpret the coefficients in the context of this application.

d   Carry out the four diagnostic checks. Are any of the four assumptions violated? If so, describe the nature of these violations.

e   Are you surprised at your results for checking the randomness assumption in (d), in light of your analysis in (a)? Why or why not?

In parts (f) to (i), assume that the diagnostic checks are satisfactory.

f   What is the standard deviation of the volume measurements? What is the standard deviation of residuals? Based on the regression output alone, what is the correlation between VOLUME values and FITTED VOLUME values?

g   Find an approximate 95% confidence interval for β_1. Interpret this interval.

h   Using the regression equation, find the predicted VOLUME in a month when WEIGHT is (i) 10,000,000, (ii) 20,000,000, and (iii) 30,000,000. Are any of these predictions extrapolations?

i   What are the 95% prediction intervals for the predictions in (h)?

j   If any of the diagnostic checks done in (d) were not satisfactory, what implications do these violations have for your answers in (g) to (i)?

9.7   Since the late 1970s, the *Financial Times* of Canada has been rating the forecasting performance of "Canada's major economists." Two ratings were on 11 July 1988 (page 7) and 7 September 1987 (page 4). The ratings combine performance on forecasting eight economic variables: change in real GDP, change in the CPI, unemployment rate, change in pre-tax profits, housing starts, current account balance, exchange rate of the Canadian dollar, and prime rate. In the 11 July 1988 issue, the error rating was described as follows:

> Each of the (eight) 1987 forecasts was assigned a penalty that varied according to how far off it was from Statistics Canada's final numbers. That penalty was then divided by the standard deviation (a statistical device for measuring volatility) for the variable being forecast, and multiplied by 100. The error rating... is the average penalty for each forecaster over the eight variables. The lowest error average wins.

[You should interpret the phrase *penalty that varied according to how far off it was* to mean that the penalty equals the absolute difference between the forecast and Statistics Canada's final number.]

Some of the data from the 1986 and 1987 ratings are stored in ASCII file ECON-FORE.DAT. These data are as follows:

Forecaster	Forecast of GDP Change		Error Rating	
	1987	1986	1987	1986
Caisse de Depot	2.4	4.1	41.2	61.1
Conference Board	2.0	4.0	43.4	50.8
Toronto Dominion Bank	3.7	3.7	45.4	44.7
Richardson Greenshields	3.2	3.0	47.4	63.0
Central Capital Inc.	2.4	*	48.4	*
Data Resources of Cda.	3.1	3.5	50.8	23.0
Bank of Commerce	2.5	2.9	53.2	38.2
Crown Life	2.3	*	54.0	*
McLeod Young Weir	2.2	2.8	55.1	39.2
Wefa Group	2.2	3.6	56.8	51.6
Nesbitt Thomson	2.1	4.3	57.4	60.7
Bank of Montreal	2.6	4.0	59.9	50.8
Informetrica Ltd.	2.3	4.2	60.4	72.4
Midland Doherty Ltd.	3.0	3.5	60.6	49.2
Wood Gundy Inc.	2.9	3.5	62.8	70.3
Bank of Nova Scotia	1.7	3.5	63.5	50.0
Dominion Securities	0.7	3.2	66.0	43.2
Royal Bank of Cda.	2.4	3.3	66.6	36.2
Burns Fry Ltd.	2.3	3.4	67.3	45.8
Coopers & Lybrand	2.4	3.7	68.9	37.2
National Bank	2.9	3.0	71.8	47.2
G.A. Pedderson & Assoc.	1.6	3.8	79.5	58.3

Asterisks imply no rating that year.

The first two columns list the forecast change in real GDP in % for 1987 and 1986, provided by 22 economists. The actual changes in real GDP for 1987 and 1986, as reported by Statistics Canada, were 4% and 3%, respectively. The last two columns list the error rating described above for these 2 years.

a Assuming that the 22 economists whose ratings for 1987 are given are a sample, briefly describe the population from which this sample was drawn.

b Was this a random sample? If not, how was the sample selected? If not, is it reasonable to treat the sample as if it were random?

c Given your answer in (b), how reliable are generalizations from the sample to the population?

d As described above, "the error rating . . . is the average *penalty* for each forecaster over the eight variables." For the 1987 error rating, can you compute the contribution to this average made by real GDP change for the first two economists? If yes, do so. If no, carry out the calculations that are possible and indicate how you would compute the missing information.

e Is there a relationship between the 1987 and 1986 error ratings? Carry out a regression of the 1987 on the 1986 error rating, and do the diagnostic checks. Briefly summarize your major findings.

f Given your findings in (e), which economist's forecasts would you rely on for 1988? Does the one who was ranked first for the 1987 forecasting performance seem to be the best choice? Is there another clear-cut choice?

g Suppose you were to award a prize to one of the 22 economists in order to encourage good *future* forecasting performance. To which economist would you award this prize based on your findings in (e) and (f)? Justify your choice.

h Given your conclusions in (g), what do you think about picking the winner of the prize *at random* from the 22 economists (that is, treating the awarding of the prize as a lottery)?

i Given that the awarding of the prize is to encourage good future forecasting performance, do you think that the awarding scheme you described in (g) is preferable to the lottery described in (h)?

j If you could award partial prizes, how would you allot the prizes to the 22 economists?

k Given your answer in (c), what qualitative generalizations can be made from the model in (e)?

9.14

SUPPLEMENTARY EXERCISES

9.8 This problem relates charges for a company's bank services to annual sales for the company. Data are available on a sample of 40 companies in a large city. The two variables to be analyzed are average monthly bank charges (in dollars), CHARGES, and annual sales (in millions of dollars), SALES. The data for the 40 companies, stored in the ASCII file BANKCHG.DAT, are as follows.

ROW	CHARGES	SALES	ROW	CHARGES	SALES
1	4550	146	21	14290	889
2	2470	342	22	2570	489
3	6980	403	23	5400	365
4	7920	311	24	4570	115
5	3520	362	25	5960	469
6	8990	597	26	3150	200
7	2010	226	27	4300	194
8	5730	351	28	1020	455
9	4940	460	29	3810	133
10	3010	208	30	5020	301
11	6550	383	31	1430	75
12	6460	494	32	13790	853
13	3990	337	33	2420	234
14	6750	520	34	13690	826
15	12500	811	35	6070	192
16	1180	277	36	1430	31
17	5900	406	37	3810	193
18	2190	273	38	15040	874
19	2500	256	39	3390	245
20	1330	464	40	5780	279

a What's a typical figure for CHARGES? What's the standard deviation of CHARGES? Is the distribution of bank charges approximately normal?

b Obtain a scatterplot of the data. Describe the nature of the relationship between SALES and CHARGES.

c   Find the least squares regression equation, linking $y = $ CHARGES to $x = $ SALES, and plot it on the scatterplot obtained in (b). Interpret the coefficients in the context of this application.

d   Carry out the four diagnostic checks. Are any of the four assumptions violated? If so, describe the nature of these violations.

e   What is the estimated standard deviation of residuals? Contrast this with the standard deviation computed in (a).

f   Find an approximate 95% interval for β_1. Interpret it. Does it include 0?

g   Using the regression equation computed in (c), what are the predicted CHARGES for another company from this town with SALES of $435 million?

h   What is a 95% prediction interval for CHARGES for the company in (g)? A 99% prediction interval? Interpret these intervals.

i   What is the correlation between CHARGES and SALES in the sample of 40 companies? What is the correlation between *actual* bank charges and *fitted* values from the regression equation obtained in (c)?

j   If any of the diagnostic checks done in (d) were not satisfactory, what implications do these violations have for your answers in (e) to (i)?

Present your results and conclusions for (a) to (j) in a summary report and attach your briefly annotated output.

9.9   A company was interested in determining how the sales performance of its sales force was related to performance on a test of mathematical ability. The study was conducted by randomly selecting 50 people from the company's sales force. For each person, last year's sales performance was recorded in the variable SALES (the value of SALES was measured on a scale on which values below 100 indicate a *below average* performance), and the score on the mathematics test was recorded as the variable MATH. The data are stored in columns 1 and 5 of ASCII file PERFORM.DAT. (You must read in 5 columns from the file.)

a   What are the unit, the population, and the response variable?

b   What's a typical figure for SALES? What's the standard deviation of SALES? Describe the shape of the distribution of SALES.

c   Obtain a 90% confidence interval for the population average of SALES. Obtain a 99% confidence interval. Interpret these intervals in the context of the study.

d   The variable SALES, as described above, is scaled such that a score of 100 indicates average performance. Is the value 100 contained in the confidence intervals you obtained in (c)? What are the implications for your study if this value is contained in the confidence intervals? What are the implications for your study if this value is not contained in the confidence intervals?

e   Obtain a scatterplot of SALES vs. MATH. Describe the nature of the relationship.

f   Find the least squares regression line and plot it on the scatterplot obtained in (e). Interpret the coefficients in the context of this application.

g   Carry out the four diagnostic checks. Are any of the four assumptions violated? If so, describe the nature of these violations.

To answer (h) to (m), assume that the four diagnostic checks are satisfied.

h   What is the estimated standard deviation of residuals? Contrast this with the standard deviation obtained in (b).

i   Find an approximate 95% interval for the population coefficient of MATH. Does it include 0? Interpret this interval in the context of this study.

j   Using the regression line computed in (f), what are predicted SALES for another member of the sales force whose MATH score is 25?

k   What is a 95% prediction interval for SALES for the employee in (j)? A 99% prediction interval? Interpret these intervals in the context of this study.

l   What is the probability that sales performance for the employee in (j) exceeds 100?

m   Suppose that the math score for a *prospective* employee is 25. Can you use the results in (j) and (k) as point and interval predictions for this employee's sales? Briefly discuss the pros and cons.

n   If any of the diagnostic checks done in (g) were not satisfactory, what implications do these violations have for your answers in (h)–(l)?

Present your results and conclusions for (a) to (n) in a summary report and attach your briefly annotated output.

10

MULTIPLE REGRESSION ANALYSIS

This chapter will help you solve the following kinds of problems:

- A store manager wants to compare the relative efficacy of in-store and out-of-store advertisements for a frequently purchased product: Using weekly data and controlling for price, what are the relative effects on sales of end-of-aisle displays and store flyers?

- A real estate broker wants to obtain a prediction model for the market price of homes: What is the relationship between market price and several readily measured variables for homes in a given neighborhood?

10.1

INTRODUCTION

In the last chapter, you learned the simple regression model that relates a quantitative response variable y to a predictor variable x. A manager may be interested in such a relationship to understand how y and x are related in the population or process, or to predict the unknown value of y from a known value of x. Such prediction problems arise when the predictor variable is easy or relatively inexpensive to measure, but the response variable—which is the variable of interest—is difficult or relatively expensive to measure.

We saw (1) how the relationship between y and x can be estimated from a sample, (2) how the estimated relationship can be evaluated, and (3) how it can be used for inference and prediction purposes.

Often not just *one* but *several* predictor variables are available. Then two questions arise:

1. Which predictor variables, if any, are related to the response variable?

2. What is the relationship between the response variable and the important predictor variables?

In determining which predictor variables to use in the prediction equation for the response variable, there are two competing demands:

1. Use as many predictor variables as possible so that no auxiliary information is ignored when predicting the response variable.

2. Use a parsimonious set of predictor variables for the response variable so that the resulting relationship is simple yet useful.

Very often, the second demand is ignored and all available predictor variables are included in the regression equation. But the demand for *simplicity* and *parsimony* is important: The fewer predictor variables that are used, the easier it is to understand the relationship between the selected predictor variables and the response variable, and the easier it is to explain this relationship to others and to convince them of the usefulness of the relationship. Suppose including a particular predictor variable leads to a regression relationship that is only slightly better than when not including it. Then, it is often advisable to opt for the simpler and more parsimonious relationship that excludes this particular predictor variable.

Many of the issues relating to multiple regression analysis are the same as for simple regression analysis. But there are some new issues as well, on which we will concentrate. In this chapter, you first learn how to use the multiple regression model for cross-sectional data and how to assess the assumptions underlying this model. You then learn how to estimate and evaluate the relationship between the response variable and the predictor variables, and finally how to decide which predictor variables to include and which ones to exclude.

The next section introduces the multiple regression model and illustrates it with an example. Section 10.3 discusses diagnostic checks, followed by an evaluation of the estimated model in Section 10.4, and prediction in Sections 10.5. Predictor variables can be quantitative, but they can also be categorical; Section 10.6 discusses how to use categorical variables. Section 10.7 shows how to model a curvilinear relationship with multiple regression. Section 10.8 discusses how to model a multiplicative relationship. Section 10.9 discusses the choice of predictor variables to be included in the multiple regression equation. Section 10.10 presents an example that illustrates the use of some of the regression tools introduced in this chapter.

10.2

THE MULTIPLE REGRESSION MODEL

Let us demonstrate the usefulness of multiple regression with the following example:

EXAMPLE 10.1

For a sample of 70 residences sold in a midsize North American city, five variables were measured.

MARKET, the amount (in $1,000) for which the residence was sold

AREA, the living area (in square feet) for the residence

ASSESS, the assessed value (in $1,000)

BASEMENT, a categorical variable indicating the presence of a basement (0 = no basement, 1 = basement)

BEDROOMS, the number of bedrooms

LOCATION, a categorical variable indicating geographical location in the neighborhood (there are three locations labeled 1, 2, and 3)

The managerial questions were:

1. Are any of the variables AREA, ASSESS, BASEMENT, BEDROOMS, and LOCATION related to the market value of a residence?

2. If so, what is a model linking these variables to market value?

3. How good is the model in (2) for prediction?

Figure 10.1 shows a partial listing of the data for the 70 residences and some summary statistics. The data are stored in ASCII file REALNEW.DAT.

The Regression Model and Its Assumptions

The simple regression model, described in Section 9.3, is

$$y = \beta_0 + \beta_1 x + \epsilon$$

FIGURE 10.1 Real Estate Data on 70 Residences

ROW	MARKET	AREA	ASSESS	BASEMENT	BEDROOMS	LOCATION
1	139	952	128	0	1	2
2	172	1255	101	0	1	2
3	178	1663	88	0	1	1
4	180	1575	110	0	1	3
5	183	1209	125	0	1	3
.						
.						
.						
66	255	2270	125	1	4	3
67	260	2275	128	1	4	2
68	262	2186	165	1	4	1
69	266	2319	176	1	4	3
70	275	2272	130	1	4	3

(a) Raw data

	N	MEAN	MEDIAN	TRMEAN	STDEV	SEMEAN
MARKET	70	214.93	214.50	215.42	31.19	3.73
AREA	70	1653.0	1619.5	1653.0	332.0	39.7
ASSESS	70	137.66	135.00	138.15	26.00	3.11
BEDROOMS	70	2.643	3.000	2.661	1.022	0.122

	MIN	MAX	Q1	Q3
MARKET	139.00	275.00	191.00	238.50
AREA	952.0	2319.0	1425.7	1882.7
ASSESS	79.00	185.00	123.00	163.50
BEDROOMS	1.000	4.000	2.000	3.250

(b) Descriptive statistics for quantitative variables

BASEMENT	COUNT	PERCENT	LOCATION	COUNT	PERCENT
0	18	25.71	1	25	35.71
1	52	74.29	2	20	28.57
N=	70		3	25	35.71
			N=	70	

(c) Descriptive statistics for categorical variables

where $\beta_1 x$ captures the effect of the predictor variable and ϵ captures the effect of unmeasured or unknown background variables. Note that these two effects are additively combined. The simplest way of generalizing this model to more than one predictor variable is to add terms for additional predictor variables:

The *postulated* **multiple regression model** is

$$y = \beta_0 + \beta_1 x_1 + \beta_2 x_2 + \cdots + \beta_k x_k + \epsilon$$

where

y is the *response* variable

$x_1, \ldots, x_k$ are the k *predictor* variables

β_0 is the *constant coefficient*

$\beta_1, \ldots, \beta_k$ are the *slope coefficients of* $x_1, \ldots, x_k$

ϵ is the *residual*. It expresses the variation in y that is not accounted for by the information contained in $x_1, \ldots, x_k$. In order to reduce the size of the residual, *additional* information is needed beyond what is presently available through the k predictor variables used.

Typically, the regression parameters $\beta_0, \ldots, \beta_k$ cannot be known, but must be estimated from a sample. Even if they were known, the relationship between y

and $x_1, \ldots, x_k$ would not be perfect, because of the variation around the regression equation, expressed by the residual ϵ.

Assuming that $\beta_0, \ldots, \beta_k$ are known, the following assumptions regarding ϵ are made in the regression model. (These assumptions parallel the assumptions made in the simple regression model; see Section 9.3.)

Multiple Regression Assumptions   These assumptions are basically the same as for the simple regression model in Section 9.3, except that they are stated in terms of more than one predictor variable.

Assumption 1: Linearity   For any given values of $x_1, \ldots, x_k$, the expected value (that is, the mean) of the residual ϵ is 0.

Assumption 2: Constant Standard Deviation (Homoscedasticity)   For any given values of $x_1, \ldots, x_k$, the standard deviation of the residual ϵ is σ, a constant that does *not* depend on the numerical values of $x_1, \ldots, x_k$.

Assumption 3: Randomness Knowing the value of the residual for one unit is totally uninformative for predicting the value of the residual of another unit. (In a time series context, we would say that successive residuals are random.)

Assumption 4: Normality   For any given values of $x_1, \ldots, x_k$, the distribution of the residual values around the regression equation is normal.

The multiple regression model fits into our usual modeling framework,

$$\text{Actual} = \qquad \text{Systematic Part} \qquad + \text{Residual}$$

or

$$y \quad = \beta_0 + \beta_1 x_1 + \beta_2 x_2 + \cdots + \beta_k x_k + \quad \epsilon$$

linearity   Assumption 1 (linearity) restates, in terms of residuals, the obvious requirement that the Systematic Part of the prediction relationship is captured by $\beta_0 + \beta_1 x_1 + \beta_2 x_2 + \cdots + \beta_k x_k$. In other words, having accounted for the variation in $x_1, \ldots, x_k$, the average effect of all other variables (whether known or unknown) on y is 0.

constant standard deviation   Assumption 2 (constant standard deviation) says that the variability around the multiple regression equation is the same, regardless of the values of $x_1, \ldots, x_k$. In other words, having accounted for the variation in $x_1, \ldots, x_k$ through the Systematic Part, the residual effect of all other variables (whether known or unknown) on y does not depend on $x_1, \ldots, x_k$.

randomness   Assumption 3 (randomness) captures the requirement that, given currently available information, all systematic information, including any time series pattern, be captured in the Systematic Part. Only unpredictable or random variability should remain in the residual.

normality   Finally, assumption 4 (normality) states that the prediction for y given particular values for $x_1, \ldots, x_k$ (that is, $\beta_0 + \beta_1 x_1 + \beta_2 x_2 + \cdots + \beta_k x_k$) is only a best guess and that the uncertainty associated with this guess can be described by a normal distribution. Using assumptions 1 and 2, this normal distribution has mean 0 and standard deviation σ.

The approach to regression modeling outlined so far is summarized in the flowchart of Figure 10.2.

FIGURE 10.2 Flowchart for Regression Modeling

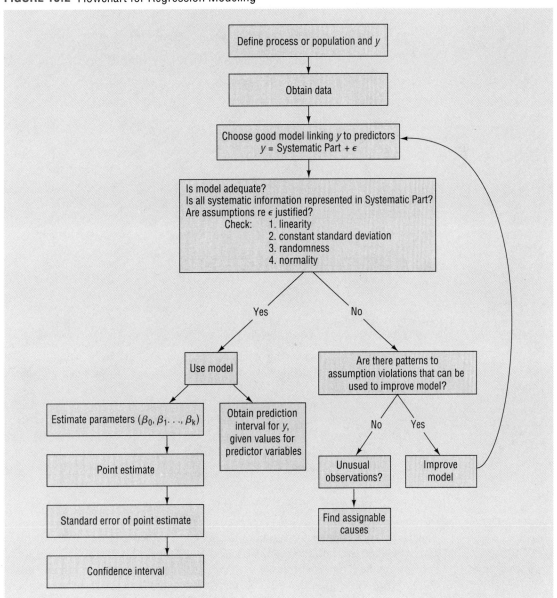

The Estimated Relationship

When only sample data are available, the postulated relationship between y and $x_1, \ldots, x_k$ must be estimated. The estimated relationship is represented by the **estimated regression equation**

estimated model

$$y = b_0 + b_1x_1 + \cdots + b_kx_k + e$$

where

b_0 is the sample estimate of the constant coefficient β_0

$b_1, \ldots, b_k$ are the sample estimates of the slope coefficients $\beta_1, \ldots, \beta_k$

e is the sample estimate of the residual ϵ: $e = y - (b_0 + b_1x_1 + \cdots + b_kx_k)$

The estimated Systematic Part, $b_0 + b_1x_1 + \cdots + b_kx_k$, is often called the *fitted value* for y, abbreviated $\hat{y}$ and said "y hat." Thus,

$$\hat{y} = b_0 + b_1x_1 + \cdots + b_kx_k$$

so that we have

$$y \quad = \quad \hat{y} \quad + \quad e$$

or

Actual = Fitted + Estimated Residual

The criterion for choosing good estimates $b_0, b_1, \ldots, b_k$, is again the **least squares criterion** (see Section 9.4). The values for $b_0, \ldots, b_k$ are readily obtained with Minitab.

Returning to Example 10.1, let us first examine the relationship between the MARKET value of a residence and two predictor variables, living AREA and ASSESSed value. The usefulness of the BASEMENT, BEDROOM, and LOCATION predictor variables are examined later. The postulated model for the *population* of residences is

MARKET = $\beta_0 + \beta_1$(AREA) + β_2(ASSESS) + ϵ

and the number of predictor variables here is $k = 2$. Since data for all residences in the population are not available, we must next *estimate* the values of the coefficients from the sample of 70 residences for which data were given in Figure 10.1.

Figure 10.3 gives the Minitab regression output for the real estate sample data. Much of the remainder of this chapter discusses this output. The best-fitting

FIGURE 10.3 Regression Output for the Real Estate Example

```
The regression equation is
MARKET = 53.6 + 0.0646 AREA + 0.396 ASSESS

Predictor        Coef       Stdev    t-ratio        p
Constant       53.582       9.620       5.57    0.000
AREA         0.064625    0.005708      11.32    0.000
ASSESS        0.39609     0.07290       5.43    0.000

s = 13.38       R-sq = 82.1%   R-sq(adj) = 81.6%

Analysis of Variance

SOURCE          DF          SS          MS        F        p
Regression       2       55140       27570   153.96    0.000
Error           67       11998         179
Total           69       67139

SOURCE          DF      SEQ SS
AREA             1       49853
ASSESS           1        5287

Unusual Observations
Obs.     AREA     MARKET      Fit   Stdev.Fit    Residual   St.Resid
  1       952     139.00   165.80        4.01      -26.80      -2.10R
 13      1610     172.00   202.78        2.27      -30.78      -2.33R
```

multiple regression equation is

$$\hat{y} = 53.6 + 0.0646(AREA) + 0.396(ASSESS)$$

Diagnostic checks must be carried out before we can reliably interpret this equation.

10.3

DIAGNOSTIC CHECKS

Diagnostic checks are carried out to see if the assumptions underlying the multiple regression model are justified. When there are several predictor variables, it can be very difficult to check the assumptions. It is essential to carefully examine them using a variety of plots. For each plot, you should ask yourself

- What would you expect to see if the assumptions were justified?
- Is there a pattern to the deviation from what you expected to see?

As in the simple regression model, the diagnostic checks are based on the residuals (see Section 9.5). In the case of multiple regression, however, experience has shown the *standardized residuals* to be preferable to the residuals. Figure 10.4

FIGURE 10.4 Data and Summary Statistics for the Real Estate Example

ROW	MARKET	AREA	ASSESS	FITTED	RESIDUAL	ST.RES
1	139	952	128	165.804	-26.8044	-2.09959
2	172	1255	101	174.691	-2.6913	-0.20604
3	178	1663	88	195.909	-17.9090	-1.40190
4	180	1575	110	198.936	-18.9359	-1.43884
5	183	1209	125	181.225	1.7753	0.13548
6	183	1689	81	194.817	-11.8166	-0.93852
7	198	1330	147	197.758	0.2418	0.01847
.						
.						
.						
66	255	2270	125	249.791	5.2086	0.41198
67	260	2275	128	251.303	8.6972	0.68589
68	262	2186	165	260.206	1.7935	0.13769
69	266	2319	176	273.159	-7.1585	-0.55654
70	275	2272	130	251.901	23.0989	1.81681

	N	MEAN	MEDIAN	TRMEAN	STDEV	SEMEAN
MARKET	70	214.93	214.50	215.42	31.19	3.73
AREA	70	1653.0	1619.5	1653.0	332.0	39.7
ASSESS	70	137.66	135.00	138.15	26.00	3.11
FITTED	70	214.93	210.47	214.94	28.27	3.38
RESIDUAL	70	-0.00	0.69	0.16	13.19	1.58
ST.RES	70	-0.000	0.052	0.012	1.009	0.121

	MIN	MAX	Q1	Q3
MARKET	139.00	275.00	191.00	238.50
AREA	952.0	2319.0	1425.7	1882.7
ASSESS	79.00	185.00	123.00	163.50
FITTED	165.33	273.16	191.56	241.66
RESIDUAL	-30.78	24.71	-9.22	8.90
ST.RES	-2.334	1.870	-0.707	0.697

lists the following variables for several residences:

> MARKET y, the market value for the residence
>
> AREA x_1, its living area
>
> ASSESS x_2, its assessed value
>
> FITTED $\hat{y}$, the fitted value
>
> RESIDUAL   the estimated residual, $e = y - \hat{y}$
>
> ST.RES   the standardized residual

It also shows some summary statistics for these variables.

To see how the values are related, consider residence 1 (row 1) for which living area (x_1) was 952 square feet and the assessed value (x_2) was 128 ($128,000).

Applying these values in the estimated regression equation,

$$\hat{y} = 53.6 + 0.0646(\text{AREA}) + 0.396(\text{ASSESS})$$

the fitted value is

$$\hat{y} = 53.6 + 0.0646(952) + 0.396(128) = 165.80$$

The actual market value is lower than the fitted value, and so the estimated residual (e) is

$$\text{RESIDUAL} = e = \text{MARKET} - \hat{y} = 139 - 165.80 = -26.80$$

As a consequence of using the least squares criterion for line fitting, the mean residual is 0.

standardized residual

Finally the residual for residence 1 can be standardized using the usual standardization formula,

$$z = \frac{\text{RESIDUAL} - \text{Mean RESIDUAL}}{\text{Standard Deviation of RESIDUAL}}$$

Since the mean Residual value is 0, this reduces to

$$z = \frac{\text{RESIDUAL}}{\text{Standard Deviation of RESIDUAL}}$$

For example, we can standardize the Residual for residence 1,

$$z = \frac{-26.80}{13.19} = -2.032$$

The standardized residuals (ST.RES) given in Figure 10.4 are obtained by dividing RESIDUAL by a standard deviation that is *approximated* by the standard deviation of all estimated RESIDUALs, 13.19. For theoretical reasons, it does not quite equal 13.19. (See, for example, Draper and Smith, 1981, p. 144.) For example, the standardized residual for project 1, given in Figure 10.4, is

$$\text{ST.RES} = -2.09959$$

which is not much different from $z = -2.032$, given above.

Unlike our approach in simple linear regression, we use the standardized residuals (ST.RES) to carry out the diagnostic checks, rather than the unstandardized residuals (RESIDUAL). It is preferable to use the standardized residuals in simple regression as well, but the advantages of the standardized residuals are not as pronounced. The diagnostic checks for multiple regression closely parallel those for simple regression, discussed in Section 9.5 (p. 395). (You may now wish to review the extensive discussion there.) Furthermore, violations of the assumptions, as uncovered with the diagnostic checks, have implications as described in Section 9.6 for the case of simple regression (p. 414).

In the remainder of this section, we discuss the four diagnostic checks in turn. We use the following statistical tools:

Assumption	Diagnostic Check
1. Linearity	Standardized residual vs. fitted plot;
	Standardized residual vs. predictor variable plots
2. Constant Standard Deviation	Standardized residual vs. fitted plot;
	Standardized residual vs. predictor variable plots
3. Randomness	Sequence plot; Control limits; Runs test
4. Normality	Normal probability plot

Diagnosic Check 1: Adequacy of the Linearity Assumption

This diagnostic check examines the adequacy of assumption 1, *linearity:*

For any given values of $x_1, \ldots, x_k$, the expected value (that is, the mean) of the residuals is 0.

standardized residual vs. fitted plot   The appropriate diagnostic tools are a *plot of standardized residual vs. fitted values* and plots of the standardized residuals vs. each predictor variable.

Why cannot we use a scatterplot of y vs. x or of e vs. x, as we did in Section 9.5? Since there is more than one predictor variable, we cannot graphically represent the relationship between y and the k predictor variables. When $k = 2$, a three-dimensional "scattercloud" could be obtained, but when $k > 2$, it is impossible to obtain a graph. Since we cannot generally graph the scattercloud, we cannot directly see how well the regression equation represents the relationship. We must find different graphs that help us assess the adequacy of the regression assumption.

One implication of the linearity assumption is that the fitted value should represent the scattercloud well: At any particular fitted value, some of the residuals should be negative, some positive, but on average they should be 0. This is operationalized in the plot of standardized residual vs. fitted values. Figure 10.5 gives it for the real estate data.

How to carry out diagnostic check 1 with Figure 10.5? Draw a horizontal line at 0 representing the regression equation. Then subdivide the plot into four vertical strips containing an approximately equal number of points (about 18 in this example). According to assumption 1, the standardized residuals should average out to 0 in *each* vertical strip. Indeed, the standardized residuals average out to roughly 0 in each vertical strip. There is no systematic relationship between the standardized residuals and the fitted values. From this we can conclude that the model passes diagnostic check 1.

FIGURE 10.5 Real Estate Example: Diagnostic Checks 1 and 2

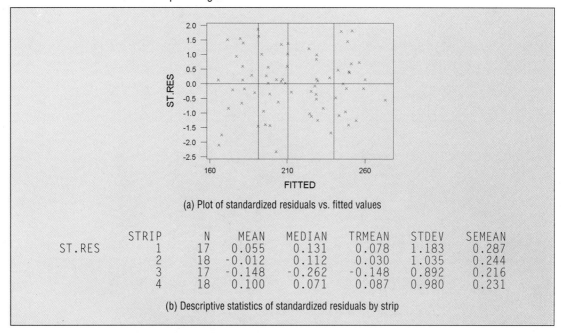

(a) Plot of standardized residuals vs. fitted values

	STRIP	N	MEAN	MEDIAN	TRMEAN	STDEV	SEMEAN
ST.RES	1	17	0.055	0.131	0.078	1.183	0.287
	2	18	-0.012	0.112	0.030	1.035	0.244
	3	17	-0.148	-0.262	-0.148	0.892	0.216
	4	18	0.100	0.071	0.087	0.980	0.231

(b) Descriptive statistics of standardized residuals by strip

When judging the adequacy of the plot, keep in mind that it is a plot of *sample* data. Remember the possibility of sampling variability: Slight deviations from what we would expect under assumption 1 may very well be due to sampling error and should be discounted. The important question is: Is there a *pattern* in the plot that deviates from what we expect? Figure 10.5 does not reveal anything noteworthy. The descriptive statistics support this visual impression: None of the means is larger than 0.148 in absolute value, which is relatively small compared to the overall variability in standardized residuals (about 1).

If more data had been available, more vertical strips should have been used to carry out this diagnostic check. A *minimum of three strips* is needed.

A few similar plots must also be examined, in which the standardized residual is plotted against each predictor variable. Figure 10.6 gives a plot of ST.RES vs. living AREA. Figure 10.7 gives a plot of ST.RES versus ASSESSed value.

We must examine both plots along the same lines as the standardized residuals vs. fitted values plot. Again, you should draw the "0-line" in each and subdivide each plot into four vertical strips. Both plots are adequate. The descriptive statistics support this visual impression.

Summarizing the information contained in Figures 10.5 to 10.7, we conclude that diagnostic check 1 is passed: Assumption 1 (linearity) is justified.

When diagnostic check 1 is not passed, we must return to the drawing board and obtain an improved model. The diagnostic checks may point to how the model can be improved. If the plot of ST.RES vs. a predictor variable is adequate, the effect of that predictor variable on *y* is adequately represented in the equation.

FIGURE 10.6 Diagnostic Checks 1 and 2, Continued

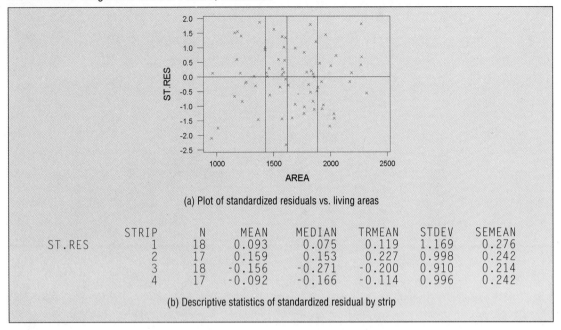

(a) Plot of standardized residuals vs. living areas

	STRIP	N	MEAN	MEDIAN	TRMEAN	STDEV	SEMEAN
ST.RES	1	18	0.093	0.075	0.119	1.169	0.276
	2	17	0.159	0.153	0.227	0.998	0.242
	3	18	-0.156	-0.271	-0.200	0.910	0.214
	4	17	-0.092	-0.166	-0.114	0.996	0.242

(b) Descriptive statistics of standardized residual by strip

FIGURE 10.7 Diagnostic Checks 1 and 2, Continued

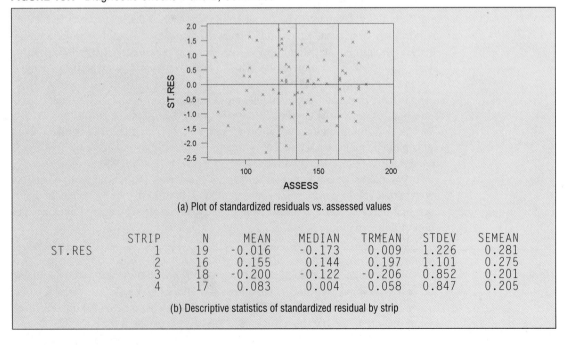

(a) Plot of standardized residuals vs. assessed values

	STRIP	N	MEAN	MEDIAN	TRMEAN	STDEV	SEMEAN
ST.RES	1	19	-0.016	-0.173	0.009	1.226	0.281
	2	16	0.155	0.144	0.197	1.101	0.275
	3	18	-0.200	-0.122	-0.206	0.852	0.201
	4	17	0.083	0.004	0.058	0.847	0.205

(b) Descriptive statistics of standardized residual by strip

Diagnostic Check 2: Constancy of Standard Deviation of Residuals

When diagnostic check 1 is passed, we can proceed to diagnostic check 2, which examines the adequacy of assumption 2, *constant standard deviation:*

> For any given values of $x_1, \ldots, x_k$, the standard deviation of the residuals around the multiple regression equation is a constant that does *not* depend on the numerical values of $x_1, \ldots, x_k$.

We also check assumption 2 with the plot of standardized residuals vs. fitted values and the plots of standardized residuals vs. predictor variable values for all predictor variables. We now check whether the variability around 0 is the same in all vertical strips, rather than whether the standardized residuals in each vertical strip average to 0.

When judging the adequacy of the plots, keep in mind that each is a plot of *sample* data. Thus, we must remember the possibility of sampling variability: Slight deviations from what we expect under assumption 2 may very well be due to sampling error and should be discounted. The important question is: Is there a *pattern* in a plot that deviates from what we expect? Examining Figures 10.5 to 10.7 in this light, there is nothing noteworthy that would lead us to question the adequacy of assumption 2. The respective descriptive statistics support this view: None of the standard deviations of the residuals is far from 1.

Diagnostic Check 3: Randomness of the Residuals

When diagnostic checks 1 and 2 are passed, we can proceed to diagnostic check 3. This is essential when the data constitute a *time series.* It is not required for *cross-sectional* data, but it is still recommended.

Diagnostic check 3 examines the adequacy of assumption 3, *randomness:*

> Knowing the value of the residual for one unit is totally uninformative for predicting the value of the residual of another unit. (In a time series context, we would say that successive residuals are random.)

Figure 10.8 gives a sequence plot and a runs test for the standardized residuals to illustrate the kind of diagnostic tool used for this check. In order to check for randomness,

- Inspect the sequence plot visually for constant level and random variation around it

- Supplement the visual impression with results from the runs test

- Ensure that all standardized residuals are between -3 and $+3$.

Since the real estate data are cross-sectional and are a random sample, there is, of course, no concern regarding randomness of the sequence: It is built in because of the sample selection procedure.

FIGURE 10.8 Real
Estate Example:
Diagnostic Check 3

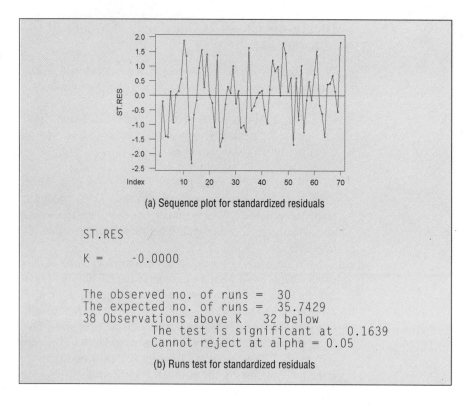

(a) Sequence plot for standardized residuals

```
ST.RES

K =      -0.0000


The observed no. of runs =   30
The expected no. of runs =   35.7429
38 Observations above K    32 below
          The test is significant at   0.1639
          Cannot reject at alpha = 0.05
```

(b) Runs test for standardized residuals

You should remember that the 3-standard-deviation control limits are used to alert you to observations that are potentially subject to special causes of variation. False alarms are always possible, so it is necessary to carefully check an observation once it has been flagged. (The reverse is unfortunately also possible: An observation that is within the control limits may have been subject to special causes of variation: Such an observation will not be flagged.)

**unusual
observations**

Minitab flags observations as unusual when the absolute value of their standardized residual is 2 or greater. Two residences were flagged in Figure 10.3; their standardized residuals are −2.10 and −2.33, respectively. Since their absolute values are well below 3, they need no further investigation.

Diagnostic Check 4: Normality of Residuals

This diagnostic check examines the adequacy of assumption 4, *normality:*

> For any given values of $x_1, \ldots, x_k$, the distribution of the residual value around the regression equation is normal.

The appropriate diagnostic tool is the normal probability plot of standardized residuals, shown in Figure 10.9. The line expected under normality fits the plot

FIGURE 10.9
Real Estate Example:
Diagnostic Check 4
(Normal Probability
Plot of Standardized
Residuals)

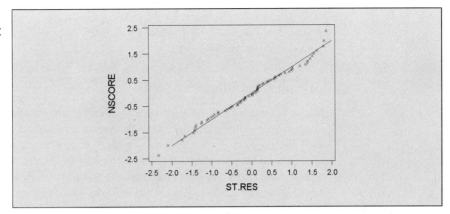

pretty well. There is a little concern at the upper end of the plot, but overall the assumption of normality is reasonable.

Summary of Diagnostic Checks

In the four diagnostic checks, we look for patterns of deviations from what we expect to see. When no such pattern exists, the corresponding check is passed. When there are problems with the diagnostic checks, some of the regression interpretations and uses are not reliable. The extent of the lack of reliability depends on the severity and nature of the violations of the assumptions. Often, the failure of a model to pass a check produces an insight about how to improve the model.

As mentioned in Section 9.5, there are two types of unusual observations: outliers and influential observations. For the real estate data, neither outlier flagged in Figure 10.3 is serious, and Minitab flags no influential observations. No observation appeared to be unusual in any of the diagnostic graphs.

The diagnostic checks are satisfactory. The linearity check suggests that the effect of the two predictor variables is adequately represented in the regression equation. The constant standard deviation check is adequate. The randomness check is passed. This is no surprise since the data are cross-sectional. Finally, the normality check is satisfactory as well.

Given that all assumptions are reasonable, we can now interpret the model fitted in Figure 10.3.

10.4

FURTHER EVALUATION OF THE MULTIPLE REGRESSION MODEL

When all diagnostic checks have been passed, we can use the regression model for estimation and prediction. When some of the diagnostic checks are failed, caution is required. See the remarks at the end of Section 9.6 (p. 414).

The regression output for the real estate example, given in Figure 10.3, is reproduced in Figure 10.10, including pointers to where the various parts of the regression output are discussed.

Overall Evaluation

In the real estate example, suppose that the regression relationship between market value and the other predictor variables was *not* available and that information was available *only* for the sample of 70 market values, given in Figure 10.1. In that case, the sample mean of market values, $\bar{y} = 214.9$, would be a good indicator of a typical residence's market value, and the sample standard deviation, $s_y = 31.2$, would be a good summary for the deviation of actual market values around this typical value.

When additional information on the residences is available in the form of other variables, differences in the residences, as measured by these predictor variables, can be accounted for by using the multiple regression equation

$$\hat{y} = 53.6 + 0.0646(\text{AREA}) + 0.396(\text{ASSESS})$$

FIGURE 10.10 Regression Output for the Real Estate Example

```
The regression equation is
MARKET = 53.6 + 0.0646 AREA + 0.396 ASSESS

Predictor       Coef        Stdev      t-ratio        p
Constant      53.582       9.620          5.57    0.000
AREA        0.064625    0.005708         11.32    0.000
ASSESS       0.39609     0.07290          5.43    0.000
             p. 462      p. 460      pp. 461, 488   p. 461

s = 13.38        R-sq = 82.1%        R-sq(adj) = 81.6%
   p. 459           p. 460                 p. 491

Analysis of Variance

SOURCE         DF         SS        MS          F        p
Regression      2      55140     27570     153.96    0.000
Error          67      11998       179
Total          69      67139

SOURCE         DF   SEQ SS
AREA            1    49853
ASSESS          1     5287

Unusual Observations
Obs.    AREA    MARKET        Fit   Stdev.Fit    Residual   St.Resid
  1      952    139.00     165.80        4.01      -26.80      -2.10R
 13     1610    172.00     202.78        2.27      -30.78      -2.33R
                              p. 456
```

FIGURE 10.11
Real Estate
Example, Continued

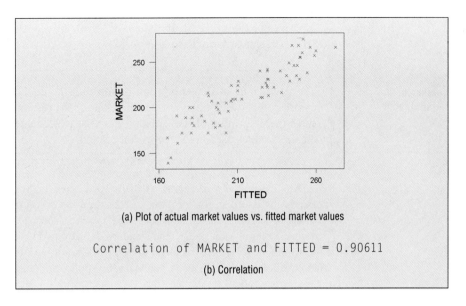

(a) Plot of actual market values vs. fitted market values

Correlation of MARKET and FITTED = 0.90611

(b) Correlation

to get a "typical" value. The residences then do not all have the same typical value, because of the differences in predictor variables. But residences with the *same* values for the predictor variables have the *same* typical value.

standard deviation of residuals

One measure of the goodness of the multiple regression equation is the standard deviation around the multiple regression equation—that is, the standard deviation of residuals—which summarizes the deviation of actual market values around the multiple regression equation. This standard deviation is given in Figure 10.10 as $s = 13.38$.[1] (It is quite a bit lower than the standard deviation ($s_y = 31.2$) that would have resulted if the regression relationship had *not* been used.)

Another useful measure of the goodness of the multiple regression equation is how well the fitted values predict the actual values on the response variable. Figure 10.11 plots the actual values of MARKET vs. the FITTED values for the real estate example.

The correlation between $y =$ MARKET and $\hat{y} =$ FITTED,

$$R_{y,\hat{y}} = R = 0.906$$

---

[1] The standard deviation of residuals in Figure 10.10, $s = 13.38$, is slightly higher than the standard deviation of residuals in Figure 10.4, 13.19, which was obtained from the *Stat ▶ Basic Statistics ▶ Descriptive Statistics* menu. The standard deviation in Figure 10.10 is obtained from the formula

$$s = \sqrt{\Sigma(y_i - \hat{y}_i)^2/(n - k - 1)}$$

where k equals the number of predictor variables (here $k = 2$), whereas the standard deviation in Figure 10.4 is obtained from the formula

$$\sqrt{\Sigma(y_i - \hat{y}_i)^2/(n - 1)}$$

The standard deviation formula used in Figure 10.10 is preferable in the multiple regression context. See footnote 2 in Chapter 9.

is also given in Figure 10.11. Its square, $R^2 = (0.906)^2 = 0.821$, is given in Figure 10.10 in percentage form, R-sq = R^2 = 82.1%.

coefficient of determination

> The **coefficient of determination** or **multiple R^2** equals the square of the correlation between fitted and actual values of the response variable. It measures the proportion of the variation in y that is accounted for by the k predictor variables used in the regression equation.

R^2_{adj}, also given in Figure 10.10, is discussed in Section 10.9. Of the two measures discussed in this section, the standard deviation of residuals and R^2, the standard deviation of residuals is preferred.

In any regression model, the standard deviation of residuals should ideally be close to 0, and R^2 should be close to 100%. It is not possible to specify, however, what is "close enough": This depends on the application and on the intended use of the regression model.

Estimation of Coefficients: Large Samples

The output for the estimated coefficients in the multiple regression equation parallels that for simple regression, discussed in Section 9.6. The relevant section of Figure 10.10 is reproduced here:

```
Predictor       Coef       Stdev     t-ratio          p
Constant      53.582       9.620        5.57      0.000
AREA        0.064625    0.005708       11.32      0.000
ASSESS       0.39609     0.07290        5.43      0.000
```

Let us concentrate on the coefficient for the variable AREA. Its estimated value is $b_1 = 0.0646$, and the estimated standard error, given under "Stdev," is 0.0057. The standard error is a measure of how well b_1 estimates the population regression coefficent β_1. It can be used to obtain confidence intervals for the coefficient β_1.

confidence interval for coefficient

The confidence interval for regression coefficients follows the usual formula:

$$\begin{matrix}\text{Point}\\\text{Estimate}\\\text{for Coefficient}\end{matrix} \pm \text{Multiple} \begin{pmatrix}\text{Estimated}\\\text{Standard Error}\\\text{for Coefficient}\end{pmatrix}$$

When large samples are available for estimation—that is, when n exceeds about 30—the multiple is obtained from Table 4.1 or from the *Calc ▸ Probability Distributions ▸ Normal* menu in Minitab.[2] For example, the 95% confidence inter-

---

[2] For small sample results, see Section 10.11.

val for the coefficient of AREA, β_1, is

$$0.0646 \pm 2(0.0057) \qquad \text{or} \qquad \text{between } 0.0532 \text{ and } 0.0760$$

The 95% confidence interval for β_1 is moderately wide, but it does not include the value 0, suggesting that, based on statistical grounds, AREA is useful for predicting MARKET in the population of residences to which we are trying to generalize.

Note that when $\beta_1 = 0$, the term $\beta_1(\text{AREA}) = 0$ regardless of the value of AREA. The model equation,

$$\text{MARKET} = \beta_0 + \beta_1(\text{AREA}) + \beta_2(\text{ASSESS}) + \epsilon$$

then reduces to

$$\text{MARKET} = \beta_0 + \beta_2(\text{ASSESS}) + \epsilon$$

Thus, $\beta_1 = 0$ implies that the predictor variable AREA is useless for predicting MARKET in the population of residences.

Of course, we do not know the value of β_1 since all we have is sample data. We might still wonder if $\beta_1 = 0$ so that the sample coefficient $b_1 = 0.0646$ is different from 0 due to chance alone. However, the 95% confidence interval for β_1 *not* including 0 suggests that b_1 is different from 0 *not* due to chance alone, and we say

statistical significance

that the difference between b_1 and 0 is *statistically significant:* We conclude that an important reason for the difference is the predictor variable AREA's association with MARKET in the population of residences.

Standardization is another statistical way of expressing the statistical significance of a difference between a sample regression coefficient and 0. The resulting

t-ratio

standardized value is called a **t-ratio,** and it is computed as

$$t = \frac{b - 0}{\text{Standard Error of } b}$$

The t-ratio is reported in the Minitab output in Figure 10.10. Here, b (without subscript) refers to any one of the sample regression coefficients and Standard Error of b refers to its standard error, found in the Stdev column in the Minitab regression output.

For the coefficient of AREA, the t-ratio is $(0.064625 - 0)/0.005708 = 11.32$. We again conclude that the difference between the sample regression coefficient of AREA (0.0646) and 0 is statistically significant. When a predictor variable's t-ratio is close to 0, the variable is not statistically significant.

p-value

The **p-value** gives exactly the same message as the t-ratio, but the numerical scale is different. For the large sample situation discussed in this section, the p-value is found approximately by

- Dropping the negative sign from the t-ratio, if there is one

- Using Minitab or Table 4.1 to find the probability that the resulting positive

t-ratio is exceeded

- Doubling this probability

For example, when the t-ratio equals 1, Table 4.1 yields $1 - 0.8413 = 0.1587$ to be the probability that 1 is exceeded. Doubling this probability, the resulting p-value is 0.3194. When the t-ratio is 2 (or -2), the resulting p-value is 0.0456.

We thus have that t-ratios that are far away from 0 correspond to p-values that are close to 0, and t-ratios close to 0 correspond to p-values close to 1.

Interpretation of Coefficients

We have briefly discussed the estimated coefficients, concentrating on how to express uncertainty about the numerical values of the coefficients. This section concentrates on how to interpret the estimated coefficient, but the uncertainty about its numerical value must *always* be kept in mind.

Section 10.2 gave the regression model as

$$y = \beta_0 + \beta_1 x_1 + \beta_2 x_2 + \cdots + \beta_k x_k + \epsilon$$

For the real estate example, the postulated relationship in the *population* of residences between MARKET and the $k=2$ predictor variables AREA and ASSESS is

$$\text{MARKET} = \beta_0 + \beta_1(\text{AREA}) + \beta_2(\text{ASSESS}) + \epsilon$$

We estimated the relationship with a sample from the population by

$$\text{MARKET} = b_0 + b_1(\text{AREA}) + b_2(\text{ASSESS}) + e$$

For the sample of 70 residences, this estimate was

MODEL 1: $\text{MARKET} = 53.6 + 0.0646(\text{AREA}) + 0.396(\text{ASSESS}) + e$

Let us concentrate on how to interpret the estimated coefficient of AREA, 0.0646. Suppose there are two residences. Both residences have the *same* assessed value, and the living area for the second residence is **1** square foot higher than that for the first residence. Then the fitted value for the second residence would be estimated to be 0.0646 higher than that for the first residence.

The following *causal* interpretation may now be appealing: If the owner of the second residence *increased* the living area by **1** square foot, leaving the assessed value unchanged, then the market value could be expected to increase by 0.0646. Unfortunately, this causal interpretation has a *serious* flaw.

To illustrate this flaw, suppose we had postulated and estimated a model relating the market value to *one* predictor variable only, say, living area. Let us call this model 2. For the 70 sample residences, the estimated model can be obtained with

Minitab (output not shown),

MODEL 2:   MARKET $= 81.1 + 0.0810(\text{AREA}) + e$

In the case of model 2, the estimated coefficient of AREA is 0.0810. If we apply this estimated relationship to two residences, the second of which has living area 1 square foot larger than the first, then the second residence's market value would be estimated to be 0.0810 higher.

Why does the estimated coefficient of AREA equal 0.0810 in model 2, when it was 0.0646 in model 1, where we had explicitly taken into consideration the influence of ASSESS? Notice that, in estimating model 2, we have *not* taken into consideration that the assessed values may differ among the residences; that is, we have *not* controlled for assessed value. But the scatterplot of AREA vs. ASSESS in Figure 10.12 suggests that residences with high assessed value *also* tend to have high living area. Saying that the effect of AREA on MARKET is measured by the coefficient 0.0810 (from model 2), we tacitly ignore the fact that houses with larger AREA also tend to have a higher ASSESSed value. To describe this phenomenon, **confounding**   we say that the effects of variables AREA and ASSESS on MARKET are partially confounded in model 2, where we *ignore* the influence of variable ASSESS.

The coefficient of AREA in model 2 thus measures two effects:

1. The direct effect of variable AREA on the response variable

2. The indirect effect on the response variable of *other* variables (such as ASSESS) not included in the regression model, but correlated with AREA

FIGURE 10.12
Real Estate
Example, Continued

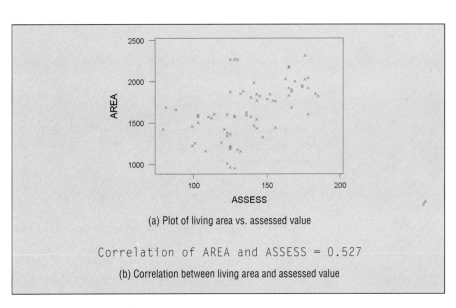

(a) Plot of living area vs. assessed value

Correlation of AREA and ASSESS = 0.527

(b) Correlation between living area and assessed value

When the indirect effect of such other variables cannot be ruled out—that is, when there is a possibility of partially confounding the effect of these other variables with AREA—then a *causal* interpretation for the estimated coefficient of AREA is not appropriate.

When such confounding is possible, we must *not* interpret model 2 as implying that an increase in AREA by 1 square foot tends to increase MARKET by 0.0810.

Let us now return to estimated regression model 1 for market value with two predictor variables:

$$MARKET = 53.6 + 0.0646(AREA) + 0.396(ASSESS) + e$$

We can now better interpret the estimated coefficient of AREA, 0.0646:

> Let us again look at two residences. If the living area in the second were 1 square foot higher than that in the first, but the other predictor variables *in* the regression were the same, then MARKET for the second residence would be expected to be 0.0646 higher than for the first residence. This difference can be ascribed to (1) the direct effect of AREA on MARKET, and (2) the *indirect* effect of variables correlated with AREA, but *not* included in the regression model.

Interpretation of coefficients: The regression coefficients are *net* coefficients, where *net* implies that the effect of other variables has been accounted for. They account for *only* the other variables *included* in the regression model, *not* for those variables *excluded* from the regression model. The possibility of confounding with the effects of (perhaps unidentified) variables not included in the regression model must not be ruled out. Such confounding can only be ruled out in a carefully designed experimental study, where randomization is properly used.

The discussions in Sections 10.2 to 10.4 have given partial answers to the three managerial questions in Example 10.1 (p. 444). We did find a model linking certain variables to market values:

$$\hat{y} = 53.6 + 0.0646(AREA) + 0.396(ASSESS)$$

We have also seen that a model with these two predictor variables yields much better predictions than a model without them.

The next few sections obtain point and interval predictions with this model. They also consider use of the remaining two predictor variables, BASEMENT and BEDROOMS.

10.5

PREDICTION OF INDIVIDUAL OBSERVATIONS: LARGE SAMPLES

This section discusses prediction of individual observations. Let us consider the market value for another residence from the same population from which the sample of 70 residences was chosen. For this residence the living area is 2,000 square feet and the assessed value is $160,000 (AREA = 2,000 and ASSESS = 160). Let us answer the following questions:

> What is a point prediction of this residence's market value? What is a prediction interval for it?

The results in this section are limited to cases in which large samples ($n >$ 30) are used. Discussion for smaller samples is given in Section 10.11.

point prediction   Based on the sample regression equation, we can predict the market value as:

$$\hat{y} = 53.6 + 0.0646(\text{AREA}) + 0.396(\text{ASSESS})$$

$$= 53.6 + 0.0646(2,000) + 0.396(160) = 246$$

This residence's actual market value, however, does not necessarily equal $246,000, and we are uncertain how close the actual value is to the prediction. The measure of how far an actual value can deviate from the regression equation is

standard error of prediction called the *standard error of prediction*. When the sample size is large, the standard deviation of residuals, $s = 13.38$, roughly estimates the standard error of prediction.

When the sample size is large (n exceeds about 30), we can obtain the multiples for prediction intervals from Table 4.1 or with Minitab. Using the point predic-

prediction interval tion of this residence's market value, $\hat{y} = 246$, and the standard error of prediction, $s = 13.38$, we can make the following statements:

> The probability is about 95% that the residence's market value falls within the limits $246 \pm 2(13.38)$, or 246 ± 27, or between 219 and 273.

The probability is about 97.5% that the residence's market value exceeds $246 - 2(13.38)$, or $219,000.

Figure 10.13 gives the Minitab output for the residence for which AREA = 2,000 and ASSESS = 160. For example, the 95% prediction interval extends from 219.06 to 273.35, which coincides with the interval obtained above.

Summarizing, a prediction interval refers to the unknown response variable value y for an *individual* unit. For regression, one approximate formula for the prediction interval is

$$\hat{y} \pm z\,s$$

FIGURE 10.13 Real Estate Example: Prediction of Another Residence's Market Value
(AREA = 2,000, ASSESS = 160)

```
The regression equation is
MARKET = 53.6 + 0.0646 AREA + 0.396 ASSESS

Predictor        Coef       Stdev     t-ratio          p
Constant       53.582       9.620        5.57      0.000
AREA         0.064625    0.005708       11.32      0.000
ASSESS       0.39609      0.07290        5.43      0.000

s = 13.38       R-sq = 82.1%     R-sq(adj) = 81.6%

Analysis of Variance

SOURCE          DF          SS          MS        F         p
Regression       2       55140       27570    153.96    0.000
Error           67       11998         179
Total           69       67139

SOURCE          DF      SEQ SS
AREA             1       49853
ASSESS           1        5287

Unusual Observations
Obs.      AREA      MARKET        Fit   Stdev.Fit   Residual   St.Resid
  1        952      139.00     165.80        4.01     -26.80      -2.10R
 13       1610      172.00     202.78        2.27     -30.78      -2.33R

R denotes an obs. with a large st. resid.

    Fit   Stdev.Fit            95% C.I.                95% P.I.
 246.21        2.40   ( 241.42,  250.99)  ( 219.06,  273.35)
```

This formula leads to intervals that are a little tight.[3] If all four assumptions for regression analysis are met, it is easy to interpret this interval: For any given predictor variable values used to compute $\hat{y}$, the probability that the response variable value for the unit is in the interval depends on z and can be obtained from Table 4.1 or with Minitab.

prediction interval vs. confidence interval
  Let us contrast the interpretation of a prediction interval for an individual unit with the interpretation of a confidence interval. Confidence intervals are computed for unknown population or process *parameters,* such as the mean μ_y or the regression coefficients $\beta_0, \beta_1, \ldots, \beta_k$. Their general form is

Point Estimate $\pm$ z(Standard Error of Point Estimate)

Their interpretation is: The probability that the parameter being estimated falls within the interval depends on z and can be obtained from Table 4.1 or with

---

[3] If only small samples are available for obtaining the sample regression line, this formula leads to intervals that are quite a bit too tight. Then the results in Section 10.11 must be used.

Minitab. In order for this probabilistic statement to be reliable, the first three assumptions for regression analysis must be met. As long as the sample size exceeds about 30, the normality assumption is not needed. For further remarks on the difference between confidence and prediction intervals, see the end of Section 9.7.

In this section, we have discussed prediction results for large samples ($n > 30$). Small sample results are discussed in Section 10.11.

10.6

USING CATEGORICAL VARIABLES IN MULTIPLE REGRESSION MODELS

So far, we have only discussed the use of *quantitative* predictor variables. Let us now turn to the use of **categorical predictor variables.** As we will see, a variable with two categories can be directly used as a predictor variable. When there are more than two categories, the approach is less direct.

In the real estate example, there are two categorical variables,

1. BASEMENT has two categories (0 = no basement, 1 = basement)

2. LOCATION has three categories (1, 2, and 3, indicating geographical location in the neighborhood)

Let us first consider predictor variables with two categories and then predictor variables with more than two categories.

Categorical Variables With Two Categories

Let us first gain some graphical understanding of regression modeling in the simplest case when there is one categorical predictor variable, x_1, with two categories, arbitrarily coded 0 and 1, and one quantitative predictor variable, x_2. The regression model is

$$y = \beta_0 + \beta_1 x_1 + \beta_2 x_2 + \epsilon$$

Since x_1 is either 0 or 1, the term $\beta_1 x_1$ is either 0 or β_1. Thus we can rewrite the regression model as

$$y = \beta_0 + \qquad \beta_2 x_2 + \epsilon \quad \text{when } x_1 = 0$$
$$y = \beta_0 + \beta_1 + \beta_2 x_2 + \epsilon \quad \text{when } x_1 = 1$$

Figure 10.14 shows that the regression model can be represented as two *parallel* lines, relating y to the quantitative predictor variable x_2. The y-intercept is β_0 when the categorical variable is $x_1 = 0$; it is ($\beta_0 + \beta_1$) when $x_1 = 1$.

When there are k predictor variables and x_1 is again categorical with two categories, the situation readily generalizes: There are two *parallel* regression equations linking y and $x_2, \ldots, x_k$, one for $x_1 = 0$ and one for $x_1 = 1$.

parallel regression equations

FIGURE 10.14
Categorical Predictor Variables in Multiple Regression

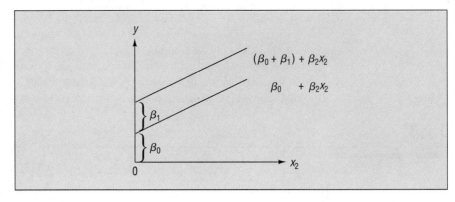

FIGURE 10.15 Real Estate Example: Regression with the Predictor Variables AREA, ASSESS, and BASEMENT

```
The regression equation is
MARKET = 67.2 + 0.0539 AREA + 0.316 ASSESS + 20.4 BASEMENT

Predictor       Coef        Stdev      t-ratio          p
Constant        67.184      8.339         8.06      0.000
AREA            0.053898    0.005106     10.56      0.000
ASSESS          0.31578     0.06213       5.08      0.000
BASEMENT        20.439      3.646         5.61      0.000

s = 11.10        R-sq = 87.9%    R-sq(adj) = 87.3%

Analysis of Variance

SOURCE          DF            SS          MS          F         p
Regression      3          59010       19670     159.71     0.000
Error           66          8128         123
Total           69         67139

SOURCE          DF        SEQ SS
AREA            1          49853
ASSESS          1           5287
BASEMENT        1           3870

Unusual Observations
Obs.    AREA     MARKET        Fit  Stdev.Fit    Residual   St.Resid
 48     1824     268.00     244.35       2.86       23.65      2.21R
 52     1992     216.00     239.51       2.02      -23.51     -2.15R
 70     2272     275.00     251.13       3.47       23.87      2.26R

R denotes an obs. with a large st. resid.
```

Consider the real estate example with three predictor variables, AREA, ASSESS, and BASEMENT. Figure 10.15 gives the regression output.

The estimated regression equation is

$$\hat{y} = 67.2 + 0.0539(\text{AREA}) + 0.316(\text{ASSESS}) + 20.4(\text{BASEMENT})$$

and the standard deviation of residuals is $s = 11.10$. The diagnostic checks for this model (not shown) are adequate. A 95% confidence interval for the population coefficient of BASEMENT is

$$20.4 \pm 2(3.646) \qquad \text{or} \qquad 20.4 \pm 7.3$$

The interpretation of $b_3 = 20.4$ is:

> Accounting for variation in the predictor variables AREA and ASSESS, the average market value for houses with a basement is by 20.4 ($20,400) higher than the average market value for houses without a basement.

We have 95% confidence that this sample estimate is within $7,300 of the population coefficient.

Our model implies that the $20,400 difference in means between houses with and without basements holds true whether we look at houses with small AREA and small ASSESSed value, houses with large AREA and small ASSESSed value, or houses with any other set of values for AREA and ASSESS.

confounding   Let us review the idea of confounding in multiple regression. Recall that the $20,400 figure is the mean additional market value for houses with a basement *after* accounting for variation in AREA and ASSESS.

Consider the following partial Minitab output describing the sample of $n = 70$ residences:

	BASEMENT	N	MEAN	STDEV
MARKET	0	18	178.00	19.88
	1	52	227.71	23.17
AREA	0	18	1362.7	277.0
	1	52	1753.4	289.1
ASSESS	0	18	118.33	19.70
	1	52	144.35	24.65

There were 18 residences without basements and 52 with basements. The mean difference in market value between these two groups was

$$227.71 - 178.00 = 49.71$$

This value is far higher than the value 20.4 obtained after accounting for AREA and ASSESS.

Notice, though, that AREA and ASSESS are positively associated with MARKET value; both mean AREA and mean ASSESS are higher for houses with a basement than for houses without a basement. So part of the 49.71 value can be accounted for by the fact that houses with a basement tend to be larger and tend to have higher assessed value than houses without a basement: The effects of AREA and ASSESS on MARKET are partially confounded with the effect of BASE-MENT on MARKET. Therefore, the $20,400 estimate is a more acceptable assessment of the effect on MARKET value of having a basement. Caution is required in attributing the $20,400 to BASEMENT alone: There may be other variables that have not been included in the regression that might account for some or all of this value.

Categorical Variables With More Than Two Categories

Let us now discuss how to use variables with more than two categories as predictor variables in multiple regression. We will again use the real estate example. Consider a regression model linking the response variable y = MARKET to the predictor variables AREA, ASSESS, and LOCATION. Since LOCATION can take on three values (1, 2, and 3) that have been *arbitrarily* assigned to three locations, these numerical values are meaningless as numbers; they are merely convenient for coding. Thus, it would be *wrong* to add the term $\beta_{\text{LOCATION}}(\text{LOCATION})$ to a regression model. Instead we must create two new predictor variables,

1. LOC_1, which equals 1 if the residence is in the location labeled LOCATION = 1, and 0 otherwise

2. LOC_2, which equals 1 if the residence is in location 2, and 0 otherwise.

It is *not* necessary to create a third predictor variable which equals 1 if the residence is in location 3. Since there are only three locations, a residence must be in location 3 when both LOC_1 = 0 and LOC_2 = 0. The relationship between LOCATION, LOC_1, and LOC_2 is best seen in the following table:

LOCATION	LOC_1	LOC_2
1	1	0
2	0	1
3	0	0

Let us now use LOC_1 and LOC_2 as two predictor variables in addition to AREA and ASSESS:

$$y = \beta_0 + \beta_1(\text{AREA}) + \beta_2(\text{ASSESS}) + \beta_3(\text{LOC\_1}) + \beta_4(\text{LOC\_2}) + \epsilon$$

The regression output estimating this model is given in Figure 10.16. The diagnostic checks (not shown) are adequate.

The estimated regression equation is:

$$\hat{y} = 49.8 + 0.0670(\text{AREA}) + 0.383(\text{ASSESS}) - 0.11(\text{LOC\_1}) + 5.85(\text{LOC\_2})$$

FIGURE 10.16 Real Estate Example: Regression with the Predictor Variables AREA, ASSESS, and LOCATION

```
The regression equation is
MARKET = 49.8 + 0.0670 AREA + 0.383 ASSESS - 0.11 LOC_1 + 5.85 LOC_2

Predictor          Coef         Stdev      t-ratio          p
Constant          49.75         10.56         4.71      0.000
AREA           0.067041      0.005943        11.28      0.000
ASSESS          0.38304       0.07303         5.24      0.000
LOC_1            -0.112         3.841        -0.03      0.977
LOC_2             5.849         4.197         1.39      0.168

s = 13.32        R-sq = 82.8%      R-sq(adj) = 81.8%

Analysis of Variance

SOURCE           DF           SS           MS          F          p
Regression        4        55606        13902      78.35      0.000
Error            65        11532          177
Total            69        67139

SOURCE           DF       SEQ SS
AREA              1        49853
ASSESS            1         5287
LOC_1             1          121
LOC_2             1          345

Unusual Observations
Obs.    AREA     MARKET      Fit   Stdev.Fit   Residual   St.Resid
  1      952     139.00   168.45        4.34     -29.45      -2.34R
 10     1377     216.00   189.07        2.95      26.93       2.07R
 13     1610     172.00   201.24        3.02     -29.24      -2.25R
 24     1010     145.00   170.43        4.03     -25.43      -2.00R

R denotes an obs. with a large st. resid.
```

The portion

$$-0.11(\text{LOC\_1}) + 5.85(\text{LOC\_2})$$

measures the effect of LOCATION on MARKET, after accounting for variation in AREA and ASSESSed value. The value of this term is given in the following table:

LOCATION	LOC_1	LOC_2	$-0.11(\text{LOC\_1}) + 5.85(\text{LOC\_2})$
1	1	0	−0.11
2	0	1	5.85
3	0	0	0

Since $-0.11(\text{LOC\_1}) + 5.85(\text{LOC\_2}) = 0$ for location 3, we can think of location 3 as a baseline location with which the other locations are compared. After accounting for AREA and ASSESS, it appears that locations 1 and 3 have similar effects on MARKET value, whereas location 2 is different from the two. Note, however, that the standard errors for the coefficients of LOC_1 and LOC_2 are 3.841 and 4.197, respectively. Thus there is a fair amount of uncertainty about the numerical values of these estimates.

indicator variable

In this example, the variable LOCATION had 3 categories, and we created 2 variables each equaling 0 or 1. Such variables are called *indicator* variables or *dummy* variables. The variable BASEMENT was also an indicator variable. In general, when a categorical variable has c categories, we must create $c - 1$ indicator variables, which can then be used in a regression equation.

In this section we have examined the use of categorical variables. In the next section, we will discuss another important type of predictor variable.

10.7

USING MULTIPLE REGRESSION TO MODEL A CURVILINEAR RELATIONSHIP

Consider an industrial investigation into the performance of a product.[4] The response variable y was a measure of performance and the predictor variable x was the level of an input variable that was coded so that the minimum and maximum values were -1 and $+1$, respectively. The managerial question to be addressed was:

What should be the input level x so that product performance y is maximized?

The data are stored in ASCII file INDUSTRY.DAT. Figure 10.17 lists the data.

The scatterplot in Figure 10.18 displays a **curvilinear relationship** between y and x. As the value of the input variable increases, the performance measure at first tends to increase, but later it tends to decrease again. The dashed superimposed line is the least squares line; it certainly does not describe this relationship well. The superimposed quadratic curve describes it much better. In this section, you will learn how to use multiple regression to model a quadratic relationship.

quadratic model

The quadratic model is

$$y = \beta_0 + \beta_1 x + \beta_2 x^2 + \epsilon$$

This model can be captured with multiple regression by using the values of the variable x as the first predictor variable and the values of x^2 as the second pre-

---

[4] The data are from O. L. Davies, editor, *Design and Analysis of Industrial Experiments,* Oliver and Boyd, Edinburgh, 1956, p. 333. A revised edition was published in 1978 by the Longman Group, New York.

FIGURE 10.17 Industrial Example

ROW	Y	X	ROW	Y	X	ROW	Y	X
1	159	-1	10	260	-1	19	146	-1
2	395	0	11	454	0	20	417	0
3	149	1	12	112	1	21	150	1
4	25	-1	13	98	-1	22	103	-1
5	255	0	14	422	0	23	455	0
6	251	1	15	270	1	24	172	1
7	184	-1	16	237	-1	25	195	-1
8	363	0	17	362	0	26	492	0
9	378	1	18	363	1	27	278	1

(a) Data

	N	MEAN	MEDIAN	TRMEAN	STDEV	SEMEAN
Y	27	264.6	255.0	265.1	129.8	25.0
X	27	0.000	0.000	0.000	0.832	0.160

	MIN	MAX	Q1	Q3
Y	25.0	492.0	150.0	378.0
X	-1.000	1.000	-1.000	1.000

(b) Descriptive statistics

FIGURE 10.18
Industrial Data:
Scatterplot of
Performance (y)
vs. Input Level (x)

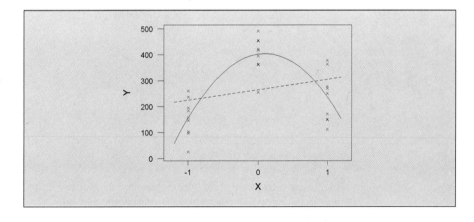

dictor variable. Note that there is a mathematical relationship between the two predictor variables. For the industrial experiment, the resulting data and the regression output are given in Figure 10.19. The diagnostic checks are carried out in Figures 10.20 and 10.21. You should carefully check them.

The standardized residual vs. fitted plot in Figure 10.20(a) is adequate, so the assumptions of linearity and constant standard deviation are reasonable. The randomness check was not carried out, since this was a randomized experimental study and the order of the observations does not represent the order in which the experi-

FIGURE 10.19 Industrial Data: Regression Output

```
ROW      Y     X    X**2        ROW      Y     X    X**2
              X₁    X₂                         X₁    X₂

 1      159   -1     1          15      270    1     1
 2      395    0     0          16      237   -1     1
 3      149    1     1          17      362    0     0
 4       25   -1     1          18      363    1     1
 5      255    0     0          19      146   -1     1
 6      251    1     1          20      417    0     0
 7      184   -1     1          21      150    1     1
 8      363    0     0          22      103   -1     1
 9      378    1     1          23      455    0     0
10      260   -1     1          24      172    1     1
11      454    0     0          25      195   -1     1
12      112    1     1          26      492    0     0
13       98   -1     1          27      278    1     1
14      422    0     0

              N     MEAN    MEDIAN   TRMEAN    STDEV   SEMEAN
    Y        27    264.6    255.0    265.1    129.8    25.0
    X        27    0.000    0.000    0.000    0.832    0.160

             MIN     MAX      Q1       Q3
    Y       25.0   492.0    150.0    378.0
    X     -1.000   1.000   -1.000    1.000


The regression equation is
Y = 402 + 39.8 X - 206 X**2

Predictor        Coef       Stdev    t-ratio        p
Constant       401.67      26.88      14.95    0.000
X               39.78      19.00       2.09    0.047
X**2          -205.56      32.92      -6.24    0.000

s = 80.63      R-sq = 64.4%     R-sq(adj) = 61.4%
. . .
```

ment was carried out. The normal probability plot in Figure 10.21 is also adequate, and so the normality assumption is reasonable as well.

We can therefore use the fitted model,

$$\hat{y} = 401.7 + (39.8)x - (205.6)x^2$$

to answer the managerial question. The standard deviation of residuals is $s = 80.6$, considerably lower than the standard deviation of y values, $s_y = 129.8$. It is possible to obtain the value for x at which $\hat{y}$ is maximized, which is 0.10.[5] Therefore, if the

---

[5] Using calculus it can be found that the equation $\hat{y} = b_0 + b_1 x + b_2 x^2$ has an extreme point at $x = -b_1/[2b_2]$. This point is a maximum if b_2 is negative.

FIGURE 10.20 Industrial Data: Diagnostic Checks 1 and 2

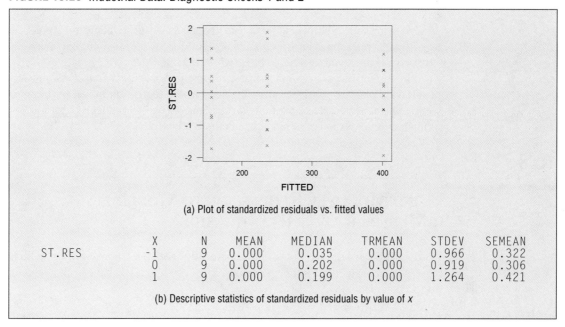

(a) Plot of standardized residuals vs. fitted values

	X	N	MEAN	MEDIAN	TRMEAN	STDEV	SEMEAN
ST.RES	-1	9	0.000	0.035	0.000	0.966	0.322
	0	9	0.000	0.202	0.000	0.919	0.306
	1	9	0.000	0.199	0.000	1.264	0.421

(b) Descriptive statistics of standardized residuals by value of x

FIGURE 10.21
Industrial Data:
Diagnostic Check
for Normality

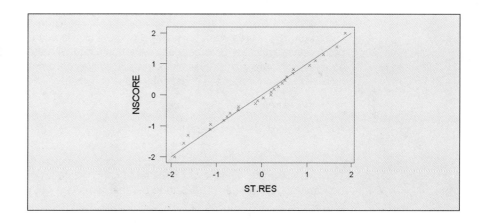

input level is set at $x = 0.10$, product performance will tend to be maximized. A point prediction for product performance is then

$$\hat{y} = 401.7 + 39.8(0.10) - 205.6(0.10^2) = 403.6.$$

There is, of course, considerable variation in performance measures. A 95% prediction interval is

$$403.6 \pm 2(80.6) \qquad \text{or} \qquad \text{from 242.4 to 564.8}$$

If the input level is set at its maximizing value $x = 0.10$, then 95% of products are estimated to have performance measures between 242 and 565.

When using multiple regression to model quadratic relationships, practical experience suggests not to drop the linear term, b_1x, while retaining the quadratic term, b_2x^2, if b_1 should turn out to be insignificant.

In this section, we have seen that it is sometimes useful to consider a transformation of a predictor variable to be included in the regression model. In the next section, we consider transformations further, and we see, in particular, that a transformation of the response variable is sometimes advisable.

10.8

USING MULTIPLE REGRESSION TO MODEL A MULTIPLICATIVE RELATIONSHIP

In this section, we discuss how to model a **multiplicative** relationship with multiple regression. Consider the following example, in which the data have been altered to protect confidentiality.

EXAMPLE 10.2

Scanner data are obtained at the checkout counter of many stores. Large amounts of data are created this way, but stores have started only recently to investigate these data for store purposes. In December 1991, a North American chain of franchised grocery stores started investigating how to use scanner data to evaluate its promotional activities. Scanner data were combined with data on promotions, such as in-store displays and flyer distribution activities. In order to get an idea of the amount of scanner data the chain of stores is collecting, it should be realized that

- There are many franchised stores.

- In each store, data are collected on thousands of individual products.

- Data are collected on a weekly basis.

As a starting point, it was decided to concentrate on one store and one product category, beverages. The data to be analyzed were obtained since the summer of 1991. Promotions changed weekly, and they were mainly of two types: flyers that were distributed outside the stores and in-store displays. Data on the following variables were measured each week on one particular beverage brand:

SALES, sales in units (abbreviated as S in our discussion)

PRICE, price in dollars (abbreviated P)

FLYER, flyer promotion (1 = yes, 0 = no)

DISPLAY, display promotion (1 = yes, 0 = no)

Data for 63 weeks are stored in ASCII file BEVERAGE.DAT. They are listed in Figure 10.22.

FIGURE 10.22 Beverage Data

ROW	SALES	PRICE	FLYER	DISPLAY	ROW	SALES	PRICE	FLYER	DISPLAY
1	323	1.01	0	1	32	904	0.98	1	1
2	48	1.55	0	1	33	113	1.23	0	0
3	58	1.52	0	0	34	26	1.57	0	1
4	1612	0.88	1	1	35	41	1.67	0	0
5	122	1.13	0	0	36	1265	0.88	1	1
6	27	1.67	0	0	37	215	1.05	0	0
7	31	1.66	0	0	38	62	1.48	0	0
8	115	1.37	0	0	39	60	1.54	0	0
9	280	1.09	0	1	40	47	1.51	0	0
10	24	1.67	0	1	41	75	1.40	0	0
11	70	1.45	0	0	42	799	0.99	1	1
12	80	1.37	0	0	43	2064	0.88	1	1
13	16	1.73	0	0	44	250	1.14	0	0
14	42	1.55	0	0	45	17	1.76	0	0
15	15	1.82	0	0	46	63	1.37	0	0
16	1155	0.97	1	1	47	1645	0.88	1	1
17	155	1.10	0	0	48	294	0.97	0	1
18	1892	0.85	1	1	49	40	1.69	0	1
19	481	0.95	0	1	50	32	1.69	0	1
20	62	1.35	0	1	51	1167	0.99	1	1
21	58	1.35	0	1	52	116	1.24	0	0
22	139	1.35	0	0	53	46	1.54	0	0
23	76	1.46	0	0	54	1568	0.88	1	1
24	841	0.99	1	1	55	283	1.00	0	0
25	204	1.28	0	0	56	56	1.55	0	0
26	77	1.37	0	0	57	83	1.43	0	0
27	29	1.61	0	0	58	31	1.53	0	0
28	58	1.70	0	0	59	1165	0.95	1	0
29	1098	0.99	1	1	60	29	1.83	0	1
30	34	1.68	0	0	61	24	1.83	0	1
31	20	1.64	0	0	62	1846	0.85	1	1
					63	359	1.01	0	0

(a) Data listing

	N	MEAN	MEDIAN	TRMEAN	STDEV	SEMEAN
SALES	63	381.4	77.0	318.9	566.7	71.4
PRICE	63	1.3241	1.3700	1.3221	0.3088	0.0389

	MIN	MAX	Q1	Q3
SALES	15.0	2064.0	41.0	359.0
PRICE	0.8500	1.8300	0.9900	1.5700

FLYER	COUNT	DISPLAY	COUNT
0	49	0	37
1	14	1	26
N=	63	N=	63

(b) Descriptive statistics

The managerial question to be addressed was:

Accounting for price, do flyer and display promotions have an effect on sales? If so, is one of the two promotional activities more effective?

At this preliminary stage, interest focused on identifying models that describe the relationship between sales and the other variables. As a starting point, two types of models were considered, additive and multiplicative models.

Let us first look at the relationship betwen sales and price during the 36 weeks when there was neither a flyer nor a display promotion. An additive model relating SALES to PRICE is:

additive model $S = \beta_0 + \beta_1 P + \epsilon$

which is the familiar regression model.

Figure 10.23 gives a scatterplot of S vs. P for the 36 weeks without promotional activities for the beverage. It is clear that the superimposed estimated regression line does not fit the data well. The relationship between sales and price appears to be curvilinear: Sales tend to decrease as price increases, but less and less so.

The *multiplicative* model often captures this type of relationship,

multiplicative model $S = \alpha \, P^\gamma \eta$

Here α and γ are the parameters of the multiplicative model, and η is a multiplicative error term whose distribution is centered around 1. The model part for the multiplicative model is

$$\alpha P^\gamma$$

When $P = 1$, the model part reduces to α; that is, sales are estimated to be α when the price equals 1.

FIGURE 10.23
Plot of Sales vs. Price for the Weeks Without Flyer and Display

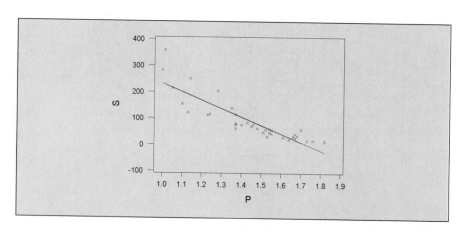

By taking logarithms on both sides of the equation, this model can be reformulated as a regression model,

logarithmic transformation

$$\log(S) = \log[\alpha\, P^{\gamma}\eta]$$
$$= \log(\alpha) + \gamma \log(P) + \log(\eta)$$

Now, letting $y = \log(S)$, $\beta_0 = \log(\alpha)$, $\beta_1 = \gamma$, $x_1 = \log(P)$, and $\epsilon = \log(\eta)$, the reformulated multiplicative model reduces to the familiar regression model,

$$y = \beta_0 + \beta_1 x_1 + \epsilon$$

Figure 10.24 gives a scatterplot of $y = \log(S)$ vs. $x_1 = \log(P)$ for the 36 weeks with neither promotional activity. The superimposed estimated regression line fits the data much better than in Figure 10.23. The output for the regression of $y = \log(S)$ vs. $x_1 = \log(P)$ for the 36 weeks with neither promotional activity is given in Figure 10.25. The diagnostic checks are given in Figure 10.26. There is some concern about the middle strip of the standardized residual vs. fitted plot: The residuals tend to be too high, and there is less variability. The other checks are adequate.

We can use the estimates of β_0 and β_1 from Figure 10.25, $b_0 = 5.842$ and $b_1 = -4.674$, to estimate α and γ in the multiplicative model. Denoting these estimates by a and g, we get

$$a = e^{b_0} = e^{5.842} = 344.5 \quad \text{and} \quad g = b_1 = -4.674$$

The resulting fitted value for sales is

$$\hat{S} = a\, P^{-g} = e^{b_0} P^{-b_0} = 344.5(P^{-4.674})$$

FIGURE 10.24
Plot of Log(S) vs. Log(P) for the Weeks Without Flyer and Display

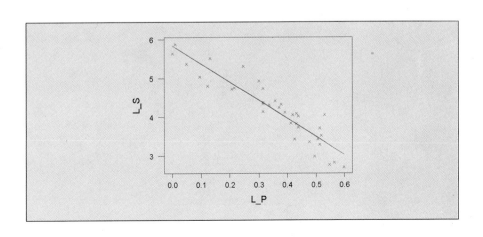

FIGURE 10.25 Regression of Log(*S*), L_S, on Log(*P*), L_P, for the Weeks Without Flyer and Display

```
The regression equation is
L_S = 5.84 - 4.67 L_P

Predictor        Coef       Stdev      t-ratio        p
Constant       5.8420      0.1271       45.98      0.000
L_P           -4.6742      0.3274      -14.28      0.000

s = 0.3139      R-sq = 85.7%      R-sq(adj) = 85.3%

Analysis of Variance

SOURCE          DF          SS          MS         F        p
Regression       1      20.087      20.087    203.86    0.000
Error           34       3.350       0.099
Total           35      23.437

Unusual Observations
Obs.       L_P         L_S         Fit   Stdev.Fit   Residual   St.Resid
 14      0.247      5.3181      4.6882      0.0629     0.6300      2.05R
 17      0.531      4.0604      3.3618      0.0781     0.6987      2.30R

R denotes an obs. with a large st. resid.
```

FIGURE 10.26 Diagnostic Checks: Regression of L_S on L_P for the Weeks Without Flyer and Display

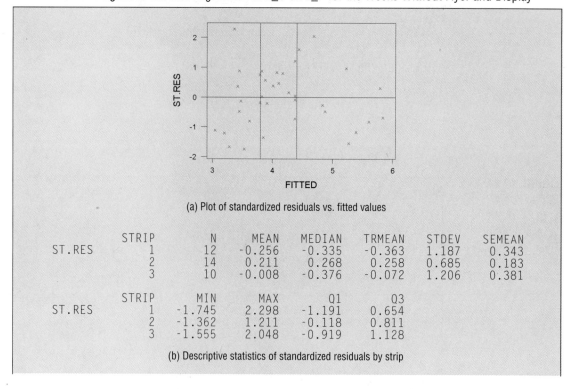

(a) Plot of standardized residuals vs. fitted values

	STRIP	N	MEAN	MEDIAN	TRMEAN	STDEV	SEMEAN
ST.RES	1	12	-0.256	-0.335	-0.363	1.187	0.343
	2	14	0.211	0.268	0.258	0.685	0.183
	3	10	-0.008	-0.376	-0.072	1.206	0.381

	STRIP	MIN	MAX	Q1	Q3
ST.RES	1	-1.745	2.298	-1.191	0.654
	2	-1.362	1.211	-0.118	0.811
	3	-1.555	2.048	-0.919	1.128

(b) Descriptive statistics of standardized residuals by strip

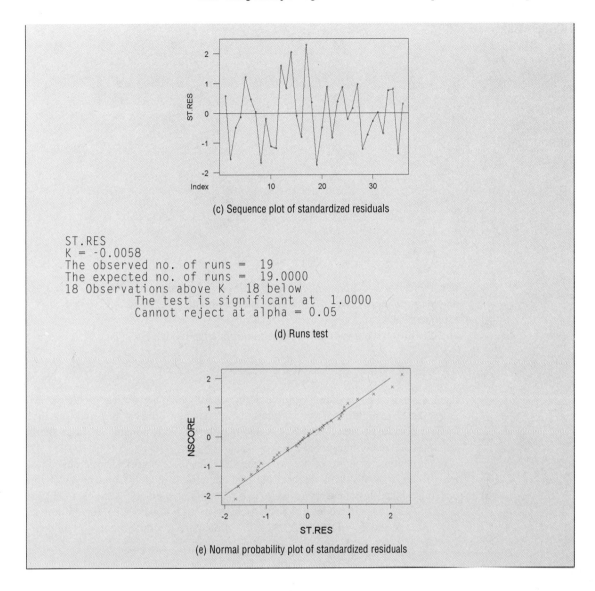

(c) Sequence plot of standardized residuals

```
ST.RES
K = -0.0058
The observed no. of runs =   19
The expected no. of runs =   19.0000
18 Observations above K   18 below
          The test is significant at  1.0000
          Cannot reject at alpha = 0.05
```

(d) Runs test

(e) Normal probability plot of standardized residuals

The fitted value is superimposed on the sales vs. price scatterplot in Figure 10.27. This curve fits better than the line superimposed in Figure 10.23, suggesting that a multiplicative model is more appropriate than an additive model. Let us interpret the two estimated coefficients of the multiplicative model. When $P = 1$, we have that $\hat{S} = e^{b_0} = 344.5$; that is, $\hat{S}$ is the estimated weekly sales value when $P = 1$. Since price values around \$1.00 were observed in the sample data, this estimate does not require any extrapolation and is thus reasonable.

elasticity   There is also a very convenient interpretation for the exponent of P, $g = b_1 = -4.674$, in the multiplicative model. It is the price *elasticity* of sales, and approxi-

FIGURE 10.27
Plot of Sales vs.
Price for the Weeks
Without Flyer and
Display
(Multiplicative
Model Curve
Superimposed)

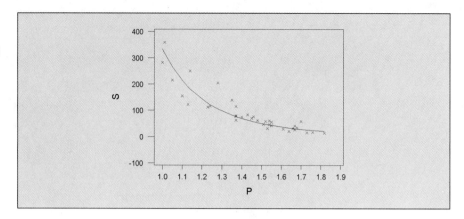

mately measures the percent change in sales when price changes by 1%. In this example, a 1% increase in price is associated with an approximate 4.67% decrease in estimated sales.

In the above formulation of the multiplicative model,

$$S = \alpha P^\gamma \eta$$

there was only one predictor variable, P. In general, there are several predictor variables that are multiplicatively related. We can again convert the multiplicative model into a regression model by taking logarithms. The exponents of the predictor variables are again interpreted as elasticities.

When one or more of the predictor variables are categorical, it is best, however, to incorporate them directly into the regression model. Consider again the beverage example where there were two categorical predictor variables, FLYER and DISPLAY. Again we let $y = \log(\text{SALES})$ and $x_1 = \log(\text{PRICE})$. In addition, let $x_2 = \text{FLYER}$ and $x_3 = \text{DISPLAY}$. We will estimate the multiple regression model,

$$y = \beta_0 + \beta_1 x_1 + \beta_2 x_2 + \beta_3 x_3 + \epsilon$$

using all the data in Figure 10.22.

The corresponding regression output is given in Figure 10.28. The diagnostic checks are given in Figure 10.29.

In the standardized residual vs. fitted plot, there is again some concern about the linearity check in the second vertical strip where the average standardized residual is a little high; there are problems with the check for constant standard deviation. The plots of ST.RES vs. each of the predictor variables are not given, but their message is similar. The randomness check is fine, as is the normality check. We will have to be careful interpreting interval estimates.

The estimated regression equation is

Fitted L_S = 5.804 − 4.568(L_P) + 1.037(FLYER) − 0.0341(DISPLAY)

FIGURE 10.28 Beverage Data: Regression Output for Full Model

```
The regression equation is
L_S = 5.80 - 4.57 L_P + 1.04 FLYER - 0.0341 DISPLAY

Predictor       Coef       Stdev      t-ratio        p
Constant     5.80402     0.08767       66.20      0.000
L_P          -4.5679      0.2119      -21.56      0.000
FLYER         1.0374      0.1331        7.80      0.000
DISPLAY     -0.03409     0.08540       -0.40      0.691

s = 0.2759      R-sq = 96.7%      R-sq(adj) = 96.5%

Analysis of Variance

SOURCE        DF          SS         MS         F        p
Regression     3     130.928     43.643    573.35    0.000
Error         59       4.491      0.076
Total         62     135.419

SOURCE        DF      SEQ SS
L_P            1     125.706
FLYER          1       5.210
DISPLAY        1       0.012

Unusual Observations
Obs.       L_P         L_S        Fit   Stdev.Fit   Residual   St.Resid
  25     0.247      5.3181     4.6764      0.0508     0.6417       2.37R
  28     0.531      4.0604     3.3801      0.0589     0.6803       2.52R
  31     0.495      2.9957     3.5443      0.0544    -0.5485      -2.03R

R denotes an obs. with a large st. resid.
```

FIGURE 10.29 Beverage Data: Diagnostic Checks for Full Model

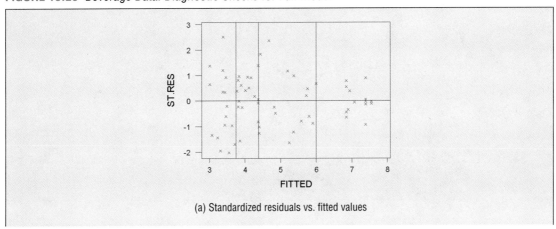

(a) Standardized residuals vs. fitted values

	STRIP	N	MEAN	MEDIAN	TRMEAN	STDEV	SEMEAN
ST.RES	1	16	-0.240	-0.408	-0.309	1.351	0.338
	2	17	0.250	0.390	0.295	0.729	0.177
	3	15	-0.075	-0.485	-0.142	1.211	0.313
	4	15	0.045	-0.023	0.054	0.533	0.138

	STRIP	MIN	MAX	Q1	Q3
ST.RES	1	-2.028	2.524	-1.423	0.863
	2	-1.573	1.393	-0.159	0.868
	3	-1.650	2.366	-1.023	0.991
	4	-0.935	0.908	-0.349	0.558

(b) Descriptive statistics of standardized residuals by strip

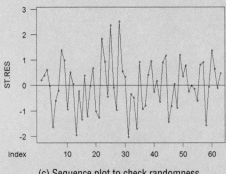

(c) Sequence plot to check randomness

```
ST.RES
K = -0.0007
The observed no. of runs =  33
The expected no. of runs =  32.4286
30 Observations above K   33 below
         The test is significant at  0.8843
         Cannot reject at alpha = 0.05
```

(d) Runs test

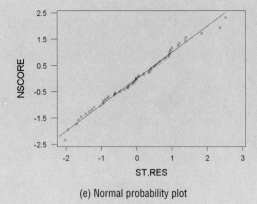

(e) Normal probability plot

Note that both FLYER and DISPLAY are categorical variables with two categories each, so the discussion on categorical variables in Section 10.6 applies here. Since there are four combinations of values for FLYER and DISPLAY, there are four distinct regression equations linking L_S and L_P. The following table lists them:

FLYER	DISPLAY	Fitted (L_S)
0	0	$5.804 - 4.568(\text{L\_P})$
0	1	$5.770 - 4.568(\text{L\_P})$
1	0	$6.841 - 4.568(\text{L\_P})$
1	1	$6.807 - 4.568(\text{L\_P})$

Note that DISPLAY has a small effect, whereas FLYER has a large effect.

Let us convert the equation relating log(sales) to the other predictor variables into an estimate of the multiplicative model by exponentiating both sides,

$$\hat{S} = e^{5.804} P^{-4.568} e^{1.037 \text{ FLYER}} e^{-0.0341 \text{ DISPLAY}}$$

$$= 332(P^{-4.568})(2.821)^{\text{FLYER}}(0.966)^{\text{DISPLAY}}$$

Since there are four combinations of values for FLYER and DISPLAY, there are four distinct equations linking estimated sales, $\hat{S}$, and price, P. The following table lists them:

FLYER	DISPLAY	$\hat{S}$
0	0	$332(P^{-4.568})$
0	1	$320(P^{-4.568})$
1	0	$936(P^{-4.568})$
1	1	$904(P^{-4.568})$

Note that neither FLYER nor DISPLAY has an effect on the elasticity; they only effect the multiplier of the price term. It is again clear that the effect of DISPLAY is negligible, whereas the effect of price is considerable.

The equations for FLYER = 0 and FLYER = 1, with DISPLAY = 0, are superimposed on the graph in Figure 10.30, again showing the large effect of FLYER on sales. Figure 10.30 uses different printing symbols depending on which FLYER/DISPLAY combination was used in a week. The following table lists the printing symbol for each combination. It also lists in parentheses the number of weeks for each combination.

FLYER	DISPLAY 0	1	Total
0	○ (36)	+ (13)	(49)
1	▽ (1)	× (13)	(14)
Total	**(37)**	**(26)**	**(63)**

FIGURE 10.30
Plot of SALES vs.
PRICE with
Superimposed
Curves for FLYER
= 1 (Dashed) and
FLYER = 0 (Solid).
See text for
explanation of ○,
+, ▽, and ×.

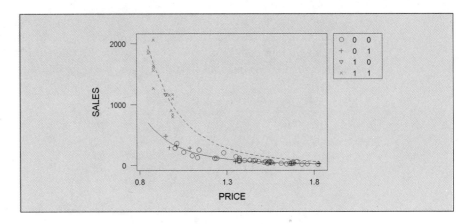

Note that there was only 1 week when there was a flyer, but no display promotion. Figure 10.30 clearly shows the effectiveness of the flyer promotion. It also indicates, however, that price tended to be low when there was a flyer promotion and high when there was not. In order to estimate the relationships better, it would have been good for both price ranges to be overlapping.

Let us interpret the coefficients of the predictor variables. Accounting for FLYER and DISPLAY, the price elasticity of sales is -4.568; that is, a 1% increase in price is associated with an approximate 4.568% decrease in estimated sales. When FLYER = 0 (that is, in a week without a flyer), the value of $(2.821)^{FLYER} = 1$, and when FLYER = 1, the value of $(2.821)^{FLYER} = 2.821$. Thus, accounting for variation in price and display activity, presence of a flyer almost triples estimated sales. Note, when DISPLAY = 0 (that is, in a week without a display), the value of $(0.966)^{DISPLAY} = 1$, and when DISPLAY = 1, the value is 0.966. Thus the estimated effect of DISPLAY is entirely negligible.

On account of the poor showing of diagnostic check 2, the standard errors of the coefficients in Figure 10.28 are not well estimated. Nevertheless, it is clear that the price elasticity of sales is definitely less than -4; the effect of FLYER is considerable; and the effect of DISPLAY is very uncertain, but certainly less.

We can now answer the managerial question:

Accounting for price, do flyer and display promotions have an effect on sales? If so, is one of the two promotional activities more effective?

Promotions with flyers have a very considerable effect on sales, but promotions with displays appear to have a negligible effect on sales, a surprising result.

The multiplicative model is appropriate when the predictor variables and the residual have a multiplicative effect on the response, that is, when we can think of their effects, after having accounted for the other predictor variables, on the response variable in terms of percentage changes. For example, the multiplicative effect of a flyer in the above example was $e^{1.037} = 2.82$, so the effect of a flyer was to *multiply* estimated sales by a factor of 2.82, or to increase sales by 182%. The effect of a 1% increase in price was to decrease estimated sales by about 4.6%, regardless of whether the price is high or low or some value in between.

In this section, we have seen how the logarithmic transformation arises from a model that has an intuitive interpretation, the multiplicative model. Of course, the response and predictor variables could be transformed in other ways than logarithmically. In that case, the interpretation of the resulting model may not be as clear. You should always strive to find models, and thus transformations, that have useful interpretations and can be justified from the context.

In this and the previous two sections, we have expanded the possibilities of modeling with multiple regression by including indicator variables, curvilinear relationships, and logarithmic transformations. You are now able to model a wide variety of situations with multiple regression. In Chapter 11, we will introduce one more type of predictor variable that is important in time series analysis, *lagged variables*.

The next section will help you choose among predictor variables.

10.9

CHOOSING VARIABLES FOR MULTIPLE REGRESSION MODELS

This section briefly discusses how to choose variables for the multiple regression equation. (We did not address this issue in Chapter 9 since we only had one predictor variable there.) As indicated in the introduction to this chapter, we should build *simple* and *parsimonious* models that include only a few essential variables. Since simple models are easily communicated, we should not incorporate a large number of variables when the additional precision of predictions is not much improved. A rough rule of thumb relating the number of predictor variables to the sample size is:

> The sample size divided by the number of predictor variables (n/k) should definitely exceed 5; ideally this ratio should exceed 15.

In the real estate example, the sample size was $n = 70$. With $k = 2$ predictor variables, the ratio $n/k = \frac{70}{2} = 35$, which is large enough.

When developing a multiple regression model, we usually only have limited ideas of which predictor variables will prove useful. At the same time, we typically have a large number of *potential* predictor variables available to us that might be related to the response variable and on which we could gather data. We should then choose predictor variables that are useful for predicting the value of the response variable.

Before using a predictor variable, we should have some basis for assuming that the value of the response variable is related to it. We must not use every conceivable predictor variable available and go on a "fishing expedition." Often, of course, we will be surprised in that a predictor variable we thought to be important turns out not to be so (and vice versa).

A few practical rules for choosing predictor variables should be kept in mind:

1. Choose sensible predictor variables.

2. Keep the purpose of the model in mind.

3. Whenever possible, test the preferred model with a second sample. Alternatively, split your sample randomly into two parts, develop the model for the first subsample and test it with the second.

This section only gives *statistical* guidance to the choice of variables. You must always use subject matter knowledge as well to choose a good set of predictor variables. A variable not considered important on statistical grounds may nevertheless be important on practical grounds and should then be included.

To illustrate, let us start with a model incorporating all available predictor variables in the real estate example. The predictor variables are

AREA   living area (in square feet)

ASSESS   assessed value (in $1,000)

BASEMENT   0 = no basement, 1 = basement

BEDROOMS   number of bedrooms

LOC_1   an indicator variable equaling 1 if the residence is in location 1 and 0 otherwise

LOC_2   an indicator variable equaling 1 if the residence is in location 2 and 0 otherwise

The resulting Minitab output is given in Figure 10.31. Note that the ratio $n/k = \frac{70}{6} = 11.7$ exceeds 5. All four diagnostic checks were carried out (not shown), and they were satisfactory. We can proceed to an evaluation of this model.

The standard deviation of residuals is $s = 10.70$; the $R^2 = 89.3\%$. The model using the predictor variables seems preferable to a model that does not use regression. But are all six predictor variables necessary?

A predictor variable whose coefficient is close to 0 should not be incorporated because its effect is not statistically significant. The relationship between a coefficient being "close to 0" and statistical insignificance must be carefully examined: Just because an estimated coefficient is close to 0 in *absolute* terms, it is not necessarily negligible—if the values for the variable that it will be multiplied by are very large, the product would not be negligible.

t-ratio   In Section 10.4, we discussed how the *t*-ratio can be used to check the *statistical* significance of the difference between a sample regression coefficient and 0 (page 461). The *t*-ratio expresses how many estimated standard errors the estimated coefficient is away from 0. If this ratio is close to 0, then the corresponding variable is not statistically significant. But when is a *t*-ratio close to 0? The following rules of thumb should serve as guidelines, at least in those examples when the sample size is between 20 and 100.

FIGURE 10.31 Real Estate Example: Regression with All Six Predictor Variables

```
    The regression equation is
    MARKET = 61.5 + 0.0566 AREA + 0.291 ASSESS + 21.8 BASEMENT
              + 0.21 BEDROOMS + 1.28 LOC_1 + 8.90 LOC_2

    Predictor       Coef         Stdev      t-ratio        p
    Constant       61.501        8.705        7.07       0.000
    AREA          0.056618      0.005377     10.53       0.000
    ASSESS        0.29104       0.06166       4.72       0.000
    BASEMENT      21.843        3.554         6.15       0.000
    BEDROOMS       0.209        1.538         0.14       0.892
    LOC_1          1.278        3.141         0.41       0.686
    LOC_2          8.901        3.432         2.59       0.012

    s = 10.70      R-sq = 89.3%      R-sq(adj) = 88.2%
    . . .

    Unusual Observations
    Obs.     AREA     MARKET      Fit Stdev.Fit    Residual    St.Resid
     1        952     139.00    161.76     3.98      -22.76      -2.29R
    49       1957     268.00    245.41     2.75       22.59       2.19R
    52       1992     216.00    238.00     2.74      -22.00      -2.13R
    70       2272     275.00    250.65     3.66       24.35       2.42R

    R denotes an obs. with a large st. resid.
```

1. If the absolute value of t is less than 1, we generally do not retain the variable.

2. If it is greater than 2, we generally retain the variable.[6]

3. Retention of a variable whose absolute value of t is between 1 and 2 is resolved on the basis of judgment in each application. You should base your judgment both on the desire for parsimony and on the plausibility of the usefulness of the variable in question given background information. Other things being equal, we prefer regression models with fewer predictor variables.

Figure 10.31 lists the output for the regression model with all six predictor variables. Using the rule of thumb, the variables BEDROOMS and LOC_1 are candidates for deletion because their t-ratios are 0.14 and 0.41, respectively. We should only delete one of these variables at this stage since the joint effect of the two may be considerable on account of confounding. Let us delete the variable BEDROOMS. Prediction of market value can just be based on the remaining five predictor variables.

---

[6] In common statistical usage, a coefficient is considered to be "significantly different from 0" when the absolute value of t exceeds 2. *We shall not take statistical significance literally since the number 2 is arbitrary.*

Figure 10.32(a) gives output for the regression of market value on the five predictor variables AREA, ASSESS, BASEMENT, LOC_1, and LOC_2. (The diagnostic checks were satisfactory, but the results are not given here.) The standard deviation of residuals for the model with five predictor variables is 10.61, which is lower than the standard deviation of residuals for the model with all six predictor

FIGURE 10.32 Real Estate Example: Regression Output for Reduced Models

```
The regression equation is
MARKET = 61.4 + 0.0569 AREA + 0.293 ASSESS + 21.8 BASEMENT + 1.20 LOC_1
         + 8.96 LOC_2

Predictor        Coef       Stdev     t-ratio        p
Constant        61.422      8.619       7.13      0.000
AREA          0.056868    0.005012     11.35      0.000
ASSESS         0.29269     0.05999      4.88      0.000
BASEMENT        21.844      3.526       6.19      0.000
LOC_1            1.202      3.068       0.39      0.697
LOC_2            8.955      3.382       2.65      0.010

s = 10.61       R-sq = 89.3%      R-sq(adj) = 88.4%
. . .

Unusual Observations
Obs.     AREA     MARKET       Fit Stdev.Fit   Residual   St.Resid
  1       952     139.00    161.98      3.62     -22.98      -2.30R
 49      1957     268.00    245.49      2.67      22.51       2.19R
 52      1992     216.00    237.82      2.38     -21.82      -2.11R
 70      2272     275.00    250.52      3.51      24.48       2.44R

R denotes an obs. with a large st. resid.
```

(a) Predictor variables: AREA, ASSESS, BASEMENT, LOC_1, and LOC_2

```
The regression equation is
MARKET = 62.5 + 0.0566 AREA + 0.292 ASSESS + 21.7 BASEMENT + 8.30 LOC_2

Predictor        Coef       Stdev     t-ratio        p
Constant        62.529      8.090       7.73      0.000
AREA          0.056639    0.004946     11.45      0.000
ASSESS         0.29241     0.05960      4.91      0.000
BASEMENT        21.749      3.495       6.22      0.000
LOC_2            8.295      2.913       2.85      0.006

s = 10.54       R-sq = 89.2%      R-sq(adj) = 88.6%
. . .

Unusual Observations
Obs.     AREA     MARKET       Fit Stdev.Fit   Residual   St.Resid
  1       952     139.00    162.17      3.56     -23.17      -2.33R
 49      1957     268.00    246.00      2.31      22.00       2.14R
 52      1992     216.00    238.33      1.97     -22.33      -2.16R
 70      2272     275.00    250.97      3.29      24.03       2.40R

R denotes an obs. with a large st. resid.
```

(b) Predictor variables: AREA, ASSESS, BASEMENT, and LOC_2

variables, 10.70. This is no coincidence:

> There is an important relationship between the absolute value of t for a pre-dictor variable and the sample standard deviation of residuals. If a predictor variable whose absolute t-value is less than 1 (greater than 1) is dropped from the regression model, then the resulting simpler model will have a smaller (larger) sample standard deviation of residuals.

Since the standard deviation of residuals measures the uncertainty around the regression equation, it should be low. Hence the rule of thumb given above.

Let us review the *coefficient of determination:*

> The **coefficient of determination, R^2,** measures the proportion of the total variation in y that is accounted for by the k predictor variables. It is the square of the correlation between the response variable y and the fitted value from the regression equation, $R_{y,\hat{y}}$. A good regression model should have high values for R^2.

Notice the values of R^2 in Figures 10.31 and 10.32(a): They are both 89.3%. [The value in Figure 10.32(a) is in fact slightly smaller than the value in Figure 10.31.] R^2 never increases when a predictor variable is dropped from a regression model. Conversely, R^2 never decreases when a predictor variable is added to a regression model. Even if the additional predictor variable consisted purely of random data, the resulting R^2 value would not decrease. In a sense, the R^2 measure is a "greedy" measure of goodness: The more predictor variables, the better. R^2, unlike the standard deviation of residuals, does *not* reward parsimonious models.

To circumvent this disadvantage, an adjusted version of R^2 is available whose quantitative behavior is like that of the standard deviation of residuals.

adjusted R^2

> The **adjusted R^2** measure is a slightly adjusted version of R^2:
>
> $$R^2_{\text{adj}} = R^2 - \frac{k-1}{n-1}(1-R^2)$$
>
> The larger the number of predictor variables k is relative to the sample size n, the larger is the downward adjustment.
>
> The adjusted R^2 has the following property:
>
> > If a predictor variable whose absolute t-ratio is less than 1 (greater than 1) is dropped from a regression model, then the resulting smaller model will have a larger (smaller) adjusted R^2 value.

Choice based on the adjusted R^2 leads to the same regression model as choice based on the standard deviation of residuals, s. Often, s is preferred because it is easier to interpret.

Moving from the regression model in Figure 10.31 to that in Figure 10.32(a), the R^2_{adj} increases from 88.2% to 88.4% because the variable dropped (BEDROOMS) had an absolute t-ratio less than 1 in Figure 10.32. Thus, based on the standard deviation of residuals and R^2_{adj}, the model in Figure 10.32(a) is preferred to the model in Figure 10.30.

The t-ratio of LOC_1 in Figure 10.31(a) is still less than 1 in absolute value. Let us drop it as well. Figure 10.31(b) gives the resulting output for the model with four predictor variables, AREA, ASSESS, BASEMENT, and LOC_2. The value of s, 10.54, is again slightly lower than the standard deviation of residuals for the model in Figure 10.31(a). Likewise, R^2_{adj} slightly increases. None of the t-ratios in Figure 10.31(b) is less than 1 in absolute value.

We can now complete our discussion of the statistical tools for choosing among predictor variables. The following table gives summary information for the four models with six, five, four, and two predictor variables (see Figures 10.31, 10.32, and 10.3).

Model Figure	$k = 6$ 10.31	$k = 5$ 10.32(a)	$k = 4$ 10.32(b)	$k = 2$ 10.3
Coefficient				
Constant	61.5	61.4	62.5	53.6
AREA	0.0566	0.0569	0.0566	0.0646
ASSESS	0.291	0.293	0.292	0.396
BASEMENT	21.8	21.8	21.7	—
BEDROOMS	0.209	—	—	—
LOC_1	1.28	1.20	—	—
LOC_2	8.90	8.96	8.30	—
s	10.7	10.6	10.5	13.4
R^2	0.893	0.893	0.892	0.821
R^2_{adj}	0.882	0.884	0.886	0.811

Notice how the coefficient of AREA, for example, changes as we move from the model with $k = 6$ predictor variables to that with $k = 2$ predictor variables. (You may want to review the interpretation of coefficients in Section 10.4 now.) A coefficient of a predictor variable measures both the direct effect of that variable on the response, net of the effect of predictor variables *included* in the model, and the *indirect* effect of predictor variables *not* included in the model. Such an indirect effect usually exists for a variable that is not included as a predictor, but is correlated with the predictor variable in question.

Based on statistical grounds alone, one may want to choose the model with $k = 4$ predictor variables in Figure 10.32(b) because its standard deviation of residuals is the lowest. This answers the three managerial questions for the real estate example (p. 444).

A good statistical approach to finding a parsimonious set of predictor variables can be summarized by the following algorithm (backward elimination):

1. Start with a sensible set of predictor variables.

2. Run a regression with the predictor variables presently under consideration.

3. Consider the predictor variable with the *t*-ratio whose absolute value is smallest.

a. If this absolute value is 1 or less, drop the predictor variable from the set of predictor variables under consideration. (Note: Drop one predictor variable at a time.) Return to step 2.

b. If this absolute value exceeds 1, stop.

This simple statistical approach to finding a parsimonious regression model is not the only variable-selection strategy. There are several others; see, for example, Kleinbaum et al. (1988).

10.10

EXAMPLE: ANALYSIS OF DRAFTING TIMES

The following example uses some of the regression analysis tools introduced so far.

Background

Industrial Product Inc. (IPI) designed and built an industrial product.[7] The drawings were produced in the drafting department. A full set of drawings consisted of one general arrangement (GA) drawing and between six and 30 detail drawings, depending on the number of accessories that were ordered as part of the industrial product. GA drawings were always on size D paper, detail drawings could be on A, B, C, or D size paper. D paper was twice the size of C paper, which in turn was twice the size of B paper, which in turn was twice the size of A paper; that is, D paper was 8 times the size of A paper. After the drawings were done, revisions were often required.

Summary

Managerial Questions.   IPI's sales department wanted to know how much time was spent on the drawings for the industrial product so that the delivery date of an order and the labor costs for the drawings could be estimated more accurately. Predicting the time spent on an order was also important for scheduling different jobs. A study was done to answer five questions:

1. Are there any trends in the time spent on the GA drawings, the detail drawings, and the revisions?

---

[7] The data are real, but the name of the company is withheld to protect confidentiality. This study was introduced in Section 2.11.

2. Is the variability in the time variables small?

3. Can any of the three time variables be predicted from the number of detail drawings, taking into consideration that the latter can be of different sizes?

4. Can the time to do GA drawings be used to predict the time to do detail drawings?

5. Are some jobs done too quickly? Is there an indirect relationship between the time to do the detail drawings and the time spent on revisions?

Data Collection.   To answer these questions, appropriate data were collected for the 71 orders completely processed in IPI's drafting department between May 1989 and June 1990.

Findings.   The study found no trends in any of the time variables. Their variability was much larger than expected. None of the three time variables was well predicted by the number of detail drawings. The time to do GA drawings was not a good predictor of the time to do the detail drawings. There was no relationship between the time to do the detail drawings and the time spent on revisions.

Recommendations.   It was surprising that none of the expected relationships could be found. There were also four unusual orders that had to be discarded from the analysis. This points to the fact that the process is not as well understood as was at first thought. In order to estimate order completion better and to improve scheduling, other influencing factors must be identified.

Statistical Details

Statistical Questions.   The statistical questions corresponding to the above questions were:[8]

1. Is a random process generating

  a. The time to do the GA drawings?

  b. The time to do the detail drawings?

  c. The time to do the revision?

---

[8] Before analyzing the data, it had been expected that the time series for all three time variables would be random, in spite of the recent introduction of computer-aided drafting. It had also been expected that the time to do the detail drawings would be strongly related to the overall size of all detail drawings taken together. (Note that this overall size could be computed by multiplying the number of size A, B, C, and D drawings by 1, 2, 4, and 8, respectively, and adding these four products.) The means for the time variables had been expected to be around 104, 26, and 1 hour for the detail drawings, the GA drawings, and the revisions, and the standard deviations for the time variables had been expected to be quite small (20, 3, and 1 hour, respectively).

2. Is the standard deviation of each time variable less than 15% of its mean?

3. Is there an adequate regression model relating

   a. The time to do the detail drawings to the four kinds of detail drawings?

   b. The time to do the detail drawings to the overall size of the detail drawings?

   c. The time to do the GA drawing to the overall size of the detail drawings?

   d. The time to do the revisions to the overall size of the detail drawings?

4. Is the time to do the GA drawings a useful additional predictor variable in the regression models in 3(a) and 3(b)?

5. Is there a negative correlation between the time to do the detail drawings and the time spent on revisions?

Statistical Unit.   The unit in the study was a customer order to IPI's drafting department that required a GA drawing.

Description of Process.   The process consisted of the 12 draftpersons preparing orders arriving at IPI's drafting department during 1989 and 1990.

Sampling Scheme.   Data were collected for the 71 orders completely processed in the drafting department between 1 May 1989 and 30 June 1990 and having a GA drawing as part of the order. The orders were listed by time of receipt.

Description of Variables.   Seven variables were measured on each order:

   The amount of time (in hours) spent on

   1. The detail drawings (TIME_DET)

   2. The GA drawing (TIME_GA)

   3. The revisions (TIME_REV)

   The number of drawings of size

   4. A

   5. B

   6. C

   7. D

A further variable (SIZE) was created by obtaining the weighted sum of the numbers of drawings of sizes A, B, C, and D, where the weights were in relation to their size; that is, the weights were 1, 2, 4, and 8. All variables were quantitative. The variable of main interest was the time spent on the detail drawings. The data are stored in ASCII file DRAFTING.DAT.

Process Characteristics of Interest.

- Statistical questions 1(a–c) required knowing whether the process was random.

- For question 2, the means and standard deviations of the three time variables were needed.

- Question 3(a) required the standard deviation of residuals and the regression coefficients of the predictor variables A, B, C, and D in a multiple regression model whose response variable was TIME_DET.

- For questions 3(b–d), the standard deviation of residuals and the regression coefficients of the predictor variable SIZE were of interest in the simple regression models whose response variables were TIME_DET, TIME_GA, and TIME_REV, respectively.

- For question 4, the regression coefficient of variable TIME_GA was of interest.

- For question 5, the correlation between TIME_DET and TIME_REV was needed.

Data.   A partial listing of the 71 observations is given in Figure 10.33, and descriptive statistics are given in Figure 10.34. (As described below, only 67 observations were used in the analysis.) The data are stored in ASCII file DRAFTING.DAT. Four units were excluded from the analysis—orders 21, 36, 51, and 62. Order 21 was excluded from the analysis since contradictory information about the customer's requirements cost a great deal of extra time. Orders 36 and 51 were very unusual. There were many anomalies with order 62, some of which were due to misunderstandings between sales and drafting with respect to a component of the industrial product. During the analysis, several other unusual observations were examined, but there were no assignable causes for any of them. They were included in the analysis. For example, the times spent on revisions for orders 9 and 23 were quite high, but it was not considered wise to exclude these orders from the

FIGURE 10.33
Drafting Times
Data

ROW	TIME_DET	TIME_GA	TIME_REV	A	B	C	D
1	104.68	20.00	15.25	6	7	7	6
2	97.59	48.50	2.25	8	8	6	6
3	185.00	25.50	6.58	8	7	5	8
4	216.90	56.00	5.50	9	7	5	7
5	70.00	11.00	3.00	3	7	4	6
6	153.26	24.50	3.50	3	8	6	5
7	103.70	26.00	5.95	7	7	6	7
.							
.							
.							
66	106.08	12.41	0.00	4	2	0	5
67	115.00	45.27	2.00	3	5	3	6
68	103.15	20.49	16.00	6	6	8	7
69	144.94	26.00	25.00	6	6	8	7
70	53.40	13.10	6.00	6	5	9	5
71	52.03	64.00	0.00	6	7	3	6

FIGURE 10.34 Drafting Times Data: Descriptive Statistics

	N	MEAN	MEDIAN	TRMEAN	STDEV	SEMEAN
TIME_DET	67	116.78	111.00	114.93	42.97	5.25
TIME_GA	67	32.54	26.50	31.64	16.66	2.04
TIME_REV	67	13.48	8.50	11.91	14.38	1.76
A	67	5.418	5.000	5.393	2.356	0.288
B	67	7.254	7.000	7.180	3.091	0.378
C	67	4.075	3.000	4.066	1.980	0.242
D	67	5.687	6.000	5.689	1.479	0.181

	MIN	MAX	Q1	Q3
TIME_DET	35.57	230.90	84.41	145.60
TIME_GA	9.10	73.50	22.50	40.00
TIME_REV	0.00	67.93	3.25	18.95
A	1.000	10.000	3.000	7.000
B	0.000	17.000	6.000	9.000
C	0.000	9.000	3.000	6.000
D	2.000	9.000	5.000	7.000

analysis since the time spent on revisions can sometimes be quite high; although order 53 was an outlier in some of the models, there was no reason to exclude it from the analysis.

Data Analysis. Based on information not shown here, the processes generating the three time variables, TIME_DET, TIME_GA, and TIME_REV, were judged to be random. One observation, order 9, was above the upper control limit for TIME_REV; this observation was examined for an assignable cause, but none was found, and so it was kept for the analysis. Given that the distribution of the variable TIME_REV was positively skewed, it was not considered surprising to find one observation in 71 slightly above the upper control limit.

Figure 10.35 gives the Minitab output for the regression model relating the time to do the detail drawings, TIME_DET, to the four predictor variables regarding the numbers of size A, B, C, and D drawings. The unusual observations 21, 36, 51, and 62 were examined in detail, assignable causes were found as described above, and these observations were excluded from the analysis. (Observation 4 was not examined in detail since its standardized residual was only 2.13.)

Let us answer questions 1(a–c):

Is a random process generating each of the three time variables?

Figure 10.36 gives sequence plots and runs tests for TIME_DET, TIME_GA, and TIME_REV. It suggests randomness for all three time variables. All observations were within the control limits, except for observation 9, which was examined above.

Let us next answer question 2:

Are the standard deviations of the time variables less than 15% of their mean?

FIGURE 10.35 Drafting Times Data: Regression of TIME_DET on Four Predictor Variables Using All Data

```
The regression equation is
TIME_DET = 22.4 + 0.26 A + 5.20 B + 3.26 C + 7.75 D

Predictor       Coef       Stdev      t-ratio         p
Constant       22.35       18.34         1.22     0.227
A               0.256       2.433        0.11     0.917
B               5.200       1.857        2.80     0.007
C               3.261       2.605        1.25     0.215
D               7.750       3.908        1.98     0.051

s = 40.96      R-sq = 34.6%     R-sq(adj) = 30.7%

Unusual Observations
Obs.      A    TIME_DET      Fit Stdev.Fit   Residual   St.Resid
  4     9.0     216.90    131.61      8.56      85.29      2.13R
 21     9.0     264.30    148.43     12.92     115.87      2.98R
 36     9.0     183.61    214.51     20.33     -30.90     -0.87 X
 51    14.0      85.38    175.52     20.46     -90.14     -2.54R
 62     7.0     264.66    122.64      7.13     142.02      3.52R

R denotes an obs. with a large st. resid.
X denotes an obs. whose value gives it large influence.
```

FIGURE 10.36
Time Series Plots
and Runs Tests for
Drafting Data

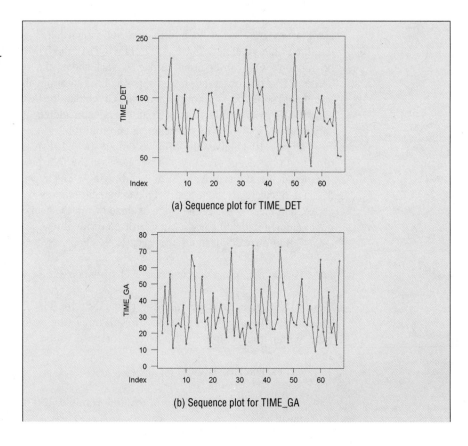

(a) Sequence plot for TIME_DET

(b) Sequence plot for TIME_GA

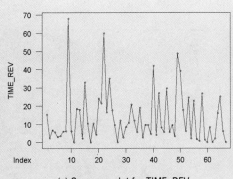

(c) Sequence plot for TIME_REV

```
TIME_DET

K = 116.7754

The observed no. of runs =  33
The expected no. of runs =  33.8955
29 Observations above K   38 below
        The test is significant at  0.8223
        Cannot reject at alpha = 0.05


TIME_GA

K =  32.5393

The observed no. of runs =  36
The expected no. of runs =  31.8060
24 Observations above K   43 below
        The test is significant at  0.2611
        Cannot reject at alpha = 0.05


TIME_REV

K =  13.4803

The observed no. of runs =  30
The expected no. of runs =  31.8060
24 Observations above K   43 below
        The test is significant at  0.6284
        Cannot reject at alpha = 0.05
```

(d) Runs tests

FIGURE 10.37 Drafting Times Data: Regression of TIME_DET on Four Predictor Variables, Excluding Four Cases

```
The regression equation is
TIME_DET = 14.2 + 0.38 A + 6.01 B + 1.37 C + 9.03 D

Predictor         Coef        Stdev      t-ratio          p
Constant         14.21       16.68         0.85      0.398
A                0.378        1.996        0.19      0.850
B                6.011        1.552        3.87      0.000
C                1.370        2.144        0.64      0.525
D                9.028        3.817        2.37      0.021

s = 32.66         R-sq = 45.7%        R-sq(adj) = 42.2%

Unusual Observations
Obs.       A    TIME_DET         Fit  Stdev.Fit   Residual   St.Resid
  4      9.0      216.90      129.73       7.79      87.17      2.75R
 32      6.0      230.90      161.92       8.92      68.98      2.20R
 67      6.0       52.03      116.83       4.98     -64.80     -2.01R
```

Figure 10.34 can be used to obtain the ratio of standard deviation to mean for each of the three time variables:

Variable	Ratio
TIME_DET	0.36
TIME_GA	0.51
TIME_REV	1.07

None of these ratios is less than 0.15.

Question 3(a) was:

> Is there an adequate multiple regression model relating the time to do the detail drawings to the four kinds of detail drawings?

Figure 10.37 displays results for the regression of TIME_DET on the four predictor variables, A, B, C, and D. Before using the regression output to answer question 3(a), we must do the diagnostic checks. None of the unusual observations flagged in Figure 10.37 is of concern. Figure 10.38 gives the residual vs. fitted plot and the residual vs. predictor variable plots. The linearity check is satisfactory, and the check for constant standard deviation is adequate. Note, however, that there is somewhat higher variability in standardized residuals for larger values of the number of size D drawings. The randomness and normality checks (graphs not shown) were adequate.

Since the diagnostic checks were adequate, we can now use the regression output in Figure 10.37 to answer question 3(a). The standard deviation of residuals

FIGURE 10.38 Drafting Times Data: Diagnostic Checks

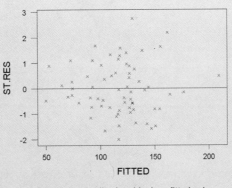

(a) Plot of standardized residual vs. fitted value

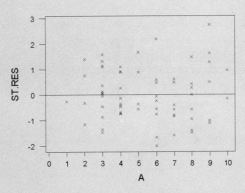

(b) Plot of standardized residual vs. number of size A drawings

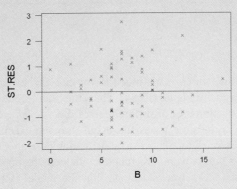

(c) Plot of standardized residual vs. number of size B drawings

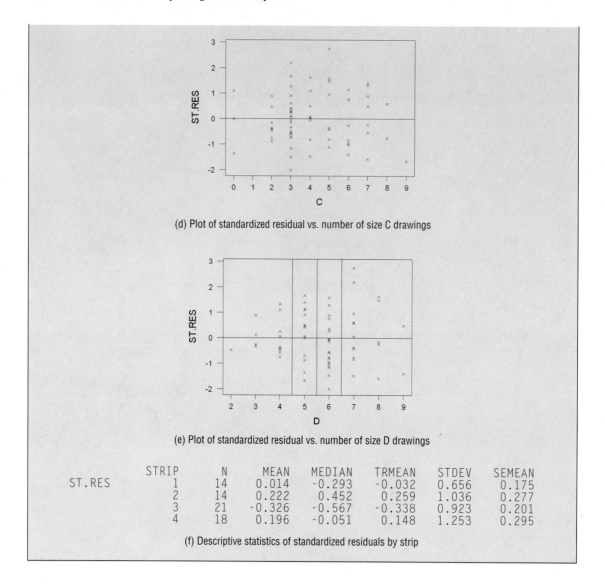

(d) Plot of standardized residual vs. number of size C drawings

(e) Plot of standardized residual vs. number of size D drawings

	STRIP	N	MEAN	MEDIAN	TRMEAN	STDEV	SEMEAN
ST.RES	1	14	0.014	-0.293	-0.032	0.656	0.175
	2	14	0.222	0.452	0.259	1.036	0.277
	3	21	-0.326	-0.567	-0.338	0.923	0.201
	4	18	0.196	-0.051	0.148	1.253	0.295

(f) Descriptive statistics of standardized residuals by strip

is $s = 32.66$, which is not much lower than the standard deviation of TIME_DET, 42.97, given in Figure 10.34. Thus the four predictor variables describing the numbers of drawings of different sizes did not appear to account for much of the variation in the time to do the detail drawings. This was also reflected in some small t-ratios. Dropping predictor variables one at a time, as long as their absolute t-ratios were less than 1, yielded the model in Figure 10.39(a). The diagnostic checks were adequate, but the model is really no better than the one in Figure 10.37.

FIGURE 10.39
Drafting Times
Data: Regressions

```
The regression equation is
TIME_DET = 17.2 + 5.88 B + 10.0 D

Predictor        Coef       Stdev     t-ratio          p
Constant        17.20       15.83        1.09      0.281
B                5.881       1.520        3.87      0.000
D               10.008       3.176        3.15      0.002

s = 32.26        R-sq = 45.3%       R-sq(adj) = 43.6%
```

(a) Regression of TIME_DET on predictor variables B and D

```
The regression equation is
TIME_DET = 3.9 + 0.366 TIME_GA + 5.79 B + 10.4 D

Predictor        Coef       Stdev     t-ratio          p
Constant         3.93       17.86        0.22      0.827
TIME_GA        0.3656      0.2365        1.55      0.127
B               5.785       1.505        3.84      0.000
D              10.373       3.151        3.29      0.002

s = 31.92        R-sq = 47.3%       R-sq(adj) = 44.8%
```

(b) Regression of TIME_DET on predictor variables B, D, and TIME_GA

To answer question 3(b),

Is there an adequate regression model relating the time to do the detail drawings to the overall size of the detail drawings?

the response variable TIME_DET was regressed on the predictor variable SIZE. (The regression output is not shown.) As in the model relating TIME_DET to predictor variables A, B, C, and D, the diagnostic checks were adequate, but SIZE did not account for much variation in the response variable.

To answer questions 3(c–d),

Is there an adequate regression model relating the time to do the GA drawing to the overall size of the detail drawings?

Is there an adequate regression model relating the time to do the revisions to the overall size of the detail drawings?

the respective response variables, TIME_GA and TIME_REV, were regressed on the four predictor variables. (The regression output is not shown.) The predictor variables hardly accounted for any variation in these two response variables.

Let us next answer question 4,

Is the time to do the GA drawings a useful additional predictor variable in the regression models in 3(a) and 3(b)?

The variable TIME_GA was added as a predictor variable to model 3(a), described in Figure 10.39(a). The results are given in Figure 10.39(b). The diagnostic checks (not shown) were adequate. Since the t-ratio of the coefficient of TIME_GA is 1.55, this variable is not very useful in accounting for variation in TIME_DET beyond what was already accounted for by variables B and D in Figure 10.39(a). Using information not given here, a similar conclusion was reached regarding the usefulness of GA drawings in model 3(b).

To answer question 5,

Is there a negative correlation between the time to do the detail drawings and the time spent on revisions?

Figure 10.40 displays the plot of time spent on the detail drawings vs. time spent on revisions. The correlation between the two variables was 0.107.

Conclusions. Question 1: The processes generating the three variables TIME_DET, TIME_GA, and TIME_REV were all random. Thus, there were no time trends in these variables.

Question 2: The ratios of standard deviation to mean exceeded 0.15 for all three variables. Thus, the relative variability in these variables was higher than expected, most important, for the time spent on revisions.

Question 3: The time to do the detail drawings was not well predicted from the numbers of detail drawings of various sizes. The regression model obtained, though statistically adequate, was not considered precise enough for practical purposes. Other factors must be taken into account to obtain good enough predictions of the time variables. Because the relationship among the sizes of the four kinds of

FIGURE 10.40

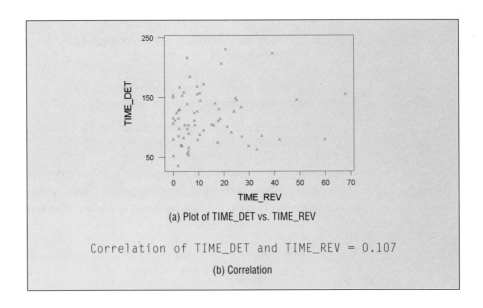

(a) Plot of TIME_DET vs. TIME_REV

Correlation of TIME_DET and TIME_REV = 0.107

(b) Correlation

detail drawings was 1:2:4:8, the relationship among the coefficients of the predictor variables was expected to be close to the ratio 1:2:4:8. Figure 10.37 does not support this expectation: The relative sizes of the four kinds of detail drawings were thus not very important in determining the total time spent on them. Time spent on the GA drawing was not related to these four predictor variables nor was the time spent on revisions.

Question 4: The variable time spent on GA drawings did not help much in predicting time spent on detail drawings.

Question 5: There appeared to be no relationship at all between the time to do the detail drawings and the time spent on revisions.

Surprises.   The results from this study were quite surprising. If the conditions underlying the process were to remain unchanged, it may be reasonable to expect the results to hold in the future as well. It should be remembered, however, that four of the 71 original orders had been discarded from the analysis, and so the results could not be applied to orders that are comparable to these four.

10.11

ADDITIONAL RESULTS

This section discusses some additional results that are sometimes needed, in particular, when the sample size is small. This section can be skipped without loss of continuity.

Evaluation of Coefficients: Small Samples

When the regression equation is based on small samples (say, $n < 30$), the confidence intervals given in Sections 9.6 and 10.4 are too narrow.

confidence interval for coefficient

The general formula for finding confidence intervals is again

$$\begin{matrix} \text{Point Estimate} \\ \text{for} \\ \text{Coefficient} \end{matrix} \quad \pm \quad \text{Multiple} \quad \left(\begin{matrix} \text{Estimated Standard} \\ \text{Error for} \\ \text{Coefficient} \end{matrix} \right)$$

but now the appropriate multiple comes from a t-table with $n - k - 1$ degrees of freedom, where k is the number of predictor variables in the multiple regression at hand.

For example, the multiple for a 95% confidence interval for a coefficient in the industrial product-performance example of Section 10.7 (see Figure 10.19, page 474) is obtained from a t-distribution with $n - k - 1$, here, $27 - 2 - 1 = 24$ degrees of freedom. Using Figure 7.24, the appropriate multiple is 2.064. Thus the 95% confidence interval for the coefficient of the quadratic term, predictor variable x_2, is

$$-205.56 \pm 2.064(32.92) \quad \text{or} \quad -206.6 \pm 67.9$$

The 95% confidence interval is moderately wide, but it does not include the value 0, suggesting that, based on statistical grounds, the quadratic term is useful for predicting performance, y.

Estimation of the Regression Equation

This section is concerned with estimating the value of the population or process regression equation,

$$\beta_0 + \beta_1 x_1 + \beta x_2 + \cdots + \beta_k x_k$$

at given values for the predictor variables. This is equivalent to estimating the *mean* on the response variable y for a *large* number of observations, all of which have the *same* values on the predictor variables. The difference between this problem and the one discussed in Section 10.5 is that, in Section 10.5, we predicted the value of the response variable for *one* observation at given values of the predictor variables, whereas in this section, we estimate the mean value of the response variable for a *large* number of observations, all of which have the same set of values for the predictor variables.

A point estimate of this mean can be obtained from the estimated regression equation. In the industrial example in Section 10.7, performance (y) was estimated to be maximized when the value of the input level is $x = 0.10$. Suppose there was a large number of products, all of which have the same input level, $x = 0.10$. What is an estimate for their mean performance and what is a confidence interval for this mean? The resulting Minitab output is given in Figure 10.41.

FIGURE 10.41
Industrial Example: Estimation and Prediction (Input = 0.10, $x_1 = 0.10$, $x_2 = 0.01$)

```
The regression equation is
Y = 402 + 39.8 X - 206 X**2

Predictor        Coef       Stdev     t-ratio         p
Constant       401.67       26.88       14.95     0.000
X               39.78       19.00        2.09     0.047
X**2          -205.56       32.92       -6.24     0.000

s = 80.63       R-sq = 64.4%      R-sq(adj) = 61.4%

Analysis of Variance

SOURCE        DF          SS          MS          F         p
Regression     2      281999      141000      21.69     0.000
Error         24      156015        6501
Total         26      438014

SOURCE        DF      SEQ SS
X              1       28481
X**2           1      253519


    Fit Stdev.Fit          95% C.I.          95%   P.I.
   403.6      26.7     ( 348.5, 458.7)     ( 228.3, 578.9)
```

Since $x = 0.10$, the values of the two predictor variables in the regression model are $x_1 = x = 0.10$ and $x_2 = x^2 = (0.10)^2 = 0.01$. A point estimate of mean performance is

$$\hat{y} = 401.7 + 39.8(x) - 206(x^2)$$
$$= 401.7 + 39.8(0.10) - 206(0.01) = 403.6$$

That is, it is the same as the point prediction for *one* product's performance with these values for the predictor variables.

Since we are estimating this mean (that is, the point on the regression equation at $x_1 = 0.10$ and $x_2 = 0.01$) from the sample of 27 products, we should also give an expression for its standard error. This standard error comes about because we used the *sample* coefficients $b_0, b_1, \ldots, b_k$ as point estimates of the corresponding population coefficients in the regression equation. In Sections 10.5 and earlier in this section, we discussed how to express sampling uncertainty about the population coefficients $\beta_0, \beta_1, \ldots, \beta_k$ individually. Here we need to combine these sources of sampling uncertainty.

standard error for regression equation

The resulting estimated standard error for the regression equation at $x_1 = 0.10$ and $x_2 = 0.01$ is given in Figure 10.41 as Stdev.Fit = 26.7.

As noted earlier, we can interpret the regression equation value as the mean of a large number of observations that all have the same values on the predictor variables. We can obtain a confidence interval for this mean with the usual formula,

confidence interval for regression equation

Point Estimate $\pm$ Multiple(Estimated Standard Error)

where the Multiple comes from a t-distribution with $n - k - 1$ degrees of freedom.

In the industrial example, the degrees of freedom are $27 - 2 - 1 = 24$, and the t-value for a 95% interval is 2.064 from Figure 7.24 or Minitab. A 95% confidence interval for the regression equation is thus

$$403.6 \pm 2.064(26.7) = 403.6 \pm 55.1$$

or between 348.5 and 458.7.

This 95% confidence interval is also given in the last line of Figure 10.41. It is a rather wide interval. We are 95% certain that mean performance at the input level $x = 0.10$ is within 55.1 of the point estimate 403.6.

In deriving the confidence interval for the regression equation, we used the standard error for the regression equation, as given in the Minitab output (Stdev.Fit). This standard error is difficult to compute, in particular, when the number of predictor variables is $k > 1$. In the case of simple regression, where $k = 1$, this standard error is

$$\sqrt{s^2 \frac{1}{n} + s^2 \frac{(x - \bar{x})^2}{\sum_{i=1}^{n}(x_i - \bar{x})^2}} = s\sqrt{\frac{1}{n} + \frac{(x - \bar{x})^2}{\sum_{i=1}^{n}(x_i - \bar{x})^2}}$$

where

> n is the size of the sample on which the regression line estimate is based
>
> x is the value of the predictor variable at which the regression line is to be estimated
>
> $\bar{x}$ is the sample mean for the predictor variable
>
> $\sum_{i=1}^{n} (x_i - \bar{x})^2$ is the sum of squared deviations of the predictor variable values in the sample from their sample mean

The second part of this term, involving $(x - \bar{x})^2$, measures the extent of extrapolation: The further x is away from $\bar{x}$ (that is, the more extrapolation there is), the larger this term is.

Prediction of Individual Observations: Small Samples

This section is a continuation of Section 10.5, where prediction of individual observations was discussed. In that section, we gave an approximate formula for the *standard error of prediction,*

> Standard Error of Prediction $= s$

where s is the standard deviation of residuals. This formula always underestimates the correct standard error of prediction, but when the sample size is *large,* it is reasonably close to the correct value. In this section, we give an exact formula for the standard error of prediction.

Let us continue the industrial example discussed in Section 10.7. Suppose we need to predict performance for another product. For this product, the value of the input level is $x = 0.10$, so the values of the two predictor variables are $x_1 = 0.10$ and $x_2 = 0.01$. Based on the sample regression equation, a prediction of performance was $\hat{y} = 401.7 + 39.8(0.10) - 206(0.01) = 403.6$.

The actual performance for this product will not necessarily equal 403.6. There is uncertainty about how close the actual value will be to this prediction. A measure of this uncertainty is the standard error of prediction. In principle, there are two sources contributing to this uncertainty.

1. One source is due to the inherent imperfection in the regression model, expressed by the residual ϵ in the model

$$y = \beta_0 + \beta_1 x + \beta_2 x^2 + \epsilon$$

This part of the uncertainty can be described by the standard deviation σ of residuals around the multiple regression equation. From the sample of 27 products, this standard deviation was estimated to be $s = 80.63$.

2. The second source is due to the fact that the values of β_0, β_1, and β_2 had to be estimated from the sample.

This second source of the uncertainty is measured by the standard error of the regression equation which is tedious to compute except when the number of predictor variables is $k = 1$. The Minitab output in Figure 10.41 gives this value under Stdev.Fit; it is 26.7.

When the sample size is at least moderate and the amount of extrapolation is moderate, this second source of uncertainty is negligible in comparison to the inherent variability around the regression equation, described in source 1 above.

standard error of prediction

In summary, the *standard error of prediction* is computed from the two sources of uncertainty, given above,

$$\sqrt{s^2 + (\text{Stdev.Fit})^2}$$

Ignoring the second source of uncertainty, the standard error of prediction approximately equals the standard deviation of residuals. This approximation always is an *underestimate* of the accurate standard error of prediction, but, under the conditions given for the second source, the amount of underestimation is not large.

In the industrial example, the standard error of prediction is thus estimated to be

$$\sqrt{80.63^2 + 26.7^2} = 84.9$$

Computation of the standard error of prediction is difficult, except when there is only one predictor variable (when $k = 1$). In that case, the computational formula is

$$\sqrt{s^2 + s^2\frac{1}{n} + s^2\frac{(x - \bar{x})^2}{\sum_{i=1}^{n}(x_i - \bar{x})^2}} = s\sqrt{1 + \frac{1}{n} + \frac{(x - \bar{x})^2}{\sum_{i=1}^{n}(x_i - \bar{x})^2}}$$

where

n is the size of the sample on which the regression line estimate is based

x is the value of the predictor variable for the new observation in question

$\bar{x}$ is the sample mean for the predictor variable

$\sum_{i=1}^{n}(x_i - \bar{x})^2$ is the sum of squared deviations of the predictor variable values in the sample from their sample mean

prediction interval

Having obtained a point prediction for the product's performance value, we can now also obtain prediction intervals. As usual, prediction intervals are obtained from the formula

$$\hat{y} \pm \text{Multiple}(\text{Standard Error of Prediction})$$

where the Multiple comes from the t-distribution with $n - k - 1$ degrees of freedom. In the industrial example, the degrees of freedom are $27 - 2 - 1 = 24$. We can thus make the following statements:

> The probability is about 95% that the product's performance value falls within the limits $403.6 \pm 2.064(84.9)$, or 403.6 ± 175.2, or between 228.4 and 578.8

> The probability is about 97.5% that the product's performance value exceeds $403.6 - 2.064(84.9) = 228.4$.

Predictive information can also be obtained with Minitab. Figure 10.41 gives the details for the product for which $x_1 = 0.10$ and $x_2 = 0.01$. For example, the 95% prediction interval given by Minitab extends from 228.3 to 578.9, which agrees with the 95% PI computed above.

10.12

SUMMARY AND OUTLOOK

This chapter introduced basic concepts underlying multiple regression analysis, where the quantitative response variable, y, is related to k predictor variables. There is a wealth of material on regression analysis that we could not cover. See Kleinbaum, Kupper, and Muller (1988) for further details.

Multiple regression relationships are useful for explanation and prediction. This chapter stressed the predictive aspect: When it is hard to get the value on the response variable for a particular unit of interest and it is easier to measure the values of related (predictor) variables for that particular unit, it may be possible to use the relationship between the response variable and the predictor variables for predictive purposes. In such a case, the predictor variables can be any information on the unit of interest that is available at the time a prediction for the response variable has to be made. If categorical, a predictor variable can take on only the values 1 or 0 (1 if a particular characteristic is present and 0 if it is absent). A predictor variable can be a transformation (square root, log, etc.) of a particular background variable. The number of possibilities is indeed large.

We must bear in mind that it is *highly* desirable on practical grounds not to have a large number of predictor variables in a particular regression model. Having simple and parsimonious models is essential, and it is imperative to choose a reasonably small number of predictor variables for any multiple regression model. The sample size divided by the number of predictor variables *(n/k)* should preferably exceed 15.

The next chapter introduces the analysis of time series with regression analysis. There, *lagged* values of the response variable are introduced as predictor variables. When carrying out time series analysis with multiple regression, it will be very important to check the third assumption underlying the regression model, the randomness assumption.

Key Terms and Concepts

multiple regression model
  assumptions: linearity, constant
  standard deviation, randomness,
  normality
diagnostic checks
estimated regression equation
  least squares criterion, s, coefficient
  of determination, R^2, adjusted R^2,
  t-ratio, p-value

categorical predictor variables
curvilinear relationships
multiplicative model
choosing among predictor variables

References

Chatterjee, S., and Price, B. (1991), *Regression Analysis by Example,* 2nd Edition, Wiley, New York.

Dielman, T. E. (1991), *Applied Regression Analysis for Business and Economics,* Duxbury Press, Belmont, CA.

  This is written at the level of this book. It uses many applied problems and has extensive computer output.

Draper, N., and Smith, H. (1981), *Applied Regression Analysis,* 2nd Edition, Wiley, New York.

  This is an excellent advanced text for most aspects of regression analysis.

Kleinbaum, D. G., Kupper, L. L., and Muller, K. E. (1988), *Applied Regression and Other Multivariable Methods,* 2nd Edition, Duxbury Press, Belmont, CA.

  This is an introduction to regression and some other techniques, emphasizing applications.

10.13

USING MINITAB FOR WINDOWS

This section shows how several of the graphs in this chapter were generated with Minitab for Windows.

Figure 10.1

Choose *File* ▸ *Other Files* ▸ *Import ASCII Data*
In the *Import ASCII Data* dialog box,
    Under *Store data in column,* type **C1-C6**
    Click *ok*
    In the *Input Text From File* dialog box,
        Choose and click data file *realnew.dat,* click *ok*

Choose *Window* ▸ *Data*

In the *Data* window,

In the boxes immediately under *C1* to *C6,* type **MARKET AREA ASSESS BASEMENT BEDROOMS LOCATION**

Click any empty cell

Choose *Window* ▸ *Session*

In the *Session* window,

Type **PRINT C1-C6**

Choose *Stat* ▸ *Basic Statistics* ▸ *Descriptive statistics*

In the *Descriptive statistics* dialog box,

Under *Variables,* type **C1-C3 C5**

Click *ok*

TALLYING CATEGORICAL VARIABLES

Choose *Stat* ▸ *Tables* ▸ *Tally*

In the *Tally* dialog box,

Under *Variables,* type **C4 C6**

Click the box next to *Percents*

Click *ok*

Figure 10.3

REGRESSION OUTPUT, STANDARDIZED RESIDUALS

Choose *Stat* ▸ *Regression* ▸ *Regression*

In the *Regression* dialog box,

Click the box next to *Response,* type **C1**

Click the box next to *Predictors,* type **C2 C3**

Under *Storage,* click the boxes next to *Standard. resids.* and *Fits*

Click *ok*

(The standardized residuals are now stored in C7 as SRES1, and the fitted values are stored in C8 as FITS1.)

Figure 10.16

CREATING INDICATOR VARIABLES FROM A CATEGORICAL VARIABLE

Choose *Calc* ▸ *Make Indicator Variables*

In the *Make Indicator Variables* dialog box,

Under *Indicator variables for,* type **C6**

Under *Store results in,* type **C7-C9**

Click *ok*

Choose *Window* ▸ *Data*

In the *Data* window,

In the boxes immediately under *C7* to *C9,* type **LOC_1 LOC_2 LOC_3**

Click any empty cell

10.14

PROBLEMS FOR CLASS DISCUSSION

10.1 Waste Management Company[9]

A waste management company had experienced significant growth over the past several years. Cash requirements were growing rapidly, making cash management ever more important. Management had become concerned about the bad debt experience and had done a study to examine several managerial questions. One of them was:

> Is there a causal relationship between bad debt experience and other variables, including the size of the accounts receivable (AR) balance, gross revenue, gross margin, and AR turnover? (Note that AR turnover is defined as gross revenue divided by AR.)

Four variables were measured in each of the 35 months between January 1987 and November 1989: (1) BAD debt (in $1,000), (2) the total outstanding AR balance (in $1,000), (3) gross REVENUE (in $million), and (4) gross MARGIN (gross revenue minus direct selling costs, in $million). The data are stored in ASCII file ACC_REC.DAT.

Use the Minitab output in Figure 10.42 to answer the above question. Assume that the diagnostic checks for all three regression models are satisfactory.

FIGURE 10.42

```
MTB > Read 'C:\MTBWIN\DATA\ACC_REC.DAT' C1-C4
      35 rows read from file C:\MTBWIN\DATA\ACC_REC.DAT
MTB > NAME C1 'BAD' C2 'AR' C3 'REVENUE' C4 'MARGIN'
MTB > PRINT C1-C4


  ROW      BAD       AR    REVENUE    MARGIN

    1     2062    19310      1440       252
    2     2479    19210      1437       276
    3     2774    21260      2052       365
    .
    .
    .
   34     3124    67730      3291       557
   35     8857    69040      3912       659
```

---

[9] The data were slightly altered to protect confidentiality.

FIGURE 10.42

```
MTB > Describe C1-C4

                N      MEAN    MEDIAN    TRMEAN    STDEV    SEMEAN
BAD            35      3769      3130      3645     1813       306
AR             35     38273     35400     37556    13704      2316
REVENUE        35      2432      2256      2391      708       120
MARGIN         35     449.2     409.0     441.4    134.0      22.7

               MIN       MAX        Q1        Q3
BAD            964      8857      2701      4304
AR           19210     69040     28370     45420
REVENUE       1437      4118      1910      2940
MARGIN       252.0     826.0     358.0     537.0

Model 1

MTB > Regress C1 3 C2-C4

The regression equation is
BAD = - 960 - 0.0649 AR + 4.21 REVENUE - 6.72 MARGIN

Predictor      Coef       Stdev
Constant      -960.0      804.9
AR          -0.06495     0.04366
REVENUE        4.208      1.816
MARGIN        -6.721      7.100

s = 1278       R-sq = 54.7%      R-sq(adj) = 50.3%

Model 2

MTB > Regress C1 2 C2 C3

The regression equation is
BAD = - 904 - 0.0458 AR + 2.64 REVENUE

Predictor      Coef       Stdev
Constant      -903.8      801.4
AR          -0.04577     0.03862
REVENUE       2.6416      0.7473

s = ?   R-sq = ?   R-sq(adj) = ?

Model 3

MTB > Regress C1 1 C2

The regression equation is
BAD = 764 + 0.0785 AR

Predictor      Coef       Stdev
Constant       763.5      752.3
AR           0.07853     0.01854

s = 1481       R-sq = 35.2%      R-sq(adj) = 33.3%

MTB > Stop
```

10.2 Oiling of Eggs[10]

In recent years, increasing quality problems in the processing of shell eggs have arisen, and are thought to be due to more complex processing and distribution operations. In order to improve these operations, an experiment was run at the Central Experimental Farm in Ottawa. This *controlled* and *randomized* experiment was to address the following questions:

1. Is quality retention significantly greater when spraying eggs with a vegetable-oil–based emulsion than when following the current practice of not oiling eggs?

2. Does the answer to question 1 depend on the timing of the oiling? Eggs can be oiled either immediately after being laid or after being washed and graded (which is done after a storage period of between 1 and 6 days).

3. What is the quality deterioration of eggs after being stored for 1, 2, or 3 weeks?

In all, 180 eggs laid on the same day by a homogeneous commercial strain of hens were used. In order to answer the questions, eggs were treated in various ways as follows:

Oiling or no oiling immediately after lay

Storage for 2, 4, or 6 days

Washing and then oiling or no oiling

Storage for 1, 2, or 3 weeks

Grading for quality

Thus each egg was described by four predictor variables and a response variable:

1. OIL_LAY, oiling immediately after lay. This was coded as 1 if the egg was oiled immediately after lay, and as 0 if not.

2. STORE_1, the length of the storage period immediately after lay. This could be 2, 4, or 6 days.

3. OIL_STOR, oiling after the first storage period. This was coded as 1 if the egg was oiled after the first storage period, and as 0 if not.

4. STORE_2, the length of the second storage period. This could be 1, 2, or 3 weeks.

5. QUALITY, as measured in Haugh units, a commonly used quality measure of the freshness of eggs. At the end of the second storage period, each egg was broken and its quality was measured.

Quality was the variable of main interest: the objective was to examine the effect of the four predictor variables on quality. The data were collected as follows: There are two distinct values for the variable OIL_LAY, three for STORE_1, two for OIL_STOR, and three for STORE_2. Thus there are (2)(3)(2)(3) = 36 distinct ways in which these variable values can be combined. Five eggs were randomly assigned to each of these 36 possibilities, so 180 eggs were used in all. The data are stored in ASCII file EGGSPART.DAT.

To answer questions 1 and 2, suppose that "significantly greater" means "an average increase of 4 or more Haugh units."

Use the Minitab output in Figure 10.43 to answer the three questions.

---

[10] The data were kindly supplied L. R. Hillier.

FIGURE 10.43

```
MTB > Read 'C:\MTBWIN\DATA\EGGSPART.DAT' C1-C5
    180 rows read from file C:\MTBWIN\DATA\EGGSPART.DAT
MTB > NAME C1 'QUALITY' C2 'OIL_LAY' C3 'STORE_1' C4 'OIL_STOR' C5 'STORE_2'
MTB > PRINT C1-C5                    # Note: Selected rows are printed here only.

ROW    QUALITY   OIL_LAY   STORE_1   OIL_STOR   STORE_2
  1     83.66       0         2          1          1
  6     78.83       0         4          1          1
 11     61.44       0         6          1          1
 16     79.01       0         2          0          1
 21     69.71       0         4          0          1
 26     77.99       0         6          0          1
 31     91.44       1         2          1          1
 36     83.68       1         4          1          1
 41     82.35       1         6          1          1
 46     78.46       1         2          0          1
  .
  .
  .
166     85.96       1         2          0          3
171     83.35       1         4          0          3
176     88.00       1         6          0          3
180     72.73       1         6          0          3


MTB > Describe C1-C5

              N      MEAN     MEDIAN    TRMEAN     STDEV     SEMEAN
QUALITY     180    73.656    73.875    73.710     8.326     0.621
OIL_LAY     180    0.5000    0.5000    0.5000     0.5014    0.0374
STORE_1     180    4.000     4.000     4.000      1.638     0.122
OIL_STOR    180    0.5000    0.5000    0.5000     0.5014    0.0374
STORE_2     180    2.0000    2.0000    2.0000     0.8188    0.0610

              MIN      MAX        Q1        Q3
QUALITY     52.180   91.440    67.635    78.973
OIL_LAY     0.0000   1.0000    0.0000    1.0000
STORE_1      2.000    6.000     2.000     6.000
OIL_STOR    0.0000   1.0000    0.0000    1.0000
STORE_2     1.0000   3.0000    1.0000    3.0000


MTB > Regress C1 3 C2-C4 C10 C11

The regression equation is
QUALITY = 70.2 + 7.68 OIL_LAY - 0.236 STORE_1 + 1.04 OIL_STOR


Predictor      Coef      Stdev     t-ratio        p
Constant     70.240      1.658      42.36      0.000
OIL_LAY       7.682      1.105       6.95      0.000
STORE_1      -0.2363     0.3385     -0.70      0.486
OIL_STOR      1.041      1.105       0.94      0.347


s = 7.415      R-sq = 22.0%      R-sq(adj) = 20.7%
 . . .
```

```
Unusual Observations
Obs. OIL_LAY    QUALITY       Fit Stdev.Fit   Residual    St.Resid
 15   0.00      85.240     69.863   1.172     15.377       2.10R
 27   0.00      85.410     68.822   1.172     16.588       2.27R
 66   0.00      52.180     70.336   0.957    -18.156      -2.47R
 94   1.00      59.720     78.491   1.172    -18.771      -2.56R
112   1.00      59.380     76.977   0.957    -17.597      -2.39R
164   1.00      59.240     77.546   1.172    -18.306      -2.50R
```

R denotes an obs. with a large st. resid.

```
MTB > NAME C10 'ST.RES' C11 'FITTED'
MTB > Plot C10*C11  ------->
```

Note: Descriptive statistics for ST.RES are given for each of the 12 distinct values of FITTED.

	FITTED	N	MEAN	MEDIAN	TRMEAN	STDEV	SEMEAN
ST.RES	68.82	15	-0.076	-0.187	-0.134	1.072	0.277
	69.29	15	0.035	0.070	0.022	1.054	0.272
	69.77	15	0.105	0.237	0.118	0.890	0.230
	69.86	15	0.055	0.023	0.011	0.920	0.238
	70.34	15	-0.311	-0.255	-0.257	1.154	0.298
	70.81	15	0.193	0.161	0.124	0.834	0.215
	76.50	15	-0.193	0.025	-0.208	0.873	0.226
	76.98	15	0.214	0.615	0.312	1.223	0.316
	77.45	15	-0.086	-0.038	-0.046	0.930	0.240
	77.55	15	0.266	0.450	0.361	1.184	0.306
	78.02	15	-0.040	0.004	-0.015	0.833	0.215
	78.49	15	-0.162	-0.324	-0.125	1.157	0.299

```
MTB > DotPlot C10;
SUBC>   By C2.
```

```
MTB > Describe C10;
SUBC>    By C2.


              OIL_LAY       N      MEAN    MEDIAN    TRMEAN    STDEV   SEMEAN
ST.RES           0         90     0.000     0.018    -0.009    0.979    0.103
                 1         90    -0.000     0.009     0.034    1.031    0.109

MTB > DotPlot C10;
SUBC> By C3.

 STORE_1                              . .
 2                         : : :       :           .
           .        . .. .    .: ::::::: ..:::::::..::.. .. : .
         +---------+---------+---------+---------+---------+---------ST.RES
 STORE_1                  .       . :.     . :...
 4         ..      . ..::...: : : :. :: ::::..:..::::: : . .
         +---------+---------+---------+---------+---------+---------ST.RES
                                     :
 STORE_1              :           :.:....
 6       .          .. .::  :.............. . .: .:. . . .
         +---------+---------+---------+---------+---------+---------ST.RES
        -3.0      -2.0      -1.0       0.0       1.0       2.0

MTB > Describe C10;
SUBC>    By C3.

              STORE_1       N      MEAN    MEDIAN    TRMEAN    STDEV   SEMEAN
ST.RES           2         60     0.013    -0.117     0.025    0.947    0.122
                 4         60    -0.025     0.035     0.005    1.065    0.138
                 6         60     0.013    -0.013     0.010    1.008    0.130

MTB > DotPlot C10;
SUBC> By C4.


                              :   .   :
 OIL_STOR           : : :    :: ::.:   .:. . :.
 0          .     ..:..:::...: ::: :::::::..:::::::.:   . .
         +---------+---------+---------+---------+---------+---------ST.RES
                            .: . . :
 OIL_STOR                 ..:::::: : :.    :.     . .
 1        .:     . ..:::... ..::::::::::: :::..::::  .: : . ..
         +---------+---------+---------+---------+---------+---------ST.RES
        -3.0      -2.0      -1.0       0.0       1.0       2.0

MTB > Describe C10;
SUBC>    By C4.

              OIL_STOR      N      MEAN    MEDIAN    TRMEAN    STDEV   SEMEAN
ST.RES           0         90    -0.000     0.041     0.007    0.995    0.105
                 1         90     0.000    -0.072     0.022    1.016    0.107
```

```
MTB > NScores C10 C12
MTB > NAME C12 'NSCORE'
MTB > Plot C12*C10
```

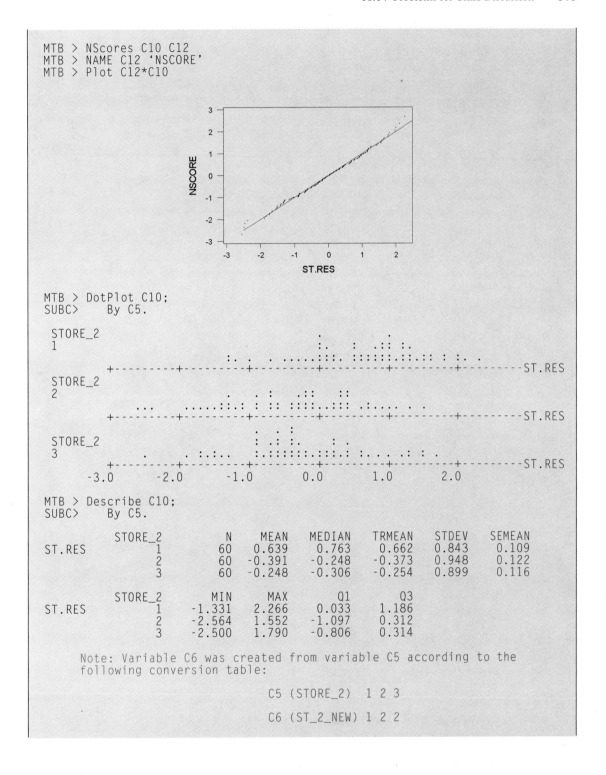

```
MTB > DotPlot C10;
SUBC>    By C5.
```

```
  STORE_2
  1                                           .            .
                                         :.     :   .:: :.
                  :. .  . .....::::. :::::::::.:.::: : :.. .
      +---------+---------+---------+---------+---------+---------ST.RES
  STORE_2
  2                          .    .  .     .:: .   ::
                  ...  .....::.:.: : :: ::::..:: .:....  . .
      +---------+---------+---------+---------+---------+---------ST.RES
  STORE_2                             . .  :
  3                          :  .:: :.      .   . .
             .       . .:.:.. .:::::::.::.::.:. :.....:: : .
      +---------+---------+---------+---------+---------+---------ST.RES
     -3.0      -2.0      -1.0       0.0       1.0       2.0
```

```
MTB > Describe C10;
SUBC>    By C5.
```

	STORE_2	N	MEAN	MEDIAN	TRMEAN	STDEV	SEMEAN
ST.RES	1	60	0.639	0.763	0.662	0.843	0.109
	2	60	-0.391	-0.248	-0.373	0.948	0.122
	3	60	-0.248	-0.306	-0.254	0.899	0.116

	STORE_2	MIN	MAX	Q1	Q3
ST.RES	1	-1.331	2.266	0.033	1.186
	2	-2.564	1.552	-1.097	0.312
	3	-2.500	1.790	-0.806	0.314

Note: Variable C6 was created from variable C5 according to the
following conversion table:

C5 (STORE_2) 1 2 3

C6 (ST_2_NEW) 1 2 2

```
MTB > Regress C1 4 C2-C4 C6 C10 C11

The regression equation is

QUALITY = 81.9 + 7.68 OIL_LAY - 0.236 STORE_1 + 1.04 OIL_STOR
          - 7.02 ST_2_NEW

Predictor       Coef       Stdev     t-ratio        p
Constant      81.947       2.293       35.74    0.000
OIL_LAY       7.6824      0.9891        7.77    0.000
STORE_1      -0.2363      0.3028       -0.78    0.436
OIL_STOR      1.0413      0.9891        1.05    0.294
ST_2_NEW      -7.024       1.049       -6.70    0.000

s = 6.635      R-sq = 37.9%     R-sq(adj) = 36.5%
. . .

MTB > Regress C1 3 C2 C4 C6 C10 C11

The regression equation is
QUALITY = 81.0 + 7.68 OIL_LAY + 1.04 OIL_STOR - 7.02 ST_2_NEW

Predictor       Coef       Stdev     t-ratio        p
Constant      81.002       1.945       41.65    0.000
OIL_LAY       7.6824      0.9880        7.78    0.000
OIL_STOR      1.0413      0.9880        1.05    0.293
ST_2_NEW      -7.024       1.048       -6.70    0.000

s = 6.627      R-sq = 37.7%     R-sq(adj) = 36.6%
. . .

MTB > Regress C1 2 C2 C6 C10 C11

The regression equation is
QUALITY = 81.5 + 7.68 OIL_LAY - 7.02 ST_2_NEW

Predictor       Coef       Stdev     t-ratio        p
Constant      81.522       1.882       43.33    0.000
OIL_LAY       7.6824      0.9883        7.77    0.000
ST_2_NEW      -7.024       1.048       -6.70    0.000

s = 6.630    R-sq = 37.3%     R-sq(adj) = 36.6%
. . .

Unusual Observations
Obs.  OIL_LAY   QUALITY        Fit Stdev.Fit   Residual   St.Resid
  37     1.00    68.290     82.181     0.988    -13.891     -2.12R
  56     1.00    66.760     82.181     0.988    -15.421     -2.35R
  66     0.00    52.180     67.474     0.781    -15.294     -2.32R
  94     1.00    59.720     75.156     0.781    -15.436     -2.34R
 112     1.00    59.380     75.156     0.781    -15.776     -2.40R
 113     1.00    88.390     75.156     0.781     13.234      2.01R
 135     0.00    81.930     67.474     0.781     14.456      2.20R
 161     1.00    90.650     75.156     0.781     15.494      2.35R
 164     1.00    59.240     75.156     0.781    -15.916     -2.42R

R denotes an obs. with a large st. resid.

Note: The diagnostic checks are satisfactory.

MTB > Stop
```

10.15

EXERCISES

Although answers are given in Appendix C, do not turn to them right away if you cannot find an answer on your own. Return to the exercise the next day and try again before turning to Appendix C.

10.3 This problem is a continuation of Exercise 9.8 where bank charges for 40 companies were related to their sales. Average monthly bank charges (in dollars) are to be related to three background variables: (1) yearly sales in $millions, (2) the average daily number of disbursements, and (3) the average daily number of deposits. The data are as follows:

ROW	CHARGES	SALES	DISBURSE	DEPOSITS
1	4550	146	840	723
2	2470	342	1270	59
3	6980	403	210	692
4	7920	311	360	3503
5	3520	362	110	361
6	8990	597	1010	67
7	2010	226	110	26
8	5730	351	140	675
9	4940	460	570	43
10	3010	208	80	157
11	6550	383	150	725
12	6460	494	310	70
13	3990	337	1220	35
14	6750	520	630	42
15	12500	811	830	408
16	1180	277	100	66
17	5900	406	40	359
18	2190	273	80	139
19	2500	256	350	344
20	1330	464	20	103
21	14290	889	2070	604
22	2570	489	10	66
23	5400	365	300	673
24	4570	115	950	744
25	5960	469	290	44
26	3150	200	120	16
27	4300	194	320	285
28	1020	455	110	17
29	3810	133	760	708
30	5020	301	110	153
31	1430	75	170	193
32	13790	853	990	408
33	2420	234	20	181
34	13690	826	1140	369
35	6070	192	1690	458
36	1430	31	90	212
37	3810	193	950	750
38	15040	874	2110	590
39	3390	245	40	142
40	5780	279	400	368

The data are stored in ASCII file BANKCHG.DAT.

a Obtain the estimated multiple regression equation for CHARGES where the three predictor variables are SALES, DISBURSE, and DEPOSITS.

   i Do the diagnostic checks. (The following questions should be qualified appropriately if one or more of the diagnostic checks are not satisfactory.)

   ii Interpret the estimated coefficients. Can any one of the three variables be dropped from this model?

   iii Find approximate 95% confidence intervals for the coefficients of SALES, DISBURSE, and DEPOSITS. Does any of these intervals contain 0? Interpret.

   iv What is the standard deviation of residuals? What is the adjusted R^2?

   v Suppose another company from this town had the following values on the predictor variables: SALES = 435, DISBURSE = 2,100, and DEPOSITS = 600. What is a 95% prediction interval for its bank charges?

b Suppose now that you are given additional information: Companies 16, 20, 22, and 28 bank with a subsidiary of a particular foreign bank, whereas the remaining companies bank with the same, well-established bank. A fifth variable, BANK, contains this information: it has the value 1 if a company banks with the foreign subsidiary, and 0 otherwise. Answer the questions in (a) above, and contrast your results with those in (a). [The company in (v) banks with the well-established bank.]

c Is the additional information in (b) useful?

10.4 This problem is a continuation of Exercise 9.5 (Dispatch function at IBM). Investigate whether introduction of the predictor variable CALLS changes your assessment of how useful STAFF is as a predictor variable for the response variable WAIT. Remember that STAFF is the staff level, which can be set by management, but that CALLS is the number of calls received, and cannot be influenced by management. (Introduction of the predictor variable CALLS allows you to control for its influence when examining the effect of STAFF on WAIT.)

a Obtain a sequence plot for CALLS. What do you see?

b Obtain scatterplots of WAIT vs. CALLS and CALLS vs. STAFF. Describe any relationship you see.

c Find the least squares regression equation relating WAIT to STAFF and CALLS. Carry out the four diagnostic checks. Are any of the four assumptions violated? If so, describe the nature of these violations.

d What is the standard deviation of the WAIT measurements? What is the standard deviation of residuals? Comment.

e Interpret the coefficients of the regression equation in the context of this application. In particular, interpret the coefficient of STAFF and contrast this with the interpretation of the coefficient of STAFF in Exercise 9.5.

f Find an approximate 95% interval for β_{STAFF}. Interpret this.

g Using the regression equation, find the predicted value for WAIT on a day when STAFF is 30 and CALLS is (i) 2,000, (ii) 2,500, and (iii) 3,000. Are any of these predictions extrapolations?

h What are the 95% prediction intervals for the predictions in (g)?

i If any of the diagnostic checks done in (c) were not satisfactory, what implications do these violations have on your answers in (f) to (h)?

j Remembering that STAFF, the number of operators on duty, can be influenced by management, what implications do your conclusions have for management? [Contrast this with your answer to Exercise 9.5.]

10.5 This problem relates to a simple random sample of 50 from 1,585 parcels of residential land in the town of Woodruff, Wisconsin, in 1975. (The data were collected to answer some questions regarding property tax equalization.) Four variables were measured on each parcel in the sample:

IMPROV   1 if parcel is improved, 0 if parcel is vacant

WATERF   1 if parcel has water frontage, 0 otherwise

ASSESS   assessed value of parcel (for tax purposes), given in dollars

APPRAISE   appraised value of parcel (approximation to the market value), given in dollars.

The data are stored in ASCII file WOODRUFF.DAT. Two additional variables are used in the analysis:

L_APPR   the natural logarithm of APPRAISE

L_ASSESS   the natural logarithm of ASSESS

The following questions relate to Minitab output from the Session window, which is given in Figure 10.44 at the end of this problem. Your answers should focus on the statistical aspects of the analysis.

a Assuming that appraised values are normally distributed, estimate the proportion of parcels in Woodruff whose appraised value is between $10,000 and $20,000.

b How reasonable is the assumption of normality made in (a)? Do you have to make any assumptions in addition to normality to compute the proportion in (a)? If so, what are they and how reasonable are they?

c Obtain a 95% confidence interval for the mean appraised value of all parcels in Woodruff. Interpret this interval in the context of this application.

d Do you have to make any assumptions to compute the results in (c)? If so, what are they and how reasonable are they?

e Obtain a point estimate and a 98% confidence interval for the difference in mean appraised value between improved and vacant parcels in Woodruff. Interpret the interval in the context of this application.

f Do you have to make any assumptions to compute the results in (e)? If so, what are they and how reasonable are they?

g Obtain a point estimate and a 90% confidence interval for the proportion of improved parcels in Woodruff. Interpret the interval in the context of this application.

h Do you have to make any assumptions to compute the results in (g)? If so, what are they and how reasonable are they?

i Using the available information, carry out the diagnostic checks for regression model 1.

j The value for s is not given in model 1. Is it less than, the same as, or more than the value of s in model 2? Why?

All the remaining questions relate to model 2. Assume that the diagnostic checks for model 2 are adequate.

k Does the constant coefficient have a practical interpretation? If yes, what is it? If no, why not?

l Give a practical interpretation for the coefficient of the predictor variable IMPROV.

m Obtain a 95% confidence interval for the coefficient of the predictor variable IMPROV. Interpret this interval.

n Why are the point estimate you derived in (e) and the coefficient of IMPROV different? How do their interpretations differ?

o Give a practical interpretation for the coefficient of the predictor variable L_ASSESS.

p Obtain a 95% interval for the appraised value (in dollars) of another parcel in Woodruff that is improved and has an assessed value of $25,000. If all necessary information is not given to compute this interval, make reasonable approximations and justify these approximations.

FIGURE 10.44

```
MTB > Read 'C:\MTBWIN\DATA\WOODRUFF.DAT' C1-C4
Entering data from file: C:\MTBWIN\DATA\WOODRUFF.DAT
     50 rows read.
MTB > NAME C1 'IMPROV' C2 'WATERF' C3 'ASSESS' C4 'APPRAISE'
MTB > PRINT C1-C4

ROW IMPROV WATERF ASSESS APPRAISE     ROW IMPROV WATERF ASSESS APPRAISE

  1     1      1    5200    17100      26     0       0     500     2000
  2     1      1    7500    18500      27     0       1    3000     9500
  3     1      0    4100    13300      28     1       0    1600     4000
  4     1      0    5700    18500      29     1       0    4000    12100
  5     1      1    9000    16700      30     0       0    1100     4500
  6     0      0     800     2400      31     1       1   13300    25300
  7     1      0   14100    26300      32     1       0    4700    16000
  8     0      0     800     4000      33     0       0    1000     4000
  9     0      0     600     2000      34     1       0   31500    35500
 10     1      1   21300    37000      35     1       0   15500    24500
 11     1      0   17400    23300      36     1       0    5100    15600
 12     0      0    1000     2500      37     1       0    5600     7100
 13     0      0    1500     2000      38     1       1   27300    40100
 14     0      0    1200     4000      39     1       0    6600    10600
 15     1      1   20900    29900      40     1       1    9600    12200
 16     0      0    1000     4500      41     1       1   27800    41700
 17     1      0    6600    15800      42     1       1   20000    30600
 18     0      0     800     3500      43     0       0     500     3500
 19     0      0     500     2500      44     0       0     500     3000
 20     1      0   18000    27500      45     1       0    1300    18800
 21     1      0   19500    26300      46     1       0    7600    11100
 22     1      1   10800    14400      47     0       0     700     2000
 23     0      0    3200     8000      48     0       0     800     4000
 24     1      0    5000     8800      49     0       0    1800     9100
 25     1      1   11100    23000      50     0       0    1000     4500


MTB > Describe C1-C4

               N      MEAN    MEDIAN    TRMEAN     STDEV    SEMEAN
IMPROV        50    0.6000    1.0000    0.6136    0.4949    0.0700
WATERF        50    0.2600    0.0000    0.2273    0.4431    0.0627
ASSESS        50      7600      4850      6634      8314      1176
APPRAISE      50     14062     11600     13143     11265      1593

               MIN       MAX        Q1        Q3
IMPROV      0.0000    1.0000    0.0000    1.0000
WATERF      0.0000    1.0000    0.0000    1.0000
ASSESS         500     31500      1000     11650
APPRAISE      2000     41700      4000     23075
```

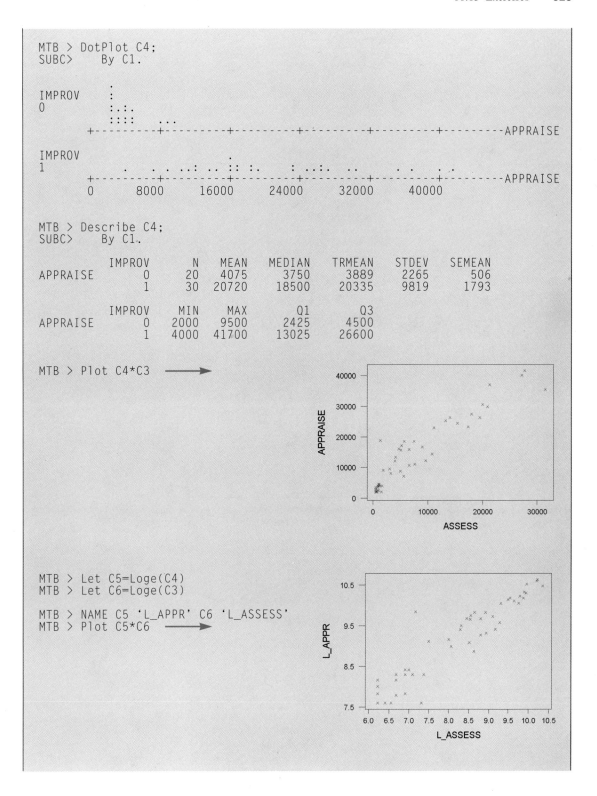

```
MTB > DotPlot C4;
SUBC>    By C1.


IMPROV      :
0           :.:.
            ::::   ...
       +---------+---------+---------+---------+---------+--------APPRAISE

IMPROV                        .
1         .   . . ..: .. :: :.    : ..:.  ..   .  . . ..:
       +---------+---------+---------+---------+---------+--------APPRAISE
       0       8000     16000     24000     32000     40000


MTB > Describe C4;
SUBC>    By C1.

            IMPROV     N    MEAN   MEDIAN   TRMEAN   STDEV   SEMEAN
APPRAISE       0      20    4075     3750     3889    2265      506
               1      30   20720    18500    20335    9819     1793

            IMPROV    MIN     MAX      Q1       Q3
APPRAISE       0     2000    9500    2425     4500
               1     4000   41700   13025    26600

MTB > Plot C4*C3 ──────►
```

```
MTB > Let C5=Loge(C4)
MTB > Let C6=Loge(C3)

MTB > NAME C5 'L_APPR' C6 'L_ASSESS'
MTB > Plot C5*C6 ──────►
```

```
Model 1

MTB > Regress C5 3 C1 C2 C6 C10 C11

The regression equation is
L_APPR = 4.54 + 0.380 IMPROV + 0.114 WATERF + 0.532 L_ASSESS

Predictor        Coef        Stdev      t-ratio          p
Constant       4.5367      0.5190         ?              ?
IMPROV         0.3799      0.1844         ?              ?
WATERF         0.1144      0.1293         ?              ?
L_ASSESS      0.53215     0.07527         ?              ?

s = ?
...

Unusual Observations
Obs.    IMPROV      L_APPR        Fit Stdev.Fit      Residual     St.Resid
 13       0.00      7.6009     8.4285    0.0839       -0.8276        -2.55R
 45       1.00      9.8416     8.7322    0.1471        1.1094         3.68R

R denotes an obs. with a large st. resid.

MTB > NAME C10 'ST.RES' C11 'FITTED'
MTB > Plot C10*C11
```

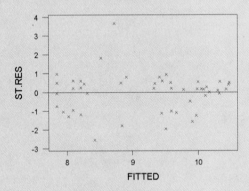

```
MTB > Plot C10*C6
```

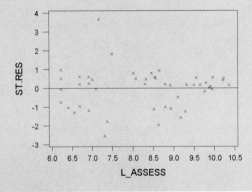

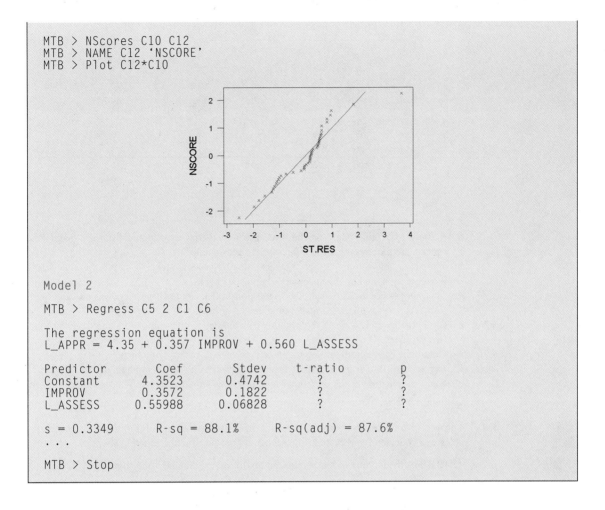

```
MTB > NScores C10 C12
MTB > NAME C12 'NSCORE'
MTB > Plot C12*C10
```

Model 2

```
MTB > Regress C5 2 C1 C6

The regression equation is
L_APPR = 4.35 + 0.357 IMPROV + 0.560 L_ASSESS

Predictor      Coef        Stdev       t-ratio        p
Constant       4.3523      0.4742         ?           ?
IMPROV         0.3572      0.1822         ?           ?
L_ASSESS       0.55988     0.06828        ?           ?

s = 0.3349      R-sq = 88.1%      R-sq(adj) = 87.6%
. . .

MTB > Stop
```

10.16

SUPPLEMENTARY EXERCISES

10.6 An experiment was run to examine the influence of temperature, concentration, and pressure on the by-product yield of a chemical reaction, in which this yield was to be low. Data characterizing 24 batches are as follows. They are stored in ASCII file EVOP.DAT. (Source: G. E. P. Box and N. Draper, *Evolutionary Operation*, 1969, pp. 79–91.)

YIELD   by-product yield (which should be low)

TEMP   temperature (degrees Fahrenheit) -175; will be -5 or 5

CONC   concentration (measured as a percent) -25; will be -3 or 3

PRESS   pressure (measured in psi) -35; will be -5 or 5

YIELD	TEMP	CONC	PRESS	YIELD	TEMP	CONC	PRESS
3.9	−5	−3	−5	3.3	−5	−3	5
4.3	5	−3	−5	5.5	5	−3	5
3.4	−5	3	−5	2.8	−5	3	5
3.8	5	3	−5	4.4	5	3	5
3.7	−5	−3	5	3.6	−5	−3	−5
5.2	5	−3	5	5.1	5	−3	−5
2.9	−5	3	5	2.7	−5	3	−5
4.7	5	3	5	3.7	5	3	−5
4.2	−5	−3	−5	3.6	−5	−3	5
5.1	5	−3	−5	4.6	5	−3	5
2.5	−5	3	−5	2.7	−5	3	5
3.3	5	3	−5	4.0	5	3	5

a Regress by-product yield on the three predictor variables. Judging from the diagnostic checks, are the four regression assumptions reasonable?

b Which variable is unimportant in determining by-product yield? Drop this variable, rerun the regression, and do the necessary diagnostic checks.

c Interpret the coefficients from the regression in (b). Contrast these coefficients and their standard errors with the corresponding values in (a).

d Based on the regression in (b), obtain 95% confidence intervals for the coefficients of the two variables.

e Obtain the correlations among the three predictor variables. Comment.

f If you were to use the results from the regression in (b) for implementation purposes, what combination of the predictor variable values would you use? What concerns do you have about these settings?

10.7 This problem relates to a process in which steel bars are ground. Information on four variables was collected for 100 orders consecutively produced in the grinding shop:

1. HOURS, the number of hours required by the order in the grinding shop

2. NUMBER, the number of steel bars in the order

3. DIAMETER, the diameter (in tenths of inches) of a steel bar prior to grinding

4. TOLERANC, the required tolerance or maximum allowable spread (in thousandths of an inch)

Assume that the process is stable. The response variable HOURS is to be related to the other three variables. The data are stored in file STEELWAR.DAT.

a Obtain a 90% confidence interval for the process average of the number of hours it takes to grind an order. Interpret it.

b For the interval in (a) to be valid, is it necessary to assume a normal distribution for the number of hours it takes to grind an order? Briefly justify your answer.

c Obtain a 90% prediction interval for the number of hours it takes to grind another order from the same process.

d Obtain a regression of HOURS on the three predictor variables. Carry out the diagnostic checks. Comment.

e Does the coefficient of TOLERANC have a meaningful interpretation? If yes, give an interpretation. If no, why not?

f A new order has come in, and you are to use the regression model in (d) to predict the value of HOURS for this order. The following information is given for this order:

NUMBER = 9 (units)

DIAMETER = 2 (tenths of an inch)

TOLERANC = 1 (thousandths of an inch)

Find a point prediction and a 90% prediction interval. Will this order be completed within 3 hours?

g Transform all four variables logarithmically. Obtain a regression of the log of HOURS on the logs of the other three variables. Carry out the diagnostic checks. Comment.

h Do (f), but use the model in (g).

i Given your assessment of the diagnostic checks, how reliable is your answer in (f)? What about your answer in (h)?

j Do you prefer the model in (d) or (g)? Briefly justify your answer.

10.8 This is a continuation of Example 2.8 (p. 31). A company was interested in the picking and packing activities of its shipping department.[11] Once an order has been received and entered into the order-entry system, a pick slip is sent to the distribution department so that the order can be prepared and shipped. A study was undertaken to answer the following questions.

1. Is there a relationship between the time taken to pick and pack an order and certain other characteristics of the order?

2. Is it possible to predict accurately the time required to pick and pack an order for shipment to a customer?

The data were collected as follows. Using the order entry system, 98 orders were randomly picked from all orders shipped in October 1988. Six variables were measured for each order:

1. the total WEIGHT of the order (in standard weight units)

2. the total number of ITEMS in the order

3. the number of LINES on the order (this equals the number of distinct products and may not agree with (2) since the order may contain different numbers of each product ordered)

4. the dollar VALUE of the order

5. the amount of TIME taken to prepare the order for shipment

6. an indicator of whether the order had CONSUMER products in it or not.

The data are stored in ASCII file PICKPACK.DAT.

a Find a good regression model relating TIME to the other predictor variables. If you plan to consider transformations, you should only look at logarithmic transformations. Do the diagnostic checks for this model.

---

[11] The name of the company is omitted to protect confidentiality. The data are real.

b In your preferred regression model, how do you interpret the coefficient of variable (6), the indicator of whether the order had consumer products in it or not? Be specific.

c Can you use the model in (a) to answer the two questions in the study?

Present your results and conclusions for (a) to (c) in a summary report and attach your briefly annotated output.

10.9 This problem relates to salaries of management and their job evaluations in a midwestern industrial plant in the early 1970s. Data for 67 managers are stored in ASCII file MM.DAT. The variables are:

1. Functional classification (0 = top management; 2 = major division 1; 3 = major division 2; 4 = major division 3; 5 = engineering; 7 = administration; and 10 = sales)

2. Job evaluation component "know-how"

3. Job evaluation component "problem-solving"

4. Job evaluation component "accountability"

5. Job evaluation total (total of variables 2–4)

6. Salary (in dollars)

For several reasons, a regression model is to be built relating some of the variables to salary. One reason is to see if there is a strong relationship, another if the model can be used to indicate if any salaries are out of line. You should omit top management from your analysis.

a Can you find a good regression model? Do the diagnostic checks. In finding the model, you should think about possibly using the square root or logarithmic transformation on the response and the predictor variables. Briefly describe your model. What are your concerns about the best model you could find?

b How would you use the model in (a) to determine if any of the managers' salaries are out of line? Discuss. Using your criterion, are any salaries out of line?

Present your results and conclusions for (a) and (b) in a summary report and attach your briefly annotated output.

10.10 A company was interested in determining how the sales performance of its sales force was related to their performance on certain tests. The study was conducted by randomly selecting 50 people from the company's sales force. For each person, the sales performance during the last year was recorded in the variable SALES (the value of SALES was measured on a scale on which values below 100 indicate a *below average* performance). Next, each subject in the sample was administered four aptitude tests: creativity, mechanical reasoning, abstract reasoning, and mathematics. The scores on each test were recorded in the variables CREAT, MECH, ABSTR and MATH, respectively. The data are stored in ASCII file PERFORM.DAT, where the variables SALES, CREAT, MECH, ABSTR, and MATH are in columns 1 to 5.

a Obtain a regression model relating SALES to the four aptitude scores. Does this model make intuitive sense? If not, what bothers you about this model?

b Carry out the diagnostic checks for the model estimated in (a) to decide if it is appropriate (that is, whether the assumptions of the regression model are reasonable here). Can this model be used for predicting SALES on the basis of CREAT, MECH, ABSTR, and MATH? If your answer is yes, briefly outline how the model can be used; if your answer is no, explain why this question cannot be answered with the model.

c   What do the values of s and R^2 imply about the model estimated in (a)?

d   Obtain a regression model relating SALES to the predictor variables CREAT, MECH, and ABSTR, and do the diagnostic checks. Briefly discuss the pros and cons of dropping the variable MATH from the model in (a).

Questions (e) to (h) relate to the model in (d). Assume that all diagnostic checks are satisfactory.

e   Obtain a 99% confidence interval for the coefficient of ABSTR. Give an interpretation of this interval in the context of the current study.

f   Suppose a prospective employee is asked to take the four tests. His scores are: CREAT = 13, MECH = 16, ABSTR = 5, MATH = 25. Obtain a point prediction for his sales performance and interpret it in the context of the current study.

g   Suppose the company decides that the employee described above should be offered a job only if the probability of his sales performance being above average (that is, exceeding 100) is at least 70%. If the model in (d) were used to estimate this probability, would the employee be offered the job?

h   Discuss briefly some advantages and disadvantages of using the test scores to evaluate prospective employees as outlined in parts (f) and (g) above.

i   Drop the predictor variable CREAT from the model in (d). Assuming all the diagnostic checks are satisfactory for this new model, discuss briefly the advantages and disadvantages of dropping CREAT from the model in (d).

10.11   This exercise relates to data on the maturing German pudding-with-topping market for the 18 bimonthly periods from December 79/January 80 to October/November 1982. The specific product was the "125 g pudding with topping cup," whose market was dominated by four national brands that together accounted for about 70% of the market. The remaining 30% were shared by about 30 regional and local competitors. Gervais-Danone was the market leader. In the 3-year period under study, extensive competitive activity had taken place, with regard to both price and advertisement. Furthermore, some modifications to the product had been introduced by several competitors. The variables used in the analysis of the data are defined as follows:

GD_SHARE, Gervais-Danone's market share (percentage of industry sales)

GD_PRICE, Gervais-Danone's average retail price per 125 g cup (in Deutschmarks, DM)

GD_AD, Gervais-Danone's advertising expenditures (in 1,000 DM)

IND_SAL, total industry sales (in millions of 125 g cups)

IND_PRIC, average volume-weighted industry price per 125 g cup (in DM)

IND_AD, total industry advertising expenditures (in 1,000 DM)

GD_REL_P, Gervais-Danone's relative price, GD_PRICE/IND_PRIC

GD_REL_A, Gervais-Danone's relative amount of advertisement, GD_AD/IND_AD

The following questions relate to Minitab output in Figure 10.45. The answers will focus on the statistical aspects of the analysis.

a What is the statistical unit in this problem?

b If you were *only* given the fitted equation for model 1,

Fitted IND_SAL = 241 − 239(IND_PRIC) + 0.00110(IND_AD)

and no information in addition to this whatsoever, could you judge which one of the two variables, IND_PRIC or IND_AD, accounts for more variation in the response variable IND_SAL? Briefly justify your answer.

c In model 1, obtain a 95% confidence interval for each predictor variable coefficient. What conclusions can you draw about how useful each predictor variable is in accounting for variation in the response variable?

d Does the constant coefficient for model 2 have a practical interpretation? If so, what is it?

e Interpret the coefficient of GD_PRICE in model 2.

f The value of R^2 is not given for model 2. Can you determine if this R^2 is greater than, equal to, or less than the R^2 in model 1? If yes, what is their relationship and why? If no, briefly indicate why.

g The value of R^2 is not given for model 2. Can you determine if this R^2 is greater than, equal to, or less than the R^2 in model 3? If yes, what is their relationship and why? If no, briefly indicate why.

h Can you conclude from model 3 that Gervais-Danone's market share is very sensitive to its relative price? Briefly justify your answer.

FIGURE 10.45

```
MTB > Describe C1-C8

                  N      MEAN     MEDIAN     TRMEAN     STDEV
GD_SHARE         18    34.456    34.275     34.412     2.107
GD_PRICE         18   0.66833   0.66000    0.66688   0.02383
GD_AD            18     385.8     370.0      380.1     331.1
IND_SAL          18     86.49     89.05      86.70      6.05
IND_PRIC         18   0.65264   0.64886    0.65224   0.02033
IND_AD           18       997       808        951       541
GD_REL_P         18    1.0240    1.0243     1.0240    0.0125
GD_REL_A         18    0.3677    0.3964     0.3635    0.3030


Model 1

MTB > Regress C4 2 C5 C6

The regression equation is
IND_SAL = 241 - 239 IND_PRIC + 0.00110 IND_AD

Predictor         Coef         Stdev
Constant        241.48         29.04
IND_PRIC       -239.17         43.89
IND_AD        0.001101      0.001649

s = 3.597       R-sq = 68.8%       R-sq(adj) = 64.7%

The diagnostic checks for this model are adequate.
```

```
Model 2

MTB > Regress C1 2 C2 C3

The regression equation is
GD_SHARE = 26.2 + 12.0 GD_PRICE + 0.00061 GD_AD

Predictor      Coef
Constant       26.21
GD_PRICE       11.99
GD_AD       0.000614

s = 2.218      R-sq = ?       R-sq(adj) = ?

The diagnostic checks for this model are adequate.

Model 3

MTB > Regress C1 2 C7 C8

The regression equation is
GD_SHARE = 125 - 88.1 GD_REL_P - 0.45 GD_REL_A

Predictor      Coef        Stdev
Constant       124.80      38.65
GD_REL_P       -88.06      37.66
GD_REL_A       -0.451      1.552

s = 1.920      R-sq = 26.7%  R-sq(adj) = 16.9%

The diagnostic checks for this model are adequate.

MTB > Stop
```

i   Suppose you worked for Gervais-Danone. Furthermore, suppose that you had to

1. Forecast Gervais-Danone's market share in December 82/January 83

2. Indicate by how much this forecast could be in error

   Could you use model 3 to do this? If yes, how would you do this? If no, why can you not do this?

10.12   In this problem you will analyze the manufacturing lead time and the production cost for a medium-size mold at a Canadian mold maker.[12] (This exercise is a continuation of Problem 9.1, p. 428). The process of manufacturing molds is very labor intensive. First, product designers initiate an idea for a product through making a prototype with wood or wax. This prototype is then given to potential customers and marketing agents for approval. Then a

---

[12] The data were slightly altered to protect confidentiality.

production mold is designed and manufactured using modern manufacturing technologies, such as Computer-Aided Design/Computer-Aided Manufacturing (CAD/CAM). The manufacturing lead time for a mold greatly affects the production schedule for the product, so the turnaround time for a production mold is a major concern for both mold maker and customer. A study was carried out to examine the operations lead time required for the manufacturing of a medium-size mold at the mold maker. Several managerial questions were to be addressed. One of them was:

> How well can the cost of a medium-size mold be predicted from the times it takes to carry out the major operations?

Data were collected on 38 medium-size molds consecutively produced between March 1987 and April 1989. Seven variables were measured for each mold: (1) CAD/CAM programming hours, (2) DESIGN hours, (3) CNC machining hours, (4) CONVENTional machining hours, (5) HANDWORK hours, (6) total HOURS, and (7) mold manufacturing COSTs (in $1,000). The data are stored in ASCII file MOLDS.DAT.

In parts (a) to (g), you will examine the variable COST without relating it to any other variables.

a Is a stable process generating COST values? What is the standard deviation of COST values?

b Is the distribution of COST values normal?

In parts (c) to (e), assume that a stable process is generating COST and that the distribution of COST values is normal.

c Obtain a 90% confidence interval for the process mean of COST values. Interpret this interval.

d Obtain a 90% prediction interval for another mold's COST value. Interpret this interval.

e Are the two intervals in (c) and (d) necessarily the same, or are they different? Justify your answer.

f Given your answers in (a) and (b), how reliable is your answer in (c)? Briefly discuss the effect of your concerns in (a) and (b), if any, on the numerical answer in (c).

g Given your answers in (a) and (b), how reliable is your answer in (d)? Briefly discuss the effect of your concerns in (a) and (b), if any, on the numerical answer in (d).

The remaining parts of this problem relate to a regression of COST on the three predictor variables CNC, CONVENT, and HANDWORK.

h Obtain a regression of COST on the three predictor variables CNC, CONVENT, and HANDWORK. Do the diagnostic checks and discuss them. How well can the cost of a medium-size mold be predicted from the times it takes to carry out these three major operations?

In (i) to (k), assume that the regression assumptions are appropriate.

i Does the coefficient of CNC have a meaningful interpretation? If yes, give an interpretation. If no, why not?

j Suppose that the CNC machining hours, the CONVENTional machining hours and the HANDWORK hours for another medium-size mold are 1,000 hours each. Using the regression output, obtain a point prediction and a 90% prediction interval of COST for this mold.

k For the mold described in (j), can you find the probability that its COST value will exceed $150,000? If yes, obtain this probability. If no, why not?

l Given your answers in (h), how reliable is the point prediction in (j) and how reliable is the prediction interval in (j)?

10.13 Star Petroleum was a privately owned petroleum-retailing company. Gasoline was sold through more than 250 franchise operations. In order to aid the company's expansion decision, management wanted to know what kind of acquisition to make in the future, full-serve or self-serve stations. Experience had shown that it was more costly to establish a self-service station since more pumps and thus more land were needed. The company obviously wanted to operate profitable stations. Franchisees were paid on the basis of the weekly number of liters sold in excess of 50,000 liters. Several questions were to be addressed.

1. Which type of gas station is more profitable, full-serve or self-serve?

2. Which type of station makes the most efficient use of its pumps?

3. Is profit related to volume, number of pumps, or type of station?

It was expected that full-serve stations would be more profitable. It was also expected that the volume of gas sold at full-serve stations would be about 1.5 times as high as at self-serve stations.

Data were collected for 54 gas stations for the financial year ending 31 December 1989.[13] Two samples were obtained: 24 self-serve stations were randomly selected from the set of all self-serve stations, and 30 full-serve stations were randomly drawn from the set of all full-serve stations. Four variables were measured for each selected station: (1) net PROFIT before taxes generated from the sale of petroleum (in dollars), (2) the total VOLUME sold (in liters), (3) the number of PUMPS, and (4) the TYPE of station (0 = self-serve, 1 = full-serve). One measure of profitability was the ratio of profit and volume (PROF/VOL). The data are stored in ASCII file STAR.DAT. During the analysis of the data, it was found that stations 14 and 40 used pumps whose number of hoses differed from the remaining stations. It was decided that these two pumps should be excluded from the analysis.

a Is this a cross-sectional or a time series study? If it is a cross-sectional study, describe the population. If it is a time series study, describe the process. What is the unit?

b Using PROF/VOL as a measure of profitability, consider the difference between the population means of the full-serve and the self-serve stations. Obtain a point estimate and a 90% confidence interval for this difference. Briefly interpret this interval.

c Consider the same difference as in (b). What is the degree of confidence in a one-sided interval for this difference that covers all positive values?

d Use your answers in (b) and (c) to address question 1: "Which type of gas station is more profitable?"

---

[13] The data have been slightly altered to protect confidentiality.

e   Consider the difference between the population means for PROFIT between the full-serve and the self-serve stations. Obtain a point estimate and a 90% confidence interval for this difference. Briefly interpret this interval.

f   Consider regression model 1, which relates PROFIT to the predictor variables VOLUME, PUMPS, and TYPE. Do the four diagnostic checks for this model. What is your overall evaluation of the adequacy of model 1?

g   Consider regression model 2, which relates PROFIT to the predictor variables VOLUME and TYPE. Do the four diagnostic checks for this model. What is your overall evaluation of the adequacy of Model 2?

Questions (h) to (n) relate to regression model 2. Assume that the regression assumptions are appropriate.

h   Using the output from model 1, what suggested an examination of model 2? Briefly justify your answer.

i   Does the coefficient of VOLUME have a meaningful interpretation? If yes, give an interpretation. If no, why not? What about the coefficient of TYPE?

j   Obtain a 90% confidence interval for the population coefficient of TYPE. Briefly interpret this interval.

k   Having accounted for the variation in VOLUME, is TYPE a useful predictor variable for PROFIT? Briefly justify your answer.

l   Contrast the intervals in (e) and (j). Are they different? If yes, can you account for these differences?

m   Suppose the VOLUME for another full-serve station was 3,000,000 liters. What is the probability that this station's profit is positive?

n   How large must a full-serve station's VOLUME be so that the probability of a positive profit is at least 95%?

o   Using all the available information, answer question 3: "Is profit related to volume, number of pumps, or type of station?"

10.14   The Canadian Task Force on Cervical Screening recommended that all women who have ever been sexually active, or who are 18 years or older, have annual Papanicoulaou (Pap) smears. A woman whose Pap smear is abnormal is typically referred to a colposcopy clinic, where her cervix is examined with a microscope (colposcope). Many of the women who attend a colposcopy clinic are very frightened and poorly informed about the significance of an abnormal Pap smear and the need for treatment. As a result, these women may not return for treatment or follow-up visits if the initial examination is not a positive experience, which may put them at an increased risk of developing invasive cervical cancer.

A study was done to compare two methods of teaching women with abnormal Pap smears, an intensive (and expensive) method and a nonintensive method. Intensive teaching consists of a 20-minute personal interview with the colposcopy nurse, followed by a detailed discussion in the examining room with the physician. The physician interactively demonstrates the examination to the patient and explains the relevant anatomy using a video display. Nonintensive teaching consists of being handed a five-page information sheet on the disease, colposcopy, and treatment. Any questions asked in the examination room will be answered directly, but without background or supporting information.

Two managerial questions were to be answered by this study.

1. Is intensive pretreatment instruction for new patients a better management strategy than nonintensive teaching?

2. Does age or level of education influence the answer to the above question?

The two methods were to be compared on a pain score that ranged from 0 (low pain) to 100 (high pain). During October and November of 1991, 79 patients were randomly assigned to one of the two methods as they arrived at the colposcopy clinic, and information was gathered on them in their order of arrival.[14] Four variables were measured on each patient: (1) type of teaching METHOD (0 = intensive, 1 = nonintensive), (2) AGE (in completed years), (3) EDUCATN (highest level of formal education expressed in years), and (4) PAIN score. The data are stored in ASCII file COLPOSC.DAT.

In this randomized controlled study, a difference in means of 10 or more on the pain score was considered important enough to warrant the additional cost of the intensive teaching method.

a Was this study done as a cross-sectional study or a time series study? If it was a cross-sectional study, briefly describe the population; otherwise, briefly describe the process. Describe the unit. What is the response variable?

b Is the process generating pain scores random?

c Obtain a point estimate for the difference between the process means of the pain scores for nonintensively and intensively taught women.

d Obtain a 98% confidence interval for the difference in (c). Interpret this interval in the context of this study.

e What is the degree of confidence in an interval for the difference in (c) that covers values 10 or greater?

f A difference in means of 10 or more was considered important. What light do your answers in (c), (d), and (e) shed on the difference in process means being 10 or more?

The remaining questions relate to the regression of PAIN on METHOD, AGE, and EDUCATN.

g Carry out the four diagnostic checks and describe your findings. Overall, are there any serious problems with the diagnostic checks? Be brief.

For the remainder of this problem assume that all the diagnostic checks are satisfactory.

h Does the constant coefficient have an interpretation in the context of this study? If so, give an interpretation. If no, why not?

i Does the coefficient of AGE have an interpretation in the context of this study? If so, give an interpretation. If no, why not?

j Obtain a 98% confidence interval for the process coefficient of AGE. Briefly interpret this interval in the context of this study.

k What is the degree of confidence in an interval for the process coefficient of EDUCATN that covers positive values only?

l Does the coefficient of METHOD have an interpretation in the context of this study? If so, give an interpretation. If no, why not?

m Obtain a 98% confidence interval for the process coefficient of METHOD.

n The confidence intervals in (d) and (m) are not quite the same. Briefly explain why they are different. Which confidence interval do you prefer? Why?

o Using your answer in (m), answer the first managerial question.

p Answer the second managerial question.

---

[14] The data have been slightly altered to protect confidentiality.

10.15   Carry out the analysis for Exercise 8.3 with regression analysis. Let the 20 yields represent values on the response variable y, and let the predictor variable x be 0 if the standard process was used and 1 if the modified process was used. Using Minitab, plot y vs. x, then regress y on x, and do the diagnostic checks.

a   Find point estimates for the intercept and the slope. Interpret them in the context of the example.

b   Find a 95% confidence interval for the slope.

c   Contrast your answers to (a) and (b) with your answers to Exercise 8.3(b).

Present your results and conclusions for (a) to (c) in a summary report and attach your briefly annotated output.

TIME SERIES ANALYSIS WITH AUTOREGRESSION

This chapter will help you solve the following kinds of problems:

- You want to understand the time series pattern underlying the movement of the Standard & Poor Composite Stock Index. You have monthly data on Standard & Poor's Index and want to use the time series pattern to predict next month's value.

- In order to predict the number of commercial housing starts in her metropolitan area, a developer has collected monthly data on commercial housing starts. Can a model be developed to predict housing starts in the near future?

11.1

INTRODUCTION

In the last chapter, you learned the basics of the multiple regression model, in which a response variable y is related to one or more predictor variables. The two main reasons for estimating such a relationship were to gain understanding of the underlying relationship and to use it for prediction. In this chapter, you learn how many time series can be modeled successfully with regression analysis.

In this and the next chapter, you learn more about time series. In Chapter 5, you learned the simplest time series model, the random process. In Chapter 6, you then learned the random walk model, but you also saw that it is not applicable to most situations. The regression analysis approach discussed in this chapter does not cover all situations where time series modeling is required, but it should yield reasonably good models for many situations.

Two time series discussed in this chapter are the Standard & Poor Composite Stock Index and monthly mortgage sales data for a financial institution.

11.2

AN EXAMPLE: THE STANDARD & POOR COMPOSITE STOCK INDEX

Sixty monthly closing values for the Standard & Poor composite stock index, SP, for the period from January 1980 to December 1984 are listed in Figure 11.1.[1] The data are stored in ASCII file SP_MONTH.DAT. Since *any* analysis of a time series should start with a sequence plot, this is also given in Figure 11.1.

The managerial questions to be answered are:

What is a forecast for the SP index for the *next* month (that is, for January 1985)? How reliable is this forecast?

Figure 11.1 shows that the time series is not random. The runs test confirms this impression. A model for predicting 1 month ahead should rely more heavily on the most recent values rather than earlier values. *Lagging,* discussed in the next section, is a useful tool to build forecasting models that use previous observations for prediction purposes.

11.3

LAGGING AND AUTOCORRELATION

In order to use regression analysis for understanding the SP time series, the idea of **lagging** must be reviewed. This is best done with an example. Suppose you wanted to describe the extent to which the month-end SP values are related to the SP values at the end of the previous month. In order to do so, you would want to plot each SP value against the *previous* SP value. In a scatterplot, you always need two vari-

---

[1] The SP data were already analyzed in Chapter 6. The analysis here is independent of that in Chapter 6. Section 11.6 compares the two approaches.

FIGURE 11.1 SP Data: Data Values, Sequence Plot, and Runs Test

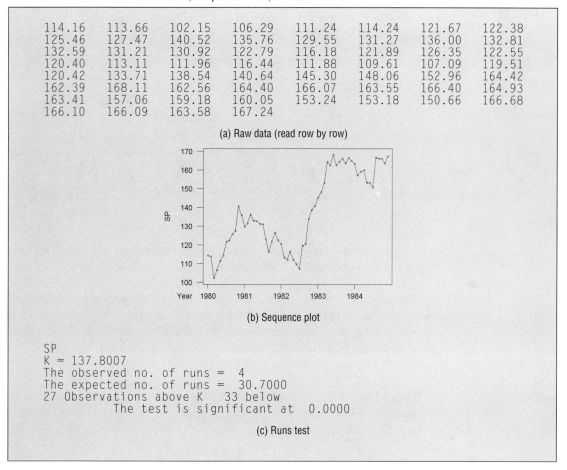

114.16	113.66	102.15	106.29	111.24	114.24	121.67	122.38
125.46	127.47	140.52	135.76	129.55	131.27	136.00	132.81
132.59	131.21	130.92	122.79	116.18	121.89	126.35	122.55
120.40	113.11	111.96	116.44	111.88	109.61	107.09	119.51
120.42	133.71	138.54	140.64	145.30	148.06	152.96	164.42
162.39	168.11	162.56	164.40	166.07	163.55	166.40	164.93
163.41	157.06	159.18	160.05	153.24	153.18	150.66	166.68
166.10	166.09	163.58	167.24				

(a) Raw data (read row by row)

(b) Sequence plot

```
SP
K = 137.8007
The observed no. of runs =    4
The expected no. of runs =   30.7000
27 Observations above K    33 below
          The test is significant at   0.0000
```

(c) Runs test

ables; each point on the plot is obtained by plotting the value on the first variable in a *particular* row against the value on the second variable in *that* row. In a scatterplot of each SP value against the previous SP value, you thus need two variables: (1) the variable containing the SP values, and (2) a newly created variable containing the previous SP values.

This newly created variable is called the *first lag* of SP or the **lag of order 1.** In Figure 11.2, consider the value for SP in row 60, 167.24. You would want to plot it against the previous value, i.e., SP in row 59, 163.58. Thus the value for SP in row 60 is 167.24, and the value of the first lag of SP in row 60 is 163.58. The value for SP in row 2 is 113.66, and the value of the first lag of SP in row 2 is 114.16 (the value for SP in row 1). Note that there is no value for the first lag in row 1. In general, denote the first lag of a variable y as y_{-1}, where the subscript "-1" is to indicate the first lag. Since Minitab does not use subscripts, in Minitab we denote the first lag of SP by SP-1.

ROW	SP	SP-1	SP-2
1	114.16	*	*
2	113.66	114.16	*
3	102.15	113.66	114.16
4	106.29	102.15	113.66
5	111.24	106.29	102.15
.			
.			
.			
55	150.66	153.18	153.24
56	166.68	150.66	153.18
57	166.10	166.68	150.66
58	166.09	166.10	166.68
59	163.58	166.09	166.10
60	167.24	163.58	166.09

A plot of SP versus SP_{-1} is given in Figure 11.3(a): The association between month-end SP values and the SP values at the end of the previous month is quite strong.

Sometimes we may want to relate each value of a time series variable, y, to the previous value but 1. This leads to the **second lag** of y, or **the lag of order 2,** denoted y_{-2}. Figure 11.2 also contains the second lag for the SP data. In general, we define the pth lag of a variable as follows:

lagging

> The **pth lag** of a time series variable y associates with each y-value the y-value p periods earlier. The pth lag is denoted y_{-p} and is also called the lag of order p.

Figure 11.3(a) shows strong association between SP and its first lag, SP_{-1}: When SP_{-1} is low, SP also tends to be low, and when SP_{-1} is high, SP also tends to be high. A convenient one-number summary for the strength of the relationship is the correlation coefficient. Figure 11.3(b) gives the correlation to be $r_{SP,SP_{-1}} = 0.964$.

This correlation is called an *autocorrelation:*

autocorrelation

> **Autocorrelation:** The correlation $r_{y,y_{-1}}$ between a variable y and its **first** lag y_{-1} is called the **first-order autocorrelation.** The correlation between a variable y and its **pth** lag, y_{-p} is called the **pth-order autocorrelation.**

Minitab can compute autocorrelations of several orders and list them in an *autocorrelogram,* a plot of the first few autocorrelations. Figure 11.3(c) is an autocorrelogram that gives the autocorrelations of first to 17th order for the SP data. The lag 1 autocorrelation is 0.937, the lag 2 autocorrelation is 0.875, etc. In the

FIGURE 11.3 SP Data

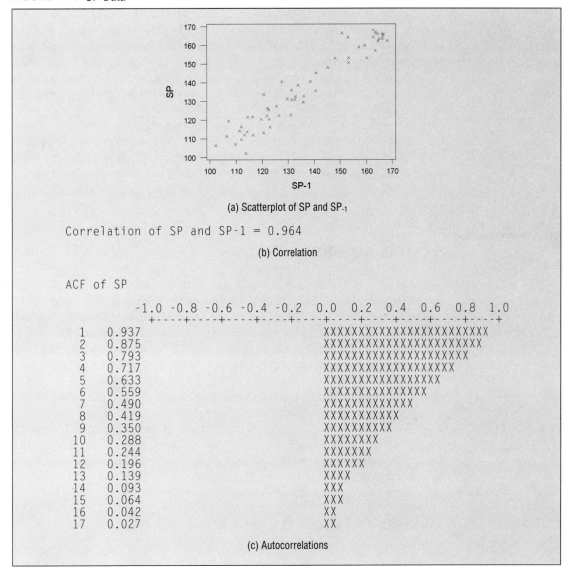

(a) Scatterplot of SP and SP$_{-1}$

Correlation of SP and SP-1 = 0.964

(b) Correlation

ACF of SP

```
              -1.0 -0.8 -0.6 -0.4 -0.2  0.0  0.2  0.4  0.6  0.8  1.0
               +----+----+----+----+----+----+----+----+----+----+
    1   0.937                                XXXXXXXXXXXXXXXXXXXXXXXXXX
    2   0.875                                XXXXXXXXXXXXXXXXXXXXXXXX
    3   0.793                                XXXXXXXXXXXXXXXXXXXXXX
    4   0.717                                XXXXXXXXXXXXXXXXXXX
    5   0.633                                XXXXXXXXXXXXXXXX
    6   0.559                                XXXXXXXXXXXXXX
    7   0.490                                XXXXXXXXXXXX
    8   0.419                                XXXXXXXXXX
    9   0.350                                XXXXXXXXX
   10   0.288                                XXXXXXX
   11   0.244                                XXXXXX
   12   0.196                                XXXXX
   13   0.139                                XXXX
   14   0.093                                XXX
   15   0.064                                XXX
   16   0.042                                XX
   17   0.027                                XX
```

(c) Autocorrelations

right part of the autocorrelogram, the magnitude of the autocorrelations is graphically displayed to provide a visual aid for the interpretation of the autocorrelogram. The size of positive autocorrelations is graphically represented by a bar consisting of X's that extends from 0 to the right. For negative autocorrelations, the bar extends from 0 to the left. For theoretical reasons, autocorrelations are computed slightly differently from the usual correlations, so the numerical values for the lag 1 autocorrelations given in Figure 11.3(b) (0.964) and Figure 11.3(c) (0.937) differ slightly.

Each autocorrelation given in Figure 11.3(c) summarizes one scatterplot. For example, the first-order autocorrelation (0.937) summarizes the plot of SP vs. its first lag, SP_{-1}, the second-order autocorrelation (0.875) summarizes the plot of SP vs. its second lag, SP_{-2}, etc. Note that some of the autocorrelations are quite high, particularly the first few.

Since the *current* observation is the *first lag* of the next observation, it may be possible to use the current value to *predict* the next value if there is a relationship between the first lag of a variable and the variable itself.

Of course, if a sequence is random there is no time series relationship, and so it is not possible to use lags for prediction. In a random series, the autocorrelations of *any* order equal 0. (Even if the process generating the data is random, the sample autocorrelations may well be slightly different from 0 due to chance variation.)

11.4

AUTOREGRESSION

Autoregression is a regression in which the predictor variables are lags of the response variable. Figure 11.4 contains Minitab output for the autoregression of SP on its first lag, SP_{-1}. It might appear from Figures 11.1 and 11.3 that higher lags, such as the second, should have been included in the autoregression. That would have been possible, but it is not necessary as will be shown with the diagnostic checks, in particular, diagnostic check 3.

Before interpreting the output further, we should carry out the diagnostic checks. Figure 11.5 is a plot of the standardized residuals vs. fitted values for this autoregression. It is quite acceptable, and diagnostic checks 1 and 2 are passed.

randomness check
When discussing assumption 3 (randomness of the residuals) in Chapters 9 and 10, we did not pay much attention to the appropriate diagnostic checks when the data were cross-sectional. When dealing with time series regression, it is imperative that close attention be paid to assumption 3.

Remembering our usual model specification,

$$\text{Actual} = \text{Systematic Part} + \text{Residual}$$

or

$$y = \text{Systematic Part} + \epsilon$$

violation of assumption 3 indicates that some systematic time series information is contained in the residuals, rather than in the systematic part. The model needs to model this time series information better in the systematic part. Assumption 3 is satisfied if the residuals are random over time. In Chapter 5, we discussed two statistical tools to assess randomness,

1. A visual impression of the time series plot, including control chart limits

2. The runs test as supporting evidence

FIGURE 11.4 Autoregression of SP on Its First Lag

```
The regression equation is
SP = 4.95 + 0.971 SP-1

59 cases used 1 cases contain missing values

Predictor        Coef      Stdev     t-ratio        p
Constant        4.948      4.890        1.01    0.316
SP-1          0.97051    0.03523       27.55    0.000

s = 5.545        R-sq = 93.0%    R-sq(adj) = 92.9%

Analysis of Variance

SOURCE         DF          SS         MS        F        p
Regression      1       23334      23334   758.97    0.000
Error          57        1752         31
Total          58       25086

Unusual Observations
Obs.    SP-1          SP      Fit Stdev.Fit    Residual   St.Resid
  3      114     102.150   115.257    1.102     -13.107     -2.41R
 11      127     140.520   128.660    0.801      11.860      2.16R
 34      120     133.710   121.817    0.935      11.893      2.18R
 40      153     164.420   153.398    0.908      11.022      2.02R
 56      151     166.680   151.166    0.862      15.514      2.83R

R denotes an obs. with a large st. resid.
```

FIGURE 11.5
SP Data: Plot of Standardized Residual vs. Fitted for Autoregression

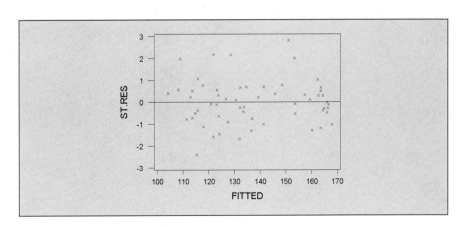

FIGURE 11.6 SP Data: Sequence Plot, Runs Test, and Autocorrelations for Standardized Residuals from the Autoregression

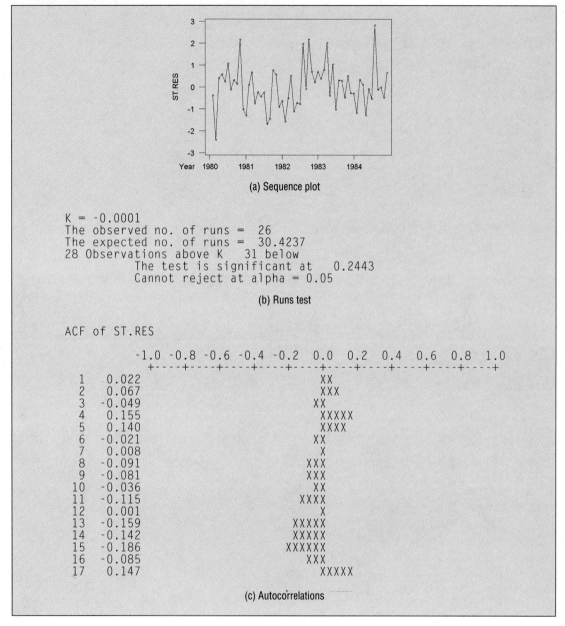

(a) Sequence plot

```
K = -0.0001
The observed no. of runs =  26
The expected no. of runs =  30.4237
28 Observations above K    31 below
          The test is significant at    0.2443
          Cannot reject at alpha = 0.05
```

(b) Runs test

```
ACF of ST.RES

             -1.0 -0.8 -0.6 -0.4 -0.2  0.0  0.2  0.4  0.6  0.8  1.0
             +----+----+----+----+----+----+----+----+----+----+
   1   0.022                               XX
   2   0.067                               XXX
   3  -0.049                               XX
   4   0.155                               XXXXX
   5   0.140                               XXXX
   6  -0.021                               XX
   7   0.008                               X
   8  -0.091                              XXX
   9  -0.081                              XXX
  10  -0.036                               XX
  11  -0.115                             XXXX
  12   0.001                               X
  13  -0.159                            XXXXX
  14  -0.142                            XXXXX
  15  -0.186                           XXXXXX
  16  -0.085                              XXX
  17   0.147                               XXXXX
```

(c) Autocorrelations

We now also have a third statistical tool to assess randomness:

3. The autocorrelation function for the standardized residuals

If the runs test is inconclusive, we must rely on the other tools.

Figure 11.6 contains the time series plot and the runs test for the standardized residuals from the autoregression in Figure 11.4. Figure 11.6 also contains the first- to 17th-order autocorrelations for the standardized residuals from the autoregression of SP on its first lag, SP_{-1}. If assumption 3 were met, the standardized residuals for this model would be a random series, and if the standardized residuals came from a random process, then all autocorrelations would be close to 0. The sample autocorrelations are all small. There is really no pattern in which, for example, all autocorrelations are either positive or negative. Thus, examination of these autocorrelations supports the assumption that the residuals come from a random series. Overall, Figure 11.6 indicates that there is little of the time series pattern left in the residuals: Assumption 3 is justified.

The final diagnostic check examines the normality of the residuals. The normal probability plot (Figure 11.7) looks adequate, though the top five observations are somewhat far away from the line expected under normality.

outlier

In regression, there are two types of "unusual observations", *outliers* and *influential observations*. When discussing unusual observations in Section 9.5 (p. 404), we saw that Minitab flags observations whose standardized residuals exceed 2 in absolute value. It is useful to know which observations are somewhat far away from the bulk of the data, but in this book we do not consider an observation to be a serious outlier unless its standardized residual exceeds 3 in absolute value. There is no such outlier in the SP example.

influential observation

An influential observation is one that has a great influence on the values of the coefficients in the regression equation—that is, the numerical values of these coefficients would change considerably if an influential observation were dropped. There is no influential observation in the SP example.

Summarizing, the autoregression model of SP on its first lag is an excellent model and needs no improvement. We can now use this model to answer the ques-

FIGURE 11.7
SP Data: Normal Probability Plot of Standardized Residuals

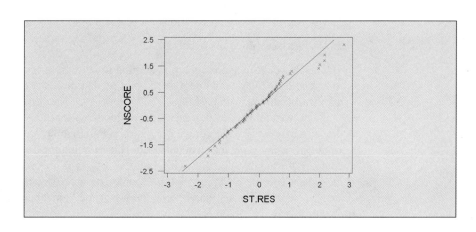

tion raised at the beginning of Section 11.2 regarding a forecast of the SP value in January 1985.

Using Figure 11.4, the prediction model is

$$\hat{y} = 4.95 + (0.971)SP_{-1}$$

prediction   A point prediction for January 1985 is

$$4.95 + 0.971(\text{Value in Dec. 1984}) = 4.95 + 0.971(167.24) = 167.34$$

Since the sample size is large, the standard error of prediction is well approximated by the standard deviation of residuals, $s = 5.545$, so a 3-standard-deviation prediction interval extends approximately $3s = 3(5.545) = 16.64$ around the point prediction,

$$\hat{y} \pm 3s \quad \text{or} \quad 167.34 \pm 16.64$$

or from 150.70 to 183.98, rather a wide interval. Since the diagnostic check of normality in Figure 11.7 was adequate, we can interpret this prediction interval as a 99.7% interval.

11.5

EVALUATION OF FORECASTING MODELS

In the last section we discussed the autoregression model for the Standard & Poor Composite Index. In this section, we will discuss some statistical methods to evaluate the goodness of forecasting models. We will do this by comparing the autoregression model with two **naive forecasting models:**

1. Use the mean of all observations for prediction.

2. Use the last value for prediction.

The mean would be a good point prediction if the time series were random or close to it. The last value would be a good point prediction if the time series were a random walk with mean change of 0.

How could we develop measures of goodness for these two naive models and the autoregression? One simple way is to summarize how the forecasting models would have done on the available data: For the autoregression model we would compare the actual values, y, with the fitted values from the autoregression, $\hat{y}$. For the naive "Use the mean" model, we would compare the actual values, y, with the sample mean, $\bar{y}$. For the naive "Use the last value" model, we would compare the actual values, y, with the first lag, y_{-1}.

FIGURE 11.8 Evaluation of Three Forecasting Models

ROW	y	$\bar{y}$	y_{-1}	$\hat{y}$	$y - \bar{y}$	$y - y_{-1}$	$y - \hat{y}$
1	114.16	137.801	*	*	-23.6407	*	*
2	113.66	137.801	114.16	115.742	-24.1407	-0.5000	-2.0820
3	102.15	137.801	113.66	115.257	-35.6507	-11.5100	-13.1068
4	106.29	137.801	102.15	104.086	-31.5107	4.1400	2.2038
5	111.24	137.801	106.29	108.104	-26.5607	4.9500	3.1359
⋮							
55	150.66	137.801	153.18	153.611	12.8593	-2.5200	-2.9515
56	166.68	137.801	150.66	151.166	28.8793	16.0200	15.5142
57	166.10	137.801	166.68	166.713	28.2993	-0.5800	-0.6134
58	166.09	137.801	166.10	166.151	28.2893	-0.0100	-0.0605
59	163.58	137.801	166.09	166.141	25.7793	-2.5100	-2.5608
60	167.24	137.801	163.58	163.705	29.4393	3.6600	3.5352

mean absolute deviation (MAD)

mean squared deviation (MSD)

Figure 11.8 gives a partial listing of the SP values (y), the mean of the SP values ($\bar{y}$), the first lag of the SP values (y_{-1}), and the fitted values from the autoregression ($\hat{y}$). It also lists the differences between the actual values and the values obtained from each of the three forecasting models. We will use two summary measures of goodness, the *mean absolute deviation* (MAD) and the *mean squared deviation* (MSD). For the "Use the mean" model, the mean absolute deviation is

$$\text{MAD}(\bar{y}) = \frac{\sum_{i=1}^{n}|y_i - \bar{y}|}{n}$$

and the mean squared deviation is

$$\text{MSD}(\bar{y}) = \frac{\sum_{i=1}^{n}(y_i - \bar{y})^2}{n}$$

For the "Use the last value" model, mean absolute deviation and mean squared deviation are

$$\text{MAD}(y_{-1}) = \frac{\sum_{i=2}^{n}|y_i - y_{i-1}|}{n - 1} \quad \text{and} \quad \text{MSD}(y_{-1}) = \frac{\sum_{i=2}^{n}(y_i - y_{i-1})^2}{n - 1}$$

For the autoregression model, they are

$$\text{MAD}(\hat{y}) = \frac{\sum_{i=2}^{n} |y_i - \hat{y}_i|}{n - 1} \quad \text{and} \quad \text{MSD}(\hat{y}) = \frac{\sum_{i=2}^{n} (y_i - \hat{y}_i)^2}{n - 1}$$

The divisor $n - 1$ is used above since only $n - 1$ predictions are available.

The following table lists MAD and MSD for all three models:

	MAD	MSD
$\bar{y}$	18.49	427.60
y_{-1}	4.24	30.88
$\hat{y}$	4.17	29.70

Both MAD and MSD tell the same story: The "Use the mean" model fares very badly; the "Use the last value" and the autoregression models are about equally good. The easiest model to use may be the "Use the last value" forecasting model.

When evaluating a forecasting model, it is best to do so with new data. For example, the autoregression model for SP was estimated to be

$$\hat{y} = (0.971)\text{SP}_{-1} + 4.95$$

based on data for January 1980 to December 1984. In order to evaluate this model, we should check how well it forecasts SP values in the future (that is, after December 1984). We have not done so above, however: We have used the model to retrospectively "predict" the actual values that were used to estimate the model.

Since values for SP after December 1984 are available, we could have applied the forecasting models to *future* cases. Let us use the SP values for January 1985 to December 1987 to compare these models. Since the "Use the mean" model is obviously bad for this time series, we will only compare the "Use the last value" and the autoregression models. The following table sets out the comparison in terms of MAD and MSD:

	MAD	MSD
y_{-1}	11.15	272
$\hat{y}$	11.59	274

Again, the two models are close, both in terms of MAD and MSD. But note that the "Use the last value" model is slightly better. This is a feature of many forecasting models: Simple models often do very well!

In the SP example, we had available "future" data, but this may not always be so in practice. We may have to use the data that were used to build the model for the purpose of evaluating the model, too.

11.6

THE RANDOM WALK MODEL VS. AUTOREGRESSION: THE STANDARD & POOR INDEX

You should skip this section if you did not read Chapter 6. Many time series are not well modeled by a random walk. We saw in Section 6.2, however, that the random walk is a good model for the SP series. Let us compare the random walk model for the SP data with the autoregression model discussed in Section 11.4: Which model gives better predictions? Which model is simpler?

In this example, the response variable is y, monthly closing value for the SP composite index. There are 60 values from January 1980 to December 1984. Figure 11.9 shows the SP values (stored in variable SP), the lag 1 differences (D_SP), and their first lag (SP$_{-1}$).

FIGURE 11.9 SP Data: Descriptive Statistics

	N	N*	MEAN	MEDIAN	TRMEAN	STDEV	SEMEAN
SP	60	0	137.80	133.26	137.97	20.85	2.69
SP-1	59	1	137.30	132.81	137.44	20.67	2.69
D_SP	59	1	0.900	0.710	0.710	5.530	0.720

	MIN	MAX	Q1	Q3
SP	102.15	168.11	120.40	161.80
SP-1	102.15	168.11	120.40	160.05
D_SP	-11.510	16.020	-2.520	4.460

(a) Descriptive statistics

ROW	SP	SP-1	D_SP
1	114.16	*	*
2	113.66	114.16	-0.5000
3	102.15	113.66	-11.5100
4	106.29	102.15	4.1400
5	111.24	106.29	4.9500
.			
.			
.			
55	150.66	153.18	-2.5200
56	166.68	150.66	16.0200
57	166.10	166.68	-0.5800
58	166.09	166.10	-0.0100
59	163.58	166.09	-2.5100
60	167.24	163.58	3.6600

(b) Selected values of SP, first lag (SP-1), and first differences (D_SP)

Our general form for a model is

$$y = \text{Systematic Part} + \epsilon$$

For both the random walk and autoregression models, the following table sets out

- The Systematic Part. For the random walk model, the relevant process parameter is μ, the process mean of the lag 1 differences. For the autoregression model, the relevant process parameters are the two regression coefficients, β_0 and β_1

- Its estimate from the data, the fitted value $\hat{y}$

- A point prediction for January 1985 that uses the value for December 1984 as the first lag, 167.24

- The relevant standard deviation giving a measure of uncertainty in the point prediction. For the random walk model, this is the standard deviation of lag 1 differences (see Figure 11.9). For the autoregression model, it is the standard deviation of residuals around the regression line (see Figure 11.4).

- A 3–standard-deviation prediction interval for January 1985

	Random Walk	Autoregression
Systematic Part	$\text{SP}_{-1} + \mu$	$\beta_1 \text{SP}_{-1} + \beta_0$
$\hat{y}$	$\text{SP}_{-1} + 0.90$	$0.971(\text{SP}_{-1}) + 4.95$
Point prediction	$167.24 + 0.90 = 168.14$	$0.971(167.24) + 4.95 = 167.34$
Standard deviation	5.530	5.545
Prediction interval	168.14 ± 16.59	167.34 ± 16.64

For the two models, the point predictions, standard deviations, and prediction intervals are very similar. It thus does not matter, in this example, whether we use the random walk model for prediction or the autoregression model. In the equation for the fitted value, $\hat{y}$, the coefficient for the first lag is 1 in the random walk, but 0.971 in the autoregression model. The random walk model is preferred in this application: It is easier to explain that a point prediction is obtained by adding 0.90 to the current value than by adding 4.95 to the current value multiplied by 0.971.

This discussion points out one useful fact: In many investigations there are several satisfactory models that can be identified. As long as they all lead to similar predictions, it does not much matter which one is used. If they do not lead to similar predictions, one should be very careful in using any one of them for prediction. It might be advisable to first examine the reasons for the discrepancies.

In this section, we have seen that a process that can be described by a random walk model can also be described by an autoregression model. This is true in general. When both an autoregression model and a random walk model fit the data equally well, the random walk model is preferable since it has a simpler interpretation. It is not generally true, however, that every process that is well-described by an autoregression model can be modeled as a random walk.

11.7

RANDOM SERIES

This section discusses the **random process** further. In Chapter 5, we introduced the use of

- Visual impression
- The runs test
- Control chart limits

to check the randomness of a process.

We now add the

- **Autocorrelations**

as a further tool to check the randomness of a process.

We use several examples to illustrate the use of the autocorrelations to check the randomness of a process. The first process is the time series of the Standard & Poor Composite Index; the second process generates the bendclip diameter data, discussed in Chapter 5; and the third process generates the residuals from the autoregression of the SP Index on its first lag.

The autocorrelation function for a time series that is generated by a *random* process has the following property:

> **Random process:** In a process that generates observations randomly, all autocorrelations equal 0.

Typically, we cannot observe all data generated by a process since it is ongoing: Only a sample sequence can be observed. In such a case the sample autocorrelations do not necessarily equal the process autocorrelations because of sampling variability.

random process and autocorrelations

> **Sampling from a random process:** When a process is random, the autocorrelations for a sample are all expected to equal 0, but they may slightly deviate from 0. A measure of the extent to which any autocorrelation may deviate from 0 is the **standard error,** which is approximately $1/\sqrt{n}$ for all sample autocorrelations, where n is the length of the sample time series.

In order for a process to be judged random based on the sample autocorrelation function,

- All sample autocorrelations should be close to 0.

- There should be no pattern to the deviations from 0. Positive and negative sample autocorrelations should be *well mixed.*

Let us first examine the SP data again. The autocorrelations for the SP series were given in Figure 11.3(c). Do the autocorrelations support the view that the process generating the SP series is random? In other words, are these autocorrelations close to 0, the expected value for each sample autocorrelation if the series were random? The standard error for each autocorrelation approximately equals $1/\sqrt{n} = 1/\sqrt{60} = 0.13$. A 2-standard-error limit around 0 extends from approximately -0.26 to 0.26. Several sample autocorrelations are outside these limits, in particular, the first few. Thus some autocorrelations are not close to 0. In addition, there is a distinct pattern to the sizes of these autocorrelations: All sample autocorrelations of order 1 to 17 are positive, and they are decreasing. Thus based on the autocorrelations, we cannot conclude that the SP series is random.

The 2-standard-error limit used in the previous paragraph is merely a guideline for judging the randomness of a time series, and it should be used in conjunction with other relevant information.

Given our visual impression of the meandering behavior of the SP series in Figure 11.1(b), the conclusion of nonrandomness is, of course, no surprise. Note that examination of the autocorrelations should always supplement a visual impression of the data, in addition to the runs test and the control limits. Since the process generating the SP data is not random, we should exploit the time series pattern for prediction purposes (as we did in Section 11.4).

Let us now turn to our second example. In Chapter 5, we used our visual impression of the sequence plot, the runs test, and the control limits to conclude that the bendclip diameter series was random. Does the autocorrelation function support this conclusion? Figure 11.10 lists the sample autocorrelation function for the 40 bendclip diameters. If the bendclip diameter data were random, all sample autocorrelations would be close to 0. The standard error for each autocorrelation would be $1/\sqrt{n} = 1/\sqrt{40} = 0.158$. As can be seen from Figure 11.10, all autocorrelations are well within 2 standard errors of 0. In addition, there is no pattern to the way in which the autocorrelations deviate from 0. Their signs are well mixed. Thus, the autocorrelations support our assessment of randomness for the process generating the bendclip diameter data.

A third example examines the randomness of the residuals from a regression. Recall that the regression model assumes *all* systematic information to be modeled in the systematic part of the model. This implies, for example, that there is no time series information contained in the sequence of the residuals. In other words, the residuals are assumed to be random in sequence (Regression assumption 3 in Sections 9.3 and 10.2). We will use the autocorrelations as a *supplementary* tool to check the randomness of the residuals. As an example, consider the autoregression

FIGURE 11.10 Bendclip Diameter Data: Autocorrelations

```
ACF of DIAMETER

                  -1.0 -0.8 -0.6 -0.4 -0.2  0.0  0.2  0.4  0.6  0.8  1.0
                   +----+----+----+----+----+----+----+----+----+----+
    1   -0.200                          XXXXXX
    2   -0.009                               X
    3   -0.050                              XX
    4   -0.146                          XXXXX
    5   -0.099                            XXX
    6    0.084                               XXX
    7    0.100                               XXXX
    8   -0.019                               X
    9   -0.255                        XXXXXXX
   10    0.153                               XXXXX
   11   -0.279                       XXXXXXXX
   12    0.120                               XXXX
   13    0.107                               XXXX
   14   -0.162                         XXXXX
   15   -0.028                              XX
   16    0.084                               XXX
```

of the SP data, discussed in Section 11.4. We had estimated the model

$$SP = \beta_0 + \beta_1 \, SP_{-1} + \epsilon$$

In Figure 11.4, the systematic part for this model, $\beta_0 + \beta_1 \, SP_{-1}$, was estimated to be

$$\hat{y} = 4.95 + (0.971)SP_{-1}$$

Thus, the estimated residuals, e, can be obtained as

$$e = SP - \hat{y}$$

As stated in Chapters 9 and 10, there are theoretical reasons to use the standardized residuals for checking assumption 3, rather than the residuals, e. The autocorrelations for the standardized residuals from the regression of SP on its first lag were given in Figure 11.6(c). They indicate that there is little time series pattern left in the standardized residuals. In particular, the autocorrelation function conforms to what we would expect from a random series: The autocorrelations are all within 2 standard errors $[2(1/\sqrt{60}) = 2(0.13) = 0.26]$ of 0, and the signs of the autocorrelations are reasonably well mixed. So assumption 3 was justified.

11.8

THE DURBIN-WATSON STATISTIC

The Durbin-Watson statistic gives a quick preliminary impression of the adequacy of regression assumption 3. It should be determined for any regression in which observations were obtained over time.

> The **Durbin-Watson statistic,** DW, is a rudimentary tool to check the adequacy of regression assumption 3, *randomness* of residuals. It is closely related to the lag 1 sample autocorrelation of residuals. An approximate computational formula is
>
> $$DW = 2[1 - (\text{lag 1 autocorrelation})]$$
>
> Thus, the lag 1 autocorrelation approximately equals $1 - (DW/2)$.

The Durbin-Watson statistic is discussed here since it is often the *only* diagnostic check for the assumption of randomness of residuals that is reported in published analyses. It is far better, however, to use the tools introduced earlier in this chapter—visual inspection, runs test, control limits, and autocorrelation function.

Figure 11.11 gives the Durbin-Watson statistic as 1.94. This implies that the first-order autocorrelation of residuals approximately equals $1 - 1.94/2 = 1 - 0.97 = 0.03$. Thus the Durbin-Watson statistic suggests no problems with autocorrelation of residuals.

The Durbin-Watson statistic gives no information about higher-order sample autocorrelations. Even if the Durbin-Watson statistic is satisfactory, there may be time series information contained in the residuals such that second- or higher-order

FIGURE 11.11
SP Data: Autoregression of SP on Its First Lag (Durbin-Watson Statistic)

```
The regression equation is
SP = 4.95 + 0.971 SP-1

59 cases used 1 cases contain missing values

Predictor        Coef        Stdev     t-ratio        p
Constant        4.948       4.890        1.01     0.316
SP-1          0.97051     0.03523       27.55     0.000

s = 5.545       R-sq = 93.0%      R-sq(adj) = 92.9%
. . .

Durbin-Watson statistic = 1.94
```

autocorrelations do not equal 0. Therefore, the Durbin-Watson statistic should only be a *preliminary* diagnostic check of assumption 3.

The two tools discussed in this and the previous section give additional information about when a time series can be taken to have been generated by a random process. In the next section, we look at another example where autoregression is useful.

11.9

ANOTHER EXAMPLE OF AUTOREGRESSION: MORTGAGE SALES AT A FINANCIAL INSTITUTION

Let us examine a time series of sales of a financial institution:

EXAMPLE 11.1

An important area of business for a certain financial institution (FI Ltd.) is its residential mortgage portfolio. In order to provide prudent financial management, it is vital to match deposits with funding—that is, FI Ltd. must carefully manage its risk against sudden changes in depositors' preferences to ensure continuous and adequate sources of money to fund its residential mortgage portfolio. An important basis for management's decisions is an accurate prediction of the demand for future funds. The following question was to be addressed:

Can a reliable prediction model be found for next month's mortgage sales?

To answer this question, monthly data were collected on dollar sales (in $1,000) of mortgage money by FI Ltd. for the 60-month period from August 1984 to July 1989.[2] The data, stored in ASCII file MORTGAGE.DAT, are given in Figure 11.12.

The sequence plot in Figure 11.12(b) reveals a monthly pattern superimposed on the overall upward drift in the data. These two aspects of the time series pattern are also reflected in the autocorrelogram, where the first and 12th autocorrelations are high, the first representing the overall upward drift and the 12th the monthly pattern.

Let us now examine an autoregression of mortgage SALES on its first and 12th lags. There are $k = 2$ predictor variables, and so the n/k ratio introduced in Section 10.9 is $\frac{48}{2} = 24$, which exceeds 15. The first lag is used to capture the upward drift and the 12th lag to capture the monthly pattern. Figure 11.13 gives descriptive statistics for SALES and the two lags considered. There are 12 missing values for the 12th lag, $SALES_{-12}$, and the descriptive statistics for SALES and its first and 12th lags are fairly similar.

---

[2] Some of the data were slightly altered to protect confidentiality.

FIGURE 11.12 Mortgage Sales: Data and Sequence Plot

58853	61493	56989	56639	36038	68946	107670	58553
74113	107214	109987	108810	102668	91780	85058	84536
60065	88739	86588	82550	164840	212245	211123	141241
133560	142182	123480	91560	66016	117614	180257	214752
264302	211900	171118	172942	157508	150772	179821	120899
102875	70687	126677	263315	242054	232625	167657	193222
196196	226829	158078	196384	157333	167290	212944	248012
195562	242152	279226	237466				

(a) Monthly sales data (read row by row)

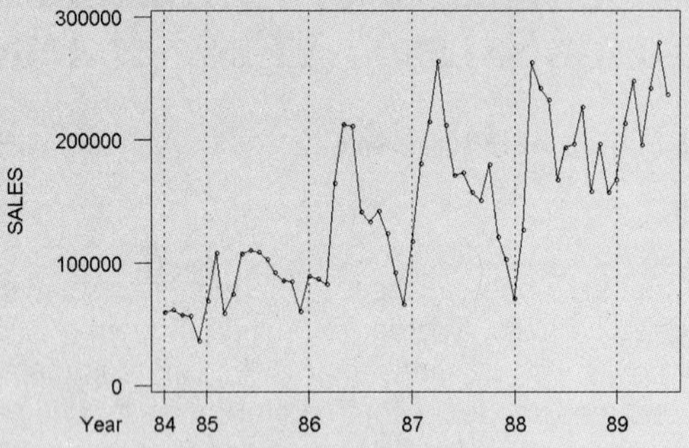

(b) Sequence plot

```
ACF of SALES

              -1.0 -0.8 -0.6 -0.4 -0.2  0.0  0.2  0.4  0.6  0.8  1.0
              +----+----+----+----+----+----+----+----+----+----+
   1   0.784                           XXXXXXXXXXXXXXXXXXXXX
   2   0.546                           XXXXXXXXXXXXXX
   3   0.384                           XXXXXXXXXX
   4   0.317                           XXXXXXXXX
   5   0.252                           XXXXXXX
   6   0.223                           XXXXXXX
   7   0.194                           XXXXX
   8   0.213                           XXXXX
   9   0.267                           XXXXXXX
  10   0.377                           XXXXXXXXXX
  11   0.463                           XXXXXXXXXXXX
  12   0.445                           XXXXXXXXXXXX
  13   0.352                           XXXXXXXXXX
  14   0.246                           XXXXXX
  15   0.130                           XXXX
  16   0.011                           X
  17  -0.088                         XXX
```

(c) Autocorrelations

FIGURE 11.13 Mortgage Sales: Descriptive Statistics

	N	N*	MEAN	MEDIAN	TRMEAN	
SALES	60	0	145533	141712	143991	
SALES-1	59	1	143975	141241	142227	
SALES-12	48	12	129469	113800	127142	
	STDEV	SEMEAN	MIN	MAX	Q1	Q3
SALES	65244	8423	36038	279226	87126	196337
SALES-1	64669	8419	36038	279226	86588	196196
SALES-12	60675	8758	36038	264302	83046	172486

Figure 11.14 presents output from the autoregression. The regression equation for SALES is

$$\text{Fitted SALES} = 37{,}671 + (0.462)\text{SALES}_{-1} + (0.396)\text{SALES}_{-12}$$

The value of the Durbin-Watson statistic is 1.72, so the first order autocorrelation of the residuals is about $1 - 1.72/2 = 0.14$. The Durbin-Watson statistic thus suggests no problems with the diagnostic checks of the randomness assumption. But we should also look at the other diagnostic checks of randomness. Figures 11.15 to

FIGURE 11.14 Mortgage Sales: Autoregression Output

```
The regression equation is
SALES = 37671 + 0.462 SALES-1 + 0.396 SALES-12

48 cases used 12 cases contain missing values

Predictor      Coef      Stdev     t-ratio        p
Constant       37671     15612      2.41       0.020
SALES-1        0.4620    0.1317     3.51       0.001
SALES-12       0.3962    0.1295     3.06       0.004

s = 37180       R-sq = 63.4%      R-sq(adj) = 61.8%
.
.
.

Unusual Observations
Obs.  SALES-1    SALES     Fit Stdev.Fit   Residual  St.Resid
 43     70687   126677  141744    17999     -15067    -0.46 X
 44    126677   263315  181277    15533      82038     2.43R

R denotes an obs. with a large st. resid.
X denotes an obs. whose X value gives it large influence.

Durbin-Watson statistic = 1.72
```

FIGURE 11.15
Mortgage Sales
Example: Standar-
dized Residual vs.
Fitted Plot

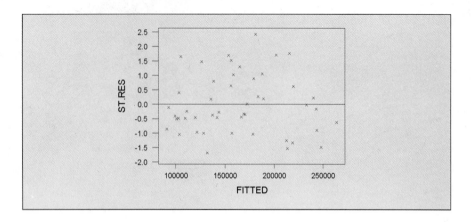

FIGURE 11.16 Mortgage Sales Example:
Sequence Plot, Runs Test, and Autocorrelations for Standardized Residuals

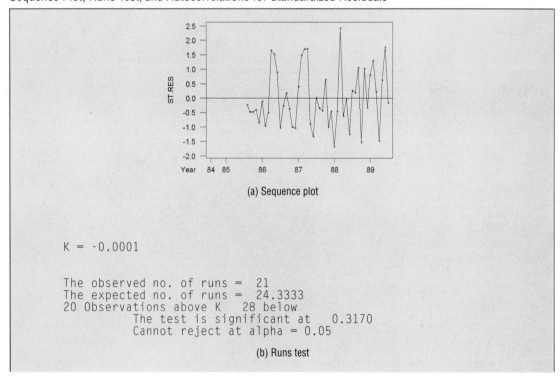

(a) Sequence plot

```
K = -0.0001


The observed no. of runs =  21
The expected no. of runs =  24.3333
20 Observations above K   28 below
        The test is significant at   0.3170
        Cannot reject at alpha = 0.05
```

(b) Runs test

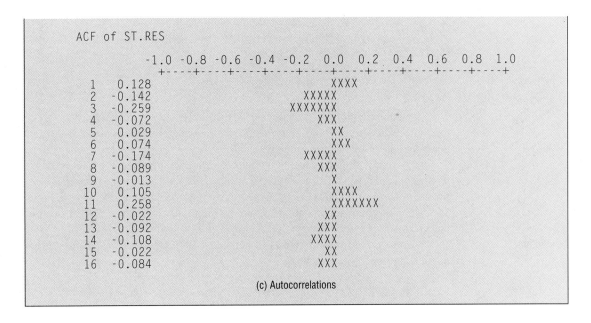

```
ACF of ST.RES

                -1.0 -0.8 -0.6 -0.4 -0.2  0.0  0.2  0.4  0.6  0.8  1.0
                +----+----+----+----+----+----+----+----+----+----+
     1    0.128                              XXXX
     2   -0.142                           XXXXX
     3   -0.259                         XXXXXX
     4   -0.072                            XXX
     5    0.029                             XX
     6    0.074                             XXX
     7   -0.174                          XXXXX
     8   -0.089                            XXX
     9   -0.013                              X
    10    0.105                              XXXX
    11    0.258                              XXXXXX
    12   -0.022                             XX
    13   -0.092                            XXX
    14   -0.108                           XXXX
    15   -0.022                             XX
    16   -0.084                            XXX
```

(c) Autocorrelations

11.17 give information for all the diagnostic checks. You should carefully study them to determine which diagnostic checks are satisfactory.

The deviations from what we expect in the diagnostic checks are minor, so we can use the model for prediction purposes. The randomness assumption, in particular, is justified. Figure 11.16(a) suggests randomness, which is supported by the runs test in Figure 11.16(b). All standardized residuals are within the control limits. Assuming that randomness holds, the standard error for each autocorrelation is approximately $1/\sqrt{60} = 0.13$, so none of the autocorrelations is large. Furthermore, the signs of the autocorrelations are well mixed.

FIGURE 11.17
Mortgage Sales:
Normal Probability
Plot for Residuals

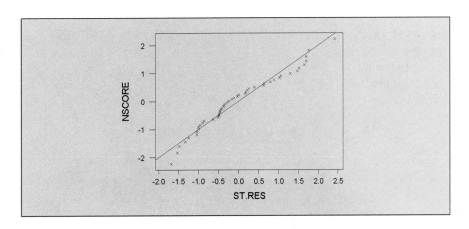

To see how well this autoregression model tracks the time series, Figure 11.18 gives a sequence plot of the actual sales (solid line) and the fitted sales (dashed line), obtained from the regression equation,

$$\text{Fitted SALES} = 37,671 + (0.462)\text{SALES}_{-1} + (0.396)\text{SALES}_{-12}$$

A sequence plot of residuals (dotted line) is also given in the figure. Although the fitted values track the time series pretty well, there is still considerable uncertainty, as shown by the size of the residuals.

An overall summary for the goodness of this autoregression model is the extent to which the standard deviation of residuals is less than the standard deviation for the original time series. The standard deviation of SALES is 65,244 (see Figure 11.13) and the standard deviation around the regression line is $s = 37,180$ (see Figure 11.14). This autoregression is reasonably good.

prediction
A prediction for mortgage sales in August 1989 can be obtained from the estimated autoregression equation,

$$\text{Fitted SALES} = 37,671 + (0.462)\text{SALES}_{-1} + (0.396)\text{SALES}_{-12}$$

The first lag for the August 1989 period is the July 1989 period. The 12th lag for the August 1989 period is August 1988 (that is, 1 year earlier). The sales values for these lagged periods are $\text{SALES}_{-1} = 237,466$ and $\text{SALES}_{-12} = 196,196$. The fitted value for sales in August 1989 is

$$37,671 + 0.462(237,466) + 0.396(196,196) = 225,074$$

Using the estimated standard deviation around the regression equation in Figure 11.14, $s = 37,180$, we can construct a 95% prediction interval,

$$225,074 \pm 2(37,180)$$

or between 150,714 and 299,434.

FIGURE 11.18
Mortgage Sales: Sequence Plots of Sales, Fitted Values, and Residuals

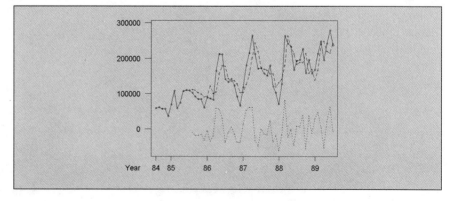

The multiple used is from a z-table. Since the standard deviation around the regression equation was used to approximate the standard error of prediction, this 95% prediction interval is a little bit tight. From the Minitab output in Figure 11.19, the 95% prediction interval extends from 148,079 to 302,135. The Minitab results are close to the point prediction and the prediction interval computed above.

The 95% prediction interval is quite wide, so the above prediction model for mortgage sales is somewhat inaccurate. In order to improve the model, it is necessary to collect information on other variables that are related to mortgage sales. But even such *leading indicators* may not help much to remove the remaining uncertainty.

model comparison   Let us finally examine how well this autoregression model does in comparison to the two naive forecasting models introduced in Section 11.5 plus another naive forecasting model. The two naive models from Section 11.5 were the "Use the mean" model ($\bar{y}$) and the "Use the last value" model (y_{-1}). The third naive model, "Use the value 12 months ago" (y_{-12}), may be useful for monthly data. Rather than giving the mean absolute deviation (MAD) and the mean squared deviation (MSD) for the four models, the following table lists two ratios for each naive model:

1. MAD divided by MAD for the autoregression model [MAD/MAD($\hat{y}$)]

2. MSD divided by MSD for the autoregression model [MSD/MSD($\hat{y}$)]

FIGURE 11.19 Mortgage Sales: Prediction for August 1989 (SALES$_{-1}$ = 237,466, SALES$_{-12}$ = 196,196)

```
The regression equation is
SALES = 37671 + 0.462 SALES-1 + 0.396 SALES-12

48 cases used 12 cases contain missing values

Predictor        Coef        Stdev      t-ratio          p
Constant        37671       15612         2.41      0.020
SALES-1        0.4620      0.1317         3.51      0.001
SALES-12       0.3962      0.1295         3.06      0.004

s = 37180       R-sq = 63.4%       R-sq(adj) = 61.8%
...

Unusual Observations
Obs. SALES-1      SALES      Fit Stdev.Fit      Residual  St.Resid
  43    70687     126677   141744     17999       -15067     -0.46 X
  44   126677     263315   181277     15533        82038      2.43R

R denotes an obs. with a large st. resid.
X denotes an obs. whose X value gives it large influence.

    Fit    Stdev.Fit         95% C.I.           95% P.I.
 225107         8923  ( 207130, 243083)  ( 148079, 302135)
```

Values of either ratio close to 1 suggest that a naive model does about equally as well as the autoregression model.

	$\dfrac{\text{MAD}}{\text{MAD}(\hat{y})}$	$\dfrac{\text{MSD}}{\text{MSD}(\hat{y})}$
$\bar{y}$	1.89	3.22
y_{-1}	1.02	1.21
y_{-12}	1.51	2.35

Not surprisingly, the autoregression model does better than the three naive models. Note, however, that the "Use the last value" model does quite well in comparison to the autoregression model.

11.10

MODELING

Sections 9.3 and 10.2 discussed modeling in the context of regression analysis. This chapter discusses time series modeling with regression analysis. The remarks made in Sections 9.3 and 10.2 are valid here as well. In particular, it is important to check the four regression assumptions with the diagnostic checks. In time series modeling, diagnostic check 3 (randomness of residuals) is particularly important. Several tools are available for diagnostic check 3: the sequence plot, the runs test, the control chart limits, and the autocorrelations.

In this chapter, we used the autocorrelations in two different ways:

1. The autocorrelations for the variable for which a prediction model is to be found can be used to identify which lags should initially be included in the prediction model.

2. The autocorrelations for the standardized residuals from the prediction model can be used for the diagnostic check of randomness. If some of these autocorrelations are not close to 0, they may point to ways of improving the prediction model.

Some implications for violations of the assumptions were discussed at the end of Section 9.6 (p. 414). They are relevant here as well. If one or more diagnostic checks are not satisfactory, we must revise the model, and the diagnostic checks may point to how to do so. The new model should also be checked, which may lead to another iteration in the model formulating process. [The iterative nature of modeling was discussed in Section 2.2 (p. 12).]

Once a satisfactory model has been found, it should ideally be tested on data that were not used to build it. This approach avoids creating models that are representative only of the particular data set at hand and not of new data.

This chapter also discusses ways to compare autoregression models with naive forecasting models that are very simple to use. If one of these models does well in comparison to the autoregression model, the simple model should possibly be used instead.

When the diagnostic checks are satisfactory and the model closely represents the data-generating process, the model can be used for prediction. Just as in regression models, it is necessary, however, that the values of the predictor variables be *known* at the time the prediction is to be made.

Sometimes, there are several equally acceptable models for a prediction situation, all of which have satisfactory diagnostic checks. All of these models should then lead to quite similar predictions, and choice among them should be guided by considerations of simplicity. If they do not lead to similar predictions, the reasons for discrepancies should be identified before using any one of them for prediction purposes.

11.11

SUMMARY AND OUTLOOK

This chapter discussed modeling of time series. You now have a set of tools available with which you can model many time series reasonably well. These models should help you (1) understand how a time series is generated over time, and (2) get short-term point and interval forecasts.

Modeling a time series is usually an iterative procedure: You postulate a model, estimate it, and carry out diagnostic checks to see if the model is adequate or needs improvement. The diagnostic checks usually give hints as to how to improve the postulated model.

The time series modeling tools discussed so far range from differencing to autoregression. These two tools need not be used in isolation, but can be combined. This may be necessary, for example, when the differences are not random, but still display a time series pattern. To model this pattern in the differences, an autoregression could be carried out linking the differences to one or more lags thereof. This approach is discussed more fully in the next chapter.

In this chapter, we discussed time series modeling only where no auxiliary information is available from *other* variables. Sometimes such additional variables are available that could be useful as predictor variables. (Such predictor variables are often called *leading indicators* in economics and finance.) In such cases, you should, of course, always carry out the diagnostic checks and study them carefully.

Key Terms and Concepts

lagging
autocorrelation
autoregression
random process
  standard error of autocorrelation,
  Durbin-Watson statistic

naive forecasting models
  "Use the mean"; "Use the last
  value"; "Use the value 1 year ago"

Reference

Cryer, J. D. (1986), *Time Series Analysis,* Duxbury Press, Belmont, CA.

> This text builds on the material discussed in this book. Its level is comparable to this book's. Minitab is used extensively.

11.12

USING MINITAB FOR WINDOWS

This section shows how several of the graphs in this chapter were generated with Minitab for Windows.

Figure 11.3

Choose *File ▸ Other Files ▸ Import ASCII Data*
In the *Import ASCII Data* dialog box,
   Under *Store data in column,* type **C1**
   Click *ok*
   In the *Import Text From File* dialog box,
      Choose and click data file *sp_month.dat,* click *ok*
Choose *Window ▸ Data*
In the *Data* window,
   In the box immediately under *C1,* type **SP**
   Highlight rows 61 to 144 of C1
   Choose *Edit ▸ Cut Cells*

LAGGING A VARIABLE

Choose *Stat ▸ Time Series ▸ Lag*
In the *Lag* dialog box,
   Click the box next to *Series,* type **C1**
   Click the box next to *Store lags in,* type **C2**
   Click *ok*
Choose *Window ▸ Data*
In the *Data* window,
   In the box immediately under *C2,* type **SP-1**
   Click any empty cell

Choose *Graph ▸ Plot*
In the *Plot* dialog box,
   Under *Graph variables,* type **C1** under *Y* and type **C2** under *X*
   Click *ok*
Choose *Stat ▸ Basic Statistics ▸ Correlation*

In the *Correlation* dialog box,
> Under *Variables*, type **C1 C2**
> Click *ok*

AUTOCORRELATIONS

Choose *Stat* ▸ *Time Series* ▸ *Autocorrelation*
In the *Autocorrelation Function* dialog box,
> Click the box next to *Series*, type **C1**
> Click the circle next to *Nongraphical ACF*
> Click *ok*

Figure 11.9

DIFFERENCING

Choose *Stat* ▸ *Time Series* ▸ *Differences*
In the *Differences* dialog box,
> Click the box next to *Series*, type **C1**
> Click the box next to *Store Differences in*, type **C3**
> Click *ok*
Choose *Window* ▸ *Data*
In the *Data* window,
> In the box immediately under *C3*, type **D_SP**
> Click any empty cell

Choose *Stat* ▸ *Basic Statistics* ▸ *Descriptive Statistics*
In the *Descriptive Statistics* dialog box,
> Click the box under *Variables*, type **C1-C3**
> Click *ok*
Choose *Window* ▸ *Session*
In the *Session* window,
> Type **PRINT C1-C3**

Figure 11.11

DURBIN-WATSON STATISTIC

Choose *Stat* ▸ *Regression* ▸ *Regression*
In the *Regression* dialog box,
> Next to *Response*, type **C1**
> Next to *Predictors*, type **C2**
> Click *Options*
> In the *Regression Options* dialog box,
>> Click the box next to *Durbin-Watson statistic*
>> Click *ok*
> Click *ok*

Figure 11.18

Choose *File* ▸ *Other Files* ▸ *Import ASCII Data*

In the *Import ASCII Data* dialog box,

    Under *Store data in column*, type **C1**

    Click *ok*

    In the *Import Text From File* dialog box,

        Choose and click data file *mortgage.dat*, click *ok*

Choose *Window* ▸ *Data*

In the *Data* window,

    In the box immediately under *C1*, type **SALES**

    Click any empty cell

Choose *Stat* ▸ *Time Series* ▸ *Lag*

In the *Lag* dialog box,

    Click the box next to *Series*, type **C1**

    Click the box next to *Store lags in*, type **C2**

    Click *ok*

Choose *Stat* ▸ *Time Series* ▸ *Lag*

In the *Lag* dialog box,

    Click the box next to *Series*, type **C1**

    Click the box next to *Store lags in*, type **C3**

    Click the box next to *Lag*, type **12**

    Click *ok*

Choose *Window* ▸ *Data*

In the *Data* window,

    In the boxes immediately under *C2 C3*, type **SALES-1 SALES-12**

    Click any empty cell

Choose *Stat* ▸ *Regression* ▸ *Regression*

In the *Regression* dialog box,

    Next to *Response*, type **C1**

    Next to *Predictors*, type **C2 C3**

    Under *Storage*, click the box next to *Residuals*

    Under *Storage*, click the box next to *Fits*

    Click *ok*

        (Residuals are stored under the name RESI1 and fitted values under the name FITS1)

OVERLAYING TIME SERIES

Choose *Graph* ▸ *Time Series Plot*

In the *Time Series Plot* dialog box,

    Under *Graph variables*, type **C1** in the first box under *Y*

    Under *Graph variables*, type **FITS1** in the second box under *Y*

    Under *Graph variables*, type **RESI1** in the third box under *Y*

    Click the box next to *Frame*, click *Multiple Graphs*

In the *Multiple Graphs* dialog box,
  Click *Overlay graphs on the same page*
  Click *ok*
Under *Time scale,* click the circle next to *Calendar*
Under *Time scale,* click the down arrow in the box next to *Calendar,* click *Month Year*
Click the *Options* box
In the *Time Series Plot Options* dialog box,
  Under *Start time,* type **8** in the box under *Month* and type **84** in the box under *Year*
  Under *Display,* click the first box so that the cross disappears, click *ok*
Click *ok*

11.13

PROBLEM FOR CLASS DISCUSSION

11.1   Analysis of Tourist Visits to Israel

The time series to be analyzed consists of 60 monthly values of the number of tourist arrivals by air in Israel for 1972 to 1976. Almost all these tourists arrived at Tel Aviv's airport. Can the time series be used to forecast the number of tourist arrivals in January 1977? Is there a bound to the forecast error? (Note: In the output from the Minitab Session window, in Figure 11.20, *y* is the number of tourist arrivals.)

FIGURE 11.20

```
MTB > Read 'C:\MTBWIN\DAT\TOURISTS.DAT' C1
    252 rows read


MTB > Delete 1:192 C1
MTB > NAME C1 'Y'
MTB > PRINT C1

Y

    29482    39182    72632    59304    58557    54678    83326    55635
    47129    58466    30179    38543    27648    35019    48774    72864
    54622    53095    84695    58486    51665    16991    20599    37058
    24304    34303    52551    59562    41172    41899    67668    52789
    37486    47071    29685    37633    21844    27238    49300    39941
    36983    40420    65322    51421    41860    50924    31195    51948
    28079    37503    62344    78792    55087    51165    80145    64743
    50699    61261    44111    57668

MTB > Describe C1

                N       MEAN     MEDIAN     TRMEAN      STDEV     SEMEAN
    Y          60      48246      50000      47910      15944       2058

              MIN        MAX         Q1         Q3
    Y        16991      84695      37165      58481
```

```
MTB > TSPlot C1
```

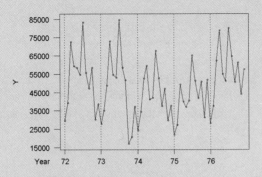

```
MTB > ACF C1

ACF OF Y

        -1.0 -0.8 -0.6 -0.4 -0.2  0.0  0.2  0.4  0.6  0.8  1.0
         +----+----+----+----+----+----+----+----+----+----+
    1   0.392                          XXXXXXXXXXX
    2   0.154                          XXXXX
    3   0.156                          XXXXX
    4   0.007                          X
    5  -0.212                     XXXXXX
    6  -0.438              XXXXXXXXXXXXX
    7  -0.200                     XXXXXX
    8  -0.090                       XXX
    9   0.077                          XXX
   10   0.053                          XX
   11   0.201                          XXXXXX
   12   0.506                          XXXXXXXXXXXXXX
   13   0.217                          XXXXXX
   14   0.023                          XX
   15  -0.032                         XX
   16  -0.082                       XXX
   17  -0.230                    XXXXXXX

MTB > Lag 1 C1 C4
MTB > Lag 12 C1 C9
MTB > Regress C1 2 C4 C9 C10 C11;
SUBC> Predict 57668 28079;
SUBC> DW.

The regression equation is

Y = 7835 + 0.270 LAG 1 + 0.578 LAG 12

48 cases used 12 cases contain missing values

Predictor      Coef          Stdev        t-ratio          p
Constant       7835          6572          1.19        0.239
LAG 1          0.2699        0.1117        2.42        0.020
LAG 12         0.5778        0.1130        5.11        0.000

s = 11708      R-sq = 47.9%     R-sq(adj) = 45.6%
...
```

```
Unusual Observations

Obs.    LAG 1          Y        Fit Stdev.Fit    Residual    St.Resid
 22     51665       16991      55565      2154      -38574      -3.35R
 52     62344       78792      47743      2652       31049       2.72R

R denotes an obs. with a large st. resid.

Durbin-Watson statistic = 1.76

     Fit   Stdev.Fit        95% C.I.          95% P.I.
   39627       3143    ( 33295,  45958)   ( 15205,   64048)
MTB > Plot C10*C11
```

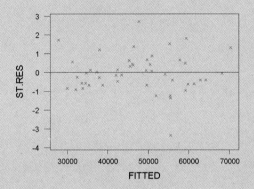

```
MTB > TSPlot C10
```

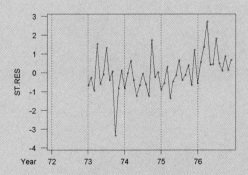

```
MTB > Copy C10 C13;
SUBC>   Use 13:60.
MTB > Runs C13

    C13

    K =  0.0011
    The observed no. of runs =   24
    The expected no. of runs =   24.8333
    22 Observations above K   26 below
           The test is significant at   0.8066
           Cannot reject at alpha =  0.05
```

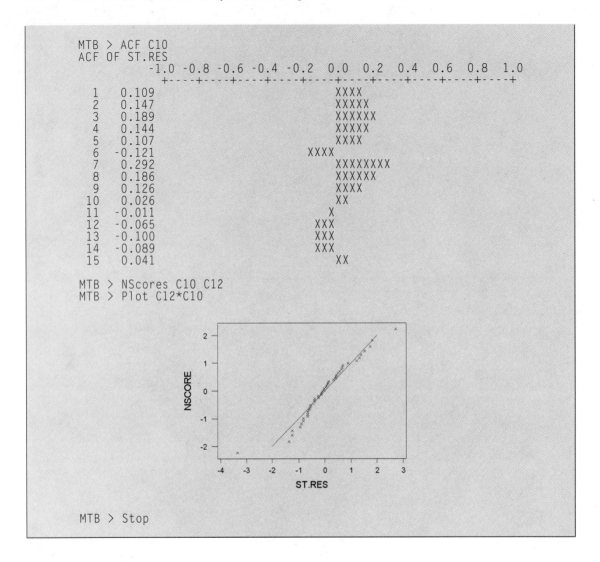

```
MTB > ACF C10
ACF OF ST.RES
                  -1.0 -0.8 -0.6 -0.4 -0.2  0.0  0.2  0.4  0.6  0.8  1.0
                   +----+----+----+----+----+----+----+----+----+----+
     1    0.109                              XXXX
     2    0.147                              XXXXX
     3    0.189                              XXXXXX
     4    0.144                              XXXXX
     5    0.107                              XXXX
     6   -0.121                          XXXX
     7    0.292                              XXXXXXXX
     8    0.186                              XXXXXX
     9    0.126                              XXXX
    10    0.026                              XX
    11   -0.011                             X
    12   -0.065                           XXX
    13   -0.100                           XXX
    14   -0.089                           XXX
    15    0.041                             XX

MTB > NScores C10 C12
MTB > Plot C12*C10
```

MTB > Stop

11.14

EXERCISES

Although answers are given in Appendix C, do not turn to them right away if you cannot find an answer on your own. Return to the exercise the next day and try again before turning to Appendix C.

11.2 This problem continues Exercise 6.6. It relates to the number of telex terminals in the CNCP Telex Network. The data are quarterly from the first quarter in 1971 to the fourth quarter in 1981 (there are 44 quarters). This analysis focuses on how the number of terminals develops over time and on prediction of that number for the first quarter in 1982. The data for NUM-

BER, the number of telex terminals connected at the end of a quarter, are given in Exercise 6.6; they are stored in ASCII file TELEX.DAT.

a Do the NUMBER data come from a random walk? Are the lag 1 differences normal?

b Let R_NUMBER be the square roots of values of NUMBER. Do the R_NUMBER data come from a random walk? Are the lag 1 differences normal?

c Using a random walk model for NUMBER, get a point prediction and a 95% prediction interval for the number of connected telex terminals in the first quarter 1982. In light of your answer to (a), how reliable are this prediction and this 95% interval?

d Using the random walk model for R_NUMBER, get a point prediction and a 95% prediction interval for the number of connected telex terminals in the first quarter 1982. In light of your answer to (b), how reliable are this prediction and this 95% interval?

e Which of the two random walk specifications do you prefer, (a) or (b)? Is your best choice satisfactory?

f Obtain a good autoregression model for NUMBER. Do the diagnostic checks. Using this model, get a point prediction and a 95% prediction interval for the number of connected telex terminals in the first quarter 1982. In light of the diagnostic checks, how reliable are this prediction and this interval?

g Contrast the prediction models for NUMBER in (a) and (f). Which one would you prefer for prediction?

11.3 Consider data on the VALUE of industrial building permits (in $1,000) in the Metropolitan Toronto Area. The data to be analyzed are the 44 quarters from 1 July 1977 to 30 June 1988. They are stored in the first 44 rows of column 5 in ASCII file INVEST.DAT. (Note: This file has 48 rows.) A 1-quarter-ahead forecasting model is to be found.

a Based on the time series plot and the autocorrelogram of VALUE, describe its important time series features.

b Obtain regression model 1, where VALUE is related to its first lag. Do the diagnostic checks, and briefly evaluate the model.

c Obtain regression model 2, where VALUE is related to its first and fourth lags. Do the diagnostic checks, and briefly evaluate the model.

d What statistical justification is there to prefer model 2 to model 1?

e Using regression model 2, find a 98% confidence interval for the coefficient of the first lag of VALUE. Interpret this interval.

f Why are the sample coefficients of the first lag of VALUE *not* exactly the same in the two regression models?

g Using regression model 2, find a point prediction and a 90% prediction interval for the value of industrial building permits in the third quarter of 1988.

h Does your evaluation of the diagnostic checks call into question the reliability of your estimates in (e) and (g)? Why or why not?

11.4 Consider data for the real gross national product (in billions of dollars), GNP, and for the unemployment rate, UNEMPL, in the United States for the years from 1890 to 1974, which are stored in columns 2 and 3 of ASCII file US_ANN.DAT. Relevant Minitab output from the Minitab Session window is given in Figure 11.21 at the end of this exercise.

a Consider the regression model with D_GNP as the response variable and D_UNEMP as the predictor variable. Here D_GNP and D_UNEMP are the lag 1 differences for the GNP and UNEMPL variables, respectively. Assuming this regression model is appropriate, what does the model say about the relationship between D_UNEMP and D_GNP? Describe the relationship in the *context* of this study, and comment on the strength of the relationship.

b Carry out the four diagnostic checks for this model.

For parts (c) to (f), assume that all four diagnostic checks are satisfactory.

c   Calculate the 97% confidence interval for the coefficient of D_UNEMP. Give an interpretation of this interval in the context of this study.

d   Does the constant coefficient in this model have a meaningful interpretation? If yes, what is it? If no, explain why not.

e   The U.S. unemployment rate for 1975 was 8.5%. Using this information, calculate a 95% prediction interval for the value of GNP in 1975.

f   If our main interest were predicting GNP, would this regression model be useful? Justify your answer.

g   Given your answers in (b), how confident are you in your numerical answers in (c) and (e)?

FIGURE 11.21

```
MTB > Read 'C:\MTBWIN\DATA\US_ANN.DAT' C1-C3
     101 rows read

MTB > NAME C1 'YEAR' C2 'UNEMP' C3 'GNP'
MTB > Delete 86:101 C1-C3  Note: These data are missing.
MTB > PRINT C1-C3
```

ROW	YEAR	UNEMP	GNP	ROW	YEAR	UNEMP	GNP
1	1890	4.0	52.7	44	1933	24.9	141.5
2	1891	5.4	55.1	45	1934	21.7	154.3
3	1892	3.0	60.0	46	1935	20.1	169.5
4	1893	11.7	57.5	47	1936	16.9	193.0
5	1894	18.4	55.9	48	1937	14.3	203.2
6	1895	13.7	62.6	49	1938	19.0	192.9
7	1896	14.4	61.3	50	1939	17.2	203.4
8	1897	14.5	67.1	51	1940	14.6	227.2
9	1898	12.4	68.6	52	1941	9.9	263.7
10	1899	6.5	74.8	53	1942	4.7	297.8
11	1900	5.0	76.9	54	1943	1.9	337.1
12	1901	4.0	85.7	55	1944	1.2	361.3
13	1902	3.7	86.5	56	1945	1.9	355.2
14	1903	3.9	90.8	57	1946	3.9	312.6
15	1904	5.4	89.7	58	1947	3.9	309.9
16	1905	4.3	96.3	59	1948	3.8	323.7
17	1906	1.7	107.5	60	1949	5.9	324.1
18	1907	2.8	109.2	61	1950	5.3	355.3
19	1908	8.0	100.2	62	1951	3.3	383.4
20	1909	5.1	116.8	63	1952	3.0	395.1
21	1910	5.9	120.1	64	1953	2.9	412.8
22	1911	6.7	123.2	65	1954	5.5	407.0
23	1912	4.6	130.2	66	1955	4.4	438.0
24	1913	4.3	131.4	67	1956	4.1	446.1
25	1914	7.9	125.6	68	1957	4.3	452.5
26	1915	8.5	124.5	69	1958	6.8	447.3

```
ROW   YEAR   UNEMP     GNP      ROW   YEAR   UNEMP     GNP

 27   1916    5.1    134.3       70   1959    5.5    475.9
 28   1917    4.6    135.2       71   1960    5.5    487.7
 29   1918    1.4    151.8       72   1961    6.7    497.2
 30   1919    1.4    146.4       73   1962    5.5    529.8
 31   1920    5.2    140.0       74   1963    5.7    551.0
 32   1921   11.7    127.8       75   1964    5.2    581.1
 33   1922    6.7    148.0       76   1965    4.5    617.8
 34   1923    2.4    165.9       77   1966    3.8    658.1
 35   1924    5.0    165.5       78   1967    3.8    675.2
 36   1925    3.2    179.4       79   1968    3.6    706.6
 37   1926    1.8    190.0       80   1969    3.5    725.6
 38   1927    3.3    189.8       81   1970    4.9    722.5
 39   1928    4.2    190.9       82   1971    5.9    746.3
 40   1929    3.2    203.6       83   1972    5.6    792.5
 41   1930    8.7    183.5       84   1973    4.9    839.2
 42   1931   15.9    169.3       85   1974    5.6    821.1
 43   1932   23.6    144.2

MTB > Difference 1 C2 C4
MTB > Difference 1 C3 C5
MTB > NAME C4 'D_UNEMP' C5 'D_GNP'
MTB > Describe C2-C5

                  N      N*     MEAN    MEDIAN   TRMEAN    STDEV   SEMEAN
UNEMP            85       0    7.045     5.100    6.530    5.433    0.589
GNP              85       0    278.0     189.8    262.5    215.6     23.4
D_UNEMP          84       1    0.019    -0.250   -0.104    2.899    0.316
D_GNP            84       1     9.15      6.85     9.23    16.30     1.78

                MIN       MAX       Q1        Q3
UNEMP         1.200    24.900    3.800     7.950
GNP            52.7     839.2    121.6     409.9
D_UNEMP      -5.900     8.700   -1.750     1.175
D_GNP        -42.60     46.70    -1.10     18.72

MTB > Regress C5 1 C4 C10 C11;
SUBC>    DW.

The regression equation is
D_GNP = 9.21 - 3.32 D_UNEMP

84 cases used 1 cases contain missing values

Predictor       Coef       Stdev     t-ratio         p
Constant       9.211       1.444        6.38     0.000
D_UNEMP      -3.3179      0.5010       -6.62     0.000

s = 13.23        R-sq = 34.8%      R-sq(adj) = 34.1%

Analysis of Variance

SOURCE        DF          SS         MS        F        p
Regression     1      7681.1     7681.1    43.85    0.000
Error         82     14362.3      175.2
Total         83     22043.4
```

```
Unusual Observations

Obs.  D_UNEMP    D_GNP       Fit  Stdev.Fit    Residual    St.Resid
  4      8.70    -2.50    -19.65       4.58       17.15     1.38 X
  5      6.70    -1.60    -13.02       3.65       11.42     0.90 X
 32      6.50   -12.20    -12.36       3.55        0.16     0.01 X
 42      7.20   -14.20    -14.68       3.88        0.48     0.04 X
 43      7.70   -25.10    -16.34       4.11       -8.76    -0.70 X
 57      2.00   -42.60      2.58       1.75      -45.18    -3.44R
 77     -0.70    40.30     11.53       1.49       28.77     2.19R
 83     -0.30    46.20     10.21       1.45       35.99     2.74R
 84     -0.70    46.70     11.53       1.49       35.17     2.67R

R denotes an obs. with a large st. resid.
X denotes an obs. whose X value gives it large influence.

Durbin-Watson statistic = 1.09

MTB > NAME C10 'ST.RES' C11 'FITTED' C12 'NSCORE'
MTB > Plot C10*C11
```

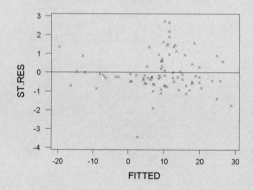

```
MTB > TSPlot C10
```

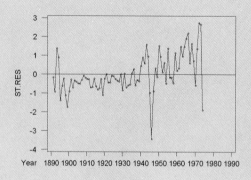

```
MTB > Copy C10 C13;
SUBC>   Omit 1.
MTB > Runs C13

     C13

     K = -0.0004
     The observed no. of runs = 23
     The expected no. of runs = 40.6190
     32 Observations above K  52 below
               The test is significant at 0.0000

MTB > ACF C10

ACF of ST.RES
               -1.0 -0.8 -0.6 -0.4 -0.2  0.0  0.2  0.4  0.6  0.8  1.0
               +----+----+----+----+----+----+----+----+----+----+
   1   0.434                            XXXXXXXXXXXX
   2   0.166                            XXXX
   3   0.182                            XXXXX
   4   0.204                            XXXXXX
   5   0.109                            XXXX
   6   0.148                            XXXX
   7   0.316                            XXXXXXXXX
   8   0.185                            XXXXXX
   9   0.161                            XXXXX
  10   0.136                            XXXX
  11   0.155                            XXXXX
  12   0.149                            XXXXX
  13   0.137                            XXXX
  14   0.148                            XXXXX
  15   0.075                            XXX
  16   0.097                            XXX
  17   0.077                            XXX
  18   0.078                            XXX
  19  -0.032                           XX

MTB > NScores C10 C12
MTB > Plot C12*C10
```

```
MTB > Stop
```

11.15

SUPPLEMENTARY EXERCISES

11.5 Consider a process that generates observations randomly. Why is it useless to use autoregression for predicting future observations from this process? Would predictions based on a random walk model for the process be useful?

11.6 In ASCII file US_RTRN.DAT, weekly rates of return are given for five stocks: Imperial Oil, Monsanto, Exxon, Union Carbide, and Du Pont. The data are for 1990 and 1991. They were obtained from the Center for Research in Security Prices database.

a Is it reasonable to conclude that the data for each stock are generated by a random process? Do the diagnostic checks.

b What are the implications of your conclusions in (a) for forecasting weekly returns?

Present your results and conclusions in a summary report and attach your briefly annotated output.

11.7 Consider Example 11.1 regarding the prediction model for next month's (August 1989) mortgage sales at a financial institution. To make this prediction, monthly data were gathered on three variables in addition to sales for the 60-month period from August 1984 to July 1989. Thus data were collected on four variables: (1) mortgage sales (SALES) in $1,000, (2) the TSE 300 index (TSE), (3) residential housing starts (STARTS) in 1,000 units, and (4) the 5-year mortgage rate (RATE). Mortgage sales were the dollar sales of mortgage money by FI Ltd. The value of the TSE 300 index was obtained at the end of each month. Residential housing starts were defined to be the number of single detached dwellings started in a month in urban centers, as calculated by the Central Mortgage and Housing Corporation of Canada through a survey of building permits issued by local municipalities and by observational confirmation. The 5-year mortgage rate was an average of the rates charged on the last Wednesday of each month by the big six banks (Royal Bank, Bank of Nova Scotia, CIBC, Bank of Montreal, TD Bank, and National Bank of Canada). The data are given in file MORTGAGE.DAT.

a Can you find a reliable prediction model for next month's mortgage sales, using no more than five predictor variables and preferably fewer? Report results on your preferred model only. Discuss the diagnostic checks for this model.

b If any of the three additional variables were not used in your preferred model in (a), can you give a rationalization for this? Use a contextual argument here.

c Using your preferred model in (a), obtain a point prediction and a 90% prediction interval for mortgage sales in August 1989. In light of the diagnostic checks, how reliable are these predictions?

11.8 This problem is a continuation of Exercise 3.22 (Abitibi-Price); see also Exercises 5.20 and 9.6 (p. 437). Consider the time series of weight/volume ratios for the spruce data, given as column 3 in ASCII file ABITIBI.DAT. Find a good time series model for the data. What concerns do you have about your model?

Before doing the analysis, think of two or three reasonable models based on the nature of the data and the sequence plot. Then analyze these models and present results for your *preferred* model only. Don't go on a "fishing expedition" trying out many different models. (Given the tools we have learned so far, you will probably not find a perfect model, but you should be able to find a pretty good one.)

11.9 Data on residential housing starts in Southern Ontario are stored in column 3 of ASCII file MORTGAGE.DAT (which contains four variables in total). Monthly values are given for the 60-month period from August 1984 to July 1989, and housing starts are given in thousands of units.

a You are to obtain a regression model linking housing starts to its first two lags. Do the diagnostic checks.

b Assuming there is no problem with the diagnostic checks, obtain a point prediction and a 98% prediction interval for housing starts in August 1989.

c In light of your diagnostic checks in (a), are your results in (b) reliable? Briefly discuss this.

d If the diagnostic checks in (a) suggested that the model can be improved, obtain a better model, which should contain no more than three predictor variables. Do the diagnostic checks, and obtain the predictions required in (b). How reliable are these predictions in light of the diagnostic checks?

12

FURTHER TOOLS FOR TIME SERIES ANALYSIS

This chapter will help you solve the following kinds of problems:

- As part of a larger forecasting system involving monthly shipments, unfilled orders, inventory, and new orders from Canadian manufacturers of plastic products, a manager wants to obtain a forecasting model for inventory.

- Quarterly sales data are available for Marshall Field & Company. What is a prediction of sales for the next quarter?

12.1

INTRODUCTION

In the last chapter, you learned how some time series can be modeled successfully with autoregression, in which the response variable in a multiple regression model is related to lags of itself. In this chapter, you learn how to analyze a broader range of time series. You learn, in particular,

- How to use *differencing* and what its relationship is to the autocorrelations

- How to use predictor variables that are different from lags in time series multiple regression

Unfortunately, some time series will remain whose satisfactory analysis will elude you, but you should get reasonably good models for many situations.

12.2

USING DIFFERENCING AS A BUILDING BLOCK FOR TIME SERIES

This section will show how differencing can be used to build models for some time series. We already encountered differencing in Chapter 6 and Section 11.6, where we used lag 1 differencing to build a random walk model. That model yielded a forecasting model for the SP time series that was similar to the autoregression model, and was actually preferable because it was simpler to interpret.

When a random-process model is not quite adequate to describe the lag 1 differences of a time series, a random walk model will not work. When this happens, we can sometimes develop a different but still simple time series model. This section shows how we do so for one particular forecasting problem. We will develop a two-step model:

1. We first ask whether a random walk model is appropriate. If it is not appropriate because the lag 1 differences are not quite random, we proceed with step 2.

2. We next try to build an autoregression model using the lag 1 differences analyzed in step 1 as the response variable.

Lag 1 differencing is indicated whenever there is a high first-order autocorrelation and the following autocorrelations slowly decrease in magnitude. Consider the autocorrelogram of the SP data in Figure 12.1. The first-order autocorrelation is close to 1 (0.937), and the autocorrelations of higher order decrease slowly in mag-

FIGURE 12.1 SP Data: Autocorrelogram

```
ACF of SP

               -1.0 -0.8 -0.6 -0.4 -0.2  0.0  0.2  0.4  0.6  0.8  1.0
                +----+----+----+----+----+----+----+----+----+----+
    1   0.937                            XXXXXXXXXXXXXXXXXXXXXXXXXX
    2   0.875                            XXXXXXXXXXXXXXXXXXXXXXXX
    3   0.793                            XXXXXXXXXXXXXXXXXXXXXX
    4   0.717                            XXXXXXXXXXXXXXXXXXX
    5   0.633                            XXXXXXXXXXXXXXXXX
    6   0.559                            XXXXXXXXXXXXXXX
    7   0.490                            XXXXXXXXXXXXX
    8   0.419                            XXXXXXXXXXX
    9   0.350                            XXXXXXXXXX
   10   0.288                            XXXXXXXX
   11   0.244                            XXXXXXX
   12   0.196                            XXXXXX
   13   0.139                            XXXX
   14   0.093                            XXX
   15   0.064                            XXX
   16   0.042                            XX
   17   0.027                            XX
```

nitude. This suggests lag 1 differencing. The resulting lag 1 differences for the SP data are well modeled by a random process. Thus, the SP data are well modeled by a random walk.

But consider the following example:

EXAMPLE 12.1

A forecasting model was needed for the inventory of Canadian manufacturers of plastic products. Monthly data were available on total month-end inventory (in $millions Canadian) for the period from January 1985 to February 1991. The data are not seasonally adjusted. Their source is Statistics Canada's "Monthly Survey of Manufacturing" (Publication 31-001). The data are stored in ASCII file MANUFACT.DAT. As part of a larger forecasting system involving monthly shipments, unfilled orders, inventory, and new orders, the questions to be addressed here are:

How can inventory be forecast? What is a forecast for March 1991?

As a first step to building a forecasting model, we ask: Does a random walk model fit? The data are listed and graphed in Figure 12.2. Note that y denotes total inventory. There is a meandering tendency to the time series plot, without a stable mean. This suggests a random walk model for the inventory data. The autocorrela-

FIGURE 12.2 Plastic Products Data: Inventory

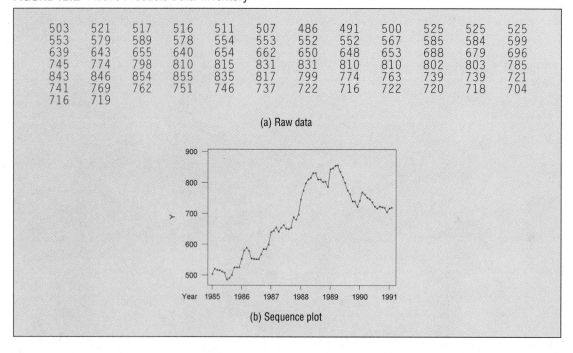

503	521	517	516	511	507	486	491	500	525	525	525
553	579	589	578	554	553	552	552	567	585	584	599
639	643	655	640	654	662	650	648	653	688	679	696
745	774	798	810	815	831	831	810	810	802	803	785
843	846	854	855	835	817	799	774	763	739	739	721
741	769	762	751	746	737	722	716	722	720	718	704
716	719										

(a) Raw data

(b) Sequence plot

FIGURE 12.3 Plastic Products Data: Autocorrelogram for Inventory

```
    ACF of Y

                 -1.0 -0.8 -0.6 -0.4 -0.2  0.0  0.2  0.4  0.6  0.8  1.0
                 +----+----+----+----+----+----+----+----+----+----+
      1   0.970                                XXXXXXXXXXXXXXXXXXXXXXXXX
      2   0.938                                XXXXXXXXXXXXXXXXXXXXXXXX
      3   0.900                                XXXXXXXXXXXXXXXXXXXXXXX
      4   0.859                                XXXXXXXXXXXXXXXXXXXXXX
      5   0.815                                XXXXXXXXXXXXXXXXXXXXX
      6   0.771                                XXXXXXXXXXXXXXXXXXXX
      7   0.728                                XXXXXXXXXXXXXXXXXXX
      8   0.688                                XXXXXXXXXXXXXXXXXX
      9   0.648                                XXXXXXXXXXXXXXXXX
     10   0.612                                XXXXXXXXXXXXXXXX
     11   0.573                                XXXXXXXXXXXXXXX
     12   0.528                                XXXXXXXXXXXXXX
     13   0.476                                XXXXXXXXXXXXX
     14   0.424                                XXXXXXXXXXXX
     15   0.374                                XXXXXXXXXX
     16   0.319                                XXXXXXXXX
     17   0.259                                XXXXXXX
```

differencing

tion function in Figure 12.3 supports this view, since the first-order autocorrelation is close to 1 and the autocorrelations decrease very slowly. A graph of the lag 1 differences, D_Y, and descriptive statistics are given in Figure 12.4. There appears to be a constant level, but there still appears to be some modest time series pattern. For example, the January values tend to be high, and the December values tend to be low. The control limits are UCL = 2.96 + 3(17.19) = 54.53 and LCL = −48.61, and the 49th value, January 1989, exceeds the UCL. The runs test does not support randomness. The autocorrelation function for the lag 1 differences of inventory, given in Figure 12.5, also supports the impression that a random walk

FIGURE 12.4 Plastic Products Data: Lag 1 Differences

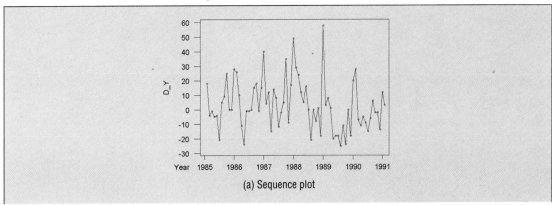

(a) Sequence plot

```
K =        2.9589

The observed no. of runs =   23
The expected no. of runs =   36.9452
32 Observations above K    41 below
          The test is significant at   0.0009
```

(b) Runs test

```
                    N        N*      MEAN     MEDIAN    TRMEAN    STDEV    SEMEAN
Y                  74         0     680.0      710.0     681.0    112.5      13.1
D_Y                73         1      2.96       0.00      1.97    17.19      2.01

                  MIN       MAX        Q1         Q3
Y               486.0     855.0     575.3      774.0
D_Y            -25.00     58.00     -9.00.     13.00
```

(c) Descriptive statistics

model does not capture all time-series information. Note, however, that the standard deviation of the lag 1 differences, 17.2, is considerably lower than the standard deviation of y, 112.5.

Since the random walk model is not quite adequate, we now turn to step 2

autoregression
of our modeling approach: Can we build an **autoregression** model for the lag 1 differences, D_Y? The autocorrelogram in Figure 12.5 suggests that the twelfth lag, D_Y_{-12}, should be used in an autoregression. The resulting Minitab output

FIGURE 12.5 Plastic Products Data: Autocorrelations for Lag 1 Differences

```
    ACF of D_Y

                 -1.0 -0.8 -0.6 -0.4 -0.2  0.0  0.2  0.4  0.6  0.8  1.0
                 +----+----+----+----+----+----+----+----+----+----+
      1    0.263                           XXXXXXX
      2    0.169                           XXXXX
      3    0.087                           XXX
      4    0.061                           XXX
      5   -0.078                        XXX
      6   -0.236                  XXXXXXX
      7   -0.128                     XXXX
      8   -0.020                        X
      9    0.006                        X
     10    0.106                           XXXX
     11    0.177                           XXXXX
     12    0.498                           XXXXXXXXXXXXX
     13    0.250                           XXXXXXX
     14   -0.023                       XX
     15    0.074                           XXX
     16   -0.015                        X
     17   -0.168                     XXXX
     18   -0.295                 XXXXXXX
```

FIGURE 12.6 Plastic Products Data: Autoregression for Lag 1 Differences

```
The regression equation is
D_Y = - 0.03 + 0.181 D_Y-1 + 0.501 D_Y-12

61 cases used 13 cases contain missing values

Predictor        Coef        Stdev     t-ratio          p
Constant       -0.033       1.974       -0.02      0.987
D_Y-1          0.1814      0.1077        1.68      0.097
D_Y-12         0.5014      0.1075        4.66      0.000

s = 14.86        R-sq = 33.0%      R-sq(adj) = 30.7%

Unusual Observations
Obs.    D_Y-1        D_Y        Fit Stdev.Fit   Residual   St.Resid
29      -15.0      14.00     -14.79      3.80      28.79      2.00R
49      -18.0      58.00      21.27      6.00      36.73      2.70RX
50       58.0       3.00      25.03      6.29     -22.03     -1.64 X
61      -18.0      20.00      25.78      6.86      -5.78     -0.44 X

R denotes an obs. with a large st. resid.
X denotes an obs. whose X value gives it large influence.
```

(not shown) uncovered problems with several diagnostic checks, and these pointed to adding the first lag, D_Y_{-1}, to the autoregression. (Note that the first-order autocorrelation was also somewhat high on Figure 12.5.) The resulting autoregression model is given in Figure 12.6.

How does this autoregression model stand up to our diagnostic checks? The residual vs. fitted plot in Figure 12.7 does not point to any problem with the linearity check. There is a slight tendency for the variability in the standardized residuals to increase with higher fitted values, but it is not serious. The descriptive statistics at the bottom of Figure 12.7 support these visual impressions. Figure 12.8 presents information about the randomness check for the residuals. The visual impression supports randomness: all standardized residuals are within the control limits; the runs test supports randomness; the autocorrelations are small and their signs are well mixed. Finally, the normal probability plot of the standardized residuals in Figure 12.9 supports normality. Thus all assumptions underlying the regression model are met, so the autoregression model estimated in Figure 12.6 is adequate.

How good is this autoregression model? The standard deviation for total inventory y is 112.5, and the standard deviation for lag 1 differences is 17.19. The standard deviation of residuals in Figure 12.6 is 14.86. Thus the autoregression model does not account for much of the variation in the lag 1 differences. This is also supported by the adjusted R^2, 30.7%.

Are predictor variables lag 1 and lag 12 both statistically significant? The t-ratio for the 12th lag is quite high, and a one-sided confidence interval for the process coefficient of the 12th lag, covering only positive values, has almost 100% confidence, since the value 0 standardizes to $z = (0 - 0.5014)/0.1075 = -4.66$. A one-sided confidence interval for the process coefficient of the first lag, covering

FIGURE 12.7 Plastic Products Data: Diagnostic Checks 1 and 2

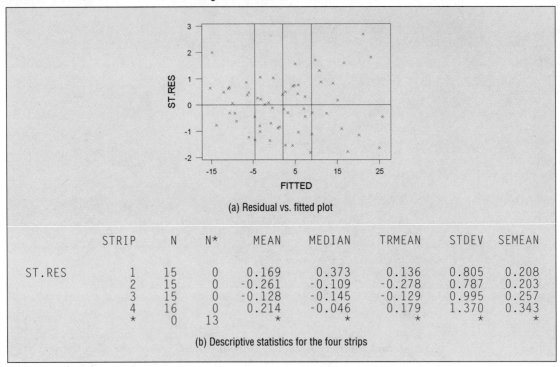

(a) Residual vs. fitted plot

	STRIP	N	N*	MEAN	MEDIAN	TRMEAN	STDEV	SEMEAN
ST.RES	1	15	0	0.169	0.373	0.136	0.805	0.208
	2	15	0	-0.261	-0.109	-0.278	0.787	0.203
	3	15	0	-0.128	-0.145	-0.129	0.995	0.257
	4	16	0	0.214	-0.046	0.179	1.370	0.343
	*	0	13	*	*	*	*	*

(b) Descriptive statistics for the four strips

FIGURE 12.8 Plastic Products Data: Randomness Check for Residuals

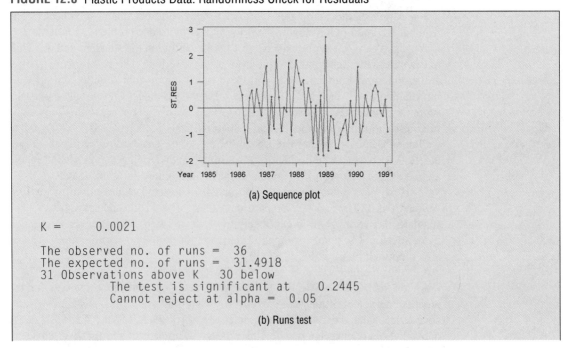

(a) Sequence plot

```
K  =      0.0021

The observed no. of runs  =   36
The expected no. of runs  =   31.4918
31 Observations above K    30 below
          The test is significant at     0.2445
          Cannot reject at alpha  =   0.05
```

(b) Runs test

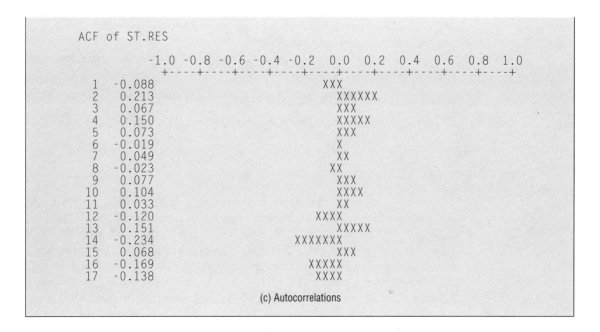

```
        ACF of ST.RES

                     -1.0 -0.8 -0.6 -0.4 -0.2  0.0  0.2  0.4  0.6  0.8  1.0
                     +----+----+----+----+----+----+----+----+----+----+
         1   -0.088                             XXX
         2    0.213                             XXXXXX
         3    0.067                             XXX
         4    0.150                             XXXXX
         5    0.073                             XXX
         6   -0.019                             X
         7    0.049                             XX
         8   -0.023                            XX
         9    0.077                             XXX
        10    0.104                             XXXX
        11    0.033                             XX
        12   -0.120                         XXXX
        13    0.151                             XXXXX
        14   -0.234                      XXXXXXX
        15    0.068                             XXX
        16   -0.169                        XXXXX
        17   -0.138                         XXXX
```

(c) Autocorrelations

FIGURE 12.9
Plastic Products
Data: Normal
Probability Plot
for Residuals

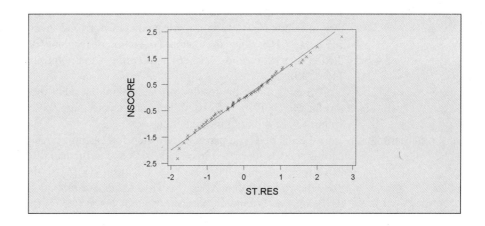

only positive values, has 95.2% confidence, since the value 0 standardizes to $z = (0 - 0.1814)/0.1077 = -1.68$. Therefore both lags, in particular, the 12th, are statistically significant: It is unlikely that the difference between each sample coefficient and 0 is due to chance alone.

      The discussion in the last two paragraphs reminds us of a useful distinction: **statistical vs. practical significance** The statistical significance of one or more predictor variables does not necessarily imply that the relationship between the response variable and the predictor variables is strong. Statistical significance answers the question: Given the data, can the difference between the sample regression coefficient of a predictor variable and 0 be attributed to chance alone? Strength of a relationship (*practical* significance) answers a different question: Is much of the variation in the response variable y accounted for by the predictor variables?

Let us now use the model to predict future inventory. As described above, the forecasting model resulted from two steps:

1. At first, we obtained the lag 1 differences for inventory, D_Y.

2. We then estimated the autoregression model for the lag 1 differences

$$\text{Fitted D\_Y} = -0.03 + (0.181)\text{D\_Y}_{-1} + (0.501)\text{D\_Y}_{-12}$$

with $s = 14.86$.

In order to obtain a prediction for inventory, y, in March 1991, we must carry out these two steps in reverse. We must first obtain a point prediction of the lag 1 difference, D_Y, in March 1991. To do this, we need the lag 1 differences 1 period earlier (in February 1991) and 12 periods earlier (in March 1990). Using the data in Figure 12.2, the lag 1 difference in February 1991 is $719 - 716 = 3$, and the lag 1 difference in March 1990 is $762 - 769 = -7$. Using these two lag 1 differences in the autoregression, the point prediction of the lag 1 difference in March 1991 is

$$-0.03 + 0.181(3) + 0.501(-7) = -3$$

That is, total inventory in March 1991 is estimated to be 3 lower than total inventory in February 1991, so a point prediction for total inventory in March 1991 is $719 - 3 = 716$. Since the standard deviation of residuals is $s = 14.86$, a 95% prediction interval extends $2(14.86) = 30$ around the point prediction (the interval is 716 ± 30).

Summarizing the results for the example, a point prediction for total inventory in March 1991 is \$716 million, and chances are 95% that the exact value is within \$30 million of this prediction.

model comparison   Let us now compare this two-step forecasting model with the "naive" forecasting models discussed in Section 11.5 and at the end of Section 11.9. The three naive forecasting models were "Use the mean" ($\bar{y}$), "Use the last value" (y_{-1}), and "Use the value 12 months ago" (y_{-12}). Again, we first compute the mean absolute deviation (MAD) and the mean squared deviaton (MSD) for each model. For each naive model, we then compute the ratio of MAD to MAD for the two-step model; likewise for MSD. The resulting ratios are listed in the following table:

	$\dfrac{\text{MAD}}{\text{MAD}(\hat{y})}$	$\dfrac{\text{MSD}}{\text{MSD}(\hat{y})}$
$\bar{y}$	8.17	59.47
y_{-1}	1.08	1.43
y_{-12}	6.65	38.04

The table clearly shows that the "Use the mean" and "Use the value 12 months ago" naive models are much worse than the two-step forecasting model. The "Use the last value" model, however, compares quite favorably; it may be simpler to use this naive model than the two-step model. Note, however, that the "Use the last value" model is very closely related to the random walk model for total inventory. As we had discussed above, the random walk model was the first step in the two-step model for inventory, and the autoregression model of the second step did not much improve on this first step.

The main point of this section is that differencing and autoregression are tools that can be used in conjunction to build a forecasting model.

12.3

SEASONAL DIFFERENCING

This section introduces *seasonal differencing* with another example, quarterly dollar sales (in U.S. $million) of Marshall Field & Company for the first quarter in 1961 (denoted 1961:1) through the fourth quarter in 1975 (denoted 1975:4).[1] The data and a sequence plot are given in Figure 12.10. They are stored in ASCII file MFIELD.DAT.

---

[1] The data are from G. Foster, *Financial Statement Analysis,* Prentice-Hall, 1978, p. 82. In his Chapter 4, Foster uses the data to illustrate a number of statistical tools that are useful in accounting.

FIGURE 12.10 Marshall Field & Company Example

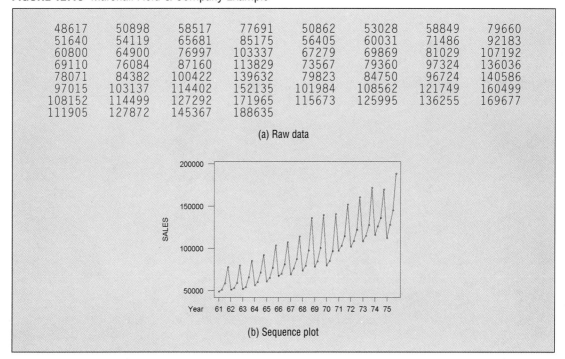

48617	50898	58517	77691	50862	53028	58849	79660
51640	54119	65681	85175	56405	60031	71486	92183
60800	64900	76997	103337	67279	69869	81029	107192
69110	76084	87160	113829	73567	79360	97324	136036
78071	84382	100422	139632	79823	84750	96724	140586
97015	103137	114402	152135	101984	108562	121749	160499
108152	114499	127292	171965	115673	125995	136255	169677
111905	127872	145367	188635				

(a) Raw data

(b) Sequence plot

FIGURE 12.11
Marshall Field
Example: Sequence
Plot of Quarterly
SALES

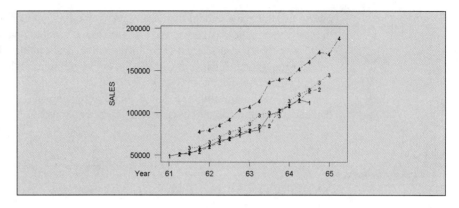

The questions to be addressed are:

What is a prediction of sales in the next period (the first quarter of 1976)? How reliable is this prediction?

There is a strong seasonal pattern. The variability of quarterly sales in each year increases as sales volume increases. In Figure 12.11, successive first quarters, second quarters, etc., are connected, effectively treating successive first quarters, successive second quarters, etc., as sub–time-series. The seasonal nature of the time series becomes quite apparent: Sales in the fourth quarter are much higher than in the other quarters. Figure 12.12 lists the autocorrelations for SALES. It also reveals a strong quarterly pattern, since the fourth-order autocorrelation is very high.

FIGURE 12.12 Marshall Field Example: Autocorrelations of SALES

```
                -1.0 -0.8 -0.6 -0.4 -0.2  0.0  0.2  0.4  0.6  0.8  1.0
                  +----+----+----+----+----+----+----+----+----+----+
    1   0.577                              XXXXXXXXXXXXXXX
    2   0.458                              XXXXXXXXXXXX
    3   0.503                              XXXXXXXXXXXXX
    4   0.842                              XXXXXXXXXXXXXXXXXXXXXXX
    5   0.456                              XXXXXXXXXXXX
    6   0.351                              XXXXXXXXX
    7   0.393                              XXXXXXXXXX
    8   0.696                              XXXXXXXXXXXXXXXXXX
    9   0.323                              XXXXXXXXX
   10   0.220                              XXXXX
   11   0.263                              XXXXXXX
   12   0.542                              XXXXXXXXXXXXXX
   13   0.197                              XXXXX
   14   0.098                              XXX
   15   0.135                              XXXX
   16   0.394                              XXXXXXXXXX
   17   0.078                              XXX
```

FIGURE 12.13 Marshall Field Example: Preliminary Regression Model Including Only the First Lag of SALES

```
The regression equation is
SALES = 34603 + 0.660 SALES-1

59 cases used 1 cases contain missing values

Predictor         Coef        Stdev     t-ratio        p
Constant         34603        10843        3.19    0.002
SALES-1         0.6603       0.1083        6.10    0.000

s = 26672      R-sq = 39.5%      R-sq(adj) = 38.4%
. . .

Unusual Observations
Obs.   SALES-1      SALES       Fit Stdev.Fit   Residual   St.Resid
 52     127292     171965    118650     4938      53315       2.03R
 53     171965     115673    148146     9041     -32473      -1.29 X
 57     169677     111905    146636     8813     -34731      -1.38 X
 60     145367     188635    130584     6477      58051       2.24R

R denotes an obs. with a large st. resid.
X denotes an obs. whose X value gives it large influence.
```

In order to show what happens to the diagnostic checks in an *incorrect* model specification, the first lag of SALES was used to produce the autoregression results in Figure 12.13. This model completely ignores the strong quarterly aspect of the data. The sequence plot of the standardized residuals in Figure 12.14 reveals this: The residuals do not display the upward drift of Figure 12.11 (which is represented in the model by the first lag). They are definitely not random as required by the third regression assumption, since the quarterly pattern is still present in them. This pattern should be represented in the model, suggesting that the fourth lag of SALES should be considered as a predictor variable.

Let us now find a good forecasting model. We will employ the two-step approach introduced in the last section. Here, however, we use lag 4 differencing

FIGURE 12.14
Marshall Field
Example: Sequence
Plot for
Standardized
Residuals from
Preliminary Model

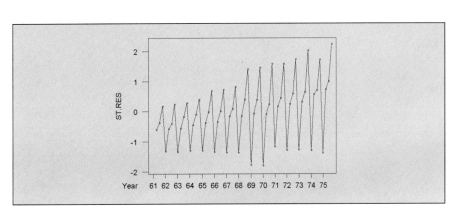

since the fourth-order autocorrelation is high and the eighth-, 12th-, 16th-, etc., order autocorrelations are decreasing slowly. Differencing at the seasonal lag is to capture the quarterly effect on sales. Here the two-step approach is:

1. Examine the lag 4 differences of SALES. Are they random? If yes, use SALES 4 quarters ago for prediction. If no, proceed with step 2.

2. Build an autoregression model for the lag 4 differences of SALES.

seasonal differencing

Whenever the autocorrelation at a *seasonal* lag is close to 1 and the autocorrelations at the *multiples* of this seasonal lag decrease slowly, **seasonal differencing** is indicated. For quarterly data, the seasonal lag is the fourth, and its multiples are the eighth, 12th, 16th, etc. For monthly data, the seasonal lag is the 12th, and its multiples are the 24th, the 36th, etc.

Let us proceed with the first step for building a forecasting model: Are the lag 4 differences random? Figure 12.15 gives a sequence plot of the lag 4 differences of sales, D4_S. The sequence plot does not look random: It seems that the variability in D4_S increases over time. Comparing this plot with Figure 12.10(b), we see that variability tends to increase as the magnitude of sales increases. As we had seen earlier (see Sections 4.8 and 6.3), a transformation can often help obtain more satisfactory models where the variability remains roughly constant. Both a square root and a logarithmic transformation of sales were attempted; the latter was more useful. The natural logarithms of SALES are stored in variable LS. A sequence plot of LS is given in Figure 12.16: The increasing variability has disappeared.

In the remainder of this chapter, we discuss models for the *log of SALES, LS,* rather than SALES itself. Once predictions for LS are obtained, they can be converted easily into predictions of sales by taking antilogs, (that is, by exponentiation). We will again use the two-step approach, and this time we will find a satisfactory model.

Consider first the differencing step: Figure 12.17 lists the autocorrelogram for LS. The fourth-order autocorrelation is quite large, and the eighth, 12th, 16th, etc.,

FIGURE 12.15
Marshall Field Example: Sequence Plot of the Fourth Differences of Sales, D4_S

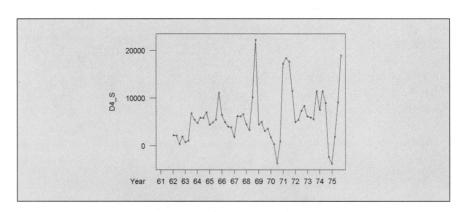

FIGURE 12.16 Marshall Field Example: Examining the Log of SALES, LS

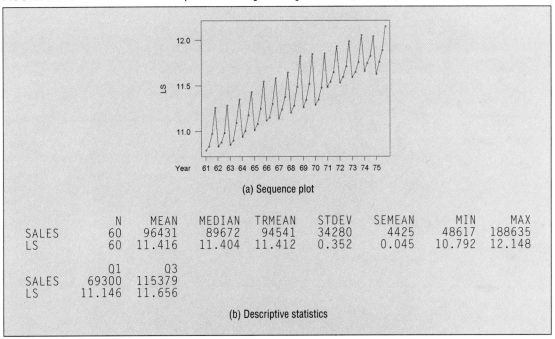

(a) Sequence plot

	N	MEAN	MEDIAN	TRMEAN	STDEV	SEMEAN	MIN	MAX
SALES	60	96431	89672	94541	34280	4425	48617	188635
LS	60	11.416	11.404	11.412	0.352	0.045	10.792	12.148

	Q1	Q3
SALES	69300	115379
LS	11.146	11.656

(b) Descriptive statistics

FIGURE 12.17 Marshall Field Example: Autocorrelogram of LS

```
    ACF of LS

              -1.0 -0.8 -0.6 -0.4 -0.2  0.0  0.2  0.4  0.6  0.8  1.0
               +----+----+----+----+----+----+----+----+----+----+
      1  0.640                           XXXXXXXXXXXXXXXXX
      2  0.507                           XXXXXXXXXXXXX
      3  0.559                           XXXXXXXXXXXXXX
      4  0.849                           XXXXXXXXXXXXXXXXXXXXXXX
      5  0.513                           XXXXXXXXXXXXX
      6  0.389                           XXXXXXXXXX
      7  0.434                           XXXXXXXXXXX
      8  0.694                           XXXXXXXXXXXXXXXXXX
      9  0.368                           XXXXXXXXXX
     10  0.247                           XXXXXX
     11  0.292                           XXXXXXX
     12  0.534                           XXXXXXXXXXXXXX
     13  0.229                           XXXXXX
     14  0.114                           XXXX
     15  0.155                           XXXXX
```

FIGURE 12.18 Marshall Field Example: Examining the Lag 4 Difference of LS

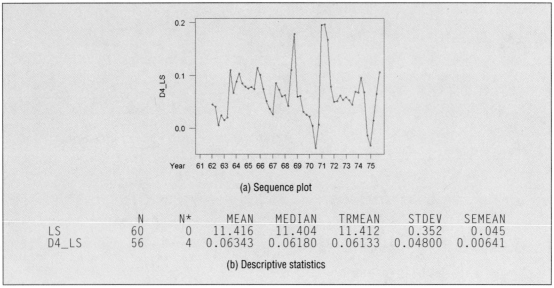

(a) Sequence plot

	N	N*	MEAN	MEDIAN	TRMEAN	STDEV	SEMEAN
LS	60	0	11.416	11.404	11.412	0.352	0.045
D4_LS	56	4	0.06343	0.06180	0.06133	0.04800	0.00641

(b) Descriptive statistics

order autocorrelations are slowly decreasing. Therefore seasonal differencing for LS is in order. The resulting lag 4 differences of LS are stored in variable D4_LS and plotted in Figure 12.18. This plot does not suggest randomness, but the impression of increasing variability from Figure 12.15 has disappeared. The autocorrelogram in Figure 12.19 also suggests that D4_LS was not generated by a random process: The first-order autocorrelation is high, but possibly a few others are as well.

FIGURE 12.19 Marshall Field Example: Autocorrelogram of D4_LS

```
ACF of D4_LS

          -1.0 -0.8 -0.6 -0.4 -0.2  0.0  0.2  0.4  0.6  0.8  1.0
           +----+----+----+----+----+----+----+----+----+----+
  1   0.559                              XXXXXXXXXXXXXXX
  2   0.065                              XXX
  3  -0.227                       XXXXXXX
  4  -0.298                      XXXXXXXX
  5  -0.174                         XXXXX
  6  -0.144                         XXXXX
  7  -0.223                       XXXXXXX
  8  -0.176                         XXXXX
  9   0.061                              XXX
 10   0.178                              XXXXX
 11   0.205                              XXXXXX
 12   0.102                              XXXX
 13  -0.077                           XXX
 14  -0.180                         XXXXXX
 15  -0.179                         XXXXX
```

To capture the time series information in the lag 4 differences, we next find an autoregression model for D4_LS. The first four lags of D4_LS are stored in variables D4_LS$_{-1}$, D4_LS$_{-2}$, D4_LS$_{-3}$, and D4_LS$_{-4}$, respectively. Figure 12.20 lists some of the data. Note, for example, that the value for LS in quarter 60 is 12.1476, and in quarter 56 it is 12.0417. Thus the value of D4_LS in quarter 60 is 12.1476 − 12.0417 = 0.1059. The value of D4_LS in quarter 59 is 0.0647, which is also the value of the first lag of D4_LS (D4_LS$_{-1}$) for quarter 60. Note the missing values for the lags in the first few rows.

Figure 12.21 gives the results for regression model 1, an autoregression of D4_LS on its first four lags. (The n/k ratio is satisfactory if these four predictor variables are used.) The diagnostic checks (not shown) for this model are satisfactory, but note (1) the outlier in quarter 41, the first quarter 1970, and (2) the low t-ratios on two of the predictor variables. It is not clear what caused the outlier, so a search for an assignable cause is in order now. Since we cannot do this, we must keep the outlier and its impact on the regression output in mind. The absolute value of the t-ratio of the third lag of D4_LS is less than 1 and closest to 0. So we drop it from regression model 1, yielding regression model 2 in Figure 12.22(a). The t-ratio for none of the predictor variables is less than 1 in absolute value. Note, however, that the t-ratio for D4_LS$_{-4}$(−1.24) is not far away from 0. To simplify the model, this predictor variable was dropped also. The resulting model is given in Figure 12.22(b). (As we move from model 2 to model 3, the resulting value of s increases very slightly only.)

FIGURE 12.20 Marshall Field Example: Additional Variables

ROW	SALES	LS	D4_LS	D4_LS-1	D4_LS-2	D4_LS-3	D4_LS-4
1	48617	10.7917	*	*	*	*	*
2	50898	10.8376	*	*	*	*	*
3	58517	10.9771	*	*	*	*	*
4	77691	11.2605	*	*	*	*	*
5	50862	10.8369	0.045142	*	*	*	*
6	53028	10.8786	0.040997	0.045142	*	*	*
7	58849	10.9827	0.005657	0.040997	0.045142	*	*
8	79660	11.2855	0.025028	0.005657	0.040997	0.045142	*
9	51640	10.8521	0.015181	0.025028	0.005657	0.040997	0.045142
10	54119	10.8989	0.020366	0.015181	0.025028	0.005657	0.040997
53	115673	11.6585	0.067229	0.069003	0.044522	0.053245	0.058722
54	125995	11.7440	0.095676	0.067229	0.069003	0.044522	0.053245
55	136255	11.8223	0.068045	0.095676	0.067229	0.069003	0.044522
56	169677	12.0417	-0.013394	0.068045	0.095676	0.067229	0.069003
57	111905	11.6254	-0.033117	-0.013394	0.068045	0.095676	0.067229
58	127872	11.7588	0.014788	-0.033117	-0.013394	0.068045	0.095676
59	145367	11.8870	0.064734	0.014788	-0.033117	-0.013394	0.068045
60	188635	12.1476	0.105918	0.064734	0.014788	-0.033117	-0.013394

FIGURE 12.21 Marshall Field Example: Regression Model 1, Autoregression

```
The regression equation is
D4_LS = 0.0512 + 0.704 D4_LS-1 - 0.298 D4_LS-2 - 0.058 D4_LS-3 - 0.121 D4_LS-4

52 cases used 8 cases contain missing values

Predictor       Coef         Stdev       t-ratio        p
Constant      0.05115      0.01287        3.98      0.000
D4_LS-1        0.7036       0.1450        4.85      0.000
D4_LS-2       -0.2981       0.1761       -1.69      0.097
D4_LS-3       -0.0579       0.1764       -0.33      0.744
D4_LS-4       -0.1208       0.1483       -0.81      0.420

s = 0.03839    R-sq = 42.6%      R-sq(adj) = 37.7%
 .
 .
 . .

Unusual Observations
Obs.  D4_LS-1       D4_LS      Fit  Stdev.Fit    Residual    St.Resid
33      0.178     0.05942  0.13369    0.01510    -0.07427      -2.10R
39      0.004    -0.03752  0.04231    0.01017    -0.07983      -2.16R
41      0.007     0.19505  0.06420    0.01319     0.13086       3.63R
42      0.195     0.19635  0.18802    0.02328     0.00833       0.27 X
43      0.196     0.16786  0.13532    0.02354     0.03254       1.07 X
44      0.168     0.07895  0.09863    0.02419    -0.01968      -0.66 X

R denotes an obs. with a large st. resid.
X denotes an obs. whose X value gives it large influence.
```

FIGURE 12.22 Marshall Field Example: Regression Models 2 and 3

```
The regression equation is
D4_LS = 0.0509 + 0.714 D4_LS-1 - 0.335 D4_LS-2 - 0.149 D4_LS-4

52 cases used 8 cases contain missing values

Predictor       Coef         Stdev       t-ratio        p
Constant      0.05092      0.01273        4.00      0.000
D4_LS-1        0.7143       0.1400        5.10      0.000
D4_LS-2       -0.3345       0.1354       -2.47      0.017
D4_LS-4       -0.1490       0.1198       -1.24      0.220

s = 0.03804    R-sq = 42.5%      R-sq(adj) = 38.9%
 .
 .
 .
```

(a) Regression model 2

```
The regression equation is
D4_LS = 0.0386 + 0.779 D4_LS-1 - 0.376 D4_LS-2

54 cases used 6 cases contain missing values

Predictor      Coef       Stdev     t-ratio        p
Constant    0.038632    0.009245      4.18     0.000
D4_LS-1       0.7791      0.1311      5.94     0.000
D4_LS-2      -0.3756      0.1310     -2.87     0.006

s = 0.03810    R-sq = 41.2%      R-sq(adj) = 38.9%
   .
   .
   .

Unusual Observations
Obs.  D4_LS-1     D4_LS      Fit  Stdev.Fit  Residual  St.Resid
 33    0.178    0.05942  0.13606    0.01368  -0.07663   -2.15R
 34    0.059    0.06136  0.01799    0.01626   0.04337    1.26 X
 41    0.007    0.19505  0.05803    0.01198   0.13703    3.79R
 42    0.195    0.19635  0.18804    0.02289   0.00831    0.27 X
 43    0.196    0.16786  0.11835    0.01701   0.04951    1.45 X
 44    0.168    0.07895  0.09566    0.01579  -0.01671   -0.48 X

R denotes an obs. with a large st. resid.
X denotes an obs. whose X value gives it large influence.
```

(b) Regression model 3

The diagnostic checks for model 3 are given in Figures 12.23 through 12.25. You should study them carefully, noting (1) any patterns in the deviations from what you expect to observe, and (2) how serious these deviations are. The outlier in quarter 41 is noticeable on all diagnostic plots. The other unusual observations flagged in Figure 12.22(b) also show up in some of the diagnostic plots. They occur during a short period of time in the middle of the time series. It might be instructive

FIGURE 12.23
Marshall Field Example: Plot of Standardized Residual vs. Fitted for Regression Model 3

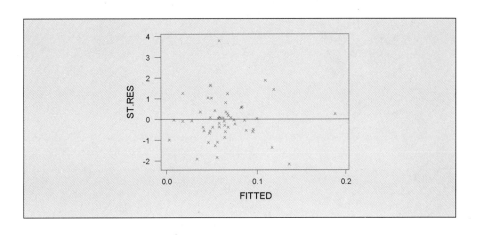

FIGURE 12.24 Marshall Field Example: Regression Model 3, Randomness Check for Residuals

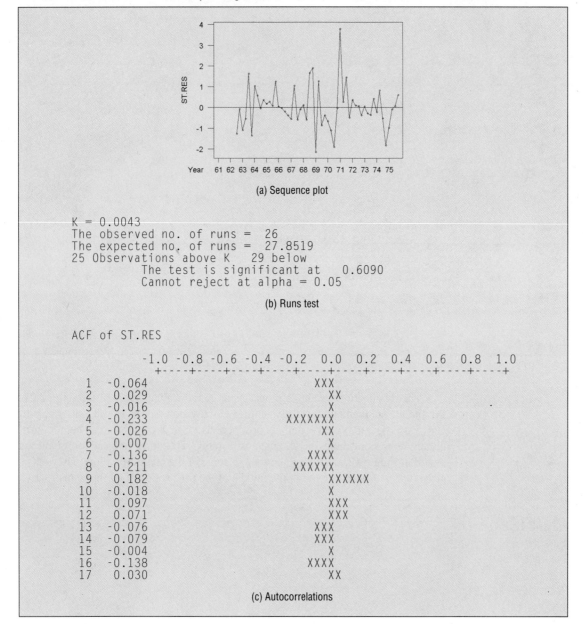

(a) Sequence plot

```
K = 0.0043
The observed no. of runs =  26
The expected no. of runs =  27.8519
25 Observations above K   29 below
        The test is significant at    0.6090
        Cannot reject at alpha = 0.05
```

(b) Runs test

```
ACF of ST.RES

         -1.0 -0.8 -0.6 -0.4 -0.2  0.0  0.2  0.4  0.6  0.8  1.0
          +----+----+----+----+----+----+----+----+----+----+
  1  -0.064                            XXX
  2   0.029                             XX
  3  -0.016                             X
  4  -0.233                        XXXXXXX
  5  -0.026                             XX
  6   0.007                             X
  7  -0.136                           XXXX
  8  -0.211                         XXXXXX
  9   0.182                             XXXXXX
 10  -0.018                             X
 11   0.097                             XXX
 12   0.071                             XXX
 13  -0.076                           XXX
 14  -0.079                           XXX
 15  -0.004                             X
 16  -0.138                           XXXX
 17   0.030                             XX
```

(c) Autocorrelations

FIGURE 12.25
Marshall Field
Example:
Regression Model
3, Normal
Probability Plot for
Residuals

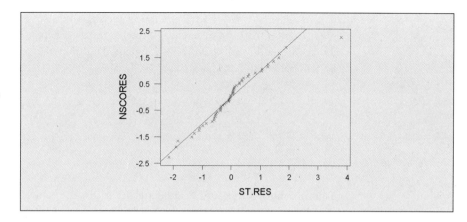

to check if there were special causes for them. The ST.RES vs. FITTED plot is satisfactory, suggesting that diagnostic checks 1 and 2 are adequate. (The plots of ST.RES vs. D4_LS$_{-1}$ and ST.RES vs. D4_LS$_{-2}$ are similar to this plot, and so they are not shown.) The sequence plot of ST.RES suggests randomness, but there is a somewhat unusual pattern between quarters 33 and 41 (1969:1 and 1971:1). The runs test and the autocorrelogram of ST.RES suggest randomness, too. Except for the outlier, the normal probability plot is satisfactory. Summarizing, the diagnostic checks for model 3, which relates D4_LS to its first two lags, are satisfactory except for the outlier.

Let us evaluate the goodness of autoregression model 3. The standard deviation of residuals in Figure 12.22(b) is $s = 0.0381$. This is somewhat lower than the standard deviation of D4_LS, given to be 0.0480 in Figure 12.18. The two lags of D4_LS thus do not account for a lot of the variation in D4_LS. The standard deviation of D4_LS, however, is considerably lower than the standard deviation 0.352 of the log of sales, LS, as given in Figure 12.18. The seasonal differencing accounts for a *considerable* amount of the variation in LS.

Since we have found model 3 to be satisfactory, let us get a prediction of sales for the first quarter 1976. From Figure 12.22(b), the prediction equation is

$$\text{Fitted D4\_LS} = 0.0386 + (0.779)\text{D4\_LS}_{-1} - (0.376)\text{D4\_LS}_{-2}$$

Since the first quarter 1976 corresponds to quarter 61 in our data, the first and second lags of D4_LS correspond to its values in quarters 60 and 59. These are given to be 0.1059 and 0.0647, respectively, in Figure 12.20. Substituting these values in the prediction equation, we get

$$\text{Fitted D4\_LS} = 0.0386 + 0.779(0.1059) - 0.376(0.0647) = 0.09677$$

A 95% prediction interval for D4_LS in quarter 1976 is thus $0.09677 \pm 2 \, s$, where $s = 0.03810$ [from Figure 12.22(b)]. The 95% prediction interval extends from 0.02057 to 0.17297.

Remember: We want a prediction for *sales* in quarter 61. So far, we have a prediction for the lag 4 difference of the log of sales in quarter 61. But the lag 4 difference of the log of sales, D4_LS, equals the difference between the log of sales, LS, and its fourth lag, LS_{-4}, i.e.,

$$D4\_LS = LS - LS_{-4}.$$

We can rewrite this as

$$LS = LS_{-4} + D4\_LS$$

Thus, the fitted value for LS in quarter 61 is just the value of LS four quarters earlier, that is, in quarter 57, plus the fitted value for D4_LS from model 3,

$$\text{Fitted } LS_{61} = LS_{57} + \text{Fitted } D4\_LS_{61}$$

$$= 11.6254 + 0.09677 = 11.7222$$

In order to get a point prediction for LS_{61}, we must add $LS_{57} = 11.6254$ to the point prediction for $D4\_LS_{61}$, 0.09677. Likewise, in order to get a 95% prediction interval for LS_{61}, we must add $LS_{57} = 11.6254$ to both ends of the 95% prediction interval for D4_LS (which extends from 0.02057 to 0.17297). Therefore, the 95% prediction interval for LS_{61} extends from 11.6254 + 0.02057 to 11.6254 + 0.17297, or from 11.6460 to 11.7984.

Having obtained a point prediction for LS_{61} and a 95% prediction interval for it, we can now take antilogs to obtain a point prediction and a 95% prediction interval for *sales* in quarter 61. The point prediction is $e^{11.7222} = 123{,}278$, and the 95% prediction interval extends from $e^{11.6460}$ to $e^{11.7984}$, or from 114,234 to 133,039.

This point prediction and the prediction interval answer the questions raised at the beginning of this section. From a statistical point of view, they are reasonably reliable since the diagnostic checks of the regression assumptions were acceptable. We had, however, expressed some concern about the outlier in period 41 and a few unusual observations a few quarters before it. A search for assignable causes would be a good idea.

Let us finally compare the two-step forecasting model for Marshall Field sales with the naive forecasting models discussed in Section 11.5 and at the end of Section 11.9. The three naive forecasting models were "Use the mean" ($\bar{y}$), "Use the last value" (y_{-1}), and "Use the value 4 quarters ago" (y_{-4}). Again, we first compute the mean absolute deviation (MAD) and the mean squared deviaton (MSD) for each model. For each naive model, we then compute the ratio of MAD to MAD for the two-step model; likewise for MSD. The resulting ratios are listed in the following table:

	$\dfrac{\text{MAD}}{\text{MAD}(\hat{y})}$	$\dfrac{\text{MSD}}{\text{MSD}(\hat{y})}$
$\bar{y}$	10.84	81.5
y_{-1}	8.88	57.1
y_{-4}	2.47	4.5

Among the three naive models, the "Use the value 4 quarters ago" model does best, but none of them does well in comparison to the two-step forecasting model.

12.4

FURTHER COMMENTS ON MODELS USING DIFFERENCING

In the last two sections, we introduced a two-step forecasting model:

1. Examine the differences or seasonal differences. If they are random, you have a simple prediction model. If not, proceed to step 2.

2. Obtain an autoregression model for the differences examined in step 1.

Let us now contrast this two-step model with a model that combines both steps into one autoregression model.

In the last section, we obtained a prediction model for LS based on using lag 4 differences. The estimated regression equation was

$$D4\_LS = b_0 + b_1(D4\_LS_{-1}) + b_2(D4\_LS_{-2}) + e$$

where the values of the estimated coefficients b_0, b_1, and b_2 were given in Figure 12.22(b), and e is the estimated residual whose standard deviation is s, the standard deviation around the regression equation. We can write this equation differently by remembering that

$$D4\_LS = LS - LS_{-4}$$

that is, that D4_LS is the lag 4 difference of LS. The first lag of this lag 4 difference can then be expressed as the difference between the first lag of LS and the fifth lag of LS,

$$D4\_LS_{-1} = LS_{-1} - LS_{-5}$$

and the second lag of D4_LS can be similarly expressed:

$$D4\_LS_{-2} = LS_{-2} - LS_{-6}$$

We can now use these expressions for D4_LS and its first two lags in the estimated regression equation for D4_LS,

$$D4\_LS = b_0 + b_1(D4\_LS_{-1}) + b_2(D4\_LS_{-2}) + e$$

We get

$$(LS - LS_{-4}) = b_0 + b_1(LS_{-1} - LS_{-5}) + b_2(LS_{-2} - LS_{-6}) + e$$

We can finally rewrite this as an equation for LS,

$$LS = b_0 + b_1(LS_{-1}) + b_2(LS_{-2}) + LS_{-4} - b_1(LS_{-5}) - b_2(LS_{-6}) + e$$

This equation relates LS to its first, second, fourth, fifth, and sixth lags. The coefficients of the first and fifth lags are the same, but they have opposite signs. A similar result holds for the coefficients of the second and sixth lags. Finally, the coefficient of the fourth lag equals 1.

Summarizing, based on model 3 the coefficients for the relevant lags of LS are:

Lag	Coefficient
1	$b_1 = 0.7791$
2	$b_2 = -0.3756$
4	1
5	$-b_1 = -0.7791$
6	$-b_2 = 0.3756$

We could, of course, also have obtained a regression model directly for LS by using its first, second, fourth, fifth, and sixth lags. But it would have been difficult to identify these lags as the appropriate ones from the autocorrelogram of LS in Figure 12.17. With *hindsight,* an estimated regression equation can be found linking LS to these lags. The resulting model output (not shown) yields the following coefficients:

Lag	Coefficient
1	0.7741
2	−0.3704
3	0.9860
4	−0.7717
5	0.3757

These coefficients do not differ much from the ones we obtained with model 3.

The iterative approach using differencing is preferable in general. It has been found in practice to be *far superior* to trying to identify the appropriate lags directly. You should follow this practice of seasonal differencing when the autocorrelation at the seasonal lag is high and the autocorrelations at the multiples of the seasonal lag are slowly decreasing.

12.5

A SECOND ANALYSIS OF SALES OF MARSHALL FIELD & COMPANY

In the previous sections we saw that autoregression with differencing yields a satisfactory model for the sales data of Marshall Field & Company. An alternative approach to autoregression (where the predictor variables are lags) is sometimes suggested: It consists of using deterministic **predictor variables for time and season-ality,** rather than lags or differences. This approach, though somewhat popular, rarely produces models that are as good as autoregression and related models. To show this and to illustrate this approach, let us define a few additional variables,

TIME, a variable indexing the period; here TIME takes on the values 1, 2, ..., 60

QUARTER, a variable indicating the quarter in a year;[2] it can take on the values 1, 2, 3, and 4

indicator variables Q1, Q2, Q3, and Q4, indicator variables taking on values 0 or 1; for example, Q1 = 1 if the quarter in question is a first quarter, and Q1 = 0 if the quarter in question is not a first quarter.

The data are listed in Figure 12.26. Study them carefully to understand the values of the variables TIME, Q1, Q2, Q3, and Q4.

---

[2] Note that QUARTER, as used here, is a categorical variable, where the quarters are the distinct categories. This variable cannot be used directly, and it must be converted into the four indicator variables Q1, Q2, Q3, and Q4. For a discussion of categorical variables, see Section 10.6.

FIGURE 12.26 Marshall Field Example: List of Additional Data

ROW	SALES	LS	TIME	QUARTER	Q1	Q2	Q3	Q4
1	48617	10.7917	1	1	1	0	0	0
2	50898	10.8376	2	2	0	1	0	0
3	58517	10.9771	3	3	0	0	1	0
4	77691	11.2605	4	4	0	0	0	1
5	50862	10.8369	5	1	1	0	0	0
6	53028	10.8786	6	2	0	1	0	0
7	58849	10.9827	7	3	0	0	1	0
8	79660	11.2855	8	4	0	0	0	1
⋮								
56	169677	12.0417	56	4	0	0	0	1
57	111905	11.6254	57	1	1	0	0	0
58	127872	11.7588	58	2	0	1	0	0
59	145367	11.8870	59	3	0	0	1	0
60	188635	12.1476	60	4	0	0	0	1

	N	MEAN	MEDIAN	TRMEAN	STDEV	SEMEAN
SALES	60	96431	89672	94541	34280	4425
LS	60	11.416	11.404	11.412	0.352	0.045
TIME	60	30.50	30.50	30.50	17.46	2.25
QUARTER	60	2.500	2.500	2.500	1.127	0.146
Q1	60	0.2500	0.0000	0.2222	0.4367	0.0564
Q2	60	0.2500	0.0000	0.2222	0.4367	0.0564
Q3	60	0.2500	0.0000	0.2222	0.4367	0.0564
Q4	60	0.2500	0.0000	0.2222	0.4367	0.0564

Let us examine a model for the log of sales, LS, that relates LS to the predictor variables TIME, Q1, Q2, and Q3. In this model we do not need variable Q4. To see this, note the following table,

Indicator Variables

Q1	Q2	Q3	Quarter
1	0	0	1
0	1	0	2
0	0	1	3
0	0	0	4

When Q1 = 1, but Q2 = Q3 = 0, the quarter in question is quarter 1, and when Q1 = Q2 = Q3 = 0, the quarter in question is quarter 4: It is superfluous to explicitly use Q4 in the regression equation and it should not be done. Minitab output for model 4, a regression of the response variable LS on TIME, Q1, Q2, and Q3, is given in Figure 12.27.

The diagnostic checks for regression model 4 must be carried out at this point. We report results here only for diagnostic check 3, the randomness of standardized residuals. The Durbin-Watson statistic in Figure 12.27 is 1.10: There seem to be problems with the randomness of residuals, since their first-order autocorrelation is high. Further results relating to the randomness of standardized residuals from model 4 are given in Figure 12.28. You should study the results carefully, noting (1) any patterns to the deviations from what you expect to see, and (2) how strong these patterns are.

FIGURE 12.27 Marshall Field Example: Regression Model 4

```
The regression equation is
LS = 11.2 + 0.0168 TIME - 0.446 Q1 - 0.395 Q2 - 0.271 Q3

Predictor        Coef          Stdev       t-ratio
Constant       11.1815        0.0134        835.70
TIME          0.0167961     0.0002841        59.13
Q1             -0.44553       0.01391       -32.03
Q2             -0.39506       0.01390       -28.43
Q3             -0.27133       0.01389       -19.54

s = 0.03803     R-sq = 98.9%     R-sq(adj) = 98.8%
. . .

Unusual Observations
Obs.     TIME        LS       Fit Stdev.Fit    Residual    St.Resid
 32      32.0   11.8207   11.7190    0.0098      0.1017        2.77R
 38      38.0   11.3475   11.4247    0.0101     -0.0772       -2.11R
 39      39.0   11.4796   11.5652    0.0101     -0.0856       -2.33R
 56      56.0   12.0417   12.1221    0.0120     -0.0804       -2.23R

R denotes an obs. with a large st. resid.
Durbin-Watson statistic = 1.10
```

FIGURE 12.28 Marshall Field Example: Regression Model 4, Diagnostics for Standardized Residuals

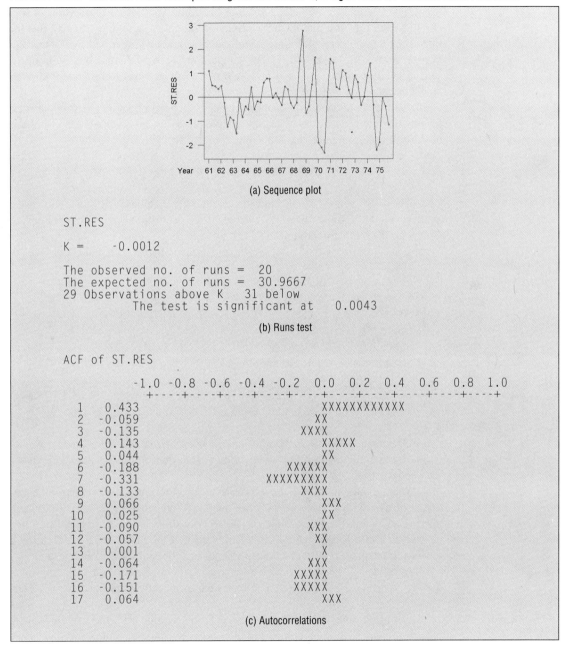

(a) Sequence plot

```
ST.RES

K =    -0.0012

The observed no. of runs =  20
The expected no. of runs =  30.9667
29 Observations above K   31 below
        The test is significant at    0.0043
```

(b) Runs test

```
ACF of ST.RES

          -1.0 -0.8 -0.6 -0.4 -0.2  0.0  0.2  0.4  0.6  0.8  1.0
          +----+----+----+----+----+----+----+----+----+----+
   1  0.433                              XXXXXXXXXXXX
   2 -0.059                            XX
   3 -0.135                          XXXX
   4  0.143                              XXXXX
   5  0.044                            XX
   6 -0.188                        XXXXX
   7 -0.331                    XXXXXXXXX
   8 -0.133                          XXXX
   9  0.066                             XXX
  10  0.025                            XX
  11 -0.090                          XXX
  12 -0.057                           XX
  13  0.001                            X
  14 -0.064                          XXX
  15 -0.171                        XXXXX
  16 -0.151                        XXXXX
  17  0.064                             XXX
```

(c) Autocorrelations

Diagnostic check 3, the check for randomness of the residuals, cannot be passed. The sequence plot does not look random. This visual impression is supported by the runs test and the autocorrelation function. Note, in particular, that the first-order sample autocorrelation is high, as was already suggested by the Durbin-Watson statistic in Figure 12.27. The standard error for each autocorrelation of the standardized residuals is $1/\sqrt{n} = 1/\sqrt{60} = 0.13$, so two of the autocorrelations are further than 2 standard errors away from 0.

In order to understand this modeling approach better, let us interpret the coefficients. (We will do this here for illustrative purposes, in spite of the fact that the diagnostic checks are not passed.) From Figure 12.27, fitted model 4 is

Fitted LS = 11.2 + (0.0168)TIME − (0.446)Q1 − (0.395)Q2 − (0.271)Q3

The coefficient of TIME indicates that the fitted values of LS for 2 successive quarters are 0.0168 units apart on average, after controlling for seasonal effects as done with the indicator variables Q1, Q2, and Q3.

The contribution to the fitted value of LS made by Q1, Q2, and Q3 is

(−0.446)Q1 − (0.395)Q2 − (0.271)Q3

which equals

0	for a fourth quarter, because Q1 = Q2 = Q3 = 0
−0.446	for a first quarter, because Q1 = 1 and Q2 = Q3 = 0
−0.395	for a second quarter, because Q2 = 1 and Q1 = Q3 = 0
−0.271	for a third quarter, because Q3 = 1 and Q1 = Q2 = 0

Of course, all these coefficients are *net* coefficients, net of the other variables in the regression equation. For a review of how to interpret regression coefficients, see Section 10.4.

We can thus interpret the coefficients of Q1, Q2, and Q3 as comparing a particular quarter with a base quarter, here, quarter 4. The coefficient of Q1, for example, indicates that the fitted value of LS is 0.446 units lower on average in a first quarter than in a fourth quarter, net of the effect of the variable TIME. In a sense this is a fixed quarterly effect that is the same regardless of the year in question.

In model 4, quarter 4 was arbitrarily chosen as the base quarter. Any other quarter could have been chosen as a base quarter as well. (See Exercises 12.8 and 12.10.)

Let us compare the model discussed in this section with the two-step model of the previous section by comparing their mean absolute deviation and their mean squared deviation. The ratio of mean absolute deviation values (model from this section vs. two-step model) is 1.07, and the ratio of mean squared deviation values is 1.18. Thus the two-step model of the last section performs better.

Although the modeling approach briefly discussed in this section appears to lead to intuitive interpretations, it usually does not capture the time series information as well in practice as the autoregression approach does.

12.6

SUMMARY

The time series modeling tools discussed in this course range from differencing and seasonal differencing to autoregression. You can now model a wide variety of time series reasonably well, but you will not always be fully successful. There are many other tools available to modeling time series. For further information, see, for example, Cryer (1986).

In this and the previous chapter we discussed only time series modeling where no auxiliary information is available from other variables. Sometimes such additional variables are available that can be used as predictor variables. In such cases it is imperative, as always, that the diagnostic checks be carried out and studied carefully.

Key Terms and Concepts

time series
    differencing, seasonal
    differencing, autoregression

indicator variables for seasons
statistical vs. practical significance

References

Cryer, J.D. (1986), *Time Series Analysis,* Duxbury Press, Belmont, CA.

> This is an introductory text to time series modeling. It uses the Minitab software package.

12.7

USING MINITAB FOR WINDOWS

This section shows how several of the graphs in this chapter were generated with Minitab for Windows.

Figure 12.15
Choose *File* ▸ *Other Files* ▸ *Import ASCII Data*
In the *Import ASCII Data* dialog box,
    Under *Store data in column,* type **C1**
    Click *ok*
    In the *Import Text From File* dialog box,
        Choose and click data file *mfield.dat,* click *ok*
Choose *Window* ▸ *Data*
In the *Data* window,
    In the box immediately under *C1,* type **SALES**
    Click any empty cell

DIFFERENCING AND SEASONAL DIFFERENCING

Choose *Stat* ▸ *Time Series* ▸ *Differences*
In the *Differences* dialog box,
    Click the box next to *Series,* type **C1**
    Click the box next to *Store differences in,* type **C2**
    Click the box next to *Lag,* type **4**
    Click *ok*

Choose *Window* ▸ *Data*
In the *Data* window,
    In the box immediately under *C2,* type **D4_S**
    Click any empty cell
Choose *Graph* ▸ *Time Series Plot*
In the *Time Series Plot* dialog box,
    Under *Graph variables,* type **C2** in the first box under *Y*
    Under *Time scale,* click the circle next to *Calendar*
    Under *Time scale,* click the down arrow in the box next to *Calendar,* click *Quarter Year*
    Click the *Options* box
    In the *Time Series Plot Options* dialog box,
        Under *Start time,* type **1** in the box under *Quarter* and type **61** in the box under *Year*
        Under *Display,* click the first box so that the cross disappears, click *ok*
    Click *ok*

12.8

PROBLEMS FOR CLASS DISCUSSION

There are two problems for class discussion. The first relates to real estate activity in Metropolitan Toronto. A regression model used for it includes not only lags of the response variable but also lags of another variable. This is straightforward to do in multiple regression. The second problem obtains a forecasting model for the monthly shipments of mobile homes in the United States.

12.1 Real Estate Activity in Metropolitan Toronto

A real estate company had been growing rapidly in the past few years. Due to new requirements by the Ontario Securities Commission, the lead time for a new real estate prospectus had increased to about 7 months and the minimum cost of preparation to $250,000. Therefore more careful planning was needed for new real estate deals. To help in this planning effort, a study was done to answer several managerial questions. One of them was:

How can residential real estate activity in the Metropolitan Toronto area be predicted in the near future?

Data were collected for the 48 quarters from the third quarter in 1977 to the second quarter in 1989 on two variables: (1) RATE, a Canadian Chartered Bank's prime lending rate at the end of the quarter, and (2) RESIDENT, total value of residential building permits in the metropolitan areas of Ontario (in $1,000). The data are stored in ASCII file INVEST.DAT.

Use the Minitab Session window output in Figure 12.29 to answer the managerial question. Note that the variable R_RESI denotes the square root of RESIDENT, R_RESI_{-1} denotes the first lag of R_RESI, etc.

FIGURE 12.29

```
MTB > Read 'C:\MTBWIN\DATA\INVEST.DAT' C1-C3
Entering data from file: C:\MTBWIN\DATA\INVEST.DAT
   48 rows read.
MTB > NAME C1 'RATE' C3 'RESIDENT'
MTB > PRINT C1 C3

ROW    RATE  RESIDENT    ROW    RATE  RESIDENT

  1    8.25     83694     25   11.00    148354
  2    8.25     69453     26   11.00    118466
  3    8.42     42071     27   11.17    102278
  4    9.25    118737     28   12.00    156786
  5    9.75     97971     29   13.17    144974
  6   11.33     70529     30   11.92    120409
  7   12.00     48385     31   11.42    117530
  8   12.00    101056     32   10.58    230653
  9   12.67    109937     33   10.33    242379
 10   14.92     85725     34   10.00    196900
 11   15.25     52824     35   12.00    219605
 12   14.58     90722     36   10.58    290686
 13   12.25     99276     37    9.75    286374
 14   14.92    113971     38    9.75    303299
 15   18.08    106542     39    9.08    401908
 16   19.25    212947     40    9.42    411085
 17   21.67    131916     41    9.83    415195
 18   18.17    133732     42    9.75    314713
 19   16.67     58439     43    9.75    351332
 20   17.42     82505     44   10.42    500730
 21   16.08     98301     45   11.25    443127
 22   13.08    135282     46   11.92    372941
 23   11.67    117823     47   12.83    396184
 24   11.00    161456     48   13.50    425797

MTB > Let C4=Sqrt(C3)
MTB > NAME C4 'R_RESI'
MTB > Describe C1 C3 C4

                N     MEAN   MEDIAN   TRMEAN    STDEV   SEMEAN
RATE           48   12.278   11.545   12.089    3.052    0.440
RESIDENT       48   190312   132824   184107   127782    18444
R_RESI         48    413.8    364.4    410.6    139.5     20.1

              MIN      MAX       Q1       Q3
RATE        8.250   21.670    9.872   13.417
RESIDENT    42071   500730    98545   289608
R_RESI      205.1    707.6    313.9    538.1
```

```
MTB > Lag 1 C4 C5
MTB > Lag 4 C4 C6
MTB > Lag 2 C1 C7
MTB > NAME C5 'R_RESI-1' C6 'R_RESI-4' C7 'RATE-2'
```

Model 1

```
MTB > Regress C4 3 C5-C7 C10 C11
```

The regression equation is
R_RESI = 79.3 + 0.534 R_RESI-1 + 0.455 R_RESI-4 - 4.52 RATE-2

44 cases used 4 cases contain missing values

Predictor	Coef	Stdev	t-ratio	p
Constant	79.32	51.74	?	?
R_RESI-1	0.5343	0.1032	?	?
R_RESI-4	0.4553	0.1034	?	?
RATE-2	-4.515	2.729	?	?

s = 48.68   R-sq = 88.5%   R-sq(adj) = 87.6%

Analysis of Variance

SOURCE	DF	SS	MS	F	p
Regression	3	726415	242138	102.18	0.000
Error	40	94790	2370		
Total	43	821205			

SOURCE	DF	SEQ SS
R_RESI-1	1	676394
R_RESI-4	1	43533
RATE-2	1	6488

Unusual Observations

Obs.	R_RESI-1	R_RESI	Fit	Stdev.Fit	Residual	St.Resid
16	326	461.46	323.49	10.18	137.97	2.90R
19	366	241.74	325.48	25.34	-83.74	-2.01R
20	242	287.24	336.54	26.13	-49.30	-1.20 X

R denotes an obs. with a large st. resid.
X denotes an obs. whose X value gives it large influence.

```
MTB > NAME C10 'ST.RES' C11 'FITTED'
MTB > Plot C10*C5
```

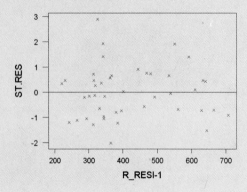

MTB > Plot C10*C6

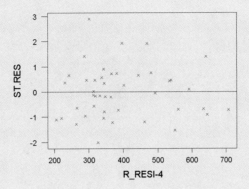

MTB > Plot C10*C7

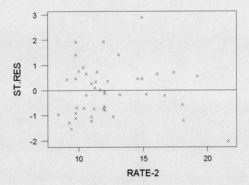

MTB > Plot C10*C11

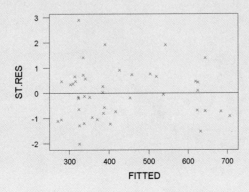

```
MTB > TSPlot C10
```

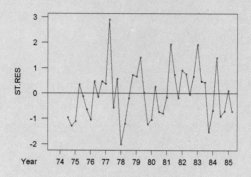

```
MTB > Copy C10 C14;
SUBCv    Omit 1:4.
MTB > Runs C14


    C14

    K = -0.0127

    The observed no. of runs =  23
    The expected no. of runs =  22.9545
    21 Observations above K   23 below
            The test is significant at  0.9889
            Cannot reject at alpha = 0.05

MTB > ACF C10

ACF of ST.RES

           -1.0 -0.8 -0.6 -0.4 -0.2  0.0  0.2  0.4  0.6  0.8  1.0
            +----+----+----+----+----+----+----+----+----+----+
  1   0.189                          XXXXX
  2  -0.002                          X
  3  -0.141                        XXXX
  4  -0.047                         XX
  5  -0.185                        XXXXX
  6  -0.011                          X
  7   0.012                          X
  8   0.215                          XXXXX
  9  -0.073                         XXX
 10  -0.178                        XXXXX
 11  -0.133                        XXXX
 12   0.009                          X
 13  -0.193                        XXXXX
 14  -0.040                         XX
 15   0.051                          XX
 16   0.187                          XXXXX
```

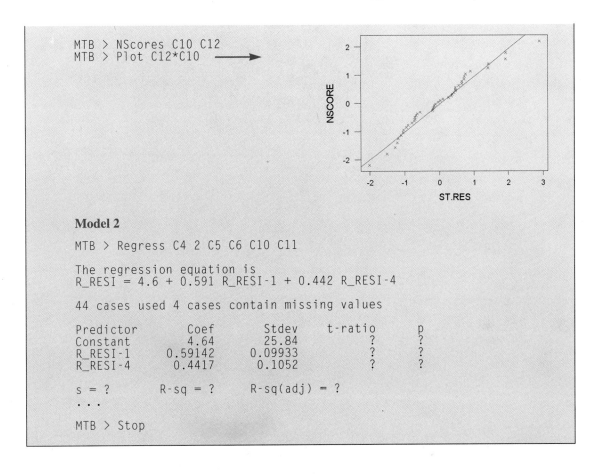

```
MTB > NScores C10 C12
MTB > Plot C12*C10
```

Model 2

```
MTB > Regress C4 2 C5 C6 C10 C11

The regression equation is
R_RESI = 4.6 + 0.591 R_RESI-1 + 0.442 R_RESI-4

44 cases used 4 cases contain missing values

Predictor       Coef        Stdev      t-ratio        p
Constant        4.64        25.84         ?           ?
R_RESI-1      0.59142      0.09933         ?           ?
R_RESI-4       0.4417      0.1052          ?           ?

s = ?         R-sq = ?     R-sq(adj) = ?
. . .

MTB > Stop
```

12.2   Shipments of Mobile Homes

The data to be analyzed are monthly shipments of mobile homes, given in 1000s of units, in the United States for the period from 1968 to 1972. (The data are taken from the U.S. *Survey of Current Business.*) The output in Figure 12.30 is to be used for predicting mobile home shipments in future months.

FIGURE 12.30

```
MTB > Read 'C:\MTBWIN\DATA\MOBILE.DAT' C1
Entering data from file: C:\MTBWIN\DATA\MOBILE.DAT
    168 rows read.          Note: The last 60 rows contain the relevant data.
MTB > Delete 1:108 C1
MTB > NAME C1 'Y'
MTB > PRINT C1
```

```
Y
   19.0  21.2  24.0  27.1  27.6  26.5  27.2  30.5  29.9  33.5  27.6
   24.0  27.1  29.4  32.5  36.0  34.6  36.4  35.2  38.1  40.1  43.4
   32.7  27.2  23.9  24.1  29.5  39.9  32.9  35.6  37.1  39.4  41.4
   40.8  30.5  27.0  24.5  28.7  35.6  42.8  40.9  47.3  45.2  49.5
   53.5  50.4  39.5  34.4  33.3  40.0  49.1  53.7  51.8  55.0  48.5
   52.1  49.1  54.4  50.7  38.0
```

MTB > TSPlot C1

MTB > Describe C1

```
            N     MEAN   MEDIAN   TRMEAN    STDEV   SEMEAN
Y          60    36.68    35.60    36.55     9.66     1.25

          MIN      MAX       Q1       Q3
Y       19.00    55.00    27.88    43.25
```

MTB > ACF C1

ACF of Y

```
             -1.0 -0.8 -0.6 -0.4 -0.2  0.0  0.2  0.4  0.6  0.8  1.0
             +----+----+----+----+----+----+----+----+----+----+
  1  0.841                              XXXXXXXXXXXXXXXXXXXXXXX
  2  0.641                              XXXXXXXXXXXXXXXXX
  3  0.448                              XXXXXXXXXXXX
  4  0.343                              XXXXXXXXX
  5  0.309                              XXXXXXXXX
  6  0.299                              XXXXXXXX
  7  0.231                              XXXXXX
  8  0.209                              XXXXX
  9  0.220                              XXXXXX
 10  0.321                              XXXXXXXXX
 11  0.416                              XXXXXXXXXX
 12  0.450                              XXXXXXXXXXXX
 13  0.335                              XXXXXXXXX
 14  0.183                              XXXXX
 15  0.012                              X
 16 -0.061                           XXX
 17 -0.076                           XXX
```

```
MTB > Lag 1 C1 C2
MTB > Lag 12 C1 C3
MTB > NAME C2 'Y-1' C3 'Y-2'
MTB > Regress C1 2 C2 C3 C10 C11;
SUBC>   DW.
```

The regression equation is
Y = 3.29 + 0.456 Y-1 + 0.537 Y-2

48 cases used 12 cases contain missing values

Predictor	Coef	Stdev	t-ratio	p
Constant	3.291	2.823	1.17	0.250
Y-1	0.45630	0.09930	4.60	0.000
Y-2	0.5366	0.1138	4.72	0.000

s = 4.193   R-sq = 79.1%   R-sq(adj) = 78.1%

Analysis of Variance

SOURCE	DF	SS	MS	F	p
Regression	2	2986.5	1493.3	84.92	0.000
Error	45	791.3	17.6		
Total	47	3777.8			

SOURCE	DF	SEQ SS
Y-1	1	2595.4
Y-2	1	391.2

Unusual Observations

Obs.	Y-1	Y	Fit	Stdev.Fit	Residual	St.Resid
35	40.8	30.500	39.455	0.674	-8.955	-2.16R
51	40.0	49.100	40.646	0.621	8.454	2.04R

R denotes an obs. with a large st. resid.

Durbin-Watson statistic = 1.05

```
MTB > NAME C10 'ST.RES' C11 'FITTED'
MTB > Plot C10*C11
```

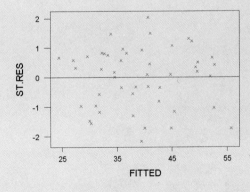

```
MTB > TSPlot C10
```

```
MTB > Copy C10 C12;
SUBC>   Omit 1:12.
MTB > Runs C12


    C12

    K =    -0.0054

    The observed no. of runs =   12
    The expected no. of runs =   23.9583
    29 Observations above K    19 below
            The test is significant at   0.0003

MTB > ACF C10

ACF of ST.RES

             -1.0 -0.8 -0.6 -0.4 -0.2  0.0  0.2  0.4  0.6  0.8  1.0
             +----+----+----+----+----+----+----+----+----+----+
     1    0.433                          XXXXXXXXXXXX
     2    0.283                          XXXXXXXX
     3    0.138                          XXXX
     4   -0.020                          X
     5    0.007                          X
     6    0.114                          XXXX
     7   -0.035                         XX
     8   -0.005                          X
     9   -0.057                         XX
    10   -0.029                         XX
    11    0.013                          X
    12    0.063                          XXX
    13   -0.166                      XXXXX
    14   -0.176                      XXXXX
    15   -0.440              XXXXXXXXXXXX
    16   -0.408               XXXXXXXXXXX
```

```
MTB > Difference C1 C2
MTB > NAME C2 'D_Y'
MTB > TSPlot C2
```

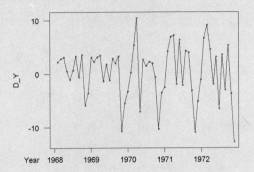

```
MTB > ACF C2

ACF of D_Y

              -1.0 -0.8 -0.6 -0.4 -0.2  0.0  0.2  0.4  0.6  0.8  1.0
               +----+----+----+----+----+----+----+----+----+----+
    1   0.169                           XXXXX
    2  -0.007                           X
    3  -0.300                     XXXXXXXX
    4  -0.273                      XXXXXXX
    5  -0.111                        XXXX
    6   0.217                           XXXXX
    7  -0.135                        XXXX
    8  -0.145                        XXXXX
    9  -0.300                     XXXXXXXX
   10  -0.048                          XX
   11   0.197                           XXXXX
   12   0.609                           XXXXXXXXXXXXXXXX
   13   0.162                           XXXXX
   14   0.097                           XXX
   15  -0.342                     XXXXXXXXXX
   16  -0.244                       XXXXXX
   17  -0.061                          XXX

MTB > Lag 12 C2 C3
MTB > NAME C3 'D_Y-12'
MTB > Regress C2 1 C3 C10 C11;
SUBC>   DW.

The regression equation is
D_Y = - 0.054 + 0.871 D_Y-12

47 cases used 13 cases contain missing values

Predictor        Coef       Stdev    t-ratio          p
Constant      -0.0536      0.5196      -0.10      0.918
D_Y-12         0.8715      0.1124       7.75      0.000

s = 3.553      R-sq = 57.2%      R-sq(adj) = 56.2%
```

```
Analysis of Variance

SOURCE         DF          SS             MS          F        p
Regression      1       758.42         758.42      60.08    0.000
Error          45       568.10          12.62
Total          46      1326.52

Unusual Observations
Obs.     D_Y-12            D_Y        Fit  Stdev.Fit      Residual     St.Resid
 28        3.5          10.400      2.997     0.629         7.403        2.12R
 35      -10.7         -10.300     -9.378     1.344        -0.922       -0.28 X
 47      -10.3         -10.900     -9.030     1.302        -1.870       -0.57 X
 58       -3.1           5.300     -2.755     0.646         8.055        2.31R
 59      -10.9          -3.700     -9.553     1.365         5.853        1.78 X
 60       -5.1         -12.700     -4.498     0.801        -8.202       -2.37R

R denotes an obs. with a large st. resid.
X denotes an obs. whose X value gives it large influence.

Durbin-Watson statistic = 2.01

MTB > NAME C10 'ST.RES' C11 'FITTED'
MTB > Plot C10*C11
```

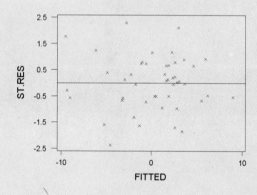

```
MTB > TSPlot C10
```

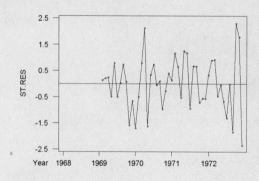

```
MTB > Copy C10 C14;
SUBC>   Omit 1:13.
MTB > Runs C14

    C14

    K = 0.0005

    The observed no. of runs =  22
    The expected no. of runs =  24.4043
    25 Observations above K   22 below
            The test is significant at  0.4766
            Cannot reject at alpha = 0.05

MTB > ACF C10

ACF of ST.RES

          -1.0 -0.8 -0.6 -0.4 -0.2  0.0  0.2  0.4  0.6  0.8  1.0
           +----+----+----+----+----+----+----+----+----+----+
    1 -0.061                        XXX
    2 -0.231                    XXXXXXX
    3  0.079                        XXX
    4 -0.173                      XXXXX
    5 -0.056                         XX
    6  0.053                         XX
    7 -0.062                        XXX
    8  0.070                        XXX
    9  0.079                        XXX
   10  0.008                          X
   11 -0.001                          X
   12 -0.038                         XX
   13 -0.065                        XXX
   14  0.180                        XXXXX
   15 -0.178                      XXXXX
   16 -0.224                    XXXXXX

MTB > NScores C10 C12
MTB > NAME C12 'NSCORE'
MTB > Plot C12*C10
```

```
MTB > Stop
```

12.9

EXERCISES

Although answers are given in Appendix C, do not turn to them right away if you cannot find an answer on your own. Return to the exercise the next day and try again before turning to Appendix C.

Exercise for Section 12.2

12.3 The data to be analyzed in this problem are quarterly Canadian GNP values from the first quarter in 1972 to the third quarter 1993. A 1 quarter–ahead forecasting equation is to be found. The 87 data values, given in millions of current dollars and not seasonally adjusted, are stored in the last 87 rows of Column 2 of ASCII file CND_QRT.DAT.

    a Obtain a time series plot of GNP. Obtain the autocorrelogram. What do you see, and what kind of model is suggested?

    b Obtain the lag 1 differences of GNP, D_GNP. What is the rationale for examining this variable? Obtain a time series plot and the autocorrelogram for D_GNP.

    c Obtain a regression of the response variable D_GNP on its fourth lag. Do the diagnostic checks and comment. (What is peculiar about the plot of ST.RES vs. FITTED? Can you explain this?)

    d Use the regression model in (c) to obtain a point prediction and a 95% prediction interval for GNP in the fourth quarter 1993. Given the diagnostic checks in (c), how reliable are these predictions?

Exercises for Section 12.3

12.4 Consider the SP data, and assume that you want to get a point prediction and a 95% prediction interval of the value of the SP index for February 1985—that is, 2 months ahead. Use a variant of the random walk model to do this by considering *lag 2* differences. Use the Minitab output in Figure 12.31 in conjunction with Figure 11.1 (page 541).

12.5 The data to be analyzed in this problem relate to quarterly net sales (SALES) and net income (INCOME) for Marshall Field & Company. The data cover the period from 1961:1 to 1975:4. They are stored in ASCII file MFIELD.DAT. The variable of interest here is a financial ratio, net income to sales (RATIO). The following questions relate to Minitab output in Figure 12.32.

    a Briefly describe the time series pattern for RATIO.

    b What does the runs test for RATIO tell you? Do you find this surprising in light of your observations in (a)? Had you expected a different result in light of (a)? If so, what had you expected?

    c What do the autocorrelations for RATIO tell you? Do you find this surprising in light of your observations in (a)? Had you expected something different in light of (a)? If so, what had you expected?

    d Compute the *t*-ratios for model 1. If you cannot do this, briefly indicate what additional information you need.

FIGURE 12.31

```
MTB > Read 'C:\MTBWIN\DATA\SP_MONTH.DAT' C1
MTB > NAME C1 'SP'
MTB > Delete 61:144 C1
MTB > Difference 1 C1 C2
MTB > Difference 2 C1 C3
MTB > NAME C2 'D1_SP' C3 'D2_SP'
MTB > PRINT C1-C3

 ROW        SP      D1_SP        D2_SP

   1    114.16         *            *
   2    113.66    -0.5000           *
   3    102.15   -11.5100     -12.0100
   4    106.29     4.1400      -7.3700
   5    111.24     4.9500       9.0900
 . . .

  59    163.58    -2.5100      -2.5200
  60    167.24     3.6600       1.1500

MTB > Describe C1-C3

              N     N*    MEAN    MEDIAN    TRMEAN    STDEV    SEMEAN
SP           60      0  137.80    133.26    137.97    20.85      2.69
D1_SP        59      1   0.900     0.710     0.710     5.530     0.720
D2_SP        58      2   1.78      0.91      1.75      7.91      1.04

             MIN      MAX       Q1        Q3
SP        102.15   168.11   120.40    161.80
D1_SP     -11.510   16.020   -2.520     4.460
D2_SP     -14.74    18.12    -4.30      8.00

MTB > Stop
```

e Why did we run the regression leading to model 2?

f Do you think the value for s in model 1 is higher than, the same as, or lower than the value for s in model 2? Briefly justify your answer.

g What is the approximate value of the Durbin-Watson statistics for model 2?

h What information do the diagnostic checks provide about the adequacy of model 2?

i Using model 2, obtain a point prediction and a 95% prediction interval for the lag 4 difference of RATIO in the first quarter 1976. What assumptions do you have to make to compute these predictions?

j In light of your answers in (h), how reliable is the point prediction computed in (i)? How reliable is the prediction interval?

k Using model 2, obtain a point prediction for RATIO in the fourth quarter 1976. If you cannot do this, briefly indicate what information is needed.

l Do you think the point prediction in (k) is equally as reliable (or unreliable) as that computed in (i)? If not, what are the differences?

FIGURE 12.32

```
MTB > Read 'C:\MTBWIN\DATA\MFIELD.DAT' C1 C2
MTB > NAME C1 'SALES' C2 'INCOME' C3 'RATIO'
MTB > Let C3=C2/C1
MTB > PRINT C1-C3
  ROW     SALES    INCOME     RATIO

    1     48617       993    0.0204
    2     50898      1167    0.0229
    3     58517      2319    0.0396
...

   56    169677      9063    0.0534
   57    111905       637    0.0056
   58    127872      3347    0.0261
   59    145367      5226    0.0359
   60    188635     10116    0.0536

MTB > TSPlot C3  ──────────►
```

```
MTB > Runs C3

     RATIO
     K =     0.0388

     The observed no. of runs =   30
     The expected no. of runs =   29.8000
     24 Observations above K   36 below
              The test is significant at  0.9567
              Cannot reject at alpha = 0.05

MTB > ACF C3

ACF of RATIO

          -1.0 -0.8 -0.6 -0.4 -0.2  0.0  0.2  0.4  0.6  0.8  1.0
           +----+----+----+----+----+----+----+----+----+----+
    1  -0.054                        XX
    2  -0.481              XXXXXXXXXXXXX
    3  -0.116                      XXXX
    4   0.862                         XXXXXXXXXXXXXXXXXXXXXXX
    5  -0.100                      XXXX
    6  -0.468              XXXXXXXXXXXXX
    7  -0.104                      XXXX
    8   0.771                         XXXXXXXXXXXXXXXXXXXX
    9  -0.123                      XXXX
   10  -0.468              XXXXXXXXXXXXX
   11  -0.127                      XXXX
   12   0.675                         XXXXXXXXXXXXXXXXXX
   13  -0.120                      XXXX
   14  -0.436               XXXXXXXXXXXX
   15  -0.138                      XXXX
   16   0.591                         XXXXXXXXXXXXXXXX
   17  -0.118                      XXXX
```

```
MTB > Difference 4 C3 C4  ──────▶
MTB > NAME C4 'D4_R'
MTB > TSPlot C4
```

```
MTB > Copy C4 C5;
SUBC>   Use 5:60.
MTB > Runs C5

    C5

    K = -0.0004

    The observed no. of runs =  19
    The expected no. of runs =  28.6786
    31 Observations above K   25 below
            The test is significant at   0.0084

MTB > ACF C4


ACF of D4_R

            -1.0 -0.8 -0.6 -0.4 -0.2  0.0  0.2  0.4  0.6  0.8  1.0
             +----+----+----+----+----+----+----+----+----+----+
    1   0.528                            XXXXXXXXXXXXXX
    2   0.190                            XXXXXX
    3   0.005                            X
    4   0.000                            X
    5   0.154                            XXXX
    6   0.185                            XXXXXX
    7   0.069                            XXX
    8  -0.124                        XXXX
    9  -0.183                       XXXXX
   10  -0.236                      XXXXXX
   11  -0.171                       XXXXX
   12  -0.125                        XXXX
   13  -0.004                            X
   14   0.111                            XXXX
   15   0.003                            X
   16  -0.126                        XXXX
   17  -0.218                       XXXXX

MTB > Lag C4 C5
MTB > Lag 2 C4 C6
MTB > NAME C5 'D4_R-1' C6 'D4_R-2'
```

Model 1:

```
MTB > Regress C4 2 C5 C6 C10 C11

The regression equation is

D4_R = -0.000201 + 0.603 D4_R-1 - 0.128 D4_R-2

54 cases used 6 cases contain missing values

Predictor        Coef       Stdev      t-ratio        p
Constant    -0.0002012   0.0006084          ?        ?
D4_R-1          0.6025      0.1384          ?        ?
D4_R-2         -0.1279      0.1379          ?        ?

s = ?
. . .

Unusual Observations
Obs.  D4_R-1         D4_R        Fit Stdev.Fit    Residual   St.Resid
 44  -0.0039     0.006710  -0.002528  0.000780    0.009238      2.11R
 57  -0.0085    -0.017191  -0.005400  0.001342   -0.011791     -2.78R
 58  -0.0172    -0.002866  -0.009474  0.002059    0.006608      1.67 X
 59  -0.0029    -0.000320   0.000271  0.002242   -0.000591     -0.15 X

R denotes an obs. with a large st. resid.
X denotes an obs. whose X value gives it large influence.
```

Model 2:

```
MTB > Regress C4 1 C5 C10 C11

The regression equation is
D4_R = -0.000232 + 0.528 D4_R-1

55 cases used 5 cases contain missing values

Predictor        Coef       Stdev      t-ratio        p
Constant    -0.0002319   0.0005974     -0.39    0.699
D4_R-1          0.5285      0.1160       4.55    0.000

s = 0.004418    R-sq = 28.1%    R-sq(adj) = 26.8%
. . .

Unusual Observations
Obs.  D4_R-1         D4_R        Fit Stdev.Fit    Residual   St.Resid
 16   0.0129     0.003813   0.006591  0.001654   -0.002778     -0.68 X
 44  -0.0039     0.006710  -0.002299  0.000723    0.009009      2.07R
 57  -0.0085    -0.017191  -0.004715  0.001112   -0.012476     -2.92R
 58  -0.0172    -0.002866  -0.009317  0.002038    0.006450      1.65 X

R denotes an obs. with a large st. resid.
X denotes an obs. whose X value gives it large influence.
```

```
MTB > NAME C10 'ST.RES' C11 'FITTED' C12 'NSCORE'
MTB > Plot C10*C11
```

```
MTB > TSPlot C10     ⟶
```

```
MTB > Copy C10 C14;
SUBC>   Use 6:60.
MTB > Runs C14

    C14 .

    K =      0.0034

    The observed no. of runs =   24
    The expected no. of runs =   28.0545
    31 Observations above K   24 below
            The test is significant at   0.2620
            Cannot reject at alpha = 0.05

MTB > ACF C10
ACF of ST.RES
            -1.0 -0.8 -0.6 -0.4 -0.2  0.0  0.2  0.4  0.6  0.8  1.0
            +----+----+----+----+----+----+----+----+----+----+
   1   0.064                              XXX
   2  -0.051                              XX
   3  -0.131                            XXXX
   4  -0.102                            XXXX
   5   0.137                              XXXX
   6   0.153                              XXXXX
   7   0.081                              XXX
   8  -0.162                          XXXXX
   9  -0.081                            XXX
  10  -0.181                         XXXXXX
  11  -0.027                             XX
  12  -0.097                            XXX
  13  -0.010                             X
  14   0.199                              XXXXXX
  15   0.011                              X
  16  -0.082                            XXX
  17  -0.218                         XXXXX
```

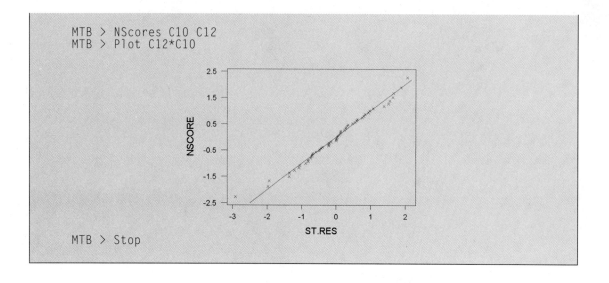

```
MTB > NScores C10 C12
MTB > Plot C12*C10
```

```
MTB > Stop
```

Exercises for Section 12.4

12.6 Suppose you are trying to model the monthly time series variable y, and suppose you have obtained a regression model linking the lag 12 difference of y, D12_Y, to its first lag, D12_Y$_{-1}$,

$$D12\_Y = 0.09 + 0.31(D12\_Y_{-1}) + e$$

Rewrite this equation in terms of y, that is, with y on the left-hand side of the equation and lags of y on the right-hand side.

12.7 Suppose you are trying to model the quarterly time series variable y, and suppose you have obtained a regression model linking the lag 4 difference of y, D4_Y, to its first four lags, D4_Y$_{-1}$, D4_Y$_{-2}$, D4_Y$_{-3}$, and D4_Y$_{-4}$

$$D4\_Y = b_0 + b_1(D4\_Y_{-1}) + b_2(D4\_Y_{-2}) + b_3(D4\_Y_{-3}) + b_4(D4\_Y_{-4}) + e$$

Rewrite this equation in terms of y; that is, with y on the left-hand side of the equation and lags of y on the right-hand side.

Exercises for Section 12.5

12.8 This problem shows that choice of base quarter in Section 12.5 was arbitrary. Using quarter 4 as a base, regression model 4 in Figure 12.27 was

$$\text{Fitted LS} = 11.2 + (0.0168)\text{TIME} - (0.446)\text{Q1} - (0.395)\text{Q2} - (0.271)\text{Q3}$$

How would the coefficients change if quarter 1 were chosen as a base quarter? (Do not use Minitab.)

12.9 This problem is a continuation of Exercise 11.2, page 572.
a Get a prediction model for NUMBER using *time* as the predictor variable in a simple regression. What does the Durbin-Watson statistic suggest? Do the diagnostic checks. What concerns do you have about this model?
b Contrast the prediction model in (a) with the random walk model in Exercise 11.2(a). Which one do you prefer? Why?

12.10

Supplementary Exercises

12.10 This problem shows that choice of base quarter in Section 12.5 was arbitrary. Using quarter 4 as a base, regression model 4 in Figure 12.27 was

$$\text{Fitted LS} = 11.2 + (0.0168)\text{TIME} - (0.446)\text{Q1} - (0.395)\text{Q2} - (0.271)\text{Q3}$$

How would the coefficients change if quarter 2 were chosen as a base quarter? (Do not use Minitab.)

12.11 Why cannot we use the variable QUARTER directly as a predictor variable in the regressions in Section 12.5? Some of the discussion in Section 10.6 may be useful to answering this question.

12.12 In this exercise, you will analyze further the sales data for Marshall Field & Company, stored in ASCII file MFIELD.DAT. This exercise can be done using the figures in Section 12.3. Assuming that the lag 4 differences of the log of sales come from a random series and that their histogram is well approximated by a normal distribution, get a point prediction and a 95% prediction interval for sales in the first quarter 1976. In light of the diagnostic checks carried out in Section 12.3, how reliable are these predictions?

12.13 In this problem, you will examine the yearly number of dwelling starts in Canada for the period from 1948 to 1976. The 29 data values are taken from *Historical Statistics of Canada*, 2nd Edition, Series A1. They are stored in column 4 of ASCII file CND_ANN.DAT. The data are:

90,194	90,509	92,531	68,579	83,246	102,409
113,527	138,276	127,311	122,340	164,632	141,345
108,858	125,577	130,095	148,624	165,658	166,565
134,474	164,123	198,878	210,415	190,525	233,653
249,914	268,529	222,123	231,456	273,203	

a Without doing any transformations, obtain a good time series model for the number of dwelling starts. You may want to consider differencing. Do the diagnostic checks.

    b Interpret the coefficients of the predictor variables, and obtain 95% confidence intervals for the corresponding process coefficients.

    c Using your model in (a), obtain a point prediction and a 95% prediction interval for the number of dwelling starts in 1977.

    d Using your model in (a), what is the probability that the number of dwelling starts will exceed 300,000 in 1977?

    e In light of your diagnostic checks in (a), are your answers to (b), (c), and (d) reliable? Describe your concerns if you have any.

Present your results and conclusions for (a) to (e) in a summary report, and attach your briefly annotated output. (Note: This report should refer to the *one* good model you identified in (a). Do *not* report your results for other models.)

12.14 Quarterly personal expenditures in Canada, given in millions of current dollars, from the first quarter of 1972 through the third quarter of 1993 are stored in the last 87 rows of column 5 of ASCII file CND_QRT.DAT. The data are as follows.

14,118	15,912	15,559	17,432	16,148	18,065	17,737	20,119
18,826	21,156	20,998	23,251	21,708	24,159	24,330	27,369
24,966	28,032	27,683	30,819	28,179	30,607	30,938	33,831
31,237	34,190	34,435	37,565	35,026	38,290	38,178	41,896
38,864	42,378	43,172	48,002	44,681	49,126	48,851	53,533
48,098	52,692	52,509	57,210	52,624	57,563	58,103	63,162
58,676	62,975	61,944	68,050	63,025	68,268	68,425	74,785
68,757	74,336	74,269	80,116	73,739	80,664	80,604	87,762
80,342	87,228	87,096	95,271	86,626	95,578	95,034	101,695
94,272	99,842	99,533	106,029	96,030	103,640	102,734	107,946
98,950	104,871	104,781	110,934	101,112	108,433	108,065	

    a Obtain a good prediction model for expenditures. In finding this model, consider whether it is necessary to transform the data. Briefly describe any concerns the diagnostic checks reveal about your model.

    b Give a point prediction and a 95% prediction interval for expenditures in the fourth quarter 1993.

    c How reliable are your predictions in (b), given your concerns in (a)?

Present your results and conclusions for (a) to (c) in a summary report, and attach your briefly annotated output.

12.15 This problem concerns sales of motor homes by Winnebago Industries during a time period in which the value of the company's common stock went from virtually nothing to nearly a billion dollars (at the price level of the early 1970s). The data are monthly unit sales from

November 1966 to February 1972. The data, stored in ASCII file WINNEBAG.DAT, are as
follows:

61	48	53	78	75	58	146	193
124	120	134	99	130	166	168	267
314	432	355	384	232	235	293	242
248	236	209	358	352	406	562	389
416	493	409	328	222	195	156	439
671	874	558	621	628	652	495	344
405	586	403	700	837	1,224	1,117	1,214
762	846	1,228	937	1,396	1,174	628	1,753

a   Use the untransformed data to obtain an autoregression model using the first and 12th
lags. Carry out the diagnostic checks.

b   Using a natural log transformation, obtain an autoregression model using the first and
12th lags. Carry out the diagnostic checks.

c   Using your most satisfactory model from (a) and (b), find a prediction for sales in March
1972. Get both a point prediction and a 90% prediction interval. How reliable is this prediction in light of the diagnostic checks?

12.16   Column 1 of ASCII file CND_MNTH.DAT contains the variable CREDIT, the monthly
amount of outstanding consumer credit (in millions of dollars), for department stores in
Canada. The data cover the period from September 1983 to July 1989. The data source is Series B122 in the Bank of Canada Review. Obtain the appropriate Minitab output to answer
the following questions.

a   Would a random walk model be reasonable for these data? Be specific and do the diagnostic checks.

b   Assuming the random walk model is appropriate and assuming normality, provide a
point prediction and a 95% prediction interval for August 1989.

c   On the basis of the time series plot and autocorrelation plot for the lag 1 differences of
credit, D_C, which lags should be considered for inclusion in an autoregression model?

d   Obtain regression model 1 in which D_C is regressed on its 12th lag. Do the diagnostic
checks for this model. What concerns do you have?

e   Assuming regression model 1 is appropriate, calculate a 95% prediction interval for outstanding consumer credit in August 1989.

f   Given the concerns you expressed in (a) and (d), how accurate do you think the results in
(b) and (e) are? Which one of the prediction intervals is more accurate?

g   Obtain regression model 2 in which CREDIT is regressed on its first, second, 12th and
13th lags. Do the diagnostic checks for this model. What concerns do you have? Contrast
this model with the forecasting approach of regression model 1.

h   Assuming all the diagnostic checks are passed for regression model 2, calculate a 95%
prediction interval for August 1989.

i   Assume all the diagnostic checks are passed for regression model 2. Can you calculate a
point prediction for September 1989? Can you obtain a 95% prediction interval for September 1989?

j Assuming all the diagnostic checks are passed for regression model 2, can you estimate the probability that the amount of outstanding consumer credit in August 1989 will exceed the amount in July 1989? If yes, obtain the probability. If no, what additional information do you need?

12.17 Consider the data for U.S. sales (in $1,000) of Lydia E. Pinkham Medicine Company for 1907 to 1960, stored in column 1 of ASCII file LYDIA.DAT.
  a Obtain regression model 1, where sales are related to its first three lags. Do the diagnostic checks, and briefly evaluate the model.
  b Obtain regression model 2, where sales are related to its first two lags. Do the diagnostic checks, and briefly evaluate the model.
  c What statistical justification is there to prefer model 2 to model 1?
  d Using regression model 2, find a 95% confidence interval for the coefficient of the first lag of sales. Interpret this interval.

12.18 A forecasting model was developed for monthly sales of a large hardware store. Sales were known to be quite seasonal. Sales, denoted y, were measured in $1,000. It was found that the 12th difference of y, $D12\_Y = y - y_{-12}$, could be well modeled by an autoregression that uses the first and third lags of $D12\_Y$ as predictor variables. Denoting these lags by $D12\_Y_{-1}$ and $D12\_Y_{-3}$, the estimated autoregression equation was

$$\text{Fitted } D12\_Y = 18.0 + 0.25(D12\_Y_{-1}) + 0.30(D12\_Y_{-3})$$

and the standard deviation around the regression equation was $s = 80$. Sales for the 24-month period from July 1991 to June 1993 were

1,380	1,260	1,250	1,670	1,970	890	790	1,000	1,200	1,670	1,600	1,470
1,390	1,370	1,360	1,740	2,200	980	1,040	860	1,380	1,850	1,660	1,730

Assuming that the usual regression assumptions are justified, answer the following questions.
  a Using the forecasting model, obtain a point prediction for sales in July 1993 and a 90% prediction interval.
  b What is the probability that sales in July 1993 will exceed sales in June 1993?
  c Rewrite the estimated autoregression equation for $D12\_Y$ as an equation linking y to its relevant lags. In particular, list the relevant lags of y and their coefficients.

12.19 ASCII file DAYTON.DAT contains quarterly financial data of Dayton-Hudson Corporation, a U.S. retailing firm. The data cover the period from 1975 to 1983. The fiscal year end is January 31; the first quarter covers February through April; etc. The data are given in George Foster, *Financial Statement Analysis,* 2nd Edition, Prentice-Hall, 1986, page 219. Data are available on two variables, (1) revenues and (2) net earnings, both in millions of dollars. Obtain a 1-quarter-ahead forecasting model for the net earnings data.

USING THE MENUS
IN MINITAB

Minitab is a very user-friendly statistical software package. Releases 9 and 10 for Windows have added powerful high-resolution graphics. If you are using an earlier release of Minitab, these high-resolution graphics may not be available to you, but you will still be able to use Minitab's many features for the analysis of data. The main purpose of this appendix is to describe how to use Minitab's menus in Release 10. Menus were also available in Releases 8 and 9. There are very few differences in the structure of the menus between Releases 9 and 10 that are relevant to this book. There are, however, several differences betweeen Releases 8 and 10. If you are using Release 8, it will not be difficult to adapt to these differences.

We will assume that you have loaded Minitab Release 10 for Windows into the default directory, C:\MTBWIN. You should next load all the data files on the diskette accompanying this book into the default data subdirectory, C:\MTBWIN\DATA. If this subdirectory contains other files, they were put there during the installation of Minitab, and they are not needed for this book. All the files on the data diskette are ASCII files with the extension: .DAT. Once these data files are stored in the subdirectory C:\MTBWIN\DATA, you are ready to start using Minitab in Windows.

Minitab can be run with menu commands or session commands. This book mainly uses menu commands.

There are four main windows in Minitab: Session, Data, History, and Info. An additional window will be created during your session for each high-resolution graph you generate.

1. The *Session* window lists the results of your Minitab session, including any output, *except for high-resolution graphics.* If you run Minitab with menus, Minitab records the equivalent commands in the Session window. You can also bypass the menus and dialogue boxes by typing commands directly in the Session window.

2. The *Data* window contains the data you are analyzing in your Minitab session in the form of a simple worksheet. The worksheet consists of rows and columns. The columns are labeled C1, C2, etc. Each column contains the values for a variable in your data set; it consists of several rows, each containing a value on the variable for a particular unit in your sample. If necessary, the data can be easily modified in the Data window.

3. The *History* window contains all the commands from the Session window. You can copy and paste commands from the History window into the Session window to enter commands previously executed in your session.

4. The *Info* window contains summary information on your current worksheet in the Data window.

In Minitab, you can choose from nine menus—File, Edit, Manip, Calc, Stat, Graph, Window, Editor, and Help:

1. The *File* menu allows you to select files for the worksheet in the Data window, to save worksheets into a file, to print files and windows, and to exit Minitab.

2. The *Edit* menu lets you edit cells in the worksheet.

3. The *Manip* menu lets you manipulate entire columns in the worksheet.

4. The *Calc* menu allows you to do mathematical calculations with the columns. You can compute simple statistics, both by column and by row. You can also generate random data from certain distributions.

5. In the *Stat* menu, you can invoke a large variety of statistical methods. Some of these are discussed in this book.

6. High-resolution graphics are generated in the *Graph* menu.

7. You can use the *Window* menu to display the windows and to choose a window to be active.

8. The *Editor* menu gives you additional editing capabilities.

9. You can use the *Help* menu to get on-line help on Minitab.

We use several typographical conventions in this book:

File ▸ Exit   denotes a menu command, in this case, open the *File* menu and choose *Exit*. Another example is: *Stat ▸ Calc ▸ Column Statistics* means open the *Stat* menu, then open the *Calc* submenu, then choose *Column Statistics*.

ALL CAPITALS   denotes a Minitab session command or subcommand, such as READ.

Most figures in this book were generated with Minitab. The Minitab menu or session commands necessary to generate some of these figures are given in the section "Using Minitab for Windows" at the end of most chapters. Whenever new commands are introduced, they are briefly annotated.

The following list contains the Minitab commands in Release 10 for Windows that were introduced in this book. Minitab has many other commands. Each submenu introduced in the book is listed under the corresponding main menu with a brief explanation and a page reference to related material in the text.

File

Save Worksheet As   page 88

[save data in ASCII, Minitab, or other formats]

Other Files

Import ASCII Data   page 86

[enter data into the Minitab worksheet from an ASCII file]

Manip

Sort   page 197

[sort the data in a column and rearrange the rows in other columns accordingly]

Copy Columns   page 252

[copy columns to other columns. You can specify which rows to copy or which rows to omit, if necessary.]

Code Data Values   page 427

[recode the values of a variable]

Unstack   page 148

[unstack columns into several smaller columns]

Calc

Random Data   page 253

[generate random data from a variety of probability distributions]

Sample From Columns   page 118

[obtain a random sample of rows from a set of columns]

Normal   page 253

[generate random data from any normal distribution]

Integer   page 118

[generate random data from any given set of consecutive integers]

Probability Distributions

Normal   page 128

[compute cumulative distribution values, inverse cumulative distribution values, etc., for a normal distribution]

      NAME

        [name variables. Always, always name your variables.]

      PRINT   page 198

        [print out columns on your worksheet onto the terminal screen]

    Data

        [move to Minitab's Data window, where you can operate on the data worksheet]

The following list refers to pages in the book where certain Minitab tasks are described:

"One must learn by doing the thing; for though you think you know it, you have no certainty until you try."
—Sophocles, ca. 450 B.C.E.

DESCRIPTION OF TERM PROJECT[1]

B.1

GENERAL INSTRUCTIONS FOR THE TERM PROJECT

General Comments

The ideas of statistics are very practical and a good way to learn them is by application. Hence work on an applied project on a problem of your own choosing will be important in this course.

The project will be completed in two installments. The first installment will emphasize design and planning; the second installment will emphasize data analysis and conclusions.

Setting for Projects

To obtain full value from a project, you should be close to the data so that you can understand the background and investigate problems pointed out by statistical analysis.

Your project should apply the ideas of the course in a business or other organizational setting. Such a project brings you into contact with "people problems" as well as data problems, which is desirable. You are expected to find the organization you will study, to contract with them, particularly with respect to access and time required of the organization's members, issues of confidentiality and deliverables.

---

[1]Thanks to Harry Roberts and Douglas Zahn for many ideas regarding this project description.

Letters of identification or assurances of confidentiality can be requested of the course instructor if required.

When thinking about a possible project, keep in mind that statistical tools are to be used in the project and that your solution is to be based on *quantitative* data. Your sample should contain *at least* 30 units, preferably 40 to 70, and every unit must be measured on at least two variables. (When the response variable is categorical—in particular, when it is dichotomous—you should try to have at least 100 units.)

The project should be based on a live, real-time application in a company or other organization—not on historical data for which most current employees are already hazy about background information. You should show initiative in getting into such a project. Your readings in the course, combined with your imagination, are likely to suggest interesting and unique possibilities.

One possibility for an organizational project is to investigate a quality-improvement question. Opportunities for a company to improve quality often appear first as problems: customers not receiving the right order, slow service, or needed items not being in inventory. Other examples of quality problems are discourteous service, customers receiving cold pizza, employees not receiving instruction on a new check-out procedure, and absenteeism. Some questions to ask in order to come up with this kind of a project are: Where in the process are there specifications for output or services? Are the specifications being met? Where can customers be served better? Where is scrap or waste being produced? Where is rework occurring on a regular basis?

Another possibility is to compare individual performance measures at successive periods of time. Thus sales, or perhaps per capita sales, for each of a number of territories this quarter may be compared against the corresponding sales last quarter. The aim is to see which territories are improving, which are holding their own, and which are losing ground.

Yet another possibility is to study the extent to which a process for which you are responsible is stable. This would entail operationally defining an important quality characteristic, obtaining a sequence of measurements for it, and analyzing the resulting time series.

If you choose a time series analysis, you must carry out the following steps:

1. Tentative model identification (for example, random walk).

2. Statistical fitting of the model (such as with regression).

3. Diagnostic checking of the fit (such as runs checks on residuals). Return to step 1 if not satisfied.

4. Control charts: retrospective identification of assignable causes in past data.

5. Prediction.

If any of the concepts just mentioned are unfamiliar, be assured that they will be covered in the course.

In some instances it may be possible to go beyond analysis to conduct actual experiments. If so, it is highly desirable to do so. Such experiments can be carried out to examine if a factor thought influential is really important.

Examples of Previous Term Projects

The following are titles of term projects done for this course in past years.

A Study of Clean Room Airborne Particulates

Customer Service in a Dispatch Operation at IBM

Analysis of Weight and Volume Data at Abitibi-Price

Document Translation for the Workers' Compensation Board

Order Processing at Cannon Book Distribution Ltd.

Supervisory Prediction Ability of Daily Harvest Completion Time

Absenteeism in the Medical Records Department at a Hospital

Study on Quality Control of the Production of Medical Oxygen

Invoice Discounting at Transamerica Commercial Finance

Analysis of Lease Turnaround Times

Effects of Oiling on Shell Egg Quality

Analysis of a Concrete Testing Program

A Study of Project Margins at a Construction Company

The Effect of a Short-Term Consumer Contest on Magazine Sales

Examining Trends in Project Size and Compliance with Budgets

Comparative Analysis of Gut Sutures from Italy and the United States

Information Security Compliance at Northern Telecom

Other potential term projects are:

Quality of Apartment Laundry Facilities

Delivery Service Experience with a Pizza Restaurant

Articles Stolen at Hotels

Length of Wait in Check-Out Line

Information about some of these projects and many others can be found in many examples and problems used in this book. A partial list is as follows:

Studies 1 to 5 in Chapter 1

Examples 2.6, 2.8; Section 2.11; Exercises 2.17, 2.26, 2.27

Examples 3.1, 3.2; Sections 3.7 and 3.11; Exercises 3.4, 3.14, 3.18, 3.22, 3.23

Examples 4.1, 4.2; Problem 4.2

Example 5.2; Section 5.11; Problems 5.1 and 5.2; Exercises 5.15, 5.27–5.32

Section 7.8; Problem 7.1; Exercise 7.32

Section 8.6; Problem 8.2; Exercises 8.12, 8.13, 8.16

Problem 9.1

Section 10.10; Problem 10.2; Exercises 10.8, 10.12–10.14

Section 11.9; Exercise 11.7

Problem 12.1

Examples of write-ups for the first installment are given in Section 3.7; examples for the last installment are given in Sections 5.11, 7.8, 8.6, and 10.10.

Housekeeping Details about the Project

In approaching your application, use the statistical tools available at the time each installment is due. However, fit the tools to your objective; you do not necessarily have to use all the tools we have studied. Also there is no penalty for reading ahead to tools we have not yet covered.

Before you start writing the first installment, make sure that the *data gathering effort is manageable*. It's best if *you* control this effort so that you won't depend on the efforts and time of others. You should gather data on *at least two, but no more than about five* variables, with the sample size being between 40 and 70, unless the response variable is categorical, in which case you'll need a sample size of at least 100.

If you will be late on any due date, a *written* "IOU" is expected *before* the due date in which you set an alternate date at which you will hand in the assignment.

Almost all students will do reasonably well on these projects and some will do outstanding work. The main hazard is procrastination: What is easy to digest in frequent small snacks can be indigestible in a single orgy, especially when data collection and computation are on the menu.

Preparation of Each Installment

Each installment should be typed, double spaced, on 8.5 × 11 inch paper, stapled flat, without using paper clips or binders, and it should have proper margins. Number all pages consecutively. If you use Minitab or other statistical software on this project, all relevant computer output is to be cut out and taped (or inserted with a word processor) onto regular paper. In any case, be sure to label the axes. Label your output as "Figure 1," "Figure 2," etc., and refer to it in the text as "Figure 1," "Figure 2," etc. Submission of computer output alone is *not* acceptable.

The installments are to be neat and legible, clearly written, and *concise*. (Some students are carried away by the ease with which the computer permits them to produce long papers; resist the temptation! Don't pad, ramble, regurgitate, or bluff.) Follow the rules of good writing within the context of the outlines provided in later sections. Include carefully edited computer output that will permit your instructor to check essential steps in reaching your conclusion; the essence of your work should be clear from the output alone, without reading your text. Do not hand in output from false starts, procedural mistakes, trips into statistical blind alleys, or statistical models that didn't pan out. Above all, don't give a play-by-play account of your experiences!

When you use Minitab, you may want to use the command OUTFILE to record the output from your main statistical analysis, then write or type most or all explanatory text onto the computer output. Use of a word processor is convenient for this purpose; you can also correct procedural errors in the computer output at the same time that you are typing in the text.

Be careful in handling and saving your data files. When you save a worksheet repeatedly, you will rewrite the old file if you give the same name. Usually you will want to do this, but if not, give a different name.

B.2

INSTRUCTIONS FOR THE PROJECT PROPOSAL (INSTALLMENT 1)

Even though the following outline may not suit your writing style perfectly, you must follow it point by point to simplify your report. Note that terms with precise statistical interpretations are **bold** in the following outline. When using a term that has a statistical meaning, be sure that your use is appropriate with this statistical meaning.

Project Title

1. Summary

   1.1   What is the real-world problem you propose to study? Describe the organizational setting and give sufficient background information. (What part of what process in what system do you propose to study?)

   1.2   What managerial questions (stated in question format and using nonstatistical terminology) relating to this problem do you propose to study? If there are several managerial questions, number them so that you can refer to them in later sections.

   What statistical questions correspond to these managerial questions? These questions should use precise statistical terminology, and they should be operational. List either the **population** or the **process, variables,** and **parameters** in these questions. Their description is not necessary here. (Sometimes it may be convenient to have several statistical questions correspond to one managerial question.)

   1.3   Of what use is it to a manager to study these questions?

1.4 For each managerial question, what is your current best guess at an answer?

2. Statistical Details

2.1 Most likely, you will be doing either a **cross-sectional** study of a **population** or a **time series** study of a **process.**

If you are doing a **cross-sectional** study, give an **operational definition** of the **population** you will study to address the managerial questions. Be sure to specify:

i The **unit** in the **population** (To help you think about what this unit is, remember that you will have measurements for two or more **variables** on each unit in your **sample.**)

ii The location of your **population of units** in time and space

iii Whether the **population size** is known or unknown, giving its value if it is known

Note that your answers to (i)–(iii) may differ from one managerial question to another.

If you are doing a **time series** study, give an **operational definition** of the **process** you will study to address the managerial questions. Be sure to specify:

i The **unit** in the **process** (To help you think about what this unit is, remember that you will have measurements for two or more **variables** on each unit in your **sample.**)

ii The location of your **process of units** in time and space

Note that your answers to (i) and (ii) may differ from one managerial question to another.

2.2 For each statistical question, state how many **variables** you will measure on each **unit,** mention each variable name, and briefly describe its use. (Is it the **response variable**—that is, the primary variable of interest? Is it a variable that should be **accounted for** because it may influence the response variable and thus your conclusions?) The total number of variables measured should agree with (3.5).

2.3 For each statistical question, what statistical aspects of either your **population** or **process** (such as **distribution shape, parameters, percentiles**) are of interest to you? What is your current best *numerical* guess about these aspects?

3. Data Collection Plans

3.1 If you are doing a **cross-sectional** study and are not taking a **census,** you should obtain your sample of units by **simple random sampling.** Describe how you will accomplish this. Saying you will take a random sample is not enough. Describe the **frame.**

If you are doing a **time-series** study, describe how you will obtain your sample.

What **sample size** will you use? How did you select this number? (In *all* projects, the sample size should be at least 30, and preferably 40 to 70. If your **response variable** is **categorical,** your sample size should be at least 100.) Are you going to do an **experimental** or an **observational** study? If you are doing an experimental study, how will you use **randomization**?

3.2 Give **operational definitions** for each of your **variables.** How will you measure your variables with as much reliability and validity and as little bias as possible? (You should measure at least two variables, but not more than about five.) If data are collected by more than one observer, how will you verify that all observers are measuring in the same way throughout the study? For each variable, give the **scale of measurement** (**categorical, ordinal,** or **quantitative**), and indicate the possible range of values on that scale.

3.3 If you plan to use a questionnaire, describe how you will get it to your **subjects.** If you propose to gather data directly from people by telephone interview, face-to-face interview, or some other method, describe explicitly how you will approach these individuals and what you will say to them. Give a verbatim script. Include a copy of your questionnaire.

   i Clearly inform potential participants about the nature of the study before starting your interview. Use no deceit. Do not place your participants at risk in any way.

   ii In *all* cases, clearly offer the potential participant a chance *not* to participate.

If you do *not* plan to use a questionnaire, describe in enough detail how you will collect your data so that another person could read your description and gather the same data.

3.4 Critique your data collection plans. (Might you encounter problems of confounding? Does somebody else have control over the data gathering efforts? etc.) What do you think is the greatest weakness at this time in your proposed study?

3.5 Present a table with fictional data on all variables for several units, where the numbers are such as might result from your study. (This table should look like a Minitab worksheet.)

4. Data Analysis Plans

    4.1 For each statistical question, what **graphical** procedures do you plan to use to describe your data? Be specific. State what procedures you will use with what variables. Using fictional data, present a mock-up of each graph you propose to use in an appendix, with the *axes labelled.*

    4.2 For each statistical question, what numerical **descriptive statistics** do you plan to compute for what variables?
        Using appropriate tools discussed so far in the course, *be sure to indicate how data from all variables you propose to measure will be used.* If you are gathering data, use it. If you cannot see how to use it, do not gather it.

5. Data Collection

Are you going to collect your data on the premises of or from the records of a business?
    If yes, give the business's name and address, and, if applicable, give the name, title, and phone number of the person who has given you permission to collect and use the data.
    If no, how will you collect your data?

6. Appendixes

The project proposal should be followed by separate appendixes for

    Questionnaire (if appropriate)

    Verbatim script (if appropriate)

    (Mock-up) Sample of values

    (Mock-up of) Graphs

B.3

INSTRUCTIONS FOR THE FINAL REPORT (INSTALLMENT 2)

When preparing your final report, you should follow the instructions on page 642.
    The cover page of the final report should contain the project title and the following signed statement:

I (we), the undersigned, certify that I (we) gathered the data analyzed in this report in the manner I (we) have described. I (we) also certify that the actual composition of this report and the associated computer work were done by me (us) and are my (our) original work.

Typed Name(s)   Signature(s)

An outline for the final report is as follows. To guide you in your final analysis and to help in reading your report, you must follow this outline point by point. Note that terms with a precise statistical interpretation are bold in the following outline. When using a term that has a statistical meaning, be sure that your use is appropriate with this statistical meaning.

Part I   Executive summary, single-spaced (a report to an effective, intelligent manager who has ***not*** taken a statistics course.)

Prepare a summary (less than *one page*) of your project and its findings, answering the following questions in numbered paragraphs:

1. Briefly describe the setting of your project, and then state the managerial questions you studied. Number these questions so that you can refer back to them if necessary.

2. How did you study them?

3. What are your findings? How do they compare to what you expected to find in installment 1? Comment on any differences seen.

4. What action(s) do you recommend on the basis of your study and its findings?

Part II.   Statistical summary, double-spaced. (This part should be about five to 15 pages long, not counting appendixes, tables and figures. It should be a report to your statistician supervisor who has taken a course on statistics like this one. Be concise.)

Address each of the following questions or requests in numbered paragraphs. If there are multiple questions or requests, answer only the relevant one(s). If you give several managerial questions in (I.1), you should have answers to each within each paragraph.

1. For each managerial question listed in (I.1), give the corresponding statistical question(s), making sure that they are in operational terms. Refer to the parameters, etc. discussed in (II.6) below.

2. Describe the **unit** in your study. (To help you think about what this unit is, remember that you will have measurements for two or more variables on each unit in the sample. Each unit is usually described by one row in a Minitab worksheet.)

3. If you did a **cross-sectional** study, briefly describe your **population.** Where is it located in time and space, and what is the **population size**? What is the **frame**? Was the population from which you sampled identical to the population of interest?

If you did a **time-series** study, briefly describe your **process** and where it is located in time and space.

4. What sampling scheme did you use? Describe it. (Was your **sample** actually a **census**? Did you use **simple random sampling** from a frame? Did you sample consecutive units generated by a **process**? etc.) If you used a questionnaire, include it as an appendix.

5. How many **variables** were measured on each **unit**? (Remember that you should have at least two, but no more than about five variables.) Briefly describe them. How were the variables measured (in dollars, thousands of dollars, kilograms, etc.)? Which variable(s) were of main interest?

6. If you did a **cross-sectional** study, what were the **population parameters** of interest for which variables? (For example, were you interested in the **mean, standard deviation, difference between two means, coefficients in a regression equation,** etc.? Remember that, unless a **census** was taken, a **parameter** is a number that is unknown and must be estimated from a **random sample.**) What other aspects of the population (for example, **distribution shape**) were you interested in?

   If you did a **time-series study,** what were the **process parameters** of interest for which variables? (See the examples of parameters in the last paragraph.) Remember that a process parameter is useful in a **model** of the process, but that it is unknown and must be estimated from a **sample.** What other aspects of the process (for example, **distribution shape** or **random** process) were you interested in?

7. Describe your **sample of units.** How many units are in your sample? In an appendix, give a listing of all the data you used (and only the data you did use) to answer the statistical questions listed in (II.1). (Units should correspond to rows and variables to columns. This listing should be followed by **dotplots** and **descriptive statistics** for all **quantitative** variables, and by **tallies** for all **ordinal** and **categorical** variables.) Did you discard any units for the purposes of your analysis? Which ones and why? (Data on discarded units must be included in the listing.)

8. Describe and discuss your data analysis, calculations, graphs, and figures, and present them in an appendix. You should only describe the analysis relevant to answer the questions listed in (II.1). (Any outlier or any observation outside the control limits should be examined for a **special cause,** and the results should be discussed. If a process is **not random,** the nonrandom pattern should be described and reasons for it should be sought.)

   Do *not* hand in output from false starts, procedural mistakes, trips into statistical blind alleys, or statistical models that did not pan out. Above all, don't give a play-by-play account of your experiences!

   Remember to number all figures and tables, and to label the axes of your figures. (See p. 642 for detailed instructions.)

9. First, describe your conclusions about the statistical questions listed in (II.1), and then describe how these conclusions help you answer the corresponding managerial question.

   Using technical statistical terminology, state the generalizations you can make from your **sample,** that is, how does your work in (II.8) help you with answering the statistical questions described in (II.1)? (If an **inferential** statement will help answer your questions, give the **point and interval estimates,** if possible. If a forecast or **prediction** will, give the **point prediction and a prediction interval.**)

   Discuss the implications of having discarded units, as mentioned in (II.7). Discuss the implications of having a nonrandom process.

   What limitations are there on these generalizations? Does your **model** make sense? (For example, is there a contextual rationale for any **predictor variables** you may have used in a **regression**?)

10. Describe any notable events that occurred throughout your study and may have influenced the interpretation of your data analysis.

11. Suppose that at some time in the future you confront a question similar to the one that gave rise to this project. What have you learned from this project that will influence your approach to the future question? Would you use such a modified approach in the future, even if it was not part of a course requirement?

   Unless your instructor advises otherwise, you should hand in one copy of Installment 2, to be graded and returned to you, and copies of both installments for your instructor's files.

Solutions to Selected Exercises

Chapter 2

2.4 **a** The total number of men was $710 + 520 + 198 + 204 = 1{,}632$; the total number of men hired was $710(.394) + 520(.354) + 198(.126) + 204(.118) = 513$. Therefore, the proportion of men hired was $513/1{,}632 = 31.4\%$. A similar calculation can be made for the women.

      b For example, the advertisements could be geared differentially to men and women.

2.5 The results should be stratified by subscriptions category:

	Gift	Previous Renewal	Direct Mail	Subscription Service	Catalog Agent	Overall
			Renewals (%)			
Jan.	81%	79	60	21	8.7	51
Feb.	80	76	51	14	4.4	64

Therefore, there is no reason to be pleased: Renewal rates are down in every category.

2.6 **a** The population was regular drinkers of Coca-Cola in 1976. The unit (subject) was a regular Coca-Cola drinker. The response variable was preference for Coke or Pepsi.

      b None was explicitly mentioned. There was an order effect: all drank Coke *first, then* Pepsi.

      c This was an experimental study, in which each subject was given two stimuli to be compared. Because of the order effect, it is a very poorly conducted experimental study with no control group.

      d There was an order effect. All subjects drank Coke first and then Pepsi.

      e Use two experimental groups to avoid the order effect. The first group would drink Q first and then M, and the second group would drink M first and then Q. If subjects were randomly assigned to the two groups, the study would be experimental, controlling for the order effect.

2.7 The scale here is ordinal. Once responses have been recorded, all that is known is which ordered category they were in. It does not make sense to talk about numerical differences among the ordered categories.

2.8 a You are interested in the number of visits to a showroom on the various days of the week. In order to plan for proper staffing at the showroom, you would be interested in the busiest day, the least busy day, etc. Here the coding of days from 1 to 7 is entirely arbitrary; a coding of Monday = 2, Tuesday = 5, Wednesday = 1, Thursday = 4, Friday = 3, Saturday = 7 and Sunday = 6 would have been just as good.

  b A task is started each Monday morning, and it is to be completed by Sunday. The completion day is recorded. Here completion day is actually a proxy for the number of days it took to complete the task.

2.9 a The population was readers of Ann Landers' column when it was run who are parents. The unit (subject) was a reader who is a parent. The response variable was "would do it again" (yes, no). The sample is not a random sample. Self-selection was used.

  b Since the sample selection procedure (self-selection) was likely to be biased, the sample probably is, too. People with negative feelings can be expected to respond more than others, so 70% may be too high.

2.10 a The population is the public, but it is difficult to pin down precisely what this means. The unit (subject) is a "member of the public." This is not random sampling, but self-selection.

  b They are probably biased because of the self-selection. People with strong views are more likely to respond than others. It is not clear that positive and negative views will cancel out correctly.

2.11 a The population consists of the households in the particular telephone-book area. The unit is a household. (It may also be reasonable to view the person who answers the phone as the unit.)

  b Several groups of people may be underrepresented. Among them, (1) people without phones (they may be poorer on average), (2) people without a listing (they may be wealthier), (3) people who have new phone numbers because they recently moved (the mobile segment of the population may not be a cross-section, since some groups may be over-represented, such as young adults who move more).

  c i Random dialing can reach people with unlisted numbers, but may be illegal.

    ii Going from household to household may be difficult.

2.12 a The population consists of applicants for public housing during a particular time period. The unit (subject) is an applicant. The response variable is family stability.

  b The factor mentioned was "accepted to live in public housing (yes, no)." Other factors are the selection method for successful applicants, household size, and single parent (yes, no).

  c This is not an experimental study. The applicants were (presumably) *not* randomly accepted for public housing.

  d The treatment is "lives in public housing." The control is "does not live in public housing."

  e The selection method for successful applicants may rely on judgments about family stability; that is, only applicants judged to be stable are accepted.

2.13 a The unit is a document. The population consists of all documents translated between October 86 and October 87. The frame is a list of all 12,411 documents.

  b Turnaround time is the response variable. Document type is used for stratification. Document length and complexity may have an effect on the response variable.

2.14 a The unit is a document. The process consists of translation of documents at the translation bureau.

  b As in 2.13(b).

2.15 *Study 1:* Depending on the setup, this study could be viewed as either cross-sectional or time series. Overall, however, a time series study is more appropriate.

a   The process consists of keeping the clean rooms free of dust particles. Cleanliness is to be achieved day in and day out. The unit would be a day or other such time period, with separate data collected for every clean room. Due to measurement problems, it is not economically feasible (nor is it necessary) to count the number of particles in a whole room. A small part of the room, say 1 cubic meter, could be examined instead.

b   The response variable is the particle count.

Study 3:   This is a cross-sectional study.

a   The population consists of the 9,000 part-time registrants at Durham College during the fall semester 1989, and the frame is a listing of these 9,000 registrants. A unit (subject) is one of these registrants.

b   The important variables measure the responses to the five questions asked. It is not clear from the description if any one of these five variables is the response; all variables could possibly be considered response variables.

2.16 **a**   The population consists of voters in the legislator's district. The variable measured is "in favor/not in favor of abortion bill." The sample consists of self-selected constituents. A source of probable bias is the self-selection of the sample: People with strong views are more likely to write to their legislator.

b   The population consists of Chinese residents of the large city. Several variables related to police service are measured. The sample consists of adults at 500 addresses chosen. Sources of probable bias are (1) The sample is not random as it represents only those people living in predominantly Chinese neighborhoods. Chinese residents of other parts of the city are excluded. (2) The survey is administered by a police officer, which may affect the candor of responses.

2.17   This is a study of the population of the 96 markets in 1987/1988. Thus a market is the unit. Even though two yearly measurements were made on each market (that is, there is a time element), it's best to view this study (as carried out) as characterizing the 96 markets as a cross-section.

2.18   This study examines a process for which a time series of the most recent 50 units was observed. The unit is a printing order, and the categorical variable is "new or repeat printing order." The company is not interested in only these 50 units, but wants to say something about units in the near future. If there is, for example, an increasing trend to the proportion of new orders, the company would want to know this and would want to project this trend into the future.

Chapter 3

3.2   The "Others" category includes the countries for which data are not specifically given, and should be on the *right* of the Pareto diagrams. The major change between 1961 and 1981, evident from the diagrams, is the increased importance of Asian immigration.

3.3 **a**   The variable of interest, income, is suitable for a histogram in which midpoints are $20,000 apart. The variable is therefore quantitative, and there is an implied order to the ranges. A Pareto diagram would be inappropriate.

b   The variable "color" is a categorical variable here, so a Pareto diagram would be suitable, listing the colors in the order 4, 5, 2, 1, and 3.

c   Satisfaction is an ordinal variable, and it would be inappropriate to list the categories in any other order. A Pareto diagram would be inappropriate.

d   The variable "day of the week" is a categorical variable here, so the order of the days of the week can be arbitrarily rearranged in such a way that a Pareto diagram would result: Saturday, Friday, Wednesday, Thursday, Tuesday, Monday.

3.4   **a**   The unit is a market. This is a census of all markets in Ontario in 1987 and 1988.

b,c There is a fairly strong positive relationship, but it is in no way perfect. It does appear that row 86 is unusual: the market share exceeds 200% in both years, so it may be wise to ignore this market. Even then the correlation is still high, but there appear to be several markets that are somewhat different from the bulk of the markets. Whether a correlation of 0.879 is "high enough" is a judgment question that cannot be answered by the data.

d   There is considerable bunching towards the smaller values, so the distribution is probably positively skewed.

3.5   The average is greater than the median. This is typical of positively skewed distributions.

3.6   **a**   Data set B is identical to data set A, except that there are three additional observations at the mean. Thus the standard deviation for data set B is smaller.

b   Data set A: $s = 19.36$; data set B: $s = 15.81$

3.7   The mean is 14, the median is 14, the mode is 14, the standard deviation is $\sqrt{58/8} = 2.693$, the variance is 7.25, and the range is $20 - 11 = 9$. Given the small size of the data set, it's difficult to tell if there is skewness or not. There may be a little positive skewness. The 10th percentile corresponds to observation $10(9 + 1)/100 = 1$, that is, its value is 11. The 25th and 60th percentiles are 12 and 14, and the 75th percentile is between 14 and 16.

3.8   **a**   Using the empirical rule for the standard deviation, 68% of observations are within 1 standard deviation of the mean, i.e., within 0.5 of 6.0 (between 5.5 and 6.5 mg).

b   The interval between 5.0 and 7.0 mg is the interval that extends 2 standard deviations around the mean. Therefore the empirical rule suggests that 95% of observations would fall within it.

c   Using the result in (b), 5% of values are outside the interval from 5 to 7 mg in a symmetrical way, so 2.5% are below 5 mg. Therefore 97.5% are less than or equal to 7 mg, and 7 mg is the 97.5 percentile.

3.9   The units are: (a) square meter, (b) dollar squared, (c) dollar, (d) square meter, and (e) unit-free.

3.10   In the following table, useful summaries are denoted by an asterisk:

	Categorical	Ordinal	Quantitative
Mean			*
Median		*	*
Mode	*	*	*
St.Dev.			*

3.11   The results are as follows:

a $2 + 3 + 7 = 12$

b $2^2 + 3^2 + 7^2 = 62$

c $(2 - 4) + (3 - 4) + (7 - 4) = 0$

d $|2 - 4| + |3 - 4| + |7 - 4| = 6$

e $(2 - 4)^2 + (3 - 4)^2 + (7 - 4)^2 = 14$

3.12   **a**   The population consists of provinces; the unit is a province. It's not clear that either variable is the response variable; in a sense they both are.

b,e The correlation is $r = -0.627$.

c,d Since there is one unusual province among the 9 (British Columbia), the value of the correlation may have been considerably affected by this outlier.

3.13
a We do not know. It could be either a sample or a population. The unit is a student who graduated with an accounting major. The response variable is annual starting salary (in $1,000).
b The mean, mode, and median are 25.9, 26.4, and 25.9, respectively.
c The standard deviation is 0.962.
d The following table gives the frequencies:

Midpoint	Frequency	Midpoint	Frequency
24,250	1	26,250	4
24,750	3	26,750	2
25,250	1	27,250	0
25,750	3	27,750	2

e The 25th percentile corresponds to observation $25(16 + 1)/100 = 4.25$; that is, it is between 24.9 and 25.4. The 75th percentile is between 26.4 and 26.5.

3.14
a The process consists of arriving calls at the dispatch center. The unit is a day. (Note that the unit is *not* an individual call since data were not collected by call. The automatic equipment at IBM aggregated the data for all calls in a day, and it recorded only the aggregate values.) The response variable is total waiting time (WAIT).
b The time series pattern is nonrandom; it is at first decreasing and then increasing. Given this nonrandomness, the cross-sectional summaries in (c), (d), (e), and (g) are not really useful.
c There is slight positive skewness.
d The mode is 22, the median is 23, and the mean is 24. This relationship is to be expected for a positively skewed distribution of values.
e The range is $48 - 9 = 39$; the standard deviation is $s = 8.61$.
f The target is rarely met.
g Using the counting method, we find 13 of the 70 days to be below target, i.e., $\frac{13}{70} = 18.6\%$. Thus the percentage above target is $100 - 18.6 = 81.4$.
h This question cannot be answered since the data were not gathered by call; they were aggregated by day.
i The correlation between WAIT and STAFF is -0.579. All other correlations are small. It's hard to use any of these variables as an aid to future staffing.

Chapter 4

4.3
a We must standardize the value $540, yielding $z = (540 - 450)/90 = 1$. From Table 4.1, we have $F(1) = 0.8413$, so the answer is $1 - 0.1587$.
b The answer is the same as in (a), since the probability is negligible that an average monthly account balance value is exactly equal to $540.000000000...
c First find the probability that the balance is less than $495 by standardizing $495, $z = (495 - 450)/90 = 0.5$. From Table 4.1, we find that $F(0.5) = 0.6915$ is the desired probability. The probability that the balance is less than $585 is found similarly. Standardize $585, yielding $z = (585 - 450)/90 = 1.5$. From Table 4.1, the desired probability is $F(1.5) = 0.9332$. Therefore the answer is $0.9332 - 0.6915 = 0.2417$.
d We must standardize $405 and $585, yielding -0.5 and 1.5, respectively. Using Table 4.1, the required answer is $F(1.50) - F(-0.5) = 0.9332 - 0.3085 = 0.6247$.

4.4 **a** We must standardize 120, yielding $z = (120 - 100)/15 = 1.33$. Table 4.1 yields $F(1.33) = 0.9082$, so the answer is $1 - 0.9082 = 0.0918$.

       b Since the probability of running out of stock is to be just 1%, we must find the 99th percentile of the demand distribution. The 99th percentile from Table 4.1 is 2.33, so the required value is 2.33 standard deviations above the mean, $100 + 2.33(15) = 135$.

4.5 **a** Standardizing Eleanor's score, we get $(700 - 500)/100 = 2$. Standardizing Gerald's score, we get $(24 - 18)/6 = 1$. If the two populations are comparable, Eleanor has the higher score since her standardized score is higher.

       b **i** We must standardize 800, $z = (800 - 500)/100 = 3$. The proportion of scores above $z = 3$ is 0.0013 or 0.13%.

           ii Standardizing 400 yields $(400 - 500)/100 = -1$, and standardizing 500 yields 0. The required proportion now is $F(z = 0) - F(z = -1) = 0.50 - 0.16 = 0.34$ or 34%.

       c The proportion above $z = 1.65$ is 5%. Hence the cut-off point is $500 + 1.65(100) = 665$.

4.6 We need to find out for each shop: (1) what proportion of washers is usable, and (2) how much it is expected to cost to get, say, 1,000 usable washers. *Shop A:* To get the proportion usable, we must first standardize the specification limits, 0.45 and 0.55: $(0.45 - 0.50)/0.025 = -2.00$ and $(0.55 - 0.50)/0.025 = 2.00$. Using Table 4.1, we find that the usable proportion is $0.9772 - 0.0228 = 0.9544$. Since 1,000 washers cost \$1.00, 1,000 usable washers are expected to cost $1.00/0.9544 = \$1.048$. *Shop B:* The standardized specification limits are $(0.45 - 0.50)/0.028 = -1.79$ and $(0.55 - 0.50)/0.028 = 1.79$. Thus the usable proportion is $0.9633 - 0.0367 = 0.9266$. The expected cost is $0.90/0.9266 = \$0.9712$. Therefore Shop B offers a better deal.

4.7 In order for normality to be appropriate, 95% of values must be within 2 standard deviations of the mean, and 5% of values must be more than 2 standard deviations away from the mean, of which 2.5% are lower than a value 2 standard deviations below the mean. Similarly, almost all values are within 3 standard deviations of the mean. If the variable cannot have negative values and it has a normal distribution, then the value 0 must be sufficiently far below the mean; that is, the value 0 must standardize to about -3 or less. If 0 standardizes to -3 or less, then we have that $z = (0 - \text{Mean})/\text{St.Dev.} < -3$ or $\text{Mean}/\text{St.Dev.} > 3$. Normality thus cannot apply if the mean is less than 3 times the standard deviation.

4.8 C1 contains 100 values drawn randomly from a normal distribution; C2 contains 10 values drawn randomly from a normal distribution; C3 contains 100 values drawn randomly from a positively skewed distribution. This distribution is such that the logarithms are normal; C4 contains 100 values drawn randomly from a positively skewed distribution. This distribution is such that the square roots are normal; C5 contains 70 values randomly drawn from a negatively skewed distribution; C6 contains 49 values drawn randomly from a normal distribution. One outlier was added to them; C7 contains 70 values randomly drawn from a *Cauchy distribution,* a distribution that is extremely thick-tailed; C8 contains 40 values randomly drawn from an *exponential distribution.* (Such a distribution has a histogram that is highest at 0 and then decreases to the right—negative values are impossible. It is thus positively skewed); C9 contains 40 values, each randomly drawn from two different normal distributions; C10 contains 100 values drawn randomly from a *uniform distribution.* (Such a distribution has a histogram that has the same height over a given range. It is thin-tailed.)

4.9 (See the answers to Exercise 4.8.)

       a A logarithmic transformation works for C3. It does not work for C4, C5, C6, and C8.

       b A square root transformation works for C4. It does not work for C3, C5, and C8.

4.10 **a** Since the mean and standard deviation of the transformed values are 50 and 10, the 10th percentile of the transformed values is $50 + (-1.28)(10) = 37.2$, where -1.28 is obtained from Table 4.1. Transforming back to original units, the 10th percentile is $37.2^2 = 1,384$.

b   The untransformed value 3,000 transforms to $\sqrt{3,000} = 54.77$, which standardizes to $z = (54.77 - 50)/10 = 0.48$. Using Table 4.1, the proportion of values above 0.48 is $1 - 0.6844 = 0.3156$, which is the answer to the question.

Chapter 5

5.3   The numbers of runs are: (a) 6, (b) 5, (c) 3, and (d) 4.

5.4   The sequence of plus and minus signs is $+ + - + - - + - + +$; there are 7 runs.

5.5   An oscillating series is characterized by units close together in time tending to be far apart in value. This implies that, if successive values are connected, there are many *crossings* of the mean level, so the number of runs can be expected to be higher than for a random series.

5.6   The data are definitely not random. There is a very strong quarterly pattern. The runs test does not detect this pattern, but the test is overridden by the strong visual impression. The fact that the data are quarterly should alert you to the possibility of this cyclical pattern.

5.7   **a**   The limits 1.99 and 2.01 standardize to $z = (1.99 - 2.00)/0.005 = -2$ and 2. We can use Table 4.1 to find the proportion outside these limits to be $0.0228 + 0.0228 = 0.0456$.
   b   Using the new process mean, the limits 1.99 and 2.01 standardize to $z = (1.99 - 2.015)/0.005 = -5$ and -1, so the proportion inside these limits is $0.1587 - 0.0000 = 0.1587$.

5.8   **a**   The value 499 ml standardizes to $z = (499 - 500)/1.2 = -0.83$, so we can use Table 4.1 to find the proportion above 499 ml to be $1 - 0.21 = 0.79$.
   b   Yes, the variable "amount filled" must have a normal distribution. Otherwise, we could not have used the normal table.

5.9   (Read the answers to Exercise 4.8, which describe how the data were generated.)
   C1: Visual impression, control limits, and runs test all suggest randomness; C2: As for C1; C3: Visual impression and runs test suggest randomness, but there are values outside the control limits. Recall from Exercise 4.8 that the data are skewed, but their logarithms are normal. For the logarithmically transformed data, visual impression, control limits, and runs test all suggest randomness. This is an indication of the frequent problem in which data from a random process with a *skewed* histogram fall outside the control limits much more frequently than would be expected if the data followed a normal distribution; C4: As for C3, except that the square root transformation leads to normality; C5: Visual impression and runs test suggest randomness, but there are values outside the control limits. This is a negatively skewed distribution, and you see that data from a random process with a *negatively skewed* histogram can fall outside the control limits much more frequently than would be expected if the data followed a normal distribution; C6: The only noteworthy feature is that there definitely is one outlier; C7: Visual impression and runs test suggest randomness, but data fall outside the control limits. These data, however, were randomly drawn from an extremely thick-tailed distribution for which one would expect more data values to be far away from the mean than under a normal distribution; C8: Visual impression, runs test, and control limits all suggest randomness; C9: Visual impression suggests a level shift, but the runs test and control limits do not detect this. The data are not random; C10: Visual impression, runs test, and control limits all suggest randomness.

5.10   **a**   The visual impression is one of randomness. The runs test result is in the gray area, but all observations are within the control limits: $UCL = 1.42 + 3(3.405) = 11.64$, $LCL = -8.80$. Therefore, a random process is a useful model to describe the process generating the DIFFRNCE values.
   b   The normality assumption is reasonable, even though there is a slight indication of negative skewness.
   c   Estimates for the process mean and process standard deviation are 1.42 and 3.405, respectively, so the

value 0 standardizes to $z = (0 - 1.42)/3.405 = -0.42$. From the normal table, the percentile corresponding to $z = -0.42$ is 33.72%, and so the answer is $1.0000 - 0.3372 = 66.28\%$.

5.11 **a** The sequence plot of WAIT reveals a slightly downward pattern up to observation 50, and then a somewhat stable pattern for the last 20 observations. Thus the sequence does not appear random. The runs test result (p-value $= 0.0373$) is in the gray area.

b No. Judging from the normal probability plot, the distribution of WAIT is slightly positively skewed.

c The mean of WAIT is 24; the UCL is $24 + 3(8.6) = 49.8$; and the LCL $= -1.8$. [WAIT cannot take on negative values, but the LCL is negative, suggesting that the normal distribution is not adequate, as indicated in (b).]

d **a** The sequence decreases to about observation 20, and then it gently increases. The impression of nonrandomness is not strong. The runs test supports randomness with a p-value of 0.47.

b Normality looks OK, except for two outliers at low end.

c The mean of CALLS is 2,731; the UCL is $2,731 + 3(241) = 3,454$; the LCL is 2,008. Observation 20 is below the LCL. This also calls the randomness of the sequence into question: The process is judged not to be stable.

e **a** There appear to be three distinct segments to the sequence plot, observations 1 to 14, 15 to 28, and 29 to 70, suggesting nonrandomness. There is otherwise no unusual observation. The runs test supports nonrandomness with a p-value of 0.

b The normal probability plot suggests normality.

c The mean of STAFF is 25.7, the UCL is $25.7 + 3(3.0) = 34.7$, the LCL is 16.7, with no observations outside the control limits. Given the nonrandomness of the data, the control limits cannot be used for prediction purposes.

5.12 In order to do the analysis, we must obtain the difference in number of invoices paid between the new and the old processes. Since the data are recorded by clerk, this requires a little rearranging. Every day we want to subtract the number of invoices paid by the clerk using the old process from the number of invoices paid by the other clerk, who is using the new process. Process used is coded 0 (old) or 1 (new). If we change the coding for the old process from 0 to -1, the required difference can easily be found. Suppose the process used by clerk 1 is stored in variable PROC_1. Then the expression $[2(PROC\_1) - 1]$ will change PROC_1 $= 0$ to -1 and will leave PROC_1 $= 1$ unchanged. Letting PROC_2 be the process used by clerk 2, and INV_1 and INV_2 be the numbers of invoices paid by clerks 1 and 2, respectively, we can compute the required difference, DIFF_INV, as

$$DIFF\_INV = [2(PROC\_1) - 1]INV\_1 + [2(PROC\_2) - 1]INV\_2$$

The sequence plot of DIFF_INV does not reveal any time series pattern and suggests randomness. The runs test supports this (p-value $= 0.5448$). All values are within the control limits, UCL $= 12.24 + 3(10.01) = 42.27$ and LCL $= -17.79$. The dotplot of DIFF_INV suggests that the difference is mostly positive. The normal probability plot reveals that the distribution is roughly normal. So we can easily estimate the proportion of times when the new process is likely to lead to a larger number of invoices paid than the old process. Standardizing 0, we get $z = (0 - 12.24)/10.01 = -1.22$. From Table 4.1 or Minitab, we find $F(-1.22) = 0.1112$. Thus the proportion of times when the new process is likely to lead to a larger number of invoices paid is $1 - 0.1112 = 89\%$. Ignoring any costs of implementing the new procedure, choose the new procedure.

5.13 **a** The unit is a unit of time, a day.

b The mean is 20.7, the UCL is $20.7 + 3(2.49) = 28.17$, and the LCL is 13.23.

c The sequence does not look random. There seems to be a dip at the beginning of the series. The runs test is in the gray area.

d The mean and standard deviation of RENTED are 20.7 and 2.49, respectively. The value of RENTED corresponding to NSCORE = -1.2 is Mean + NSCORE(Std.Dev.) = $20.7 - 1.2(2.49) = 17.7$, and the value corresponding to NSCORE = 1.2 is 23.7. The data distribution is slightly negatively skewed.

e   For a random process, the best guess would be at the mean, 20.7. Given the dip at the beginning, however, the mean is too low. Note that, after the initial dip, the process seems to have continued at a constant level. The overall sample mean is lower than the sample mean for the part of the series after the dip, and if this characterized the random part of the series, then prediction should *exclude* the data corresponding to the dip.

f   A 95% PI is $20.7 \pm 2(2.49)$, or 20.7 ± 5, or from 15.7 to 25.7. This is not quite reliable, since the checks in (c) and (d) were not quite satisfactory. If the part after the dip characterizes the random part of the series, then the sample standard deviation for this part alone is a little smaller than for the entire series, including the dip. Then the prediction interval would be a little narrower than computed.

5.14   a   The unit is a calendar year. It may have been better to define the unit as containing the entire "winter season" (the period extending from July to June in the following year).

b   Yes, the process is random, as suggested by the sequence plot. The runs test does not call this into question. The control limits are UCL = $142.2 + 3(31.9) = 237.9$ and LCL = 46.5; all observations are within these limits. Randomness implies that we can treat the data as if they were cross-sectional, and we can then find prediction intervals for the amount of snowfall, using either the normal distribution—if applicable—or the counting method. If the data are not random, then prediction becomes more difficult.

c   Yes, the normal probability plot is good.

d   Assume that $\mu = 142.2$ and $\sigma = 31.9$. *100% refund:* We must first compute 20% of the average, $0.2(142.2) = 28.4$; standardizing this value, we get $z = (28.4 - 142.2)/31.9 = -3.57$. From Table 4.1, we get $F(z = -3.57) = 0$, hence the probability that snowfall will be less than 28.4 cm is approximately 0. *50% refund:* 40% of average is $0.4(142.2) = 56.9$; this standardizes to $z = (56.9 - 142.2)/31.9 = -2.67$. Hence, the desired probability, 0.0038, is also small. No additional assumptions are needed.

e   There is some uncertainty about the accuracy of the mean and the standard deviation used. However, the sample size of 43 is large enough to make the assumptions reasonable.

5.15   a   Based on a visual impression, it seems that the figures in July and August of any year are always high. We should investigate why this was so. Is it because July and August are vacation months? This pattern is not strong, however. The runs test and the control limits support randomness. Proceeding as if the attendance process were random may not be too misleading.

b   No, the normal distribution is not appropriate. We have to base our estimate on the raw data and use the counting method; the raw data are not given in the output, however.

c   If the process is indeed random, this is "tinkering with the process." What is needed is to analyze the underlying common causes for variation. If the process is random, then you will have low attendance months once in a while, just due to chance.

d   As in (a).

e   The relationship is moderately positive, but there is one unusual month with the lowest attendance in MAIN and very high attendance in PLANET. What happened in that month?

5.16   a   The unit is a unit of time, a month.

b   Since the mean is 3, the control chart limits are UCL = $3 + 3(9.8) = 32.4$, and LCL = $3 - 3(9.8) = -26.4$. No values are outside the control limits. It appears that the standard deviation is higher in the first half of the time series plot than in the second. However, this impression is influenced by very few data points, and the process could in fact be random. The runs test supports randomness (p-value > 0.1). If the data did behave like a random process, it would imply that the time series of the returns can be treated like cross-sectional data (that is, it does not contain any time related information), and hence charting to predict future returns would be useless.

c   Since the mean and standard deviation are $\bar{y} = 3$ and $s = 9.8$, respectively, a 1-standard-deviation interval is $\bar{y} \pm s$, that is, it extends from -6.8 to 12.8. There are 43 observations (out of 60) or 71.6% in this interval. A 2-standard-deviation interval is $\bar{y} \pm 2s$, that is, it extends from -16.6 to 22.6. There are 58 observations or 96.7% in this interval. Hence, the actual probabilities are a bit high.

    d   The normality assumption is reasonable for the stock return data. There is one unusual value, December 1983, at the lower end.

5.17 **a**   The process is not random. There is a definite nonrandom time series pattern to the data, characterized by lower standard deviation in the beginning and higher standard deviation later on. The observed significance for the runs test is 0.2819, so the results from the runs test would support randomness. The control limits are UCL $= 3.667 + 3(3.634) = 14.6$ and LCL < 0. At least one observation is above UCL, again suggesting that the process is not random.

    b   The distribution of response time is definitely not normal, and so the normal table cannot be used to estimate the required proportion by standardizing 10, etc. The raw data must be used to give an approximate answer. From the dotplot, we find that 5 of the 60 response times exceeded 10 hours, so an estimate of the required proportion is $\frac{5}{60}$ or 8.33%.

    c   No. The unit here is an individual service call. No data are available on the daily number of calls. (A very rough estimate could be obtained if we knew on how many days the 60 calls were received.)

5.18 **a**   The unit is a can of cocoa powder. The response variable is weight of contents.

    b   The value 500 g must be standardized: $z = (500 - 505)/2 = -2.5$. From Table 4.1 we get that 0.62% of cans weigh less than 500 g: The regulation is not being met.

    c   The 0.5 percentile is 2.58 standard deviations below the mean. If 500 is to be the 0.5 percentile, then the mean must be set 2.58 standard deviations above it, at $500 + 2.58(2) = 505.16$ g.

    d   An assumption of normality is necessary, and is quite reasonable for such a weighing process.

Chapter 6

6.1 **a**   The unit is a unit of time, a month.

    b   There is an upward drift. The mean is 245.

    c   There does not appear to be a time series pattern. The mean is 27.9.

    d   The mean of SALES (245) is a point prediction. A prediction interval is: (Point prediction) $\pm$ 3(St.Dev. of SALES) or $245 \pm 3(120.6)$, or 245 ± 362. (This interval covers negative values, so the result is questionable.)

    e   A point prediction is $385 +$ Mean of D_SALES $= 385 + 27.9 = 412.9$. A prediction interval is: (Point Prediction) $\pm$ 3(St.Dev. of D_SALES), or $412.9 \pm 3(60.5)$ or 413 ± 182.

    f   The prediction based on the random walk is more reasonable.

6.2 **a**   The random walk model is definitely not appropriate for GDP. The visual impression of the sequence plot of lag 1 differences does not suggest randomness. This is supported by the runs test (p-value $= 0.0000$). All observations are within the control limits, which are -212.8 and 458.6.

    b   The standard deviation of the lag 1 differences (111.8) is considerably less than the standard deviation of the undifferenced series (1,544). This is necessary for a random walk.

    c   A point prediction for GDP in 1991 is $5,423.4 + 122.9 = 5,546.3$.

        i   A 95% PI is $5,546.3 \pm 2(111.8)$, or from $5,322.7$ to $5,769.9$.

        ii   We must first standardize 5,500: $(5,500 - 5,546.3)/111.8 = -0.41$. From Table 4.1 or Minitab, the probability that this value is exceeded is $1 - 0.34 = 66\%$.

    d   The distribution of lag 1 differences must be normal in order to compute the prediction interval and the probability. The normal probability plot suggests strong positive skewness.

    e   The answers are completely unreliable.

    f **a**   The random walk model for the log of GDP, L_GDP, is much better than that for GDP. The first differences seem to have a slight meandering pattern, and the variation appears to be somewhat larger early on. The runs test would support randomness. All observations are within the control limits, UCL = 0.1656, and LCL = −0.021.

b   The standard deviation of DL_GDP is considerably less than that for L_GDP, 0.0311 vs. 0.952.

c   The point prediction for L_GDP in 1991: 8.5985 + 0.0723 = 8.6708. The 95% PI is 8.6708 ± 2(0.0311), or from 8.6086 to 8.733. Thus the point prediction for GDP is $e^{8.6708}$ = 5,830. Likewise, the 95% PI for GDP extends from 5,479 to 6,204. We must standardize log(5,500) = 8.6125, which is (8.6125 − 8.6708)/0.0311 = −1.87. From Table 4.1 or Minitab, the probability that this value is exceeded is 1 − 0.035 = 96.5%.

d   The distribution of lag 1 differences (DL_GDP) must be normal in order to compute the prediction interval and the probability. The normal probability plot for DL_GDP suggests normality.

e   The answers are not great. Because of the meandering pattern in DL_GDP and the higher variation earlier on, a better prediction model should be found.

6.3   **a**   No, there is increasing variability in the lag 1 differences of Winnebago sales. This can be seen from a sequence plot of these lag 1 differences.

b   No, there is still increasing variability in the lag 1 differences of $\sqrt{\text{sales}}$, but it is less pronounced than in (a).

c   Yes.

   i   There is fairly constant variability in the lag 1 differences of log(sales).

   ii   A visual inspection of the sequence plot of these lag 1 differences suggests that they vary unpredictably around a constant level, so the lag 1 differences behave as if they were random.

   iii   The runs test for these lag 1 differences has a p-value of 0.373, so this test supports the observation of randomness made in (ii). [Note: If you were to examine the lag 1 differences in (a) or (b) along the lines of (ii) and (iii), you would observe increasing variability around the constant level.]

d   Prediction for sales in March 1972 should be based on logs. [If you are hazy on logs, see the prediction based on square roots below.] *Point prediction:* Estimate of log(sales) = log(1,753) + [Mean of the lag 1 differences of log(sales)] = 7.47 + 0.0533 = 7.522; *Interval prediction:* A 3-standard-deviation interval for log(sales) is: (Point prediction) ± 3[Std.Dev. of the lag 1 differences of log(sales)] = 7.522 ± 3(0.3528), or from 6.464 to 8.58. For practical application, it is *easier* to interpret values in original sales units (dollars) than in logs, and so we have to transform back from logs to original units. This is done by taking antilogs. Therefore a point prediction of sales is $e^{7.522}$ = 1,849, and a 3-standard-deviation interval for sales extends from $e^{6.464}$ to $e^{8.58}$ or from 642 to 5,328. Note that this interval is quite wide.

Using square roots, the following predictions are obtained:
Point prediction: Estimate of $\sqrt{\text{sales}}$ = $\sqrt{1,753}$ + (Mean of the lag 1 differences of $\sqrt{\text{sales}}$) = 41.87 + 0.541 = 42.410; *Interval prediction:* A 3-standard-deviation interval for $\sqrt{\text{sales}}$ is: (Point prediction) ± 3(Std.Dev. of the lag 1 differences of $\sqrt{\text{sales}}$) = 42.410 ± 3(3.977) or from 30.479 to 54.341.
Therefore, a point prediction of sales is 42.410^2 = 1,799, and a 3-standard-deviation interval for sales extends from 30.479^2 to 54.341^2, or from 929 to 2,953. This interval, however, is much too narrow since its computation assumes that there is constant variability in the lag 1 differences. As noted in (b) above, however, this variability has been higher in recent months than in earlier months, so our prediction into the future should make allowances for this increasing variability.

Chapter 7

7.2   **a**   The probability for each of the 9 possible samples is the same, $\frac{1}{9}$. The possible samples are (4,4), (4,6), (4,10), (6,4), (6,6), (6,10), (10,4), (10,6), and (10,10).

b   The sample means for these samples are 4, 5, 7, 5, 6, 8, 9, 8, and 10.

c   The sampling distribution is:

$\bar{y}$	Probability
4	$\frac{1}{9}$
5	$\frac{2}{9}$
6	$\frac{1}{9}$
7	$\frac{2}{9}$
8	$\frac{2}{9}$
9	0
10	$\frac{1}{9}$

The mean is $6\frac{2}{3}$.

d The population mean is $\mu_y = 6\frac{2}{3}$, the same as in (c), as it should be.

e The probability is $\frac{5}{9}$ that $\bar{y}$ is 7, 8, 9, or 10.

f **a** The probability for each of the 6 possible samples is $\frac{1}{6}$. The 6 possible samples are (4,6), (4,10), (6,4), (6,10), (10,4), and (10,6).

  b The sample means are 5, 7, 5, 8, 7, and 8.

  d The population mean is $\mu_y = 6\frac{2}{3}$.

  e The probability is $\frac{4}{6}$.

  c The sampling distribution is:

$\bar{y}$	Probability
5	$\frac{2}{6}$
6	0
7	$\frac{2}{6}$
8	$\frac{2}{6}$

The mean of the sampling distribution is $6\frac{2}{3}$.

7.3 **a** The unit is a family. The distribution is not normal since normality would imply a considerable proportion of negative incomes: The $0 value standardized is $z = (0 - 10{,}400)/6{,}800 = -1.53$, so the proportion of negative incomes would be about 6% if incomes were normally distributed.

b **i** The standard error of the mean is $6{,}800/\sqrt{400} = 340$. The value $11,000 standardizes to $(11{,}000 - 10{,}400)/340 = 1.76$, so the probability is 0.96 that $\bar{y}$ is less than $11,000. The value $9,000 standardizes to $(9{,}000 - 10{,}400)/340 = -4.12$, so the probability is close to 0 that $\bar{y}$ is less than $9,000. Therefore, the probability that $\bar{y}$ is between $9,000 and $11,000 is 0.96.

  ii The required interval is $10{,}400 \pm 2(340)$, or $10{,}400 \pm 680$.

  iii We need the 99th percentile of the sampling distribution of the mean. Since its shape is normal, we can use $z = 2.33$, so the 99th percentile is $10{,}400 + 2.33(340) = \$11{,}192$.

7.4 **a** The value 88 mm standardizes to $z = (88 - 100)/6 = -2$, and 104 mm standardizes to $z = (104 - 100)/6 = 0.67$. Therefore the proportion of diameters meeting the specification is $0.75 - 0.02 = 0.73$. The additional assumption is that diameters are normally distributed.

b The value 112 mm standardizes to 2. Therefore the proportion is 0.95.

c The value 102 mm standardizes to $(102 - 100)/6 = 0.33$, and 98 mm standardizes to -0.33. Therefore the probability is $0.63 - 0.37 = 0.26$.

d The standard error of $\bar{y}$ is $6/\sqrt{36} = 1$. Therefore 98 mm standardizes to $(98 - 100)/1 = -2$, and 102 mm standardizes to 2. The probability is then 0.95. Since the sample size exceeds 20, the sampling distribution of $\bar{y}$ is normal regardless of the shape of the population distribution. So no additional assumptions are needed.

e Part (c) refers to an individual diameter, and (d) refers to the sample mean for 36 diameters.

f The standard error is $8/\sqrt{36} = 1.33$. Therefore 98 mm standardizes to $(98 - 102)/1.33 = -3$, and 102 mm standardizes to 0. The desired probability is $0.5000 - 0.0013 = 0.4987$.

7.5 **a** The population consists of all retail stores in metropolitan Toronto. The unit is a retail store. The response variable is after-tax profit per dollar revenue.

b A point estimate of the population mean is $\bar{y} = 4.8$. Using solely this estimate tells us nothing about how good this estimate is.

c The 95% CI is $4.8 \pm 2(1.6/\sqrt{100})$, or 4.8 ± 0.32, or from 4.48 to 5.12. Since n is large, it is not necessary to assume that the response variable values are normally distributed. For large n, the sampling distribution of the mean is normal regardless of the shape of the population distribution.

d We need a 95% prediction interval, which is $\bar{y} \pm 2(1.6)$, or 4.8 ± 3.2, or from 1.6 to 8. It is necessary to assume that the response variable has a normal distribution.

e The intervals are different, and they should be. The confidence interval in (c) is a statement about a population mean, and the prediction interval in (d) is a statement about an individual unit.

7.6 **a** Concentrate on the sample mean, $8,000, first. Assume that this sample mean was obtained from a random sample of size $n = 100$. From Exercise 7.3, we know that the sampling distribution of the mean is roughly normal, with mean $10,400 and standard error $6,800/\sqrt{n} = 6,800/\sqrt{100} = 680$. In other words, the observed sample mean standardizes to $(8,000 - 10,400)/680 = -3.53$. Such a value is quite unusual, and it raises questions about the reasonableness of treating the sample as random. Since we haven't talked about the sampling distribution of the standard deviation, we cannot say whether 5,000 is quite a bit different from 6,800 or not.

b No, the nonresponse rate is 50% and is quite high. It's not clear that nonresponse can be ignored when a survey relates to income.

7.7 The mean of the 10 numbers is the *population* mean, so no inferences are required. A confidence interval is useful when generalizing from a sample mean to the mean of the population the sample was drawn from randomly, and no such generalization is necessary here.

7.8 The sample size cost function is $1,000 + 500n = 19,000$, so $n = 36$. The standard deviation of monthly sales is $\sigma = \sqrt{10,000} = 100$. The confidence interval is of the form $\bar{y} \pm 76/2$ or $\bar{y} \pm 38$. The confidence interval formula is $\bar{y} \pm z\sigma/\sqrt{n}$, so $z\sigma/\sqrt{n} = 38$ in this example, or $z = 38(\sqrt{36}/100) = 2.28$, that is, the confidence interval extends 2.28 standard errors around the sample mean. From the normal table, we find that $F(z = 2.28) = 0.9887$. Since this is a two-sided confidence interval, the degree of confidence is $0.9887 - 0.0113 = 0.9774$ or 97.74%.

7.9 **a** The estimated standard error is $0.06/\sqrt{35} = 0.01$. The point estimate of μ_y is 99.68, so the 95% confidence interval is $99.68 \pm 2(0.01)$, or 99.68 ± 0.02.

b The prediction interval is $99.68 \pm 2(0.06)$, or 99.68 ± 0.12.

c The confidence interval in (a) refers to uncertainty about the population mean. The prediction in (b) refers to uncertainty about another unit.

d The value 100 standardizes to $(100 - 99.68)/0.06 = 5.33$, and 99.6 standardizes to $(99.6 - 99.68)/0.06 = -1.33$. Thus the probability is $F(z = 5.33) - F(z = -1.33) = 1 - 0.092 = 0.908$.

e The answer is the same as in (d).

f Normality must be assumed for (b), (d), and (e), since they are statements about the population distribution of oxygen content.

7.10 **a** The population consists of all individuals who have taken the GMAT test. The subject (unit) is an individual who has taken the GMAT test. The response variable is the GMAT score.

b GMAT scores are normally distributed in the population of persons taking the GMAT, but they are probably not normally distributed among the students in question, since the GMAT is used as one criterion for acceptance into the program. Therefore, there is a cutoff below which few students would be expected.

c The 90% CI is $580 \pm 1.65(80/\sqrt{25})$, or 580 ± 26. The sample size is moderate, so the multiple 1.65 is a little small for a 90% CI. Therefore this interval is a little tight.

d The 90% CI is $600 \pm 1.65(100/\sqrt{36})$, or 600 ± 28.

e The estimated standard error of the difference is $\sqrt{80^2/25 + 100^2/36} = 23.1$. Thus the 90% CI for the difference in the two population means is $(580 - 600) \pm 1.65(23.1)$, or -20 ± 38, or from -58 to 18.

There is considerable uncertainty about the value of the difference. Furthermore, the interval covers the value 0, so there is not much evidence to suggest that the population means at the two business schools are different: The difference between the two sample means, -20, may well be due to chance.

f   The value 0 standardizes to $[0 - (-20)]/23.1 = 0.866$, so the degree of confidence in the interval covering all negative values is $F(z = 0.866) = 0.81$, and the degree of confidence in the interval covering all positive values is $1 - 0.81 = 0.19$. The data do not strongly suggest that the difference is either positive or negative; see the conclusion in (e).

7.11   **a**   This is a population study, but it is not clear what the population is. It seems to consist of tubercular patients, but their location, etc., are not known. They do not seem to have been randomly selected from whatever the population is. It may be reasonable to assume, however, that selection was neutral with respect to the effect of the treatment, so it may be reasonable to treat the sample as if it were random. The subject (unit) is a tubercular patient. The response variable is degree of improvement.

b   To ascertain how well the data establish the effectiveness of streptomycin, obtain a 99% confidence interval for the difference between the means of the treated and untreated patients.

	$\bar{y}$	s	n
1. Treated	0.673	1.733	55
2. Untreated	-0.865	1.727	52

The 99% CI for the difference in means is $(\bar{y}_1 - \bar{y}_2) \pm 2.57 \sqrt{s_1^2/n_1 + s_2^2/n_2}$, or $0.673 - (-0.865) \pm 2.57\sqrt{1.733^2/55 + 1.727^2/52}$, or $1.538 \pm 2.57(0.335)$, or 1.54 ± 0.861. This interval does not include 0, and therefore streptomycin can be concluded to be effective (with 99% confidence). To get the degree of confidence in the interval that covers all positive values, we must standardize 0, i.e., $z = (0 - 1.538)/0.335 = -4.59$, so we have almost 100% degree of confidence that the difference is positive and streptomycin is effective.

c

	$\bar{y}$	s	n
1. Treated	0.164	3.190	55
2. Untreated	-2.57	4.585	52

The 99% CI is $2.914 \pm 2.57(0.768)$, or 2.91 ± 1.97. The CI covering all positive values is such that 0 standardizes to $z = (0 - 2.914)/0.768 = -3.79$. We draw the same conclusion as in (b).

7.12   **a**   The population consists of all people who are eligible to vote in the next election. The response variable is "party the subject would vote for." It is quite possible that the response variable is whether the subject would vote for the party in power or not; in this case, the response variable values are "yes" and "no." The measurement scale is categorical.

b   This is difficult to decide from the information given. But since the time of the next election is typically not known, the term "eligible to vote" is difficult to operationalize. However, the results from sampling the population of currently eligible voters should be pretty similar to results from sampling the target population.

d   The point estimate of the population proportion π is $p = 380/900 = 0.422$. The 95% CI for π is $p \pm 2\sqrt{p(1-p)/n}$, or $0.422 \pm 2\sqrt{0.422(0.578/900)}$, or $0.422 \pm 2(0.0165)$, or 0.422 ± 0.033. One interpretation is: This kind of estimate is within 3.3% of the correct proportion 19 times out of 20. The 90% CI is $0.42 \pm 1.65(0.0165)$, or 0.42 ± 0.027.

7.13 A 95% CI for π is $0.60 \pm 2\sqrt{0.6(0.4/100)}$, or 0.60 ± 0.098. The estimate of the population proportion of television set owners who have color sets is 60%; chances are 95% that this estimate is no more than 9.8 percentage points in error.

7.14 a   This is a population study. The unit is a billing. The response variable is correctness of billing (yes or no).

   b   A 95% CI for π is $0.12 \pm 2\sqrt{0.12(0.88)/100}$, or 0.12 ± 0.065. Among the day's billings, 12% are estimated to be in error. Chances are 95% that this estimate is no more than 6.5 percentage points from that day's overall proportion of billings in error.

7.15 a   Let us estimate $\pi_2 - \pi_1$. A point estimate is $0.0778 - 0.0455 = 0.0323$. The standard error is $\sqrt{0.0778(1 - 0.0778)/90 + 0.455(1 - 0.0455)/110} = 0.0345$. Thus, a 95% confidence interval is $0.0323 \pm 2(0.0345)$, or 0.0323 ± 0.0690. Chances are 95% that the difference between batch proportions is within 0.069 of the point estimate, 0.032. This is a pretty wide interval, reminding us that sample sizes have to be in the several hundreds to achieve small standard errors when estimating proportions.

   b   We must standardize the value 0: $z = (0 - 0.0323)/0.0345 = -0.94$. Using Table 4.1 or Minitab, we find the quantile corresponding to $z = -0.94$ to be $F(-0.94) = 0.1736$. Thus chances are $1 - 0.1736 = 83\%$ that the difference between the two batch proportions is covered by an interval consisting of positive values only. (Note: When the difference $\pi_2 - \pi_1$ is positive, proportion π_2 is larger than π_1.)

7.16 The rule of thumb contains two cutoff values: 0.10 and 0.01. They refer to the probabilities in both tails of a z distribution. Thus the corresponding probabilities in the lower tail are 0.05 and 0.005. From Table 4.1 or Minitab, the corresponding z values are -1.64 and -2.58. Thus, if the absolute observed z value is less than 1.64, the hypothesis is not called into question. When it exceeds 2.58, it is called into question. In between, the results are inconclusive.

7.17 From the answers to Exercise 7.11(b), a point estimate for the difference is 1.538, the standard error for this estimate is 0.335. Thus the point estimate is $z = (1.538 - 0)/0.335 = 4.59$ standard errors away from the hypothesized value of the difference when the population means are equal (0). This is a very large value for z; the resulting p-value is virtually 0. So the data do not support at all that the two means are the same.

7.18 The sample proportion of incorrect billings is $p = 0.12$. If the hypothesis were true, the standard error would be $\sqrt{0.05(0.95)/100} = 0.0218$. Using $\pi_0 = 0.05$, the sample proportion standardizes to $z = (0.12 - 0.05)/0.0218 = 3.05$. This is quite a large value. The p-value is $2(0.0011) = 0.0022$; i.e., it is less than 0.01. Therefore, the data do not support the manager's past experience.

7.19 a   The desired probability can be obtained from the sampling distribution of the mean, where $\mu_y = 50$ and the standard error of the mean is $\sigma_y/\sqrt{n} = 40/\sqrt{100} = 4$. This sampling distribution is definitely normal, because of the large sample size ($n = 100$). The desired probability is thus that $\bar{y}$ exceeds 58, or that a standard normal variable exceeds $z = (58 - 50)/4 = 2$. This probability is 0.0228.

   b   This is the same situation as in (a), except that the mean of the sampling distribution is now assumed to be $50 + 10 = 60$, and not 50. So the desired probability is that $\bar{y}$ exceeds 58, or that a standard normal variable exceeds $z = (58 - 60)/4 = -0.5$. This probability is 0.6915.

   c   If the sample can be viewed as a random sample and if the distribution of warranty costs per appliance is normal, then a 95% confidence interval for the mean warranty costs per applicance is $58 \pm 2(24/\sqrt{16})$; that is, it extends from 46 to 70 and is quite wide. [The multiple 2 is small: Since the sample size is small, a t-multiple would be more appropriate, so this 95% interval is a little tight. The appropriate degrees of freedom value is $n - 1 = 15$; the t-multiple is thus 2.13.] The hypothesized value for the mean, $50, is well within this interval, so the data do not really rule out the $50 claim, but there is a lot of uncertainty.

7.20   **a**   There is not a lot of information, but the wording of the exercise suggests that the unit is a single-family house (or at least a house with one heating bill only), so the population consists of all single-family homes in the particular neighborhood. The response variable is "heating bill for last year."

      b   The 98% CI for μ_y is $2{,}247 \pm 2.33(1{,}157/\sqrt{60})$, or $2{,}247 \pm 348$, or from 1,899 to 2,595. Chances are 98% that the population mean is covered by this confidence interval. Note that the value \$2,000 is not ruled out by the data at the 98% confidence level.

      c   No additional assumptions are needed. It is not necessary that the distribution of heating bills be normal, since the sample size is large.

      d   Since the 98% CI covers the value \$2,000 and values less than it, such values are not ruled out given the sample results and the desired degree of confidence. Given the wording of the exercise, "should be opened only...," the new office should not be opened. (We can also look at this differently and find the degree of confidence in an interval that is \$2,000 or less. Standardizing 2,000, we get $z = (2{,}000 - 2{,}247)/(1{,}157/\sqrt{60}) = -1.65$, so the degree of confidence would be 0.05, which is small, but may not be small enough to warrant opening the new office.)

      e   We must assume normality for the distribution of heating bills here. Standardizing the value \$2,000, we get $z = (2{,}000 - 2{,}247)/1{,}157 = -0.21$, so we get the answer from Table 4.1, $1.00 - 0.42 = 0.68$ or 68%.

      f   Normality is not quite reasonable, so the answer in (e) is *very* approximate only. Based on the counting rule, there are 32 bills among the 60 less than \$2,000, or 53.3%

      g   The standard error of the difference is $\sqrt{8^2/35 + 7^2/25} = 1.946$, so the 90% CI is $(34 - 36) \pm 1.65(1.946)$, or -2.00 ± 3.21. The one-sided CI covering all negative values has degree of confidence 85%, since $z = [0 - (-2)]/1.946 = 1.03$, and $F(z = 1.03) = 0.85$.

      h   No assumptions were needed.

      i   The implication would be that the sample data do not rule out the possibility of the two population means being the same at a 90% confidence level.

      j   The implication would be that the sample data suggest the two population means to be different at a 90% confidence level.

      k   No. The confidence interval extends from -1.21 to 5.21, and so it covers \$0.

7.21   **a**   This is a cross-sectional study of a population, where the population is the large shipment of components. The unit is a component. The response variable is the important internal dimension.

      b   The 98% CI is $40 \pm 2.33(3/\sqrt{36})$, or 40 ± 1.17. We can be 98% confident that this interval covers the population mean.

      b   No additional assumptions were needed. Since the sample size is large $(n = 36)$, the sampling distribution of the mean is approximately normal. So we do not have to assume that the population distribution of diameter values is normal.

      c   No. This is not simple random sampling from the entire population. (In simple random sampling, every conceivable sample of size $n = 36$ has the same chance of being drawn. Here, for example, a sample consisting of 36 units from the first location cannot possibly be obtained.)

Chapter 8

8.3   **a**   There may be a problem with the order in which batches were run. Ideally, the standard and modified batches should have been run in random order since there may have been changes in the production environment over time. A time effect could be confounding the results since all 10 standard batches were run first, followed by the modified batches.

      b

process	mean	st.dev
standard	84.24	2.90
modified	85.54	3.65

A point estimate for the difference between the two process means, $\mu_1 - \mu_2$, is $84.24 - 85.54 = -1.3$. The estimated standard error of this estimate is $\sqrt{2.90^2/10 + 3.65^2/10} = 1.47$. Thus, the 95% CI for the difference is $-1.3 \pm 2(1.47)$, or -1.3 ± 2.9, or from -4.2 to 1.6. Since the sample sizes are both quite small, the multiple 2 is too small, so the 95% CI is too tight. Minitab uses the correct multiple and obtains an interval from -4.41 to 1.80, which is indeed somewhat wider.

c   This is a reasonable assumption, particularly if process conditions remained unchanged and if these conditions can readily be replicated in the future.

d   A point estimate for the difference is -1.3. This suggests that the modified process is superior, though there is a lot of uncertainty, given the confidence interval in (b). But if the change could be done at no expense, this should be done given the results from the point estimate.

8.4   Using the hypothesized difference 0, we must standardize the observed sample difference, -1.3: $z = (-1.3 - 0)/1.47 = -0.88$. The p-value is $2(0.1894) = 0.3788$. Thus the data do not contradict the hypothesis of no difference.

8.5   **a**   The standard deviation 6.466 refers to the standard deviation of the $4(24) = 96$ readings. It measures the overall variation around the mean 55.124. The pooled standard deviation, 5.686, is based on the 24 subgroup standard deviations. Each such standard deviation measures the variation around the corresponding subgroup mean. There is no reason why the two should coincide.

b   The control limits are $55.124 \pm 3(5.68/\sqrt{4})$, or LCL $= 46.60$ and UCL $= 63.65$. The values in June 1985, July 1985, and June 1986 are outside the control limits. (After some investigation, it turned out that the temperature for the test room was cooler in the summer.) Therefore, the process was not random.

c   The observed significance for the runs test is 0.0277, so it is inconclusive.

d   Visual inspection of the sequence of standard deviations suggests randomness. From the s chart, the control limits are UCL $= 11.91$ and LCL $= 0$. The standard deviation for the 11th subgroup, 11.63, is close to the UCL, but it is just within the control limits. Thus the process of standard deviations appears stable.

e   Not really, since the $\bar{y}$ chart suggests that the process is not random. A search for assignable causes is in order. See the answer to (b).

f   No. The process is not random. Even if it had been random, it would not have been possible, since the sampling distribution of the $\bar{y}$ values does not necessarily have the same shape as the distribution of the individual adhesion numbers.

8.6   **a**   The unit is a day, and the response variable is the number of incorrect billings.

b   There were 152 incorrect billings in the 20-day period, so the estimate of the process proportion is $152/3,000 = 0.051$. The control limits are UCL $= 0.051 + 3\sqrt{0.051(0.949)/150} = 0.051 + 0.054 = 0.105$, and LCL $= 0.051 - 0.054 = 0$. Therefore, days 9 and 11 are outside the control limits, so the process is not random.

c   The 95% CI for process proportion π is $0.051 \pm 2\sqrt{0.051(0.949)/3,000}$, or 0.051 ± 0.008. Chances are 95% that the process proportion of incorrect billings is within 0.008 of the point estimate, 0.051.

d   Exclude days 9 and 11. The estimate of the process proportion based on the remaining days is $125/2700 = 0.0463$, so the 95% CI for π is: $0.0463 \pm 2\sqrt{0.0463(0.9537)/2,700}$, or 0.0483 ± 0.0080. Both estimates are very precise, but the second is a little lower than the first.

8.7   **a**   The unit is a weekday. The response variable is the number of incomplete shipments. There were 271 incorrect shipments in the 30-day period, so the estimate of the process proportion is $271/2,250 = 0.12$. The control limits are UCL $= 0.12 + 3\sqrt{0.12(0.88)/75} = 0.12 + 0.11 = 0.23$, and LCL $= 0.12 - 0.11 = 0.01$. None of the observations is outside the control limits.

b   The observed significance for the runs test is 0.1878, so it would support a visual impression of randomness.

c   There seems to be an upward trend to the number of incorrect shipments. This impression is not strong, and it is not reflected in the control limits or the runs test. There is some doubt about the stability of the process. An investigation of the reason for the upward trend might be in order.

8.8 **a** The general formula for a CI for μ_y is $\bar{y} \pm z$(Standard Error). Thus, $5 = z$(Standard Error), where (Standard Error) $= s_y/\sqrt{n} = 18/\sqrt{36} = 3$. Thus we have: $5 = z(3)$, or $z = \frac{5}{3} = 1.667$, so the degree of confidence is $0.9515 - 0.0485 = 0.9030$: this is a 90.3% CI for μ_y.

   b No. Because of the large sample size, a normality assumption for individual weights is not needed.

8.9 **a** The point estimate for the process mean of DIFFRNCE, μ, is 1.424. The standard error for this estimate is $3.405/\sqrt{46} = 0.502$. A 95% CI for μ is $1.424 \pm 2(0.502)$, or 1.424 ± 1.004, or from 0.420 to 2.428. Chances are 95% that the process mean is within 1 of the point estimate 1.4.

   b No, the confidence interval in (a) does not contain 0. A "yes" answer would imply that the data do not rule out the mean difference to be 0; in this case, both the portfolio and the Value Line index would be performing the same on average. A "no" answer would imply that the data suggest the process mean difference to be different from 0 so that, on average, either the stock portfolio would be outperforming the Value Line index or vice versa.

   c Using the hypothesized value, 0, we must standardize the observed sample mean, $z = (1.424 - 0)/0.502 = 2.84$. The p-value is $2(0.0023) = 0.0046$. The hypothesized value 0 for the process mean of DIFFRNCE is not supported by the data.

8.10 **a** This is a time series study of a process, the unit is a printing order, and the categorical response variable is "new order or not."

   b The point estimate is $p = \frac{24}{50} = 0.48$, so the 98% CI for the process proportion is $0.48 \pm 2.33\sqrt{0.48(0.52)/50}$, or 0.48 ± 0.14. Chances are 98% that the unknown population proportion is within 0.14 of the point estimate 0.48. We have to assume that the process is stable. The sequence plot looks random, and the runs test supports this impression, so the assumption is reasonable.

   c The formula for the CI is $p \pm z\sqrt{p(1-p)/n}$, that is, the half-width of the CI is $z\sqrt{p(1-p)/n}$. So the width of the confidence interval depends on p, the sample proportion, which won't be observed until *after* the sample has been collected. Note, however, that the quantity $p(1-p)$, which appears in the standard error formula, has its maximum at $p = 0.5$, so the maximum half-width is $z(0.5/\sqrt{n})$. The half-width was to be no more than 0.01, and then we have that $z(0.5/\sqrt{n}) = 0.01$, or $n = [z(0.5/0.01)]^2$. Since $z = 2.33$, we have that $n = [2.33(0.5/0.01)]^2 = 13{,}572$, a truly enormous sample size that suggests that the required accuracy is quite unreasonable.

Chapter 9

9.2 **b** Using $x = 50$ in the regression equation, we get the point prediction for y, $5.0 + 0.9(50) = 50$. Since $\sigma = 10$, a 95% prediction interval extends $2(10) = 20$ around the point prediction, i.e., from 30 to 70. We can standardize the value 55, using the point prediction and σ, $z = (55 - 50)/10 = 0.5$. Using Table 4.1 or Minitab, we find that 0.5 corresponds to the 0.6915 quantile, so the desired probability is $1 - 0.6915 = 30.85\%$.

   c We can use the answer in (b), since the average value of y for all these products is 50, i.e., the proportion is 30.85%.

   d When $x = 60$, the point prediction is $5.0 + 0.9(60) = 59$, and the 95% prediction interval extends $2(10)$ around it, that is, from 39 to 79. Standardizing 55, we get $z = (55 - 59)/10 = -0.4$; the desired probability is $1 - 0.3446 = 66\%$.

   e We are looking for an x value so that the 0.01 quantile of y is 55. The 0.01 quantile of a z distribution is $z = -2.33$. Thus 55 is 2.33 standard deviations below the regression line, i.e., $55 = (5.0 + 0.9x) - 2.33(10)$, or $0.9x = 73.3$, or $x = 73.3/0.9 = 81.444$. The desired value for the proxy variable is 81.4.

9.3 The intercept equals 100, and the slope equals 2.

9.4 **a** A linear model looks reasonable, but there appears to be a slight curvilinear relationship. The increase in y when x increases from 0 to 1 is not quite as large as when x increases from -1 to 0.

b *Check 1:* The means of the residuals in the first and third strips are slightly less than 0, and the mean in the middle strip is a little higher than 0. This supports the concerns raised in (a). *Check 2:* The standard deviation of residuals seems to be a little less in the third strip than in the other two. *Check 3:* There is an increasing pattern to the residuals, but note that this is not a time series study. (Further investigation re-vealed that there were other predictor variables that were ignored here, but that are important.) *Check 4:* Normality is OK. Overall, the concern raised in (a) is supported by these checks.

c Constant = 29.88: When detergent level is at the coded value 0, average washing performance is 29.88. Slope = 6.91: As coded detergent level increases by 1 unit, washing performance tends to increase by 6.91 on average.

d 95% CI for β_0: 29.88 ± 2(1.29), or 29.9 ± 2.6. Chances are 95% that the model coefficient β_0 is no more than 2.6 away from the point estimate, 29.9. 95% CI for β_1: 6.91 ± 2(1.584), or 6.91 ± 3.17, or from 3.74 to 10.08, so this interval does not cover 0. Thus the sample data suggest that detergent level has an influence on washing performance.

e The point prediction is $\hat{y}$ = 29.88 + 6.91(0.5) = 33.34. The 90% PI is: $\hat{y} \pm z\,s$, or 33.34 ± 1.65(6.72), or 33.3 ± 11.1. When detergent level is at 0.5, chances are 90% that washing performance is within 11.1 of 33.3.

f The answers in (c) to (e) should be taken with a grain of salt. (An improved model should be found, but we need the tools in Chapter 10 to find one.)

9.5

a There seems to be an abrupt change in STAFF between days 28 and 29. The WAIT sequence plot is a lit-tle bathtub-shaped, where the bottom is around days 30 to 45. The 98% CI for mean of WAIT is 23.99 ± 2.33(8.61/$\sqrt{70}$), or 24.0 ± 2.4. It's not clear what this "process mean" represents here, since the *se-quence* of WAIT values is *not random*. It is certainly not possible to use the results derived here for pre-diction purposes, so there is no real use for this confidence interval. The WAIT values are slightly posi-tively skewed. Once again, since the sequence of WAIT values is not random, the histogram is not useful for prediction purposes.

b There seems to be an indirect relationship between WAIT and STAFF: As STAFF increases, WAIT tends to decrease.

c The estimated regression equation is: Fitted WAIT = 67.0 − 1.67 STAFF. *Slope coefficient* of STAFF, −1.67: On 2 days for which STAFF levels differ by 1 operator, the WAIT values tend to differ by 1.67, and the day with the higher STAFF tends to have the lower WAIT. *Constant coefficient* or intercept, 67.0: It doesn't really have a useful interpretation since considerable extrapolation would be required.

d *Check 1* (residual vs. x plot) looks OK. *Check 2* (residual vs. x plot): As x increases, the dispersion in residuals also tends to increase, i.e., there is no constant dispersion. *Check 3:* The sequence plot of resid-uals has a bathtub shape whose bottom is around days 25 to 30; i.e., there seems to be a slight time series pattern. The runs test doesn't pick this up, it looks OK. *Check 4* (normal probability plot): There is a slight deviation from normality. Overall, checks 2 and 3 are not passed, so the model in (c) is not accept-able for prediction purposes, and we should go back to the drawing board. The remaining parts of this problem *must* be interpreted with this in mind.

e The standard deviation of the response variable WAIT is 8.61, the standard deviation of residuals is s_e = 7.068; i.e., there is not much reduction in variation when using STAFF for prediction. The correlation between WAIT and Fitted WAIT is the square root of the R^2, i.e., $\sqrt{0.335}$ = 0.579.

f 95% CI for β_1: −1.67 ± 2(0.285), or −1.67 ± 0.57. Chances are about 95% that this interval covers the true, but unknown, value of β_1.

g **i** STAFF = 30: Fitted WAIT = 67 − 1.67(30) = 16.9

ii STAFF = 50: Fitted WAIT = −16.6. This is extrapolation, and the result, a negative value, does not make sense.

h **i** The approximate 95% prediction interval is $\hat{y} \pm 2s$. Here it is 16.9 ± 2(7.068), or 16.9 ± 14.1, or from 2.8 to 31.0.

ii The approximate PI is −16.6 ± 2(7.068), or −16.6 ± 14.1, or from −30.7 to −5.5.

i The conclusion in (d) was: Back to the drawing board, and so none of the answers in (e) to (h) is reliable. You were to find them in the context of this example to show what the implications would have been if (d) had been satisfactory.

j Based on the scatterplot in (b), there is a weak indirect relationship between WAIT and STAFF, i.e., the higher the STAFF level the lower the WAIT, but this is not pronounced. STAFF level does not seem to affect WAIT much.

9.6 **a** There is constant level, but a seasonal pattern (10 months per year). VOLUME and WEIGHT tend to move together.

b There is a strong linear relationship (possibly slightly curved).

c Fitted VOLUME = 2,713 + (0.0011876) WEIGHT. Constant coefficient, 2,713: It has no real physical meaning. Extrapolation to small WEIGHT values is dangerous. Slope coefficient, 0.0011876: For 2 months in which WEIGHT differs by 1 unit, VOLUME tends to differ by 0.0011876 units. This is an approximate relationship that has been observed. We cannot interpret the coefficients as reflecting a causal relationship. For example, we cannot say that if WEIGHT were to increase by 1 unit, then VOLUME would tend to increase by 0.0011876 units. There may be confounding factors—not measured or not known—that might account for some of the effect.

d *Check 1:* The residuals for low and high WEIGHT values tend to be less than zero. *Check 2:* Variability in residuals is NOT constant. *Check 3:* There is a slight 10-month seasonal time series pattern, even though this is unconfirmed by the runs test. *Check 4:* The distribution of residuals is positively skewed.

e This is not really surprising. In (d) there is still a time series pattern, which is just not captured by looking at VOLUME and WEIGHT alone.

f The standard deviation of VOLUME is 13,214, the standard deviation of residuals is $s_e = 2,030$. Thus WEIGHT accounts for a large amount of the variation in VOLUME. The correlation between VOLUME and FITTED is high at $\sqrt{R^2} = \sqrt{0.977} = 0.988$.

g 95% CI for β_1: $0.0011876 \pm 2(0.0000254)$, or from 0.0011368 to 0.0012384. Chances are 95% that the model slope coefficient is between 0.0011368 and 0.0012384. This interval is quite narrow; i.e., β_1 is accurately estimated.

h **i** The point prediction is $\hat{y} = 2,713 + 0.0011876(10,000,000) = 14,589$.
  ii $\hat{y} = 26,465$
  iii $\hat{y} = 38,341$
  None of these predictions is an extrapolation.

i **i** The approximate 95% prediction interval is $\hat{y} \pm 2s$, or $14,589 \pm 2(2,030)$, or from 10,529 to 18,649.
  ii The approximate PI extends from 22,405 to 30,525.
  iii The approximate PI extends from 34,281 to 42,401.

j None of the checks is really adequate, so all results are called into question and should be viewed with great caution! (Back to the drawing board: Find a better model. In later chapters, we will discuss some statistical tools that will enable us to find a better model.)

9.7 **a** The population consists of all reputable forecasters in Canada.

b This was not a random sample, and it is not reasonable to treat the sample as if it were random: The 20 best forecasters in 1987 were selected.

c This sample can never be used to generalize about the population, in particular with respect to means, standard deviations, etc.

d For the Caisse de Depot, the contribution is $100(2.4 - 4)/s$, and for the Conference Board, it is $100(2 - 4)/s$, where s is the standard deviation of GDP change for the last 10 or 20 years.

e The R^2 is near 0! This implies that there is either no relationship whatsoever or a nonlinear relationship. The diagnostic checks will reveal which is the case. The diagnostic checks are OK. (There is 1 outlier on the normal probability plot.) Therefore, performance in 1986 is uninformative about that in 1987!

f There is no clear-cut choice.

g,h Random assignment looks OK.

i We doubt that you can find a scheme that is much better than random assignment.

j Give everybody the same proportion.

k The result in (e) is probably generalizable, at least qualitatively.

Chapter 10

10.3 **a** The estimated regression equation is Fitted CHARGES $= -1,334 + 12.26$(SALES) $+ 1.431$(DIS-BURSE) $+ 4.391$(DEPOSITS)

  i *Check 1:* In the plot of ST.RES vs. FITTED, the ST.RES values to the left tend to be above the 0 line, and the ST.RES values in the center tend to be below the 0 line; there appears to be a cluster of five observations with large values for FITTED. The ST.RES vs. SALES plot looks a little bit like this, too, but the impression is not as strong. The ST.RES vs. DISBURSE plot suggests that ST.RES values to the left tend to be below the 0 line, and in the center, they tend to be above the 0 line. The ST.RES vs. DEPOSITS plot looks like this, too. Overall, there are problems with the linearity check. *Check 2:* Given the inadequacy of Check 1, Check 2 was not done. *Check 3:* The results, not given, look fine. This is a cross-sectional study. *Check 4:* The normal probability plot suggests negative skewness, in particular, at the bottom end.

  ii Constant coefficient, $-1,334$: It has no physical meaning; the negative value reflects the danger of extrapolating for values of SALES, DISBURSE, and DEPOSITS close to 0. Coefficient of SALES, 12.26: It means that, accounting for the variation in DISBURSE and DEPOSITS, two companies with SALES differing by 1 unit tend to have CHARGES differing by 12.26 units. The coefficients of DISBURSE (1.431) and DEPOSITS (4.391) have a similar interpretation. Because of the problems with the linearity check, none of these numbers is very reliable.

  iii 95% confidence interval for the coefficient of SALES: $12.26 \pm 2(1.26)$, or 12.3 ± 2.5; DISBURSE: $1.431 \pm 2(0.528)$, or 1.43 ± 1.06; DEPOSITS: $4.391 \pm 2(1.013)$, or 4.39 ± 2.03. None of these intervals includes 0. Because of the failure of Check 1, these intervals are not very reliable.

  iv The standard deviation of residuals is $s = 1,508$, the adjusted $R^2 = 84.1\%$. Because of problems with Check 1, s and R^2 are unreliable.

  v The point prediction for this company is $\hat{y} = -1,334 + 12.26(435) + 1.431(2,100) + 4.391(600) = 9,639$. The approximate 95% prediction interval is $\hat{y} \pm 2s$, or $9,639 \pm 2(1,508)$ or from 6,623 to 12,655; this is a rather wide interval. (The 95% PI obtained with Minitab is a little wider; it extends from 6,199 to 13,080.)

  b The estimated regression equation is Fitted CHARGES $= -762 + 13.36$(SALES) $+ 0.828$(DIS-BURSE) $+ 3.412$(DEPOSITS) $- 3,606$(BANK)

  i *Check 1:* The impression is similar to (a) above, but not as strong. The two dotplots for ST.RES stratified by the two values of BANK are fine. *Check 2:* The variability of ST.RES decreases for high values of FITTED. The ST.RES vs. SALES plot is similar to this. The other two plots, ST.RES vs. DISBURSE and ST.RES vs. DEPOSITS, look fine. The dotplots involving BANK look fine. *Check 3:* This is as in (a) above. *Check 4:* The normal probability plot looks fine.

  ii The interpretations are similar to those in (a). The coefficient of BANK is $-3,606$: Accounting for variation in SALES, DISBURSE, and DEPOSITS, the average charges for firms banking with the foreign subsidiary are \$3,606 lower than the average charges for firms banking with the well-established bank.

  iii SALES: $13.36 \pm 2(0.95) = 13.4 \pm 1.9$; DISBURSE: $0.828 \pm 2(0.405)$, or 0.83 ± 0.81; DEPOSITS: $3.412 \pm 2(0.769)$, or 3.41 ± 1.54; BANK: $-3,606 \pm 2(648)$, or $-3,606 \pm 1,296$. None of the confidence intervals contains 0.

  iv The standard deviation of residuals is $s = 1,114$; the adjusted $R^2 = 91.3\%$.

  v The point prediction is $\hat{y} = -762 + 13.36(435) + 0.828(2,100) + 3.412(600) - 3,606(0) = 8,836$. The approximate 95% PI is $8,836 \pm 2(1,114)$, or $8,836 \pm 2,228$ or from 6,608 to 11,064. Again, this is a wide interval. (Using Minitab, the 95% PI extends from 6,277 to 11,397.)

  Model (b) is better than model (a).

  c Yes, the new information is useful.

10.4

a There seems to be a slight upward tendency, with possibly a few unusual values at the beginning. Other than that, the plot suggests randomness.

b There seems to be no real association in either plot; the corresponding correlations support this view.

c The estimated equation is Fitted WAIT = 35.31 − 1.800(STAFF) + 0.01282(CALLS). All diagnostic checks are improvements of the corresponding checks in Exercise 9.5. It's possible to use this model for estimation and prediction.

d The standard deviation of WAIT is 8.62, the standard deviation of residuals is $s = 6.41$. STAFF and CALLS do not account for a lot of the variation in WAIT.

e The coefficient of STAFF, 1.80, has the following interpretation: On 2 days for which STAFF levels differ by 1 operator and CALLS volume is the same, the WAIT values tend to differ by 1.80, and the day with the higher STAFF tends to have the lower WAIT. (Here we have controlled for CALLS.)

f 95% CI for coefficient of STAFF, β_{STAFF}: $-1.80 \pm 2(0.261)$, or -1.80 ± 0.52. Chances are about 95% that this interval covers the true, but unknown, value of β_{STAFF}.

g i The point prediction is Fitted WAIT = 35.31 − 1.80(30) + 0.01282(2,000) = 6.95.
   ii The point prediction is 13.36.
   iii The point prediction is 19.77.
      Locating the points (CALLS = 2,000, STAFF = 30), (2,500, 30) and (3,000, 30) on the scatterplot of CALLS vs. STAFF, it becomes clear that the prediction at (2,000, 30) is possibly an extrapolation.

h i The approximate 95% PI is $6.95 \pm 2(6.41)$, or 6.95 ± 12.82 or from -5.85 to 19.77. (The Minitab 95% PI is from -7.03 to 20.9.) The PI covers negative values, so it's not too reliable. Note from (g) that this prediction may represent extrapolation.
   ii Using Minitab, the 95% PI extends from 0.18 to 26.6.
   iii Using Minitab, the 95% PI extends from 6.63 to 32.9.

i The diagnostic checks are satisfactory, though not perfect, so the answers in (f) to (h) are reliable as given.

j Controlling for the number of calls, the average total waiting time differs by -1.80 for 2 days for which staff differs by 1, with the day with the larger staff having the lower average waiting time. This appears to be a very small decrease! Note, however, that confounding is possible with other, unmeasured, variables.

10.5

a The value $10,000 standardizes to $z = (10,000 - 14,062)/11,265 = -0.36$, and $20,000 standardizes to 0.53. Using Minitab or Table 4.1, the desired proportion is $F(0.53) - F(-0.36) = 0.70 - 0.36 = 0.34$.

b It's quite unreasonable, since it would imply a considerable proportion of appraised values to be negative. Note that the value $0 standardizes to $(0 - 14,062)/11,265 = -1.25$! No additional assumptions are necessary.

c 95% CI for μ_y: $14,062 \pm 2(11,265/\sqrt{50})$, or $14,062 \pm 3,186$. Chances are 95% that the population mean is no more than $3,186 away from its point estimate, $14,062.

d Normality need not be assumed. Since the sample size is large ($n = 50$), the sampling distribution of $\bar{y}$ is approximately normal.

e 98% CI for $\mu_{improved} - \mu_{vacant}$: $(20,720 - 4,075) \pm 2.33\sqrt{9,819^2/30 + 2,265^2/20}$, or $16,645 \pm 4,340$. Chances are 98% that the difference between the two means is no more than $4,340 away from $16,645. It is quite clear that the mean appraised value for improved lots is quite a bit larger than the mean appraised value for vacant lots.

f No. The sampling distribution of $\bar{y}_{improved} - \bar{y}_{vacant}$ is normal because of the large sample sizes.

g The point estimate of the population proportion of improved lots, π, is $p = \frac{30}{50} = 0.6$. The 90% CI for π is $0.6 \pm 1.65\sqrt{0.6(0.4)/50}$, or 0.6 ± 0.11. Chances are 90% that the proportion of improved lots is no more than 11 percentage points away from the point estimate, 60%. This interval is quite wide!

h No. Because of the large sample size, the sampling distribution of p is normal.

i *Checks 1 and 2:* Using four vertical strips on the ST.RES vs. FITTED plot, these checks are acceptable, though there is somewhat lower variability in the fourth strip. There is an outlier, observation 45, which was flagged in the regression output. A similar conclusion is reached from the plot of ST.RES vs. L_ASSESS. *Check 3:* No information is given. This is a cross-sectional study, so an examination of check 3 was not necessary. *Check 4:* The outlier is clearly visible on the normal probability plot. Otherwise, normality is a reasonable assumption.

j   The value of s is larger in model 1, since the variable dropped from model 1 (WATERF) has a t-ratio = $0.1144/0.1293$, which is less than 1.

k   Not really, it's just the intercept. For it to have a practical interpretation, there would have to be considerable extrapolation.

l   The average difference in L_APPR between improved and unimproved lots is 0.357, after controlling for L_ASSESS. Of course, the underlying model linking APPRAIS and ASSESS is multiplicative. The estimated multiplicative model 2 is Fitted APPRAIS = $77.66(1.429)^{\text{IMPROV}}\text{ASSESS}^{0.56}$. Thus, accounting for assessed value, the estimated appraised value of an improved lot tends to be $1.429^1 = 1.429$ times that of an unimproved lot; i.e., it is 42.9% higher on average.

m   95% CI for β_{improv}: $0.357 \pm 2(0.1822)$, or 0.357 ± 0.364. There is a fair amount of uncertainty regarding β_{improv}. Chances are 95% that the average difference estimated in (l) is no more than 0.364 from β_{improv}.

n   The point estimate in (e) refers to the mean difference in appraised value between improved and unimproved lots. The point estimate in (l) refers to the mean difference in log(appraised value) between improved and unimproved lots, after controlling for L_ASSESS.

o   Two lots, both of which are either improved or not, tend to have a difference in L_APPR of 0.56 when their values for L_ASSESS differ by 1 unit. Of course, we can also interpret 0.56 as an elasticity: Accounting for the predictor variable IMPROV, a 1% difference in assessed value is associated with a 0.56% difference in estimated appraised value.

p   The point prediction for L_APPR is $4.3523 + 0.3572(1) + 0.5588\log(25,000) = 10.379$. The standard error of prediction is approximated by $s = 0.3349$. Thus, an approximate 95% PI for L_APPR is: $\hat{y} \pm 2s$, or $10.379 \pm 2(0.3349)$, or 10.379 ± 0.6698, or from 9.7094 to 11.049.

These estimates are given in terms of log(appraised value). In terms of appraised value, a point prediction for this parcel is $e^{10.379} = \$32,183$. A 95% PI for this parcel's appraised value extends from $e^{9.7094} = \$1,647$ to $e^{11.049} = \$62,881$. Note that this interval is pretty wide!

Chapter 11

11.2   **a**   Yes, a random walk model is reasonable. The lag 1 differences are random, since the sequence plot looks random, the runs test is OK, and the autocorrelogram is acceptable. The normal probability plot of the lag 1 differences is acceptable.

b   For the R_NUMBER series, the answers are very similar to (a).

c   The mean of the lag 1 differences is 31.7; their standard deviation is 10.23. The point prediction for a random walk model is Point prediction = Current value + Mean of lag 1 differences = 2,365 + 31.7 = 2,397. The 95% prediction interval is Point prediction $\pm$ 2(Standard deviation of lag 1 differences), or 2,397 $\pm$ 2(10.23), or 2,397 $\pm$ 20, or from 2,377 to 2,417. The point prediction and 95% PI are quite reliable because the diagnostic checks, discussed in (a), are fine.

d   The mean and standard deviation of the lag 1 differences of R_NUMBER are 0.3955 and 0.1205. Thus a point prediction of R_NUMBER for the first quarter in 1982 is $\sqrt{2,365} + 0.3955 = 49.027$. The 95% PI is $49.027 \pm 2(0.1205)$, or from 48.786 to 49.268. By squaring the point prediction and the limits of this PI, we re-express the results in terms of NUMBER: Point prediction: $49.027^2 = 2,404$; 95% PI: from $48.876^2 = 2,380$ to $49.268^2 = 2,427$.

e   The NUMBER specification is simpler and the diagnostic checks are just as good, so it is preferred. The point predictions and prediction intervals are not all that different.

f   Relate NUMBER to its first lag, NUMBER$_{-1}$. The estimated regression model is: Fitted NUMBER = $20.6 + (1.007)\text{NUMBER}_{-1}$. All four diagnostic checks are pretty good. Point prediction: $\hat{y} = 20.6 + 1.007(\text{NUMBER in period 44}) = 20.6 + 1.007(2,365) = 2,402$. 95% PI: $\hat{y} \pm 2s$ or $2,402 \pm 2(9.975)$, or $2,402 \pm 20$. The point prediction and 95% PI are quite reliable since the diagnostic checks are OK.

g The two models yield similar results, but (a) is simpler to interpret, so it is preferred.

11.3 **a** There appears to be a quarterly pattern that is superimposed on a gentle upward drift. This suggests that an autoregression model using the first and fourth lags might be a good starting point.

b The fitted model is: Fitted VALUE $= 9,063 + 0.627(\text{VALUE}_{-1})$. *Check 1:* The ST.RES vs. FITTED plot is satisfactory. *Check 2:* Use the same plot as for check 1. There appears to be moderate increasing variation in ST.RES as FITTED increases. *Check 3:* This is not satisfactory. The sequence plot clearly shows a quarterly pattern. The runs test is acceptable, but the autocorrelogram is not. The standard error of each autocorrelation is $1/\sqrt{44} = 0.15$, so there are several autocorrelations for ST.RES that are more than 2 standard errors away from 0, in particular, the fourth and the eighth. This is not surprising given our assessment in (a). *Check 4:* There are two values above the line at the bottom and four below the line at the top. Normality is marginal at best.

c The fitted model is: Fitted VALUE $= 3,322 + 0.380(\text{VALUE}_{-1}) + 0.547(\text{VALUE}_{-4})$. *Check 1:* This is satisfactory. Three plots used were: ST.RES vs. FITTED, ST.RES vs. VALUE_{-1}, and ST.RES vs. VALUE_{-4}. *Check 2:* Use the same plots as for check 1. There appears to be moderate increasing variation in ST.RES as FITTED increases. *Check 3:* This is fine based on the sequence plot of ST.RES, the runs test, and the autocorrelogram. *Check 4:* The normal probability plot is marginal at best. There are two values above the line at the bottom and four below the line at the top.

d The diagnostic checks for model 2 are better than those for model 1, in particular, the randomness check of ST.RES.

e The 98% CI for the process coefficient of VALUE_{-1} is $0.3799 \pm 2.33(0.1208)$, or 0.38 ± 0.28. This interval is pretty wide, but it only covers positive values, suggesting that the effect of VALUE_{-1}, net of the effect of VALUE_{-4}, is positive. Chances are 98% that this net effect is no more than 0.28 away from the point estimate, 0.38.

f Regression coefficients are net of the other predictor variables used *in* the regression. VALUE_{-1} is the only predictor variable in model 1, but VALUE_{-4} is also included in model 2. Since VALUE_{-1} and VALUE_{-4} are related to each other and to VALUE, the coefficient of VALUE_{-1} in model 2 measures the direct effect of VALUE_{-1} and the indirect effect of VALUE_{-4} (in addition, of course, to the indirect effect of possibly many other variables, known or unknown).

g The relevant values of the first and fourth lags are 33,066 and 48,947, respectively, so the fitted value is: Fitted VALUE $= 3,322 + 0.380(33,066) + 0.547(48,947) = 42,661$. The 90% prediction interval is $42,661 \pm 1.65(7,454)$, or $42,661 \pm 12,299$. Thus the best guess for the value of industrial housing starts in the third quarter of 1988 is 42,661. Chances are 90% that the actual value is no more than 12,299 away from this value. Note the wideness of this interval. To reduce it, other predictor variables must be found. (In practice, this turned out to be very difficult, so the real estate company who was interested in this forecast had to live with the uncertainty.)

h Yes. The point prediction is adequate since check 1 was fine. But the PI is only very approximate because of checks 2 and 4.

11.4 **a** This model relates the change in GNP to change in unemployment. The fitted model is: Fitted D_GNP $= 9.21 - 3.32(\text{D\_UNEM})$; i.e., the larger the increase in the unemployment rate, the lower the change in GNP, a reasonable model. The standard deviation around the regression line is $s = 13.23$, which is somewhat lower than the standard deviation of D_GNP, 16.30. Thus D_UNEM seems to be a moderately useful predictor variable.

b There is one outlier, observation 57 (Year 1946). *Check 1:* Not OK. The residuals for values of FITTED between 10 and 20 tend to be positive. *Check 2:* This is hard to evaluate in light of failing check 1. *Check 3:* The sequence plot does not look random. After about 1940, the variation in ST.RES increases and the ST.RES tend to be positive. The runs test does not support randomness, nor does the autocorrelogram. *Check 4:* The outlier clearly sticks out on the normal probability plot, which is not well approximated by a line. Overall, the model is bad. It seems advisable to treat the data as two distinct subseries, before World War II and after. The remaining results are thus only useful to practice the mechanics of multiple regression.

c 97% CI for process coefficient of D_UNEM: $-3.32 \pm 2.17(0.50)$, or -3.32 ± 1.09. Consider 2 years with the increase in the unemployment rate 1 unit higher in one of them. Then the improvement in GNP will tend to be by 3.32 units lower in the year for which the increase in the unemployment rate was higher. The CI quantifies the accuracy of the estimate -3.32.

d Yes. In years when the unemployment rate remains constant, GNP tends to increase by 9.21.

e First, all figures have to be expressed as changes. The change in the unemployment rate for 1975 is $8.5 - 5.6 = 2.9\%$, so the point prediction for the change in GNP in 1975 is $9.21 - 3.32(2.9) = -0.42$. A 95% PI for this change is $-0.42 \pm 2(13.23)$ or from -26.88 to 26.04, a very wide interval. Since GNP in 1974 was 821.1, the 95% PI for GNP in 1975 is from $(821.1 - 26.88)$ to $(821.1 + 26.04)$, or from 794.2 to 847.1. This PI is quite wide.

f No. If you're trying to predict the change in GNP from this year to *next* year, this model requires that you *know* the change in the unemployment rate from this year to *next* year, clearly an impossibility. The model is not useful for prediction; it is possibly useful for gaining understanding of economic facts.

g The model is bad. Thus all estimates derived from it are bad. It might be best to treat the data after World War II separately from the data before World War II.

Chapter 12

12.3 **a** There is a quarterly pattern superimposed on an upward drift. The variability in each year seems to be increasing. The autocorrelations decrease slowly. A model using differencing seems to be in order, but somehow the quarterly effect must be captured, too.

b The first-order autocorrelation was high, and the autocorrelations are decreasing slowly. There is a strong quarterly pattern to these lag 1 differences. This is supported by the high fourth-order autocorrelation of D_GNP, and the autocorrelations at multiples of 4 decreasing slowly. (It looks like we should do lag 4 differencing on this time series! That could be done, but we shall use an autoregression approach here.) Note that the runs test quite erroneously suggests randomness. During the first 10 years, the variability in D_GNP values is increasing. (A log or square-root transformation of the GNP data is probably in order!)

c There are no unusually large residuals. The first two checks of linearity and constant standard deviation are fine. There appear to be two clusters in the ST.RES vs. FITTED plot. In light of the sequence plot of D_GNP, this is not surprising: The values for quarters 2 and 3 are always on the high side, and the values for quarters 1 and 4 are always on the low side. Thus the FITTED values for quarters 2 and 4 tend to be high, and those for quarters 1 and 3 tend to be low. To do the check of randomness of the ST.RES, we obtained: (1) a time series plot of ST.RES (which suggests increasing variation over time), (2) the runs test of ST.RES (the observed significance at 1.00 suggests randomness), (3) the control chart limits (all ST.RES are within them), and (4) the autocorrelogram and the standard error of each autocorrelation, $1/\sqrt{87} = 0.11$ (the signs are well mixed, the autocorrelations are pretty small, but the fourth, eighth, and twelfth autocorrelations are somewhat high at -0.37, 0.242, and -0.276). Thus randomness is not really OK, and an improved time series model must be found. The normality check seems OK, except for the upper end where there are several somewhat high values. Overall then, this model should be improved.

d Given the diagnostic checks, the following predictions should be improved upon by using a better model. The fitted equation for the lag 1 difference of GNP, D_GNP, is: Fitted D_GNP $= 34 + 0.988(\text{D\_GNP}_{-4})$, and the fourth lag corresponding to quarter 88 is $169,056 - 173,226 = -4,170$. Thus, Fitted D_GNP $= 34 + 0.988(-4,170) = -4,086$. The 95% prediction interval for D_GNP is $-4,086 \pm 2s$, or $-4,086 \pm 2(5,953)$, or $-4,086 \pm 11,906$, or from $-15,992$ to 7,820. Now, note that the lag 1 difference is D_GNP $= \text{GNP} - \text{GNP}_{-1}$. Rewriting this, we get GNP $= \text{GNP}_{-1} + \text{D\_GNP}$, so Fitted GNP $= \text{GNP}_{-1} + \text{Fitted D\_GNP}$. Thus we only need to add the first lag of GNP corresponding to quarter 88 to the fitted value of D_GNP, and we have the required predictions. The first lag of GNP in quarter 88 equals the value of GNP in quarter 87(177,883). The point prediction for GNP in quarter 88 is thus $177,883 - 4,086 = 173,797$, and the 95% prediction interval for GNP in quarter 88 extends from $177,883 - 15,992$ to $177,883 + 7,820$, or from $161,891$ to $185,703$. The diagnostic checks were not acceptable, so these predictions must be improved upon.

12.4 A point prediction for February 1985 should be based on the value 2 periods before (i.e., in December 1984), which is 167.24. To this should be added the mean of the *lag 2* differences, D2_SP, which is 1.78, so the point prediction is $167.24 + 1.78 = 169.02$. A 95% PI is (Point prediction) $\pm 2s$, where s is the standard deviation of the *lag 2* differences, 7.91; that is, the PI is $169.02 \pm 2(7.91)$, or 169.02 ± 15.82.

12.5 **a** There is a very strong quarterly pattern. It appears as if each quarter's time series, taken separately, is meandering around a constant level.

b The runs test does not support the visual impression in (a). It seems that the runs test is not good at picking up this kind of nonrandomness, and its result should be ignored.

c The fourth-order autocorrelation is highest, and this supports the visual impression in (a). Since the fourth-order autocorrelation is high, it is not surprising that the 8th, 12th, etc., order autocorrelations are also high.

d The t-ratio for the constant coefficient is $-0.000201/0.0006084 = -0.33$. The t-ratios for the coefficients of D4_R$_{-1}$ and D4_R$_{-2}$ are $0.6025/0.1384 = 4.35$ and $-0.1279/0.1379 = -0.93$, respectively.

e Because the t-ratio for variable D4_R$_{-2}$ in model 1 was less than 1 in absolute value.

f The value for s in model 1 is expected to be higher since the variable dropped has t-ratio less than 1 in absolute value.

g The first-order autocorrelation of ST.RES for model 2 is 0.0064. The DW statistic is approximately $2[1 - (\text{first-order autocorrelation of ST.RES})] = 2(1 - 0.0064) = 1.9872$. This is close to 2, suggesting no problem with the randomness of the ST.RES of model 2.

h *Checks 1 and 2:* The ST.RES versus FITTED plot looks fine regarding the linearity and constant standard deviation assumptions. *Check 3:* The time series plot of ST.RES looks random, the runs test supports this visual impression, all ST.RES are within the control limits, and all autocorrelations are close to 0 with their signs well mixed. *Check 4:* The normal probability plot looks OK, but there is some indication of negative skewness.

i The fitted equation is $\hat{y} =$ Fitted D4_R $= -0.000232 + 0.528(\text{D4\_R}_{-1})$, with a value for $s = 0.004418$. Thus a point prediction for the lag 4 difference is: $\hat{y} = -0.000232 + 0.528(0.0536 - 0.0534) = -0.0001264$.

A 95% PI for the lag 4 difference is: $\hat{y} \pm zs$, or $0.0001264 \pm 2(0.004418)$, or 0.0001 ± 0.0088. Since the sample size is large, $s = 0.004418$ is a good approximation for the standard error of prediction. We have to assume that all diagnostic checks were OK, which was pretty well the case, except for a hint of negative skewness.

j Since check 1 was fine, the point prediction is reliable. The prediction interval is to be interpreted with very slight caution due to the hint at negative skewness.

k The predictions for the value of RATIO in the first quarter 1976 are obtained by adding its fourth lag, the value in quarter 57 (0.0056) to the values in (i). The point prediction for RATIO in the first quarter 1976 is thus $0.0056 - 0.0001264 = 0.0055$, and a 95% prediction interval is from $0.0055 - 0.0088$ to $0.0055 + 0.0088$, or from -0.0033 to 0.0143.

l Just as the estimates in (i), these predictions are quite reasonable.

12.6 Since the 12th lag is D12_Y $= y - y_{-12}$, we have $y = 0.09 + (0.31)y_{-1} + y_{-12} - (0.31)y_{-13} + e$.

12.7 The first eight lags are involved, and the resulting equation is $y = b_0 + b_1 y_{-1} + b_2 y_{-2} + b_3 y_{-3} + (1 + b_4)y_{-4} - b_1 y_{-5} - b_2 y_{-6} - b_3 y_{-7} - b_4 y_{-8} + e$.

12.8 The equation is most conveniently rewritten as: Fitted LS $= 11.2 - (0.446)Q1 - (0.395)Q2 - (0.271)Q3 + (0)Q4 + (0.0168)\text{TIME}$, where Q1, Q2, Q3, and Q4 are either 0 or 1. If quarter 1 is chosen as a base quarter, then the coefficient of Q1 should be 0. Compared to Q1, the coefficient of Q4 is 0.446 higher, so the coefficient of Q4 in the (base quarter 1) equation is 0.446. In the base quarter 4 equation, the coefficient of Q2 is $[-0.395 - (-0.446)] = 0.051$ higher than the coefficient of Q1, so the coefficient of Q2 in the base quarter 1 equation is 0.051. Likewise, the coefficient of Q3 in the base quarter 1 equation is $[-0.271 - (-0.446)] = 0.175$. Not accounting for the effect of TIME the value of Fitted LS for quarter 1 is: $11.2 - 0.446(1) - 0.395(0) - 0.271(0) + 0(0) = 10.754$. If quarter 1 is chosen as base, the constant coefficient should then be 10.754. Overall, the base quarter 1 equation is: Fitted LS $= 10.754 + (0)Q1 + (0.051)Q2 + (0.175)Q3 + (0.446)Q4 + (0.0168)TIME = 10.754 + (0.051)Q2 + (0.175)Q3 + (0.446)Q4 + (0.0168)TIME$. You should obtain Fitted LS for 1 or 2 quarters to convince yourself that the two equations give identical prediction results.

12.9 **a** The estimated regression equation is: Fitted NUMBER $= 927 + (32)TIME$. *Checks 1 and 2:* There are definite patterns in the ST.RES vs. FITTED plot. Therefore, both checks 1 and 2 are failed. *Check 3:* The sequence plot of residuals and a runs test suggest nonrandomness. Therefore, this is a poor model.

  b The random walk model is preferable.

INDEX